RUGBY

RUGBY

A NEW ZEALAND HISTORY

RON PALENSKI

AUCKLAND
UNIVERSITY
PRESS

'If it hadn't been for rugby, I'd still be a country boy living in Te Kuiti going to the sales once a week. This is the story of the game and the men who made it. Wilson Whineray and Don Clarke, Fred Allen and Kel Tremain. Good men that all New Zealanders should know about. And a great game that I still love.'

— SIR COLIN MEADS

Contents

Acknowledgements

It would be neither possible nor practical to thank everyone who, wittingly or otherwise, contributed to my ability to write this book. People involved in rugby one way or another nurtured my knowledge and enthusiasm for years, from my earliest memories of watching a test match while crouched on the grass not far from the touchline. From my knee-high view then to looking down on games from the heights of grandstands, my interest in the game and all it means has never wavered.

The book would not have happened but for the suggestion that it should from Dr Sam Elworthy of Auckland University Press. Of all the many books about rugby published in New Zealand, there has never been an overall narrative history. This is an attempt to fill that gap. It is not an academic history, though I have included endnotes so readers can delve further and to add provenance. I have referred to academic historians when I have felt the need, although comparatively few in New Zealand have ever bothered much about rugby, for all its influence on the country's history and social life. Greg Ryan in Christchurch is a notable exception.

I have tried to avoid reusing all the old sources which just get perpetuated, sometimes misleadingly, especially when it is so easy and convenient to 'research' via Google or Wikipedia. I did use the old sources – Arthur Swan's two-volume *History of New Zealand Rugby Football* for example – as a reference point but then tried to go further. The Bibliography provides a comprehensive list.

Very few letters or diaries by or about rugby players seem to have survived, but I used some I tracked down. The National Library's website Papers Past (http://paperspast.natlib.govt.nz/cgi-bin/paperspast) has rapidly become an indispensable tool for any historian, historical writer or family researcher; it is not so much what is revealed (because that can still be found in bound volumes or on microfilm) but the speed at which it is revealed. This is matched in Australia by Trove (https://trove.nla.gov.au/newspaper) and in France by the French National Library (http://gallica.bnf.fr). There are similar, although more limited, websites for British and American newspapers. I was fortunate enough to be able to supplement those with my own extensive collections of clippings and tour scrapbooks which were started in 1921 by an ardent rugby follower in Wellington, Henry Magnussen, and continued until 1984. Many of the later volumes come with match programmes and photographs and many of the latter are included here.

Among those I thank directly are Clive Akers for his knowledge and chronicling of players; Max Cryer for advice on a variety of matters; Tim Curnow for permission to use lines of poetry from his father Allen; Peter du Chateau for helping out with a piece of his family history; Sean Fagan in Sydney for his expertise on the early days of Australian rugby (http://jottingsonrugby.wordpress.com); Brian Finn for his expertise and interest; Tony Gilbert for sharing his knowledge and astute observations; John Griffiths in Britain for his knowledge of all things rugby and correcting some of my errors; Owen and Michael Harvey for information about their relative, Ernest Denis Hoben; Frédéric Humbert in Paris for his help with illustrations and answering questions about French rugby (http://www.rugby-pioneers.com); Lindsay Knight for responding to questions about players, games and people; Max Lambert for similar advice and for tracking down service records in Wellington; Bruce Leadley at Timaru Boys' High School for help about Rex King; Lynn

McConnell for pointing me in some directions; Brian Moloughney for his encouragement and interest in rugby; Mark Pirie for steering me in the direction of some rugby poems, including one of his own; Lee Richards in London for hunting out documents in the UK National Archives; Peter Sinclair for his yarning about football days; Bill Sutton for the use of some of his lines; Alison Waghorn for the use of diaries and other documents kept by her father, Bill Dalley. The risk in naming people in this way is unwittingly omitting some; if I have, I apologise.

Thanks, as always, are due to the ever-helpful staffs at the Hocken Collections and the Central, Law and Medical Libraries at the University of Otago; at the Alexander Turnbull Library, especially the now-retired David Colquhoun; Archives New Zealand; Births, Deaths and Marriages at the Department of Internal Affairs; the Barr Smith Library, University of Adelaide.

I also thank the photographers whose works supplement the words; some of them are known and acknowledged, some not because they could not be traced – all are thanked.

Gratitude is due to Sam Elworthy and his staff, especially Anna Hodge and Katrina Duncan, for putting it together; and to my family, especially Kathy, for their continued support.

A word about words

Errors, odd spellings or misspellings in quotations have been kept as they appeared originally; if explanations or corrections seemed necessary, they have been added within square brackets or included in the endnotes. This applies to the singular or plural use of the word Māori and the use of macrons and other diacritic marks.

The word rugby is not capitalised when it is referring to the game but is capitalised when it is the school or, as in Rugby rules, in relation to the school.

The word football may to some readers mean different things. Not to me. Football covers a variety of games: rugby is one, soccer or association football is another; others are rugby league, Australian rules (AFL) or American or Canadian football.

Ron Palenski
Dunedin, March 2015

Two boys, one football, an empty street. Even spectators. An ideal chance for a bit of footy in Bell Street in Wanganui in 1906. This photo was taken by Frank Denton, about whom *Truth* once rhymed: '. . . the photos he takes, are no failures or fakes . . .'. This is the evidence. 1/1-017498-G, ALEXANDER TURNBULL LIBRARY.

Introduction

Out in the field the forwards are a-lining,
The backs are crouched already in their place
Cold and grey, with a wink of sun shining
It's just the day for scrum, and rush, and pace[1]

When the New Zealand Rugby Football Union marked its seventy-fifth anniversary in 1967, it chose the Chief Justice of the day, Sir Richard Wild, to deliver the keynote address. Wild was more than just a formidable presence off the bench. He was a good enough rugby player as a young man to represent Wellington and was in the New Zealand Universities team that broke new ground by touring Japan in 1936. A younger brother, Peter, had also played first-class rugby and became a member of the national union council and manager of the Under 23 team that beat the All Blacks in 1973.

The anniversary was a grand affair because the union was conscious that it had not been able to do justice to its fiftieth anniversary, which had fallen in 1942 when the country was at war. All former All Blacks and national administrators were invited to the function in the Overseas Terminal on Oriental Parade in Wellington, and a test match against New Zealand's most enduring foe, Australia, was played that afternoon. The old players marched around Athletic Park before the game, grouped by years with the three survivors of 1905 in the van – Billy Wallace, George Nicholson and Bunny Abbott. That night, they all went off to the dinner. The Prime Minister, Keith Holyoake, was there. He had played eighteen games for Golden Bay–Motueka in his trimmer days. (If only he knew, he'd chuckle that a statue of himself in garter robes now stands outside New Zealand rugby headquarters in Wellington – surely the only statue anywhere of a hooker.)[2]

At the dinner, the three 1905 men sat in isolated splendour at a table of their own. The Australian players mingled with the All Blacks, young and old. Sir Richard Wild exchanged legal banter with his Australian counterpart, Sir Leslie Herron, who had been a Sydney flanker in his youth; Don Clarke and Billy Wallace chatted while they posed for photos, famous fullback and famous fullback; father and son All Blacks Ned and Kevin Barry shared a beer; Richard ('Tiny') White, a formidable lock in the 1950s, towered over one of the smallest men to play for New Zealand, halfback Ponty Reid; there was Tom French, who lost an arm in the first war a couple of weeks after playing in an army 'test'; Alex Bruce, a member of the 1919 army team that was the first New Zealand team to go to South Africa; Ian Botting, who played for both New Zealand and England, and who was dressed in the 'uniform' of a Church of England minister; so many names, so many faces, all in the name of rugby . . .

Wild's address went for 45 minutes, punctuated by laughter, table-thumping approval and cries of 'hear, hear'. At one point he trailed off into his own poetry (although he attributed it to a ten-year-old boy ill in bed):

> Oh, I could tell you some tales
> Of matches in Wales,
> Or at Twickenham, Newlands and Sydney,
> Of Williams and Wooller and Morkel and Muller,
> Or players of similar kidney.

There was absolute silence when he tried, in the ringing tones that usually echoed off panelled courtroom walls, to explain why rugby had taken such a hold on New Zealand:

> Rugby exactly suited our climate and our soil. It matched the temperament of the New Zealander and in large measure has moulded our national character. It is the team element which provides a spur to the weaker spirit, a curb for the selfish and discipline for all. It treats every man as an equal from whatever background he comes. There's no yielding to status in a rugby tackle, there's no privilege in a scrum.[3]

He was neither the first nor the last to try to pin down why rugby took such a hold in New Zealand.

Don Clarke did more than just kick six penalty goals for New Zealand's 18–17 win against the British Isles in Dunedin in 1959. That is Lions wing Peter Jackson he has wrong-footed while other All Blacks wait to see what happens next. They are lock Nev MacEwan, halfback Roger Urbahn, first five-eighth Ross Brown and wing Pat Walsh.

As mythical as the tale of rugby's beginnings is, All Blacks and others still feel as if they are treading in the footsteps of history when they go to Rugby School in Warwickshire. These are some of the 1963–64 All Blacks training on the school ground, with Rugby boys lined up to watch. The school's chapel is in the background and just visible, between the boys and the chapel, are goalposts which once stood at Twickenham.

No one has a definitive answer why, of the various forms of football that were played haphazardly in the nineteenth century, rugby should have emerged to gain such a hold on the psyche of a nation.

In tracing the arrival and development of the game in New Zealand, I reached back further into its antiquarian roots of ball games in ancient China, Greece and Rome, but found none that could be positively identified as a football antecedent. The word 'football' itself has come to mean different things to different people at different times and, most recently, has been requisitioned by the soccer governing body, FIFA, and its adherents, as its own. But that form of football has no greater claim to the ownership of the word than rugby has. Football in the beginning was played in different areas according to different rules. The advent of railways made it easier for one group or town or school to see what another was playing, and eventually men who had recently been boys met in London to see if they could find a common set of rules. They could not. From the generic football emerged the Football Association and, a few years later, the Rugby Football Union. To argue that rugby evolved from soccer is to misunderstand or misinterpret the reality. Of course, the perpetuation of the myth surrounding William Webb Ellis – the boy 'who took the ball in his arms and ran with it' – does nothing to bring clarity to the issue. In football's evolution, Ellis was nothing more than a belated red herring. The belief that all forms of football involved only kicking until

The First XV from Christ's College in Christchurch in 1878. The captain with the ball is Herbert William Williams, who followed his father and grandfather and became Bishop of Waiapu, and a noted Māori scholar. Second from left is Harry Beswick, a lawyer who became mayor of Christchurch in 1896. Most of the team also played for Canterbury. ½-029526-F, ALEXANDER TURNBULL LIBRARY

Ellis happened along is a myth. The American president, John F. Kennedy, once said: 'For the great enemy of truth is very often not the lie – deliberate, contrived and dishonest – but the myth; persistent, persuasive and unrealistic.'[4]

Rugby came to New Zealand with men who had played it at schools or clubs or in the army in the United Kingdom (not only England), and native-born New Zealanders took to it instead of the various forms of football (the Victorian game, the Harrow game, the Eton game or combinations thereof) played occasionally since 1840. The first game of rugby in New Zealand was reportedly played in Nelson in 1870, but there is evidence pointing to at least one, and perhaps more, games in Wanganui before that. Wherever the game was first played, it spread throughout the country remarkably quickly, particularly by those who saw the value of provincial teams and, within fourteen or fifteen years of the first game, a national team. The structure that was erected in the 1870s and 1880s continues today, with some changes wrought by the switch to professionalism in 1995. Māori took to the game as if it were their own. They mounted the first significant overseas tour, they played the game in a manner that was copied by others, they introduced the black jersey with the silver fern and they were indirectly responsible for the coining of the name, All Blacks.

It is the success of the All Blacks, from their first tour in 1893 and their first British visit, in 1905, that has underpinned the success and strength of New Zealand rugby. The history of the game in New Zealand is in large measure the history of the All Blacks. The national team's record is phenomenal by any standards in any sport. But the team's enduring success has been predicated on a strong and enthusiastic domestic game, at club and provincial level, allied of course with popular support. One level of rugby depends upon the other; and vice versa.

The answer to 'why rugby?' comes in two parts: that rugby clubs and unions organised themselves quicker than did any other competing winter sport

Big government departments had their own rugby teams based on branch offices or sections. This team of engineers from Christchurch went south to play the Dunedin equivalent at Carisbrook in 1918.

A good example of a cobbled-together social team during the Second World War (probably 1944) and hence the fact the team is two short.

and provided a national team first. Having done that, the national team was successful and proved to be better than any other in the limited rugby world.

It was the success of the early national teams and the competition between provinces that led to rugby having a standing in the community like no other sport. In the suburbs of the cities and in towns and villages, rugby teams provided a focal point, a sense of community, a sense of belonging, a sharing of identity. They inculcated a tribal allegiance that went beyond a sporting competition that lasted a whole afternoon in the early days, then an hour or two. Clubs or the pubs where clubs met became centres not just for the players but for the community as a whole, and it is only in relatively recent, more mobile, years that that has waned. But, in some areas, not a lot is different.

Club rugby remains important to its followers; in one corner of New Zealand, the Seddon Shield is as significant and as revered by an ardent follower of the West Coast or Buller as the Bledisloe Cup is by followers on a national scale.

Rugby has been a man's game, and sometimes derided for so being, since its rudimentary beginnings. The women's game was established in New Zealand (and elsewhere) late in historical terms, but women were agitating to play, and did so, much earlier than has hitherto been thought. They also followed the game avidly. Their story is told here for the first time.

Alan Mulgan, a journalist and essayist, once remembered his days following matches at Potter's Park in Auckland before Eden Park became the main ground. He talked of the old days and the old ways:

> The wait before play; the thrill at the appearance of the teams; the excitement and the barracking; the grandstand changing into a tidal rip when a try was scored. The chatter at halftime; the smell of damp grass and orange peel; the gathering dusk . . . the final bell, the surge of the cheering crowd out to the gates – you remember these things, I know.[5]

To later generations, the sounds of rugby would be the staccato of sprigs pounding on concrete as players warmed up by running on the spot or as they half-trotted down a tunnel to the ground; the smell would be of liniment that was liberally wiped over legs and sometimes shoulders; the noise would be the roar of the crowd as the teams emerged, with echoes throughout the game as the favoured team scored. Different generations take different memories to their old age; it remains one of the attractions of rugby. It did not matter if it was club rugby, a school match, a rep game or the ultimate, a test match.

Alan Mulgan's son John was a writer, editor and observer of life. Reminiscing about his young days, John Mulgan remarked: 'Rugby football was the best of all our pleasures: it was religion and desire and fulfilment all in one.'[6] He wrote this during the Second World War when he served with an English regiment and observed that the New Zealand attitude of playing to win and of an 'exaggerated attention' to games was deprecated by a lot of thinkers.

The game must go on. A heavy snowfall in the south of the South Island in August 1939 stopped many things, but not rugby and certainly not the Ranfurly Shield. Southland repulsed Manawatu's challenge 17–3 and despite the weather, a crowd of about 5000 still found its way to Rugby Park in Invercargill. In this photo, Southland halfback Jack Purdue whips round the blind side to kick for the line. The other Southlander is Ray Mahony (13). Manawatu players facing the camera are Jack Finlay, Bernard O'Dea and Bill Little. The referee, Ivan Dillon, became a casualty of war three years later.

No matter the level, different generations take different memories to their old age.

> But to be frank . . . I found in wartime that there was a considerable virtue in men who had played games like professionals to win, and not, like public-school boys and amateurs, for exercise . . . they looked on war as a game and a game to New Zealanders is something that they play to win, against the other side, and the referee, if necessary.[7]

Rugby is much different now from what it was; enormous changes have taken place since the philosophical base of the game was overturned by the decision to go professional. But the foundation remains the same as it evolved in the nineteenth century, the way tours were organised and how the pyramid of aspiration of club to national team was erected. Along the way, the game has faced many threats. Its steadfast clinging to amateurism was a constant battle through the twentieth century; so too the equally steadfast desire to play against South Africa. Through it all, rugby has had, and continues to have, a pervasive influence in New Zealand. It is so pervasive that it is difficult to categorise in the way league is said to be a working-class game or rugby in Australia an upper-middle-class game; those types of tags could never cling to rugby in New Zealand. The World Cup in 2011 was the most overt manifestation of that, when almost everyone in the country it seemed entered into the spirit of the occasion. Rugby since the nineteenth century has been a part of what New Zealand is and what New Zealanders are.

A former director of art at Rugby School, Bob Nicolson, depicts the mythical moment when William Webb Ellis supposedly first ran with the ball. Nicolson took the title for his painting ('. . . with a fine disregard for the rules') from the plaque at the school that remembers a moment no one could recall seeing.

1 A fork in the football road

The broad philosophy of football you can understand if you will. Come along with me a little nearer, and let us consider it together.[1]

Among the crowd of about seven thousand at the Grange Road ground for the All Blacks' match against Cambridge University in November 1905 was a tall, thin man with a flourishing white moustache. His name was Herbert Giles and he was professor of Chinese at the university; a renowned sinologist, he gave his name to half of the accepted way then of rendering Chinese script into English, the Wade-Giles method.[2] As he watched the All Blacks beat the university by 14 points to nil – a scoreline that set Cambridge feet a-dancing because it was not like the 47–0 thrashing delivered by the All Blacks to Oxford two days before – Giles cast his mind back more than two thousand years: 'I began to wonder if anyone would take an interest in, or even believe, the fact that football was played by the Chinese several centuries before Julius Caesar landed in Britain.'[3]

The date of the New Zealand–Cambridge match was 9 November, a date of no special significance now but one that was then celebrated as the King's Birthday. The All Blacks after the match went back to London by train, where they had a semi-formal dinner put on by expatriate New Zealanders at the Trocadero restaurant in Shaftesbury Avenue followed by a show at the Palace Theatre. All that the players would have wanted, like players of any era, would have been to get back to their hotel, the Manchester, in Aldersgate in the City, because this was Thursday night and they had another game on the Saturday. In Cambridge, students celebrated long into the night, partly because of the unexpected low score against them and partly because of the expected high jinks associated with the annual holiday. The All Blacks' vice-captain, Billy Stead, recalled the excesses: 'About 2000 students, out to do any damage they can, are very difficult to control and, despite an extra hundred police imported for the occasion, they damaged property to the value of £300. As we left at 8pm, we only saw the start of proceedings.'[4]

It is unlikely Giles would have seen any of the students' mayhem either. He much more likely would have gone home and started to compose, in his fertile mind at least, the article about the beginnings of football in pre-imperial China that was published in a magazine, *The Nineteenth*

Century and After, the following January when the All Blacks were on their way to the last leg of their tour in North America.

There is a general belief, fostered by some histories, that football's origins were in ancient Greece and Rome. Giles winds the clock back still further. This is a history of the game in New Zealand, not a history of the game globally, but not to write about how and where the generic football was played would be akin to writing a general history of New Zealand without mentioning Britain. Games, like most things, evolved into today's form rather than being manufactured and presented in a finished state to an anticipatory populace.

Before delving too far into the ancient past, though, vocabulary needs to be clarified, particularly one word: football. Football, despite what soccer enthusiasts may say, is a generic term rather than the name of a specific game. In various versions and with various spellings, football had been played for centuries, and it was only late in the nineteenth century that football gave birth to two distinct offshoots, Rugby (as in the school in Warwickshire) rules and Association (as in Football Association) rules. They became, more simply, rugby and soccer (the word soccer deriving from the second syllable in 'association'), and it is only in relatively recent years that adherents of soccer claim it to be the One True Faith and that rugby was really a splinter game.

Soccer has no more claim to the ownership of the word football than rugby has. (But as sports marketing and image-conscious people became involved, rugby gradually has been quietly dropping the f-word from its titles. The New Zealand Rugby Football Union as a name was perfectly adequate for more than a hundred years; for the last ten or so, it has been the New Zealand Rugby Union.) To further cloud the issue, people in Victoria, Tasmania, South Australia and Western Australia, as well as in the United States and in Canada, have entirely different games in mind when their ears prick up at the word football. Their games too were children of the same parent. Soccer, rugby, Australian rules, American and Canadian football (and a few others) are blood brothers or cousins. (In February 2012 the *Age* newspaper in Melbourne carried a headline on its front page: 'Like it or lump it, football is back.'[5] It was not about soccer. A month later, the *Press* in Christchurch had a similar headline but about a different game.[6])

The issue of who 'owns' the name of football has been around as long as there have been uniform rules. Previewing the 1880 season, a writer in *The Times* related that soccer followers claimed a monopoly on the word football because they had eliminated handling. But he said there was no more legitimate or scientific form of football than the dropkick or dribbling (then a big part of rugby).[7] When people say, 'But rugby is a branch of football and it's football that was the original game,' the 'Y' argument should be employed. Imagine a capital Y. The bottom is the distant past when all sorts of games with balls were played in different countries for centuries. Travel up the Y and you reach the crossroads erected in the 1860s when rugby went one way and soccer the other.

In 1905, Giles was inspired by the All Blacks' match to seek out the foot of the Y. Giles traced football back to the third millennium BC when it formed part of the military curriculum. 'It is generally admitted to have been originally a military exercise and a handbook on football, in twenty-five chapters, is said to have been in existence under the Han dynasty, say two thousand years ago,' Giles wrote.[8]

He quoted the man generally regarded as China's first historian, Sima Qian (Giles used his romanisation method, which transcribed the name as Ssu-ma Ch'ien). Qian, who was described as The Great Historian, wrote of the rich and powerful town of Linzi (Lin-tzu): 'There were none among its inhabitants who did not perform on the pipes, or on some stringed instrument, fight cocks, race dogs, dice or play football.'

Football was known as tsu-chu in the Wade-Giles method but is now romanised under the pinyin system as zu qiu.[9] (Some soccer followers, including the governing body, FIFA, render it incorrectly as 'cu ju'.) The *History of the Han Dynasty* (206 BC to AD 25) mentioned football several times, including a comment: 'Tsu is to kick with the foot; chu, the ball, is made of leather and stuffed and is kicked about for amusement.' One emperor, Cheng of the Jin dynasty, was said to be fond of football, but officers told him it was both exhausting and unsuitable to the imperial dignity. Cheng apparently replied: 'We like playing and what one chooses to do is not exhausting.'

Giles also unearthed a poet, Li Yu, who lived between 50 and 130 AD and wrote perhaps the first football poem:

> A round ball and a square wall,
> Suggesting the shapes of the Yin and the Yang;
> The ball flying across like the moon,
> While the two teams stand opposed.
> Captains are appointed, and take their places,
> According to unchanging regulations.
> No allowances are made for relationship;
> There must be no partialities.
> But there must be determination and coolness,
> Without the slightest irritation at failure . . .
> And if all this is necessary for football,
> How much more so for the business of life!

Six years after the All Blacks' visit to Cambridge, Giles summarised what he had learnt about the Chinese origins of football. 'Football was played in China at a very early date,' he wrote, 'originally with a ball stuffed full of hair; from the fifth century AD, with an inflated bladder covered with leather. A picture of the goal, which is something like a triumphal arch, has come down to us. . . .'[10] Giles recorded that winners were rewarded with flowers, fruit and wine 'and even with silver bowls and brocades, while the captain of the losing team was flogged and suffered other indignities'. The game thereafter disappeared for several centuries and was revived only towards the end of the nineteenth century as the Chinese empire faded and was eventually replaced by the republic.

Historical accounts frequently overlook the early Chinese role in the development of football and settle instead on ancient Greece and Rome for their ball game beginnings. The Greeks played a game called *episkyros* that involved two teams of up to fourteen or fifteen players, each defending a white line over which the opposing team tried to kick or throw a ball. Once the line was crossed, the game ended. So it was a game for possession rather than for points. And that, according to one classicist, is all that can be said about the game with confidence.[11] Some rugby hearts beat faster when their owners learned of *episkyros* and saw a similarity with rugby, but another classicist, Harold Harris of the University of Wales (and being Welsh, likely to know something about rugby), slowed the pulse rates down again when he wrote there was not the slightest evidence that kicking played any part in the game.[12] The Roman game of *harpastum*, which has its claimants as an antecedent of rugby, came from the Greek *phaininda*, which meant intercepting. In this game, two sides tossed a ball to each other while a hapless competitor between the two tried to grab it. Once again, hard evidence is lacking and yet another classicist, George Marindin, was among the first to suggest that looking back at ancient Greece and Rome for footballing roots was probably a waste of time. 'It will probably never be possible to lay down with certainty all the rules of any Greek and Roman game at ball,' he wrote.[13] He also added, in an ominous note for all who followed his line of study, 'it may be well to guard against the idea that football of any sort was played in ancient Greece and Rome'.[14]

Harpastum did not entirely disappear from sight. It is probably the basis for the version of football called *il calcio* in northern Italy, especially Florence, from the sixteenth century. That game

Italian students playing football, probably in Padua, in about 1590. This is an engraving from a book on national costume by Pietro Bertelli. THE LANGTON COLLECTION, 1991

should not be confused, although probably is, with the Italian name for football, *calcio* (which is Italian for kick) – the 'AC' part of AC Milan, for example, stands for *Associazione Calcio*. *Il calcio*, also known as *giuoco del calcio fiorentino* (Florentine kick game) developed as the young men of Florence adapted their game to the enclosed spaces of the inner city. It involved both handling and kicking with the ultimate aim of getting the ball over a designated spot on the perimeter of the field. Enthusiasts revived the game in the twentieth century and three matches are now played each year in the Piazza Santa Croce in Florence. The rules of the modern version are much the same, including such niceties as head-butting, punching and elbowing. For all the influence of the Florentine kick game or even of *harpastum*, the English usually get the credit for introducing modern football – that is, soccer – to Italy in the late nineteenth century with two of the first clubs, Genoa and Milan, being founded by and for English expatriates and having 'cricket' in their original titles (and hence Milan rather than Milano). As with China, the game had to go through a filtering process in Britain, or at least in England and Scotland, before heading back from whence it came.

One of the rugby personalities of the twentieth century, Danie Craven, was player, coach, manager and general ruler of white South African rugby from the mid-1930s until almost the end of the apartheid era in the early 1990s. Craven was also a highly qualified historian and anthropologist.

In 1978, while he was president of the South African Rugby Board, he completed his last doctoral thesis, in physical education, about how and where games began.[15] He arrived in the lobby of the Park Lane Hotel in Piccadilly brandishing newly bound copies of the thesis as if he were Moses waving his tablets. In it, Craven argued that sports and games in their rudimentary forms did what rats carrying diseases did – they went west from China and other parts of Asia to Greece and the Roman Empire, thence to western Europe and subsequently to Britain where the Atlantic prevented any further westward drift. And there they stayed for several hundred years until what came to be known as the games revolution when Britain, in the proud words of Sir Charles Tennyson, 'taught the world to play'.[16]

English sociologists Eric Dunning and Kenneth Sheard, who have made the most comprehensive social study of the origins and development of football, believe there is no firm evidence that a game called football was played in Britain before the fourteenth century. But they note drily: 'However, lack of data has not deterred writers from speculating about the pre-fourteenth century origins of the modern games.'[17] They even offered the theory, as sacrilegious as it may be to today's soccer fanatics, that football could have been so-named not because it involved kicking but because it was played on foot (as opposed to on horseback).[18]

What is known for sure is that football was a folk game played under various names throughout the British Isles, as well as in places such as Italy and France, from at least the Middle Ages. Folk games were played more or less spontaneously by groups of people in a particular locale according to rules passed on by word of mouth over the years. Different towns had different rules and quite often different objects in their games. The only common factor seems to have been a ball that was originally the bladder of an animal – usually a pig. Dunning and Sheard thought the bladder's size made it easier to kick than smaller, solid balls, and that could have been a reason for the name football. But it is clear that the ball was also propelled or carried forward by means other than kicking. How else to explain the disappearance of the ball into the midst of a heaving melee? Although games had their own loose sets of rules – or perhaps customs is a more appropriate word – they were wild, unruly affairs and often served as an outlet for antipathies that existed between groups, between towns or even between families. Violence was endemic. It may have been fortunate then that games were played usually on festive days such as Shrove Tuesday or Ash Wednesday. They were not regular, programmed occurrences in the manner of sporting fixtures now because their participants had more pressing things to do.

According to Joseph Strutt, an eighteenth-century English antiquarian who compiled an exhaustive record called *The Sports and Pastimes of the People of England*, forms of football did make an early appearance on British fields.[19] The Shrovetide game at Chester was said to have been in commemoration of the kicking about of the head of a captured Dane; the Derby game was supposed to have marked a local victory over the Romans. The game was supposed to have been played in the twelfth century, if William fitz Stephen is to be believed. He was the biographer of Thomas Becket and wrote in his *Description of the City of London* in 1190:

> After dinner, all the youth of the city go into the field of the suburbs and address themselves to the famous game of football. The scholars of each school have their peculiar ball; and the particular trades have most of them theirs. The elders of the city, the fathers of the parties, and the rich and the wealthy, come to the field on horseback, in order to behold the exercises of the youth, and in appearance are themselves as youthful as the youngest; their natural heat seeming to be

This was simply captioned 'The Rugby Union game' in Montague Shearman's comprehensive *Athletics and Football* edition for the *Badminton Library of Sports and Pastimes* in 1887.

> revived at the sight of so much agility, and in a participation of the diversions of their festive sons.

Whether Stephen meant football as it is now understood is a moot point. He wrote in Latin and his words were interpreted in different ways including, by an antiquarian in the eighteenth century, to mean tennis.[20] And this confusion lends credence to the Dunning and Sheard belief that it is best to be wary of any claimants for football provenance before at least the fourteenth century. But there was no doubt that Britons were using the word, whether spelt 'foot-ball', 'fute-ball' or just plain old 'football' or other variants, by at the latest the Middle Ages. What is in doubt is what the word actually meant; that is, what the game was if indeed it was a game at all.

By the fourteenth century too, authorities, from kings to councils, began to notice the game. King Edward II became the first monarch to try to ban football. The reason he did so was not because it was violent and threatened the health of his subjects but because while they were enjoying themselves at football, they were not practising their archery. There was also an element of snobbery. Montague Shearman, a lawyer, judge and co-founder of the Amateur Athletic Association in England, wrote about athletics and football for the *Badminton Library of Sports and Pastimes* in 1887.[21] 'For many centuries in England,' he wrote, 'any pedestrian sport which was not immediately connected with knightly skill was considered unworthy of a gentleman of equestrian rank, and this will account in a great measure for the adverse criticisms of football which proceed from writers of aristocratic position.'[22]

For three or four hundred years, a succession of monarchs tried to suppress football, some for the same reason as Edward II and some because it was so violent it upset other people in the towns where it was played. The fact so many kings (queens are mysteriously absent from the Dunning and Sheard list of royal disapprovers) sought an end to football was an indication of how unsuccessful they were.[23] One of the kings who failed in his football mission was Richard II who was, *Spectator* columnist Paul Johnson wrote in an impassioned pitch against modern football (soccer), 'a finicky king responsible for bringing in the pocket handkerchief and the three-pronged fork'. Richard's campaign against football may 'help to explain why he was eventually dethroned and murdered in Pontefract Castle, a dismal Yorkshire hole in what is now the heart of soccer country'.[24]

The game of football appears to have fallen from favour in England from the early seventeenth century until the early nineteenth partly because of its violence and partly because of the rise of Puritanism, whose devotees took a dislike to the game, especially since it was played on Sundays, the only time most young people had available to play. 'The political ascendancy of this ascetic creed,' Shearman wrote of the Puritans, 'was short, but the hold that it took upon the manners and feelings of the nation not only put a stop in a great measure to Sunday football, but rendered the game less acceptable upon other days.'[25]

By the late eighteenth century, Strutt thought football was disappearing: 'The game was formerly much in vogue among the common people, though of late years it seems to have fallen into disrepute and is but little practised.'[26] Strutt wrote about games and pastimes in England and did not concern himself with other parts of the British Isles. But folk football was played outside England too – *caid* in Ireland, *cnapan* in Wales, *calcio* in Italy, *la soule* in western France (also recorded in Cornwall in the thirteenth century) – but their significance has collapsed under the weight of what the word 'football' came to mean. The English language as a transmitter of ideas and concepts as well as a communications tool was also a factor in the dominance of football as seen in the English-speaking world. If more spoke Welsh or Cornish, the world might now be playing and watching *la soule* or *cnapan* instead of them being quaint relics of an almost-unknown past.

Sir Walter Scott in 1815 helped ensure that the game the Scots knew as football did not lose favour as it had south of the border. Paul Johnson in his anti-football tirade in the *Spectator* in 2000 thought Scott's intervention was to civilise the game by gentrification. But Scott was looking after his 'ain folk'. He allied himself with a team of players from the Ettrick Forest area in the Borders against a team of the men of Yarrow, who were backed by the Earl of Home. Scott, who was sheriff of the forest, wrote some verse to mark the match, of which these have since been the most-quoted lines:

Then strip lads and to it, though
sharp be the weather,
And if, by mischance, you should happen to fall,
There are worse things in life
than a tumble on heather,
And life is itself but a game of football.

This print shows that the game in parts of France, *la soule*, was similar to folk games in Britain and Ireland. Village teams of men and boys fought, sometimes literally, to get the ball into the centre of the opposing village. The game depicted is in lower Normandy. *L'ILLUSTRATION*, FRÉDÉRIC HUMBERT COLLECTION

Rugby as it was played in France in the late nineteenth century. The ball still appears more round than oval but the distinctive goalposts have appeared. This woodcut by French artist Charles Laplante was captioned: *'C'est la ce qu'on appelle une belle bousculade.'* (This is what we call a beautiful scramble.) BIBLIOTHÈQUE NATIONALE DE FRANCE

Scott foresaw the fine rugby tradition of having a drink after the game: 'And when it is over, we'll drink a blythe measure . . . to the lads that have lost and the lads that have won.'[27]

So while Scottish youth (and youth no doubt in other countries) pursued their brands of football, the game in England was in what Shearman called a state of dormancy until the games revolution took hold in the 1850s. This transformation was an offshoot of the Industrial Revolution when Victorian Britons set about changing their island state and much of the world besides. In essence, the public schools took in the folk games of the countryside, gave them rules and conventions, and then fed them via the universities back to the countryside again – and beyond to a waiting world. From this process emerged the distinct games of rugby and soccer (and along the way, Australian rules in Melbourne, American football at Yale, Canadian football at McGill in Montreal and so on). It was not just football. Hardly a sport or game exists that was not in some way devised or codified by the British. As the Mayor of London, Boris Johnson, famously remarked at the handover at the end of the Olympic Games in Beijing in 2008, 'Ping pong is coming home!' Indeed it was.

The sports revolution was set off by a few key factors. One was the advent of the railway system that dramatically cut travelling time and allowed schools to have contact with each other and therefore learn for the first time what games other boys played. Previously, travel time was determined by the speed and stamina of horses (and the ability of people to pay for their use) or the endurance of a person walking. Another factor was the enclosure movement in England, under which landowners could remove from their land what had previously been communal rights, restricting the space available for the playing of games. Schools became the best place to play.

C. L. R. James, the Trinidadian activist, essayist and cricket enthusiast, noted the wider changes in this brief period of frantic activity. He gave as examples the introduction of Benjamin Disraeli's Reform Act which introduced popular democracy to England and the defeat of the slave states in the American Civil War. James suggested in his best-known book *Beyond A Boundary*[28] that three men alone created the Victorian era: Thomas Arnold, the headmaster of Rugby; Thomas Hughes, the author of *Tom Brown's Schooldays*; and cricketer W. G. Grace.

Arnold almost single-handedly changed public schools in England and with that change cultivated the games revolution (among other things). As Dunning and Sheard showed in their sociological study of rugby, the public schools were hotbeds of rebellion in the early part of the nineteenth century and masters were practically powerless at times to control the boys. The man most associated with the turnaround in standards was Thomas Arnold, who took over as headmaster at Rugby in 1827. As his biographer in the *Oxford Dictionary of National Biography* remarked: 'When Arnold took over the headmastership Rugby School was suffering from a general decline which was widespread in public schools at the beginning of the nineteenth century. Low moral standards, harsh discipline and ossified teaching methods had shaken public confidence in them.'[29]

Arnold tightened discipline at Rugby, ensured masters had the authority and power to control boys and he inculcated in his pupils the concept of a healthy mind in a healthy body. This was the beginnings of the 'muscular Christianity' reflected in novels such as *Tom Brown's Schooldays*. By any standards at any time Hughes's novel of life at Rugby was an enormous seller and must have done much to open the eyes of the wider public to the attraction of organised sport. And then there was Grace, one of the most well-known and popular figures of his day, and considered one of the best cricketers of all time, whose technical innovations and influence on the game left an enduring legacy. As James wrote: 'That the Victorian middle classes found in these three what they had been waiting anxiously for is proved first by the extraordinary enthusiasm of the reception they gave to them, and secondly by the manner in which they took from each exactly what they needed to create a whole and rejected the rest.'[30]

Rugby mythology says that William Webb Ellis began the game of rugby at Rugby in 1823 by catching the ball and running with it. Ellis was a Lancashire lad, son of a soldier who died during the Peninsular War in 1812. Ellis senior had not been a wealthy man and it seems that whatever money he had was spent on gaining his commission. His widow, Ann, was left penniless and had to bring up two young sons on the £10 pension she was granted for each. Like other mothers in similar circumstances at the time, she moved to Rugby in Warwickshire and because young Willy was 'a town boy', he was admitted to Rugby without mother having to pay the fees. Older brother Thomas enrolled at the same time.[31] According to Sheard, most boys at the school were 'members of the clergy, gentry and aristocracy'.[32] In a class-conscious era, Ellis was of a lower class. He attended Rugby from 1816 until 1825, from the age of ten until eighteen.

Ellis went from Rugby to Brasenose College at Oxford, where his expenses were met by scholarships and he distinguished himself as a cricketer, playing for the university in the only game that really mattered to it, against Cambridge. He gained his bachelor and master's degrees and joined the Church of England. He served at various churches in south-east England, most notably St Clement Danes in the Strand in

Left: The only known published likeness of William Webb Ellis. This was published not for any role in rugby but for his views on the Crimean War. *ILLUSTRATED LONDON NEWS*, 29 APRIL 1854
Right: Matthew Bloxam, the Rugby antiquarian whose letters to the school magazine began the Ellis myth.

London (1836–55) and for the last seventeen years of his life at Magdalen Laver in Essex. A school was built at Magdalen Laver thanks to subscriptions raised by Ellis. He contracted tuberculosis and followed the fashion of the time by going to Menton, France where it was thought the clear, dry air of the Mediterranean littoral would help his lungs. (Katherine Mansfield in 1919 had the same idea.) He died there in 1872. Ellis never married and would have been known to people only within the church and his parishioners. He was not a noted national figure and the only likeness of him known to have been published was in the *Illustrated London News* in April 1854. And it was not published because of any football connection. The Anglican Church declared 6 April 1854 a fast day because of Britain's entry into the Crimean War and the *ILN* carried illustrations of clergymen who had devoted sermons to the war.[33]

Ellis had no presence at all in the published histories of football until the last decade of the nineteenth century. Shearman did not mention him in his magnum opus and the name 'Ellis' did not appear in Frank Marshall's history, *Football – the Rugby Union Game*, in 1892.[34] That was all the more remarkable because, like Ellis, Marshall was a clergyman and imbued with the 'muscular Christian' belief of the times. He was a strong believer in the role of the public schools in the formation and rounding of young Englishmen. Marshall would have relished identifying Ellis as the originator of the game, but instead he did not mention him.

The name Ellis had surfaced briefly twelve years before as the result of letters to the editor of *The Times* about the origins of rugby. By this time, rugby was a well-established, popular game. Prompted by the letters, a former pupil of Rugby and still a resident of the town, Matthew Bloxam,

Football at Rugby in 1870 as drawn by William Luson Thomas. The weekly *Graphic* in its accompanying text ventured the opinion: 'Of all the manly games which contribute so materially to make English boys what they are, we do not hesitate to assign the first place to football.' This was published a year before the formation of the (English) Rugby Football Union and the magazine commented: 'We cannot conclude without expressing our wish that means could be found of drawing up a set of football rules which might be used in common by all the public schools, whose respective games are now so various as to be quite unintelligible to each other.' GRAPHIC, 8 JANUARY 1870

wrote to the school magazine, the *Meteor*.[35] He said he had left Rugby in 1820, three years before Ellis supposedly made his mark. Ellis caught the ball and, according to the rules then applying, should have retreated to kick it because the opposing boys could advance only to the spot where Ellis caught the ball; or he could have passed the ball to someone else to kick. But, according to Bloxam, 'Ellis for the first time disregarded this rule and . . . rushed forwards with the ball in his hands towards the opposite goal with what result as to the game I know not.'

Bloxam's account of what he believed to have happened was therefore based on hearsay and more than 50 years after the event. No one else, then or earlier or later, ever supported Bloxam's account. In 1880, whether Ellis or anyone else ran with a ball, or did not, was essentially an arcane issue confined to readers of the *Meteor*. It only became a wider issue, and then one of great moment, in the 1890s when rugby split because the Rugby Football Union would not agree to demands from clubs in Yorkshire and Lancashire for compensation for players who lost working time because of rugby. Debate followed north–south and along class lines: the southern English and the well-off and well-educated wanted to retain control of 'their' game versus the more pragmatic northerners who saw betterment of the game through gate money and an approach founded on business lines, which included a fair deal for players. The views were irreconcilable and clubs from Yorkshire and Lancashire left the RFU to form the Northern Union, which later became the Rugby League.

A painting that shows boys at Rugby in their house playing uniforms. RUGBY SCHOOL

The split deprived rugby of its playing strength in the north and effectively handed over football hegemony in Britain to soccer.[36]

The southern custodians of rugby, and especially those who had been to Rugby School, did not like the way the game had spread beyond their grasp and they set up a subcommittee of the Old Rugbeian Society to establish how the game began. Bloxam had died in 1888 and Thomas Hughes, the author of *Tom Brown's Schooldays*, was asked for confirmation of the Ellis story. He rather crushed the committee by telling them he had never heard of Ellis as a footballer – he was at the school seven years after Ellis – and that '"the Webb Ellis tradition" had not survived to my day'.[37] No one could be found who knew Ellis, saw him play football or who knew first-hand of the supposed 1823 incident. Ellis himself had died in 1872. Nevertheless, the committee accepted the Bloxam version and so the myth was confirmed. The committee did not even bother itself with the origin of other distinctive features of the game such as the oval ball, H-shaped goals, scoring over the crossbar, points for tries as well as goals and, most distinctive of all, the offside law. Although a much-photographed plaque at the school records Ellis's feat (or rather, the society's version of it), the archivist at the school, Rusty Maclean, does not set much store by it. He and an academic historian, Lincoln Allison, argue that the Ellis story is not so much false 'as preposterous in its assumptions and implications and derisory in its provenance'.[38] A casual reader would read the plaque or hear the myth and think that the boys were playing non-handling soccer and that Ellis broke the rules and caught the ball and ran with

Artist Melvyn Warren Smith's 'Rugby Footballer circa 1870' was produced in a limited edition in 1995 to raise funds for a statue of William Webb Ellis at Rugby School. The knickerbockers suggest 1870, but the distinctive oval shape of the ball suggests the style of around the turn of the nineteenth century. ROBERT WILLIAM, RUGBY/PALENSKI COLLECTION

it. But soccer did not exist until forty years after Ellis's supposed act and, in any case, handling in the form of football practised at Rugby was legitimate. The Old Rugbeian Society took rules out of context and twisted facts to suit its purposes.

North of the border, the Scots knew all along that the English had made things up. They and the Irish played a carrying form of football long before the unknowing Ellis was pushed onto centre stage. The (English) Rugby Football Union perpetuated the Ellis myth in 1923 when it staged a so-called centenary match at Rugby School. Players from Scotland, Wales and Ireland were invited to share in the sham and one of them was Harry Stevenson, who played fifteen matches for Scotland late in the nineteenth century. A few years later, Stevenson recalled his own rugby researches and how it was received by English colleagues:

> Many years ago, when I had occasion to hunt for the origins of Rugby [his capital], I discovered that the High School [Royal High School in Edinburgh] played a carrying game round about 1810. This fact I mentioned to some of my old English football friends and others when we gathered at Rugby in 1923 as representatives of the carrying game to help to celebrate the centenary – so-called. When told that they have given the name 'Rugby' to the game but that they certainly did not invent it . . . some of them were very annoyed.[39]

The advertising agency for the beef stock cube, Oxo, uses marketing licence in saying rugby developed at Rugby in the eighteenth century. RUGBY SCHOOL

'Rugby School from the Close.' An etching by Walter Cox from a drawing by Thomas M. Henry, published in 1888. The teams are depicted in their house colours.

There is other evidence of the game beginning far from Rugby School and outside of England. The Edinburgh club known as Accies was founded in 1857 and calls itself the second-oldest rugby club in the world, yet it does not burden itself with the name 'rugby'. Accies' full name is Edinburgh Academical Football Club. And the oldest? None other than Dublin University Football Club, said to have been founded in 1854. It too overlooked the 'rugby' name, as did the oldest in England, Blackheath, founded in 1858 (there has been some talk of Guy's Hospital FC being founded in 1843, but there's no evidence to support that). To prove it all, Accies produced in 2008 probably the biggest and most professional history of any club – 438 pages unravelling the unbroken thread of Scottish rugby.[40] In Ireland, a mathematics lecturer, Trevor West (brother of former Irish referee John West), wrote a history of sport at Trinity College Dublin in which he spelt out the antecedents of rugby.[41]

West quotes from an epic poem written by an eighteenth-century Irish lawyer and writer, Matthew Concanen, which was published in Dublin in 1720. 'A Match at Football' tells the tale of a game between two villages, Lusk and Swords. The game begins with the ball – 'three folds of bullocks-hide' stuffed with 'finest hay' – being tossed in the air:[42]

> First Felim caught; he pois'd and felt it soft,
> Then whirld it with a sudden stroke aloft.
> With Motion smooth and swift he saw it glide,
> 'Till Dick, who stop'd it on the other side . . .

The match was neither rugby nor soccer; just another version of the folk football which, in Ireland's case, was in some areas called *caid*. The ball was kicked and carried, as in most games until football came to its parting of the ways later in the nineteenth century.

The Accies book, not surprisingly, gave Ellis short shrift. It noted that it was 23 years after Ellis's supposed big bang moment that pupils got around to writing down rules and 48 more years before a uniform set of rules was recognised nationwide (in England). Author David Barnes remarked drily that such facts rather undermine the suggestion Ellis changed the nature of the game in one single afternoon.

Rugby has its myths and it has its history. The contrived elevation of Ellis and the split in rugby came almost at the end of a sequence of events that saw the transformation of football from school and village games with different rules to two main games: rugby and soccer. During the middle years of the nineteenth century boys from the public schools went to the two great universities, Oxford and Cambridge, and took their football with them. Since they brought different rules, they tried to settle on one uniform set and establish a national game. But several games came

Visits to the Ellis plaque at Rugby School used to be obligatory for touring teams. The 1963–64 All Blacks obliged. From left, Ian Smith, John Major, Dennis Young, Ralph Caulton, Brian Lochore, Colin Meads and Paul Little. *AUCKLAND STAR*

down to two: one favoured by Old Etonians and their allies and one favoured by Old Rugbeians and theirs. The disagreement was not solely about handling or kicking. What drove the wedge more securely was about the level of violence allowed in the game. Old Rugbeians favoured the retention of hacking (kicking on the shins) and other types of 'manly' physical violence, while Old Etonians, Old Harrovians and others were keen on a more 'civilised' approach.[43] When clubs and schools met in 1863 to agree on a common set of rules, hacking was a major point of disagreement, and the Football Association was formed. The Old Rugbeians and their allies picked up their ball and left. Eight years later, the clubs and schools that did not favour the association game formed the Rugby Football Union. The fork in the footballing Y roads had been met: soccer went one way, rugby the other.

The differences in playing methods between the two games were not the sole distinction. It was differences in attitude which ultimately determined soccer to be the dominant sport in Britain. In 1872, for example, a year after the formation of the RFU, the FA comprised only fifteen clubs. It was as socially elite as rugby was. The association's first and most influential secretary, Charles Alcock, introduced the FA Cup to encourage interest in the game while the RFU was opposed to any form of organised competition between clubs. (It stayed that way in England for about a hundred years. It is only since the beginning of the World Cup that

'Football at the Wall' is a version of football unique to Eton College in Berkshire. The game is played along a wall of about 120 metres in length, which marks a boundary of the school playing fields. A line is cut in the grass about 5 metres from the wall and parallel to it, and the game is played within this narrow space. The object is to get the ball to the opponent's goal, which on the left is a door and on the right a tree that is marked in about the same size as the door. A story in the magazine the *Graphic*, which accompanied this sketch by Leslie Ward, said the game was 'of such a complicated nature that it would be all but impossible to make it intelligible to the uninitiated but for the excellent sketch . . .' Ward was noted for his caricatures under the name of 'Spy'. *GRAPHIC*, 29 JANUARY 1876

A maul in goal, part of the game long since eliminated. This is an 1881 woodcut from a drawing by a noted illustrator, William Barnes Wollen. Text which accompanies the illustration calls the maul in goal 'a critical event of the game and which fully justifies the vehement exertions of these stout young fellows'. *ILLUSTRATED LONDON NEWS*, 1 JANUARY 1882

English rugby has had premierships and proper competitions and that winners of the Six Nations have been officially acknowledged.) Over the next fifteen years, soccer was confronted with the question of paying players, just as rugby was, but Alcock and members of the FA showed a greater willingness to compromise for the good of the game. Some northern association clubs were found to have paid players and were suspended by the FA. When they threatened to form their own association, the FA backed off and allowed professionalism in certain circumstances.[44] Not to have done so would have alienated support from sport-loving people in the north of England.

Rugby a few years later, confronted with the identical issue, took an entirely different route. The shape of football in the twentieth century had been determined: soccer as the dominant code allowed payments, and had cups and gate money as well; rugby set itself against all three; Northern Union (Rugby League from 1922) eventually allowed all three. A British Labour politician and journalist, Joe (later Sir Joseph) Mallalieu, once argued that the more intransigent rugby became, the more it alienated possible supporters. 'While rugger was trying to cut its own throat, soccer became our national winter game.'[45]

A typical rugby scene around the turn of the nineteenth century. A photo by Harry Lock that appears to have been taken just before the start of a match between the two great rival clubs in Westport, White Star and Westport. Both clubs were based at the town's main ground, Victoria Square. PH-NEG-A735, AUCKLAND WAR MEMORIAL MUSEUM

2 Rugby comes to New Zealand

In dreams I play an old-time game at
Nelson; through the din
I hear the panting breaths of men all
striving hard to win![1]

People played football in New Zealand from the earliest days of European settlement. When there was time and when there was space, balls were kicked and passed. The games were impromptu rather than organised and were played on anniversary or fete days or on other special occasions. This description was typical: 'After dinner, cricket, foot-ball, and every amusement that could be devised went on . . .'[2] In Auckland, some adventurers explored caves in the Epsom area and one of them remarked they had often noticed 'the hollow sound that answers to the foot-ball'.[3]

The early football could have been a version of the folk or village games which immigrants had played in the British Isles, or it could have been a version of one of the games played at the public schools, or it could have been a mishmash of the lot. Short of having descriptions of the games played, let alone the rules written down and surviving for readers more than 170 years later, it is not possible to know what type of football followed dinner.

The Australian game, or Victorian rules, added to the football variety several years later. Miners and immigrants brought it to New Zealand, and the Australian historian, Geoffrey Blainey, thought it entirely natural that the game could have taken root in the South Island because of the links between the Victorian and Otago goldfields and because of the normal shipping route from Melbourne or Hobart to Bluff and Port Chalmers.[4] 'Many Victorian footballers went to New Zealand in the 1860s in search of gold or as clerks, bank tellers and merchants,' he wrote. One of a group of men who devised the game, Tom Wills, could also have brought it. He was with the English cricket team that the Otago merchant and entrepreneur Shadrach Jones brought to Otago and Canterbury in February 1864. Wills, one of Victoria's best cricketers, played for the Otago and Canterbury 'twenty-twos' that played the Englishmen.[5]

Rugby as a distinct form of football began to emerge in the 1860s and there are various versions of where and when the game was first played.

The only person to hold the title of historian for the New Zealand Rugby Football Union, Arthur Swan, settled on Nelson in 1870 as rugby's starting point and his conclusion has been widely accepted. Swan determined that Charles John

This drawing was captioned 'Football in the colonies' when it was published in Sydney in 1874, the year in which the Southern (later New South Wales) Rugby Union was formed. The accompanying text remarked that football in winter 'is the most popular means of recreation and amusement for the young men of the colony. It has become as fashionable in the large towns of New South Wales, Victoria and New Zealand as it ever was in any village green in Old England.' This sketch was said to be a faithful representation of a game in Sydney between the 'Die-hards' (striped jerseys and flannel trousers) and the 'Heavy Swells' (dark jerseys and knickerbockers). *ILLUSTRATED SYDNEY NEWS*, 25 JULY 1874

Monro, the son of a politician, Sir David, came home from being educated at a rugby-playing school in England, Christ's College in London, and persuaded his friends in Nelson to play the new 'manly' game. There is no doubt that a game between Nelson College Old Boys and 'Town' was played at the Nelson Botanical Reserve on 14 May 1870, thereafter followed by a game in Wellington which, in Swan's history, became the first to be played in the North Island.[6]

Swan had carefully read every newspaper story he could find about football and tried to determine from the content what form of football it was. He deduced therefore that the first game he could find that fitted all the requirements of constituting a rugby game – tries, handling, scrummages, kicking over a crossbar on goalposts – was the one in Nelson. Having found his needle, he showed little interest in what else may have been in the haystack. He turned a Nelsonian eye to other claimants prior to 1870 – and so has just about everyone else. Swan was adamant:

> In setting down this account of the evolution of the Rugby game in New Zealand, no consideration has been given to the period prior to its introduction to Nelson Club. While the banding together of sportsmen to play 'football' of various types . . . may have some bearing on the ultimate taking up of Rugby, their story finds no place in this History.[7]

The founder of the game in Nelson, Charles John Monro, pictured in 1930 and Nelson College in 1932. MONRO PORTRAIT, 223693, COOPER-SHARP COLLECTION, NELSON PROVINCIAL MUSEUM

There is ample evidence in the form of lengthy descriptions of the game and team lists which supports Swan's conclusion. There is less evidence, but still some, that in fact the first game of rugby was played the year before, in 1869, in Wanganui. The evening paper in the town was the *Herald*. It was begun by jeweller-journalist (and future premier) John Ballance, and carried an unambiguous advertisement on 2 June 1869 that read:

> FOOT-BALL MATCH
> 'Country v Town.' – Town accepts the Country's Challenge, provided the Rugby rules are attended to. Game to commence at 2 o'clock p.m. on Saturday, 12th inst.[8]

The game was delayed and both the *Herald* and its tri-weekly opponent, the *Chronicle*, reported the match would take place on John Walker's property at Aramoho on 19 June. And it did. The *Herald* had first crack at reporting the match, which was played concurrent with a trotting match on Walker's land. (It was called 'match' because it was a two-horse match race.) The trotting match was over three miles and the *Herald* reporter lamented that neither horse was very good. The report added: 'Meanwhile, a football match was going on between fifteen of the town and same number of the country. The match was very well contested and after two hours hard kicking was withdrawn, rain and darkness coming on. The match will be resumed on Saturday week.'[9]

FOOT-BALL MATCH.

"COUNTRY v. TOWN."—Town accepts the Country's Challenge, provided the Rugby Rules are attended to. Game to commence at 2 o'clock p.m. on Saturday, 12th inst.

June 2, 1869.

A pointer to rugby being played in Wanganui before it was played in Nelson. *WANGANUI HERALD*, 2 JUNE 1869

Detail of a painting by William Barnes Wollen that depicts a match between Newport (broad hoops) and Cambridge University. The painting was hung in the Royal Academy in 1879 and now hangs at Twickenham. This version of it was published in Australia in 1882 and captioned 'Spill and run'.
AUSTRALIAN TOWN AND COUNTRY JOURNAL, 20 MAY 1882

The *Chronicle*'s report was a little longer and a little more informative, including a clear implication that rugby rules were indeed, as the original advertisement required, 'attended to'. It said:

> The foot-ball match on Saturday was not terminated when night-fall brought the game to a termination. The country side, however, seemed to have the best of it, having had the ball in the neighbourhood of their goal for some considerable time, but were unable to kick it *over the horizontal* bar. The match is thus postponed for a fortnight.[10] [Italics added].

Also postponed, according to the report, was a running race 'as both the competitors were disabled in the foot-ball match'. Saturday matches seemed to become a regular thing because a month later the *Herald* reported that the match a few days previously was the best of the season. It did not include any more obvious clues about the type of game such as kicking the ball over a horizontal bar, but there were still references that lent themselves to an assumption the rugby rules prevailed. In one game, the Country boys had 'the advantage in weight, which was counterbalanced by the pluck and splendid play of the town boys'. The *Herald* talked of several disputes being resolved by umpires (who officiated as well as a referee) and reported that boys aged fifteen or sixteen indulged in oaths and bad language. 'Foul-mouthed language ought not to be cultivated by the rising generation.'[11]

In Swan's reckoning of the rugby chronology, the game was established in Wanganui three years later, in 1872. But there is a big difference between the words 'established' and 'played'. Swan thought the game began there in 1872 because of the arrival in the town of a jeweller, Alfred Drew, who had played in Nelson. The names of the teams in the first game recorded by Swan were 'Town' and 'Country', the very names adopted three years before. Another pointer to the game being first played in Wanganui came from Thomas Eyton, part-promoter and advance man for the Natives' mammoth tour of 1888–89. Eyton, who served in the British Army during the New Zealand Wars, wrote that he played in a match in Wanganui in 1871, Armed Constabulary v Wanganui. 'Probably the knowledge of Rugby Football by both Teams was only promiscuous,' he recalled.[12] Where the Wanganui argument falls down under Nelson's contemporary evidence and later passionate enthusiasm is that there are no team lists in existence and no mention of who played, so therefore no possibility of linking those 1869 players with later rugby appearances.

Ernest Denis Hoben, usually known as Denny, was a journalist who became the instigator and founding secretary of the New Zealand Rugby Football Union. He had an advantage denied to Swan: he could have, almost certainly would have, talked to those who kicked footballs around in the 1860s. In 1895, when he was 31, Hoben wrote a piece about the history of rugby for the Melbourne version of the English topical magazine *Review*

In various poses, players wait to see which way they will play. *AUSTRALIAN TOWN AND COUNTRY JOURNAL*, 20 MAY 1882

of Reviews.[13] In it, Hoben talked about a game at the Domain in Auckland in 'about 1869' between keen locals and sailors from the British warship *Rosario*. (It was really 1870.) The Auckland team was captained by a later politician and lawyer, William Lee Rees. But as Swan would no doubt have noted, there was no evidence that what they played was rugby. Hoben was on firmer evidentiary ground when he wrote that Rees and two younger colleagues, Billy James and Charles Bunny, played rugby at the Basin Reserve in Wellington in 1868. 'Only a round ball could be procured at first,' he wrote, 'but a Rugby ball was ultimately obtained from Melbourne and the inhabitants looked on in amazement at these energetic youths buffeting their treasure.'

An early history of Wellington rugby (written by Dan McKenzie, a secretary of the Wellington union) also included details of the kick-about at the Basin and even had detail about how the first (round) ball was bought from a shop called Warburton's on Lambton Quay.[14] Kicking about is one thing; playing a proper game is another. Hoben, as a journalist on the *Evening Post* specialising in politics and music in addition to his rugby duties, could have known both Rees and James. Rees by then was a Member of Parliament and James a well-known figure in legal circles. (Bunny had died in 1889.) Hoben moved in opinion-shaping circles, as a letter from an All Black friend, William McKenzie, indicated: 'Well I remember one day . . . seeing him [Hoben] striding down Lambton Quay in company with Richard Seddon – two men at that time carrying all before them by means of persistent application and all-round ability.'[15]

In September 1868, the *Wellington Independent* newspaper announced a match between the 18th Royal Irish Regiment and a team of civilians. 'The civilians could not raise a team and so two

One of the earliest photos of a representative team in New Zealand. Wellington players line up for the camera before their match against Nelson in 1875. From left, they are George Frederick Colin Campbell, a later auditor-general and NZRFU selector, manager and president; Peter Purves Webb, who played for the first New Zealand team in 1884; John Clunie Bishop; James Clarendon Ramsbottom Isherwood, a former British soldier; William Pattison James; Charles Frederick Wray Palliser, later NZRFU representative in London and briefly high commissioner; A. P. Morris; Alexander Bulwer Campbell, a lawyer who also played for Nelson, brother of George; A. Stohr; John George Blackett, later government engineer; C. France; Allan Bishop, younger brother of Clunie; George Fyfe Bishop, oldest of the Bishop brothers who was killed in 1916 when struck by a train while out walking; in front, Robert George Park, railway engineer and newspaper owner. MNZ-1037-1/4-F, ALEXANDER TURNBULL LIBRARY

companies of the regiment played each other instead,' Hoben wrote. But, again, there was no evidence the Irish squaddies played rugby. Whatever it was, it was 'played with much spirit and caused no little fun and excitement,' the paper reported.[16] The '18th Royal Irish Regiment' as described by the *Independent* was more formally known as the 18th Regiment of Foot, an Irish infantry regiment in the British Army. A kindred Irish regiment, the 14th, played in Perth on the way home from New Zealand and there have been some published claims that the match was the first rugby game in Western Australia. The 14th included 'many keen rugby players'.[17] The 18th Regiment, meanwhile, was headquartered in Wanganui and was the last British Army unit to be based in New Zealand.

Christchurch also had its advocates for rugby primacy. The Christchurch Football Club was formed in 1863 and when it marked its centenary, a club history said: 'Organised rugby football in New Zealand will be 100 years old when the Christchurch Football Club celebrates its centenary.'[18] There is no doubt the club was formed when it said it was and its first two games were against Christ's College, but there is doubt about what version of football was played. As was usually the case in the days before structured

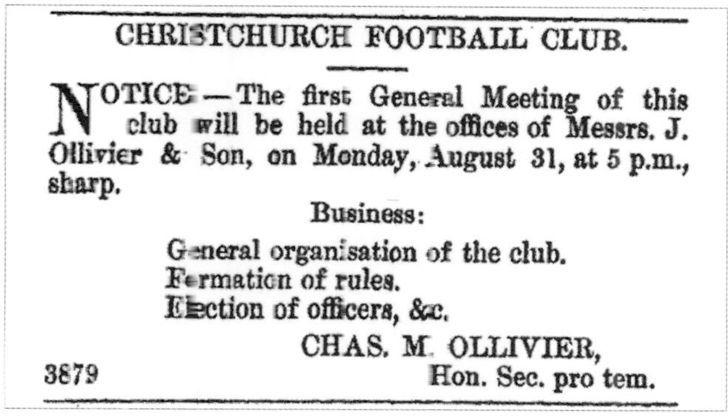

CHRISTCHURCH FOOTBALL CLUB.

NOTICE.—The first General Meeting of this club will be held at the offices of Messrs. J. Ollivier & Son, on Monday, August 31, at 5 p.m., sharp.

Business:

General organisation of the club.
Formation of rules.
Election of officers, &c.

CHAS. M. OLLIVIER,
3879 Hon. Sec. pro tem.

Evidence of the early existence of the Christchurch Football Club. *PRESS*, 29 AUGUST 1863

administration and codified laws, clubs or schools played their own version of football that may have had elements of other games added in. It is known with some clarity that the club's first opponents, Christ's, played according to 'college rules' based on a game played by one of the school committee, George Harper, at Radley, a Church of England school in Oxfordshire.[19] The college's history records tellingly: 'When Mr Croasdale Bowen, an old boy from Rugby, tried to teach the boys Rugby, they would not have it and hacked him.'[20]

A later noted figure in the Christchurch club, James Randell ('Pa') Evans, recalled that the game when he arrived from Japan in 1874 was not played according to Rugby rules, 'but according to a code of regulations the authorship and origin of which are shrouded in mystery'.[21] Swan was of the firm view that the Christchurch club adopted Rugby rules only in 1875 when it had to in order to play against the first touring team, Auckland.[22] George Macquarie, captain of the Christchurch club at the time, recalled: 'Knowing next to nothing about Rugby rules or how to play the game, I agreed to stand aside and Anderson was picked to captain our team and assist us in our practices, which he did splendidly.'[23] Anderson was John Anderson, who was raised in Canterbury and played for Scotland against England in 1872 while he was at university in Edinburgh. Some advocates of the Christchurch-first argument could be guilty of enthusiasm rather than trying to claim something that was not theirs to claim. A recent club history records that 'the long-standing contention of the Christchurch Football Club is that it was NOT [its capitals] the first rugby club in New Zealand but that it played a form of football that evolved into rugby'.[24]

The orthodox view is that rugby began in Nelson and spread out from there, a ripple from a dropped stone. But this was in an era when communication between centres of population was limited and limiting; the telegraph for communication was expensive, the post slow (sometimes letters from Auckland to Wellington still went via Sydney), and

John Anderson, the first New Zealander to play in a test match.

railways in their infancy. The Press Association, which had a significant if largely unacknowledged role in spreading and sharing information around the country, was not formed until the end of the 1870s. It seems more than possible that people with vision worked away at starting things or improving things in their own areas without knowing what was going on in other places.

Edmund Bunny, a Wellington lawyer and a man sometimes regarded as the founder of Lower Hutt, was a footballing pioneer and the brother of Charles Bunny, who had kicked the ball about with Rees and James. He recounted what he knew of rugby history and concluded: 'In my opinion there is no one who can claim to have been the founder of Rugby football in New Zealand. Each provincial district developed its own organisation and no doubt there were one or two especially active players who were responsible for the origin and development of the game in each district.'[25] Bunny was not dismissive of Monro's role in Nelson. He acknowledged that Monro introduced the rugby rules to Nelson on his return from school in London and that the game in Nelson led directly to the game in Wellington later in 1870. But he then added a cautionary rider: 'It can hardly be assumed . . . that the Nelson movement had any great influence on the early stages of the game in Auckland, Canterbury, Otago or Taranaki.' It was a valid point.

Monro's role in the formative years of the game should not be belittled. His place should be secure because evidence is on his side. Monro was not one to blow his own trumpet, although he found occasion to do so late in life when the *Dominion* in Wellington carried an interview with Robert Tennent, a friend and teammate of Monro's in those early days in Nelson.[26] Tennent had been founding secretary of the Nelson club and an occasional team captain. In the interview, Tennent described the beginnings of rugby in Wellington. Tennent's description of the game was inoffensive and in parts enlightening:

Robert Collings Tennent, one of the pioneers, founding secretary of the Nelson Football Club.

> . . . when a scrum was formed all the forwards stood opposite one another in a line. The ball was thrown in between the lines by one of the players and everyone kicked it as it passed. In those days only goals were counted. The game was very fast – much faster than it is today [1928] and the running and dropkicking of the players was quite a feature.

What annoyed Monro was that Tennent was described as the founder of the first rugby club in New Zealand, but they were the words of a *Dominion* subeditor and reporter in both heading and text, not Tennent's. Monro appeared not to notice the distinction and replied:

> I have known Mr Tennent for more than 60 years and when we were young I knew him extremely well, upon the football field and in many other relations. He has always been a man of great energy

The opening blast

A New Zealander, according to official rugby historian Arthur Swan, showed the world how to referee the game more effectively. In 1884 a Christchurch man, William Atack, tired of shouting and waving his arms around while refereeing, hit on the idea of using a whistle, previously the preserve of policemen, shepherds and steam engines.[1] A website that extols New Zealand innovation elevates Atack to an 'inventor'.[2] But a careful reading of Swan's words produces a different interpretation. Swan certainly wrote that Atack (pronounced 'ay-tack') 'is considered to have been the first to use a whistle'. He then proceeded to quote Atack, but it was in the third person, which meant Atack was either averse to using the personal pronoun about himself (most unusual for a referee) or he was talking about another referee:

> The Referee had to use his voice to stop the game, and when both sides were appealing the voice had to be exercised loudly, and he found it exhausting. Thinking it over one day, his fingers strayed into a waistcoat pocket, where they encountered a dog whistle. The inspiration came to him that it would be a fine thing to use the whistle to stop the game. The next time he refereed he called the teams together and they agreed to play to the whistle. It was a great success and was speedily adopted all over the country.

So did the 'he' and 'him' relate to Atack or someone else? Swan gave no source for the comments. Atack played and refereed in Christchurch in his younger days and became a nationally known figure as manager of the Press Association for 44 years until 1930. He was known for not holding back with opinions and had a stoush with Prime Minister William Massey during the First World War about censorship.[3] When Atack died in 1945, the morning paper in Wellington made no mention of the referee-whistle theory, but the next report in the afternoon paper mentioned 'one of his claims being that he was the first to introduce a whistle on the field, though that innovation was not recognised officially until some years later'.[4]

But whether Atack or some other referee was the first to use a whistle in 1884 becomes academic. He (or whoever) may have been the first in New Zealand, but he was not the first in this part of the world, never mind the wider world. The year before, when Queensland played New South Wales for the first time in Brisbane, the referee was William ('Monty') Arnold, who was related to Thomas Arnold of Rugby. Arnold was manager of the New South Wales team and refereed the game – with a whistle, as a report in the *Brisbane Courier* makes clear.[5]

Whistles were used the following year when a New Zealand team went to New South Wales for the first time and it seems likely that those first All Blacks went home and told referees what their colleagues across the Tasman were using instead of waving handkerchiefs and yelling. The New Zealand team's first match was on 28 May and the manager, Sam Sleigh (as 'Poster') wrote home: 'Two spells of 40 minutes each were played and the umpires used whistles on noticing any gross infringements of the rules.'[6]

During the 1880s each team provided an umpire and the host union a referee. Before whistles, they stopped play by voice commands or otherwise used hand signals and they conferred

The whistle with a story. It was originally used by Welsh referee Gil Evans in matches involving New Zealand, South Africa and Australia in the Edwardian era. He passed it on to compatriot Albert Freethy, who used it in the Olympic Games final in 1924 and to send off All Black Cyril Brownlie. It was subsequently used to ceremoniously begin each World Cup. NZ RUGBY MUSEUM

on infringements with usually the majority view prevailing. The umpires, who carried sticks which they raised in agreement or kept down in disagreement, were in effect today's touch judges. An additional official was the timekeeper who sat at a table, usually on the touchline on halfway, and rang a bell to signal the start and end of play. The first mention of a whistle in the (English) Rugby Football Union laws seems to have been in 1885: 'In any match each umpire must carry a stick and the referee must be provided with a whistle.'[7]

New Zealand can lay legitimate claim to an authentic whistle story. Each of the World Cup opening matches has been started by a blast on a whistle originally used by Welsh referee Gil Evans for New Zealand's first match against England in 1905. Evans gave the whistle to one of his successors, Albert Freethy, who used it in the last Olympic Games rugby final, in Paris in 1924, and in the All Blacks' test against England in 1925 when he sent Cyril Brownlie off (the second to be sent from the field in a test match). The whistle was later given to the New Zealand Rugby Museum in Palmerston North and its founder, John Sinclair, came up with the idea of having the whistle start the first World Cup match in 1987. The practice has been followed in each cup since.

New Zealand can claim a refereeing first for when William ('Gun') Garrard from Christchurch refereed Australia's first rugby test, against Great Britain in Sydney in 1899. He did so at the request (and expense) of the New South Wales union.[8] Australia then turned its face against so-called neutral referees and did not use another until Graeme Harrison from Wellington refereed an Australian test against France in 1981. Garrard was not the only New Zealand connection in the first Australian test: two of the players, Peter Ward and Walter Davis, were New Zealanders, as was the coach, Billy Warbrick. One of the Natives of 1888, Warbrick was also one of the touch judges (it being the practice of the time for touch judges, or line umpires, to be provided by each team). It seems to have been a commonly held view that Robbie Deans was the first New Zealander to coach the Australian team. Warbrick was there first with the first team.

> and credit is due to him for the enthusiasm with which he entered into all forms of athletic sports, greatly to the advantage of the young men living in early times in my native town of Nelson. But when he states that he was the founder of rugby football in New Zealand he is not correct. . . . Mr Tennent was simply a member of the Nelson Football Club, not one of whom had seen the rugby game, which they adopted at my instigation and played under my tutelage until familiar with the rules. No credit is due to me in the matter. My introduction of rugby to my native land was merely a coincidence – a concurrence of circumstances. Still, such as it is, I am not disposed to sit quietly down and allow my claim to be jumped by an old friend.[27]

The 'old friend' did no such thing. Tennent worked for the Bank of New South Wales and he managed branches throughout the country, taking his rugby passion with him. He could also claim a Rugby connection. His wife's mother, Emily Boor, was Emily Arnold before she was married and was a cousin of Thomas Arnold the Younger, as he was known, the youngest son of Thomas Arnold of Rugby School.[28] (Intriguingly, Thomas Arnold himself thought of moving to New Zealand. He told a friend in 1840 he owned 200 acres in New Zealand and often thought of moving 'not to return after so many years, but to live and die there'. What put him off more than anything was 'that vile population of runaway convicts'.)[29]

Monro was concerned with ensuring that the past was recorded accurately. That at least had been his motivation in 1904 when, after watching the first test to be played in New Zealand, he read an article in an *Evening Post* 'test special', published on the Saturday night, by Peter Webb, an early Wellington player and a member of the first New Zealand team in 1884. Monro wrote a letter to the editor of the *Post*, saying that Webb generally was probably the best authority, but: 'As to the genesis of the game, however, your report, like most history, is inaccurate, or perhaps I should say defective.' Monro then proceeded into some detail on how he arrived back in Nelson clutching the rugby rules, how he persuaded his mates to play the new game, and how he set about organising the first game in Wellington. He reflected on Nelson's victory against the tyro Wellingtonians:

> How we did enjoy ourselves, both victors and vanquished, and how little we thought in those remote times that football would one day become the great national game of the colony or that in the year of our Lord 1904 some of us would form part of that vast multitude who on Saturday last cheered themselves hoarse when a crack team from England was so signally defeated by our successors and fellow countrymen.[30]

In 1930, when he was 81, Monro went to Wellington for the fourth test against Great Britain and was one of the New Zealand union's special guests at the dinner afterwards. Surrounded by notables of the game such as members of the 1905 and 1924 New Zealand teams, Monro was introduced as the man responsible for arranging Wellington's first game.[31] The introduction could have been a little more detailed and precise than that, but it was nevertheless a crowning moment for Charlie and his game.

Wherever rugby was first played, it did not mean an end to other forms of football. Rather, as clubs were formed through the 1870s, it led to a period of confusion about what football they would play. In July 1871, for example, 25 footballers met at a paddock in Thorndon in Wellington to play according to the rugby rules. There was a snag, as the *Evening Post* recorded: 'Sides were chosen . . . and some brisk play began, which however, was scarcely according to the rules, only about six of those present knowing them.' Three clubs met in 1875 to reach agreement on which rules to adopt and, according to a report in the *Evening Post*, decided on a combination of 'Rugby Union

The match in this 1882 photograph of Newtown Park in Wellington was not identified, but it could have been New South Wales' second game in New Zealand, when they beat Wellington 14–2. This was also the ground two years later on which a representative New Zealand team first played. PA1-Q-120-17-2, ALEXANDER TURNBULL LIBRARY

and the Melbourne Association'. But a footballing reader disagreed and wrote to the editor saying the meeting 'adopted the Wellington [i.e. Wellington Football Club] code with the exception of the rule for running with the ball and its necessary evils, substituted the Melbourne rule by which a player, instead of keeping the ball when he has got it, is compelled to bounce it every now and again . . .'.[32] Swan noticed this extraordinary compromise between claimants for different games and said the set of rules decided on 'must be the most unique in the history of any football game'.[33]

Auckland clubs (then including Waikato and Thames) decided in 1875 to make the first big football trip and they arranged games in Wellington, Dunedin, Christchurch, Nelson and New Plymouth. The Aucklanders lost the lot, but as one newspaper writer recorded: 'The defeat of the team is doubtless a disappointment, but none can imagine the disadvantages and difficulties they had to contend against unless present.' It had been a bold and adventurous tour, especially with just fifteen players and even more especially because it was just two years since the adoption of rugby in Auckland. The earlier *Rosario* games and two or three against Thames had been under a variety of rules that seemed to owe more to Melbourne than Rugby. The arrival in Auckland of players from the Wellington club seemed to settle the issue in 1873.[34] Much of what is known about the early days of Auckland football is owed to a man hardly ever acknowledged in sporting history, Billy Robinson, an Englishman who spent 22 years in New Zealand and captained both Auckland and Thames at rugby and cricket, refereed many games and was also prominent in other sports. He emerges only occasionally and briefly from anonymity. He wrote a brief history of football in Auckland at the time of the New Zealand tour of the British Isles in 1905–06.

Auckland's bold venture forced the footballing hands of some of their opponents. In Dunedin, for example, the first two clubs, Dunedin and Union, played a mixture of soccer and Australian rules but agreed they needed to adopt the rugby rules in order to play against Auckland. In one practice match, the first half was rugby and the second soccer. In another practice match, this one solely according to rugby rules, 'the new rules manifested themselves in torn garments and bleeding noses,' according to the *Guardian*, a short-lived morning paper.[35]

One of the Auckland players in Dunedin, Fred Pilling, was a Hamilton man and played for the Hamilton club, but lived and worked in Auckland as a sharebroker. Under the elastic or non-existent rules of the time, he also played for Parnell. Two years after playing in Dunedin, he was dead. He seems to have been the first person in New Zealand to be killed while playing rugby. Pilling was playing for Parnell against Ponsonby and in the final attacking move of his life, ran with the ball towards the goal-line. He eluded all the Ponsonby players but two, James Haultain and Thomas Kerr. Haultain, eighteen-year-old son of a cabinet minister, Theodore Haultain, told the inquest that he and Pilling collided, Pilling's head

The only known likeness of Billy Robinson, Auckland footballer and cricketer. *OBSERVER*, 29 DECEMBER 1888

hitting Haultain's left arm. Other players and spectators gathered round Pilling on the ground and he was heard to say to someone that he had no feeling in his legs. Pilling was carried from the Domain to his Parnell boarding house, where he was examined by three doctors who agreed on a diagnosis of 'concussion of the spine'. His lower body remained paralysed. Pilling was said to be in no pain and told one of his visitors, in the best spirit of English pluck: 'Never mind old man, we won the game.'

In the strikingly graphic way in which such events used to be reported, Pilling was said to have complained of some pain on the Monday morning. 'At half-past nine this morning, tetanic symptoms began to develop,' a report in the *Auckland Star* said. 'A few minutes later Pilling was seized with an epileptic fit and after about three minutes violent convulsions, he expired.'

His death brought a sharp focus to the potential dangers of the game; numerous reports in the 1870s talked of spectators laughing as players were thrown into the mud or were otherwise left in undignified poses, but this time it was no joke. Even Haultain in his evidence said the game was dangerous, but this particular game was played according to the rules. 'I do not think the game should be put down,' he said. 'The charging [one player deliberately running into another] should be done away with.' One of the doctors who treated Pilling, a Dr Ellis, agreed. 'I have had six cases of injury occasioned by it within the last two years,' he said at the inquest. 'I don't think it would be possible to put down a game so universally recognised but it should be modified so as to render it less dangerous.'

The coroner, Thomas Philson, told the jury in his summing up they had the power to recommend the government prohibit the game or insist on modification of the rules to make it safer. And just so the jury was in no doubt about his views, the coroner said the game was worthy only of savages. But the jury did not go that far. It found Pilling died as the result of an accident and recommended the rules of the game should be modified to prevent similar accidents. The Hamilton club of which Pilling was a member met later in the same week and agreed not to play any more games that year.[36]

Various discussions were held then and later with no tangible result because to have 'modified' the rules to the extent suggested would have meant the game would not have been rugby any more. (Twenty years after Pilling's death, an All Black playing for Otago, Barney Armit, died after a tackle in a game against Taranaki and after lying paralysed in hospital for several weeks.)

An indication of how non-rugby people viewed the dangers of the game came in 1877 when the Bank of New Zealand told its staff that any who could not work because of football injuries would be dismissed. Rather than civil libertarian cries of outrage or threats by rugby people to take their business elsewhere, the move seemed to gain general support. That at least was the view of the *Otago Daily Times* editorial writer, who could

Barney Armit, the first All Black to die as the result of an injury in a match.

have been the editor and part-owner at the time, George Reed, an Irishman who was an ordained Presbyterian minister and journalist. The bank, the paper said, 'has given practical expression to a sentiment that is pretty generally entertained.' Stronger words ensued:

> A brutal, savage game, such as this, when conducted according to the now generally recognised rules of playing, is a disgrace to civilisation. We have before our eyes the fact that a promising youth [presumably Pilling] was very recently murdered in the game played within that province, and there is scarcely a file of papers from Home that can be opened which does not tell of some serious or fatal accident resulting from the game.

The writer went on to recite a story about a man charged with manslaughter in England for the death of a player, but the judge declared there was nothing unlawful about the death. 'That law which prohibits prize fighting and declares the cock-pit to be illegal,' the paper continued, 'is found to entirely condone the indulgence of the most brutal usage in football.'

The medical journal *Lancet* provided its view after the death of a player in England. It said that to answer the question 'is football dangerous?' it distinguished between the game as played by boys and by men. Its point generally was that boys were better suited to the rough and tumble of any form of football, even rugby, but that men, especially those in sedentary occupations, ought to be more careful. 'We would not discourage any manly sport, but we would insist that in every case the physical exertion should be adapted to the age, strength and habits of the individual.'[37]

The bank soon slipped down the slopes from the moral high ground. Within three years, the banking industry followed others and formed its own teams and competitions. This was noticed by a writer for the *Otago Witness*, the weekly version of the *ODT* that had so strongly condemned rugby:

> The fact of such a match being played shows conclusively that it's very little use trying to prevent people letting off their surplus energies in a legitimate way. I feel sure . . . every reader bar those angels in disguise, mothers, will agree in stating that football is about the best occupation a young man can have on a winter afternoon.

Patea and Hawera players plus match officials pose for a photo before they played in Patea in June 1884. Hawera beat their southern Taranaki neighbours 15–5. PH02011-2080, PUKE ARIKI, COURTESY OF ELTHAM AND DISTRICTS HISTORICAL SOCIETY

GRAND STAND AT POTTER'S PADDOCK, AUCKLAND.

Football at Potter's Paddock in Auckland, as depicted by artist Samuel Ernest Slader. *NZ GRAPHIC*, 23 AUGUST 1890

The word 'football' stood for several activities in the nineteenth century. 'Football' in a heading, and sometimes in the accompanying story, did not immediately indicate what type of football it was. Thomas Sibbin died in a practice game at Potter's Paddock in Auckland in 1891. Hands were wrung, editorials were written. But he was killed in a practice soccer match or, in the phrasing of the day, 'an Association game'.

An Auckland weekly newspaper, the *Sporting Review*, took a predictable stand that probably reflected its assumed readership, given its title. 'Of course the occasion will be improved by homilies on the dangers of football,' it said, 'but it should not be forgotten that every year presents its sad scroll of deaths due to amusement in some shape.'[38] Its view was that 'manly pursuits' would continue to be followed, as risky as some may be, 'unless we are to degenerate into a nation of milksops'. Without providing figures, it said there were fewer fatalities in football than in rowing, swimming, sailing, driving and shooting, despite football having vastly more adherents.

A poet frequently published in the North Island, especially in the *Auckland Star*, was A. W. (Augustus William) Hurry, who burst forth in rhyme from his Ponsonby home on any number of subjects. One of them was an answer to critics of rugby violence:

Long may you cling with meritorious pride
To this grand sport. In spite of some who sneer
And prate of danger. Was there yet a sport
From this one element entirely free?
Let Roman amphitheatres decide,
Or the Olympian contests. Shame on those
Who carp and jest in oft unearned repose
In their indifference or apathy.[39]

Members of the Armed Constabulary, who were both soldiers and sworn police and many of them Australians, took to rugby in their leisure hours and were involved in the formation of clubs, especially in Taranaki. The first club outside of New Plymouth was reported to have been based on an Armed Constabulary unit in Hawera. This undated photo is of an Armed Constabulary team in Taranaki in the late 1870s. PHO2002-844, PUKE ARIKI

And what type of young men risked their lives, for such was an occasional view, playing football? Were they of the Monro type, well-born and well-educated? Sometimes. Rugby was brought from its elite base in southern England, but it did not bring the base. There were people such as Rugby's George Sale and Alfred St George Hamersley, a product of another rugby school, Marlborough, who was a lawyer and part-time soldier. They encouraged the playing of rugby wherever they went, especially Sale in Dunedin and Hamersley in Timaru. In Hamersley's case, it was his ability at the game rather than his breeding, education or wealth that impressed people in New Zealand. The Dunedin footballers met a Timaru team captained by Hamersley in 1877 and one of them, Sam Sleigh, remarked: 'The Timaru men were captained by Mr Hammersley [Hamersley] and we have only to mention that this gentleman captained the English team against Scotland in 1874 to show that the Timaru Club had an advantage that no other club in New Zealand could boast of.'[40]

Hamersley played for England in the first match against Scotland in Edinburgh in 1871, the match now recognised as the first rugby international.[41] While there were undoubtedly British influences on the way rugby took shape, the role of settlers and native-born, and especially Māori, ensured that rugby in New Zealand was not merely a clone of the class-dominated game in the British Isles.

The Post and Telegraph Department regularly fielded rugby teams. This one captured by photographer Frederick James Halse is typical of the type when players provided their own gear. The team was not identified, but it is most likely to be in the Wellington area. ½-010310-G, ALEXANDER TURNBULL LIBRARY

3 Thinking nationally – sometimes

An English sport – though fair Zealandia boasts
Her crowning triumphs; for can there be found
A township named within her rugged coasts
Wherein this much-loved game doth not abound?[1]

New Zealand changed rapidly in the 1870s: the wires of the telegraph spread to capture the whole country in their web and steam engines chugged away doing their best to follow suit, though hampered by terrain in the North Island. More people travelled and learnt what the rest were doing, or not doing, more thoroughly than was possible when communities were isolated and accessible mainly by sea, by horse or on foot. And although the 1870s were a period of great immigration, the percentage of the population that was native-born was also on the rise: young men grew up knowing no other country.

It was a time of thinking nationally. Several companies which had a lasting effect on New Zealand were founded during the decade, among them the Union Steam Ship Company, and rugby took its first baby steps toward a national outlook to balance the parochial view that had hitherto ruled. The first provincial rugby unions were formed within a decade of the game taking root. But even before the first of them, Canterbury, was established, it had already played interprovincial rugby. The team went by the name of Christchurch Clubs and in 1877 met Dunedin Clubs for the first time in Cranmer Square in Christchurch. The Dunedin men wore red and black jerseys, so the Christchurch boys had to wear blue and white. Such must have been the shock at playing against their own colours, Christchurch lost by two tries to none.[2] (Blue and white were the colours of Christ's College.)

Clubs from South Canterbury, Christchurch, Temuka and Ashburton met in 1879 at the Grosvenor Hotel in Timaru to form their union. Delegates toyed with the idea of rising above their provincial status and calling their new organisation the New Zealand Rugby Union and 'to invite the other Clubs of the colony to join'. But pragmatism replaced enthusiasm. Timaru (or its environs) can lay reasonable claim to much in New Zealand sport: athlete Jack Lovelock, racehorse Phar Lap, boxer Bob Fitzsimmons. . . . It was where the Canterbury Rugby Union was formed and also was the site of the first amateur athletics club in New Zealand; it was at its instigation that the New Zealand Amateur Athletic Association took shape.

The administrative pioneers in the Grosvenor Hotel saw practical difficulties in the way of forming a New Zealand union. As the *Timaru Herald* reported:

> . . . the great disadvantage attendant on the working of an Association of the separate Clubs of the whole Colony being pointed out, it was resolved to form, in the first instance, a Canterbury Union, with which the other provinces might be conjoined to form a Union for the colony. It was shown that each Club could not send delegates to any annual meeting of the Union, if the Union embraced the Clubs of the whole colony directly, whilst a sub-association in each province could be attended and from the club delegates a certain number could be elected to represent the province at a meeting of the New Zealand Union, should one be afterwards formed.[3]

And that was pretty much how it turned out: a New Zealand union at the apex of the triangle, provincial unions in the middle and clubs at the base.

The Canterbury pioneer, Monty Lewin.

The founding secretary, Monty Lewin, was told to find out what other provinces thought. His enquiries appear to have amounted to very little because a New Zealand union was not formed until thirteen years later. Lewin was a man who liked to make things happen. He was born at Chittoor in what was known as the Madras presidency in imperial India, the son of an English member of the Indian civil service and grandson of a High Court judge in India. He was sent home to be educated and spent a year at Caius College, Cambridge, before making his way to the farthest-flung part of Victoria's empire.[4] He became a member of the Christchurch Football Club and, concerned about the prevalence of the Australian game in the city, tried in 1873 to persuade the club to switch to rugby rules. He failed then, but succeeded three years later. According to one of the Canterbury union's historians, Larry Saunders, the union was formed to keep Australian rules at bay.[5] A Victorian team apparently planned a visit to Christchurch and the Christchurch club, with Lewin to the fore, thought such a visit might deal a death blow to rugby unless a union was formed. It appears the foundation meeting was held in Timaru because it was convenient to do so the night of the annual match between South and North Canterbury ('North' then including Christchurch).

Three weeks after the Canterbury union was formed, its players were joined in Christchurch by teams representing the combined clubs of Dunedin and Wellington for a three-way tournament. During the partying that followed – with women wearing the colours of the visitors, it was disclosed – the blokes must have talked about the Canterbury union because just over a month later, the Wellington and Athletic clubs followed suit. As in Christchurch, the players led the charge. The captain of the team in Christchurch, 27-year-old Tom Cowie, who worked for the government audit department, presided over a meeting in Wellington in the Star Hotel at which the decision was made to form a union. Two of the first committee were noted cricketers as well as footballers, Charles Knapp, who was then 33, and a lawyer who had played both sports for Canterbury (or what became Canterbury), Frank Ollivier, who was 34. Knapp came from an English clerical family and worked in insurance until he moved to the Public Works Department in 1881.

Two other men involved with Wellington at the time were influential in involving New Zealand in international rugby. One was 22-year-old Arthur Bate, who was establishing himself as a sharebroker and was a busy man about town as secretary of several sports organisations, including the Wellington Football Club. He became the founding secretary of the Wellington union. Bate's influence was in organisation. The influence of the other, Joseph Astbury Warbrick, was in playing and in pushing Māori to the forefront of what became the national game. At the time of the formation of the Wellington union, Joe Warbrick was still just seventeen but had already played for both Auckland and Wellington. The second-born son of an English-born trader in Bay of Plenty, Abraham Warbrick, and his first wife, Ruhia Ngākarauna, of Ngāti Rangitihi, Warbrick was sent to school at St Stephen's in Parnell, Auckland and thereafter seemed to live a peripatetic life as a footballer and farmer, popping up in rugby teams in Tauranga and Napier as well as Wellington and Auckland.

He was not the first Māori footballer at first-class, that is, provincial, level, but he was undoubtedly among the best of the nineteenth century alongside the two Taiaroa brothers, Jack and Dick, and their cousin, Tom Ellison. Each in their own way had an influence beyond playing and, given this was at a time when the Māori race was thought to be dying out, a disproportionate influence on the way rugby in New Zealand developed and progressed.

The brothers Taiaroa, Jack and Dick.
TOITŪ OTAGO SETTLERS' MUSEUM

Bate did most to provide the stage on which Warbrick and others could perform. Within two years of the formation of the Wellington union, he talked about a combined New Zealand team – that is, a first All Black team if not in name – and bringing the other provinces into a New Zealand union. He wanted a New Zealand team, made up of players from the three provincial unions then in existence, Canterbury, Wellington and Otago, plus Auckland, to be chosen and dispatched to Sydney to play there, Newcastle and Bathurst. Bate's brainwave came in July 1881 and that was too late in the season for the people in Dunedin, who thought not enough time was left to make arrangements.

Bate tried again the following year, in 1882, but Otago came up with a different excuse for not

The 1882 New South Wales team, the first from overseas to play in New Zealand. The captain, Ted Raper, is second from the right in the front row.

wanting anything to do with it. The president of the Southern (NSW) union, John Calvert, had been in Dunedin and urged the locals to support sending a New Zealand team to Sydney. (Calvert, who was president from the union's formation in 1874 until 1915, was another early rugby man characterised as a muscular Christian. The son of the professor of divinity at Cambridge, he was a graduate of Oxford.) At the Otago union's annual meeting in May, at which Calvert's urgings were reported, one of the delegates said that since the Sydney union was the older of the two, it should travel first. And there the matter lay until the irrepressible Bate exchanged letters with William ('Monty') Arnold, who with brother Richard had founded the Wallaroos club in Sydney and had been prominent in the Southern union. The Arnolds, relatives of Thomas Arnold of Rugby, had helped organise the first interstate match with Queensland in August 1882, and they were keen on extending rugby's influence. (Another of the Arnolds, Tom – 'Thomas the Younger' – had spent some time in New Zealand and may not have been keen on extending rugby to Otago. He wrote to his mother: 'There is nothing either in the country or in the colonists which would make me wish for one moment to stop at Otago.'[6] To be fair, he wrote that in April 1848, not even a month after the first settlers arrived.)

Since Bate could not organise a team to go to Sydney, he and Arnold fell back on an alternative plan to get a New South Wales team to New Zealand, and in September 1882 it happened: the first rugby contest between New Zealand and one of the Australian colonies. Although the provinces had not been keen to support a visit to Sydney,

When mind and muscle met

After the first game in New Zealand by an overseas team, New South Wales against Auckland in 1882, the mayor of Auckland, James McCosh Clark, had to propose the toast to the visitors at a dinner in the Star Hotel. He did so with some reluctance, he told players from both sides and about forty others, because he did not understand the game of football sufficiently well to talk about it.[1]

The Ayrshire-born mayor would have been in good company. Few others throughout New Zealand, including players, could have honestly admitted to a thorough understanding of the game because even then, ten or twelve years after rugby was first played, different rules applied in different areas. Sometimes even the players would not have known what game they were playing; there were cases of Rugby (after the school) rules one half and Association (for Football Association) rules the other.

In these rudimentary playing days, the handling version of football was a heaving mass of forwards with only occasional attempts to run the ball at or past the opposition. The scrummage, or scrimmage as it was still sometimes called, was in effect the equivalent of today's rolling maul, but with most players involved. The end in rugby was the same as it has always been, to somehow get the ball over the opponents' goal-line, but the means frequently were different and confusing.

Progression was often through the forwards taking the ball upfield at their toes – the old and lost art of dribbling. An account of a move in the first match against a British side in New Zealand described the ideal: 'The . . . forwards now buckled down to their work in real earnest and gradually, inch by inch, they pushed their stalwart opponents before them, amid the cheers of the onlookers, [Bob] Martin appearing in the van with a nice dribble after the scrum broke up.'[2]

Paintings of games in the nineteenth century that portray movement and space are more a reflection of the artists' wishful thinking or of artistic licence than they are a true representation of the game. The reality was more like this description of play in the first interprovincial game, Auckland Clubs against Dunedin Clubs, in 1875: '[James] Cleverdon next got the ball pretty well clear of the scrimmage and sent it skying into the air; but on it reaching terra firma it was at once surrounded by about thirty of the players and a most exciting scrimmage took place.'[3]

Sometimes, players did not even know which rules would be applied until shortly before they played. In Wellington in 1875, one club was convinced rugby rules were the way of the footballing future, but another wanted to switch to Victorian rules. They agreed on rugby a few days before a game in Nelson and joined forces to put a combined Wellington team on the field for the first time. This was the team portrayed in an early and well-preserved photo and featured some of the notable men of early New Zealand football. Among them were George Campbell, who turned down a chance to be in the first national team, and Peter Webb, who replaced him; Charles Wray Palliser, who was briefly high commissioner in London; and three Bishop brothers who later played prominent roles.

Footballing confusion was compounded by different areas having different scoring values. In some games, points were awarded to the attacking

This was captioned 'An upcountry football match' when it was published in the *New Zealand Graphic* in 1892. Readers could have been forgiven for thinking it must have been a game out in the North or South Island backblocks. But in fact it was a game in England, sketched by William Barnes Wollen. *NZ GRAPHIC*, 17 SEPTEMBER 1892

team for force-downs, given when the defending team touched down in goal. In the Otago–Auckland game of 1875, however, a force-down early in the game was disputed. 'After some minutes' spirited play,' a report went, 'Auckland obtained a force down; but the captains not having decided whether to score for this, the points were left in dispute.'[4] The captains must have agreed at some stage because the half a point for that first force-down was Auckland's complete tally.

By 1888, general New Zealand practice was one point for a try, two points for a conversion, three points for a dropped goal and three points for a goal from a mark. A converted try was referred to as a goal. In Sydney, however, a try was worth three points and a dropped goal worth four. In Queensland, the try was worth two points and the conversion three. Then there was the field goal, an impromptu kick over the crossbar that rugby dropped in 1905. This was a description of one: 'Simpson . . . took a speculating kick at the ball as it was bounding along and, greatly to the astonishment of everyone, it went flying over the bar between the posts.'[5] (The field goal as it used to be should not be confused with a dropped goal, which is still referred to in Australia as a field goal.)

Tom Ellison, the Poneke and Wellington forward who was among the foremost of rugby thinkers, reckoned the critical time for the development of the game in New Zealand came with the visit of the first British team. New Zealanders until then believed forwards in front of the ball when it had been heeled from a scrum were offside and therefore there was a general desire to keep the ball in front of all players. But the British showed that heeling out was legitimate and back play thus developed. Forwards, it became clear, in front of the ball were not offside provided they made no attempt to play the ball when it was behind them.[6] The base of the scrum thus became a launch pad for backs to attack and this in turn led people such as Ellison to come up with different back formations, and these evolved into what is familiar today.

At the risk of making a simple game complicated, the British lesson did not mean New Zealand backs had not passed the ball before – it meant New Zealanders could be more systematic with their back play. The Natives began their tour just a couple of months after some of the players had played against the British team; it was this period, 1888–89, in which the birth of the modern New Zealand game occurred.

The British team's first match provided lessons for New Zealanders, even though it was conceded the British players were not wholly representative of the best in the game. This passage from a report of the first match shows what an eye-opener the British play was:

> Very shortly . . . it was beyond doubt that the Englishmen must win, their passing, running and dodging being alike a treat to witness and of such a calibre as we have not hitherto been accustomed to. It was not only with their hands that they passed, for their feet were occasionally employed for the same end; and it was the exception rather than the rule for a back to fail to take the ball when passed to him. The style of play indeed resembled a set of machinery pieced together, every man apparently knowing when the ball was to be passed to him and from what direction it would come – whether thrown back, horizontally, or over the shoulder.[7]

The reference to a set of machinery is interesting because it was for this type of organised, systematic play that the Natives and the 1905–06 New Zealand team came to be known.

Ellison's view that heeling out was not practised before 1888 because of a fear of being offside did not find agreement elsewhere. Irwin Hunter, an early Otago player and later writer about the game, said the ball was heeled back from an early stage. But Hunter felt that it wasn't quite in the spirit of the game unless the scrum was pressing hard on the opponents' line because 'it does away with the hard fighting and good footwork which makes forward play interesting'. Hunter was a practitioner as well as a theorist: 'I was playing football in Dunedin in 1884. Heeling out was quite legitimate then, and was often resorted to.'[8]

Andy Spence, a journalist in Dunedin and Wellington in the early years of the twentieth century, made a name for himself by writing columns about war and rugby. When the Anglo-Welsh team toured New Zealand in 1908, Spence wrote a poem for a book about the tour by a colleague, Robert Barr. Spence's verse looked back over the game's history and seemed to attribute enlightenment to the tour of 1888:

> Till '88 we played a kind
> Of ancient game of scrum and maul,
> Where muscle triumphed over mind.
> And heavy feet chased tortured ball –
> Indeed, a very stupid game
> Till '88 when Stoddart came.[9]

they stumped up willingly enough to cover the Sydney team's costs. Auckland came up with £100 and half the proceeds, Canterbury two-thirds of the proceeds, Wellington offered £50 and half the proceeds and in Otago the local union offered to pay all costs and keep all profits. The Sydney players themselves, captained by a 24-year-old lawyer, Ted Raper, paid £5 each for the privilege of being on the ground floor of trans-Tasman rugby rivalry. Only sixteen players made the trip and one didn't get beyond the first game because of injury, which meant a bare fifteen players tripped through New Zealand, winning four of their seven matches. The players wore olive-green jerseys bearing the stars of the Southern Cross in gold. Although the tour is regarded as being by New South Wales, it really was just a collection of Sydney players so was not wholly representative of either the geographical spread or the strength of the game in the colony. It was nevertheless a beginning. The captain, Raper, did not live to see the next tour. The scourge of the nineteenth century, typhoid fever, was no respecter of fitness and he died ten days after contracting the disease in February 1884.[7]

The intercolonial ice having been broken, there was now a clear obligation for the New Zealand unions to reciprocate Sydney's visit. Some people in Otago during 1883 thought it might be an idea to form a New Zealand union for the purpose, but that was talked down on the grounds that there could be only one national union, the Rugby Football Union in England, otherwise everyone would play their own games with their own rules (and some did). It was an attitude that eventually died a lingering death. Also during

The first New Zealand team. Back row, from left: James O'Donnell, Hart Udy, George Robertson, James Allan, Edward Millton, Tom Ryan, Bob Wilson. Middle row: Jack Taiaroa, George Carter, John Dumbell, William Millton, Henry Braddon, George Helmore, Peter Webb, Sam Sleigh (manager). Front row: Ned Davy, John Lecky, Joe Warbrick, Harry Roberts. Absent: Tim O'Connor. MNZ-1018-1/4-F, ALEXANDER TURNBULL LIBRARY

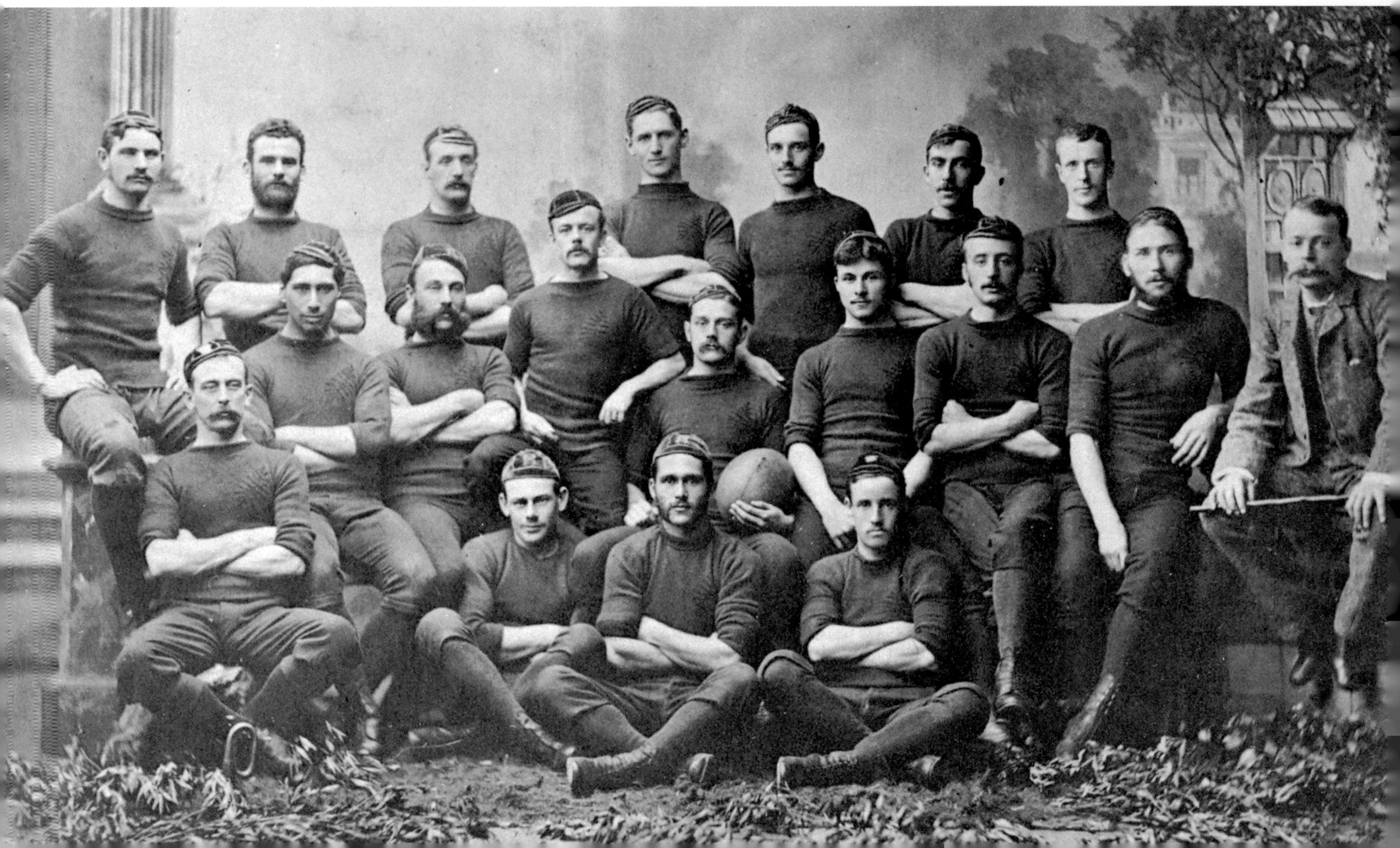

1883, Canterbury, Otago and Wellington played a triangular tournament won by Wellington and this served, in effect, as a trial for the first national team. This was the view of William Millton, who had graduated from being the founding treasurer of the Canterbury union to its secretary. It helped that he was also occasional captain of the Canterbury cricket team and during matches around New Zealand in the summer of 1883–84 he was able to play cricket by day and talk rugby by night. In December, he had written to the other unions, suggesting they act sooner rather than later otherwise the planned tour would suffer as in the past with leaving things too late. He thought the triangular interprovincial matches of 1883 so close that it was difficult to say which was the strongest, so he proposed that a New Zealand team comprise five players from each of Otago, Wellington and Auckland and four from Canterbury. He said in his letter: 'If all the unions will work together and send their contingents on some definite basis such as . . . suggested, there need be no difficulty in getting together a very strong team of thoroughly experienced players, who would drop into their respective places without a great deal of practice.'[8] The principle of selection based on provincial spread rather than wholly merit lasted, as bizarre as it may seem, for much of the amateur era of rugby, even if it was not always as overt as in the beginning. Rugby is replete with anecdotal tales of selectors' deals and trade-offs in ensuring provincial representation; there are also tales in reverse, unions complaining bitterly to the New Zealand union that they were not represented in any given team.

William Millton, the captain of the first New Zealand team.

Millton thereafter left much of the organisation of the team to Samuel Sleigh, an English-born insurance broker in Dunedin who had played for Otago and been on the Otago union's committee since its formation. It was Sleigh who co-ordinated the selection of the team, though each province told him who its players would be, and wrote to the Arnold brothers in Sydney about the itinerary, what rules would apply and what the financial arrangements would be. And it seems to have been Sleigh, in the absence of anyone else claiming responsibility, who came up with the idea that this first national team would wear a dark blue jersey and on its left breast would be embroidered a gold fernleaf. Since Sleigh's club, Dunedin, and province, Otago, both wore blue, his choice was probably not unexpected. Why or how he chose the gold fernleaf has not been handed down.

The team Sleigh thought he was taking to Sydney changed a little before it got there. Some players could not get leave from work and one asked for expenses and was told he could stay at home. But the most unusual pre-tour incident was the arrest of one of the players while on his way to assemble with the team. James O'Donnell was Irish-born and described as a 'rattling forward' and one of the fastest in the team. However, he could not outrun his creditors. The train carrying him north from Invercargill stopped at Clinton

Sale of the nineteenth century

When the Auckland and Otago players wined and dined after the first interprovincial match in New Zealand, the thoughts of the man presiding over their celebration dinner drifted back about thirty years.

He was George Samuel Sale who in 1875 was in his fourth year as the foundation professor of classics at the University of Otago. But he was at the rugby dinner on the night of 22 September in his capacity as president of the Dunedin Football Club, not as a celebrated academic. In fact, Sale chaired the dinner at the Imperial Hotel in Princes Street, just along the road from where the game had been played that afternoon, ending in fading light at five o'clock with Otago ahead 9½ points to Auckland's ½.

Sale remembered his time at Rugby School as he assembled his thoughts for his speech. At the appropriate time, he rose to propose 'The Health of Our Visitors, the Auckland team'. As an old football player, he began, he congratulated the players for the day's game. Then he mentioned that 30 years before, he took part in the framing of the rugby rules and, in the words of an *Otago Daily Times* reporter, 'he never saw a game played with better pluck and more good feeling'.[1]

The reporter did not elaborate on Sale's reference to the framing of the rules. But of all the thousands upon thousands of after-match speeches uttered and stuttered up and down the land since the game was first played, none surely could have contained such a spellbinding line.

Sale was a Rugby and rugby man through and through. He was born in the town in 1831 to Mary and her husband John, who was writing master at the school that was then presided over by Thomas Arnold.[2] Young Sale was at the school from 1839 until 1850 when he went to Cambridge, where he gained his bachelor and master's degrees and where he also taught for a time. He immigrated to Christchurch in 1860, worked briefly at Lake Coleridge Station and formed a friendship with an aspiring politician, William Rolleston. Within three months, Sale became editor of the *Press* in Christchurch, a job he held for just a few months before he chased gold in Central Otago and on the West Coast. He gained minor political positions on the Coast before the pending death of his father forced a return to England. A career in law seemed in prospect until the newly established University

George Sale, who had a hand in writing rugby's laws.

of Otago decided it wanted him for its classics chair. So he moved to Dunedin where he remained until his retirement in 1907.

His influence on the university was profound and that influence extended to the sporting fields.[3] He helped organise and play in the first rugby match in Dunedin, in 1871 between a university team and a team comprising pupils and former pupils of the High School (later Otago Boys' High School). That and a second game were the catalyst for the formation of football clubs and Sale was elected president of the first, Dunedin, in 1872. Although Dunedin did not at first wholeheartedly embrace the rugby rules, they did so eventually with some guidance from Sale. In addition to his role at the Dunedin club, he was also an energetic advocate of a club at the university.

Sale's earlier role at Rugby, to which he alluded in his 1871 speech, is still not definitively known. What is known for sure is that during 1844 and 1845 various boys at the school wrote down the rules of their version of football for the benefit of later pupils. A committee of eight boys was appointed in 1844 and they passed work on to three senior pupils the following year. One of the three was William Delafield Arnold, seventeen-year-old son of the former headmaster. They presented a compilation of 37 rules and this was approved by the Sixth Levee, the sixth-form decision-making body. The first rule book was then printed.

Sale was not one of the last drafting three, but may have been either in the first group of eight or a part of the Sixth Levee. It had to have been one or the other.[4]

By the time Sale was on his way back to New Zealand to take up his new role at the university, three other former Rugby pupils had drafted the rules of the game for the newly formed Rugby Football Union. By this time the pupils had found their vocations and, being lawyers, they submitted laws, not rules, which is why the game still has laws.

in South Otago and a policeman took him off the train and waited on the platform for one going back to Invercargill. He appeared before a magistrate that night, was freed and boarded another train the next day. Two writers of letters to the editor of the *Southland Times* wondered what on earth was going on and why O'Donnell was allowed to leave and had not paid his debts.[9] The answers were never forthcoming because O'Donnell went on tour and stayed in Sydney the rest of his life, eventually becoming a city councillor. He also played for New South Wales.[10] Less dramatically, a man regarded by many as the best footballer in the colony, Joe Warbrick, missed his ship to Wellington to join up with the rest of the team and travelled independently to Sydney.[11]

The tour in many ways established New Zealand rugby as it would continue. The team won all nine of its matches, and it was representative of all of New Zealand (at least all of the unions which contributed) rather than of a particular 'class' or occupation type. There have been occasional comments over the years about the preponderance of farmers in All Black teams or of the influence of a supposed upper middle class.[12] The 1884 team, like practically every other team to follow, was a cross-section of New Zealand society: rich and poor, rural and urban, the well educated and those who had a fleeting acquaintance with school. Also, unlike teams from other colonies or countries until well into the twentieth century, it included indigenous people. Foremost among them was Warbrick, but one who gained even more publicity was an Otago back who had just left school, Jack Taiaroa (or Teone Kerei Taiaroa). Sleigh described him as brilliant and people in Sydney must have agreed because newspapers advertised the last match of the tour with the line: 'Last great match – final appearance of TAIAROA'.[13] Members of the team are also regarded as the first All Blacks, even though the team preceded the national union by eight years. (The New Zealand union retrospectively presented the survivors with caps during the 1920s.)

Millton, the captain of the 1884 team, was, like Raper, the captain of the 1882 team, a promising young lawyer. And, like Raper, Millton was soon a victim of typhoid. A year after the tour, he married Elizabeth Anderson, youngest daughter of John Anderson and brother of John, who had played rugby for Scotland. Two years after that, in 1887, he was struck by typhoid and died.

The New South Wales team, popularly known on both sides of the Tasman as the Cornstalks rather than the Waratahs – a name that came later – toured again in 1886 and added Nelson, Wairarapa and Hawke's Bay to their list of opponents. As welcome as they may have been to provide intercolonial rugby, it was not seen as international. The first steps towards the international game came the following year, in the early summer of 1887, on the cricket fields of Australia.

Sports in the last thirty or so years of the nineteenth century largely took the shapes recognisable today, but there was also experimentation, especially within cricket. An English cricketer and entrepreneur, George Parr, sailed with a team from a tour of Australia for a series of matches in the South Island in February 1864. The local organiser was the pioneer merchant Shadrach Jones, and all he wanted was to provide entertainment. English cricket teams, some official, some not, continued to go to Australia and in the summer of 1887–88 there were two: one led by George F. Vernon and sponsored by a company in Melbourne, and the other assembled by a trio of go-getting cricketers, Alfred Shaw, Arthur Shrewsbury and James Lillywhite. They were captained by C. Aubrey Smith, later an actor in Hollywood, and were under the sponsorship of a Sydney company. Vernon's team introduced to Australia the gifted and popular Andrew Stoddart, a multi-talented cricketer and rugby player referred to as 'my dear victorious Stod' by Queen Victoria.[14] The two teams played their way around the cities and country areas

Andrew Stoddart was both a renowned cricketer and rugby player in the nineteenth century. DAVID FRITH

over the summer and agreed to settle differences and combine for one solitary test match against Australia. All the while, Shaw, Shrewsbury and Lillywhite made plans to make more money with rugby. After all, Stoddart (known by his cricket nickname of 'Drewy') was close at hand and had played for England and was once described as 'the greatest wing three there has ever been'. They decided that once the cricket was done with, they'd keep Stoddart in Australia and bring from Britain a team of rugby players to tour the Australasian colonies. The various rugby unions on both sides of the Tasman agreed, providing the team was an amateur one.

Doubts arose, however, as soon as the team was selected in England. As the players prepared to leave from Gravesend in Kent, *Illustrated London News* ran a photograph of the team. In the accompanying text, the paper remarked that in

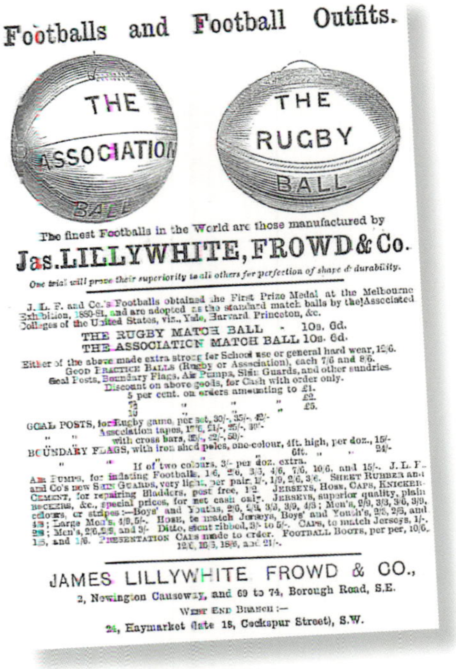

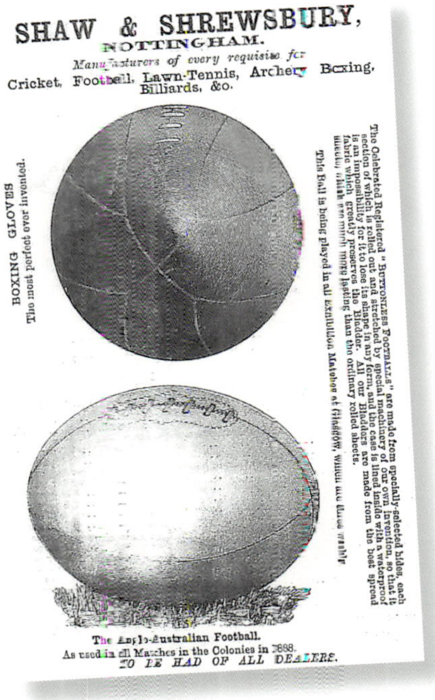

Advertising evidence of Lillywhite's sporting interests; and a Shaw & Shrewsbury sporting goods advertisement that appeared in a football yearbook in 1888.
THE FOOTBALL ANNUAL, 1888

publishing the photograph 'we desire to express no opinion one way or the other on the question of the amateur status of the team, which will doubtless be further considered by the Union at the proper time'.[15] The paper got that right.

Questions about the amateur status of the players had been raised almost as soon as the names were made public. It was not a fully representative team of England, much less the British Isles. Most players were from the north of England and only three were established internationals. More than a month before the team was due to leave Gravesend, the English union secretary, George Rowland Hill, said publicly: 'Our attitude has not changed. The undertaking has not had our support.' The *Sunday Times* made its view clear: the promoters 'have ruthlessly upset the amateur world without caring the value of a pin what the results would be, so long as they make money. Our fond hope is that they will lose heavily, *pour encourager les autres*.'[16]

The Rugby Football Union declared one of those chosen, John Clowes, who played for Halifax, a professional and told the other players that if he played, they also would be declared professional. As a result, Clowes, who was American-born of English parents, tripped through New Zealand and Australia without having to lace a boot (although he may have played in one or two of the Victorian rules games). After the team had left, a special general meeting of the RFU endorsed the action taken by Rowland Hill and his committee against Clowes and decided to discuss the tour again when it was over. Each player had to swear an affidavit saying he 'received nothing beyond their hotel and travelling expenses'. And, of course, they all did. The age of amateurism, as W. G. Grace's wealth amply demonstrated, was also the age of hypocrisy. Stoddart was said to have been paid £200 for his role in the tour.[17] More than a hundred years later modern marketing transformed the team into the first of the official British and Irish Lions teams. It was no such thing.

Statistical accounts of the tour vary, probably because about a third of their games were Victorian rules, and some of those games were not reported beyond where they were played.

The British team of 1888, the first to tour New Zealand and Australia. This photo was taken on board their ship before leaving Gravesend. *ILLUSTRATED LONDON NEWS*

An unidentified cartoonist for *Otago Punch* drew this before Otago met the first British team to visit New Zealand. It was published on the morning of the match at the Caledonian Ground. *OTAGO PUNCH*, 28 APRIL 1888

Even when they were reported, there were often variations in the scores. The most common reckoning seems to be that they played a total of 54 matches, of which they won 33, lost 14 and drew 7. Under rugby rules, they played 35 and won 27, lost 2 (Taranaki and Auckland) and drew 6. Nineteen of the 54 matches were in New Zealand and 35 in Australia. Although they lost the majority of their Victorian rules games, they nevertheless acquitted themselves well in a form of football none had seen, let alone played, before. Most of their wins in the strange game were in country areas of Victoria, but they did beat two of the leading clubs, Melbourne and Port Adelaide.

The team captain, Bob Seddon, was drowned while the side was in Maitland in New South Wales. It was the last day in Maitland before heading to nearby Newcastle, as Seddon explained

The captain who died. Bob Seddon, leader of the first British team. *ILLUSTRATED SYDNEY NEWS*, 30 AUGUST 1888

in a letter to the *Manchester Courier* found in one of his pockets. 'Today all of the team are going out driving and boating,' he wrote after recounting their activities on recent days. 'The rowing party will also enjoy themselves by stripping and having about an hour's fun in the water.'[18]

The rest of the team left for Newcastle, leaving Seddon, Stoddart and Jack Anderton, a wing from Salford, to enjoy the Hunter River. Stoddart and Anderton stayed on the banks as Seddon left in a boat for a short punt, his feet strapped in. The boat capsized, Seddon could not free himself or right the boat and Stoddart and Anderton could not reach him in time. Arthur Shrewsbury wrote of the tragedy to the Manchester sports paper, *Athletic News*:

> At first no one could realise the possibility of such an event occurring as only an hour and a half previous we had seen him standing outside his hotel at Maitland, with no hat upon his head and a cigarette in his mouth, in the very best of health and spirits . . . poor Bob stood looking the very impersonation of perfect happiness and contentment.[19]

A pall fell over the venture, according to Stoddart's biographer, David Frith. But the *Sunday Times* showed no sympathy: 'We never expressed any great partiality for the Anglo-Australian football trip and now that it has ended in the death of Seddon . . . we shall always look upon the affair with loathing, as, we think, will many others.'[20]

Stoddart took over the captaincy and led the team through its last matches in New Zealand where the play was often, according to Frith, 'outrageously rugged'. That seemed a view shared by the British players too, especially after a match against Wellington, but in the age-old rugby game of tit for tat, Wellington's players accused the British of starting it. *New Zealand Punch* published an artist's impression of rough play, though it was drawn and published before the British team had played in New Zealand.

One of the 1888 tales that has often been repeated concerns one of the first Māori to play for New Zealand, Jack Taiaroa, who went to Australia with the 1884 team. By 1888, he was a lawyer in Hawke's Bay and played against Stoddart's team. The ball went into touch and Stoddart himself, so the story went, retrieved it, bounced it back into play, regained it while the Bay players supposedly stood around watching and waiting for a lineout, and scored a try. Taiaroa was then said to say in his best fractured English to Stoddart: 'What game this, Englishman?' Stoddart explained the laws of the game. A little while later, Taiaroa was bumped into touch. The legend has it that he now knew what to do. He bounced the ball back into play, recovered it, and scored. 'My word,' he supposedly exclaimed, 'this the best game I ever played.' The story appeared in various books and papers and has been perpetuated over time, including by Alf Wiren, an early Wellington rugby historian

A colourised photo of the 1888 British team, apparently in New Zealand before its first match.
JOHN WILLIAMSON, *FOOTBALL'S FORGOTTEN TOUR* (PERTH: 2003)

and secretary. He repeated the Taiaroa story in the programme for a New Zealand Māori match against Wellington in 1934.

But Irwin Hunter saw the whole story as utter nonsense. He cited the laws of the time that did not allow such a practice and, in any case, 'Taiaroa's behaviour is that of a cheeky little Maori boy spoiled by Rotorua tourists.' In fact, according to Hunter, 'Taiaroa was a big silent Maori, a blue-blood, a man who knew how to behave himself, the peerless footballer of his day.'[21] Hunter also could have added that Taiaroa's English was as faultless as Stoddart's.

Although the British won most of their matches and complained they were under-strength when they lost to Taranaki and Auckland, the margins in all games were sufficiently narrow to encourage a view they should have played a national team. This is what the trio of promoters sought – potentially more money of course – and what some New Zealanders wanted. The Wellington union asked others what they thought of assembling a national team to play the British. In Otago, according to the *Otago Witness* columnist 'Forward' (James Hutchison), the union there was all for it and even suggested the game be played at 'some central place' such as Christchurch.

The British tour came in two parts. They played nine times in April and May before heading for the Australian section of the tour. They returned in September for another ten matches, including two against the South Island. It seems clear that the original intention was for one of the island matches, if not both, to be against a New Zealand team. But for reasons which have escaped survival, a national team did not eventuate. It was not for lack of support. The leading provincial unions were all in favour and so were some newspapers. The views of supporters were summed up in an editorial in the *Evening Post*: 'Unless the English team be pitted against a New Zealand representative team the full benefit of their visit will not be reaped by the players of this colony, nor will any real test be afforded as to the comparative strength of New Zealand as a football playing country.'[22] The most likely author of the editorial was Edward Thomas Gillon, the *Post* editor who was said to have written practically all leading articles in his twelve-year period as editor (1884–96). A writer in the Christchurch-based *New Zealand Referee*, identifying himself only as 'Drop Kick', agreed it would be a good idea to field a New Zealand team, but only if there were three matches 'in order that a thorough test of the merits of the respective teams may be got'. Such an exercise would be costly 'but . . . does not the importance of the visit of the first English football team to these distant possessions of the British Empire justify us in marking the occasion in some appropriate manner?'[23]

The talk about a New Zealand team was in May; when the British returned in September, there was nary a word. The only combined team that was fielded was the South Island, which played once in Dunedin and once in Christchurch. Both were British wins. Stoddart's men even found time to play cricket, beating Canterbury by 38 runs at Lancaster Park (Canterbury's XI included later notable statesman William Pember Reeves and lawyer Frederick Wilding, the father of tennis champion Anthony).

Shrewsbury was interviewed at length when he arrived home but made no reference to the lost prospect of playing against New Zealand. Rumours the tour had lost money, perhaps as much as £1,000, were not correct, he said. 'It had hardly answered expectations, but still there would be no loss, he and his partners have cleared their expenses,' according to a report in the London *Sporting Life* that was republished in the *NZ Referee*.[24]

For all the professed interest in New Zealand, no explanation was forthcoming about why a national team was not fielded. Since the main provincial unions were in favour of the idea, it is possible that satisfactory arrangements could not be reached with the promoters; in other words, what share of the gate the visitors would get. That could also explain why the British team did not

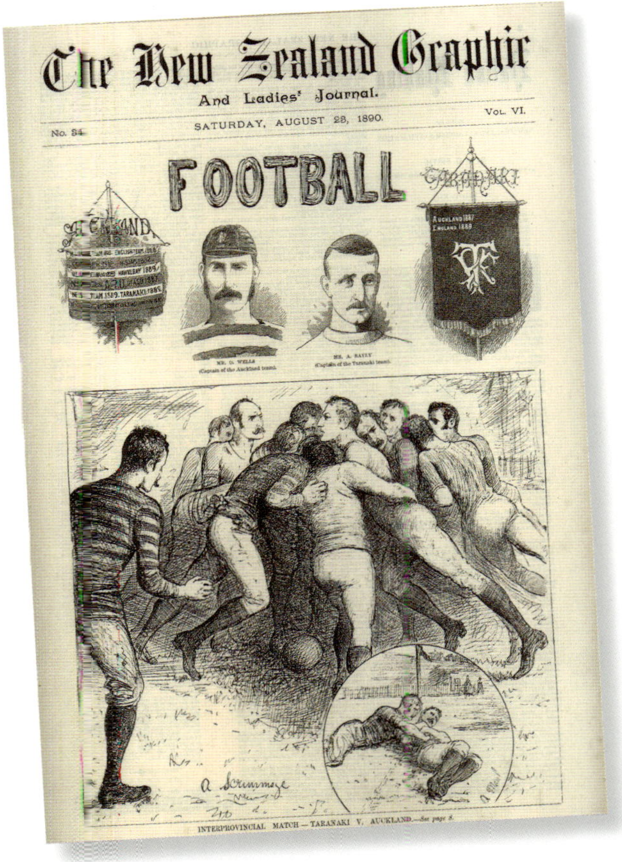

What the *New Zealand Graphic* editor thought interested his readers most in 1890. The artist was not identified, but it could have been 1884 All Black Tom Ryan, who was a regular contributor of sketches to the paper.
NZ GRAPHIC AND LADIES JOURNAL, 23 AUGUST 1890

play against the New Zealand Natives, although by the time the Natives were assembled and playing in New Zealand, the British had already moved on to Australia. When the British returned for their second leg, the Natives were well on their way to Britain; in fact, they played their first match, against Surrey, the day before Stoddart's team left Wellington for home. The supposed professionalism of the British may also have been a factor. The Natives had the support of the English union, which Stoddart's team did not, and any game between the two could have and probably would have jeopardised that support.

THE MAORI FOOTBALL TEAM: FIRST MATCH AT RICHMOND, OCT. 3—AGAINST THE SURREY CLUB.

4 The first and the greatest

The ugly duckling throve exceedingly and became the best and handsomest exponents[1]

People in England did not get what they expected when the Natives team arrived in London in September of 1888. They expected savages and they expected to win. Neither came true. But for those with a long enough memory, there was a precedent for natives taking up the white man's games. In 1868, a team of Australian Aboriginal cricketers had visited England and, viewing them in the context of cricket at the time rather than from a lofty hindsight, they proved to be better at the game than anticipated. Later writers echoed the contemporary popular journalism which had the tour as vaudevillian and a curiosity. The *Age* in Melbourne called them 'children of the forest', and *The Times* educated its readers: 'They represent the colonies of Victoria, Queenstown, South Australia, and New Zealand. Their hair and beards are long and wiry; their skins vary in shades of blackness, and most of them have broadly-expanding nostrils, but they are all of the true Australian type.'[2] Queenstown? New Zealand? No New South Wales? The tour was totally ignored when the centenary of the first test between England and Australia was marked in 1977. But these little-known pioneers played 47 matches against varying quality opposition (W. G. Grace was one opponent) and won 14, lost 14 and drew 19.[3] The cricketers were even labelled 'the All Blacks', although that may have owed more to acquired knowledge than original inspiration. The name appeared as the heading of an anonymous poem, which read:

To Britain they came from the land of the South
As strangers for honour and glory,
And now as true heroes intrepid and bold
Will their names be recorded in story.

Carl Hentschel, a Polish-born English illustrator and engraver, drew this series of sketches of the Natives in their first match in Britain, against Surrey at Richmond. It filled the front page of the *Illustrated London News* and in a story inside, the paper commented on the players: 'They are dressed in black knickerbockers and jerseys which, in the case of the Maoris, with their dusky hue of face and hands, gives them a rather sombre aspect; but they are all men of fine growth, well knit and well proportioned and are skilled adepts in all points of the game.' *ILLUSTRATED LONDON NEWS*, 13 OCTOBER 1888, 1 AND 2

For not with the sword did they covet renown,
The battle they fought was at cricket,
In lieu of grim weapons of warfare they strove
With the bat and the ball at the wicket.

The poem was included in an anthology of cricket poetry with the heading: 'Aboriginal cricketers of 1868 – the "All Blacks"'.[4]

Just two years before the Natives arrived, in 1886, a team of Parsees, as they were known at the time, began the first visit to England by cricketers from India. Captained by an Edinburgh-trained medical doctor, Dhunjishaw Patel, the players were apparently all descendants of the Parsis from Iran, the followers of the Zoroastrian religion who left Iran for India in the eleventh century to escape the advance of Islam. The team, in the time-honoured cricket phrase, did not often trouble the scorers – in fact, it won one of 28 matches and lost 19. But the tour was popular with spectators. In the last year of the nineteenth century, the ethnological showcase was polished again when a soccer team billed as the 'Basutoland Kaffirs' from Orange Free State toured the United Kingdom and played 49 matches against a variety of opposition, winning just one match.[5] Such tours were part of a culture that sought the exotic – from Buffalo Bill's Wild West Show, to the bearded ladies of travelling showmen to international exhibitions in which countries showed off their wares, including their indigenous people.

And now here were the Māori.

An editorial writer for the *Daily Telegraph*, the national daily seen then and now as a 'good' rugby newspaper, prepared his readers for the New

This is not the full complement of the Native team of 1888–89 but is probably the most complete picture. Only one player, Henry John ('Pi') Wynyard, is absent. The picture must have been taken in England, possibly at Lord Sheffield's estate in Sussex, where it is known a photograph was taken. Back row, from left: Jimmy Scott (manager), Arthur Warbrick, Sandy Webster, Wi Karauria, Heta Rewiti ('Davy') Stewart, George Williams, Wiri Nehua, Billy Warbrick, Joseph Te Rene, Alf Warbrick and Tom Eyton (co-promoter). Second row: 'Smiler' Ihimaira (Ihaimaira Karaka), Richard Maynard, William Thomas ('Tabby') Wynyard, David Gage, Joe Warbrick (captain), Tom Ellison, Charles Goldsmith (Tare Korimiti), George ('Sherry') Wynyard, William Anderson. Front row: Pat Keogh, Dick Taiaroa, William ('Mother') Elliot, Jack Lawlor (Australian football coach), Edward ('Mac') McCausland, Charles ('Barlow') Madigan, Fred Warbrick, Harry Lee.

Zealand onslaught: 'We have been invaded, and the Maori is upon us. Full five-and-twenty strong he landed at Plymouth, moved to Fenchurch St and is now encamped at Richmond, busily preparing and practising for the forthcoming fifty or sixty pitched battles to be fought in the course of the coming season.' It did not take long before the English realised there was more serious purpose than novelty, more rugby talent than showmanship, in the team. Frank Marshall, an English cleric who wrote a history of English rugby four years after the tour, noted this shift:

> In the early matches the New Zealanders appeared on the field in their native mats and headdresses, and uttered their well-known cry of 'Ake, ake, kia kaha' . . . and undoubtedly curiosity had much to do with the attendance at the games. Later, when the real merits of their play was recognised, they discarded those advertising spectacles and depended upon their genuine exhibition of football to attract spectators.[6]

Their prowess actually preceded them. A London-based writer for the *Scotsman* told his readers the Māori were 'superb players', according to 'one who has seen them'. He could barely contain his wonder when he added: 'My informant tells me, what may seem surprising to some readers, that Taiaroee [Taiaroa] at one time practised as a lawyer in Dunedin.'[7]

Once they had played a few games, a rhymester for *Punch* also saw the rugby value of the Natives beneath the layer of English expectation:

> You've come then, brother Maoris,
> At us to have a shy,
> And if we'd guard our glories,
> We'll have to mind our eye.
> Our camp you seem to flurry,
> And stir its calm content;
> You've flabbergasted Surrey,
> And scrumplicated Kent!
>
> Your kicking, brother Maoris,
> Has given us the kick;
> You're well matched all, well 'on the ball',
> And strong, and straight, and quick.
> By Jove, this is a rum age,
> When a New Zealand team,
> Licks Bull at goal and scrummage!
> It beats Macaulay's dream.
>
> You're welcome, brother Maoris,
> Here's wishing you good luck!
> With you there pace and power is,
> And skill, and lots of pluck.
> A trifle 'rough'. Why, just so!
> But that you'll mend, no doubt,
> And win, all Sportsmen trust so,
> In many a friendly bout.[8]

It certainly was many. The Natives played an extraordinary number of matches from June in 1888 in New Zealand until they returned home in August 1889. Accounts vary, but most put the total at 108. As hefty as it is, that does not tell the whole story. They also played another eleven games of Australian rules in Victoria and New South Wales on the way home. Chroniclers of the tour have mostly ignored all but the rugby. In fact, the Natives played 119 games – 82 won, 6 drawn and 31 lost. This was with just 26 players, playing three and sometimes four times a week for nothing but the glory. (They roped in five different players on three different occasions when they were caught short on the last legs in Australia and New Zealand.)

The Macaulay dream the *Punch* poet referred to was a comment by the English nineteenth-century politician and historian, Lord (Thomas Babington) Macaulay. Writing about the enduring strength of the Roman Catholic Church, he was of the opinion that it 'may still exist in undiminished vigour when some traveller from New Zealand shall . . . take his stand on a broken arch of London Bridge to sketch the ruins of St Paul's'.[9]

From Smiler, with love

Writing letters is almost a thing of the past. All Blacks are like anyone else and utilise the social media as the way of communication, even with relatives, rather than old-fashioned putting pen to paper. Among treasured memories in many New Zealand homes, and in some formal archives, are the real deal: letters which players painstakingly wrote by hand to relatives and friends.

It was not too long ago in historical terms that players on tour would go into the lounges or writing rooms of hotels – themselves more reminders of the past – to write their missives, usually in a copperplate hand they learned at school or from their parents through repetition and fear of a rap across the knuckles with a ruler.

One of the earliest surviving letters from a player on tour overseas is also one of the most delightful. It was written by one of the Natives, known as 'Smiler' Ihimaira, but more properly known as Ihaimaira Karaka by his grandfather, Te Muera Rangitaumaha.

It was written from the Glendower Hotel in Kensington in the West End of London nearly three weeks after the players arrived. This is a translation of Ihimaira's Māori:

> To Te Muera, also to Raniera
>
> Great is my affection towards you all. My inmost heart is full of love, and I cannot help keeping you constantly in remembrance. O, sirs! Salutations to you all. May God be gracious and keep you all in health who are living at that place. Here end the greetings to each of the people.
>
> And now about our travels. After Melbourne we sailed across the great water to England which we reached in a month and two weeks. I suffered most of all with seasickness, as also did Nehua. We could eat no food for over a week, but recovered when crossing the line, which divides that world (hemisphere) from this. It was terribly hot and we felt the sun in all its strength for four days, so that we could not go below at night, but lay on the steamer deck at night without blankets.
>
> We then entered the Red Sea and landed at several towns on the coast. We also saw the place where Moses crossed over with children of Israel when they were pursued by Pharoah [*sic*, Pharaoh] and his hosts who were overwhelmed and drowned in the returning waters. Then we reached the narrowest part of the Red Sea and our ship steamed into the canal dug by human hands. It is 90 miles in length and cost fifty millions. [He would have meant pounds]. The work was all done by the Arabs. After leaving Alexandria [we] crossed over to the coast of Italy near against Rome, and beheld many of the places visited by the Apostles. Eventually we arrived safely in England and on the Wednesday, four days afterwards, we met a representative team picked from ten clubs and beat them by 4 points to one in the presence of a vast multitude of people. About sixty matches in all have been arranged for us.
>
> Friends, we are all in good health and spirits. I like the travelling about greatly. I have been presented with a valuable ring by a lady of great rank. It cost at least six pounds and contains diamonds set in gold.
>
> We play our next match on the 17th October.
>
> This is all the greeting to you. May God preserve you and the tribe.
>
> From your loving grandchild,
> 'Smiler.'

But the Natives' tour had grown out of a much more practical idea. The Māori footballer Joe Warbrick dreamt of taking a team of Māori to beat the Brits at their own game. It was a dream fulfilled, a stupendous undertaking not approached in concept, size and length until the early years of the twentieth century when the New Zealanders and South Africans toured in 1905 and 1906. And the length of the Natives' tour has never been matched. It was the first visit to Britain by a rugby team from beyond its shores (a Canadian football team toured at the same time, but they played 'the Association game', as it was known).

Historian Greg Ryan argued the Natives' tour was largely forgotten and suggested that exorcising it from memories may have been deliberate.[10] But the Natives were neither forgotten nor overlooked. They had no official status because the New Zealand Rugby Football Union was formed three years after the team arrived home; yet Arthur Swan, the union's only official historian, recorded the full details of the tour in the first volume of his history (published by the NZRFU) and it was also fully covered in the *New Zealand Rugby Encyclopedia* when it first appeared in 1981. Other books have mentioned it to a greater or lesser degree. Newspapers over the years have frequently looked back on the tour and the *Dominion* in Wellington gave a full page to a story in 1988 marking the tour's centenary.

The first news of something in the wind emerged early in 1888. It was reported from Napier in January that Warbrick had written to the secretary-treasurer of the Wairarapa union, Sidney Wickerson, asking him to recommend three Māori 'experts at football to form part of a native team to meet an English team of kickists'.[11] A month later, Warbrick was more forthcoming in a letter to an Auckland player, although the intention was still for a team to play the expected British side. But whether it was still intended to be a Māori-only team was less clear. Warbrick said he was 'working up a native team' but asked his correspondent if 'Mr von Sturmer will be able to play. I would look upon him as a decided acquisition.' The von Sturmer was William Norris Ogier Von Sturmer, who worked for the Bank of New Zealand in Hamilton. His father was the second editor of the *New Zealand Herald*, Frederick John Von Sturmer, born in Oxford, England, and his mother was Catherine Jane, formerly Wasley, who had been born in Gloucester. Not a lot of Māori blood there. But there was football talent because Von Sturmer the younger was frequently

Joe Warbrick and half-brother Billy in the 1870s.
PA2-0695, ALEXANDER TURNBULL LIBRARY

Alf Warbrick as photographed by Malcolm Ross. *MELBOURNE LEADER*

mentioned in Waikato match reports in the late 1880s, though he did not play for Auckland (as Hamilton people did in those days). In any event, the bank transferred Von Sturmer to Auckland in April and that appeared to end his football career.

It is not clear when Warbrick's plan for a team to play against the British side became much grander and he reset his sights on a tour of Britain instead. Within a month of the news that he had written to various people about a team to play the British, he was in Christchurch where he said they would play the British, certainly, but then go on tour themselves. He was there as part of a recruiting trip and to seek the support of the Canterbury union and assure it the tour was not a professional venture. He ended that trip in Auckland and took ship back to Napier with three members of the team, the Wynyard brothers William ('Tabby') and George ('Sherry') and Heta Rewiti Stewart, otherwise known as Davy. Warbrick's four brothers, Alf, Arthur, Frederick and William (Billy), also joined the others in Auckland but went to Napier overland.

The passenger list for the *Te Anau*, the ship that took the players to Napier, included someone by the surname of Cuff. For a conspiracy theorist, this was intriguing. After Napier, the *Te Anau* headed for Lyttelton, Port Chalmers and Bluff before going to Melbourne. Could the Cuff have been Leonard Cuff, the founding secretary of the national athletics association and an active athlete as well as opening batsman for Canterbury and New Zealand? The question is pertinent because at some time over the summer of 1887–88 the New Zealand Amateur Athletic Association decided to award black caps to its national champions. They were of black velvet with silver piping and in silver on the front was the badge showing the interlocking letters of NZAAA.[12] This was the first known use of black and silver as national colours. Cuff's role was clear: 'Mr L. A. Cuff, the hon sec of the N.Z. Amateur Athletic Association, was kind enough to show me the Association's Standard Cap . . .' according to 'Vaulter' in the *New Zealand Referee*. The national rugby team that went to Australia in 1884 wore, as Joe Warbrick well knew, blue jerseys with a gold fernleaf embroidered on the breast. But when Warbrick's Natives first walked on to the field, they wore black jerseys with a fernleaf in white on the left breast.

Was it mere coincidence that Cuff in Christchurch and Warbrick in Napier independently but at around the same time came up with black and silver or white as colours for their national ventures? Surely that is asking too much of chance. In the small sporting world of the 1880s, it is entirely likely that Warbrick and Cuff knew each other and it is possible, but it cannot be put more strongly, that they discussed colours. If it were Cuff on the *Te Anau* heading south, and there is no way of knowing, he and the Natives would both have been saloon passengers and it would have been improbable for them not to have met and talked. Through Cuff's sporting interests and

Some Natives did not live long to tell their tales

Joe Warbrick, one of the finest rugby players in the nineteenth century and without whom the Natives' tour would not have happened, was farming at Matata on the Bay of Plenty coast in 1903 when his brother Alf got into the headlines for what Alf himself called a foolhardy stunt.

Alf Warbrick, the second oldest of the Warbrick boys, was a celebrated guide in the thermal region of the North Island and in 1903 rose to a challenge by an English adventurer, Horace Buckridge, to row across the superheated, roiling water of the Waimangu Geyser crater lake. Waimangu was then at the height of its fame, frequently belching forth the contents of its small lake more than 300 metres into the air.

'A few minutes after we put out from the shore,' Alf Warbrick wrote, 'we were immersed in steam rising in thick clouds from the boiling water, and the heat was almost intolerable. However, I succeeded in rowing safely across and about the pool, and altogether we were about twelve minutes on the water.'[1] (Buckridge was killed later in 1903 when hit by a boom while sailing a yacht west of the Chathams.)

Alf Warbrick and Horace Buckridge shrouded in steam during their row across the Waimangu crater lake.
ALF WARBRICK, *ADVENTURES IN GEYSERLAND*
(WELLINGTON: A. H. & A. W. REED, 1934)

Warbrick's stunt was reported throughout New Zealand. Joe Warbrick, then aged 41, read of it and decided to visit his brother and to see what all the fuss was about, and he hoped he would see the geyser 'play'.

Alf guided Joe and some tourists towards the geyser on Sunday, 30 August 1903. Alf knew its habits and thought 'a big shot' was likely. Three Australians watched from what Alf thought a dangerous spot and he told them they should move to a safer position. They did. But soon after, Joe and two sisters on a visit from Rangiora, Katherine, twenty, and Ruby Nicholls, nineteen, and a young man from Auckland, David McNaughton, moved down a path towards where the three men had been. Worried, Alf shouted a warning. He then appealed to the girls' mother, Helen (known as 'Nellie') who was with him. She tried to call her daughters back. 'It is all right, Mother,' one of them cried. Nellie's third daughter, Beatrice, had stayed in Auckland with relatives rather than make the trip to Rotorua.

Alf Warbrick guided the rest of his party to higher ground then went back with Nellie Nicholls for the others. Warbrick saw them in the distance and said: 'There they are . . .' Anything else he might have said was drowned out by the roar of the geyser's eruption. Mud, ash, rocks, boiling water were thrown violently into the air. Warbrick and Nellie Nicholls were covered in ash and mud but, fortunately for them, the rocks fell short; he carried her back to safety then with others from the party, returned to the scene of the eruption. About 500 metres from where they had been overwhelmed, Warbrick found his brother, dead. 'His coat had caught on a stump and had arrested further progress down the mountain torrent. After some little time I managed to lift him on to dry ground.'

A hundred metres further on, the body of one of the sisters was jammed between two big rocks. The other was found lying in sand and, further on, McNaughton's body was found. As Alf Warbrick later recalled, the geyser asserted its ferocious mana by taking toll of four lives. 'It seemed to be exacting a demoniacal revenge' (for crossing it in the boat a fortnight before).

An inquest in Rotorua two days later found no blame attached to Alf Warbrick and the jury determined his brother, the sisters and McNaughton 'were accidentally suffocated and killed by boiling water or steam, or both steam and water, combined

An eruption of the Waimangu Geyser, similar to that which claimed the lives of Joe Warbrick and three visitors.

with shock . . .'. Warbrick's body was taken to Matata for a tangi, McNaughton's to Auckland where he was buried on the following Wednesday. Nellie Nicholls, whose husband Walter had died during a visit to Britain the previous year, and daughter Beatrice were joined in Auckland by relatives and sailed with the bodies of the two sisters for Lyttelton. (Beatrice married Derrick Warner Westenra in Christchurch in 1910 and among their children was 'Jerry' Westenra, a noted fighter pilot in the Second World War. A later link in the same genealogical chain was the singer, Hayley Westenra.)

Journalist Malcolm Ross described meeting Alf Warbrick in Rotorua in 1895:

> Have you ever seen Warbrick? If not you have missed seeing as fine a type of physical and intellectual manhood as you will see in a day's march in Maoriland. He stands over 6 feet high, a powerfully limbed, deep-chested, handsome fellow, with the dark expressive eyes of his mother's people and a complexion that has caught somewhat of the fairer glow of the pakeha blood, which, united with the best and the purest of an ancient and noble people, has given to Rotorua a model guide, a brave and strong man and – a gentleman.[2]

Some of the Natives did not live even as long as Joe Warbrick to tell their tales.

The tour finished towards the end of winter in 1889; by the end of the year, two were dead; within a decade, four more had died. Another eight died within the next ten years. The causes of some of the early deaths were attributed to the tour, though there can be no way of proving that.

Sandy Webster of Auckland was the first to die, just a month after the end of the tour. He had left the team in Britain, preferring to go straight home rather than play in Australia. He spent a few days in Auckland before he went to stay with his parents William and Annabella at Wairere, Hokianga. He then took a job as manager of a

Alf Warbrick, left, and John Vigor-Brown, the mayor of Napier, centre, at Eden Park in 1925 when Auckland and Hawke's Bay drew.

company collecting guano at Long Island in the central Pacific, the eastern extremity of what is now Kiribati. He hadn't been there long when he had a foot crushed by a railway trolley that was delivering guano to the wharf. Since there were no medical facilities on the island, he was put on board the brigantine *Oamaru* to be taken to Dunedin. But the wound became infected, tetanus ('lockjaw' as it was known) set in and he died five days into the voyage.[3]

In the fond way newspaper writers spoke of players (quite often because the author was a fellow player), Webster was described as being 'of a genial, kindly nature, popular with all whose fortune it was to know him'. He was said to have kept a 'first-rate diary' of the tour but unfortunately it has never been published and is now impossible to trace.

Five of the players died from tuberculosis, or consumption as they knew it. Rudimentary medical knowledge and a lack of effective drugs (before the development of antibiotics) meant the disease was often fatal. The first to die, Wi Karauria, did not see the year out. Newspapers didn't fudge his cause of death in December. He died of consumption, they said, brought on by conditions on the rugby tour.[4] A former police inspector and Canterbury forward and contemporary of the Natives, John Cassells, agreed. Writing more than 30 years after the tour, he said: 'The unfortunate part about it was the season at Home was very miserable, with a lot of rain and sodden grounds everywhere. As a result, many of the men died from consumption on their return.'[5]

Charles Goldsmith, more properly known as Tare Korimiti, died in August 1893, but a report of his death undermined the theory that players became infected in Britain because of poor weather and cramped conditions in hotels and trains. 'He caught cold while engaged on a survey and became a victim to that fell disease, consumption,' the *Poverty Bay Herald* reported.[6] The others to succumb to tuberculosis were Charles 'Barlow' Madigan in 1896 and Warbrick brothers William (1901) and Frederick (1904).[7]

William Anderson from Thames was described by Thomas Eyton in his book of the tour as 'the hardest grafter in the team; always on the ball and did a tremendous lot of useful work'.[8] When Anderson resumed playing for Thames in the 1890 and 1891 seasons, his form was said to have been not up to the standard he reached in England. He died in early 1892, and readers of the *Thames Star* learned: 'It appears that while on the football tour in the Old Country he received a severe internal strain, from the effects of which he never recovered, and his death is attributed to this.'[9]

Richard Maynard of Poverty Bay was regarded by Eyton as 'one of our very best'. He died of typhoid fever in Gisborne in January 1897. The fact the *Poverty Bay Herald* called him the first victim of typhoid that summer was an indication it was a deadly disease with which the paper's staff was sadly familiar.[10]

Another of the Natives suffered a horrific death. The player known throughout the tour as Joseph Te Rene was killed when he tried to jump on to a moving train at Waikanae on the Kapiti coast. Te Rene, 38, was with a group of Māori, including his wife, who had been to Otaki to see the Māori king, Mahuta Tāwhiao I, who was a distant cousin. They were on their way home to Porirua when the train stopped at Waikanae. Te Rene jumped down on to the platform to speak to someone and while he was still on the platform, the train began gliding out of the station. Te Rene, according to reports, ran and tried to jump on to a viewing platform at the back of the first carriage, but was stopped by a railway guard. He then ran past the guard and tried to grab a handrail but 'spectators saw him lurch forward and fall right under the carriages'.[11]

Te Rene suffered injuries which could not have been survivable. Both legs were said to have been cut off and he also had head, arm and torso injuries. People got his body back onto the train in the hope that he would survive long enough to be seen by a doctor at Porirua, but he had died by the time the train reached Paekakariki, two stops south. One newspaper reported: 'The pitiful incident was made more melancholy by the fact that [the] deceased's wife was on the train. Frenzied with grief, she attempted to throw herself under the carriages while the cars were in motion.'

The longest-lived of the Natives, William Elliot. He was nicknamed 'Mother', according to Auckland writer Ernest Eyre, 'because of the kindly attentions he bestowed on the boys after a jovial night out'.

Five Warbrick brothers went on the tour. The second to die was Arthur who, at the age of 39 in 1902, was drowned when he was swept out to sea at the mouth of Ohiwa Harbour west of Opotiki. He was employed by the local council as a ferryman to get passengers across the broad mouth. He was alone in his boat when it was apparently overturned in heavy weather.[12]

Joe Warbrick was the third of the brothers to die and the last of them, Alf, died in 1940. Two more of the Natives, Harry Lee and Tom Ellison, died in 1904, and another, 'Davy' Stewart, died of Bright's disease (nephritis) in 1909.[13]

The last survivor of the team was 'Mother' Elliot, who died in Auckland in 1958.[14]

his job with South British Insurance, he did travel around the country. (Cuff helped rugby when he could. In 1892, when he led an athletics team to England, he talked to rugby authorities about the prospects of a New Zealand tour. One of the athletics team's constant supporters was one of the 1884 rugby players, Tom Ryan, who was on his way to studying art in Paris.)

There have been other versions of how black and a silver fernleaf became emblematic of New Zealand. The choice of black may have been simply pragmatic. Since the Natives before they left thought they were playing in each of the British countries (Ireland then being constitutionally British), it would not have made a great deal of sense to sport jersey colours which were already being used there. Sam Sleigh, who underwrote and managed the 1884 tour, had by this time gone back to Britain, where he lived in retirement. He was a member of the (English) Rugby Football Union and agreed to act as tour planner and co-ordinator for the Natives. Clashes of jersey colours were not looked kindly upon and Sleigh would have ensured Warbrick knew, if he did not know already, that Scotland wore blue, England white, Wales scarlet and Ireland green. Some of the Natives were from Wellington, which wore black, and the team was based for its first few weeks in Hawke's Bay, which had black as part of its colours. Nearly 40 years later, a reporter for the *Evening Post* in Wellington tried to establish the origins of black. He spoke to one of the surviving Natives, George Williams, otherwise known as 'Bully'. Williams told the reporter he was present when Warbrick chose black and the reason was it was 'the most suitable colour to withstand the wet and sloppy playing fields which were likely to be experienced in England'. A player who chose not to join the Natives because of family circumstances, Jack Webster, agreed. Just to add to the intrigue, when the Natives first played a warm-up game in Napier, the local paper reported their jersey colours to be blue. Whether that was just a simple mistake or

One of the most significant members of the Natives team, Tom Ellison, and his cap from the tour.
NZ SPORTS HALL OF FAME

whether they wore blue until black jerseys became available cannot be known.

The same *Evening Post* story that covered the origin of the jersey colour also came up with a novel reason for the silver fern. The Wellington team was on its way north through the Hutt Valley in 1887 on its way to play Wairarapa in Greytown and the train stopped at Hayward's Farm, an area known in Wellington now as providing a road to the coast. One of the Wellington players, Michael Hyland, said that 'Miss Hayward gave one of our boys a fernleaf and asked him to wear it for luck'. As a result, according to Hyland, two of his team-mates, Tom Ellison and Davy Gage, both members of the Natives, suggested the silver fern for the jersey. A lovely story, but spoilt by facts, especially

This is the most commonly used photograph of the 1888–89 Natives, though it does not include the whole party. It must have been taken in Auckland before the team's strength was supplemented by Pākehā, but some of the Natives are also missing. Those not included were William Anderson, William ('Mother') Elliot, Pat Keogh, Harry Lee, Charles Madigan, Edward ('Mac') McCausland, Wiri Nehua, Joseph Te Rene, Henry ('Pi') Wynyard and the team's advance man, Thomas Eyton, who may have been on his way to Melbourne when the photo was taken. Also missing is the Australian rules coach who accompanied the team, Jack Lawlor, but he would have still been with the British team at the time. Behind the players are the flags of the United Tribes and a Union Jack. The photographer was Edward Beauchamp Singleton Mercer, a son of Captain Henry Mercer, a British artillery officer killed at the Battle of Rangiriri in 1863. Mercer, who had been declared bankrupt in 1887, evidently left Auckland in 1889 and died in Bulawayo in 1905. Back row from left: Arthur Warbrick, Sandy Webster, Jimmy Scott, George Williams, Billy Warbrick, Alf Warbrick. Middle row: Ihaimaira Karaka, William ('Tabby') Wynyard, Davy Gage, Joe Warbrick, Fred Warbrick, George ('Sherry') Wynyard. Front row: Dick Taiaroa, Tom Ellison, Richard Maynard, Wi Karauria, Charles Goldsmith.

the fact the fernleaf had been used on the first team's jersey in 1884 (if in gold).[13]

The idea of the tour was Warbrick's and no one has claimed otherwise, but a former English soldier-settler who had gone back to Britain on holiday, Thomas Eyton, was of a like mind. Eyton soldiered around the North Island for much of the 1860s and gained 60 acres of prime real estate for his service with the Taranaki Militia, then moved on to the Treasury in Wellington.[14] In 1887, he took his seventeen-year-old daughter Sarah to show off his homeland and have a look at Queen Victoria's fiftieth jubilee celebrations. Father and daughter also watched some rugby in late 1887.

> I witnessed some important matches played at the Rectory Field, Blackheath, and it seemed to me that that play I saw was not vastly superior

> to that I had seen in New Zealand and that if a Team from this Colony – especially Maoris or Half-castes – could be taken back to England, and brought to up-to-date form, such a venture would prove a success in every respect.[15]

The Eytons arrived back in New Zealand in late March 1888 to find that Warbrick was well under way with organising what Eyton had wanted to plan. He wrote to Warbrick and the upshot was that he joined the venture as the advance man. Warbrick had already hired a manager, Gisborne hotelier Jimmy Scott.

Warbrick's planned match against the Seddon/Stoddart Englishmen did not come to pass, perhaps because he and the English promoters could not 'agree on terms', as the phrase of the day had it, perhaps because Warbrick did not want his team tainted by the professional rumours about the English, or perhaps simply because logistics did not allow it. The English were in New Zealand in May before going to Australia for the best part of three months, returning in early September. The Natives played their first home game in late June and by September were well on their way to Britain.

It was not quite the Native team Warbrick had envisaged. He realised during their nine matches at home that they needed strengthening in some positions, especially after he broke a bone in an ankle in a loss to Auckland. Gradually, five Pākehā were added and the Māori team, as it was originally to be named, became the Natives on the basis that all were native-born, that is, born in New Zealand. But they were not. One was an Anglo-Irishman born in Birmingham, Pat Keogh and another, 'Mac' McCausland, was born in Victoria. Nevertheless, the New Zealand Native football team they were. They also took with them to Britain an Australian rules footballer, Jack Lawlor. He was hired by Scott while the team was in Melbourne en route to Britain, and the plan was that during the tour he would teach the Natives about the Australian game so they could acquit

Pat Keogh in the full Native playing uniform.

themselves well in Victoria on their way back. But it did not work out that way. Eyton thought it was a bad idea and said so, and he was fully vindicated. The Natives were so busy playing rugby in Britain, at least three games a week and sometimes four, they had no time to practise another game, given the amount of slow train travel they had as well. Lawlor, who filled a similar role with the English team in New Zealand and Australia and with more success, cost the Natives £200.

Before, during and after their tour the Natives had to contend with the vexed and hypocritical issue of professionalism. So-called amateur cricketers demanded huge sums of money to tour yet still somehow managed to call themselves, and be called by others, amateurs. Any hint that rugby players might do the same brought down the wrath of god

The ruler of English rugby for nearly forty years, George Rowland Hill.

or George Rowland Hill of the English union, who some thought was the same thing. A news report that the Natives were to be paid, in fact that some thought they were not being paid enough, appeared a month or so before the team left. It caused some rumblings in provincial unions and Warbrick had to assure them the tour was not professional and players would not benefit financially. Sleigh delivered assurances at the other end to Rowland Hill. The tour was conducted against the background of the Clowes affair that blighted the English tour and the increasing awareness that the northern counties of England did not have the same attitude to amateurism as did the southern counties. To rugby people in New Zealand, the RFU's strict amateurism regulations were framed in England for English players in English conditions. Their application beyond the seas was not considered. Eyton wrote after the Natives' tour: 'It seems to me that in the case of teams on an extended tour, such as that of the Native team, something besides actual travelling and hotel expenses must be allowed. While not advocating an actual wage to players, I consider they should receive pocket money. . . .'[16] One of the more thoughtful of the Natives, Tom Ellison, wrote along similar lines: 'Personally, I think that these laws were never intended to apply to extended tours abroad. Such tours were never contemplated at the time the rules were framed. However, if I am wrong in this view, I think that the law should be under certain circumstances relaxed.'[17]

The Natives found themselves in the vanguard of a running battle that New Zealanders, and southern hemisphere countries generally, had with British unions and the International Rugby Board for more than a hundred years. Indeed, the determinedly Anglocentric view of international rugby is still evident to those attuned to such matters. (Rugby of course was not the only English-based amateur sport; rowing was one of the leaders when it banned professional watermen, and the amateur code dominated the Olympic Games and other multisport events for most of the twentieth century. But it is rugby that is being discussed here and it was in rugby that amateurism had its greatest effect in New Zealand.)

Far from being professional and making the players oodles of money, the Natives' tour was essentially a financial flop: too many games, not enough paying spectators. In some places, there were plenty of spectators but they were ground members and therefore watched for their annual fee rather than a match fee. The manager, Jimmy Scott, who was declared bankrupt five months after the tour, declared it to be 'a dead loss'. Greg Ryan's study concluded that it broke even. Scott's bankruptcy was one indicator; an even better one, and more poignant, came in Sydney towards the end of the tour when Joe Warbrick sold his korowai, his feather cloak or cape, for £4. He had worn it throughout the tour when standing on the touch line as either a spectator or touch judge; it would have meant much to him and to New Zealand. But instead it stayed in Sydney. It now rests in the Australian Museum.

The Natives ran head on into the pitfalls of touring that every team since has encountered one way or another. One came in their match against England. Bizarrely, Rowland Hill appointed himself referee. In modern terms, that would be like the chief executive of the New Zealand union appointing himself referee of an All Black match. Ellison and other players criticised several of Rowland Hill's decisions during the match, but the one that rankled most was when Ellison tackled Andrew Stoddart and Stoddart's shorts ripped apart. In modest manner, the Natives gathered around Stoddart to protect his dignity in case maidens in the crowd did not avert their gaze. While this was happening, one of the England players, Frank Evershed, grabbed the ball and ran and scored a try. The Natives remonstrated with Rowland Hill and three of them left the field in disgust. Rowland Hill allowed the try, signalled play to continue despite the Natives being three men down and then, back with his secretary's hat on, after the game demanded an apology from the Natives. It was delivered but relations between them and the English officials were said to be never the same again.

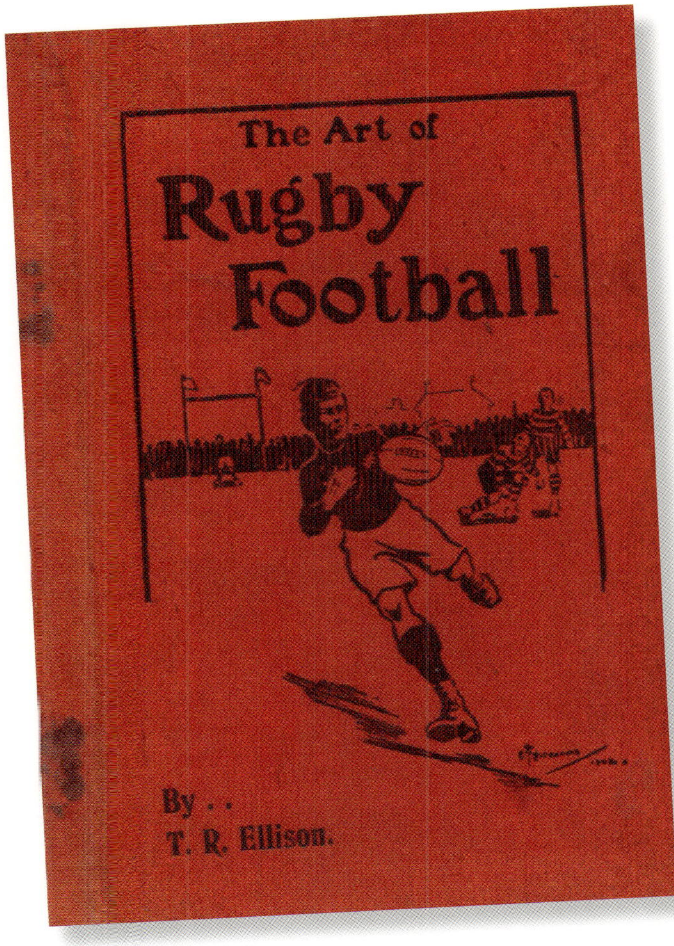

One of the earliest and now one of the rarest books on the game, Tom Ellison's *The Art of Rugby Football*.

The Natives had difficulties of an entirely different kind when they played Middlesex. The match was at the country estate of the Earl of Sheffield in rural Sussex. Yes, Middlesex in Sussex. The players were told it would be more of a social occasion than serious sport and it was intended as an opportunity for the Earl to extend his celebrated cricket patronage to rugby and for the players to have a relaxing day with the aristocracy. Without the Natives knowing, however, Middlesex officials set about choosing the best side they could find, including English and Welsh internationals. Before the game, there was a sumptuous lunch with alcohol. The Natives got stuck in – to both. The English, having seen it all before, stood back. The result of the following match was inevitable. Middlesex won 9–0 and the Natives thought they had been conned. The referee was the ubiquitous Rowland Hill. It was reported that when the Natives were required after the game for a team photo, two of them were found sound asleep in some shrubbery.

The alcohol-induced slumber may have been exacerbated by sheer exhaustion. Between the first week of October 1888 and the end of March 1889, they played 75 matches – with 11 before getting to Britain and another 33 after leaving it. Just take the first week of March as an example: on the 2nd they

The Natives and Jack the Ripper

Dickensian London was also Jack the Ripper's London when the Native team arrived there at the end of September 1888. By then, the unknown murderer who terrorised the Whitechapel area of the East End had already claimed his first two victims. Two more women died while the team was based in London before its first game and the fifth confirmed victim died after the team had left for the north.

The players, like everyone else in London, would have been well aware of the fear and loathing created in the narrow, dirty, smog-bound East End. The *Penny Illustrated Paper*, which was precisely what it sounded, warned of a 'Reign of Terror' (its capitals) in London in its issue of 6 October. Players could have read the paper in their railway carriage on the way from London to Northampton for their second game. The paper's artist had gone from Fleet Street to the East End and sketched what he was allowed to see, including a draped corpse in the mortuary.

It would have been a shocking introduction for the players to the biggest city in the world and one they would have seen as the glamorous heart of the Empire. The murders occurred in the East End and the players were staying at the Glendower Hotel in Kensington, just a few miles but a material world away in the West End. But they may have had a closer link to the murders, which were never solved and which continue to fascinate as the number of books, films and websites indicates.

One of the suspects was a member of the rugby fraternity with which the players mixed. It is in the nature of such events that the space left by an absence of proof is always happily filled by conspiracy theorists and, in the case of Jack the Ripper, there has been no shortage of suspects. One of them has been Montague John Druitt, a well-educated upper-middle-class son of a Dorset surgeon.

The Metropolitan Police take a more objective, sober view of possible suspects and still name just four on its website.[1] Druitt is one of them. Druitt has been both accused and defended by conspirators. There is no doubt he was 'in the mix', as a detective schooled in rugby clichés might have said. Druitt is assumed to have committed suicide in December 1888 after the five confirmed Jack the Ripper murders. As many as ten murders after that are regarded as possible Ripper victims. Druitt's decomposing body was found in the Thames near Chiswick in West London on the last day of December.

One of the main policemen associated with the fruitless search for the killer, Assistant Chief Constable Sir Melville Mcnaghten, named Druitt as a suspect, but the veracity of his contention was somewhat undermined when he described him as a 41-year-old doctor when in fact Druitt had been a 31-year-old lawyer. Evidence against Druitt seems scant and based almost solely on his suicide following so closely the fifth of the confirmed Ripper murders. Nevertheless, his place among the four suspects continues on the Metropolitan Police website.[2]

Bloggers, ignoring the inconvenient need for evidence and happily aware dead people cannot sue, can say what they like and there has been a welter of speculation about Druitt's physical and mental health and his sexual persuasion. What seems to be less well known about him was that he rubbed shoulders with the leaders of English rugby and was one of the directors of the Blackheath club, a bastion of amateurism in English rugby, when it made a share issue. A notice announcing the incorporation of the club lists Druitt as its honorary secretary and also as a director. Other directors were George Rowland Hill, the leading administrator of English rugby until the 1920s, and Harry Vassall, like Rowland Hill an archetypal gentleman amateur and treasurer of the English union.

Druitt's address was given as 9 Eliot Place, Blackheath, which was in fact the address of George Valentine's School where Druitt had been assistant schoolmaster. Accommodation at the school was part of his position. He apparently took the job to supplement his income as a lawyer in days when lawyers were not well paid. Druitt was dismissed from the job at the end of November for 'getting into serious trouble', according to evidence at his inquest. That was never explained. His dismissal may have been a reason for his suicide.

While it is not likely the players would have met Druitt in the brief time they were in London at the start of the tour, they certainly became well acquainted with Hill, Vassall and others, and it would scarcely be credible to suggest they did not discuss the events in East London or the suicide of Druitt. Aside from his role at the Blackheath club, Druitt was a noted cricketer (although never played a first-class game), hockey player and rugby player. He did not receive a blue for rugby at Oxford but did play for his college, New College.

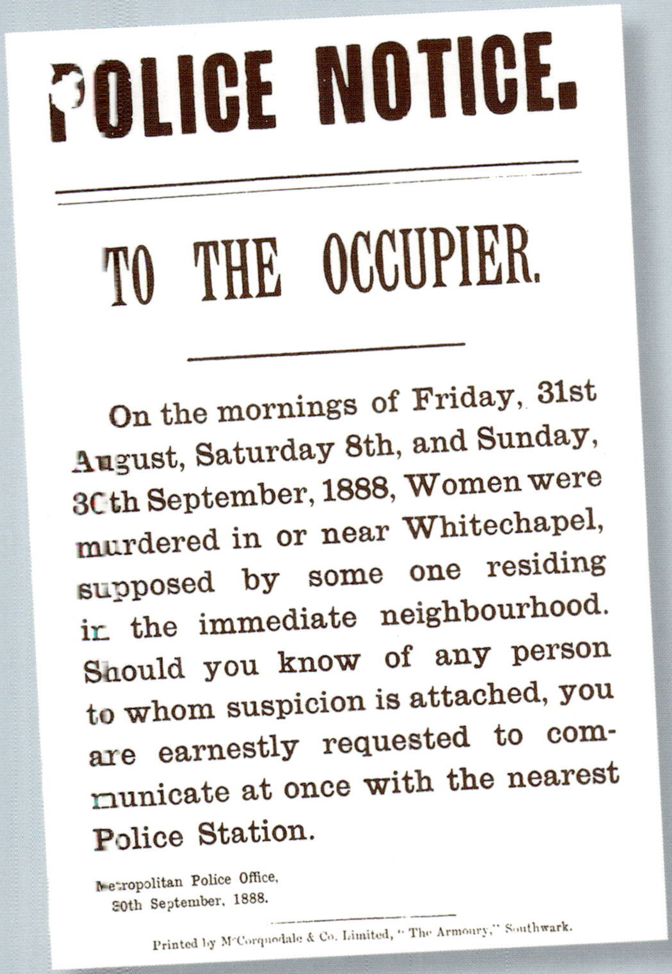
POLICE NOTICE.

TO THE OCCUPIER.

On the mornings of Friday, 31st August, Saturday 8th, and Sunday, 30th September, 1888, Women were murdered in or near Whitechapel, supposed by some one residing in the immediate neighbourhood. Should you know of any person to whom suspicion is attached, you are earnestly requested to communicate at once with the nearest Police Station.

Metropolitan Police Office,
30th September, 1888.

Printed by M'Corquodale & Co. Limited, "The Armoury," Southwark.

An example of the posters which were displayed around London when the Natives were there.
METROPOLITAN POLICE, LONDON

played Runcorn, on the 4th they were at Oldham, the following day they were at Halifax and then two days later they played Barrow and District. Two days after that, they played against Widnes. Seven days, five matches. That was a typical rather than an unusual week. All of this was with a maximum playing strength in Britain of 26 – but there were many times the Natives struggled to get the bare fifteen on to the field. Their best player and organiser, Joe Warbrick, went on tour with a broken ankle and, in Eyton's words, was 'of very little service as a player'. Warbrick himself recalled when they lost their first match in England, to Moseley in Birmingham, that within the first quarter of an hour Billy Warbrick had a collarbone broken and George Wynyard a knee dislocated. Regular, allowable injury replacements were nearly a century away, not to mention modern medical treatment. Joe Warbrick remembered how lean the playing resources were:

> Accidents multiplied rapidly and though we had 26 men in many cases we could not put more than 10 to 12 fairly sound men in the field. I remember at Liverpool [the team's 24th win] we discussed the necessity of picking some outsiders to play for us but rather than do so Maynard, who was ill in bed, offered to play, also Madigan, McCausland and G. Wynyard, who were far from fully recovered from injuries.[18]

He was proud of their record given the trying circumstances in which it was attained, as well he might have been. No other New Zealand team has done so much over such a long period with so little. Warbrick recalled with some bitterness that a Hawke's Bay paper (from which he might have expected some support) had considered before the tour the Natives were not good enough to play English schoolboys and that the Otago union secretary, John Chapman, had written to the union's man in England, Sleigh, with the view the Natives would not win a single match.

The scale of the Natives' endeavour should not be underrated. They did not gad about England beating village teams cobbled together for the occasion. The strength of English rugby then, before the split over payment, was in the north and it was mostly in the north that the Natives played. It is no exaggeration to say that sides the Natives played such as Yorkshire and Lancashire were much more formidable than they were when the 1905 All Blacks played them (because the bulk of rugby players in the two counties by then was playing rugby league). The Natives also played full international teams: they beat Ireland but lost to Wales and England. Each of the matches, as far as the opponents were concerned, was regarded at the time as a full international. In fact, the only full international England played in the 1888–89 season was against the Natives because they were in the midst of a fundamental disagreement with the recently formed International Rugby Board, and Ireland, Scotland and Wales would not play them. The disputes were about differing interpretations of rules. The rugby season, according to a writer in the *Manchester Weekly Times*, would have been exceedingly dull without the New Zealand team.[19]

In fact, the same writer thought that the autocratic Rowland Hill had had his amateur eyes opened by the Natives and realised the game could benefit by teams playing attractive rugby that the public wanted to watch. A perennial philosophical debate within British rugby until probably the 1970s was the balance between playing the game for the players' sake and playing it to attract spectators. It was not until the 1970s that English clubs were allowed to play competition matches; previously, all were 'friendly'. It was only after the outcome of the debate was clear that the IRB finally agreed to a World Cup.

A decade after the tour, Billy Warbrick, who was then playing and coaching in Sydney, said the hardest matches the Natives had were against Yorkshire and Ireland forwards –

> Big, fast men who came rushing down in a body with the ball upon their toes. To fall on the ball, or to snatch it up and run straight through was the only way to defend. To play Rugby a man must not consider his personal safety at all. The Irish had the best of it at halftime, but in the second spell, being as soft as the spuds they live upon, they were run right off their legs.[20]

The Natives did much in Britain to show that, like cricket, the game could benefit from international teams, just so long as they were still amateur and under English control of course. But they were given a painful lesson in the English attitude, or at least the RFU attitude as expressed by Rowland Hill. Jimmy Scott, the Natives' manager, had negotiated the use of the Oval at Kennington, just south of the Thames, for the match against England, reasoning it was close to central London and therefore more accessible to people who did not have unlimited finance. But Rowland Hill ruled against the Oval and said the match must be at a rugby ground and he decided on Rectory Field at more distant Blackheath. 'We can't have the game sacrificed to the gate,' he grandiloquently told Scott. The Natives' argument was they needed the greater return the Oval would have given them to pay for the tour, but such a sensible argument fell on deaf RFU ears.

There were benefits for New Zealand from the tour, however. One of the players, George Williams, wrote in 1924: 'The Natives were the first body of athletes to visit Great Britain from New Zealand and as this country was little known then, they put New Zealand on the sporting map.' (The race walker, Joe Scott, was in Britain before the Natives in 1888 and became the first New Zealander to win a world title, but he was frequently described as an Australian.) Another benefit from the Natives' tour was the trickle-down of knowledge that, until professionalism, touring engendered. A player's knowledge was widened by playing against national teams elsewhere and he imparted that knowledge to his teammates at provincial and club level. Williams commented: 'The team became a great combination after playing so much together and picked up many valuable points in rugby which were imparted to New Zealand players on our return.'

The curiosity value of the Natives dissipated as knowledge of their rugby prowess increased. After they beat Midland Counties 10–0, a writer in the *Liverpool Mercury* remarked: 'The Maoris are evidently big guns after all.'[21] There were still, however, incidents on the tour. Eyton, almost with a sense of frustration, remarked that they were often referred to as 'the Maoris' rather than as the Native football team and they were expected to be 'blackfellows'. 'We had not even a tattoo mark among the team and in their walks abroad they attracted little or no attention from the casual passer-by,' he wrote. 'In order to try and keep faith with the British public, the team on one occasion purchased some black masks and they were paraded by some of our jokers wearing them, and looking out of the railway carriage windows at the expectant crowd.'[22]

Betting was commonplace on rugby, as with most sports, in the nineteenth century and early into the twentieth and gave rise to allegations of match fixing and rigging. Inevitably, there were betting allegations against the Natives. The most publicised came after their second-last match before returning to New Zealand, against Queensland in Brisbane. They had beaten Queensland 27–0 the previous week but struggled to an 11–7 win in the rematch. It was the 74th victory of their tour. The *Courier* newspaper on the Monday fanned the sparks of rumours, which apparently had begun even during the game:

> Some of the Maoris seemed scarcely up to form in the earlier part of the game, but towards the end they all appeared to work exceedingly well. This may be accounted for by the fact that the Queenslanders were not in such perfect training as

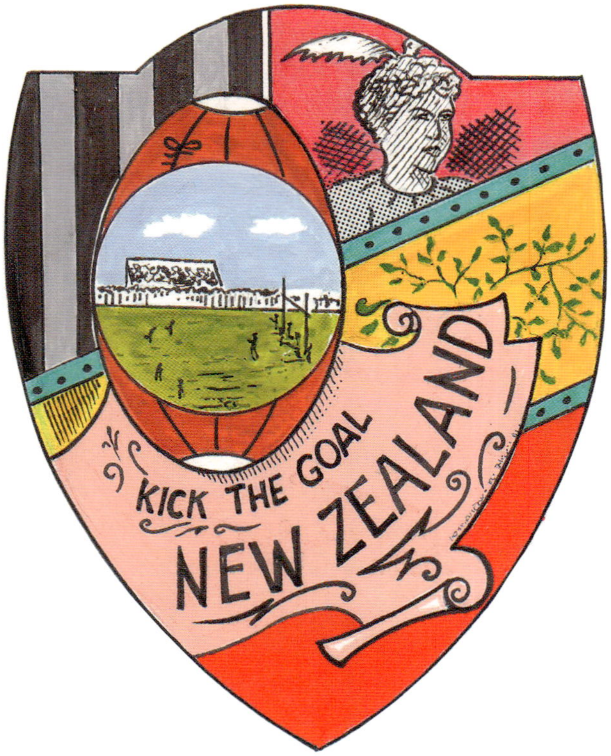

A facsimile of a typical 'play up' card of the nineteenth century, which usually were slid inside hatbands.

> their opponents and that, therefore, the excellent play of the Maoris was not so much perceptible at the beginning as at the end of the match.[23]

Amid the confusing and contradictory accusations of corruption that followed, the fact the Natives might just have had enough of touring and playing was not mentioned. By this time, they had played 110 games. It also seemed to have been quickly forgotten that the Natives' fullback, Billy Warbrick, was felled by a kick to the head early in the game and was carried off. He eventually resumed his place at fullback, but if he did not play to his usual form, it might have been understandable. It was while Billy Warbrick was off the field that his brother Joe apparently confronted the other players with the betting rumours and they found renewed endeavour when play resumed. But did that mean they had been got at? There was no clear answer.

The Sydney *Referee*'s rugby man said Joe Warbrick wanted a full inquiry and to have the bookmaker named: 'Unfortunately it's often tried in big matches of all kinds, and in this particular instance I fancy there must be some mistake, as I know of a wager 300 to 100 on the Maoris winning, taken by a private individual, so possibly in the heat of the moment things got a little mixed up.'[24]

Whatever the cause, the effect was that Joe Warbrick decided four of his players, Keogh, 'Barlow' Madigan, Charles Goldsmith and Arthur Warbrick, should not play until they had been exonerated. They missed the last match in Queensland, against Toowoomba, and the Natives then headed home for the final leg of their odyssey. Their landing point was Bluff, but it was the Otago union rather than Southland that decided to get involved. The Southland union said it could not assemble its committee in time to enquire into what happened before the Natives' match against Southland and a following one in Gore against Mataura. So while the Natives played two games without eight of their touring party – four who had gone home and the four who had been stood down – the Otago union got involved. It said it would not support any game involving the Natives until the allegations of shady practices were disproven. The Natives moved to Dunedin after their two games in Southland and on the night before they were due to play Otago, they met and resolved to ask Otago to forget all about what happened in Brisbane (if indeed anything did). The Natives asked that the four, suspended 'on suspicion' only, be returned to favour. They also pointed out that in a tour of more than twelve months, no similar accusations had ever been made against them and 'the indifferent play during part of the match on 20th July may very well be attributed to other causes'. The Otago union accepted the allegations had no factual basis and the Otago game – and the balance of the tour – went ahead.[25]

As the writer in the *Referee* noted, betting on big matches was not uncommon at the time;

gambling on most sports was the norm rather than the exception. Keogh, one of the Natives briefly under suspicion, was banned indefinitely by the Otago union about eighteen months later for his role in 'fixing' the result of a match between his club, Kaikorai, and Alhambra. The latter won the match and this gave rise to accusations of gambling and professionalism that ultimately saw the end of Keogh's career. He agreed he'd bet on the match but that he was not the only punter; he refused to name any others. He was unquestionably the leading back in Otago in his day and among the best, if not the best, in New Zealand, and it was argued he suffered from his own brilliance. If his team lost, it was because of him; if his team won, it was also because of him. The Otago union sniffed out the professionalism inherent in betting and in the words of its president, James Allen (the later wartime minister of defence and acting prime minister): 'Committee considers P Keogh a professional and that he be suspended during the pleasure of the committee.'[26] Keogh never played again, but his reputation did not suffer. When he died in 1940, the Otago union's weekly match programme paid a glowing tribute to him and called him 'one of the greatest footballers the world has seen'.[27] A bit over the top perhaps, but it conveyed a sense of the impact Keogh made during a career that lasted only from 1887 until 1891.

When the New Zealand Rugby Union marked the centenary in 2010 of the first official national Māori team, it produced a booklet highlighting the history and significance of Māori rugby. Although the Natives' tour was not official and it preceded the formation of the national union, the place of the tour was nevertheless marked and acknowledged. The booklet included a message from the Minister of Māori Affairs, Pita Sharples, who noted: 'Mai i te tīmatanga, ko te iwi Māori tētahi poutokomanawa mō te whutupōro i Aotearoa.'[28] Which was a neat way of saying that Māori have been pivotal to the development of rugby in New Zealand from the beginning. The Natives' tour provides the strength to that belief. Much of what followed in New Zealand rugby came from the Natives' tour; innovations which have been attributed to the 1905–06 New Zealand team in Britain in fact began with the Natives. Here are just two examples. It has been a common enough belief that the All Blacks of 1905–06 were the first to have designated forward positions rather than the prevailing British habit of first-there-first-down. The Natives did it first. As Tom Ellison, the thinking man's rugby player, wrote:

> In the scrum we invariably beat the English packs, not through having better men, but through our more scientific system of packing the scrum and having specialists in each position instead of merely fine all-round men; the result being, that our two front-rankers, for instance, simply buried the two Jacks-of-all-Trades who happened to be pitted against them in the different scrums.[29]

Similarly, the wing forward was the defining characteristic of the New Zealand game. The wing forward was in effect a second halfback whose duties were to put the ball into scrums and to protect his own halfback from the attentions of opponents and to allow him to get the ball away quickly. It was most famously used by the 1905–06 team and was frequently criticised as a form of cheating practised especially by the All Blacks' captain, David Gallaher. The All Blacks did play the wing forward and Gallaher did play in that position, but it did not begin with them. It did not even begin in New Zealand. The position began in northern England and the Natives brought it back. Ellison wrote of himself as the instigator of the wing forward, and in New Zealand he was. An English journalist and author, Edward Bolland Osborn, whose pen roamed far and wide until his death aged 75 in 1938, turned his attention sometimes to rugby. He wrote in 1906 – when it was all the rage – of how the wing forward moved from England to New Zealand:

> The Maoris, as they were called, were barely equal to the better club teams but among them were two players of undoubted genius – a half-back named Keogh . . . and T. R. Ellison, an incomparable forward, who also had the inventor's mind. When the latter returned to New Zealand, he took up the profession of wing forward and so adorned the post that it became an established position and the cornerstone of a new model.[30]

Ellison, who did not live to see the All Blacks in Britain, freely acknowledged that the wing forward's role was later much abused by some of its practitioners. 'The so-called wing-forwards of to-day are nothing more than aimless, off-side jostlers, who do more harm to their side than anything else,' he wrote in 1902, two years before his death.[31] This was the substance of the criticism in Britain in 1905. Played properly in the manner developed by Ellison for the Natives and for his club, Poneke, for Wellington and for New Zealand, the position was legal and effective.

Away from the actual playing of the game, the Natives also introduced the haka as a prelude to matches – although, like the 1905 team, they did not do it before all matches. Their haka was more 'war cry', as it was often described, than haka, but it was nevertheless an innovation that endured and grew. The 1884 team, of which Joe Warbrick was a member, adopted the cry, 'Kia kaha' ('Be strong!'). The Natives took it a little further and Ernest ('Denny') Hoben, the journalist who four years later cajoled the provincial unions into forming the national union, claimed a hand in it. Hoben was at the time secretary of the Hawke's Bay union and was well known to the Warbrick brothers (some of whom went to a school in Tauranga run by Hoben's mother). He recalled how Joe Warbrick wondered about a 'war cry' for their tour and told him of how Rewi Manga of Ngāti Maniapoto was supposed to have said, 'Ake, ake, kia kaha,' in response to a call for surrender from the British general at Orakau in 1864, Duncan Cameron, and that this was wrongly interpreted as meaning, 'We will fight on forever and ever.' Hoben recorded that what in fact Rewi said was: 'Ka whāwhai tonu, ake, ake, ake' ('We will fight only, for ever and ever'). He then wrote:

> 'Why not,' I suggested, 'link Orakau with the first Māori invasion of England. Take ake, ake. Add kia kaha and make it declaration and adjuration.' And so, 'Ake ake, kia kaha' ('Be strong, forever and ever') came into being as the war cry of the first Māori football team to go abroad. It rang to victory on many a British field. When the New Zealand Rugby Union was formed I had it again made the war cry of its teams and as such it was used in Australia and Britain.[32]

The haka aside, the Natives' legacy is on display every time the All Blacks play. It was substantially the Natives' playing uniform that was adopted as the new national team uniform after the formation of the New Zealand Rugby Football Union in 1892. Tom Ellison, a Wellington delegate to the first annual meeting of the union, proposed the uniform, except there was provision then for white knickerbockers (which became black shorts in 1901). But the jersey, so emblematic of the All Blacks, was what the Natives wore. Fittingly, Ellison was captain of the first national team that wore the new jersey. And it was the Natives and the team in 1893 that gave rise to the name 'All Blacks', and not the fanciful and often repeated notion that somehow an English journalist bestowed the name upon the 1905 team.

It seems something of a paradox that while historian Greg Ryan remains the only person to have written a book about the Natives' tour, he has also suggested in at least two forums that the role of Māori in rugby was ambiguous and sometimes overstated. He has argued that before the 1920s the Māori embrace of the game was 'largely confined to an educated and acculturated elite'.[33] Part of his argument is that Pākehā

Another photo of the Natives, this one taken by Henry Chapman in Swansea in the last week of December 1888 and reproduced in Frank Marshall's book on rugby. Back row: Pat Keogh, Tom Eyton (agent), Alf Warbrick, Sandy Webster, George Williams, George Wynyard, Tom Ellison, Wi Karauria, Jimmy Scott (manager), Henry Wynyard. Middle: William Anderson, Fred Warbrick, Joe Warbrick, Edward McCausland, Harry Lee, Davy Stewart. Front: David Gage, William Elliot, William Wynyard, Dick Taiaroa. FRANK MARSHALL, *FOOTBALL: THE RUGBY UNION GAME* (LONDON: CASSELL, 1892)

administrators were indifferent to Māori rugby until they realised that league was a threat to them. In terms of the Natives, Ryan points out that provincial unions supported the Natives' tour until the addition of the Pākehā players, implying, as Ryan thought, that a purely Māori team posed no threat to their authority. But the provincial unions were concerned about professionalism and hence Joe Warbrick's hasty trip to Christchurch to reassure the Canterbury union. Yes, some of the prominent Māori players were educated and since the subject here is their playing of rugby, of course they were acculturated since no one has suggested Māori invented the game. Ryan is correct when he says that Māori were ultimately expendable in the later controversies about South Africa, but the later wrong-headed decisions of largely (but not only) Pākehā administrators should not detract from Māori attraction to rugby at any level, not just the highest. Harry Dansey once wrote that when Māori first took up rugby, they found it provided the teamwork that was an essential part of Māori life and it provided legitimate hard physical contests. 'Maori rugby draws its strength and character from hidden sources,' he wrote. 'It has roots in tradition for though its flesh and bones are European, its heart and spirit are the authentic expression of the old-time

Maori love of strenuous, even violent, competitive physical activity.'[34]

Osborn's remark that the Natives were barely equal to the better club teams is worth examination. It cannot be known which games he saw and at which stage of the tour he formed his opinion (assuming he saw games at all). No one has pretended they were all-conquering but their results reflected an ability beyond the average. They were beaten by some of the leading club teams certainly (Halifax and Swinton in the north and Cardiff among others), but they also beat some (Liverpool, Newcastle, Wigan) as well as Ireland. Arthur Swan, the NZRFU's official historian, thought the fixture list was so long it was inevitable there were some substandard teams, but there were also some very good ones. He calculated that in Britain alone, 28 teams would meet modern (he was writing in 1965) criteria for being a first-class fixture. Critics of the Natives, or at least those not wholly convinced of their playing merits, should also remember how few players they had and how many matches they were expected to play. Even the train travel over such a prolonged period would have tired ordinary people, never mind chucking in games of rugby between trips. Swan's role as the national union's historian was to tend to the playing books, to keep a count of who played for New Zealand where and when. His main brief was the All Blacks, but he went beyond the official line when he wrote: 'I am going to say at the outset that the tour of the New Zealand Native team of 1888–1889 was the greatest of any.'[35]

Rugby and music often in tune

Every so often the All Blacks are criticised for mumbling their way – or even worse, just staying mum – through the national anthem before test matches. On one occasion in 2009, the captain of the time, Mils Muliaina, responded to such a view by saying there would be less clamour from the public if it were known how bad the rugby players were as singers.

'If you look at the French and compare them to us, we probably just open our lips a little bit,' Muliaina said.

Allied with the view that All Blacks do not sing well enough – the outcry would be much greater if they did not play rugby well enough – is an occasionally expressed belief that rugby and the arts do not sit happily alongside one another. One scholarly look at rugby and music ventured the view: 'Rugby songs may excite our interest because of the apparent disjunction between the values of sport and the values of an art such as music.'[1]

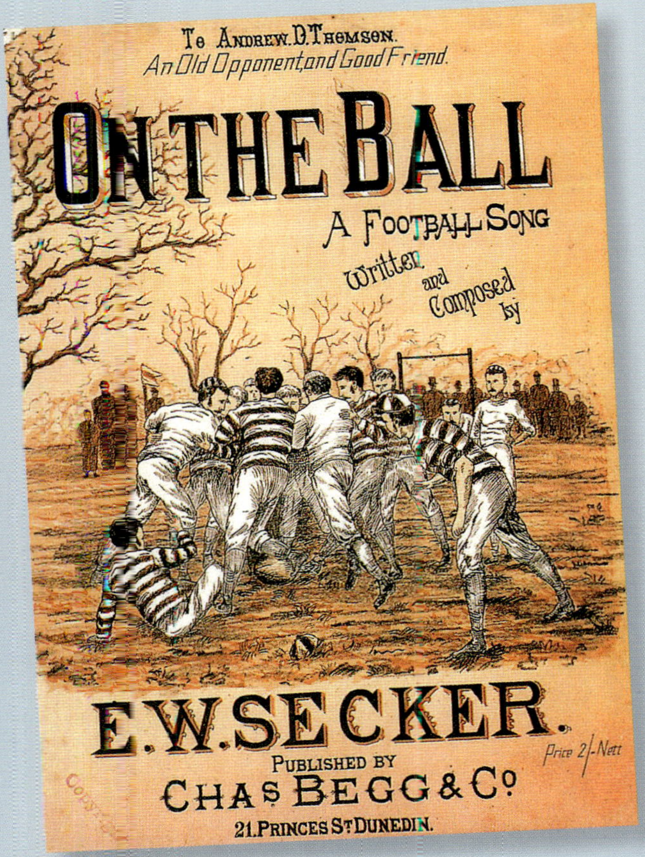

An early copy of the sheet music for 'On the Ball', after composer Edward Secker had sold the rights to Chas Begg and Co.

But Muliaina and academe may have been selling rugby and music short. It is perhaps not generally known, but there is a long and mostly harmonious link between the two. From the first bawling out on a Manawatu train of the quintessential New Zealand rugby song 'On the Ball' in the nineteenth century, to a few All Blacks in the twenty-first century recording a waiata (song) and uploading it to YouTube, rugby and music have generally got on well.

Some noted players made records that were well received even if they were not top of the pops. George Nepia of the 1924 team recorded 'Beneath the Maori Moon' and 'Pokarekare Ana'; in fact, Nepia said the composer of 'Maori Moon', Walter Smith, was an uncle of his in the small northern Hawke's Bay town of Nuhaka and wrote the song with Nepia's voice in mind.[2] Pat Vincent, captain in two tests against South Africa in 1956, had several records released of his laid-back crooning in the style of 1940s Frank Sinatra. In the modern era, a ten-year-old Māori boy sang Ben E. King's 'Stand By Me' (a favourite with All Black teams) in a 1993 video promoting support for the All Blacks. It included shots of players such as Grant Fox and Michael Jones standing ready on the field. The boy was Tamati Ellison, whose whakapapa (ancestry) includes the first official New Zealand

Original sheet music for 'On the Ball'. The handwriting on the left under the title reads, 'Written and composed by "Forward".' It was not long before 'Forward' was revealed as Edward Secker. MS-PAPERS-0573, ALEXANDER TURNBULL LIBRARY

captain, Tom Ellison. Tamati too grew up to be an All Black.

Most modern rugby followers will know that Richie McCaw is not just a competent guitarist but is also an accomplished piper. He was one of the All Blacks in the performance of the Wiremu Huata song 'Tūtira Mai Ngā Iwi' that found its way onto YouTube. He is captured both singing and playing. It is a song learnt at school and one that comes readily to rugby players when protocol requires them to render a waiata. When the Highlanders, led by Taine Randell, went to the Ngāi Tahu marae at Otākou – the place where Tom Ellison was born and is buried – to pay their respects, they sang 'Ngā Iwi'.

Away from the public gaze, rugby teams often took to music so much that it became a part of belonging to a club or a team. Many have their own club or team songs and belt them out usually in the privacy of clubrooms or a dressing room, and teams have been known to go on tour with specially prepared song sheets. Contrary to what may have been a popular view, very few of the songs were ribald. New Zealand takes its rugby too seriously for such undergraduate humour. Players who can also play guitar or piano are especially valued. Bryan Williams, the great All Black wing of the 1970s, spent hours on his guitar in hotel rooms or public lounges during tours, and it was not uncommon for locals to join the players in singing along. Every era seems to have such a player. Bill Gray, the Bay of Plenty midfield back of the 1950s, was another for whom it was a race to see which was packed first, the guitar or the boots. On the morning of the second test against South Africa in 1956, Gray half lay on his hotel room bed plucking away to himself; his roommate Ron Jarden later reported he did not mind in the least.

Players have their own ways of preparing for big matches and seldom appreciate intrusions.

But in Gray's era teams also had a public outlet for their enthusiasm for song. From the 1920s until the 1960s, community sings were a popular public entertainment usually in the bigger centres and typically in a picture theatre on a Friday lunchtime.[3] A pianist or organist would play tunes of the day or of yesterday and the public would walk in off the street to join in, usually at the cost of a donation for some charity. Touring rugby teams regularly attended. In 1959 in Dunedin on the day before the first test, members of the British Isles and New Zealand teams showed up at more or less the same time. The All Blacks stood back and let the Lions have their sing and after twenty minutes or so, the visitors left and the home team took over with such easy-to-sing standards as 'Pack Up Your Troubles', 'Bye Bye Blackbird' and 'Down by the Riverside'.

Thirty years earlier, according to one of the players, Mark Nicholls, the All Blacks sang two of their favourite songs, a Rodgers and Hart number, 'Blue Room' and 'The Mountains of Mourne', when they were travelling to matches. That was unusual in itself because teams of later eras insisted on absolute quiet in the bus on the way to games.[4]

Terry McLean, that much-travelled rugby writer whose first tour was in 1930 and last in 1987, always maintained that a team that could sing well together was a happy team and, if happy off the field, should play well on it. This was McLean lore rather than scientific fact, but it seemed to be right more often than not. He especially prized the singing of British teams (the 1977 Lions even produced a long-playing record), but one of his favourites was any South African team singing that mournful Boer War tale of a love far away, 'Sarie Marais'. McLean's eyes also lit up and his hands clasped in admiration whenever a Fijian team, or any group of Fijians, launched into 'Isa Lei'. McLean was less enthusiastic in his later years about what he considered ordinary singing performances by New Zealand teams, so he was pleasantly surprised when the 1978 All Blacks after their loss to Munster walked into the match dinner in Limerick in single file, each player with a hand on a shoulder in front, singing the work song from 'Snow White and the Seven Dwarfs': 'Hi ho, hi ho, it's off to work we go . . .' It was a copy of an act by the Scottish team in New Zealand in 1975, but no matter. It was a gesture much appreciated by the people of Munster.

The Australians used to be keen on team songs (and may still be) and they had almost a theme song for a time – a made-for-harmony reminder of university days, 'The Whiffenpoof Song'. It apparently began life before the First World War at Yale and moved from its Ivy League base into the services, from where it seemed to have been borrowed by the British Barbarians and then the Wallabies. Some lines during their 1972 tour of

The Lions of 1977 moved from rugby ground to music studio. This album of easy-listening old favourites was recorded at Waitangi on 24 July, between the second and third tests. The choirmaster was the Scottish lock, Gordon Brown.

New Zealand seemed especially apt: 'We are poor little lambs who have lost our way; Baa, baa, baa; We are little black sheep who have gone astray; Baa, baa, baa.'

The Welsh, it will come as no surprise, are the best of all. Most New Zealanders who have been to Wales will know 'the land of song' is not a dreamt-up marketing line. A group of All Blacks once went to a Welsh club on a weeknight to meet the players and have a couple of drinks. After an hour or so, one of the All Blacks asked if there was any chance of a song. The locals who were gathered in the club, players, older men, women, some children, had a hurried conversation and launched into an impromptu version of 'Ar Hyd y Nos' – 'All Through the Night' (the traditional Welsh air, not the Cyndi Lauper song of the same name). It sounded as if they had been rehearsing it for months. Bryan Williams, by happy coincidence, played his hundredth match for New Zealand in Wales and a Cardiff club official presented a memento to him before the match. Unbidden, the crowd stood and sang for him: 'We'll keep a welcome in the hillside, we'll keep a welcome in the vales; This land you knew will still be singing, When you come home again to Wales; This land of song will keep a welcome, And with a love that never fails, We'll kiss away each hour of hiraeth, When you come home again to Wales.'[5]

Rugby's association with music undoubtedly began with Ted Secker and his 'On the Ball', which became almost the signature tune of the game for the next sixty or seventy years. A book in 1970 marking the centenary of the first match in Nelson was called *On the Ball* and no one then could have wondered why. English-born Secker was a Palmerston North accountant and captain of the Manawatu team in 1887 and was said to have written the words on the eve of a match against Wanganui, and his players first sang it on the short train trip from Palmerston North. A pianist, he put his words to the tune of an English song popular at the time, 'We'll All Go A-Hunting Today'. Since there were no intellectual property lawyers to go a-hunting at the time, the song became a success. Secker dedicated the song to the Feilding captain, Andrew Thompson, and the local paper, the *Feilding Star*, called it a 'cheerful and harmonious song peculiarly adapted for Knights of the Leather on all festive occasions'. Secker was encouraged to send a copy to the musical retailers and publishers, Chas Begg and Co., in Dunedin, and it bought the rights.

Within a year, Joe Warbrick's Natives sang the song almost daily when on tour in Britain, but all the publicity came to nothing for Secker because copies of the music were not available in England. It was reported that the agent to whom copies had been sent was ill when they arrived and shortly afterward died, the unsold sheet music lying fallow among his property. The song was 'boomed', to use a word of the time, again in 1905 when the All Blacks were in England and the noted all-round sportsman and writer Charles Burgess Fry tried to buy the rights, but Secker would not sell.[6] It steadily gained ground, though, and was eventually sold in Australia, Europe and the United States, with a few minor word changes along the way. Secker's first line of 'Oh, some talk of cricket and some of lacrosse' became 'Well, some talk of soccer and some talk of league'. Secker 'longed' for the huntsman's loud call; but the Americans 'mickled' for it (some Scottish influence seemed to have crept in).

Perhaps because of the success of 'On the Ball', or perhaps just because of the dominance of rugby, the game continued to attract composers. A year after 'On the Ball' was first sung, a poem in the *Auckland Star* written by a well-published Otahuhu man, William Robert Wills, was set to music by the organist at St Matthew's in Auckland, James Phillpot, and was published as 'Zealandia's Victory'. It was around this time that Ernest Denis Hoben was making a national name for himself as the foremost advocate of a national rugby union; he was known also as a songwriter of some merit and his brother Sydney as a

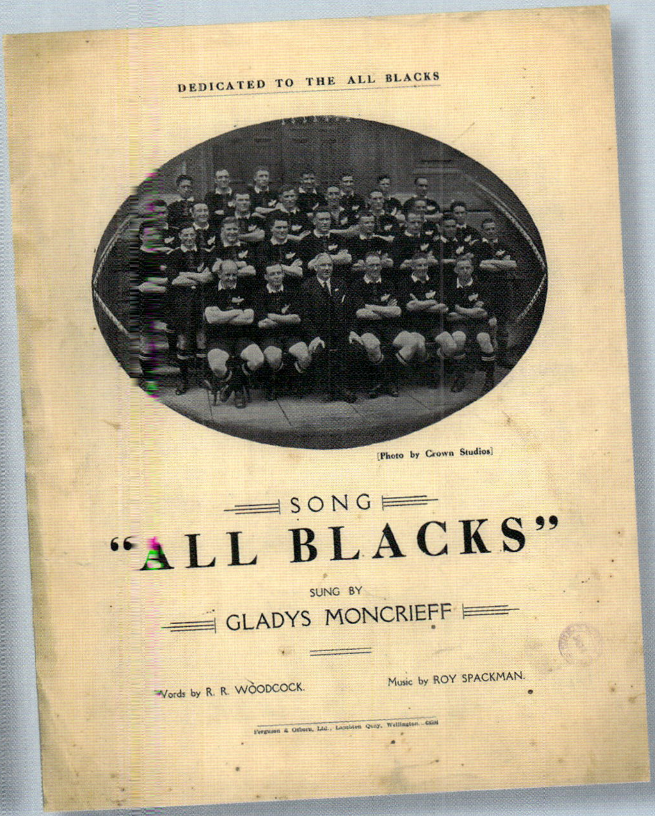

Two examples of the All Blacks being celebrated in music. An expatriate Wellingtonian, Bert Rache, greeted the New Zealand team in Sydney in 1907 with his 'Haere-mai' march (left) and the Invincibles eighteen years later were celebrated by Napier composers Rupert Woodcock and Roy Spackman.

Leipzig-trained concert pianist and organ soloist of even greater merit.

When the All Blacks went to Sydney in 1907 at the time of the rumours about a new professional team, they were entertained on their arrival in the Town Hall by the debut performance of a march written especially for them, 'Haere-Mai to the All Black Team'.[7] Its composer was a noted Sydney man of music, Bert Rache, but better known in his home town of Wellington by his birth name of Bert Rash. Composers and lyricists decided the All Blacks, like the lady riding to Banbury Cross, should have music wherever they go. The 1924 team, which toured Britain unbeaten and became known as the Invincibles, had a song written about them by Napier men Rupert Woodcock and Roy Spackman. Called simply 'All Blacks', it carried the team's photo on the front and proudly proclaimed it was sung by Gladys Moncrieff, one of the great Australian entertainers of the first half of the twentieth century.

Two Aucklanders, Elizabeth Chandler and Harry Hiscocks, also wrote about the Invincibles and were a little more adventurous with their title. Their work was called 'The All Blacks (Rugby Football Boys) – A song with a kick in it', and lyricist Chandler managed to mention each one of the players. It was first performed publicly by Chandler's son, Charles. A daughter, Nell Shepherd, wrote in a letter years later that the song was very popular and sung 'in every picture theatre in New Zealand, played in every dance hall, whistled in the streets right through New Zealand'.[8]

Many other tunes, either instrumental or for vocalists, were published about rugby generally or the All Blacks specifically, including one piano solo called 'March of the All Blacks'. The twist provided by composer Ngaire Kinder was that it was played only on the black keys.

The 'All Blacks' Football Song' was written by Paul Gregory and released in time for the third test against South Africa in Christchurch in 1956 – the match the All Blacks had to win if they were to win the series (and they did). The tune was recorded by the Woolston Brass Band in Christchurch, but it did not perform it at Lancaster Park because the brass band that played on the day was the Band of the 3rd Armoured Regiment. Nevertheless, Gregory's words were reproduced in the match programme:

> From the Cape of Northland to
> the plains of Southland
> Hear the cry, 'Come away, the Black!'
> Play it hard! Play it fast! Play it to the line
> Bury their line with our Silver Fern.

The South African players were evidently taken with rugby's association with music. The *Evening Post* reported when the team left Auckland:

> One of the most outstanding things about the Springboks and the novelties which they struck in New Zealand is that until they came here they had never heard of the football song, 'On the Ball'. Before they left for home yesterday, they were searching Auckland music shops for recordings of the song which few New Zealanders fail to learn at school.[9]

The 1950s and 1960s brought a range of rugby-associated music, some of it motivated by specific people or events or simply as local adaptations of hits from overseas. The skiffle hit by Lonnie Donegan of England, 'My Old Man's A Dustman', in New Zealand became 'My Old Man's An All Black', with a line reflecting increasing concerns about South Africa: 'Fee fi fo fum, there ain't no Hories in that scrum!' A country song written by Roy Acuff and its singer, Jimmy Dean, 'Big Bad John', became in New Zealand 'Big Bad Don' – a reference to All Black Don Clarke. Another hit borrowed and adapted was Johnny Horton's 'Sink the Bismarck' and under the skilful conducting and rewriting of Lew Pryme (a later boss of the Auckland Rugby Union) it became a celebration of Fergie McCormick scoring a record 24 points against Wales in 1969.[10]

The ball heads for the back of a lineout in New Zealand's thirteenth match of the 1905–06 tour, against Midland Counties in Leicester. Captain David Gallaher wears No. 8 and the unsuccessful jumper is Charlie Seeling. Midland Counties forward Cecil Shaw, who later played for England, scored a try in this match, just the second the All Blacks had conceded on tour. New Zealand won 21–5. MNZ-1012-1/4-F, ALEXANDER TURNBULL LIBRARY

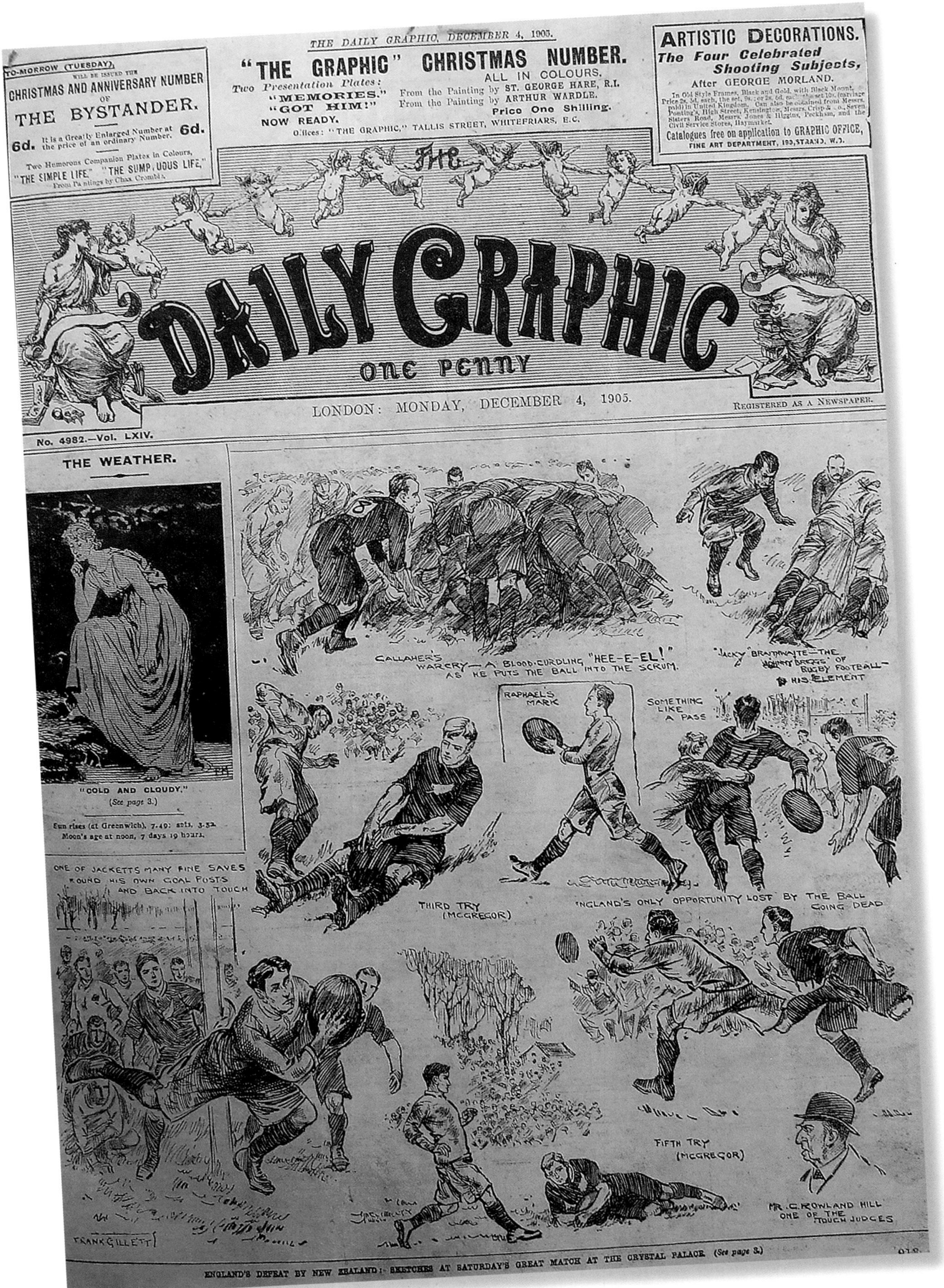

THE DAILY GRAPHIC, DECEMBER 4, 1905.

TO-MORROW (TUESDAY) WILL BE ISSUED THE
CHRISTMAS AND ANNIVERSARY NUMBER OF
THE BYSTANDER.
6d. It is a Greatly Enlarged Number at the price of an ordinary Number. 6d.
Two Humorous Companion Plates in Colours,
"THE SIMPLE LIFE." "THE SUMPTUOUS LIFE."
From Paintings by Chas Crombie.

"THE GRAPHIC" CHRISTMAS NUMBER.
ALL IN COLOURS.
Two Presentation Plates:
"MEMORIES." From the Painting by ST. GEORGE HARE, R.I.
"GOT HIM!" From the Painting by ARTHUR WARDLE.
NOW READY. Price One Shilling.
Offices: "THE GRAPHIC," TALLIS STREET, WHITEFRIARS, E.C.

ARTISTIC DECORATIONS.
The Four Celebrated Shooting Subjects,
After GEORGE MORLAND.
In Old Style Frames, Black and Gold, with Black Mount. Price 2s. 3d. each, the set, 9s.; or 2s. 6d. each, the set 10s. (carriage paid) in United Kingdom. Can also be obtained from Messrs. Ponting's, High Street, Kensington, Messrs. Crisp & Co., Seven Sisters Road, Messrs. Jones & Higgins, Peckham, and the Civil Service Stores, Haymarket.
Catalogues free on application to GRAPHIC OFFICE,
FINE ART DEPARTMENT, 190, STRAND, W.C.

THE DAILY GRAPHIC
ONE PENNY

LONDON: MONDAY, DECEMBER 4, 1905. REGISTERED AS A NEWSPAPER.

No. 4982.—Vol. LXIV.

THE WEATHER.

"COLD AND CLOUDY."
(See page 3.)

Sun rises (at Greenwich), 7.49; sets, 3.52.
Moon's age at noon, 7 days 19 hours.

ENGLAND'S DEFEAT BY NEW ZEALAND: SKETCHES AT SATURDAY'S GREAT MATCH AT THE CRYSTAL PALACE. (See page 3.)

5 The grand tour

Then to the field, goal-bound and chalky lin'd,
Comes forth a band of Britons from that isle
Deep-meadow'd, happy, Seddon-rul'd and free.[1]

Seen in isolation, the Natives' tour of 1888–89 was a stupendous undertaking, made even more remarkable by the fact that its planning and execution were the work of Māori at a time when indigenous people in other settler colonies were either marginalised or ignored. As extraordinary as that was, the tour takes on even greater significance when it is understood that it helped mould New Zealand rugby into the shape it took until late in the twentieth century.

The Natives tour led directly to the formation of the New Zealand Rugby Football Union and that itself led to the first tour of the United Kingdom, France and North America by a fully representative team in 1905–06. It also led to the playing uniform of the All Blacks, the black jersey with the silver fern, and the nickname for the national team itself. Without the Natives, there still would at some stage have been a national rugby union and there still would eventually have been a tour of Britain; the Natives' tour led to them happening sooner than they otherwise would have.

Would there still have been All Blacks if not for the Natives? The national team jersey may have remained blue, as it was in 1884.

If there are still some subscribers to the belief that rugby in New Zealand was organised and conducted only by old boys from the posh schools and universities of England, consider this: the Natives' tour was organised by Joe Warbrick, a part-Māori who combined farming and playing rugby with whatever other jobs he could find. After the tour, the heir presumptive in the development of rugby took over and he was a red-haired Aucklander of recent Irish extraction, Ernest Denis Hoben, known to all as 'Denny'. Born in Auckland in 1864, his paternal grandfather was from County Mayo and his maternal grandfather from Londonderry. He was said to be 'a firm believer in himself and he never forgot to lift his head of red hair when opportunity came'.[2] Hoben's early years were spent in New South Wales but by the time he was a teenager, he had made a mark in Tauranga as a footballer, cricketer and journalist.

Typical of the coverage that followed the All Blacks in Britain was this front-page treatment in the *Daily Graphic* on the Monday after the England test. *DAILY GRAPHIC*, 4 DECEMBER 1905

The instigator and founding secretary of the New Zealand Rugby Football Union, Ernest Denis ('Denny') Hoben.

He was captain of football and cricket teams in which the name Warbrick frequently occurred. Mother Sarah taught at schools in Tauranga and along with Denny Hoben and his younger brother, Sydney, Warbricks also appeared in the school rolls. By the mid-1880s, Hoben was in Hawke's Bay where he was similarly immersed in journalism and rugby. He worked on the *Waipawa Mail* then moved to the *Daily Telegraph* in Napier, where he also became secretary-treasurer of the four-year-old Hawke's Bay Rugby Union as well as manager of the provincial team. This put him in close contact with the leading players of the time, including Joe Warbrick. The people from the public schools and Oxbridge did play a key part in nineteenth-century New Zealand rugby, but if it were them alone, could the game have survived, never mind flourished?

As both union secretary and team manager, Hoben knew of the difficulties in arranging fixtures with other unions and knew too that different playing rules applied in some cases. He also knew that both the Auckland and Wellington unions had talked about the formation of a national union but nothing had happened. Things came to a head at the end of the Natives' tour when Hoben was in the South Island as manager of the Hawke's Bay team. He got himself into a bit of warm water with the Otago union for trying to arrange a Hawke's Bay match against the Natives in Dunedin when it looked as if Otago might call off its own match against the Natives because of supposed betting in Queensland. In the event, the Otago–Natives match was played and Hoben instead arranged for Hawke's Bay to play the Natives in Christchurch. The Bay union initially disagreed with its secretary-manager's action, but eventually and reluctantly supported him. The messy way in which the matches were arranged, though, confirmed for Hoben and his boss, Hawke's Bay chairman Frank Logan, a Napier lawyer, that a New Zealand union was needed to control and co-ordinate fixture lists.[3]

The Natives' tour fired enthusiasm for a fully representative team to follow in the Māori footsteps and various people of influence sounded out how it could come about. Among them was Logan, who on a trip to Britain in 1889 saw the secretary of the (English) Rugby Football Union, George Rowland Hill, and asked him about the prospect of a full tour. It was too soon after the Natives, Hill responded, but he could have added that he was still having trouble with his own natives (the other British countries and Ireland refused to play England in the 1888–89 season). Another footballing envoy from New Zealand was Alfred Newman, a medical doctor who worked as a businessman and politician in Wellington and who had been president of the Poneke club since its inception in 1883. Newman, who was later president of the Wellington and New Zealand unions, also made enquiries while in Britain about a tour. Sam Sleigh, the insurance broker who organised managed and financed the first New Zealand tour in 1884, was by 1888 back living in Kent (and still young enough to play fullback in 1888 for a London team that played Brussels). He and Newman discussed a full New Zealand tour and Sleigh, who had organised the British end of the Natives' tour, was also in continual contact with English officials. One of the issues in the late 1880s was that the English union needed a national union with which to negotiate rather than a collection of provincial unions, some of which were affiliated to the English union.

From the 1870s through the 1890s, sports organisations began to realise they could operate more efficiently with a central body. The quasi-military national rifle shooting association was formed first, in 1878, with impetus provided by the government. But after that it was the sportspeople themselves: lawn bowls and tennis established national associations in 1886, athletics, rowing and racing clubs followed in 1887 and, by 1890, there was a national swimming association. Rugby, already being labelled the national game, lagged behind. Frank Logan in Napier knew the importance of such organisations because he was on the committee of the tennis club that drove the formation of the national association. In 1890 and 1891, Hoben moved around the country, sometimes as manager of the Hawke's Bay team and sometimes in the company of his brother Sydney, a well-regarded Leipzig-trained concert pianist whose talents were in demand. He talked to provincial unions wherever he went and tried to persuade them of the need for a national union. It seemed obvious: far better to belong to a national organisation in New Zealand than one in England. But, for some, obdurate was the word rather than obvious.

The most vehement opponents were Otago and Canterbury (in that order). Southland was also opposed but more for the pragmatic reason that it was south of Otago and it would otherwise have been isolated. The leaders of the opposition campaign appeared to be the Otago union secretary, John Chapman, and a columnist in the *Otago Witness* writing under the name of 'Forward' (who was James Hutchison, a member of the Otago union committee, a future editor of the *Otago Daily Times* and, ironically, a future member of the New Zealand Rugby Football Union appeals council).

Provincial unions met in Wellington at the Club Hotel on Lambton Quay over two days in November 1891 and, but for Otago, agreed to establish a national union. Canterbury was not represented at the meeting because, the union said, the date was inconvenient. Everyone met again at the Club Hotel the following April and the union was formed without Otago, Canterbury and Southland.

Otago spelt out four objections: that it was premature; that Otago and other unions affiliated to the English union already had the power of county committees; that it was geographically difficult for all but unions in the southern North Island; and that as a corollary of the third objection, a national union would become nothing more than a Wellington organisation.[4] It seemed odd that a body such as the Otago union, known for its Scottish roots and in a city where Scots accents were still prevalent, should place its allegiance to the English union ahead of its commitment to the future of the game in New Zealand. Its geographical argument was equally difficult to justify: did it really think communication between Dunedin and London was quicker than it was between Dunedin and Wellington? The only argument that endured was the fourth one, and there have been many administrators over more than a hundred years, and not just from the South Island, who have quietly spluttered about the game being run by Wellington men. Ron Don, for many years the Auckland chairman, was noted for the low esteem in which he held Wellington. Delegates at annual meetings seldom elected Wellington men

The art of the footballer

Only a couple of hundred people turned up at a wet and windy Newtown Park in Wellington on Thursday, 22 May 1884 to watch a rugby landmark unfold: the first game by a national representative team. It was intended as a get-together match for the players chosen to go to New South Wales, and the plan was for the game to be played the previous day, but the weather was so bad a postponement was considered prudent.

The weather was a bit better on the Thursday than it had been on the Wednesday, although several heavy showers swept over the ground just before the start and play, according to the *Evening Post*, was 'exceedingly unpleasant'. The *Post* reporter thought the weather was the reason so few people – an estimate of 150 to 200 was given – bothered to show up to see the first All Blacks in action.

The opponents were described as 'a Wellington XV' and included two of the national team. The weather meant the game was of an hour's duration only, although the Union Steam Ship Company's ship, *Hauroto*, delayed its sailing for the players so that too may have been a factor in the short game.

One of the stars of the show was an Auckland wing, Tom Ryan, who was an expert at dropkicking goals with either foot. He demonstrated that particular skill with his right foot after 10 minutes and thus became the first person to score for New Zealand. Harry Roberts of Wellington scored

Tom ('Darby') Ryan during his days sailing and painting in the Rotorua–Taupo area.
TAUPO MUSEUM

the first – and only – try, which Ryan converted and the match ended, in the *Post*'s words, 'two goals to love' (converted tries were known as goals until well into the twentieth century).

Ryan continued as he began and played in each of the eight matches in New South Wales and was described by organiser and manager Samuel Sleigh as a splendid back. 'His grand drop-kicking fairly astonished the spectators,' Sleigh wrote.[1] 'Was supposed to be slow on his pins but the way he careered along the Australian turf gave one a decidedly contrary opinion.'

Ryan, however, deserves to be remembered for much more than his football exploits with the first New Zealand team. He was born to an Irish mother and an English father in London in 1864 and, within a year mother Mary took her son to New Zealand, young Thomas using his mother's surname. They settled in inner-city Auckland and Tom was sent to Church of England Grammar School in Parnell (the forerunner of King's College). Ryan's interest in sport went beyond football and he played cricket for the Gordon and Parnell clubs, was a member of the Auckland Athletic and Cycle Club and Auckland Rowing Club and showed a particular liking for yachting. Somewhere along the line, he acquired the nickname of 'Darby'.

He gained enduring fame as an artist. He won his first prizes while still playing rugby and during the late 1880s he worked as an illustrator for newspapers and magazines; among his assignments was a tour of New Zealand with the Governor, Lord Onslow, the products of which appeared in the *Graphic*. In 1891, he was subject rather than artist. A fellow artist, Louis John Steele, exhibited a painting, 'Starlight's Last Stand', taken from Ralph Boldrewood's *Robbery Under Arms*. Captain Starlight was pictured standing by his charger, aiming his carbine at the viewer. It was the likeness of Ryan that gazed out of the painting.[2]

Ryan decided to get some formal training as an artist and left Auckland in March 1892 with the intention of going to Florence. At a farewell in the British Hotel on the corner of Queen and Durham Streets, Ryan said he was going to London 'to see a little of life', to follow the small New Zealand athletics team on its first British tour, and then on to Florence to study the human figure with 'the highest authorities'.[3] Ryan did indeed travel around Britain with the athletes and went to Paris with them on their last leg, and there he stayed. He enrolled in the Academie Julian, where he painted and studied for a year. Among the pupils was another New Zealander, Charles Goldie, with whom Ryan formed an enduring friendship.

While in Paris, Ryan continued his rugby involvement. French rugby was then in its

A Maori Swing, a 1912 painting by Tom Ryan.
ART + OBJECT, AUCKLAND

Tom Ryan's oil painting of his wife, Mere (Mary).
ROTORUA ENERGY CHARITABLE TRUST HERITAGE COLLECTION, ROTORUA MUSEUM TE WHARE TAONGA O TE ARAWA

formative stage and clubs in Paris were small and costly and based on privilege rather than proselytising. Expatriates such as Ryan formed an Academie Julian club and it made the semifinals in the second year of the French club championship. Just five clubs took part and 'CA de l'Académie Julian', as it was known, was beaten in one semifinal by the eventual champions, Stade Français. Under a prior arrangement between all five clubs, Ryan went from player in a semifinal to referee of the final.[4] The secretary of the Auckland Art Society, Henry Sealy, toured the salons in Paris and remarked in a letter home that Ryan 'has got back to his old form again and is by far the best player in Paris'.[5] Sealy came across Ryan at an artists' fancy dress ball and remarked he was 'not the least original, in his tattoo and feathers, as a Maori chief'.

Ryan returned to Auckland in August 1893 and, to pursue his skills as a landscape artist and his interest in sailing, he moved to the Rotorua–Taupo district where he remained until failing health forced a return to Auckland in the 1920s. Ryan had gained a master mariner's certificate and ran public launch services on Lakes Taupo and Rotorua; he was captain of the *Tongariro* for about twenty years and part-owner from 1900 until 1909. When he returned to Auckland, he took up farming on Great Barrier Island. Throughout his sailing and farming days, he continued to paint and exhibit.[6]

Ryan had married Mary Faith Murray in 1903; they had a daughter Edna and a son, Thomas. Mary was a daughter of a Ngā Puhi leader, Kamariera Te Hau Takiri Wharepapa, one of thirteen northern Māori who went to England in 1863 for a lecture tour and to meet Queen Victoria.[7] While there, he married Elizabeth Reid and Mary was their third child. Elizabeth lived with her husband and growing family at Mangakahia until at least 1901, by which time they were separated and Elizabeth and some of her children moved to a house in Parnell which, according to journalist and Māori chronicler James Cowan, Wharepapa had bought for her. The whānau from the north were always welcome in Parnell, even after Elizabeth remarried. It was the connection between Ryan and Wharepapa that was reputed to have provided an entrée for Ryan's friend, Charles Goldie, to paint his memorable Māori portraits, among them being one of Wharepapa.

The New Zealand Rugby Football Union was formed in 1892, but it brought the 1884 team under its umbrella in 1925 when it decided surviving players should be awarded caps. Ryan was in Auckland Hospital in November 1926 when two rugby officials showed up and presented him with his cap. He died the next year.[8]

149 NEW ZEALAND INTERCOLONIAL FOOTBALL TEAM.

Complimentary Banquet and Smoke Concert

WILL BE HELD AT

AARONS' EXCHANGE HOTEL

—ON—

SATURDAY EVENING, JULY 8, 1893

AT 7 P.M.

ADMIT ONE.

H. C. STOCKHAM,
Hon. Sec. Entertainment Committee.

10/6.

Tom Ellison's invitation to dinner for the 1893 New Zealand team he captained. NZ SPORTS HALL OF FAME

as president of the union: there were only six in the first hundred years and none at all between Clarrie Gibbons in the seventy-fifth anniversary year of 1967 and the election of Andy Leslie in 2007.

The argument between the three southern unions and the NZRFU was essentially the past versus the future. Hoben, Logan and the others had a vision of a game run by New Zealanders for New Zealanders; Otago and Canterbury wanted the status quo, that is, the game being run from the other side of the world according to conditions applying there and not necessarily in New Zealand. It was an argument Otago and Canterbury were bound to lose. One of the costs of their stand became evident at the first annual meeting of the NZRFU. Tom Ellison, an Otago man by birth and breeding, successfully moved that no union affiliated to the NZRFU play against any non-affiliated union. This effectively condemned Otago, Canterbury and Southland to playing only each other. The attitude of Otago and Canterbury had been most peculiar, he said, and their efforts to injure the NZRFU, notorious.

Another effect of the southern stance was that their players were not eligible for the first national team under the auspices of the NZRFU, which went to Australia later in 1893. This was the team captained by Ellison and which wore the uniform he had suggested at the annual meeting in April of black jersey with silver fern and white knickerbockers: the same jersey as that worn by the Natives. This was also the first national team to be referred to collectively as the All Blacks.

The national union having been formed, its driving force and founding secretary, Denny Hoben, turned his active mind to the next big challenge: a tour of Britain. Before the NZRFU became a fact, a well-known sportsman in Christchurch, Len Cuff, led a team of athletes to Britain. Hoben asked Cuff if he could make enquiries while he was there about the chances of a rugby tour. In the meantime, Hoben lifted his sights even higher. He thought American universities might be interested in playing New Zealand and he wrote to the commissioners of the Chicago Exhibition, proposing a team could play there on the way home from Britain. But the plans came to nothing: Rowland Hill told Cuff directly and Hoben by letter that a tour would not be agreed to unless it was representative of all New Zealand. The Americans replied they were keen but could not play outdoors at the time of year proposed and would have to find an indoor stadium big enough.[5] Otago's obduracy continued and secretary Chapman thought a tour by a New Zealand team would be nothing but a paid holiday for a few players and a Wellington clique. There was a holiday, but not of the type at which Chapman sneered. Wellington had a half-day holiday on the day the first New Zealand team played a preparatory match against Wellington before heading off under Ellison's captaincy for Australia. The half-day was suggested by the mayor of Wellington, and banks, merchants and lawyers entered into the spirit of things and closed their doors for the football.

Hoben, seemingly never at a loss for words, spoke to the players on the eve of their departure and told them the first NZRFU team was more native than the Natives because only one among the travelling party was not born in New Zealand. He was not quite right. Three were born overseas – Maurice Herrold was born in Calcutta and brought to New Zealand when he was eleven; Bob Oliphant was born in Ireland and arrived in New Zealand when he was thirteen; and Angus Stuart, born in Scotland, had been a member of the English team in 1888 and stayed in Wellington until he went home in 1902. Three of the team, Tom Ellison, Davy Gage and William Thomas ('Tabby') Wynyard, had been members of the Natives.

Aucklanders head out to the football at Potter's Park in Epsom 1901, before Eden Park became the city's main rugby ground.

Spectators on the western bank at Athletic Park in Wellington watching a match early in the twentieth century. The photo was taken by Joe Zachariah, who marketed himself as 'Zak'.

The depth of feeling between supporters of the NZRFU and its opponents became apparent with the team's departure. The cabins on the Union Steam Ship Company ship, the *Wakatipu*, appeared to have been overbooked and the players were instead directed towards steerage quarters, above which several hundred sheep were penned. The players, with manager George Campbell and Hoben, refused to bunk down and instead took themselves to the saloon where a friendly steward issued blankets and the deck became their beds. A reporter in the *Evening Post* (the newspaper for which Hoben was a parliamentary and music reporter) reported the mix-up and accused the company, which was based in Dunedin, of deliberately denying players saloon cabins and of deeming

An invitation to the dinner after the first test to be played in New Zealand, against Great Britain in Wellington on 13 August 1904.

a team without Otago or Canterbury players not worthy of consideration. James Hutchison in Dunedin read about this and commented that 'no one should be surprised at the lengths to which the New Zealand union party will go'. He also talked about how the players turned up their haughty noses at the accommodation offered them. Shorn of all the rhetoric from both sides of the rugby divide, it seemed a genuine error by the shipping company.[6]

At the end of the tour, during which the All Blacks lost only to New South Wales, a half-hearted attempt was made to get the national team to play a combined South Island team in Wellington, a classic 'Them and Us' match. Hoben raised the idea with Member of Parliament James (later Sir James) Allen, who was a former Otago player and president. Allen sent a telegram to Chapman's successor as Otago secretary, Fred Horne, who replied: 'If Hoben wants match let him communicate with sister unions Otago Canterbury and Southland.' Hoben did, but to no avail. The three outcast unions met in Dunedin and decided they still did not want to be a part of the New Zealand union and it was 'not desirable' for a combined match 'because of the state of feeling in football circles'.[7] They also talked about the prospect of forming a South Island Rugby Football Union but decided against. Within a year, Canterbury broke ranks with its South Island colleagues and joined the NZRFU at the 1894 annual general meeting. Southland too applied for affiliation but withdrew when its delegates realised it would mean an end to games against Otago. Full unity came a year later when the Otago union's annual meeting in 1895 voted narrowly to affiliate; it was clear that rugby in the southern part of the South Island had become pretty boring with only Otago and Southland to watch. The diehard opponents such as Chapman and Hutchison held out, but the political wisdom of Allen, reinstated for a second stint as president, allied with pragmatism won the night. Southland also returned to the fold.

The New Zealand union then turned to its next goals: joining forces with the unions in Australia and a tour of Britain. The first never happened, despite genuine attempts on both sides of the Tasman, and the second took longer than expected. The talk of rugby federation with Australia needs a little explanation. During the 1890s there was increasing talk across the Tasman of the separate colonies joining together, although in New Zealand the temperature of the idea never got above lukewarm. There was close co-operation in sport, though. Athletics and swimming had joint championship meetings and Tasman hopping was common among sportspeople. It was not surprising that rugby should consider one trans-Tasman umbrella

All Blacks adopted by twins

A diary kept by Paddy Carolin, the vice-captain of the South African team that toured Britain in 1906, was published in 1990 after it had been gathering dust for nearly a century in an attic. Included in it was a photo of two women, one wearing a South African jersey and the other a New Zealand jersey. Inscribed on the photo is the message, 'Love from the twins, April 07.' Carolin described them as 'the New Zealand twins' and in a note the diary editors, Gideon Nieman and Lappe Laubscher, said they must have been the original rugby fanatics. They said the twins followed the All Blacks on tour in 1905 and followed suit the following year with the original Springboks.[1]

Who were these women? Diaries written during the 1905 tour talk about followers, but their names were not often given. The most complete off-the-field account was written by the vice-captain, Billy Stead, and he made no mention of 'the New Zealand twins'. Neither did the manager, George Dixon, in either his published or unpublished accounts. The 'twins' have not appeared in any of the numerous books written about the 1905 team, either at the time or later.

The Springbok jersey shown in the Carolin photo looked genuine enough, but the New Zealand jersey worn by the other sister had a disproportionately large silver fern, as if it were a jersey created by its wearer rather than left by an admirer. But the two women certainly existed and they were twins, all right. But they were not New Zealand twins. They were Australians by the names of Doris and Aileen Woods, born in 1886 in Manly in Sydney – Aileen a half an hour ahead of Doris – daughters of Maud Fitz-Stubbs and her husband, Harry Woods. Their life was one of inseparable devotion to each other and neither married.

Their musical ability came presumably from their mother who was an amateur pianist and composer in Sydney in the last two decades of the nineteenth century.[2] Their sporting interest seemed to stem from an uncle, Sammy Woods, their public servant father's brother who played cricket for both Australia and England as well as rugby for England. With Mum as accompanist and manager, the twins set out on a stage career from an early age and in 1899, when they were thirteen, were advertised as starring artistes in a 'prom' concert in the Sydney Town Hall as, 'Brilliant twins introducing the latest "coon songs" in costume . . .' ('coon songs' was the name given at the time to what later were known as Negro spirituals and still later as traditional African-American songs). They performed throughout Australia and sometimes in New Zealand until early in the twentieth century when their mother took them to Britain. By then Uncle Sammy was firmly established as the Somerset county cricket captain and, according to a later note by cricket journalist Christopher Martin-Jenkins, had even transformed his 'Seedney' accent to 'Zummerzet'.[3]

It seems they only billed themselves as 'the New Zealand twins' after they arrived in England. No reason for the name has been forthcoming, although perhaps it did have something to do with the rugby team in 1905. The stories about their close association with both the All Blacks and the Springboks came not from the pens or mouths of others, but from themselves. They jointly attached their names to an article in the *Weekly Dispatch* in London in 1907 that demonstrated an affectionate

A signed postcard of 'the New Zealand twins', among the earliest of tour supporters.

fondness for their footballing friends. They said one of their most treasured mementoes was a Marconigram (a wireless telegram specific to the Marconi company) from the All Blacks when they were crossing the Atlantic to the United States in January 1906. 'Kia ora, twins,' the message read. A New Zealand journalist in London at the time, Charles Rous-Marten, who had music as one of the great loves of his life, probably knew the twins personally. This was indicated when he wrote home: 'They also cherish two silver ferns given to them by a certain member of the All Blacks, whose blushes I will spare by refraining from publishing his name.'

'Rous', as others knew him, said the twins also had a large photograph of the team, signed by all the players, a huia feather and the ball used in the match against Newport, the third-last of the tour.

When the first Springboks to tour Britain arrived a year after the All Blacks, Rous-Marten said the twins, by then twenty, badgered their uncle Sammy to ensure they met the players. They subsequently attended several of the matches and gained a matching pair when the captain, Paul Roos, gave them the ball from the South Africans' Newport match. 'This is a trophy with which we would not part for untold gold,' they said in the *Dispatch* story. The newspaper illustrated the article with the picture of the twins each wearing rugby jerseys that was later reproduced in the South African book.

They later made a concert tour of South Africa with their mother and they also trod the boards throughout Europe, as well as in tsarist Russia. Their musical ability and their likeness seemed to attract publicity wherever they went.

When they were born, the identity issue was obvious and Doris was given a blue bow and Aileen pink so their mother could tell which was which. They seemed to have been thus colour-coded during their childhood because on one occasion, the colours were mixed and one of the twins got two doses of medicine instead of one each. They were said to have suffered identical ailments and once, when they were older, they went to a doctor and asked in unison 'Do we suffer from a weak heart, doctor?' They once suffered from the singer's dread, laryngitis, and the doctor was amazed their throats were duplicates in signs and symptoms.[4]

In a later article about them, it was said their tastes were the same in everything, from food to literature and art. 'An order for two is safe enough at a restaurant so long as one is consulted. Once or twice the girls themselves have been deceived for Aileen, catching sight of her reflection in a Bond Street mirror, thought it was Doris and waved her hand to her.' When asked about the prospect of marriage both agreed it was unlikely. 'Neither of us could go away on a honeymoon without the other,' one said.

When war began in Europe in 1914, the twins and their mother headed for Southeast Asia and they became regulars at concerts and clubs in Singapore, Malaya and India. A trip to the United States seems to have been fitted in because it was reported they had a film chance with the Vitagraph studio but turned it down, preferring to stick to the stage. After the war, in 1919, the show-business paper *New York Clipper* said they were in Vladivostok as part of a troupe entertaining American soldiers.[5] They do not seem to have returned to Europe and moved to Hong Kong with the intention of introducing cabaret singing and dancing there. They also taught singing and dancing to children. When the Japanese invaded Hong Kong in 1941, the twins and their younger sister, Valentine Winfield, were living in the home of the general manager of the Hong Kong and Shanghai Banking Corporation, Sir Vandeleur Grayburn, and his wife Mary. Doris worked for the bank. By this time, the mother was dead.[6]

They were incarcerated in the Stanley internment camp and a fellow internee, Barbara Anslow, occasionally mentioned the twins in her diary.

> The most pathetic accommodation I saw was that of twin ladies, Aileen and Doris Woods (then in their fifties), who in their younger days had been well-known singers overseas, their mother accompanying them on the piano but the mother had died pre-war and the twins never sang publicly after that although they did sing to the soldiers in hospital.
>
> When they came to our room one day [Anslow's 24th birthday] we persuaded them to give us a song and they sang a chorus of 'One Alone' from 'The Desert Song', their voices soaring throughout the entire flat. It was so wonderful to hear them.
>
> Their billet was in the science block . . . they had a little corner in part of a narrow room like a corridor, with a stone floor. Their bed was half a ping pong table. . . . They counted themselves lucky to have such a quiet spot.

Anslow also recorded that the twins had lost all their mementoes of their singing days.

On 11 November 1942, Remembrance Day but that went unremarked, Anslow recorded:

> The Woods twins are very interesting. We hadn't known them [before the war] but one day when they were visiting a friend in hospital they noticed Mabel in the ward and stared at her and shouted: 'Bette!' They explained to us that Mabel looked so like the film star Bette Davis whom they had met in Hollywood during their singing career; ever after, they called Mabel Bette.

The sisters survived the war. Doris returned to the day job she had before the war with the Hong Kong and Shanghai Banking Corporation and Aileen worked at Radio Hong Kong. Both retired on the same day in 1960 at the age of 74. A *China Mail* reporter asked a friend if they would leave the colony, as it then was, and received the reply: 'They will not leave Hong Kong.'[7]

organisation, the better to co-ordinate fixtures and make representations to whoever controlled the game in Britain. The International Rugby Football Board, formed in 1886, nominally had control; the Rugby Football Union, to which the New Zealand RFU was affiliated, had effective control.

In the year that rugby in New Zealand united, the game in England divided. Three months after Otago and Southland dragged their feet under the national union table, more than twenty clubs in the north of England met in Huddersfield and unanimously adopted the resolution: 'That the clubs here represented decided to form a Northern Rugby Football Union, and pledge themselves to push forward, without delay, its establishment on the principle of payment for bona-fide broken-time payment only.' The Natives had played all but three of the clubs seven years before; they represented the strength of rugby in Lancashire and Yorkshire. The insistence on amateurism and its accompanying ethos was at enormous cost for English rugby; it was not fatal, but it caused wounds from which the game has never recovered.[8] It has never since been close to challenging soccer's greater following.

While the RFU had its hands full with the clubs in the north, there was also a dread that a tour by a team from the colonies – whether New Zealand, Australia or South Africa – might infect England with the professionalism plague. It was that barrier, erected out of fear rather than any rational thought, which delayed for as long as it did the first colonial visit, by New Zealand in 1905. New Zealand delivered pledges and entreaties and always Rowland Hill and his committee found reasons to stall. Alfred Newman and Len Cuff assured the English of how lily-white the New Zealanders were and when those appeals fell on unresponsive ears recruited the persuasive tongues of politicians. William Pember Reeves, the agent-general (forerunner of high commissioner) in London since 1896, also called on Rowland Hill. (Reeves had played both rugby and cricket for Canterbury, so unlike some politicians who involve themselves in rugby, he knew what he was talking about. When the tour came closer to being a reality, he found out the costs of a cricket tour by Australia and told the NZRFU to use them as a guide.)

It did not help the official cause that a private New Zealander tried to organise a tour of his own. George Stephenson was a celebrated rugby player in Dunedin who, working as an auctioneer for his father (the founder of Wright Stephenson), went to England in 1891 to learn more about the woollen mills business. Working in Yorkshire, he played rugby for the Manningham club before it joined others in the split from the English union. Stephenson returned to Dunedin, continued to play rugby and when his father died, he became a wealthy man. This allowed him to indulge a passion (and a talent) for acting and he returned to England for a lengthy holiday, and he turned out again for Manningham, by then a league club. He thus became the first New Zealander to switch from rugby to league. Stephenson went on to buy and build up a theatrical company and while he was doing so, he came up with the idea of financing a rugby tour of Britain. He got an old mate, William McKenzie, who played for New Zealand in 1897 and was a journalistic colleague and friend of Denny Hoben's, to write to the NZRFU. Stephenson proposed, through McKenzie, that a team of twenty tour Britain and Australia for eight months in 1900 and that he receive 8 per cent on the amount he spent and one-fifth of the net proceeds. The players would be chosen by him and two people nominated by the NZRFU. The union sent the proposal to provincial unions, asking their views. A resounding answer was that any such tour should be organised and controlled only by the union, which was just the answer it wanted.[9]

Tom Eyton, the advance man for the Natives in 1888, contributed his experience. Clubs in England, he reminded people who may have read his book, had ground members who got into matches for nothing other than an annual fee and

Great Britain at the southern (right) end of Athletic Park kicks off on 13 August 1904 in the first test match to be played in New Zealand. Photographer Charles Martin appears to have been on the top of the western bank to take the photo, which seems not to have been published at the time. Martin's grandson, Paul, restored the plate glass image more than a hundred years later and added fragments from other images to complete what he called a jigsaw. © CHARLES MARTIN AND PAUL MARTIN (PMARTIN790@AOL.COM)

that therefore limited the gate return a visiting team might expect. He also wondered whether any New Zealander could afford to go to Britain and still adhere to the English union's rules on professionalism: 'I doubt if there is one of the front rank players in New Zealand . . . able to provide himself with pocket-money without which it would be found that the team would naturally be very discontented.'[10] He argued the New Zealand union should provide daily expenses to the players to cover 'numerous petty wants'. This was precisely what agitated the guardians of amateurism and, just as precisely, concerned thinkers such as Tom Ellison, who wrote that the laws about professionalism were framed to apply in England and it was never imagined by the framers that they should apply to tours.

As New Zealanders found, Ellison was quite right. Players in a British team in New Zealand in 1904 led by a Scot, David Bedell-Sivright, were paid 'wine money' of three shillings a day. No fuss was made of it at the time because no fuss was needed: it was accepted as a necessity of life. The fuss came later only after the Scots realised the All Blacks of 1905 were paid the same daily allowance; not only was it paid, but it was done so with the approval of the English. Delegates to the New Zealand union's annual meeting in 1904, the meeting at which they decided – but not unanimously – to send a team to Britain, wondered how some of the players would fare for so long without income. Neil Galbraith, the union's treasurer, reminded them that the British players of 1888 and 1899, the latter going only to Australia, were reimbursed for 'out of pocket' expenses. It was well known, he said, that not all the British players could afford to leave their work for 'pure sport' and he was sure the English union would allow New Zealand some discretion.

New Zealanders had been agitating for a tour of Britain since the Natives got home, so the tour of 1905–06 was a long time coming. One of the reasons was uncertainty about New Zealand's amateurism bona fides, another was the north–south divide in England and another was the Boer War. New Zealanders and Australians were also involved in the war and as a result, rugby tours were put on hold. The war lasted from October 1899 until midway through 1902, and when New Zealand reignited the tour idea with a visit to Britain by Alf de Costa, a Wellington sharebroker who preceded Galbraith as the union's treasurer,

Rowland Hill said it was too late because clubs already had their fixture lists arranged.

So 1905 it became. The national union estimated the cost at about £6,000 and set about raising the money, partly by seeking contributions from provincial unions and partly by appealing to the public. The union thought a percentage of gate receipts in Britain would make up any shortfall. Not everyone was in favour of the big adventure. Otago, which still looked on the national union with a cautious eye, was opposed on several grounds. One of its delegates at the meeting that decided on the tour, Dick Isaacs, produced a shopping list of reasons against:

1. That the visit would not benefit New Zealand football (vide Native team).
2. That the work of the New Zealand union is the conservation of football and not the advertisement of the colony.
3. That football is at such an ebb in New Zealand as to render the movement inopportune.
4. That it would be impossible to form such a team without constituting the members thereof professionals.
5. That the surplus funds of football in New Zealand will be better directed to the more frequent visits of football teams from England.
6. That such a trip may spoil the lives of many of the participants (vide Native team).
7. That there has been no invitation received from Home for a team to visit England, all the representations having been made from New Zealand.[11]

None of these reasons was sufficient enough to deter any other union from supporting the tour or to stop Otago's advocacy of one of its outstanding personalities, Jimmy Duncan, becoming the coach. There was widespread opposition to Duncan as

An invitation to the official farewell to the 1905–06 New Zealand team in Wellington.

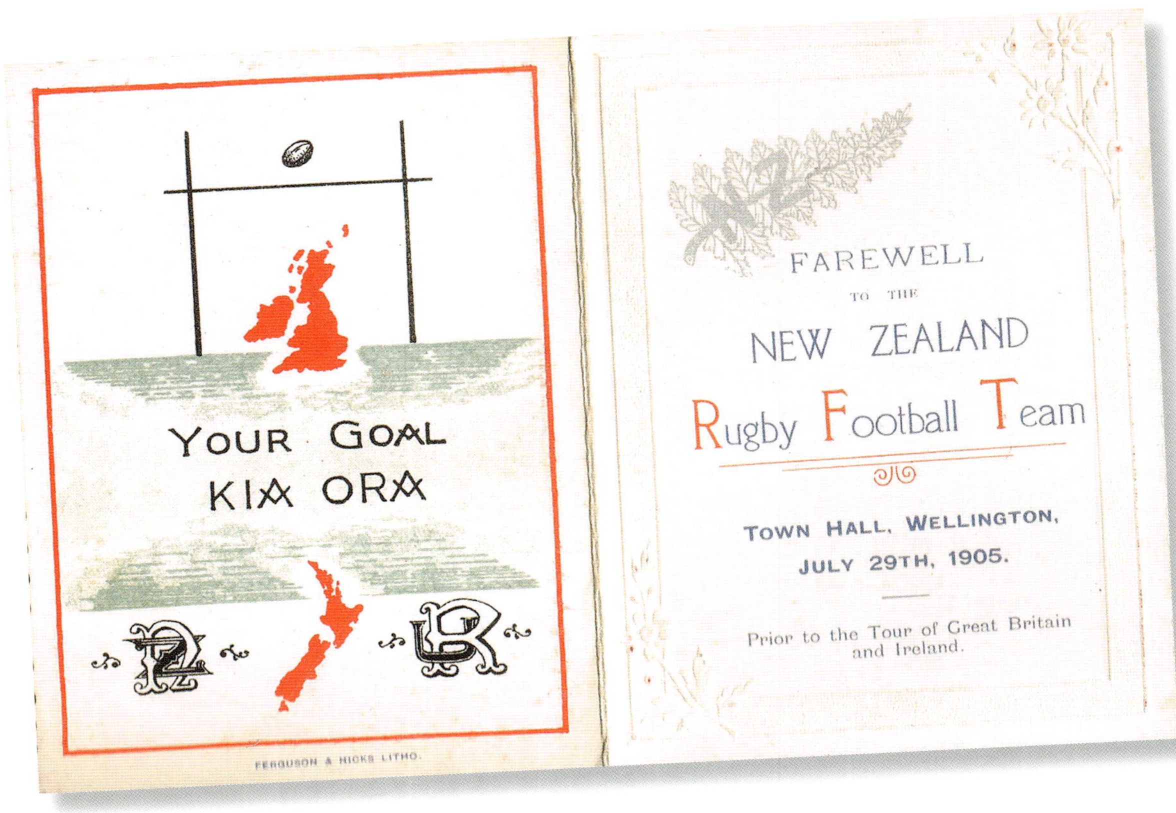

The Otago union was opposed to the tour but it still contributed four players and the coach. From left, Ernie Booth, coach Jimmy Duncan, Steve Casey and William Johnston. Alex McDonald sits in front.

coach, largely on the grounds that the money would be better spent on another player, but Otago got its way and he went anyway. There were frequent tales of a rift within the team – between those for and against Duncan – and that he was more or less ignored as a coach. He became, it appears, more of an assistant to manager George Dixon and that the coaching of the players was left to the captain, Dave Gallaher, vice-captain Billy Stead and one of the forwards, Bill Cunningham from Auckland.

The team's internal tensions were privately acknowledged but publicly denied. For all that, the 1905–06 All Blacks were extraordinarily successful, losing just the one match, the test against Wales, which itself endured as a piece of rugby folklore. It is true, as later critics have argued, that the real strength of English rugby was not met because by 1905 Yorkshire and Lancashire were 'Northern Union' bastions. George Stephenson had warned as much two years before the tour. Soccer was beating rugby out of the market in England, he said, and 'in a few years the ERU [RFU] will be as extinct as the dodo'. A New Zealand team would 'paralyse' any English team.[12] At the same time, rugby outside of the British Isles was a bit of a mystery, if a comment taken by one of the leading sportsmen and commentators of the day, Charles Burgess Fry, can be relied on. He wrote about England's influence in games for *Strand Magazine* and said 'Outside the British Isles important football is played only in America and Australia.' In rugby football, as opposed to association football, the world championship lies between the British Isles countries, he said. 'It is, perhaps,

Where it all began. Captain Dave Gallaher throws into a lineout in the first match of the 1905 tour, a 55–4 victory against Devon at Exeter.

worth mentioning that Association flourishes in Australia, New Zealand and at the Cape.'[13] Since Fry, a celebrated figure in his time, played cricket and soccer for England and once broke the world long jump record, here was ample proof that practising sportsmen were not necessarily the most knowledgeable.

The All Blacks were also criticised for the manner of their play, especially the employment of the wing forward and their method of putting the ball into the scrum. But such criticisms need to be put in context. The wing forward was not a New Zealand invention designed to harass the opposing halfback, but was developed by Tom Ellison of the Natives and others from what they saw in northern England. Many teams in Britain that opposed the All Blacks also had wing forwards. Shrewdly, they called them by other names. Dave Gallaher pointed this out:

> And what amused me throughout this phase of the bother was that nearly all our opponents themselves played wing-forwards, although they called them 'halves'. They had one half who put the ball in and took it if it came out his side, and another half on the other side who did ditto if it came out there. That is practically playing two 'wings'. But they were above suspicion, apparently, because they were called 'halves'.[14]

A well-regarded and long-time Australian writer, John Corbett Davis, wrote as 'The Cynic' in two Sydney sports papers which later merged, the *Arrow* and the *Referee*. He had his own view on British reporters' criticism of the All Blacks. He wrote after Gallaher had been killed in 1917: 'Gallaher was an infinitely greater character and sportsman than nine-tenths of his narrow-visioned critics, chagrined to find a team of Colonials

The try that never was

Billy Wallace has a lot to answer for. William Joseph Wallace, one of the outstanding players of the early twentieth century, was otherwise known as 'Carbine' for a great-hearted racehorse of the time and sometimes known as 'Will' or as 'Kill Danger' (this latter especially by his grateful teammates).

It was thanks to Wallace that the myth of the 1905 team being the first to be called the All Blacks was perpetuated. Wallace was also responsible for giving a second wind to the belief that he set up a try by Bob Deans in the test against Wales, but that it was not allowed by referee John Dallas.

Disputes about scores given or not given, the try that was disallowed, the goal that was or was not kicked, are just a part of rugby, as disagreement with officials' decisions is part of any sport. The All Blacks have won tests because of disputed decisions and they have lost them. Wales was the first contentious loss. The Deans 'try' stands supreme in scoring denial because it became a focal point between two countries for which rugby was important and stood to represent the difference between supremacy and not. It was, according to Welsh rugby historians David Smith and Gareth Williams, 'the grit in the oyster that produced a black pearl for future generations'.[1]

Part of the enduring attraction of the argument was that it could not be resolved. It was there, then it was gone forever. The fact was a try was not given and Wales won 3–0, giving the pioneering team its only loss on a distinguished tour. Deans himself did not live long enough to add spice to the argument. He came from the landholding pre-1850 Deans family in Canterbury and was a man for whom everyone seemed to have a high regard and whose integrity was never questioned. He maintained that he got the ball down over the line. But he died of complications after appendicitis just three years later. As a great-nephew, Robbie Deans, once said: 'If Bob said he scored, then he scored.'

Bob Deans . . . 'If he said he scored, he scored,' said great-nephew Robbie. MNZ-1009-1/4F, ALEXANDER TURNBULL LIBRARY

By the middle of December 1905, the All Blacks had played 27 matches and amassed 801 points for and just 22 against. It is true English rugby was not in a strong state at the time, partly because its best rugby-playing counties had formed rugby league a decade earlier, but the results were nevertheless astonishing and earned the team a level of newspaper coverage never seen before and not matched

A 1981 facsimile, accurate in all details, of the now-rare 1905 Welsh test programme.

since. Front-page photos, drawings and stories about the New Zealand team were commonplace, providing just the type of publicity for the distant colony that its premier, Richard Seddon, and his man in London, William Pember Reeves, was after. It should be understood that soccer, although widespread and popular, did not have the hold on the British sports-going public in 1905 that it later gained. Newspapers frequently ran stories under the catch-all heading of 'football' and distinguished in the body of the story between 'the Rugby game' and 'the Association game' (invariably, their capitals).

As the tour progressed, through England to Scotland, then to Ireland and back to England, the New Zealanders were shadowed by the knowledge that Wales was still to come. All Blacks of any era, even those utterly immersed in the modern, knew of the cry, 'Wait till you get to Wales!' The Welsh did not just lie in wait, planning their ambush. They scouted out their foes. Some of the players went to New Zealand matches in the south and south-west of England, especially nearby Cheltenham in early December, and their main selector, Tom Williams, was among the thousands crammed into Crystal Palace for the test match against England, won by New Zealand by five unconverted tries to nothing on a wet, muddy afternoon. Some players went off to play in club matches in England to try out their combinations. The seriousness of the Welsh challenge and the enthusiasm of the principality for the game was evident when the All Blacks arrived in Cardiff late on the Thursday night before the Saturday game. 'There was hardly room to breathe, let alone move,' Wallace recorded in his memoirs.[2] The horse-drawn carriage carrying the players the short distance from the station to their hotel was stopped several times by the press of the crowd.[3] Needless to say, the Arms Park in the centre of the city was packed on the Saturday afternoon. Smith and Williams thought there were 47,000 at the game; in the days of standing room only, any guess would do. Just to cover themselves, they called it 'the biggest rugby assembly hitherto'.[4] A *South Wales Argus* reporter put it thus: 'Never before or since can such a multitude have been shod with such suspense or quivered with such excitement.'[5]

Before the game, the pre-match ritual. In this case, though, it was the beginning of a tradition. Tom Williams had reported to the Welsh union that the New Zealanders sometimes before games uttered their 'war dance'. (The 1905 team used the Te Rauparaha haka but not before every match.) Williams saw the psychological value of the haka to the All Blacks and thought the Welsh could counter it with some emotional chest-thumping of their own. The local morning paper, the *Western Mail*, contributed its view that the Welsh players should sing 'Hen Wlad fy Nhadau' ('Land of My Fathers'), a nationalistic air composed nearly 50 years before by a Pontypridd father and son, Evan and James James.

So David Gallaher led his players out to the centre of the playing arena shortly before 2.30 p.m. while the crowd sang 'Men of Harlech'. The stirring final line, 'Cambria ne'er can yield.' had barely faded away when the All Blacks created a stir of their own: 'Ka mate! Ka mate!' The haka then was more a bit of foot shuffling and the odd stamp with the waving around of arms rather than the choreographed spectacle it later became. When the haka ended, the players moved to their positions but the Welsh stayed still in a rough semi-circle and sang their anthem – faintly at first, but the strains were picked up by the crowd and a chorus of thousands joined in, reaching the crescendo:

> *Gwlad! Gwlad! pleidiol wyf i'm gwlad.*
> *Tra môr yn fur i'r bur hoff bau,*
> *O bydded i'r heniaith barhau.*

(The English words convey none of the passion and feeling in the song, but a literal translation runs:

> Land! Land! I am true to my land!
> As long as the sea serves as a wall for this pure, dear land
> May the language endure for ever.)

It was the beginning of the ritual of anthems preceding test matches, although as far as the haka was concerned, the order changed. (To mark the centenary, the Welsh and New Zealand unions agreed that the haka could precede the Welsh anthem for the 2005 match. The Welsh tried to repeat that the following year, but the New Zealanders got the pip and did the haka in the dressing room.)

Soon after Dallas began the game, Wallace's worries were confirmed. He was concerned that too many players were stale; they'd put on weight through too much train travel and too much hotel living, and that they'd been on tour too long. Like others, he knew the hardest leg of the tour came at the wrong time. It was evident not long after the start that the backs, in particular, were well below their best form. It didn't help that they were missing their most potent finisher, speedster George Smith, who was injured, and their vice-captain and tactical general, Billy Stead, who was variously described as being ill, being rested and injured. Stead in fact was one of the touch judges (touring teams provided players to run the touch until the 1960s). From his privileged vantage point, Stead could see clearly what went wrong: 'The attempts to find the line, give or take passes or even to field a ball, were absolutely painful to watch. Never on this tour has our back play fallen to so low a standard . . .'[6]

It was no real surprise, therefore, when after 27 minutes the fastest Welsh wing, 25-year-old medical student Teddy Morgan, scored a try. The three points thus gained seemed a fair reflection, so went the majority view, of how play had developed. The All Blacks were slightly better in the second half as they tried time and again to level the scores. The best chance, it seemed, came with about ten minutes to play (although various timings have been offered over the years). Wallace retrieved the ball after a kick and set off on the type of curving run for which he was known. Rather than run down the left wing touch, Wallace angled inwards and by the time he got to halfway, he was in about the centre of the field, more or less alongside Dallas, as it happened. Wallace ran inside Gwyn Nicholls, the Welsh captain, and then straightened to run for the Welsh goal-line, but directly ahead of him, standing on about the 25-yard line (as the

Teddy Morgan, who scored for Wales against New Zealand in 1905 and who believed the All Blacks scored a try too.

22 was then), waited the best Welsh back of the day (and Nicholls's brother-in-law and business partner), the English-born Bert Winfield. Wallace advanced towards Winfield and passed to his left to Deans. 'Go Bob!' Wallace shouted. With about 30 metres to run, Deans evidently saw the chance not just of a try, but of a converted try which, if achieved, would have given New Zealand the lead. He angled his run therefore for the posts, but the curved line he took put him closer to Morgan, who was haring back in defence. Deans's angled run also gave one of the Welsh centres, Rhys Gabe, the extra time to get back to defend. As Deans approached the line, he was tackled by both Morgan and Gabe and thus began differences of opinion that have continued for more than a century.

Deans said he scored. Some versions have him being dragged back across the line into the field of play or the ball was picked up and taken back; whichever it was occurred before Dallas arrived on the scene. The referee, seeing that the ball was not over the line, ordered a scrum with a Welsh put-in. There was nothing else he could have done. Consultations with off-field officials were in an undreamt-of future.

Conflicting newspaper reports of the time have not helped resolve the issue (other than the one indisputable fact that it was not a try because the referee said it was not). Newspapers reporters were seated at a trestle table at ground level a few metres back from the touchline. How well a reporter could follow play depended on where he was seated; if he was at the end nearest the Welsh goal-line, he probably would have had a good view; if at the other, he was that much further away and his view would probably have been impeded by his colleagues, especially as they stood in moments of excitement. Not many reporters followed the team around the country – the *Daily Mail*'s John Buttery seems to have been the only one at all games apart from the first two – and so they would not necessarily have been readily able to identify who was who of the New Zealanders (even though jerseys were numbered). So there were conflicting reports that Wallace nearly scored or that Hunter nearly scored as well as Deans. Deans himself put it beyond doubt the next day when, in response to a request, he sent his famed telegram to the *Daily Mail* in which he said he scored. For some reason, the *Mail* did not publish the telegram until the end of the tour when it was included in its tour book. The telegram supported the published assertion by Buttery that Deans 'was collared, but not before he had crossed the Welsh line'.[7]

Players and some people at the ground knew of the belief a New Zealander could have scored, nearly scored, or should have scored, but people at home remained ignorant of the controversy for some weeks. An initial report of the match was cabled to New Zealand and distributed through the Press Association to all newspapers, but it made no mention of the Deans 'try'. That came

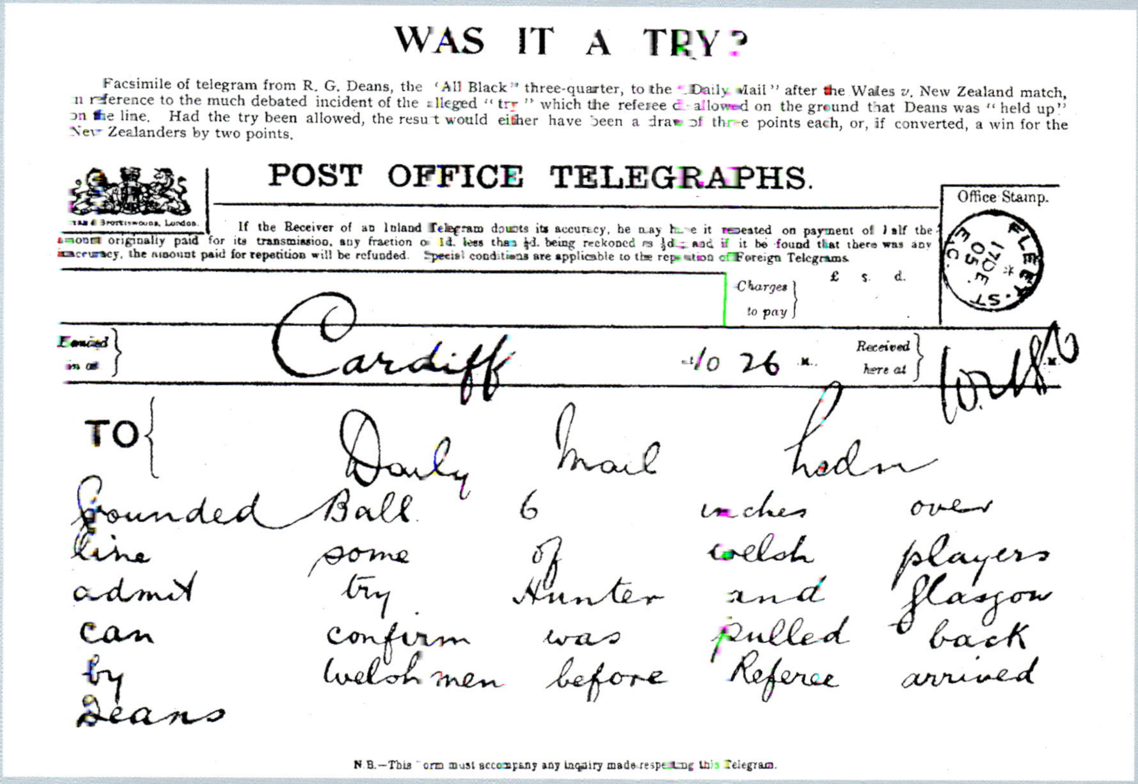

WAS IT A TRY?

Facsimile of telegram from R. G. Deans, the "All Black" three-quarter, to the "Daily Mail" after the Wales v. New Zealand match, in reference to the much debated incident of the alleged "try" which the referee disallowed on the ground that Deans was "held up" on the line. Had the try been allowed, the result would either have been a draw of three points each, or, if converted, a win for the New Zealanders by two points.

POST OFFICE TELEGRAPHS.

If the Receiver of an Inland Telegram doubts its accuracy, he may have it repeated on payment of half the amount originally paid for its transmission, any fraction of 1d. less than ½d. being reckoned as ½d.; and if it be found that there was any inaccuracy, the amount paid for repetition will be refunded. Special conditions are applicable to the repetition of Foreign Telegrams.

Office Stamp. FLEET ST. E.C. 17 DE 05

Charges to pay £ s. d.

Handed in at Cardiff 10 26 M. Received here at 10.48

TO Daily Mail Ldn

Grounded Ball 6 inches over line some of Welsh players admit try Hunter and Glasgow can confirm was pulled back by Welshmen before Referee arrived Deans

N.B.—This form must accompany any inquiry made respecting this Telegram.

A facsimile of the telegram Bob Deans sent at the request of the editor to the *Daily Mail* the day after the loss to Wales.

only several weeks later, in early 1906, when reports and newspapers arrived by ship from Britain. By the time the players arrived home in March 1906, the Deans incident had been well covered. The Premier, Richard Seddon, referred to it in his welcoming speech in the Auckland Town Hall. The All Blacks 'had not said a word against the decision but in their hearts and in the opinion of most people it was recognised it was not a defeat, but try to try'.[8] Manager George Dixon's view, as reported publicly and in his diary, was that Deans had scored a fair try but that Wales deserved their win; like most, he conceded the All Blacks had not played well enough to win. An unidentified All Black called the Deans 'try' 'as fair a try as I have ever seen scored on a football field'. The referee 'did not see the try scored and he did not consult the line umpire, who did, so he gave the benefit to the defending side . . . but there you are, it's all in the game'.

There the matter more or less lay for the next fifteen years or so until Teddy Morgan was interviewed in London by *Lloyd's Sunday News* and a copy of the article found its way to New Zealand. Morgan said the try scorer was Wallace, but in all other respects his view concurred with that of New Zealanders. He added that the Welsh touch judge, Ack Llewellin, confirmed a try had been scored (as had the other touch judge, Billy Stead). The most telling comment by Morgan was:

> I am personally convinced that Wallace grounded the ball before being pulled back into the field of play, but the referee disallowed the try on the ground that the ball had not been grounded. A number of the Welsh players, including R. T. Gabe, had no doubt that the colonial try was legitimate.

Morgan's comments were put to Wallace by a *Dominion* reporter and he was so aroused he

A drawing of Bob Deans that appeared in manager George Dixon's tour book.

sketched a plan of the movement that led to the 'try', a plan that has been the basis of all following diagrams purporting to show what happened. Wallace then described the move in the game, saying he could remember it as clearly as he could a club match the previous Saturday. 'To my certain knowledge Deans grounded the ball a foot over the Welsh line,' he said. 'As Deans fell over the line the Welsh forwards fell on top of him, through his sudden dive. Deans made a mistake in getting up off the ball, instead of laying on it until the referee arrived.'[9]

Wallace said Deans spoke to him soon after the incident: 'It is a bare-faced swindle.' Wallace also said he heard Llewellin say to nearby spectators that a try had been scored. (Why Morgan attributed the 'try' to Wallace in the London interview is a mystery. He evidently told a New Zealand colleague at Guy's Hospital, Pat McEvedy, a later president of the New Zealand union, that Deans had scored. In 1921, he was quoted in a book, *Rugby Football Up to Date*, as saying Deans had scored, yet a year later he gave it to Wallace.)[10]

Anyway, the next step in the try narrative came at the dinner in Swansea in 1924 on the night of the Invincible All Blacks' defeat of Wales. Morgan was seated at the same table as the New Zealand captain, Cliff Porter, and he asked him if he knew Wallace. Both being from Wellington, they knew each other well. Morgan accordingly took Porter's menu and wrote on it: 'To Billy Wallace. Carbine. From Teddy Morgan. Deans did score at Cardiff 1905.'

Over the years, New Zealanders arrived at the old Arms Park and asked to have pointed out to them 'the spot' where Deans scored. It was, in 1905,

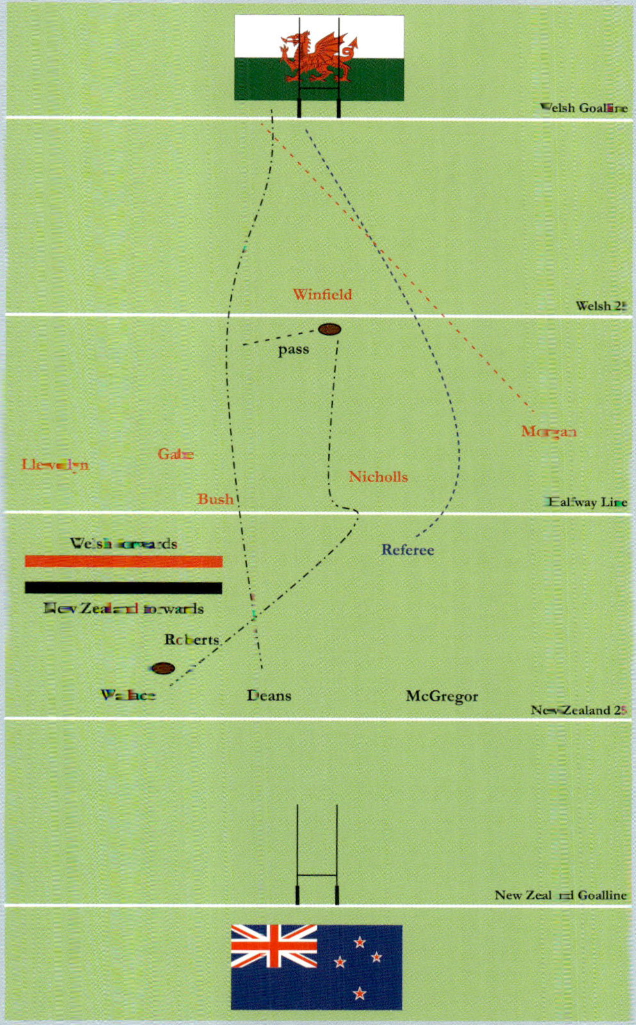

A diagram based on Billy Wallace's original sketch of the moves that led to Bob Deans's 'try' against Wales. PAUL SIDES

at the Westgate Street end – that is, the centre of the city end – of the ground and towards the Angel Hotel corner. But as the ground was redeveloped time and again, the spot was gradually covered over. That didn't stop cheeky Welshmen from pointing out to gullible New Zealanders where history was made. There have been tales of travellers grabbing handfuls of dirt in the belief they had once been fallen on by Bob Deans, and being chased out of the ground by angry groundsmen. The grit was transferred from the oyster to places of memory in New Zealand.

When the Empire Games were in Cardiff in 1958, the Arms Park was the venue for the athletics and opening and closing ceremonies. Charlie Jenkins, the sports editor of the *Evening Post* in Wellington, remarked: '. . . my seat in the press stand was almost in line with the normal goal line at the scoreboard end, the famous end. All New Zealanders who have played or watched at Cardiff Arms will remember where that is.'[11] The sports editor of the Cardiff morning paper, the *Western Mail*, was Bryn Thomas, better known as an ardent chronicler of Welsh rugby J. B. G. Thomas. When Val Sloper of Christchurch won the shot put on the first day and thus became the first gold medallist of the games he wrote: 'It is the first All Black victory at the Arms Park since 1946.'[12] (No one at the time would have needed to be told he was referring to the 2nd NZEF team's defeat of Wales and the Welsh victory over the All Blacks in 1953.)

A perception grew during and after the 1905–06 tour that New Zealanders played hard, took advantage when they thought they could get away with it, and generally did not have the same 'the game's the thing' attitude of the English. A competitive attitude, which became universal at the top level of the game, may have been behind the All Blacks' first appearance in fictional literature. This happened in the juvenile weekly, the *Magnet*, which recorded the goings-on at Greyfriars School and the gastronomic excesses of Billy Bunter. The writer Charles Hamilton, who used the pseudonym of Frank Richards, had one of his main characters blocking his ears during a match: '"Ow" roared Bob Cherry stopping his ears with his fingers, "you're not refereeing a match with the All Blacks".' Richards had painted Greyfriars as a soccer, not a rugby, school so presumably the All Blacks' style of play and the referees' impatience with it made an impact on boys beyond rugby.[13]

POSITION OF SCRUMMAGE AND LEFT WING FORWARD.

One of the most versatile cartoonists of the early twentieth century was Ecildoune Frederick Hiscocks, an Australian who moved to New Zealand as a horse breaker and artist. He drew this explanation of the wing forward for Tom Ellison's book, *The Art of Rugby Football.* TOM ELLISON, *THE ART OF RUGBY FOOTBALL* (WELLINGTON: GEDDIS AND BLOMFIELD, 1902)

coming out and teaching them how to play the game.'[15]

Rugby's laws were not always clear or universally applied in 1905. The International Rugby Board, although it was formed in 1886, did not set the playing laws of the game until the late 1920s. It was responsible only for test matches, although frequently ignored. The English union until then liked to think it decided how the game should be played, a sort of MCC or Royal and Ancient of rugby, but other countries (including New Zealand) sometimes thought otherwise. Not that the English (or, more broadly, the British) were all that squeaky clean anyway. When the British first played a test match against New Zealand, in Wellington in 1904, they lost 9–3. A noted journalist, Gordon McLean, wrote of that test: '. . . the British halves made no attempt to put the ball into the scrums properly, but shied it against the legs of the hookers, and tried to get away with it on the rebound. For these breaches, they were repeatedly penalised.'[16] This was the team that was paid 'wine money', which was more noted for its socialising than for its rugby and had four of its members staying at Government House in Wellington rather than with the rest of the players in a hotel. The captain, David Bedell-Sivright, described as a hot-headed Scotsman by McLean, had taken his team off the field in Newcastle because the referee ordered off one of the British players, Denys Dobson, for obscene language. Bedell-Sivright apparently remonstrated with the referee: 'Mr Dobson is an Oxford man and a gentleman.' Bedell-Sivright, in the words of a reporter unimpressed by his haughty manner, then 'picked up his valuable

The 1905–06 New Zealand team at Ealing during their first visit to London in early October 1905, for their match against Middlesex. Top row: Frank Glasgow, Billy Wallace, Fred Newton, Simon Mynott. Fourth row: Bob Deans, Jimmy Hunter, George Nicholson, Billy Johnston. Third row: Jimmy Duncan, Ernie Booth, John Corbett, George Tyler, Duncan McGregor, Charlie Seeling, Teddy Roberts. Second row: George Gillett, 'Bunny' Abbott, George Dixon, Bill Cunningham (standing, watch chain prominent), David Gallaher, Billy Stead, Billy Glenn, Bill Mackrell. Front row: Steve Casey, Alex McDonald, George Smith, 'Mona' Thomson, Jim O'Sullivan. Eric Harper was absent.

hyphen and marched his team off the field'. Play resumed 20 minutes later. Dobson's obscenity, it was later learned, was to enquire of the referee, after a penalty was given against him: 'What the devil was that for?'

Much has been written in the context of 1905 about a supposed physical degeneracy of the English people. After early setbacks in the Boer War, Rudyard Kipling wrote 'The Islanders', which was a plea for universal training in shooting and was scornful about devotion to sport:

Ere – ye fawned on the Younger Nations for
　the men who could shoot and ride!
Then ye returned to your trinkets;
　then ye contented your souls
With the flannelled fools at the wicket
　or the muddied oafs at the goals.[17]

The All Blacks had played six matches when a former Auckland lawyer, Percy Vaile, wrote a letter to the editor of *The Times* in which he talked about football matches as being matches between the

The Minister for Football

Politicians of whatever hue and in whatever country have always loved to latch on to sporting success. Some, such as in Eastern Europe during the communist era, valued sporting success so much they embarked on state-sponsored cheating. The vast majority are much more benign and seem to just like basking in reflected glory.

The British prime minister of the 1960s, Harold Wilson, used to happily maintain that England could win the (soccer) World Cup only under a Labour government (conveniently ignoring those of his voters in Scotland, Wales and Northern Ireland who may not have given a fig for England's soccer success). The Australian prime minister two decades later, Bob Hawke, seemed to arrange his itinerary to be instantly on hand at times of sporting success and especially when the America's Cup was won in 1983. American presidents generally contrive to throw a first ceremonial pitch every April when baseball begins. New Zealand political leaders are no different and a prime minister crowding into a dressing room for a photo opportunity with a winning All Black (or any other) team has become a visual cliché.

The first in New Zealand to readily identify himself with sporting success was Richard Seddon, the larger-than-life prime minister from 1893 until 1906. But, for Seddon, it was not just associating himself with success. It was all about the promotion of New Zealand and, by extension, its exported primary produce and the excellence of a country for both tourists and immigrants.

Seddon's two most controversial engagements with football were a telegram to the *Daily Mail* early in the 1905 tour and his decision at the end of it that the government would 'reward' the players by bringing them home through North America where they could play more games.

As to the former, Seddon only responded to an attention-grabbing ploy by the editor of the *Mail* who cabled him asking what 'New Zealand thinks of their remarkable success'. Seddon responded with his personal view rather than a collective view of the country, if such a thing were possible. He said he was not surprised by the team's success and that results were 'awaited almost as eagerly as the news of the late war in South Africa and the results are received with great enthusiasm'. Few could have quibbled with that. Seddon then gave his reason for football's success. It was an obvious plug for the benefits of living in New Zealand: 'The natural and healthy conditions of colonial life produce stalwart and athletic sons of whom New Zealand and the Empire are justly proud.'[1]

The mass-circulation *Mail* would have loved Seddon's response; the low-circulation *Westminster Gazette* did not. A paper targeted at 'clubland' in London's West End and no lover of colonials, it wondered: 'Is this really quite the sort of thing for a Premier to cable?' New Zealand newspapers, whether generally supportive of Seddon or not, happily answered the question. The *New Zealand Herald*, which was not a Seddon paper, said in an editorial:

> It is probably not quite the sort of thing that a British Premier would do, but in the case of Mr Seddon it is the most natural thing in the world. The business of a colonial Premier is to keep himself and his colony constantly before the British public, and never to miss an opportunity of advertising

French illustrator 'Mich' (Michel Liebeaux) depicts All Blacks 'Bunny' Abbott, Billy Glenn and Dave Gallaher, plus French hooker Paul Dedeyn and wing Gaston Lane, after the test in Paris on New Year's Day 1906. It was the first test match to be played by France. *LA VIE PARISIENNE*, 6 JANUARY 1906

> both. And Mr Seddon knows how to do that better than any man. He has made New Zealand and himself talked about over half the world.[2]

The *Auckland Star*, which supported Seddon, helpfully backgrounded the carping paper:

> The *Westminster Gazette*, it may be remembered, is alone among the papers of London for its consistent criticism of the doings of Mr Seddon. Its caricaturist (Mr Carruthers Gould) seems to have set the ball rolling, and the pursuit has been carried on since with a persistency that is at least a recognition of the status of the colony.[3]

Such was the success of the All Blacks in Britain in the last three months of 1905 that some wanted it to just carry on and on. There was a suggestion for an additional game at the end of the tour against a combined British team, but it fell through because the Welsh union said the proposed date was too close to its match against England. There was talk of a match against the best the All Blacks did not play, the Northern Union (league) teams, and a former All Black in Wellington, William ('Offside Mac') McKenzie, said two more matches should be played against Wales because best of three was a better way of determining who was best. As for the players, they just wanted to get home. Their only game in France was on New Year's Day 1906 and they headed back across the English Channel and, they thought, a few days' packing and sightseeing before boarding the ship for home. But when they arrived at the Manchester Hotel in London, they learned that the New Zealand Government had agreed to a return via North America and that their manager, George Dixon, had been charged with organising matches along the way.

The team's vice-captain, Billy Stead, wrote a regular newspaper column throughout the tour and said: 'Just heard with disgust that we have to play three matches in America. We had all congratulated ourselves on coming through an arduous tour, and we think it rather hard of our union to call us into the field.'[4]

John Blomfield's cartoon for the *Free Lance* depicting the return of the All Blacks encapsulates Premier Richard Seddon's promotion of the team and of New Zealand. Blomfield, a younger brother of the *Observer* cartoonist and part-owner William ('Blo'), depicts the New Zealander as a moa. This pre-dated depictions of a kiwi but showed a national independence by avoiding the lion's cub favoured by other cartoonists. *NEW ZEALAND FREE LANCE*, 10 MARCH 1906

A section of the huge crowd at the ferry terminal in Auckland that greeted the All Blacks on their return in March 1906. The *New Zealand Herald* said the eastern side of Queen Street wharf was black with people when the players returned from 'the most remarkable tour of a body of athletes that has ever been known'. Amid the throng pictured were the players and the Premier, Richard Seddon, who had been ferried in from their ship.

Dixon wrote to the New Zealand union secretary in Wellington, Edgar Wylie: 'I must confess to a feeling of disappointment when I received instructions for the American route. At that time I was fully convinced that it would be impossible because of weather and conditions to play in either Canada or America and I was looking forward to the six weeks quiet and rest of the steamer.'[5] Dixon told Wylie the players were heartily tired of football. In his unpublished diary, Dixon wrote: 'This trip is a confounded nuisance.'

But Seddon said go, so the reluctant footballers went. The *Evening Post* called the trip a picnic and a wicked waste of public money. The *Otago Daily Times*, whose editor was an opponent of long standing of the NZRFU, wrote the union was gaining the benefit rather than the players. By that, he meant the government had spared the union the expense of the North American trip but it was never the intention, until Seddon's intervention, to return by that route. As with most things involving Seddon, newspapers trod well-worn editorial lines. Critics of Seddon or of rugby, then or now, needed to know how to read between the lines.

The weekly Auckland newspaper, the *Observer*, was a frequent critic of Seddon's. It was also the employee of the team's manager, Dixon, so a William Blomfield cartoon was understandable. He depicted Seddon handing a sore-looking Dave Gallaher a ticket for a trip through Canada and the United States. It ran a caption saying:

> King Dick (to the New Zealand rugby captain): Congratulations, my fine fellow. You and your team have done splendidly. Now, I propose, by way of holiday, to send the team through Canada and America to play some more matches.
>
> Captain Davy Gallagher: Holiday, you call it. Surely, bruised and battered as we are, we have played enough football for the honour of New Zealand. Anyhow, we want to get home.

Dixon arranged three matches in the United States, but none in Canada because of frozen grounds. The first game was an unofficial exhibition in New York in which the opposition was a team grandly named 'All-New York'. Most of New York would not have known of it. In fact, it comprised eight expatriate Britons and seven of the New Zealanders, including the coach, Jimmy Duncan. Dixon was the referee. They played two games against British Columbia in San Francisco partly to demonstrate to Californians how much better (and safer) rugby was than American football.

The team arrived back in Auckland in March 1906 and the *Evening Post*, true to its recent form, again criticised Seddon, this time for meeting the players. Calling him the Minister for Football, it wondered 'by what code a football function takes precedence over the state business'.[6]

The *Post* editorial added: 'We have criticised him in many of his roles and it is with regret that we begin what we fear will be a long course of criticism of his football administration.'

But it was not. Seddon was dead within three months.[7]

THE UN-LICKED CUB.

The 'lion cub' was indeed unlicked when resident *Punch* cartoonist Bernard (later Sir Bernard) Partridge drew this in October 1905 before any of the five tests were played. The licking came in the fourth, against Wales. *PUNCH*, 11 OCTOBER 1905

manhood of nations.[18] His essential point was that the New Zealanders were winning not just because they were better than the teams they had so far played, but because New Zealanders as a national people were better. Vaile's opinion has been frequently quoted since, as if he were a spokesman for the country instead of just one man expressing an opinion. Vaile was an unrelenting self-publicist. A writer in the Wellington weekly, the *Free Lance*, called Vaile 'the hero of every sport he doesn't play' and 'the blow-hard Aucklander'. Vaile wrote of himself in a tennis book: 'Many players on whose judgment and integrity I would stake my tennis reputation have assured me that if I had started much younger and played a better game, I might easily have been a champion.'[19]

Premier Richard Seddon and Pember Reeves extolled in British newspapers the benefits of living in New Zealand, but their aim was to attract investment and immigrants rather than to praise rugby players.

After the first couple of weeks, during which wins and points piled up, newspapers in Britain doted on the All Blacks. It was not just the halfpenny-a-day, drum-beating *Daily Mail* that saw the rugby players as a circulation booster. All papers, up and down the market, devoted more space to the 1905 All Blacks than they did to any later New Zealand team. The phrase 'All Blacks' gained a full place in the language not because any of the papers coined it, but simply because of the number of them and the breadth of their coverage. One flawed theory about why the All Blacks had such commanding wins in the first part of the tour was [in] 'what became a typical All Black strategy, the New Zealanders arrived early in the season when the English were far from match fit'.[20] In fact, they arrived then because that was what the English union wanted; Rowland Hill did not want any disruption to his clubs' programmes or to the international fixtures which began in January. In the context of the first three tours of Britain, the New Zealanders also arrived unfit for matches because they had been on a ship for weeks. Teams tried to maintain some sort of fitness with regular exercises and running round the decks – and some even tried shovelling coal into the ships' boilers – but nothing was as good as actual match practice on a field.

There was no need for anyone, either then or later, to theorise and generalise about a nation's fitness or flabbiness as a reason for the All Blacks' success. If the All Blacks were fitter, both physically and mentally, it was not because

An Ernest Frater painting of a try in the 1905 match against Middlesex at Stamford Bridge, the New Zealand team's first in London. The All Blacks won 34–0 and scored eight tries. *SPHERE*, 7 OCTOBER 1905

A 'play-up' card published for the All Blacks' match in Leicester against Midland Counties.

The weekly illustrated London newspaper the *Sketch* ran this full page of All Black head shots a few days before the test against England. The caption writers were not as familiar with some of the names as they could have been. Bob Deans became 'Dubar' and, more logically, George Gillett became 'Gellett'. *SKETCH*, 29 NOVEMBER 1905

they were from New Zealand, but because they had trained themselves to be so. If the English players were not as fit, it was because they had not trained as the New Zealanders had and because it was early in their season (and that was their fault). The All Blacks also had a more systematic approach to the game than the English did at the time, having built on what the Natives had tried earlier. The All Blacks' approach was more hard-nosed. Any close observer of rugby in England – not necessarily in Britain – knows that until full professionalism, there was a noticeable difference in attitude between the English player and the New Zealander. To put it broadly, winning was what counted for New Zealanders because it was 'their' game; the playing was the key thing for the English. It was – and is – a headliner sport in New Zealand; Wales apart, in Britain it is way behind the public interest in soccer. But the difference did not encompass just rugby. A close and shrewd observer of British, and especially English, life in the years immediately before the

The All Blacks, some of them wearing running spikes, pose after training at Newton Abbot before their first game. Standing: Jim O'Sullivan, Charlie Seeling, Simon Mynott, George Gillett, Bill Cunningham, Frederick Newton, John Corbett, Bob Deans, Steve Casey and William Johnston. Sitting: Billy Glenn, Eric Harper, George Nicholson, Billy Wallace, Alex McDonald, Fred Roberts, 'Mona' Thomson, Jimmy Hunter, 'Bunny' Abbott. In front: George Smith and Ernie Booth. Captain Dave Gallaher was absent. MNZ-1009-1/4F, ALEXANDER TURNBULL LIBRARY

First World War, Guy Scholefield, worked as a journalist in London for four New Zealand newspapers. Along the way, he earned himself a doctorate at the London School of Economics so he was able to train the eye of both journalist and scholar on habits and attitudes. 'Nothing has lost the English sportsman so many good games as his conservatism,' he wrote. 'And nothing has incensed him more with his rivals.'[21] Sporting writers in England 'appeared in the role of petulant, whining complainers'. They acknowledged, he thought, the prowess of their visitors but complained bitterly they were not 'playing the game and from that they were not sports'.

Portrayal of the 1905 tour came in for caustic reappraisal in its centenary year when one historian (Caroline Daley) blamed two others (Keith Sinclair and Jock Phillips) for inventing the tradition of 1905.[22] In essence, her point was that the two highlighted what suited their arguments

Billy Stead with the ball in this sketch by Frank Gillett for the *Graphic*. Teddy Roberts has just passed the ball and wing forward and captain Dave Gallaher peers over the scrum to check progress. According to the accompanying text, Stead then passed to Bob Deans and then Duncan McGregor for one of the latter's four tries in the All Blacks' 15–0 win in the Crystal Palace test. *GRAPHIC*, 9 DECEMBER 1905

They gained a following; they already had the name

Being a Welshman and a journalist, John Buttery would surely have had a fine sense of humour, the gift of eloquence and a good deal of cynicism. Had he lived, Buttery would have chortled at the various stories that grew up about his being responsible for the New Zealand rugby team being known as the All Blacks.

But Buttery died not long after the 1905–06 tour on 23 August 1906, at the age of 39, from complications after an appendix operation (the same cause of Bob Deans's death two years later).[1] Buttery figures large in tour stories, and is sometimes given the credit for coining the name 'All Blacks', because he worked for the *Daily Mail* and it was at the forefront of the 'popular' newspapers which cashed in on the tour.

Buttery was born in Usk in Monmouthshire, about 15 kilometres north of Newport and far enough from the English border to be definitively Welsh, in late 1866 or early 1867. But he did not long remain in Wales, showing up on Census returns in Buckinghamshire in 1871 and Derbyshire in 1881. He joined the Institute of Journalists in 1889, but his first identifiable newspaper jobs were with the *Evening Star* in Sheffield in 1893 and then he moved to the Sheffield morning paper, the *Telegraph*, in 1896. He went to South Africa before the Boer War and worked for a newspaper financially supported by the Transvaal government, *Standard and Diggers' News* in Johannesburg. When the war began in late 1899, he branched out and wrote for papers in Britain as well as writing a book, *Why Kruger Made War*.[2] He was back in London the following year, 1900, when he found lodgings in the Strand – just along the road from the New Zealand Government office – and gained the job as rugby and cricket writer for the *Daily Mail*. The *Mail* had been started four years before and by then was well on its way to sales of a million copies a day, making it for a time the biggest-selling paper in the world. Its market was unashamedly – and successfully – the newly literate lower middle class.

Buttery did not see the All Blacks' opening matches against Devon on 16 September or Cornwall five days later; the *Daily Mail* report of the Devon match was written by Leonard Tosswill, a doctor who had played for England.[3] Dennis Lawry, the county secretary, filed a report of the Cornwall match.[4] Buttery soon joined the tour, however, and wherever the All Blacks went, he was sure to follow. He and the *Daily Mail* became so identified with coverage of the tour – even though other newspapers also covered it extensively – it was probably inevitable that exaggerated stories of his influence arose. Buttery knew little of that, though. His last reporting assignment seems to have been the Olympic Games in Athens in May 1906 – known as the Intercalated Games as they were outside of the four-year sequence but gained official recognition because they marked the tenth anniversary of the first of the modern games in Athens. His verdict: '. . . for nearly a fortnight we have had a daily jumble of chaotic mismanagement which would have been amusing had it not been so irritating'. Buttery wrote that he did not expect to go to another Olympic Games.[5] He didn't; he died two months after going home.

Billy Wallace reminisces about the 1905–06 tour in 1958 when he was 79. EP-1958-2523, *EVENING POST* COLLECTION, ALEXANDER TURNBULL LIBRARY

His mark had been made on rugby. It was through Buttery, though not necessarily his idea, that Bob Deans sent his telegram to the *Mail* on the day after the Welsh match, proclaiming that he had scored. The telegram was reproduced not in the paper itself, but in the paper's booklet about the tour that was edited by Buttery and published soon after the tour (and was available for sale in New Zealand before the players arrived home).[6]

Buttery has been the main person singled out as the inventor of the name 'All Blacks'. The myth says he called the team 'all backs' because of the way they played and a printer inserted an 'l'. The story has been so persistently repeated it has survived the publication of contrary evidence. The naming of the All Blacks has become one of rugby's two great myths (the other being the flawed tale about William Webb Ellis).

Whatever happened or did not happen in 1905, the team was known as the All Blacks when it arrived in Britain. There is no other way to explain this sentence in the report in the Exeter *Express and Echo* the morning after the opening match: 'The All Blacks, as they are styled by reason of their sable and unrelieved costume, were under the guidance of their captain . . .'[7] Clearly, the phrase could not have been the invention of Buttery (who was not in Exeter anyway) or anyone else in Britain. Teams in the nineteenth century were frequently popularly known by their colours – 'the Blues', 'the Blacks', 'the Blue and Whites' – and 'All Blacks' was a natural step. The first known published reference to All Blacks was in relation to the Natives who in mid-1889 were on the last leg of their 119-match odyssey. The weekly Sydney sports paper, the *Referee*, had this to say the morning after the Natives beat New South Wales (italics added): 'When I say that NSW led by 9 points to love up to the first few minutes of the second spell, it can be imagined how *the all blacks* played up during the last term to turn the tables as they did.'[8]

Two months later, the name was applied to the Wellington provincial team which used to have a uniform of black jersey and black shorts (or knickerbockers). Before a match against Auckland in 1889, a reporter wrote: 'I think the all blacks should be pleased if they can obtain a draw against the blue and whites [Auckland].'[9] Four years later, when the first official New Zealand team was in Australia, an Auckland journalist wrote of a pending match against New South Wales: 'I expect to see the all blacks come out on top with a substantial majority.'[10] There were other references to the national team as the All Blacks before 1905.

The name, perhaps because of its novelty and because it was redolent of ethnicity, became popular with the British press and so the tour gave it a much wider currency. Billy Wallace, the longest-lived of the 1905 players, believed the name came from the *Daily Mail*. He recorded in memoirs published in 1932 that when the players arrived in Taunton in Somerset, they saw posters exhorting people to 'see the wonderful All Blacks play'. Wallace wrote: 'The name 'All Blacks' had now stuck to us. It is the name with which we were christened by the *Daily Mail* and it caught on with the general public, though quite a number were misled into thinking we were a team of black fellows.'[11] In 1955, Wallace mentioned at a reunion of the 1905 team that the *Daily Mail* referred to the team as 'all backs' after the match against Hartlepool because the forwards could run and pass as effectively as the backs. 'You coves don't know,' Wallace said. 'I was on the committee and know about it. We played Hartlepool and we beat them 63–0 and the *Daily Mail* . . . wrote the New Zealand team were all backs. So we were. All our forwards could pass as good as any back and it was headed up, "The New Zealand All Backs". Wallace's memory was that a subeditor or printer must have inserted a rogue 'l' and the name was born.

A nice story maybe, but not one supported by the facts. When Wallace recounted this at the 1955 reunion, one of his teammates, Alex McDonald (who was sitting alongside Wallace), interjected: 'An 'l' of a difference.' Laughter filled the room at the Midland Hotel in Wellington.[12]

The *Northern Daily Mail*, the edition printed in Manchester to get an early exposure to the northern market, mentioned the name All Blacks – for the first time – after the Hartlepool match, but not in the context Wallace recalled. The match report went fourteen paragraphs before it said: 'A glance at the undermentioned weights of the invincible "all blacks" will convey some idea of the calibre of the team.'[13] The main paper, printed in London, said of the 63–0 win: 'This is a record in the tour, which is yet barely a month old, exceeding as it does by eight points the 55 points the "All Blacks", as the Colonials are dubbed, piled up against Devon.'[14] There was no mention in either edition of forwards running and passing like backs. The *Daily Mail*'s first usage of the name came about a month after it had first appeared in the Devon paper.

Buttery was unwittingly involved in yet another story about the naming. One of the players, Ernie Booth, was later a journalist and he recalled in 1927 that he and Buttery chatted during a training session at Ealing in London.[15] The captain, Dave Gallaher, and George Gillett both wore black belts and had elastic kneelets and anklets that had been dyed black. Buttery was said to have asked why. 'Oh,' Booth's reply was recounted, 'just to be all black.' According to Booth, Buttery said the name was a great idea and 'he boomed the name every day in the *Daily Mail* and other papers followed'.

In a cine film of the 1953–54 New Zealand tour of Britain, the narration begins with an unidentified voice saying the name has always been something to conjure with in Britain. 'The original Maori team paid a visit in 1905; calling themselves the All Blacks, they went again in 1924.' So much for pictures not telling fibs.

Just to show that myths are easier to find than evidence, the *Daily Mail* carried an online story during the World Cup in New Zealand in 2011 repeating the assertion about 'all backs' and pesky printers.

that the 1905 All Blacks helped establish New Zealand's national identity, and airbrushed out the less savoury bits (such as criticism of the wing forward, rough play, off-field misdemeanours and the like). Another Daley target was the contention the All Blacks were superior physical beings not because they were fit and well-trained rugby players, but because they came from a land that produced better physical specimens. Daley argued that the views of Sinclair and Phillips had a significant impact on the manner in which others wrote about the tour and on the writing of New Zealand's social history.

Daley had other, less significant, sallies at the tour along the way. But in tackling rugby myths,

One of the earliest examples of commercial endorsement by the All Blacks. The Jason Underwear Company in Leicester used New Zealand and Australian wool to make a range of underwear products, which it then sold throughout the Empire. The players each signed the testimonial that the brand had given 'general satisfaction' and they recommended it to all athletes and sportsmen. Even James O'Sullivan, whose writing hand was in a sling because of a broken collarbone, signed. It notes 'his mark, witnessed'. George Dixon, a stickler for adhering to the amateurism regulations, also signed. There is no reason to believe the players were paid for their endorsement, but samples of products were probably given. Vice-captain Billy Stead wrote of the players visiting factories and other businesses during the tour and being given samples, including boots and cigarettes.

Typical of the official 'mug shots' of the 1905–06 team. This one is of George Nicholson.

to use Greg Ryan's phrase, Daley sidestepped one of the game's most enduring myths: that the All Blacks gained their nickname in Britain. 'When they left New Zealand in 1905 these rugby players were referred to as "the New Zealanders"; soon after arriving "Home" they were renamed the "All Blacks". The black jerseys they wore defined them for the British press. Once New Zealanders picked up on the term, a national team was created.'[23] In a footnote to this sentence, Daley commented: 'Ron Palenski is adamant that the

A cartoon from an unknown source that typically represents New Zealand rugby dominance over British sides. This has been a recurring theme of British cartoonists from 1905 until the present. The caption on this version read: 'Poor Jones, the full back of the Old Crockonians, the night before their match with the New Zealanders, has a horrible dream, in which he attempts to stop a rush on his goal-line by the terrible "All Blacks".'

team were so named by a journalist for the *Express and Echo* in Devon the day after the first game of the tour.' Whether Palenski was adamant or not was irrelevant; what was relevant was that the Exeter newspaper published the name 'All Blacks' before any other British paper and this fact alone destroyed any fanciful notion of the team being named because of a printer's error. Ryan himself acknowledged the first use of the name All Blacks was in Exeter agrees it was common for teams to be named for their colours but then quotes unidentified 'others' as pointing out no other international rugby team has acquired a name based on its playing colours. That is hardly relevant to New Zealand but followers of 'Les Bleus' may disagree. He says: 'Of course, as Caroline Daley points out, the real significance of the name should rest not in its origin but in the fact that common usage of such an important symbol derives from the British press rather than the NZRFU or the New Zealand public.'[24] Further research has shown that the 1888 Natives team, which introduced the black jersey with the silver fern to the rugby world rather than the 1905 team, was referred to at least

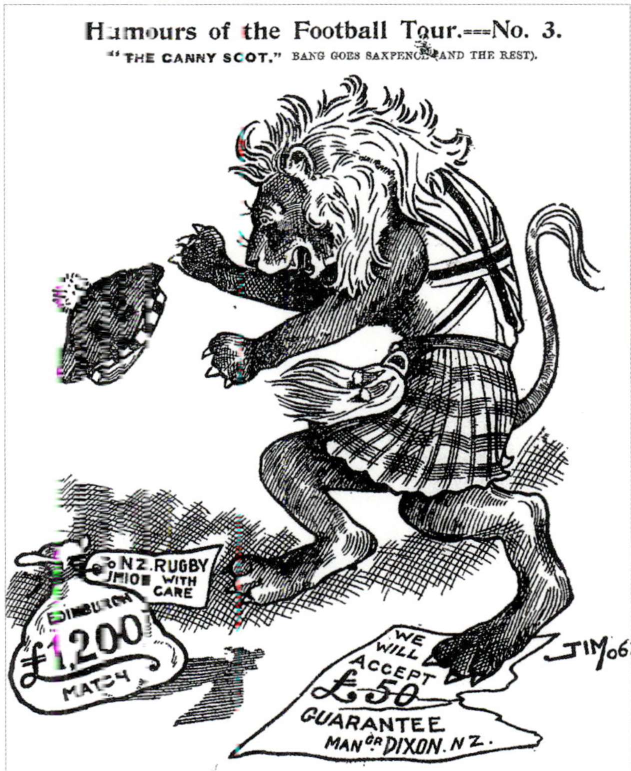

A cartoonist identified only as 'Jim' for the weekly *Otago Witness* reflects on how the All Blacks took both the test and the money when they went to Edinburgh for the first time. The small print at the bottom says, 'Enough to make any lion rampant!' *OTAGO WITNESS*, 24 JANUARY 1906

A Stuart restoration

Modern readers wanting to learn about the All Blacks' tour of 1905–06 have to wade through half-truths, speculation, fiction intended and unintended, and a touch of envy to get somewhere near the truth. The best way through the verbal maze is to find evidence and stick to it. But even then there is a risk of a wrong turning or a dead end.

Take Hamish Stuart, for example, and some of the 1905 players would have liked to have taken him far away. He was the 43-year-old Scot who wrote regularly about the team for the weekly Manchester-based *Athletic News* (mainly a soccer paper) and the *Daily Chronicle*, one of the well-read national papers of the time. He was not the main rugby writer for either paper. Stuart has drifted into history as being one of the severest of critics of the New Zealanders.

It was Stuart who wrote: 'The New Zealanders have a lower ethical idea of the game than ourselves and throw the whole moral burden of the rules on the referee.'[1] The gist of his complaint then and on other occasions was that the All Blacks played to the whistle – something the Australians complained about after the first test in 1903 – or to the letter of the law rather than its spirit. Academics reviewing the tour have pointed out that 'popular' accounts of it overlook Stuart because his strictures do not fit the usually glowing retelling that is required. But at least one academic, Welshman Gareth Williams, saw beyond that and pointed out that Stuart was also critical of Welsh and Yorkshire teams.[2]

Stuart was originally from Wick in Caithness in the northeast corner of Scotland where his father was a bank manager. He gained degrees in arts from Glasgow University and law from Edinburgh University and played both rugby and cricket – on two counts, therefore, he had the best of both worlds. While a competent rugby player, he never played for Scotland, although some reports in 1905 said he did (he was a reserve for Scotland against Ireland in Glasgow in 1882).

Billy Wallace recalled at a reunion of the 1905 team in Wellington in 1955 that Stuart had a go at the All Blacks every chance he got. Wallace thought he knew why:

> The team was training at Newton Abbot [in Devon] and he was there ahead of other reporters and tried to get the team [for the first game]. Some of the players gave him a team but it included players who were still in New Zealand. He published it and when he knew he'd been had, he had it in for us.[3]

But were Stuart's views always as black as they have been painted? Not on the evidence of an introduction he wrote early in the tour for a booklet by an Englishman, William Wills Robinson, who had spent several high-profile years in Auckland sporting circles. Among other accomplishments, he refereed the first match in Auckland by an overseas team (New South Wales in 1882).[4]

Stuart was quickly to the point in the piece he wrote for Robinson. The second sentence reads: 'It is safe to say . . . that no side has made history, or ensured a permanent place in the annals of the game, with the same dramatic suddenness as the New Zealand team now delighting the whole football community of the Mother Country with their splendidly vigorous, yet highly scientific, methods of "playing Rugby".' 'Splendidly vigorous' – that is not a phrase often used in association with

This painting by Fleet Street illustrator Arthur Morton Faulkner of the test against England at Crystal Palace in 1905 was acquired by the New Zealand High Commission in London in 1962 and sent to the New Zealand Rugby Football Union. The services of Billy Wallace, then one of five survivors of the 1905 team, were sought to identify the All Blacks. Wallace ruefully remarked that the passage of time had blurred his memory but he was reasonably confident the All Blacks pictured were, from left: Steve Casey, Frank Glasgow, Jim O'Sullivan, Charlie Seeling (reaching for ball), George Gillett (background), Jimmy Hunter, Fred Roberts, Alex McDonald, George Tyler, Bob Deans (on hands and knees), Fred Newton, Dave Gallaher (passing), Billy Wallace, Billy Stead.

Stuart's reported views of the tour. The introduction became a parade of encomiums: New Zealand had to conquer a world wedded to the soccer code 'yet within a month the world was won'; they 'made the fullest use of their unique opportunity of proving to the football community that the possibilities of the Rugby game are not to be measured by the style of play into which England has sunk'; they 'may have greater powers of perception and a superior physique than even the pick of our players can boast'; they seem framed for football'. Stuart said backing up was the secret of the All Blacks' success:

> To play this sort of game well a side must, of course, have speed and stamina. The New Zealanders are so richly endowed with both that they would play any game well. Little wonder then that they play their own game to perfection, and with such telling effect against sides of mongrel methods, inferior pace, and less individual excellence.

Stuart's nice words about the team were written and published before any of the matches in Wales, by which time the All Blacks were regarded as 'stale' – and players such as Billy Stead and Billy Wallace commented that by the last weeks of the tour players were 'stale' from constant playing, training and travelling. But not Stuart. By then, he had reverted to criticising the All Blacks and his attitude was noted by John Hoatson, a cleric in Leek in Staffordshire who had been a Canterbury selector and referee and who had been a significant contributor to the early flowering of rugby in Victoria.[5] In an article about the tour for the *Lyttelton Times*, Hoatson wrote: 'I know of only one competent critic who fails to allow for the team's staleness. That one is Hamish Stuart . . . since the upset of some of his forecasts earlier on, [Stuart] has been absolutely bitter in his comments on the New Zealanders, and any judicial faculty he may have had has gone completely by the board.'[6]

When Stuart died of tuberculosis on board a ship off Gibraltar in 1914, an unidentified columnist in the weekly *Free Lance* in Wellington reminded readers that Stuart had sometimes been unkind about the All Blacks 'but he was a good fellow all the same, although at times he appeared too serious in his writings'.[7]

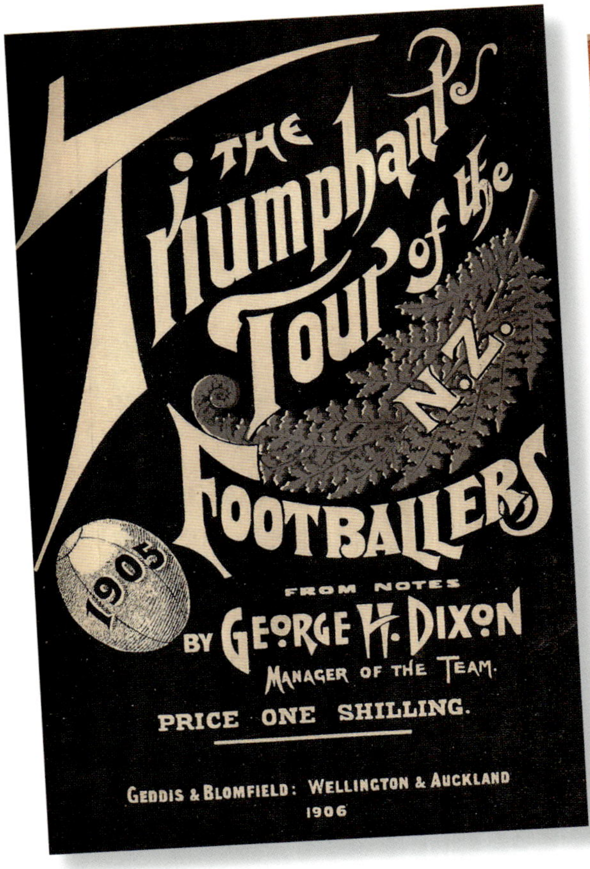

Two of the books produced about the 1905–06 tour. On the left is the book by the team manager, George Dixon, and the other was published by the *Daily Mail* and edited by its rugby writer, John Buttery. It included a contribution from the New Zealand captain, David Gallaher.

once as the All Blacks, as was the first NZRFU team in 1893.

Daley and Ryan separately also argued that much of what New Zealanders learned of the 1905 team's progress came from British sources, thus devaluing its nationalistic import. Much of it did, but so did much of it come from New Zealanders who saw the games, including at least two players. The only contemporary British book about the tour, John Buttery's *Why the All Blacks Triumphed!*, included a chapter by the New Zealand captain, Dave Gallaher. The other two books published were by New Zealanders. But even if New Zealanders did learn more about the tour from British journalists, that was no different to anything else at any other time. Even today, when news from the other side of the world is but a keystroke away, news organisations in other countries, especially the United Kingdom, remain a prime source. In 1905, most newspapers were represented in Britain by New Zealand correspondents (for example, the *New Zealand Herald*, the *Evening Post*, the *Press* and the *Otago Daily Times* combined as New Zealand Associated Press to have Charles Rous-Marten based in London at the time). At least two of the players, Billy Stead and Ernie Booth, wrote for papers during the tour. For later tours, the New Zealand Press Association (representing all daily papers) also had a resident correspondent in London. Since no New Zealand papers have their own staffs in London now, it could be argued that newspapers (mostly overseas-owned anyway) rely more on British sources now than they did more than a hundred years ago.

Rugby at the Olympics

When the All Blacks were tucked away in the artists' colony of St Ives in deepest Cornwall in 1993, some of the players were ushered into the local rugby clubrooms and shown the club's most prized possession, an Olympic silver medal.

It had been won by Tom Wedge, one of three St Ives men in the Cornwall team that played as Great Britain against Australia in the Olympic Games rugby 'final' in 1908. Cornwall were the English county champions in the 1907–08 season and when the Rugby Football Union received an invitation to compete in the Olympic Games, it decided against a formal England team but passed the invitation on to Cornwall. The Cornish didn't need to be asked twice.

The Australians, who were on their first tour of Britain, had beaten Cornwall in their third game of the tour and dealt to them again 32–3 at White City in London, the Cornish effort probably not helped by a sightseeing tour on the morning of the game and then lunch at the House of Commons with Cornish MPs. Just to be pedantic about things, it was the Australian rugby team that toured but the Australasian rugby team that played the only rugby match at the first London Olympics. New Zealand and Australia combined in their Olympian endeavours for the games of 1908 and 1912. The first New Zealand representative to win an Olympic medal, walker Harry Kerr, wore a green vest that had Australasia emblazoned across it. The rugby players stayed with their light blue New South Wales jerseys, but they were still, officially, Australasia.

The French were supposed to have played in London but they withdrew on the grounds they could not find sufficient players. Being the Olympics, the invitation should have been for a British rather than an English team, but the RFU apparently took it upon itself to decide matters.

One of several posters published for the rugby section of the Olympic Games in Paris in 1924.

It had been rugby's second appearance at the Olympics and was no more successful than the first. That had been in Paris in 1900 when three teams played. They have been recorded as France, Germany and Great Britain, although in reality they were a French club team (France's first official test was not played until 1906), a Frankfurt club team and an English team known as the Moseley Wanderers, which was made up of players from the Birmingham area. Only two games were played, France beating Germany and Britain, and the French won the Olympic title. Such was the disorganised nature of the Olympics, though, it was many years before it was determined what were official Olympic events and which were not. Rugby was retrospectively approved.[1]

Rugby seems to have been in favour because it was a game much loved by Pierre de Coubertin, the Frenchman who had the idea of reviving the ancient Olympics and inviting all countries to them (unlike several others in the nineteenth century who staged locals-only Olympic Games). Coubertin liked the 'muscular Christianity' concept of Rugby School, which he visited several times, and in 1897 he wrote:

> Football [rugby] is truly the reflection of life, a lesson in experimenting [in] the real world, a first-rate educational tool . . . football is also played under other rules for a game named football Association. [This reversal of the usual order of the two words was probably a result of the translation from French to English.] The Association is an elegant game, very subtle, but which can't be compared to Rugby.[2]

Coubertin also had an active role in rugby and was the referee of the first French club final in 1892 when Stade Français played Racing Club de France. But despite Coubertin's support for rugby, it was not played in Stockholm in 1912. It reappeared at the hastily organised games in Antwerp in 1920, when the only two competing countries were France and the United States. The American presence at Antwerp and again in Paris in 1924 was one of those historical quirks of sport.

One of the New Zealanders who toured California in 1913, Jim Wylie, had also been there with the Australian team in 1912. He stayed and enrolled at Stanford University where he spent the war years (aside from a brief period in Canada as a trainee member of the Royal Air Force) and coached the university's rugby team. Wylie and one of the Australians, Danny Carroll, who also stayed, helped to keep rugby going as a minor sport. Several of Wylie's Stanford players were among those who badgered the American Olympic Committee to get a team to Antwerp and Carroll, who had played for Australia in the Olympic match in 1908, became the player-coach. Since France were the only other team, there was only one game in the Olympic 'tournament' and that was won by the Americans 8–0.

The organisers of the next games, in Paris in 1924, made more of an effort to run a credible rugby tournament, but they still failed to get any of the established rugby countries. Timing was one obvious issue. The New Zealand union received an invitation at a meeting in March 1924 and the Olympic tournament was played over a fortnight in May. But whatever the timing, New Zealand was already committed to the tour of Britain and Ireland in 1924–25. There was also talk of a rugby tournament to coincide with the Empire exhibition at Wembley, but that didn't go ahead. The English union declined its invitation because the rugby season, as far as it was concerned, was finished by May.

The enthusiastic Americans, partly selected and coached in California by Wylie, included six who had been in Antwerp four years before and set off again for a moment in the Olympic sun. The other teams in Paris were France and Romania. France beat the Romanians 61–3 and the Americans beat them 37–0, setting up the final that had been predicted.

An incident occurred in the United States–Romania match that has seldom been reported but which relegates the All Black, Cyril Brownlie, from first to second in the list of rugby players to be sent off in internationals. The American first five-eighth, Ed Turkington, was tackled late by a Romanian after claiming a mark and Turkington punched him. Turkington explained to the referee, a Welshman who lived in France whose name was listed as Wood Leyshon, that he merely retaliated. According to American author Mark Ryan, 'With the crowd going crazy and calling for Turkington's head, there was only ever going to be one decision.' Ryan quoted an unidentified American newspaper report as saying: '. . . Turkington was put out of the game, accused of roughing up a Romanian . . . he went off the field accompanied by unjustifiable comments from the stands'.[3]

The ace in the American pack was Alan Valentine, a Rhodes Scholar who had become the first American to gain a rugby blue at Oxford. He joined the team for the warm-up matches in England and took over as virtual coach, instilling in his players the need to cover each other defensively. The halftime score was only 3–0 in favour of the Americans, but match reports said the American forwards, with Valentine prominent, took charge in the second half and they won 17–3. There was a view that the Americans were fitter than the French and had suggested 45-minute halves, figuring it would strain the French. And 45-minute halves it was.

The second half was said to be a violent affair and one Frenchman, Marcel-Frederic Lubin, was sent from the field by referee Albert Freethy for punching American Dick Hyland. The American captain, Babe Slater, implored Freethy to recall Lubin and Freethy was said to have replied, 'If you want him, go and get him.' Slater did.[4] Ryan wrote that Freethy 'was on the verge of putting the Frenchman off the field but the Americans begged him to allow Lubin to continue'.

A similar incident occurred later in the game, according to a reporter for the *Chicago Tribune* as repeated by Ryan. Hyland was 'slugged twice' by the French captain, No. 8 René Lasserre, and Freethy told him and Slater that the punching warranted dismissal. 'Let him stay in,' Slater was quoted as saying.[5]

The dismissal of Turkington in the Romania match and threats of dismissal in the final must have caused Freethy considerable thought because seven months later when he sent Cyril Brownlie from the field at Twickenham, he ignored pleas to have the All Black brought back.

The fighting at the rugby and similar crowd displeasure at the boxing prompted a writer in *The Times* to comment that the world was not yet ready for the international brotherhood promised by the Olympics. This was the other side of the 'Chariots of Fire' games, the dark side not exposed in the British film of gilded youth at play.

'The fact is that it has once more been demonstrated with dreadful clearness that the games exacerbate international bitternesses instead of soothing them,' *The Times* man wrote. This pre-dated by 21 years George Orwell's diatribe against competitive sport, of which the most quoted extract was that serious sport was 'war minus the shooting'. Less quoted has been his comment that international sporting contests led to 'orgies of hatred'.[6] The International Olympic Committee decided the following year to drop rugby, mostly because of the poor attendances and because of a move against team sports. An unofficial rugby tournament was played at the same time as the Berlin Olympics in 1936 in which France beat Germany in the final. Thereafter, rugby and the Olympics were seldom uttered in the same sentence. The Paris-based International Amateur Rugby Federation (FIRA) proposed in 1960 that rugby be readmitted to the games, but the International Rugby Board would have none of it. It was dead against tournaments of any kind.

There were also practical reasons against a proper rugby tournament being fitted into the time slot of an Olympics; at least eight teams would have been needed for it to be meaningful and players would have needed at least three or four days, preferably more, between games. When the game went professional and the Olympics became a global stage worth strutting on, sevens rugby was the obvious answer.

A section of the crowd of about 12,000 that was at Alexandra Park in Auckland
for New Zealand's 29–0 win against the Anglo-Welsh in 1908.

6 The game splinters

They may steal his name, but not his fame.[1]

Two issues rose above all others for rugby for much of the twentieth century: each in its distinctive way shaped the attitude of generations of administrators, reflected the times in which they lived and worked, and fashioned the image of both players and the rugby body politic. The first to make itself felt was amateurism, which went hand in ill-fitting glove with the rise of rugby league, and the other was South Africa in all its sporting and political manifestations.

The game's embrace of amateurism, and its reaction to the threat from a similar game in which players could be paid – but not always were – was seldom plain and straightforward. From the first, when coaches and officials could be 'rewarded' but players could not, to the last, when some of the leading figures in the game were banned for life for writing books, some of rugby's reactions to league were anachronistic.

Amateurism and the consequential emergence of rugby league was a product, like most things in modern sport, of Britain in the nineteenth century. The concept of amateurism was as much based on the English class system as it was on a belief that sport was for enjoyment rather than profit. This belief based in southern England led to clubs in Yorkshire and Lancashire wanting to compensate their players for time lost at work because of either playing or being injured. This was known as 'broken time' payment. The workers of the north (of England) could not afford time off work; for some players in the south, there was no need to work and many were at university anyway.[2] In some sports, especially cricket, 'amateurs' earned more from their sporting prowess than did the professionals because they were paid daily allowances and given expenses; professionals were paid a basic, usually minimum, wage. The Rugby Football Union, formed in 1870, turned its face against payments for players, just as it was also opposed to staging matches for the benefit of the public and charging people to watch. The essence of amateurism was that the game was for the players. This attitude lasted for nearly a hundred years and lay behind the total absence of organised competitions in England until the 1980s and abhorrence at the thought of international competitions such as a World Cup or, even worse, the Olympic Games. The decision in Paris in 1995 by the International Rugby Board to make the game 'open' (in its phrase) did not just rewrite a rule or two; it turned upside down the whole philosophical base of the game.

The two different footballs, the Rugby game and the association game, settled into their ways in the last third of the nineteenth century. The Industrial Revolution and its benefits, especially leisure time and better communications, brought about a sporting evolution as well. The 'muscular Christianity' made popular in the influential public schools inculcated in a new generation the joy of games for the sake of them and frowned upon a society that was replete with gambling in all forms of recreation. As the nineteenth century waned, Pierre de Coubertin began his idealistic re-creation of the ancient Olympic Games and, fired with enthusiasm after his visits to Rugby, chose the increasingly popular policy of no pay for play. It became a class issue because the well-off in southern England could afford to indulge a passion for sport whereas the workers of the Midlands and the north could not; they could work and they could play, but work had to come first. As noted earlier, soccer faced the same issue as rugby in the north and although its inclination was to ape the Rugby Football Union and ban payment to players altogether, it chose a pragmatic different route. The FA Cup, played first in 1872, was won for the first eleven years by amateur clubs based in the Home Counties – the last of them the Old Etonians. Blackburn Olympic became the first team from the north and the first from a working-class base to win the cup; in 1883, they beat Old Carthusians (old boys of Charterhouse School) in a semifinal and Old Etonians in the final in a win that had long-term significance for the cup itself and for the game in general. Soccer a few years later allowed broken-time payments. The Rugby Football Union, by contrast, did not agree with cup competitions and disagreed with broken time. Another fork in the footballing road had been met; soccer went onto a main highway, rugby onto a byway.

Rugby unions in New Zealand, both the provincial unions before 1892 and the national union thereafter, rarely toyed with any idea of players earning money from playing the game. Before the formation of the NZRFU, some of the provincial unions were affiliated to the RFU and were bound, happily so it seemed, by its rules and regulations. After the formation of the NZRFU, the same applied except it was the NZRFU that was represented on the RFU. Occasional suggestions that players might be paid, such as when the Natives' tour was being organised or when other British tours were talked about, were quickly quashed. It seemed not to be questioned that if New Zealand rugby wanted to tour Britain, wanted to accept tours from Britain, and wanted

The founder of league in New Zealand, Bert Baskerville, also wrote a book about rugby.

to be regarded as a legitimate rugby country, it had to be bound by the English rules. This was Home rule for rugby. The occasional cries that the rules were framed for players in England and not for those on the other side of the world, such as the contention made by Tom Ellison in 1897, gained some publicity but no discernible support.

The northern counties that broke away from the RFU formed their own game called Northern Union (later rugby league), and Dave Gallaher's All Blacks saw some games in 1905. Northern Union scouts supposedly approached some of the All Blacks with offers to stay and play, but there is no evidence of which clubs approached who or with what. The desire to pit the best of New Zealanders, Gallaher's All Blacks, against the best English rugby players – the men of the Northern Union – was the theme of a story in the *Daily Mail* by a former player, F. W. Cooper.

> What many old players like myself would like to see would be a match between a picked Northern Union team and the Colonials. . . . I have little doubt that my side would achieve a victory. The wearers of the Silver Fern have not been defeated, but they have not played the cream of English football, who are men playing under the banner of the Northern Union.[3]

Bert Baskerville in the jersey of the team he formed.
NZ SPORTS HALL OF FAME

Cooper wrote this between the All Blacks beating Yorkshire 40–0 and their next match, the Welsh test that became the only loss of the tour.

The *Daily Mail* 'quickie' book of the tour reproduced Cooper's story, and the book was for sale in New Zealand before the players arrived home.[4] It was read avidly by a 23-year-old Wellington clerk with the Post and Telegraph Department, Bert Baskerville.[5] 'This set me thinking,' he later wrote. 'Why shouldn't a New Zealand team play the Northern Unionists?'[6] He answered himself by acknowledging that the RFU would not allow amateurs to play against professionals, although in soccer the two played alongside each other and occasionally against each other; the same applied in cricket.[7] Baskerville was not just a postal clerk. He was a keen track athlete in the summer and so enamoured of rugby in the winter he wrote a book about it.[8] He set about raising a team to take to Britain and had what he called guarded conversations with some of the All Blacks when they got back. One of his confidants was undoubtedly the outstanding and versatile New Zealand wing George Smith, who had seen Northern Union while on tour with the All Blacks. Baskerville would have known Smith through both rugby and another sport they shared, athletics. He laid his plans during 1906 and Smith may have assisted

Lance Todd became one of the enduring figures of the first New Zealand league team and had an early introduction to match fixing. He had played rugby for the City club, the same club as All Black wing George Smith, and for Auckland in 1905. Todd was with the City team that went to Sydney in 1906 and when Bert Baskerville put his plans together for a 'professional' team to go to Britain, Todd was among the first chosen. Like several others, he remained in Britain after the tour and settled down to a playing career with Wigan; between 1908 and 1914, he played 186 times for Wigan and twice for Lancashire. Todd and another New Zealander with Wigan, All Black William ('Massa') Johnston, were the innocent parties in a match-fixing scandal in 1908. They had been approached by a club member and coal merchant, Edward Croston, on two successive nights and offered £5 on the first night and £20 on the second to 'go down', as the court evidence put it. 'You can do it Todd, by fumbling your passes,' Croston was quoted as saying. Todd replied he would not do it 'for all the money in Wigan' and Johnston apparently said: 'Put your money in your pocket and don't be an old fool.' Croston, charged in the Police Court under the Prevention of Corruption Act, was jailed for two months with hard labour. Todd transferred to Dewsbury in 1914 but war intervened and he enlisted with other expatriate New Zealanders in London. After nearly five years' service during which he was commissioned and mentioned in dispatches, Todd returned to Wigan where he became secretary of the Blackpool North Shore Golf Club and later the licensee of the Ship Hotel. He also became secretary-manager of the Salford club (and won three championships) at the same time as becoming a league commentator for BBC radio. Todd signed up with the Home Guard in 1940 and as a captain, became adjutant of the 43rd County of Lancaster (Salford) Battalion. He and the battalion's commanding officer, Lieutenant-Colonel Frank Sewell, were returning from duty in the early evening of 14 November 1942 when their car driven by Todd hit an electric tram pole. Both were killed. The Rugby League in 1946 instituted the Lance Todd Trophy for the man of the match in the annual Challenge Cup final.

when he went to Sydney in July that year with the City club from Auckland and settled down to a dinner and a natter with footballers from New South Wales and Queensland. Australian rugby league chroniclers Ian Heads and David Middleton called this 'great reunion' of footballers a stepping stone to the eventual formation of league on both sides of the Tasman.[9] Encouraged by the reactions of players, Baskerville wrote to each of the Northern Union clubs and reached agreement on the broad principles, including taking 70 per cent of the gross gates, of a tour.

A New Zealand journalist in London, Guy Scholefield, reproduced sentences from Baskerville's letter which had appeared, at least in part, in the Manchester paper, *Athletic News*. 'The team will include men whom you have already seen playing, if you witnessed some of the "All Blacks"' British games in 1905; others who would have been in the 1905 team but for the fact that they were not of the "stand up collar" variety of player; and some who have since made their reputations.'[10] Baskerville presumably meant some players were not chosen because they were not of the 'right class', the type who wore peaked collars, similar to those on today's dress shirts. Labourer-players such as Wallace, Gallaher, Cunningham, among others, would have laughed at such a view.

Baskerville of necessity kept quiet about what he was doing but, eventually and inevitably, news leaked out. The *Daily Telegraph* in London reported on 11 March 1907 that another New Zealand tour was in prospect, this time involving the Northern Union, and the news became public in New Zealand on 26 April.[11] It caused a flurry of indignation, denials and disbelief. A Press Association message circulated not long before this date said the Northern Union was in financial trouble and was considering going flat cap in hand back to the RFU. That may have been wishful thinking by rugby people, but Baskerville did say in his letter to the Northern Union: 'Your game would have a revival.'

The New Zealand union reacted quickly. Once it knew Baskerville was the man behind it, the Wellington union banned him for life until it realised it did not have the authority to do any such thing because Baskerville had not played any professional game. The NZRFU sought affidavits from leading players ahead of the annual interisland game declaring that they had not and would not have anything to do with the new venture. Some players complied, but Aucklanders refused to do so, saying that as amateurs they were free agents and could not be compelled to commit themselves to the NZRFU. (They later relented.) Rumours about which players had been approached and which had signed moved as quickly as the limited communications system of 1907 allowed. Most rugby writers supported the establishment position, which saw the Northern Union as a threat to the primacy of their game and its adherents as disloyal mercenaries. But the Australian-owned *Truth* spoke up for Baskerville's scheme. The unidentified *Truth* reporter seemed to have inside knowledge and wrote that people who could put up £10,000 (about $1.5 million today) 'and not miss it expressed their readiness to take the matter in hand'. He wrote that several players had expressed their willingness to tour: 'As to their identity, the writer prefers to keep "mum" at the present stage . . .'.[12] Three weeks later, the same newspaper (and presumably the same writer) commented: 'It is reported that two wealthy sportsmen in this island are willing to guarantee £500 each towards the expenses of sending a professional team to England conditionally on it being proved to them that the combination is well representative of the flower of New Zealand Rugby.'[13] (Since *Truth* was printed and published in Wellington, it is assumed 'this island' meant

A postcard from the 1907 All Blacks' tour of Australia.

How the All Blacks at the Sydney Cricket Ground in 1907 were portrayed by a Sydney artist. *BULLETIN*, 25 JULY 1907

the North Island. 'Sportsmen' at that time meant wealthy supporters of sport, not participants.)

Most newspapers opposed the venture. The *New Zealand Free Lance* was typical:

> It is the first time in the history of Rugby football in this colony that professionalism has had the hardihood to come out in the open and boldly avow itself. In fact, it is paying an undeserved compliment to this professional element to say it has had the courage to come out into the open at all. It has been rather dragged out . . .[14]

The author was not identified but George Dixon, manager of the 1905–06 All Blacks and chairman of the NZRFU, was manager of the paper. Its parent paper in Auckland, the *Observer*, was not as negative but disagreed with the professional team wearing a black jersey with a silver fern. 'Legally, there may be nothing to prevent it, but morally it is not right that they should do so.'[15]

A young Dunedin artist, Stuart Reid, who gained a later fame as a war and equine artist in Australia, drew a cartoon for the *Otago Witness* that showed the NZRFU kicking out 'the spoilsport' and a badge indicating playing for money. Reid headed the new badge with his made-up Latin, '*aurum cupidimus*', and when the newly professionalised players arrived in Sydney in August, the allusion extended when the *Sydney Morning Herald* began calling them the All Golds.[16]

Disagreement in public with Baskerville's league intentions was echoed in private, including in the Baskerville household. His youngest sister Kathleen later wrote: 'I can remember that at meal times at home talk always centred on sport, and when my brother embraced the league faith the arguments with those members of the family still favouring rugby were long and wordy.'[17]

It was not apparent which players had sided with Baskerville until two groups, one that sailed from Auckland and one from Wellington, arrived in Sydney. The group of 28 included eight who had been All Blacks, four of them on the 1905–06 tour: Duncan McGregor, Bill Mackrell, George Smith and Billy ('Massa') Johnston.

To much surprise on both sides of the Tasman, New Zealand were beaten 14–0 by New South Wales in 1907, just the second time the All Blacks had been held scoreless (the first was the Welsh test in 1905). Four days before, New Zealand had beaten New South Wales 11–3 and, three days later, beat Australia 26–6. This was the year in which two 'All Blacks' teams were in Sydney – the real one and the newly formed league team, which was frequently called the professional All Blacks or the All Golds or sometimes, as in newspaper advertisements, just the All Blacks. This cartoon by Trevor Lloyd appeared in the Auckland *Weekly News* after the 14–0 loss and was captioned: 'The Kiwi and the Kangaroo: a slight reverse.' 'Kiwi' and 'kangaroo' were names that came to be more associated with league than with rugby. The Australian rugby team was first known as the Wallabies in 1908. *WEEKLY NEWS*, 25 JULY 1907

Talks had continued among interested Australians, most notably the cricketer Victor Trumper, an entrepreneur and close friend of Trumper's, James Giltinan, and a Labor activist and real estate agent, Henry Hoyle. Together, they drummed up support for league and at a meeting on the night of 8 August formed the New South Wales Rugby Football League. The New Zealanders arrived in Sydney a few days later and played three matches during August under rugby rules and fifteen a side. Newspaper advertisements promoted the New Zealanders as 'All Blacks'. In the New South Wales side was the man acknowledged as the best Australian rugby player in his time, Dally Messenger. By the end of August, he was on the ship with the New Zealanders heading for their tour of England, having been hired as a guest player.

Earlier in the month, while the New South Wales league was being organised and while the New Zealand league players readied for their tour, Messenger had played two tests against the real All Blacks. And they included one of the soon-to-be professionals, Johnston. The All Blacks included two others who later turned to league, Charlie Seeling and Ned Hughes (although Hughes was later reinstated to rugby and played for the All Blacks again).

The success of the 1905 New Zealand team in Britain was the catalyst for the formation of the first New Zealand league team in 1907; as Baskerville said on several occasions, he wanted to take a team to pit against the northern players whom the All Blacks could not play. Baskerville's team came along at the right time for those rugby people in New South Wales who were increasingly

Amateurs cash in

In 1908, when the New Zealand Rugby Football Union emphatically and publicly had aligned itself with England and declared professionals in their sport to be beyond the pale, one of its outstanding players collected £322 – about $50,000 in today's terms – for what he had done for the game.

The happy recipient was Billy Wallace, who went from being a foundry worker to owning his own foundry. There was no secret about it; there were no whispers behind cupped hands, no euphemisms such as being 'looked after' and no stories of banknotes being stuffed into boots (which was a British peculiarity anyway).

Even a century later, he was still being talked about as one of the greatest of All Blacks. He played in the first test, against Australia in 1903, and his last was against the Anglo-Welsh in 1908. He played 51 matches for New Zealand, including 11 test matches, and scored 379 points, a record that lasted for half a century. A wing or a fullback, Wallace was central to the upward progress of the All Blacks during the Edwardian era.

A chronic knee injury ensured that his last test was the second against the Anglo-Welsh in Wellington and by the time of the third test in Auckland, men were touting for money on his behalf. The 'Wallace testimonial' became something of a talking point. Its organisers wanted a benefit match for Wallace, but the national union said that would be professionalism and could not be approved. But it made no attempt to stop Wallace from otherwise cashing in on his prowess with the rugby ball.

Wallace's payment was amply publicised while the Anglo-Welsh were touring, but there was no apparent reaction from them. George Harnett, the manager who had views on licensing laws in Invercargill and immorality in Dunedin, said nothing that was recorded about a well-known All Black making money. When the Anglo-Welsh were in Auckland, a writer in the *New Zealand Herald* reported that circulars canvassing for money for Wallace had been sent to various 'gentlemen'.[1] The writer said the rugby unions could not be involved so the testimonial had to be arranged privately. 'There is no doubt that had Wallace served himself as faithfully as he had served Rugby football in New Zealand, he would today have been a much richer man,' the *Herald* report said. 'The enormous sacrifice of time demanded of him by the tour of the All Blacks to Great Britain and Australia and those of the Otago and Wellington representative teams to different parts of the Dominion have severely drained his resources, until today he is in the position of being a comparatively poor man.'

By the beginning of December, five months after the appeal began, the Wallace Testimonial Committee had its final meeting and reported that Wallace had already received £250 and would now receive a cheque for the £72 balance in the committee's account.[2] According to the Reserve Bank's inflation calculator, £322 in 1908 was worth about $50,411 in 2013. Wallace, who had hitherto worked for the iron foundry owned by the Luke brothers in Wellington, and two workmates started up their own casting shop. (Sir John Luke was a mayor of Wellington and brother Charles a member of the Legislative Council. Wallace related a story that Charles Luke's son Ronald was in London during the 1905 tour and wired

A studio shot of Billy Wallace taken for the 1905–06 tour.

Wallace before the England test: 'Can you book me two tickets – Luke of Wellington.' A couple of the characters of the team got hold of the telegram first and altered the 'L' to a 'D' and Wallace was both puzzled and gratified that he had received a telegram from the Duke of Wellington until he noticed the changed letter.)

Wallace was later on the national union's Wellington-based management committee and manager of the All Blacks who won the Bledisloe Cup for the first time in 1932.

His earning money from the game was not an isolated case. Testimonials seemed to be common for retiring or departing rugby players and the size of the gift was determined by their status as players. Jimmy Duncan, who was captain in New Zealand's first test and coach in the first home test, received nothing from a grateful national union. His wife Isabella, however, received a handsome gold watch to acknowledge her husband's services. This helped inflate the spectre of professionalism when Duncan coached the All Blacks in 1905.[3]

It seemed not unusual for provincial rugby unions to fork out money as a gesture of appreciation. Colin Gilray played just one test, against Australia in 1905, but days before he left Dunedin in 1907 to take up a Rhodes Scholarship he was given, so it was reported, 'a purse of sovereigns by the Otago Rugby Union'.[4] This was reported without comment about the game's amateurism regulations, the New Zealand view being that an amateur – and the vast majority of sportspeople were – was one who was not paid for competing, nothing more, nothing less. In addition to the liberal interpretation of the regulations, amateurism in New Zealand also avoided the class and breeding connotations with which it was linked in Britain. (Gilray later played four tests for Scotland, the land of his birth. His father had moved to Dunedin from Scotland to take up a position at Otago University.)

As Geoff Vincent calculated for academic articles on the tour, twenty of the Anglo-Welsh players in 1908 had been educated at public schools, six were at universities and four were post-graduates at Guy's Hospital. The All Blacks who confronted them, by contrast, included a boilermaker, a blacksmith, a cooper, an engineer and a foundry worker, among others. Dave Gallaher, who captained the 1905 All Blacks and who managed the team in 1908, worked in a freezing works. Billy Stead, who captained the All Blacks in the first and third tests against the Anglo-Welsh, was a cobbler and Jimmy Hunter, the captain in the second, was a farmer.

The testimonial practice appears to have continued until at least the immediate years after the First World War. Dick McGregor, who played in New Zealand's first two tests and was described as 'one of the finest footballers to have represented Auckland and New Zealand', had tuberculosis

Sunhat and all, Billy Wallace kicks one of his nine goals against Devon in Exeter, the first game of the 1905–06 tour. This photo was reproduced on the cover of the programme when the 1979 All Blacks played in Exeter.

and moved to Queensland and then New South Wales in search of a comforting climate. Whatever the New Zealand union's view in 1908, supporters staged a benefit match at Thames for him in 1918 – before normal rugby had resumed after the war – and he gained £286 (about $31,000 today).[5] He died in Sydney in 1925, aged 50.

Rugby players who switched to league were banned, many of them for life. But the national union, following England's lead, did not have such an enduringly harsh view of other professional sports. Two celebrated All Blacks of the 1920s, Jack Steel and Jim Parker, were professional sprinters who plied their trade up and down the country during the summer. This was at a time when running for money was on the wane, but a £15 stake for a win was still common. At least one race, the Sheffield, carried prize money of £80, of which £50 went to the winner. Steel and another West Coast player, William Nahr, once ran a challenge race against each other for cash. There was one rule for players who went to league and another for those who pursued another professional sport. As early as 1903, the Transvaal union – recently resurrected after the Boer War – asked the English union if a professional boxer was an amateur according to regulations. As illogical as it may sound today, the RFU responded: 'It was decided that being a professional boxer did not interfere with his amateur status.'[6]

Players were at a disadvantage compared with those who administered the game. Several of the 1905 All Blacks relied on the generosity of fellow players such as Bob Deans and Eric Harper to get them through the long tour – despite the persistent belief of the Scots that they were professionals – and some players had to leave their jobs to tour. One Aucklander – understood to be Bill Cunningham – returned home with just a 'thrummer' (a threepenny piece) in his pocket, according to *Truth*, and the Auckland union paid for his board for the first fortnight.[7] But the manager, George Dixon, was given £100 by the national union after the tour, separate from the expenses he had to use during the tour.

Revelations about the Anglo-Welsh team's profligate spending became public around the same time as the Scottish union refused to play England because the All Blacks three years before had been given three shillings a day expenses. Amid the various stories about Harnett and his players was one that two players stayed at Government House in Sydney and submitted an account to Harnett for £8 10s in tips, and this was passed on to the New South Wales union, which paid up. The team was given £17 for tips on a ship between Melbourne and Sydney, and Harnett himself was given £1 a day.[8] When this news arrived in New Zealand, local reporters scouted around for Anglo-Welsh excesses on their side of the Tasman and found 'haughty Harnett and his burlesque team' did not use their expenses to cover drinks at meals and instead sent the accounts to Wellington.

The increasing arguments about expenses for amateur players came about because the advent of league lent focus and as a result, enquiries were made into where the whole expenses business began. This led back to a tour of Australia in 1899 by a British combination captained by a rugby-playing parson, Matthew Mullineux. The team was, evidently, the first to draw pocket money (as opposed to the 1888 team, members of which were paid fixed fees) and they were followed by the 1904 team led by a Scot, David Bedell-Sivright. He candidly agreed about the amount of three shillings a day 'wine money' except that it was 'invisible', by which he meant if a player did not claim the full amount, he never saw it. He believed that the All Blacks and the Australians in 1908 were paid £1 1s a week (i.e. three shillings a day) in addition to the expenses money but this was not so.[9] The Scottish union made no complaint about the first two tours, of which they were a part, but would have nothing to do with the third, in 1908, because of England's agreement to the All Blacks being paid three shillings a day.

The Scottish Football Union (it did not become a rugby union until 1924) famously rejected the chance to share the proceeds of the All Blacks' match in Edinburgh in 1905, believing evidently that not much money would result. Or as a rhymester sorrowfully noted in Edinburgh's *Evening Dispatch*:

> In ony case, to welcome,
> The Colonials we are blate,
> An' we've made a plain arrangement
> That we'll gie them 'a the gate.

The Inverleith ground was packed, much to the chagrin of the Scots. The Scottish union hosted no official functions for the players and the match was not deemed to be a full international. The union sought the full accounts of the tour from the hosts, the English union, to determine if the All Blacks were paid, as they believed was the case. When the accounts were eventually produced, the first entry on the debit side was plain to see: 'To daily allowance to players, £1042 9s 0d.' The Scots responded by saying they would not honour the commitment to play England in March 1909, the argument being that since the RFU sanctioned the payments to the New Zealanders, the RFU was professional as well and an amateur body such as the Scottish union could not play them. The Scottish union secretary, John ('Jock') Aikman Smith, said the Australians in 1908 were also paid a daily allowance and they too were therefore professional.[10]

The New Zealand union was represented at the time on the RFU by Charles Wray Palliser, who worked in the high commission (and was later briefly high commissioner). He wrote a letter to the editor of the *Sportsman* newspaper to protest against 'the unsportsmanlike action of Scotland's Union in seizing so frail an excuse to

The ruler of Scottish rugby for the first quarter of the twentieth century, 'Jock' Aikman Smith.

make England the scapegoat for the presumed evil doings of New Zealand'. He said he thought there was much that Scotland was not saying and the Scottish attitude went much deeper than the professed horror at the payment of daily expenses.

> That the Scottish Union has a very strongly expressed dislike for visiting teams from our colonies coming over here is most evident . . . and I have no doubt . . . that this question has long been the subject of very many discussions with the Scottish Committee, who have been waiting the opportunity for striking at England, the leader of imperialism in sport . . .[11]

In a letter to the New Zealand union secretary, Joe Avery, Palliser was blunt: 'It is, of course, obvious that the action of Scotland is a reprisal for the supposed wrongs she suffered at the hands of New Zealand.'[12]

The International Rugby Board had been in existence since 1886, but it was in effect a committee comprising representatives from only England, Scotland, Ireland and Wales and its role was to rule on any disputes about international matches between any of the four. It was not a true international governing body (and was not overhauled until the professional era). It met to discuss Scotland's disagreement with England and, predictably, Ireland sided with Scotland on the matter of the 1905 expenses so nothing was decided. But as Palliser wrote in another letter to Avery:

> A resolution was, however, unanimously carried to the effect that no daily allowance shall in future be paid to players coming here from the Colonies. . . . as far as I can see, it will make little or no difference except throwing a lot of work on the manager in paying all small extras incurred by the team which hitherto has been covered by the daily allowance.[13]

Having compromised, England's match against Scotland went ahead. Another outcome of the dispute was that two years later, the board – that is, the so-called 'home countries' – decided that any future tours should not be arranged by England alone and that each of the four should have a say in when tours took place, by which country, and even on detail such as itinerary, accommodation and travel. They also agreed that each of the four would pay a £750 guarantee for any future tour. This cosy little agreement was not adhered to by England in early 1923 when it decided to invite New Zealand for another tour. For that reason as well as some residual resentment from 1905, Scotland refused to have anything to do with the tour by the team that came to be known as the Invincibles.

Dally Messenger first beat New Zealanders, then joined them. Herbert Henry Messenger was regarded as the best rugby player in Australia in the opening decade of the twentieth century and, more than a hundred years later, is still said to be one of the greatest league players the country has produced. Messenger played in the New South Wales team that beat the All Blacks 14–0 in 1907, and soon after the other New Zealand team, the All Golds, showed up in Sydney. Messenger was signed for league by one of the new sport's great advocates, cricketer Victor Trumper, for £180 for three matches against the New Zealanders. Messenger was regarded as the outstanding player in the first Australian league team, which lost all three tests. After the third match, Dally Messenger joined the New Zealanders for the tour of Britain. He was the outstanding player on the tour and according to one report, 'returned to Sydney . . . with £2[illegible] in his pocket and well fitted out with new clothes'. From then until 1913, he was the most celebrated player in Australian league and captained the Kangaroos on several occasions. He was, according to his biographer, 'rugby league's first and greatest hero'. The annual Australian Rugby League player and coach awards have been known as the Dally M Awards since 1980 and the player of the year receives the Dally M medal.

resentful of players being out of pocket while the union happily cashed in.[18] There was also more of a professional sport culture in Australia than existed in New Zealand either then or at any other time. Amateurism had become the norm in New Zealand by the late nineteenth century; in Australia, however, it was different. Professional cycling and athletics were enormously popular then and for much of the twentieth century; Australia's cricketers had recently been through a controversial negotiation with the newly formed Board of Control about payment. There was also an element of class distinction, again something more apparent in Australia than New Zealand, and a more overt Irish influence. It may not, however, have been as black and white as a onetime leader of the Australian Labor Party, Mark Latham, painted it in 2010: 'It [league] started in Australia in 1908 as a breakaway from the toffee-nosed, tweed-coated amateur code of rugby union . . . a group of tough-minded, hard-bodied working class men in Sydney resented the elitist and parsimonious values of the rugby union establishment.'[19]

Within the political rhetoric and the clarity of hindsight, there was some truth. A Manchester-born journalist, Gordon Russell, wrote in 1907 that if the New Zealand union could devise a system under which its players could be paid for loss of time from work and not forfeit their amateur status, 'the New Zealand union would be doing a good thing in the interests of the game'. He said it was unreasonable to expect employers to continue to pay their employees while they were on a rugby tour, just as it was unreasonable to expect a player to forfeit income so he could play rugby for his country.[20] Russell was doing nothing more than echoing what Tom Ellison and Tom Eyton had said publicly towards the end of the nineteenth century: that the rules about amateurism when drawn up were intended to be applied in England. Their application elsewhere was probably not thought of at the time.

Latham's outburst, which largely reflects a populist view of the original differences between the two games, could have been applicable in Sydney or Lancashire and Yorkshire, where league did indeed become the working-class game. The difference in New Zealand was that the majority of the working class stayed with rugby. This distinction was central to a doctoral thesis on the origins of New Zealand league.[21]

The first league tour had a sad ending when its lifeblood, Bert Baskerville, died of pneumonia in

A fixtures card published in Sydney for the New Zealand tour in 1907. Such cards typically listed a team itinerary and names, heights and weights of players.

Brisbane when the team was on its last leg. He was just 25. The team's manager, Harry Palmer, and a representative group of players, captain Hercules ('Bumper') Wright, 'Jum' Turtill, Bill Mackrell and Arthur Kelly, escorted the body back across the Tasman while the rest of the team reluctantly played its remaining fixtures. The New Zealand union, bitter to the end, sent neither representative nor wreath to the funeral, but both the New South Wales and Queensland Rugby Unions sent wreaths. An editorial in *Truth* called the NZRFU absence 'one of the most cold-blooded, callous and unfeeling treatments that could possibly be meted out to anyone'. But when league was played in New Zealand for the first time a fortnight later as a benefit for Baskerville's mother, Maria ('Minnie'), several notable rugby people were there. Among them was a Member of Parliament and NZRFU vice-president, Tom Wilford, who had followed the 1905 All Blacks around Britain. He said he had mentioned earlier that several of the rules of the new game should be adopted by rugby and, now having seen the game in action, he saw no reason to change his mind. George Campbell, the president of the union, expressed a similar view, although he did not see the game at Athletic Park. They were prescient comments because, for many years afterward, New Zealand and Australian officials persistently tried to have the English union amend some laws to make the game more attractive. The argument, particularly pointed from Sydney and Auckland, was that rugby needed to be made more exciting and enticing for spectators who otherwise gained more satisfaction from rugby league. A British Labour politician and sports columnist, Joe Mallalieu (later Sir Joseph), reasoned that the English union opposed such changes 'because they did not want even to appear to be following rugby league'.[22]

This was Baskerville's legacy to rugby. He created league in New Zealand and gave it impetus in Australia; and he forced rugby to look

A cartoon from the *Sportsman* in Sydney gives the Australian view that an amateur who gained more than three shillings a day was a professional. The three shillings a day was the expenses paid to the New Zealand team in Britain in 1905. *SPORTSMAN*, SYDNEY, AUGUST 1907

at its own methods of play. As an 1890s All Black and journalist, William McKenzie, wrote in 1907: 'Baskerville's Professional team is really the firing of the first shot at the English Rugby Union's moth-eaten methods of management so slavishly followed by our own executive.'[23]

The tour by the Anglo-Welsh in 1908 has been seen by some commentators as a reaction by rugby to the threat of league. But it had been approved by the RFU in 1906, further details were discussed in March 1907 and the decision to go ahead was made in December 1907. So while the final decision was made at the time of the All Golds' tour, the principle of the tour preceded rugby knowledge of Baskerville's plans.[24] There was no suggestion in any of the speeches by the loquacious Anglo-Welsh manager, George Harnett, that the tour was motivated by anything other than reciprocating the visit by the 1905 team. The New Zealand union's treasurer, Neil Galbraith, reported at the end of the tour that there were record crowds at the majority of matches, which did not suggest rugby was in need of shoring up in the face of a threat from league.[25] In fact, rugby authorities in Britain seemed more troubled than their counterparts in New Zealand. Contemporaries said that the standoffishness of the Scottish and Irish unions was because of their disagreement with the English about daily expenses. The Scots and the Irish saw this as professionalism; yet both had sanctioned the previous tour, in 1904, when a Scot was captain, and when daily expenses were also paid. Harnett tried to laugh the disagreement off: 'Ireland said they did not object to our coming, but none of them came. We tried to get Scotland to alter their decision, whatever the reason for it was. It has been suggested that the All Blacks took away too many of their nimble sixpences from the match at Edinburgh.'[26] A report from London was more to the point: 'Ireland and Scotland refused to countenance this expedition because they are not satisfied that the proceeds of the last All Black tour have been devoted to their proper purposes.' One Scottish player, Tom Wilson, was initially chosen for the tour but the Scottish union promptly suspended him and he was replaced, whereupon the Scots lifted the suspension.

There was much about this tour, whatever its intentions, that perhaps reflected the uncoordinated state of international rugby at the time. The case of Fred Jackson was an enduring example. He played in six of the first nine tour matches, including the first test in which he converted the only Anglo-Welsh try. On the eve of the second test in Wellington Harnett received a cable from the RFU: 'Jackson suspended. Return him forthwith.' A day later, Jackson was put on a ship for Sydney and, during the voyage, newspaper accounts emerged about Jackson playing league under false names, 'John Jones' and 'Ivor Gabe'.

This novelty tablecloth was produced for the New Zealand team in Australia in 1907. Picture cards, which players were required to sign, were attached. Ernie Booth, for example, wrote his signature on a card which bore the legend, 'Love me, love my' followed by a picture of a dog. Billy Wallace's card bore the legend: 'U are 4 ME.'

A reporter put this allegation to him when he arrived in Sydney, but Jackson 'did not care to make any statement'. Jackson appears to have spent a couple of months in Sydney before exchanging his London ticket for one to return across the Tasman. The New Zealand union treasurer, Neil Galbraith, who travelled throughout the country with the Anglo-Welsh, received a letter from a contact in Sydney that read: 'Have seen Jackson and it appears he wants to return to New Zealand. He offered to hand over his ticket to London in consideration of a ticket to Wellington.' Galbraith's correspondent, who was identified only as Kelly, took Jackson to see the New South Wales union lawyers. 'They have drawn

The Anglo-Welsh lion marvels at the kiwi in this cartoon drawn by Fred Rayner. It was one of several he produced for a small book about the tour. *SKETCHER SOUVENIR*, 25 JULY 1908

up a receipt which they assure me should cover the business.'[27] Later reports said Jackson was anxious to return to New Zealand because he had met a woman he wanted to marry. That is hindsight. He was married in 1913 to a Ngāti Porou woman from Te Araroa, Horowai Henderson, who was only sixteen at the time of the Anglo-Welsh tour.

The team, while Jackson was still with it, did not get further north than Masterton. It seems likely that Jackson met his future wife after he returned from Sydney rather than her being a reason for the return. Either way, Frederick Stanley Jackson settled down to become a New Zealander – he spent some time in Dunedin immediately after his return, was reported to have gone 'up country', spent most of the 1909 rugby season on the West Coast and by the end of that year was back in Wellington, en route to Auckland. (The West Coast union asked the NZRFU if Jackson could referee while he was in Greymouth. The reply was that he could not.)[28] While he was in Dunedin, he spoke to a columnist for the *Otago Witness*, 'Full Back', a pseudonym for a local reporter, Sid Minn.[29] He said he was hoping to clear his name, evidently not realising he would have had to have returned to England to do so. 'I have seen a lot of Northern Union games,' he told Minn, 'and the Rugby Union game, if played well, is far ahead of it. What is required in the Rugby Union game is a modification of the rules and intelligence to play it.'

Jackson later captained the Auckland league team and played for the national team against a 1910 British team. One son, Everard, became an All Black, and another, Sydney ('Bully'), captained the Māori Battalion team at times during the Second World War. Fred himself was an East Coast rugby selector. He died in 1957, apparently

The Anglo-Welsh team beaten by Otago at Carisbrook in 1908. Standing: Pat McEvedy, Herbert Archer, Edgar Morgan, Rowland Griffiths, Henry Vassall, Bill Oldham, Tom Smith, Robert Dibble, John Ritson, James 'Maffer' Davey, William Morgan. Seated: John Dyke, Fred Jackson, Reg Gibbs, Fred Chapman, 'Ponty' Jones. *OTAGO WITNESS*, 3 JUNE 1908

California, here we come

Rugby in the years immediately before the First World War thought it was ready for America. But America, as rugby was soon to learn, was not ready for it.

The American flirtation with rugby centred on California where universities attempted to branch out on their own with 'the English game' rather than continue with American football, which was seen as too dangerous. An American Universities team, comprising players mainly from Stanford University and the University of California, toured Australia and New Zealand in 1910. In Australia, a game was arranged against the national Māori team then on its first tour, but on the New Zealand leg, the Americans played only provinces rather than a national universities side.

One of the leading authorities on amateur sport in California, Bill Unmack, predicted great things from the universities' tour and the *San Francisco Call* headed his story: 'Will California produce rugby world's champions?' He answered in the affirmative, but eventually the answer was negative (two Olympic gold medals notwithstanding).[1]

Australia reciprocated the universities' visit with a tour of California by the Wallabies in 1912 which (falsely) raised American hopes even more. The Australians lost to both Stanford and California and beat 'All-America' by a lucky 12–8. The poor performance by the Australians was said to have been caused more by a determination to have a good time than a winning time. One of the players, Bob Adamson, was quoted as saying: 'We were never in bed. That was the trouble. I've never had such a time in my life.'[2]

Reading of the results, but perhaps not of the social excesses, the New Zealand Rugby Football Union planned a more serious mission for the following year. The administrators decided the best possible team should be sent and that its one game against All-America would have the exalted status of a full international. The pending tour to California was also given priority over a visit to New Zealand by Australia. The Wallabies met a full New Zealand team in the first test in Wellington and were beaten 30–5. The All Blacks then left for California and the Australians were left to play a New Zealand B team in the remaining two tests and they lost them as well. (The first test in Wellington may have been the only rugby test to be played in quarters. The weather was so bad the game was stopped every 20 minutes and hot drinks were taken out to the players.)

The All Blacks were given an enthusiastic if verbose welcome to San Francisco: 'Twenty-three cleanly-built, stocky-shouldered, deep-chested (yes, and every other double-jointed adjective that might describe tip-top athletic presence) young fellows disembarked from the good ship *Willochra* yesterday and were ushered into San Francisco . . .'[3] The writer, Ed Kneass, noted the All Blacks had beaten the Australians before departure and that it was substantially the same Australian team that had visited California the year before. Any hopes Californians may have had did not last long. In twelve matches before the test, the New Zealanders gave powerful demonstrations of the gulf between them and the Americans. They scored 457 points and had only a solitary penalty goal kicked against them. The test at Berkeley just continued the trend. The All Blacks won 51–3, thirteen tries to a penalty goal. The founder of the

The kiwi, having conquered the Australians, goes in search of the 'Yankee Eagle', according to cartoonist William Macbeth, to 'kick some of the starch out of his feathers'. Starch may have been kicked during games but the players seem to have enjoyed themselves off the field. Dick Roberts, Tommy Lynch, 'Doolan' Downing and Jock McKenzie (front) dress for the occasion when they visit a 'Wild West saloon'. *FREE LANCE*, 18 SEPTEMBER 1913

Olympic club in San Francisco, Douglas Erskine wrote that the All Blacks plastered defeat on the flower of American rugby. 'It was humiliating in a way, but then it is no disgrace to be beaten by such a team as New Zealand. . . . The New Zealanders know too much about the game. They have had it grafted into their systems since they were babies . . .'[4]

The tour revealed more than just a gulf between the New Zealand and Californian rugby abilities. Contemporaries also saw a vast difference in attitude, with one reporter remarking that 'college spirit is apparently something that is but little understood by the New Zealanders'.[5] New Zealand historian Greg Ryan noted: 'To them [Californians] the only part of the game that really mattered was the Scoreboard and there at the end of 1913 they had nothing to encourage the continuation of the rugby experiment.'[6]

The All Blacks finished off their tour with three games in British Columbia, winning each of them without conceding a point. The second game, against Victoria, resulted in the death of the local fullback, Peter Ogden. It would be difficult to find a more reckless player, wrote the only New Zealand reporter on the tour, Doug Guiney:

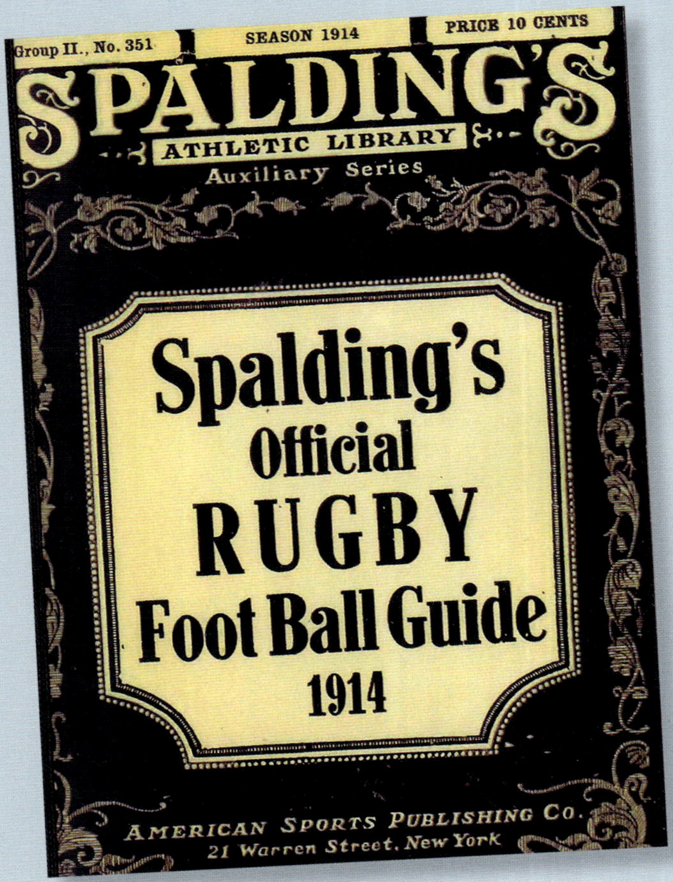

The Californian flirtation with rugby as a replacement for American football was indicated by this guide for the 1914 season produced by the American sporting goods company founded by Albert Spalding. Its usual sporting preoccupation was baseball.

> The risks that he continually entailed were great and altogether he was knocked out on three separate occasions. Each time he acted peculiarly and was badly dazed, but he answered all queries with the reply, 'I'm all right' and simply refused to quit playing. Subsequent happenings revealed the fact that Ogden received a mortal hurt the first time he went down and it was dreadful to contemplate that we were playing against a dying man for a considerable part of the game.[7]

Ogden was carried from the field shortly before the end of the game and died on the way to hospital. The New Zealand captain, Alex McDonald, and a forward, Jim Douglas, gave evidence at the inquest, which reached a conclusion of accidental death.

On the way home, New Zealand met Fiji in a rugby match for the first time, although it was an unofficial encounter. A former Otago player, Paddy Sheehan, was working in Suva as a plumber and prevailed upon manager George Mason to allow a game against a local team during their ship's brief stopover. The All Blacks won 67–3. The local team, Guiney noted, comprised white men, mostly New Zealanders. Among the ship's passengers was the poet, Rupert Brooke, who was heading for his only visit to New Zealand. There was no indication the players knew he was a fellow passenger or that he had been educated at Rugby and played the game:

> When first I played I nearly died.
> The bitter memory still rankles –
> They formed a scrum – with me inside!
> Some kick'd the ball, and some my ankles.
> I did not like the game at all,
> Yet, after all the harm they've done me,
> Whenever I came near the ball
> They knocked me down, and stood upon me.[8]

Cornwall were the English county champions in 1908 and represented Great Britain in the Olympic Games tournament in London, losing the one match to Australia. This postcard shows the mysterious Fred Jackson was a member of the Cornwall team that won the title, but by the time of the games, he was banned.

without enlightening any of his whānau about his English playing background. People in league took an interest in his case but could not advance the narrative much beyond what was published in the first place in 1908. The Jackson story has always been long on speculation and short on evidence. One of the suggestions was that, whatever his real name, he took the name Jackson and initials from a noted cricketer, Frank Stanley Jackson – usually recorded as F. S. Jackson until he was knighted for political and diplomatic services. The English union mounted an inquiry in 1909 into alleged professionalism at the Leicester club (Jackson's club), but it was cleared and Jackson was one of the players reinstated.[30]

Being young, privileged men far from home, the Anglo-Welsh players seemed to value the social aspects of touring as much as they did the football. One of their best-known players, Henry Vassall, struck up a friendship with a Wellington woman, Gwendoline Chase-Morris, on the ship to New Zealand. After the first few days in Wellington, she was among people who farewelled the players as they headed for the South Island. *Truth* reported that when the ship was 300 yards from the wharf, 'Miss Chase-Morris could not contain her admiration for the Oxonian and called out loudly, "Goodbye, Vassall" to the amusement of everybody on the wharf.' At the end of the tour, Vassall missed catching the ship from Auckland to Sydney and had to head to Wellington to catch another. (He missed that too and eventually went to Sydney a month later and missed the Australian leg of the tour. He later sent a letter of apology to the NZRFU.) The reason for his lack of punctuality in Auckland was assumed to be Chase-Morris. At least Vassall was honourable in his intentions. The pair were married in London in 1910 and spent much of their life together at various British embassies and high commissions in Africa.

One of the English forwards, Percy Down, may have wished he too had missed the ship. He was leaning over the ship's rail hand in hand with a woman who was still on the wharf when the ship moved away. As the gap between ship and shore widened, the woman let go and Down by name became down by direction. Two of the All Blacks among the thousands there to farewell the team, George Gillett and Arthur ('Bolla') Francis (the latter Dave Gallaher's brother-in-law), dived in and they were followed by a local man, identified only as Cassidy. As the New Zealanders headed toward Down, who was thrashing about and calling for help, Galbraith and one of the English players, John Jackett, lowered themselves to a pile

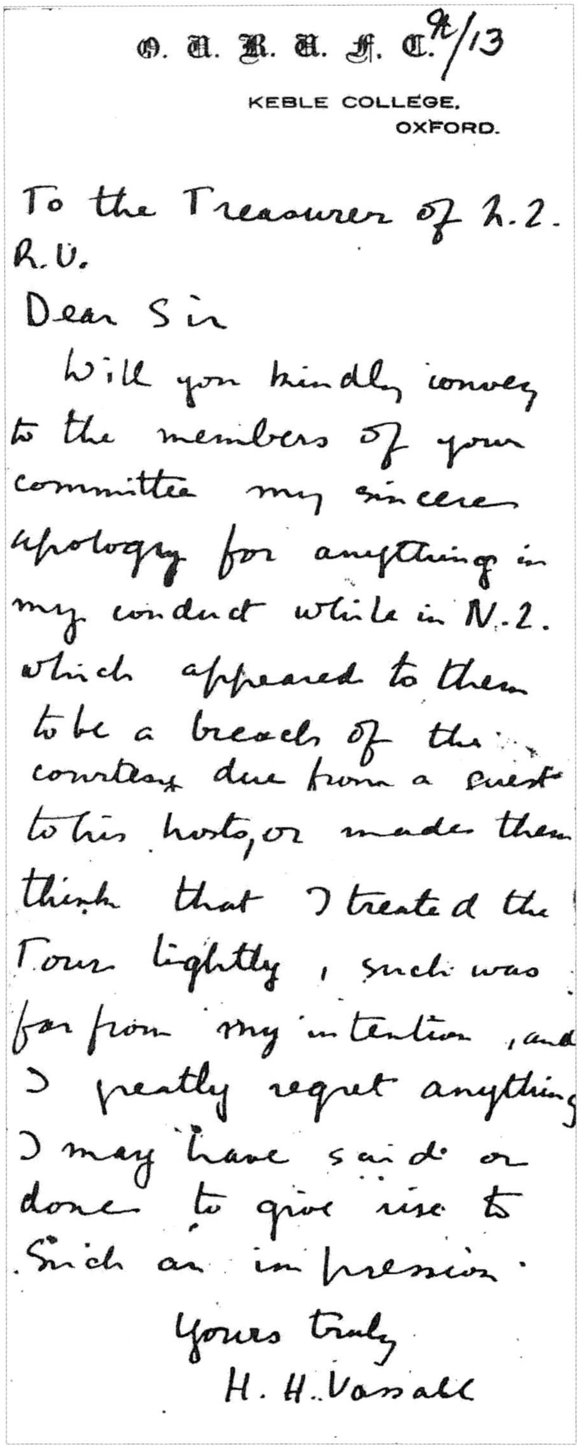

O. U. R. U. F. C.

KEBLE COLLEGE,
OXFORD.

To the Treasurer of N.Z.
R.U.

Dear Sir

Will you kindly convey to the members of your committee my sincere apology for anything in my conduct while in N.Z. which appeared to them to be a breach of the courtesy due from a guest to his hosts, or made them think that I treated the Tour lightly, such was far from my intention, and I greatly regret anything I may have said or done to give rise to such an impression.

Yours truly
H. H. Vassall

The apologetic letter Henry Vassall sent to the New Zealand union. He was sorry for any conduct that could have been seen as 'a breach of the courtesy due from a guest to his hosts'. It was never his intention, he wrote, to treat the tour lightly. Vassall later became a career diplomat.

beneath the wharf. Down was eventually dragged to safety and everyone got back on to dry land.[31]

Such antics helped confirm a belief that the Anglo-Welsh players were in New Zealand for a good time rather than a successful football tour. An unidentified writer for *Truth* thought Down's falling overboard was 'telling evidence of the condition of these much belauded alleged players' and it condemned 'sisters and daughters' in Wellington for 'gallivanting about with muddied oafs who came to this country to learn how to play Rugby'. The paper quoted the Anglo-Welsh captain, Alf Harding, as saying his players suffered through lack of training; *Truth*, however, blamed women and wine.[32] Manager Harnett caused a bit of a stir in the last week of the tour when he labelled Dunedin as the most immoral town in New Zealand – apparently because some of his players went astray – but he did not do his own standing much good when he criticised Invercargill for the fact it was 'dry'. He could not get a drink because of the licensing laws, but he said, 'I saw more drunken people in Invercargill than I have seen in any other city of the Dominion.'

On the field, the Anglo-Welsh were overwhelmed. They were beaten 32–5 in the first test in Dunedin and, as a result, the New Zealand selectors introduced six new players for the second test, presumably thinking the opposition was not a threat. The second test, played in wet and muddy conditions in Wellington, was drawn 3–3. The All Blacks were back at full strength for the third test in Auckland and won 29–0. Harding's team also lost to Wellington, Otago, Canterbury, Taranaki and Auckland. The manner of the loss to Taranaki was indicative of a difference in attitudes. An Anglo-Welsh player was being treated for an injury by two of his teammates, but as play had not been stopped, the Taranaki centre, Ernie Dive, scored what turned out to be the winning try. Harnett, who came from a refereeing background, said the Taranaki players were wrong in spirit, if not in law. But the *Taranaki Daily News* responded

Play during Wellington's 19–13 win against the Anglo-Welsh at Athletic Park in 1908. The photographer was 'Zak' (Joe Zachariah). PACOLL-4601-04, ALEXANDER TURNBULL LIBRARY

by saying that Dive had to beat Vassall to score so the latter at least continued playing. 'If two of the visitors stopped playing . . . it was their own loss,' the paper said.[33] It was neither the first, nor would it be the last, time that New Zealanders played to the whistle, to the chagrin of their opponents.

Pat McEvedy, a New Zealand doctor in the Anglo-Welsh team, later wrote to a British newspaper that in the third test in Auckland, his side 'lacked dash, there being a great want of life in all their movements'. He blamed too much use of the sulphurous baths in Rotorua in the week before the match but 'there is no getting away from the fact that the New Zealanders played magnificent football'.[34]

The Anglo-Welsh went on to Australia for a nine-match tour at the New Zealand union's expense (a reciprocal arrangement because the New South Wales union paid for the 1904 British team's tour of New Zealand). The NZRFU lost about £200 on the New Zealand tour but gained a profit of £1,200 in Australia, meaning an overall profit of £1,000. Galbraith, in reporting on the finances of the tour, noted that the union at the end of it had just enough money to meet working expenses.[35]

Critics denounced rough play by New Zealanders, but what precisely 'rough' means depends on whether it is a British or a New Zealand point of view. The local men were, it seems, hard and competitive, and this could have come across as rough against British players who had a different attitude to the game and who were not fully fit. Harnett talked in Bob Barr's book about 'a tendency to roughness' and the *Daily*

Express in London, using an unidentified source, talked of 'scientific brutality' by New Zealanders. Such accusations were not uncommon when one side played to win and the other saw the game as an extension of a social lifestyle. The All Golds in England came across the same problem. One of them, Tom Cross, was, according to halfback and part-time manager Jim Gleeson, deliberately kicked in the face; Cross retaliated with his fists and was sent from the field while the original transgressor played on.[36]

The wing forward was again a handy whipping boy. The local boy in the Anglo-Welsh team, Pat McEvedy, spoke at the formal dinner in Auckland after the third test and accused the All Blacks of 'pointing'. This now-obsolete usage meant cheating. He told the diners that 'a tendency to point was a characteristic of New Zealand players'. But an unsigned article in the *Observer* newspaper said what a lot of New Zealanders would have been thinking, that McEvedy was out of touch with developments in the game. The paper charged McEvedy with living so long in London that he had lost sight of 'vast strides' made in football in other places. 'The victory gained by the All Blacks,' it said, 'was not won by pointing, but by superior play, both individually and collectively, on the part of New Zealanders.'[37] One of the observations of British rugby, apart from the Welsh, that New Zealanders made in 1905 was that they had not developed; that they played a slow game that was unfashionably static and unadventurous. The All Blacks showed how the game could be played but the Anglo-Welsh, for whatever reason, learnt little.

No sooner had the British left for home than provincial unions began agitating for changes in the laws of the game, believing that it needed to be faster and more attractive to retain spectators who, with the introduction of league, had a choice. In the van of the campaign was the Otago union which, on the face of it, seemed unusual for such a conservative body. But Otago had never really overcome its 1890s aversion to being ruled from Wellington and its proposals for law reform were, according to a report in the Wellington newspaper, the *Evening Post*, 'deemed by many members to be an attack on the Management Committee of the New Zealand Union'.[38] Otago had tried to push through a need to change during the union's annual meeting in May 1908 and when little came of that, it successfully sought a special general meeting in October. One of its delegates, James Hutchison, said it was imperative that the game's laws be amended and if necessary by severing relations with the English union. Hutchison used the phrase 'cutting the painter', which seemed to be trotted out every time over the following years that New Zealanders felt English administrators were too slow in accepting a need for change.

Some of Otago's suggestions for change were radical, but all had been informally proposed before by provincial unions, referee bodies or newspaper writers. It wanted the wing forward to be abolished; no charge to be allowed in the case of free kicks or kicks at goal; the referee to put the ball into scrums; the throw-in from touch to be not less than five yards; a tackled player to be allowed to pass the ball from the ground providing it was done immediately. But whatever the nature of the changes, there was an underlying philosophical difference. George Dixon, the union chairman and manager of the 1905 team, put it clearly enough at the annual meeting in 1908: 'They [English union officials] looked upon things from a different standpoint from that which others took. In their opinion football was a recreation, and not a spectacle. Football should be played from a player's point of view and not from that of the spectators.' Dixon, as delegates to the annual meeting knew, was firmly in the English camp.

Changes sought by Otago, and endorsed by a majority of provincial unions, were not introduced because they did not have English union approval and it was the English union that continued to rule rugby. For a decade or so from the late

A section of the crowd at Alexandra Park in Auckland for Auckland's match against the Anglo-Welsh. Auckland won 11–0, giving the Anglo-Welsh their sixth loss on tour with a seventh, the third test, still to come.

nineteenth century the New Zealand, New South Wales and Queensland unions made various efforts to form an Australasian union, in part to modernise the game's laws and present a united antipodean face to the RFU. Advocates also saw such a union as a more practical vehicle through which to organise tours. While meetings were held in Sydney, nothing eventuated. It may be that what took it temporarily to the top of the agenda was not so much concern about the laws, but more the mood of federation that held sway in Australia at the time. Unions on either side of the Tasman continued to work together, however, and sometimes, whether by accident or design, followed similar policies. Between 1910 and 1913, for example, both the New Zealand and Australian unions independently sought to boost the rugby game in California by hosting a team and by sending their national teams there, which resulted in both countries having official tests against 'All-America'. The All Blacks played Metropolitan (Sydney) on 5 August 1914, but the crowd's attention frequently switched from the game to the scoreboard – not to check on the score, but to follow the momentous news unfolding elsewhere. The scoreboard revealed that the Australian Governor-General, Sir Ronald Munro Ferguson, had told the prime minister and the state premiers that Britain – and therefore its empire – was at war with Germany. Each of the All Blacks who toured Australia that year volunteered for war service and three of them were killed in action, three of thirteen All Blacks who died while on service during the war. Four of the Wallabies who played against New Zealand in 1914 were also killed, four of ten to die as soldiers between 1914 and 1918. Rugby in both countries was greatly curtailed in the name of the greater good and mostly only junior games were played.

League continued and has had a bad press as a result, even though the game's historian Ian Heads reckoned at least ten Australian players or officials were killed in action or died of wounds or disease. Among the first was Teddy Larkin, who had played rugby for New South Wales and Australia against New Zealand in 1903 but who became the first secretary of the new league organisation. He was killed on the first day, the day of the landing, at Gallipoli. One fairly general view was that rugby players were middle class and fitted the theory of sport, and especially rugby, being a training for war; league, however, was seen as working class with many Catholic or Irish-origin adherents who therefore were less keen to fight for Britain and its empire. (Australia did not have conscription during the war.) Larkin rather dented that theory – he was Catholic and a state Labor Party MP. The two league organisations, New South Wales and Queensland, continued as best they could, maintaining football on Saturdays and otherwise supporting the war effort. The rugby argument is that it suffered in Australia because of the war and league gained a dominance that it would never lose.

By 1920, when New Zealand again sent a rugby team to Australia, the public mood across the Tasman was clearly with league. Rugby in Queensland had practically ceased to exist, despite a bizarre two-match series between teams from the Queensland union and the Queensland league to raise money for the former. The All Blacks played three matches against New South Wales in

This advertisement makes it clear that while the All Blacks may be 'the greatest of footballers', they have not won an Olympic championship. The match against Metropolitan (Sydney) on 5 August 1914 was to raise funds to send an Australasian team to the next Olympic Games in Berlin in 1916. But as the players would have seen on the scoreboard during the match, Britain declared war on Germany.

front of crowds of 9000, 7000 and 3000. During the same winter, an England league team played a three-test series against Australia in front of crowds of 'between 20,000 and 30,000' (Brisbane) and 50,000 and 30,000 (both Sydney).

New Zealand and New South Wales officials met and agreed that for the game to survive, there would have to be annual matches against the All Blacks 'for as long as was necessary'. Among the officials who negotiated the arrangement was Sir Henry Braddon, a prominent Sydney businessman who had played for the first All Blacks in 1884 when working as a bank clerk in Invercargill. The two unions also renewed their pleas to England to change the laws in order to make their game more attractive. They drew up long lists of suggested amendments, approved on both sides of the Tasman, only to be met with a mere acknowledgement from the RFU. Some unions, including New South Wales and Auckland, went ahead with changes anyway: one of them was the 'kick into touch' rule which meant players could kick into touch on the full only from behind their 25-yard (22) lines. The International Rugby Board finally embraced this change in 1968. New Zealand and Australia could also replace injured players, but only in games between themselves. This too made it onto the international rugby statute book in 1968.

Increasing frustration in the southern hemisphere, and continual talk of 'cutting the painter', led to a slight concession from the RFU: it convened an 'Imperial Rugby Conference' at the Great Northern Hotel in London. The conference, at which New Zealand, Australia and South Africa were represented, lasted just a day and was not a resounding success. The RFU's ruling voice for 40 years, George Rowland Hill, was in the chair but would not allow any discussion about professionalism. There was a long debate about whether a player knocked the ball on if he knocked it forward but recovered it before it hit the ground. It was so complex no decision could be reached. It took another 50 years for that particular law to be adopted. The conference did agree to set up an 'Imperial Advisory Board', but once the overseas men were home, the International Rugby Board abandoned the idea. One of the New Zealand delegates, Sam Wilson, said bleakly: 'The conference could not be called a success.'[39] The IRB proposed imperial conferences at least every three years, but New Zealand said it was not interested. Stan Dean, who was the chairman from 1922 until 1948, considered such crumbs a waste of time. The IRB tried again in 1932 and said it would set up a 'Rugby Football Commission', but Dean said the NZRFU would not attend and would continue to affiliate with the RFU until New Zealand was given a seat on the IRB.[40]

Through all this period of uncertainty, there was also progress. While league consolidated its position in Australia and became the dominant game, in New Zealand it also became established as a significant sport with increasing public interest. But rugby seemed to continue an upward path and was barely affected by league. When the game was re-established after the First World War, a tour of New Zealand by South Africa, then the tour of Great Britain and Ireland in 1924, followed by the first visit to South Africa, created enormous public interest. Interprovincial matches, especially for the Ranfurly Shield, also attracted vast crowds.

From trenches to touchlines

Football has become a part of a collective, received memory of the First World War, fostered by antics such as a British officer kicking a ball ahead of his troops when they were ordered to attack. This did occur, but other tales emerged as writers sought evidence that sport was preparation for war, that striving on the sports field for one's school was but a prelude to fighting for one's country on the battlefield.[1]

Sport certainly became a part of the New Zealand military machine during the war, especially after the division moved from Egypt to northern France. As a well-travelled journalist and former All Black, Ernie Booth, noted, the division practically forced rugby on the troops.[2] He did not mean that as a criticism. 'Its efficacy for physical training was well recognised,' he wrote. 'From this, fully 90 per cent became active participants or close followers of their own brigade's or battalion's football stunts.' (Booth worked for the Australian YMCA in France and Britain during the war.) Towards the end of 1916, after the travails of the Somme, the division's commander, 'Guy' Russell, singled out one of his senior men from Gallipoli, Arthur Plugge, and told him to organise football.[3]

But even before France and 1916, the men organised their own games. There were some in Egypt before the Gallipoli campaign and the New Zealanders and Australians played at least one game on the island of Lemnos during the Gallipoli fighting. No rugby ball could be had so they used a soccer ball instead, all the scoring consisting of tries – thirteen to the New Zealanders (who included three All Blacks) and one to the Australians.[4]

The division gained in reputation as the war progressed; so too did its rugby teams. 'The players demonstrated their quality in no uncertain manner, winning 95 per cent of all matches played,' Booth wrote. As the civil and military authorities also recognised during the Second World War, sport – and for New Zealanders, especially rugby – was an essential tool in ensuring soldiers' welfare.

The soldiers who played, regardless of the level of competition, were not some cosseted elite. Whether playing for company, battalion or brigade teams, they still had to perform their primary functions as soldiers. If that meant their unit was in

English artist Richard Caton Woodville's drawing of a much-reported incident when a British army officer provided footballs for his men to kick towards the Germans while 'going over the top'. Captain Wilfred Nevill of the East Surrey Regiment gave his men two soccer balls on one of which was written, 'East Surreys v Bavarians'. More than 60 years later, it was reported that the inscription on the ball read, 'East Surreys v Barbarians', giving rise to a belated belief it was a rugby ball that was kicked. Among other football-trenches tales, there was a report of Australians dribbling a rugby ball and the Germans mistaking the ball for a new type of grenade. *ILLUSTRATED LONDON NEWS*, 27 JULY 1916

The rugby soldiers being led in a haka before the Somme Cup match in Paris in 1917. The haka leader is believed to be Roger Dansey, a captain in the Pioneer Battalion, who introduced the 'Ka mate' haka on the slopes of Chunuk Bair on Gallipoli in August 1915. BIBLIOTHÈQUE NATIONALE DE FRANCE

the front line, that was where the footballer was too. Plugge, an Auckland science teacher in peacetime and a lieutenant-colonel in war, was made director of physical training for the division. Twenty-four of the best men were assembled in Rouen in northern France in late 1916 and while they trained at football, they also had to attend various military courses and take their turn at labouring work.

Over the winter of 1916–17 they played seven matches, amassing 292 points and conceding just nine. Their only close encounter was a 3–0 win against a Welsh Division XV that included some internationals (though they were not identified in newspaper reports). That game was played in Belgium in early 1917 in front of a crowd ranging from generals to privates to a group of Trappist monks. The official New Zealand war correspondent, Malcolm Ross, was among the crowd and explained the intricacies to the monks and some watching Belgians. Ross was well qualified to do so: in his younger days, he had played for Otago and was for a time the secretary of the Otago union. 'Close at hand a great captive balloon swung in the air, and at intervals came the report of a bursting shell flung from the Boche lines,' Ross wrote.

The New Zealanders hoped to go to London to play a British army team that was unbeaten and also play against a full Welsh team. But the war was the priority. Instead, the team went to Paris in April 1917 to play France in a match organised by a newspaper, *Le Journal*, as a way of brightening Easter Sunday for Parisians. It wasn't just Parisians whose Sunday was brightened by the football. The game was played at Vincennes in the east of Paris and 60,000 were said to have been there. The French players had been on active duty and a range of French generals had to give their approval

A French player tries to break to the right in the Somme Cup match in 1917. The closest New Zealander intending to stop him is Reg Taylor, the 1913 All Black who was killed in action soon after at Messines. BIBLIOTHÈQUE NATIONALE DE FRANCE

for them to leave. Two of the players were aviators who had taken part in raids the day before.

The New Zealanders, who included several players who became All Blacks after the war, took to the field first and to the delight and amusement of the crowd, did a haka. 'As the men take up the chorus,' one writer quoted by Ross said, 'the public acclaim our guests who, without losing time, begin to give forth their terrible Komati-komati-ka-ourah.'

The game was one-sided, New Zealand winning 40–0, although Ross noted that the standard of French play had improved since they first played the All Blacks in 1906. One newspaper, *L'Image*, called the performance a masterly lesson in athletics. 'Our men . . . had to bow to world champions who beat the Irish army, the Welsh team and the British air force. The result of 40–0 was nevertheless honourable and was proclaimed in a storm of cheers and a burst of fraternal esteem.'[6]

As later New Zealand teams which played in France came to learn, the celebrating, carousing and back-slapping went on into the night. The French presented a piece by a noted sculptor, Georges Chauvel, to the New Zealand captain, Aucklander George Murray. It depicted a French soldier in the act of throwing a grenade and was formally called 'Le Lanceur de Grenades', but the New Zealanders and French dubbed it the 'coupe de la Somme' and the Somme Cup it remained.

The New Zealanders had one last match, against New Zealand Hospital at Amiens, then returned to active duty, which for most of them meant preparing for the assault on Messines. One of them, Taranaki wing forward Reg Taylor, was killed at Messines during the initial assault. Another, Tom French, never played again. Six weeks later at Passchendaele, he was shot in the left arm so badly it had to be amputated. He remained involved in rugby and was a selector, coach and administrator for the rest of his life. In 1949, he coached the New Zealand Māori team in Australia and a grateful Sydney businessman, Jack Morris, presented a cup that became known as the Tom French Cup. It is awarded annually by the New Zealand union to the best (male) Māori player.

The captain of the French team that played for the Somme Cup at Vincennes was Maurice Jean-Paul Boyau, a 29-year-old soldier who had transferred to the French Air Service and became one of the leading aces of the war with 21 barrage balloons and fourteen aircraft to his credit. Before the war, he had captained France against Ireland. He was reported missing on 16 September 1918, just a fortnight before he was due to be presented with a diamond and platinum Légion d'honneur cross bought by subscription by the athletes of France.[7]

When the war ended, sport became even more important to the military minds that were concerned not just with the welfare of the troops but also with giving them something to do until they could get them home. Representatives from various units in France and Britain met in London in November 1918 and set up an NZEF sports committee. Given the time of year, rugby was the

The soldiers who won the Somme Cup in Paris in April 1917. Standing, from left: the New Zealand Division's director of physical training, Lieutenant-Colonel Arthur Plugge, William Bright, Reg Taylor (killed in action a few weeks later), Jim Moffit, Arthur Wilson, Dick Fogarty, George Murray (captain), Les Cockroft, Tom French, C. King, Eddie Ryan, Bert Adams and Captain Tom Lawless. In front: Norman Stead, John McIntyre, George Owles, Charlie Brown, Billy Wilson, Hugh Whittington and the assistant manager, Arthur Nelson. Billy Wilson, who played league for New Zealand before and after the war, and Arthur were brothers. Arthur played for the All Blacks from 1908 until 1914. Norman Stead was a brother of the 1905 All Blacks vice-captain, Billy Stead. BIBLIOTHÈQUE NATIONALE DE FRANCE

Pat Hanna, a soldier, cartoonist and entertainer, was among the crowd estimated at between 15,000 and 20,000 at the Parc des Princes in Paris on 17 February 1918 when a New Zealand army team beat a French services team 5–3. After a scoreless first half, the French led by a try until the last minute when a gunner who played for Canterbury before and after the war, Norman Carnegie, scored a try that was converted. Hanna went on to become entertainment officer for the New Zealand Division during its occupation of Cologne in early 1919, and formed a troupe called 'The Diggers' which toured New Zealand and Australia after the war. Chanticleer, the name Hanna used for the cockerel, was the rooster in a French folk tale about Reynard the fox. The cartoon appeared in the London-based fortnightly paper, *Chronicles of the NZEF*. *CHRONICLES OF THE NZEF*, 27 MARCH 1918

dominant sport and teams were organised from various depots with the best of the players chosen for a New Zealand Army team. This team formed the basis of the side that won the King's Cup, a tournament between national services teams, and which subsequently became the first New Zealand side to make a tour of South Africa. The NZEF 'A' team – various other unit teams also played – won 35 of 40 matches with three drawn and two lost, all in a relatively short amount of time. The winning of the King's Cup and its presentation by the King, George V, was the highlight. Booth, who seldom seemed at a loss for words, wrote:

> It will be valued more than any guns, medals, flags or other souvenirs of the war and will probably find a resting place in the Houses of Parliament in Wellington. By winning . . . the team are really carrying back in the King's Cup the ashes of British rugby. This seems singularly fitting when it is remembered that New Zealand is the only country that recognises rugby as essentially its national game.[8]

It was not just rugby, but it was rugby that drew the crowds. As the manager of the team in Britain, Jim Cameron, who had the title of Sports

The army team in Paris in 1919 after it had won the King's Cup in England. The New Zealanders beat France 16–10 in this match at Colombes Stadium in Paris and, a week later in Toulouse, won again 14–13. This was the basis of the team that toured South Africa from July until September that year, but without its outstanding flanker, All Black 'Ranji' Wilson, who was part-Barbadian. He is the second uniformed New Zealand soldier from the right. BIBLIOTHÈQUE NATIONALE DE FRANCE

Officer, NZEF, later wrote: 'In all branches of sport our men did wonderfully well, but it was only the rugby teams that could bring in gate money.'[9]

Among other sports was a successful rowing eight (which included Darcy Hadfield, who was also unbeaten in single sculls and was later an Olympic bronze medallist and world champion), rifle marksman Les Loveday of Taranaki won the King's Prize at Bisley, and track athletes, among them Olympic hurdler Harry Wilson, had successes 'too numerous to mention' according to Cameron. Unlike the rugby players, the rowers and athletes competed at the American-organised Inter-Allied Games in Paris.

If the soldier-sportsmen themselves had been asked why they played, the answers would have been many and various: because they enjoyed it, because it relieved the military tedium and danger, because they were ordered to, because their mates played, because they had nothing else to do and so on. It seems unlikely that many would have subscribed to the belief fostered in academic circles, especially in Britain, that sport was part of their training for war. The main advocate of this was a well-regarded English academic historian and sociologist, J. A. (Tony) Mangan, who saw 'the public school embrace of the games cult as military preparation' and that 'English playing fields were recognised training grounds for imperial

The army forwards, without any evident serious intent, show how their scrum packs down. The photo seems to have been taken before a match, possibly in Paris in 1919. BIBLIOTHÈQUE NATIONALE DE FRANCE

battlefields'.[10] Such was Mangan's influence that a generation of historians followed his words and views and an expatriate New Zealander, Scott Crawford, edited a tribute book in 2004.[11]

The Mangan view might be called the Newbolt view, after the poet Henry whose 'Vitai Lampada' epitomised the perceived relationship between school sport and war: 'There's a breathless hush in the Close to-night/Ten to make and the match to win . . .' and so on until the boy hero becomes a man hero when, with the machine-gun jammed and the colonel dead, a schoolboy rallies the ranks: 'Play up! Play up! And play the game!' Such stirring stuff does not easily make the transition to a pragmatic world. But even if Mangan's main thesis – that the value system of how rugby and cricket should be played was transferred from school to war – held true, was it applicable everywhere? Was it even applicable to the vast majority of British soldiers whose parents could not afford to send them to a public (i.e. fees-paying) school? For all Mangan's high standing in academic circles, there is some questioning of his conclusions. Wray Vamplew, an English historian who spent eighteen years in Australian universities – and therefore saw at first hand how the other half lived – wrote that Mangan was not necessarily wrong, but that his evidence was more indicative than conclusive or compelling.[12]

Action from an army match in 1918 or 1919. Many such games were played on both sides of the Channel, especially after the 11 November 1918 armistice. The fact the New Zealanders are wearing black indicates it is one of the national combinations such as a Trench XV, but the lack of visible spectators indicates it is unlikely to be the divisional team. The photographer was Thomas Frederick Scales, the second official war photographer who was assigned primarily to documenting New Zealand activities at camps and hospitals in Britain.
½-014265-G, ROYAL NEW ZEALAND RETURNED AND SERVICES' ASSOCIATION COLLECTION, ALEXANDER TURNBULL LIBRARY

Welcome home. Thousands of people lined Wellington's inner-city streets on 16 March 1925 to welcome back the Invincibles from their tour. According to one report, the crowd was six and seven deep at some points as the morning procession, led by mounted policemen and followed by the players in cars, went from Lambton Quay to Kent Terrace and back again to the Grand Hotel in Lambton Quay. PACOLL-7985-05, ALEXANDER TURNBULL LIBRARY

7 From war to the Invincibles

Sound trumpet and drum,
For the All Blacks have come,
Bowed down 'neath their burden of glory[1]

Laurie Knight, an All Black who was a brother and a father of All Blacks, looked back on the 1920s: 'The game was well administered, there were many great players of a few years later just emerging . . . they were great players of a great era, an era of distinction and progress.' He should know. He played during that decade, was considered for the 1924–25 Invincibles and eventually received his New Zealand blazer in 1925 against New South Wales.[2] During the 1920s New Zealand rugby desired its own identity at the same time as wanting to be recognised as an international power, but to achieve the latter, it had to lose some of the former.

Auckland was the main stage upon which New Zealand briefly flexed its antipodean muscle, until it was reminded that if it wanted to play the game, it had to be according to the way it was done in England. In the period from before one war had ended until the next one started, New Zealand rugby went through a series of crises and experiments that had the cumulative effect of consolidating rugby's place in the national psyche and the country's significance to others as a rugby nation. There were extraordinary successes, such as the unbeaten tour by the All Blacks in 1924–25, and unremitting challenges, such as the two series against South Africa, one at home in 1921 and the other there in 1928. There were times of anxiety, such as the changes in playing laws aimed at making rugby more attractive than league, especially in Auckland; and when New Zealand virtually propped up Australian rugby because the game in Queensland had faded away to nothing. There were times of riches, when crowds crammed into grounds to watch the South Africans, to watch matches for the Ranfurly Shield – which after twenty years had begun to prove its worth – and times of hard-headed realisation such as the inevitable decision that the wing forward, a characteristic of the New Zealand game, had to go.

It was also the decade when politics – not politics in the benign form of Seddon cashing in on rugby's popularity but politics under the malign influence of racism – first had an impact on New Zealand rugby. The origin was South Africa, a country that New Zealanders realised during the Boer War of 1899–1902 was as enamoured with rugby as they were. At least, the white population

The team formed by New Zealand troopers during the Boer War that won the Zeerust Cup in 1901, probably the first foreign trophy to be claimed by a New Zealand rugby team. Zeerust is a farming area about 250 kilometres north-west of Johannesburg and the soldiers, part of an artillery battery, played in a tournament there. TE AWAMUTU MUSEUM COLLECTION

was. The rest were neither asked nor wanted. Dave Gallaher, the 1905 captain who had served in South Africa, wrote with his vice-captain, Billy Stead, of rugby there: 'There is something about the climate and the country that makes one feel instinctively that here is a place where Rugby football would thrive if it would anywhere in the world. One of us has had a fair experience of the country and this thought recurred over and over again.'[3] (A team of troopers led by Gallaher 'easily' beat the leading Transvaal teams and beat a Maritzburg, Natal, side by a 'record margin'.)[4] New Zealanders, whether soldiers or miners or both, formed teams in Pretoria and Durban and won the local competitions; a New Zealander was secretary of the Transvaal union in 1904.[5] The first rugby trophy to be won by a New Zealand team overseas was probably the Zeerust Cup, won by a New Zealand Battery team at Zeerust in the Transvaal in 1901 against an English team.[6] By the time of the First World War, rugby was well established in South Africa and its national team had toured Britain and Ireland twice, something New Zealand and Australia had each been allowed to do only once. What is more, the South Africans beat Wales. Former enemies of the English but now best friends, the newly named Springboks were seen as the amateur ideal and they did not question English hegemony, unlike their colonial cousins on the other side of the Indian Ocean.

The services encouraged rugby, like other sports, during the war, partly to aid fitness and partly under the banner of soldiers' welfare. They assembled the best players from various New Zealand teams in France and England into a New Zealand Army team that played the Empire Allies for a cup donated by King George V. The victorious New Zealanders went on to play France at Twickenham, before which the King presented them with his cup. Among the players who shook the regal hand was Arthur Wilson, who had played ten test matches for New Zealand. He had been born Nathaniel Arthur Wilson in Christchurch in 1886, a son of Tabatha and Joe Wilson. Tabatha was from Yorkshire, Joe from Barbados. Wilson's appearance earned him the nickname of 'Ranji', after the Indian prince who played test cricket for England in the 1890s, Kumar Shri Ranjitsinhji. (Wilson's nickname was sometimes rendered as Rangi, but that could have been because it more naturally rolled off New Zealand tongues.) Wilson was one of the leading lights in the army team and when the South African Rugby Board decided it wanted the New Zealand team to play there on the way home, he would have been one of the first chosen. Another member of the army team was Parekura ('Pare') Tureia, a promising young five-eighth from Poverty Bay.

Eighteen days before the soldiers took possession of the King's Cup, the South African board cabled the country's high commissioner in London, William Philip Schreiner – better known simply as W. P. Schreiner – who happened to be a former board president. Its message was a cost-saving to the point: 'Would it be possible to arrange representative Australian or New Zealand army rugby team break journey Cape Town stop tour union for six weeks or less stop travelling and hotel expenses paid stop pardon liberty stop reply paid stop and end.'[7]

Schreiner did as he was bid and by the middle of May told the board arrangements had been made with New Zealand providing the board agreed that it would pay all internal travel and hotels for a party of 29. The board agreed. Schreiner cabled again on 2 June advising of the travel arrangements and asking if the fixture list could be cabled. It seems to have been only at this point that it dawned on board members the composition of the New Zealand team may not be entirely to its liking. It decided by eight votes to six to again cable Schreiner: 'Confidential if visitors include Maoris tour would be wrecked and immense harm politically and otherwise would follow stop Please explain position fully and try arrange exclusion.'

The motion to send the cable had been seconded by Bill Schreiner, one of W. P. Schreiner's sons. The older Schreiner in London, who had been prime minister of Cape Colony before the Boer War, was regarded as one of the early genuinely liberal South African politicians and had argued publicly that non-whites in South Africa should be given full and equal rights. He was a younger brother of campaigner Olive Schreiner, who was equally liberal but better known internationally. The son appears not to have been as liberal. It therefore fell to Schreiner to convey the distasteful news to the army team that two of its potential members were not wanted. Schreiner had been ill for most of his time in London and he died just three weeks later. *The Times* in its obituary said of him: 'It would be cynical to say that he was too honest to be a great success as a politician; but there would be an element of truth in it nevertheless.'[8] The New Zealand High Commissioner, Sir Thomas Mackenzie, was among the mourners at his funeral.[9]

How precisely the information that they were not wanted for South Africa was conveyed to the two players cannot now be known. The fact they were excluded for racist reasons was concealed – in fact, it was reported that Tureia missed the ship taking the team to South Africa and eventually returned to New Zealand via Panama.[10] (As a serving and well-regarded soldier who was

The national Māori team that played South Africa in 1921. It was captained by Parekura Tureia, who had not been allowed to tour South Africa two years before. Back row: Turi Tangitu, Joe Kororiko, Winiata Tapsell, Jim Garlick, Arthur Grace, Ben Gemmell, Matiu Edwards, Rangi Broughton. Middle row: Edward Kuru, Wattie Barclay, Wiremu Parata (manager), Tureia, Wiremu Te Whata, Jimmy Mill. Front row: Wharepapa Mitai, Taituhu Peina, Jack Blake, Turi Carroll.

commissioned in the Second World War, this seemed unlikely but the published report went unquestioned. His service record makes no mention of missing an embarkation.)[11] He surely would have taken extra delight when he captained the Māori against the South Africans in Napier in 1921.

Wilson did in fact get to South Africa and coincidentally met up with his teammates in Durban. Some published reports have said he travelled with the team but was not allowed to go ashore.[12] In fact, Wilson left London on the troopship *Cordoba* on 18 July 1919 and the team departed two days later on a seized German liner, the *Cap Polonio*, hastily converted for use on the South Africa run. As the *Natal Witness* recorded: 'Amongst the troops on the New Zealand transport is their great forward, Ranji Wilson, who had already met and fraternised with his old comrades.'[13] The paper called Wilson a Pacific Islander and added it would be a good thing if he could be added to the team.[14]

Years later the *Evening Post* sports editor, Fred Boshier, wrote that Wilson helped select the team of which he could not be a part: 'Because of the colour situation in South Africa, one of the finest forwards in the King's Cup team, A. ("Ranji") Wilson, of Wellington, had to be left behind but, to demonstrate the spirit of a great sportsman, Wilson co-operated in the selection of the touring side.'[15] Boshier gave no source for the comment, although as a Wellington rugby writer of long standing, he almost certainly would have known Wilson.

Also many years later it was learnt that at least one of the soldier players, Alex Bruce, a Wellington teammate of Wilson's, 'always carried an ever deepening sense of guilt' about Wilson's omission. According to his son Don, Bruce felt that 'team and management had taken

Death of a captain

When the 2nd New Zealand Expeditionary Force team, the Kiwis, entered the last phase of its post-war tour in March of 1946, it took the time to visit the First World War battlefields and pay tribute to those who had gone before. Among the graves of many they visited was that of the captain of the 1905–06 All Blacks, Dave Gallaher, who was killed at Passchendaele in 1917. Two members of the Kiwis party laid a wreath at the base of Gallaher's headstone at the Nine Elms cemetery at Poperinge in the midst of an area where every corner seems to bear a signpost to a war cemetery. One was 1928 All Black Vic Butler, one of the Kiwis selectors and the team's assistant manager. He was chosen because he, like Gallaher, was from Auckland. The other was Percy Guyton, the team's masseur. He was selected because he too was a Passchendaele casualty; in fact he'd been taken to the same casualty station where Gallaher died.

Gallaher was killed on the first day of the battle of Passchendaele. For New Zealanders, Passchendaele comprised two phases – an assault on a spur of the Passchendaele ridge in Flanders that was known to the troops as Abraham's Heights; and an assault on a second ridge eight days later. By the military reckoning of the time, the first phase was a success – the deaths of 487 New Zealanders might suggest otherwise – but the second was a disaster. (The death toll of New Zealand troops on 12 October was 846; that does not account for those who were wounded on that day and died later.) One of the best-known British war correspondents, Philip Gibbs, wrote of the first day: 'It was a great day for the Australians and New Zealanders, their greatest and most glorious day.'[1] The number and names of the dead were not known until after that.

Gallaher, a sergeant in the Auckland battalion, was in the 4 October assault that began at six o'clock in the morning just as rain and a strong south-westerly wind began. Confronting the British armies of which the New Zealanders were a part on a 12-kilometre front were a German Guards division and a Bavarian division. Some reports say Gallaher was mortally wounded by shrapnel from German shells; his service record says he died of gunshot wounds to the face.[2] No matter the cause, the effect was the same. Stretcher bearers – conditions were so difficult there were six to a stretcher – took him to the nearest aid post, the 3rd Casualty Clearing Station of the Australian Imperial Force. Its war diary shows he was one of 851 wounded dealt with that day.[3]

Gallaher was buried three days later, on 7 October, one of a production line of interments. His service was conducted by an English-born and educated Anglican minister, Evelyn George Muschamp, who had immigrated to Australia. (A son, Cecil, was later rector of St Michael and All Angels in Christchurch.)[4]

Gallaher was 43 years old, though army records listed him as being 40. When he enlisted, he gave his date of birth as 31 October 1876, when in fact he had been born, as his birth certificate shows, on 30 October 1873, at Ramelton in Ireland. He had begun the fiction when he had enlisted for service in the Boer War in 1901, saying he was 25 when in fact he was 28. During the Boer War, he was also recorded as 'Gallagher' but took to spelling it without the middle 'g' when he returned home. It is presumed he did that so the name would be

Assistant manager Vic Butler and masseur Percy Guyton at Dave Gallaher's grave in the Nine Elms Cemetery in Flanders during the 2nd New Zealand Expeditionary Force team's tour in the northern winter of 1945–46. Guyton had been wounded in the same battle that cost Gallaher his life; Butler was a member of Gallaher's club, Ponsonby.

pronounced correctly rather than with a hard 'g'. When a brother, Henry, enlisted in the Australian Imperial Force in 1917, his name was listed as 'Gallagher' but with the second 'g' crossed out.

The Kiwis' masseur, Guyton, was a member of the 4th Field Ambulance of the NZEF and was serving in the same area where Gallaher was killed. It is entirely likely he spent some time as a stretcher bearer because of the great number of wounded and there were only about 200 designated bearers. Each wounded had to be carried about three kilometres over muddied ground and around shell holes so numerous they were sometimes contiguous.[5] Guyton was shot in the right knee on the day of the second New Zealand assault, the twelfth, and taken as Gallaher had been to the 3rd Australian CCS. He was transferred a day later to hospital and within a week was in hospital in England, his war over.[6]

A trained physiotherapist and masseur, Guyton joined the air force in the Second World War but was transferred to the army and commissioned so he could work on the rehabilitation of wounded soldiers. After his work on the Kiwis' tour, he was seconded to a British hospital for a year before returning to civilian life in New Zealand.

Gallaher's name was perpetuated by the Gallaher Shield for club competition in Auckland and, more latterly, the Gallaher Cup for which New Zealand and France play. (Gallaher was captain of the first All Blacks to play France.) Not long before Gallaher was killed, he wrote to an old teammate, Ernie Booth, who was with the Australian YMCA in France and Britain: 'So far I have a whole skin, though life here, on the whole, is a matter of chance. So long "Old Horse", heaps of luck and good wishes from your old pal, Dave.'[7]

'Dave was a man of sterling worth,' Booth wrote, 'slow to promise, always sure to fulfil; girded by great determination and self-control, he was a valuable friend. . . . In the huge list of fallen International Rugbyites in this gigantic fight of Right and Might, the name of Dave Gallaher among sportsmen-fighters stands out pre-eminently.'

the soft option – that a stand then on the racial issue of "coloured" inclusion would have saved humiliation of a fine man and sportsman and set the stage for later tour consideration'.[16] A stand then by the tour organisers – that is, army sports officers rather than the New Zealand Rugby Football Union – may have been a blunt statement South Africans could not ignore. But the stand was not taken.

Historian Greg Ryan wrote of the Wilson exclusion that 'it was commonly understood among rugby officials that New Zealand would acquiesce to the domestic racial policy of South Africa, as the Springboks would reciprocate when they visited New Zealand in 1921'.[17] But he gave no source for the comment and neither did he acknowledge that the army team had nothing to do with New Zealand rugby officials, whatever 'common understanding' there may have been. The army team was chosen by the army, not by the New Zealand Rugby Football Union. There may well have been some 'when in Rome' understanding later in the century when reciprocal tours had been established, but there could not have been in 1919 (the time of which Ryan was writing) because there had been minimal contact between the two unions and no tours. A South African historian, Floris Van Der Merwe, saw the tour as having a 'positive effect on the morale of civil as well as military lives' and: 'It is just a pity that a negative political stigma is attached to these events of 1919. The racial ban, and not the positive aspects . . . is all that is associated with it.'[18] For all his concern about a negative legacy, Van Der Merwe nevertheless provided a full recounting of the events that led to the exclusion of Wilson and Tureia and corrected the mistake made by other historians that Wilson travelled with the team and stayed on board the ship.

Wiremu ('Ned') Parata, the single most influential person in the fostering of Māori rugby in the twentieth century, was quoted in a newspaper story in 1932 as saying that the captain of the army team, Charlie Brown of Taranaki, was in fact part-Māori – he just did not look the part. Parata helped organise matches for the team when it arrived home.[19] At least two Māori played in South Africa in 1917 when teams from two troopships bound for England played in Durban during a refuelling stop. John Grace from Gisborne scored one of the two tries for the winning team from the *Turakina*. A teammate was Paraire ('Friday') Pirihi and both were with the Māori Contingent in the 17th reinforcement draft.[20]

The army team's experience in 1919 and the South African tour of 1921 laid down markers for a future of controversy, but rugby at the time was more concerned with the threat of league and with trying to persuade English officials to change the playing laws to make the game more attractive. Auckland felt the league threat most keenly and it proposed and in some cases adopted changes. Players started playing and spectators started watching 'the Auckland game' which, at various times, played to laws different from the rest of the country. Auckland, like New South Wales, adopted the kick into touch law that is the present law. Players in the rest of the country could kick the ball into touch on the full from wherever they were on the field with impunity. On some occasions, the referee put the ball into the scrum (which had happened in the South Island at times in the nineteenth century and later in the twentieth) and an offside line was drawn through the centre of a scrum, beyond which the wing forward could not advance until the ball was in the halfback's hands.

Players such as Laurie Knight in Auckland argued these changes led to 'fast, good handling forwards whose support of clever backlines has never been equalled'. But other observers, especially Vic Cavanagh junior, who played for Otago but was best known as a coach, thought the 'bounce-out rule' (restricting kicking into touch on the full) caused the start of a decline in New Zealand rugby.[21] Auckland's changes were approved by the New Zealand union and

This served as both tour souvenir and match programme for the first visit to New Zealand by a South African team, in 1921. The reference to 'the third Springboks' means it was the third South African team to tour overseas after two earlier tours of Great Britain and Ireland.

eventually by the English union, but they were 'dispensations', not changes. This meant that for international matches, the laws as laid down by the English union still applied.

Rugby throughout its history has struggled to achieve universal application of its playing laws and Auckland's variations in the 1920s were just one more example. Hardly a rugby year has gone by without some change to a law, or interpretation of a law, although the public (and even players) remain largely unaware of the finer points. One All Black coach, Eric Watson, used to argue the Cavanagh philosophy that rugby was a simple game; it was, but one made complex by its administrators, sometimes as a reaction to imagined threats from other games, at times to borrow from other games and occasionally because of perceived safety issues. (Some consistency to the application of the laws came after 1926 when the English union agreed the International Rugby Board, on which the English held a majority, should formulate all playing laws and that they should apply at all levels of the game. This was in effect the end of the RFU trying to be rugby's governing body like cricket's MCC or golf's Royal and Ancient.)[22]

Rugby was not as threatened by league as some people in the game thought. But the constant comparisons between the two games amounted to an obsession at times and once reached the House of Representatives. A nationally known Labour member, John A. Lee, wanted to know why rugby players who were public servants were given half-pay when on tour and league players were not. Prime Minister Gordon Coates said he knew of just one example of this apparent contradiction: a league player was not given half-pay because he received more than the equivalent from the league itself.[23]

The South African tour of New Zealand in 1921 did much to consolidate the status of rugby as the premier winter sport. Capacity crowds watched the nineteen matches and the national union gained a profit of £7,170 (about $570,000 in today's terms); but more than success as expressed by crowd numbers and revenue, the tour created a widespread interest and set a pattern for tours of New Zealand that lasted until the end of the amateur era.[24] Newspapers gave extensive coverage to the team beyond its matches and people crowded to see the players arrive in cities or at functions so the tour became more than just a series of games. But the overriding benefit of the tour was that it provided evidence for all to see of another national rugby team that was at least the

All Blacks ham it up during a training camp at Days Bay, across the harbour from Wellington, before the third test in 1921.

equal of New Zealand's. New Zealanders had read of the Springboks' two tours of Britain and how their results compared favourably with those of the 1905 All Blacks; they had read also of the strength of the opposition against the army team in 1919. The 1921 tour provided first-hand evidence; it also gave New Zealand crowds their first international rugby since 1913. More than changes in laws, the fillip of top-class competition gave rugby the boost it wanted. Flow-on effects were evident at the following annual meeting of the national union when several country areas sought recognition as provincial unions. Two of them, King Country and East Coast, were accepted. And for those who were still fixated with what league may or may not have been doing, an *Evening Post* report a week before the annual meeting said 'the league game is at present under a cloud and men are returning wholesale, like prodigal sons, to the old home'.[25]

Ultimately in rugby, as with any sport, it is what happens on the field that matters. Administrators can administer, crowds can flock, reporters can write, carpers can cavil, but it is what the players do within the white lines of a rugby field that determines the success or failure of a match or a tour. From the first game, in front of a crowd of about 10,000 at Cook's Gardens in Wanganui, the Springboks exhibited what would later be known as star quality. Their speedster on the wing, Adriaan ('Attie') van Heerden, who the year before had competed in the 400 metres hurdles at the Olympic Games in Antwerp, scored the first try. He became the centre of attraction thereafter for younger supporters, a sort of a Lomu of his day. As a writer in the *Observer* in Auckland later recalled: 'A veritable Apollo on the field, it was small wonder that the flappers fell for him, some of them mere college girls. Usually it is the schoolboys who indulge in footballer hero worship, but on this occasion they were outdone by the girls and many were the requests for autographed photos for the boudoir.'[26]

New Zealanders had a genuine local hero when New Zealand and South Africa met in a test match for the first time. It was five-all in the second half at Carisbrook in Dunedin and the All Blacks were on defence. The first five-eighth, Ces Badeley, attempted a kick across field in

The infamous 1921 cable

The first South African team to tour New Zealand beat the national Māori team 9–8 in Napier on Wednesday, 7 September 1921. Reports the day after the match were nothing exceptional and the Springboks continued on their tour to Nelson. A day later, however, the local paper, the *Daily Telegraph*, carried a report with the damning headings:

> THE NAPIER CROWD
> 'MOST UNSPORTSMANLIKE
> EVER EXPERIENCED'
> SPRINGBOKS FRANKLY DISGUSTED
> 'MOST UNFORTUNATE
> MATCH EVER PLAYED'

Its report found its way via the Press Association into other daily newspapers and all New Zealanders could read:

> The following is a copy of a message apparently forwarded to South African newspapers by someone travelling with the Springboks' team:- Most unfortunate match ever played. Only result great pressure being brought to bear on Bennett induced them to meet Maoris, who assisted largely entertainment Springboks. Bad enough having play team officially designated New Zealand natives, but spectacle thousands Europeans frantically cheering on band of coloured men to defeat members of own race was too much for Springboks, who frankly disgusted. That was not the worst. The crowd was most unsportsmanlike experienced on the tour, especially section who lost all control of their feelings. When not booing referee, they indulged in sarcastic remarks at his expense. On many occasions Africans were hurt. Crowd, without waiting for possibility of immediate recovery, shouted 'Take him off!' 'Take him off!' Their faithful coloured allies proved loyal to New Zealand, for, in addition to serious injury to Kruger's leg, Van Heerden had to stay off field for fifteen minutes. Others were limping badly. Maoris flung their weight about regardless of niceties of the game.[1] The cabled comments by the South African reporter had an immediate reaction and, longer term, they were held by various writers and historians to have lit the fuse of one of the most controversial issues in twentieth-century rugby.

But another comment in Napier may have had more of an impact on the future of rugby relations between New Zealand and South Africa.

The Hawke's Bay Rugby Union, host of the Māori match, cabled the South African manager, Harold Bennett, and asked him to disassociate himself and his team from the reported comments, but did express regret at the action of a section of the crowd. The fuss over the reporter's comments somewhat obscured the potentially more portentous item that rose at a Hawke's Bay union meeting. Union secretary John Brown said Wiremu Parata had asked Bennett if there were any chance of a Māori team visiting South Africa. The *Daily Telegraph* report then said: 'Mr Bennett had told him plainly that neither Mr Parata nor any member of his race would ever get accommodation in South Africa. Mr Bennett was also going to insist that no Maori should be included in any New Zealand team visiting Africa.'[2] There appears to have been no published reaction.

A sentence also appeared in the *New Zealand Herald* saying that the South Africans had not wanted to play against the Māori and did not enjoy it when they did so. The *Herald*'s report was filed by its 'own correspondent' (otherwise unidentified) in Wellington who added that 'the visitors come from a country where the colour line is drawn very clearly and their acquaintance with New Zealand has not been sufficiently long for them to understand the status of the Maoris in this country'.[3]

Surprisingly, this comment – buried as it was in a story about another South African complaint, about their hotel accommodation in Nelson – caused hardly any reaction. It did provoke a comment from that most eminent of Māori leaders, Te Rangi Hīroa (Sir Peter Buck who was then just plain Dr), who said if the South Africans not long being in New Zealand was sufficient excuse 'then we can only conclude that, in developing brawn and muscle to ensure success on the football field, their powers of exercising their mental faculties . . . have suffered deterioration'.[4]

Bennett did his best to repudiate the cabled comments and said the correspondent who had written the damning words was sorry he did so (though, as it turned out, he was not). Bennett said he and his players had no objection to playing against Māori and no complaints afterwards. 'We have never expressed any views like this and the cable did not represent our feelings,' he said.[5] The correspondent identified himself as C. Blackett and said he was astonished to see Bennett's remarks and his 'abject' apology.

'What I do regret,' Blackett said, 'apart from the unfortunate manner in which the message was disclosed at this end, is the mutilated and abridged form in which it was published in certain papers for reasons best known to themselves. . . . Persons who surreptitiously obtained and disseminated the cable only published those passages which could be construed as an attack on the Maoris.'[6]

A few days later the third test did much to bring the cable issue to an end. Newspapers generally took the *Herald*'s line, suggesting that South Africans did not really understand the status of the Māori. *Truth* appeared on the morning of the test with its usual eloquent outrage and its unidentified writer said the cabled message was 'too bad for words' and that its writer should be 'severely sat upon and silenced'.[7] Other newspapers reported that telegraph operators in Napier were sacked for leaking the cable but were later reinstated.[8]

Blackett was the correspondent for the Johannesburg *Star*. The fact the tour ended only a couple of weeks after the news of his cable first broke ensured the story faded away, only for it to be brought up occasionally thereafter and when Blackett himself was nowhere near New Zealand. The implication was always that Blackett was a South African, white and ignorant of the ways of New Zealand. In fact, he was an Australian and had close connections with New Zealand. His full name was Cephas Augustine Mortimer Blackett – his initials in 1921 were given as 'C. W. E.' – and he had been born in Franklin, Tasmania, in 1881, the eleventh of thirteen children. Known as Mort, he was thought to have worked in New Zealand late in the nineteenth century when some of his family moved across the Tasman. By the time of the Boer War, though, he was back in Tasmania because he enlisted in Hobart, where he gave his occupation as journalist. He stayed in South Africa when the war ended in 1902 and joined the *Star* as a junior reporter. He toured Australia in 1911 with the South African cricket team as a correspondent for the British news agency, Reuter. By then, he had gained a niche in cricket history by being roped in as a substitute to make up the numbers for South Africa in a pre-tour match against Western Province. (He was out for a duck and took one catch.)[9]

Blackett became an officer in the Natal Light Horse and fought against the Germans in South-West Africa (Namibia) in 1915 before returning to Sydney to enlist with the Australian Imperial Force. He was attached to a brigade headquarters, was on the staff of the Australian general, John Monash, by the end of the war and was made a member of the Order of the British Empire (MBE) 'for services in connection with the war'.[10] Blackett, who never married, spent the rest of his life in Johannesburg, where he died in 1938. His death was reported in New Zealand, but no mention was made of his infamous message of seventeen years before.[11]

Suggestions have been made that the 1921 match and Blackett's cable were factors in the New Zealand Rugby Football Union's subsequent policy towards South Africa, which was that Māori would be 'protected' by not being selected for tours there and that no Māori team played the 1937 South Africans. There is no evidence, however, that Blackett's cable was ever discussed formally by the NZRFU. It seems more likely that Bennett's hitherto unpublicised remark to Parata – that Māori would not get accommodation there and he would recommend Māori not be chosen – would have been much more responsible for the All Blacks being all-white. (Bennett had been president of the Griqualand West Rugby Union since 1913 and while his views on Māori may have accurately reflected the general mood in South African rugby, any personal influence he may have had after the tour was short-lived. He was killed in a car crash in February 1923.)[12]

behind the South African backs, but the kick was sliced. The second five-eighth, Mark Nicholls, took up the story:

> Before the ball landed, Jack Steel ran in and took it on the full (he jumped for it) and immediately swerved out towards the touchline. Gerhard Morkel, the Springbok fullback, didn't get within 15 yards of him. Charlie Meyer, the Springbok second five-eighth, chased Jack every yard of the way to the corner flag but could not get within tackling distance.[27]

The run for the try was variously estimated at between 50 and 70 yards, but Steel was too quick no matter what the distance. A rugby wing on the West Coast in the winter, he was a professional sprinter on the tracks in the summer. A Coast fan in the crowd rushed on to the field and shook Steel's hand, both shaker and shaken smiling broadly. 'Moke' Belliss and Percy Storey, each of whom had been in the 1919 army team in South Africa, also scored tries for a 13–5 New Zealand win.

According to Norman McKenzie, a national selector and coach and one of a remarkable set of rugby brothers, the All Blacks were confidently expected to win the second test in Auckland. But they were put up in a hotel in the centre of the city (the Royal, in Victoria Street) where they became 'the cynosure of all eyes' and 'strenuous preparations for the game were not greatly persevered with'. The South Africans won, a dropped goal by their fullback, Morkel, being the difference. The prospect of New Zealand being beaten in the three-match series then went to the front of minds. The All Blacks were dispatched to Days Bay across the harbour from Wellington for five days of intensive training. It was as concentrated and organised as anything that could be devised by any of the professional coaches of the twenty-first century. From before dawn each day, an athletics coach, 'Dorrie' Leslie, and a couple of assistants kept the players under scrutiny.[28] Three of the 1905

All Blacks Billy Stead, George Nicholson and Alex McDonald, and two selectors, Alf Griffiths (father of later national captain Jack) and Donald Stuart, put them through rugby drills. Players had to be in bed by nine at night – so strenuous were the days such an early bedtime was probably welcome – and lights out was ordered for 10 p.m. Leslie, according to the *Evening Post*, then did his rounds making sure all the players were sleeping comfortably.[29]

Among the players was Karl Ifwersen, an Auckland second five-eighth who had been recently reinstated from a stint with league, in which he also played for his country. The concentrated preparation and Wellington's weather conspired to ensure that neither All Blacks nor Springboks went away with a series win. Athletic Park was almost totally awash, constructive rugby was difficult and goal-kicking unwise: the game was a scoreless draw (one of only two in the All Blacks' ledger – the other was in 1964 against Scotland).

One of the 1905 All Blacks, Ernie Booth, had gone on to play for New South Wales and work in Australia as a journalist before returning to New Zealand in 1921 to write and coach. He called the national union's reinstatement of players such as Ifwersen 'a strong fighting factor' against the league game (because people went to see him play) and that the English union had lost a great opportunity by not doing the same thing. 'What a glorious chance it lost about the time when the union and Northern Union army men were playing together,' he wrote.[30] This was the constant challenge faced by the New Zealand union until it gained representation on the International Rugby Board after the Second World War, wanting to do one thing for the perceived good of New Zealand rugby, but having to do another to obey the dictates of the English union (and therefore still be in good standing when it came to tours). This explains why Ifwersen did not go to Britain with the 1924 team. He was one of the great players of his generation, or as Norman McKenzie wrote: 'Astuteness on the rugby field will get a man out of a lot of trouble. Karl Ifwersen was one of the most astute inside backs I have seen.'[31]

The NZRFU ruled Ifwersen ineligible for the 1924 tour because he was a reinstated player and 'ran the serious risk' of being banned either by the English union or the IRB. This was at a time an Australian, Tommy Lawton, was banned in England because he had played league in Queensland (when there was no rugby). For all that, Ifwersen went on as a replacement in one of the 1924 trials, although in everyone's full knowledge that he could not be chosen.[32] It would be easy to say about ninety years later that the NZRFU should have stuck to its principles and told England so, but the circumstances then were not what they later became. England then was still the unofficial leader of many, not just one of the pack.

Another player not wanted for the 1924 tour was Phonse Carroll. Born in Mataura to parents from Cork, Carroll was a conscientious objector during the First World War. A hooker in the old two-three-two scrum, he played for New Zealand in 1920 and 1921, but when it came time to consider players for the British tour, Carroll appeared to have been penalised for his non-military past. By then, the New Zealand union had agreed to a request from the Returned Soldiers' Association (as it then was) not to choose military defaulters. The RSA questioned the fairness of permitting military defaulters 'to take equal places with the rest of the community in the pursuits which are boasted of as being one of the greatest factors in moulding our race'.[33] It was not just a rugby issue. Other sports chose not to select players who were said to be defaulters. One letter to the editor of the *Evening Post* from 'Old Soldier' said: 'Football is not the only game which has its shirkers. They are, I believe, to be found in cricket clubs, tennis clubs, golf clubs and athletic clubs.' He said soccer had 'steadily set their faces against the continuance of such a scandal'.[34] Carroll switched to league and was a member of the national team that went to England in 1926; he was one of seven players who were banned by the New Zealand Rugby League for life for various disagreements with the team's management. The bans were rescinded in 1962.[35] (Defaulters were not always what they seemed. McKenzie was the Hawke's Bay coach in the 1920s and was told by the NZRFU and the RSA of the possible consequences if he chose a player who was a defaulter.[36] McKenzie made enquiries and found the player was a stoker on a ship bound for England at the time he was called up and since he did not respond, he was posted as a defaulter. McKenzie said stoking on a ship in a sea full of German submarines was as risky as any form of warfare, but he had to leave the player out.)[37]

There was movement throughout the country in what could be seen as a quiet evolution of the game, when men of enduring influence decided the old ways were not their ways; that the game needed to be modernised and if it were played as well as it could be, threats from other games such as league were immaterial. Some of their names are well known still, men such as Vic Cavanagh senior who coached club and provincial sides in Dunedin then reared his son to do the same. There was a lawyer and later crown prosecutor in Auckland, Vin Meredith, who after a grounding in Wellington rugby was Auckland's sole selector (and de facto coach) for much of the 1920s. There was Norman McKenzie, who almost single-handedly provided Hawke's Bay with one of its most successful periods and gave the Ranfurly Shield a cachet among provinces that the famous old trophy has never lost. In Invercargill there was a man whose name hardly ever appears in print. He was Frank Mussen, a journalist but primarily an enthusiast for the game, and when he gained a seat on the Southland Rugby Union, he ensured the union hired the 1905 All Black Ernie Booth as a coach at £6 a week. It was a bold, unprecedented move for the time, but Mussen's idea was that Booth would scour the schools for potential talent and mould a Southland team capable of beating any other in New Zealand. The national union said Booth being paid made him a professional, but he took the job anyway and found some other way of earning money. According to another born and brought up in Southland, *Truth* sports editor Morrie Mackenzie, Mussen 'lashed what he termed "the old home province" into a football crusade which brought the Ranfurly Shield to Southland for the first time and started a rugby revival of the first magnitude'.[38] In Bay of Plenty and within Māori rugby throughout the country, there was Wiremu ('Ned') Parata, who spent a lifetime promoting Māori players and spending his own money to do so.

The net effect of men such as these in the 1920s was that New Zealand rugby entered a period that was as rich in playing talent as any in the sport's history. George Nepia was one of this galaxy. He had come to the notice of both McKenzie and Parata in Hawke's Bay and had played for the province as a wing and second five-eighth. A great friend and almost as gifted as a rugby player was Lui Paewai, and it was Paewai's father who reckoned young George would be a better fullback than a wing or in the midfield. Paewai senior badgered Parata until agreement was reached and Parata put Nepia at fullback in the Northern versus Southern Māori match in 1924, one of several national trials. Nepia later recalled he wandered all over the field, knowing nothing of fullback play, and he thought his chances of being an All Black were over before they began. Parata told him: 'George, you are a certainty for the tour.' And Nepia replied: 'Ned, you are quite mad.' Nepia was chosen at fullback for the next trial, North Island Possibles against Probables, after which Stan Dean announced the first sixteen certainties for the tour. Nepia recalled:

> The moment Stan entered the clatter of knives and forks stopped dead. There was a silence which would

When the All Blacks became Invincibles

Until the era of contrived, imposed nicknames for rugby teams, popular names were acquired along the way: All Blacks was first used for the national team in 1893, but it was only during the 1905–06 tour that the name gained wide usage and acceptance. It was as a result of the New Zealand team being known as the All Blacks that the teams of South Africa and Australia followed suit and became known as the Springboks and Wallabies.

Nicknames were all the rage in other sports early in the twentieth century and they derived from popular usage. In league, for example, South Sydney gained their nickname of Rabbitohs while they were still a rugby club. Their amateur players, sporting the red and green colours for which the league club is still known, apparently used to hawk rabbits around the Souths heartland on Saturday mornings to raise a bit of cash. The cry of 'rabbitoh' accompanied them. In baseball, the Los Angeles Dodgers were once the Brooklyn Dodgers. People from Brooklyn early in the twentieth century were known elsewhere in New York as 'trolley dodgers' because of the large number of tracks for 'trolley cars' (electric trams) baseball fans had to cross to get to the Dodgers' ground. The baseball team was originally known as the 'Brooklyn Trolley Dodgers' and this was gradually shortened to just Dodgers. The name first appeared on the team's playing uniform in 1933, and when the Dodgers were sold to Los Angeles in 1957, their name went with them.

The best-known nickname for a New Zealand team after All Blacks itself is the Invincibles, the name given to the 1924–25 team that played in Britain, Ireland, France and North America without a loss. The name is not unique to rugby. There have been several Invincibles, and not just in sport. In one way or another, they are faithful to the meaning of the word – that they are unable to be beaten or overcome (or they or their adherents think they are). A chief secretary for Ireland, Lord Cavendish, and a senior Irish public servant, Thomas Burke, were assassinated in Dublin in 1882 in what became known as the Phoenix Park murders. Those involved, including five who were hanged, were members of a previously unknown Republican organisation, the Irish National Invincibles. Well before that, a French regiment at the Battle of Waterloo, the 45th Regiment of the Line, an infantry unit, was known by the British as the Invincibles. But since the French did not do too well at Waterloo, they may not have been invincible after all. Others have had much more peaceable credentials.

The first sports team to be known as the Invincibles appears to have been the English soccer club, Preston North End, which went through the 1888–89 season of 22 matches without a loss. Along the way, the club won both the league and FA Cup. In the modern era, Arsenal were sometimes referred to as the Invincibles for not losing an away match in the 2001–02 season. In cricket, Don Bradman's Australians in England in 1948 became known as the Invincibles for not losing a match. Another Australian team, the league team of 1982, was also called the Invincibles for touring Britain and France without a loss.

The Invincible All Blacks, captained by Cliff Porter of Wellington, played 32 matches between September 1924 and February 1925 and won the lot: 28 in the United Kingdom and Ireland, two in France and two in British Columbia. They

Jack Gilmour's cartoon from the *New Zealand Free Lance* of 7 January 1925 – the first known reference to the 1924–25 team as the Invincibles. Gilmour used his pen name, 'Jno Gee'. H-542-001, ALEXANDER TURNBULL LIBRARY

became known as the Invincibles and the name was so enduring that it was central to a trade-mark infringement court case in 2001. But who originated the name? A scouring of newspapers published during the tour revealed nothing. The team was feted and lauded, but no reference to their being invincible could be found – of course, because they had to finish their tour to be so. Or did they? Four days after the last match in Britain, the test win against England, the *New Zealand Free Lance*, a weekly magazine-style newspaper published in Wellington, carried a cartoon showing a kiwi kicking a ball over a crossbar labelled 'undefeated record' with a lion acting as a despairing goalkeeper. The caption read: 'Invincible New Zealand. The Kiwi beats all Rugby Records.'[2] The cartoonist was John Henry Gilmour, otherwise known as Jack, who was reasonably well known at the time but has since slipped under history's radar.

Gilmour was born in Christchurch in 1892 and in 1911 he succeeded the celebrated David Low as cartoonist for the *Canterbury Times*, a weekly publication owned by the daily *Lyttelton Times*. After war service with the Otago Mounted Rifles, during which he was a regular artist for the London newspaper for troops, *Chronicles of the NZEF*, he moved to Wellington where he found work as cartoonist for both the *Free Lance* and *NZ Truth*. For a few months in 1928, he put aside his pen and pencils to run the election campaign for the United Party, a remnant of the Liberal Party and led by the former Liberal premier, Sir Joseph Ward. Gilmour must have done something right because United formed the government after the 1928 election. He left for London in 1932 and the following year was reported to have been appointed cartoonist for *The Blackshirt*, a newspaper published by Sir Oswald Mosley's Fascist party. He seemed to have spent most of his time in London, however, as a freelance cartoonist and illustrator.[3] He died in Christchurch in 1951.[4]

The next known mention of the Invincibles in a rugby context came in 1927 when a writer in the *Auckland Star* referred to the Auckland team of the early 1900s as the Invincibles.[5] The name did not stick to that team, but it did to the All Blacks of 1924–25. In March 1928, the vice-captain of the team, Jock Richardson – by then living in Australia – was hired by newspapers in New Zealand to write a series of articles previewing the tour of South Africa that year. He began his second article: 'The "Invincibles" of 1924, twenty-nine all told, will supply to the twenty-nine chosen to try conclusions with their peers of South Africa some of the finest players they had in that never-to-be-forgotten tour.'[6]

have better filled a mortuary. Suspense. He calls out names . . . he calls out mine! I didn't give a whoop of delight. I was too staggered for that. I slumped back in my chair unable to believe my ears.[39]

Delight when the 1924 team was chosen was not universal, however. The 1905 All Black, George Tyler, wrote that the squad was 'the weakest team New Zealand has ever had – weak in the scrums, weak on defence and lacking in pace'. There was clamour by Auckland for the inclusion of its halfback, Don Wright, because of perceived deficiencies with the play of Jimmy Mill, the chosen halfback from Hawke's Bay. This led Gordon Coates, then the deputy prime minister, to phone Norman McKenzie and ask him if something could be done to take the team up to New Zealand standard. 'I replied that we thought the team was up to New Zealand standard. Furthermore, that we did not presume to interfere in politics and we would be very pleased if politicians didn't interfere with rugby. He replied, "So, is that how it is?" and I said "Yes." He retired very gracefully.'[40]

Aside from the composition of the team, there was even doubt whether the tour would go ahead. One of the reasons was that the Rugby Football Union in England, mindful of the fuss caused by Scotland in 1905 and of the souring of relations, would not agree to the New Zealanders being paid a daily allowance. Some delegates to the NZRFU annual meeting said players would suffer as a result and the tour should not go ahead. Another reason for opposition was an aversion by some delegates to reverting to the English laws. The annual meeting eventually voted in favour of the tour but some 'noes' were registered. England's apparent care at not upsetting Scotland again was academic anyway. England had already upset the Scots because the tour had been organised by the RFU and not through consultation with the other 'national' unions (i.e. Scotland, Wales and Ireland), as had been agreed after the kerfuffle involving the first New Zealand tour. As a result, Scotland refused to have anything to do with the tour and the All Blacks did not play there.

Nepia, only nineteen years of age, played in every game on the long tour of 38 matches

The selectors who chose the Invincibles pause at Oamaru railway station during their tripping around the country – from left, Norman McKenzie, Lou Carmine, Harry Davis, Arthur Geddes, Arthur Wilson, Norman's brother Ted McKenzie and Arthur Guy.

King George V is introduced to the All Blacks of 1924–25 at Twickenham before their match against Combined Services. The King and Bill Irvine shake hands with players Bert Cooke (left), George Nepia and Cyril Brownlie looking on. The manager, Stan Dean, is doing the introductions and behind is the New Zealand High Commissioner, Sir James Allen, himself a onetime rugby player and official.

that encompassed four in Australia, two in New Zealand, 28 in the British Isles, two in France and two in Canada. It was a team of much talent but, according to Norman McKenzie, no one surpassed Nepia. Ever after, when Nepia played in New Zealand or Australia, or when he played league in England and for New Zealand in the 1930s, people said he never played better than he did in 1924. Bert Cooke from Auckland, second five-eighth or centre, was also a rare player of exceptional talent. He later wrote that no one in New Zealand saw Nepia play as well as he did on the Invincibles' tour and that he touched the greatest heights in the match that mattered most to the players, the test against Wales. As another teammate, Read Masters, wrote: 'There were times when the great crowd were aroused by the sight of the scarlet jerseys sweeping down the field taking the ball at toe, but Nepia invariably dashed their hopes.'[41]

No New Zealand rugby tour of the British Isles would seem complete without some form of controversy, either real or manufactured – and All Blacks have seen plenty of both. Cyril Brownlie was one of four rugby-playing brothers from Hawke's Bay. The youngest of them, Laurence, played for New Zealand in 1921, but an injured knee forced him to retire. The father

Albert Freethy (left) and the England captain, Wavell Wakefield. Freethy was the Welsh referee who sent Cyril Brownlie from the field at Twickenham. He showed at the Olympic Games in Paris a few months earlier he was not afraid to send players off. Wakefield, one of the dominant rugby players of the 1920s, was later a Conservative member of the House of Commons and when he retired in 1963, was made Baron Wakefield of Kendal.

apparently said to two brothers, Maurice and Cyril: 'If Laurence can win New Zealand rugby honours, so can you two.' And they did, being chosen together for the Invincibles' tour. (A fourth brother, Tony, who played for Wanganui, was killed in action in Palestine in 1917.)

The final match, against England at Twickenham, began by all accounts in a manner that was regarded as vigorous and the referee, Albert Freethy, felt moved to give a general warning to both sides. This was the same Freethy who had tried to send a player off in the Olympic Games final in Paris several months earlier, but was persuaded otherwise. There would be no persuasion this day. After seven minutes, there was a bit of a melee, Freethy pointed to the grandstand and Cyril Brownlie walked alone from the pack, head bowed. What on earth had happened? Various versions emerged and the least convincing of them was Freethy's, who said Brownlie had kicked the England prop, Reg Edwards, while he was on the ground. If he kicked him, it should not have mattered whether he was on the ground or not. But some who were there said he was not on the ground at all. One of the All Blacks, Abe Munro, said Freethy was in a state of rage and was determined that Brownlie should be sent off.[42] Arthur Carman, who had taken unpaid leave from the Audit Department in Wellington to report the tour, said that Brownlie and Edwards clashed in a contest for the ball, but both were on their feet.[43] Appalled, the New Zealand captain, Jock Richardson, appealed to the England captain, Wavell Wakefield, to intervene. He evidently replied that he did not see what had happened and, in any case, he did not interfere in decisions by referees.

Bill Dalley was among the All Blacks watching from the stand. 'We blamed Wakefield as much as the referee,' he wrote in his diary. 'Richardson, who was captain on the day, appealed to Wakefield and he turned his head away. He says he did not hear Richardson appeal to him; if he had, he would have considered it.'[44] Brownlie meanwhile had reached the players' tunnel where he was met by a former Auckland mayor and cabinet

Cyril Brownlie's worst moment – sent from the field at Twickenham by Welsh referee Albert Freethy. Brownlie and Colin Meads remain the only All Blacks to be sent off in a test.

minister, Sir Arthur Myers, who had left his seat to help a fellow New Zealander in evident distress. As Sir Arthur's grandson, Douglas Myers, said years later: 'This great bear of a man was in tears, absolutely inconsolable, while my rather diminutive grandfather was placed in the position of cheering him up.'[45] Among the spectators was the Prince of Wales (later King Edward VIII) and he reportedly asked the New Zealand manager, Stan Dean, at halftime if he could help.[46] The princely offer was appreciated but declined. The fourteen-man All Blacks went on to beat England, with Cyril's brother Maurice scoring a try. New Zealand's win in the twenty-eighth match of the tour was celebrated in verse by William Pember Reeves, who was at the post-match dinner as a noted expatriate:

> Weave them a crown, for they gained it there,
> Winning achievement's aim.
> Twine them a wreath of the fern they wear,
> Famed, since they gave it fame.
> For the forest-leaves that our champions earn
> Tell best of the glory great
> Of the conquering sons of the Silver Fern
> And the Last of the Twenty-Eight.[47]

The end of the match was not the end of the affair. Freethy reported Brownlie and Edwards to their national unions. The RFU said a month later it censured Edwards for undue roughness.[48] The NZRFU, when it eventually considered the case when the players were home, decided no further action was necessary.[49] The All Black match was the eleventh test for Edwards, who was from Newport and was Welsh, but England in those days was not above cross-border raids. He did not play for England again and soon after moved to Canada where he lived the rest of his life. One of the England centres, Len Corbett, later happily

The Prince of Wales, later King Edward VIII, is presented to Cyril Brownlie before the test against England at Twickenham. Soon after, Brownlie was sent from the field and, at halftime, the prince asked if he could intervene to get Brownlie reinstated. Brownlie's brother Maurice is on his right and doing the introductions for the prince is the manager, Stan Dean.

wrote that he never attempted to establish the truth of what happened, even though he was on the field, but Freethy was the 'ablest, fairest and firmest referee it was ever my experience to play under . . .'.[50]

Tales of New Zealand resentment at Freethy's action echoed, anecdotally anyway, down the years. One New Zealand cricketer who had also been an All Black when on tour of England in 1937 was said to have remonstrated with Freethy when he met him in Swansea. Three of that cricket team had been All Blacks – 'Curly' Page, who was the captain, Bill Carson and Eric Tindill. In 1953 when the All Blacks were in Porthcawl in Wales, some of the players were said to have refused to shake hands with Freethy when introduced to him. Both these reactions were reported by long-time reporter and author Terry McLean; he did not tour with the cricket team so could not have had first-hand knowledge of the 1937 incident, but he did tour with the 1953–54 All Blacks and stayed with them at the Seabank Hotel in Porthcawl.[51]

Corbett, the England centre, rather damned the All Blacks with faint praise when he summarised their success as opportunism and their ability

A souvenir pennant produced for the first of two matches the 1924–25 team played against London Counties. The first was at Twickenham, won 31–6, and the second six weeks later at Blackheath, won 28–3.

THE LAST OF THE TWENTY-EIGHT

3rd January, 1925, 10 p.m.

Thirty-five years on the march have swung
Since I could try to play,
Yet one old fellow to-day grew young,
I was a boy to-day,
Shouting at scrimmages stark and stern,
Cheering the triumph great
Of the sinewy sons of the Silver Fern
In the Last of the Twenty-Eight.

Seven and twenty victories won!
Week upon week came tales,
Of Ireland beaten, the North o'errun,
Victories four in Wales.
Braving the music of Swansea's song
They had settled the ancient debt
And stars thrice nine in a shining throng
Wanted but one star yet.

Nothing else mattered at all we thought,
Talk of the past grew tame.
Conquered provinces counted nought
In face of that last grim game,
Twenty-seven, with *that* not won,
Left Victory's crown to fate,
And All-but-One! appeared almost none
In the pause before Twenty-Eight.

They had known bad moments: the coolest 'Black'
Feels a quiver, felt—gone again—
When an Irish pack with a gale at its back
Comes rushing in Irish rain,
When Oxford fliers, whose feet have wings,
Prove slippery triers bold,
Or Cambridge Blues, when the wet mud clings
Are desperate lads to hold.

'Twas a bath of misery, all allow,
When the hurricane loosed its breath,
And the storm above and the slime below
Were mingled on black Blackheath;
But the tightest corner of corners tight
Came after the word of fate
Left fourteen fighting a fifteen's fight
In the tussle for Twenty-Eight.

Kia Toa! young forwards tall,
Now let the Fern-leaf shine!
Fight and fall not—until you fall
Over the English line.

Kia Toa! New Zealand! see
Nepia guards the gate,
A rock and house of defence is he,
A *tino tangata* great.

Swift as a swallow's darting flight
Skimming along in air,
So flew the feet of our runners light,
Scudding and swerving there.
With flash and flicker and flash again,
Shooting a quick, short pass,
They rush, out-racing the chasing men,
Over the trampled grass.

'A Fine Machine'—so the scribes repeat
'Machine'! but when all is said,
The 'All Black' plays with his hands and feet,
But the 'All Black' wins with his head.
Thews and sinews and brawn to boot
Had in that hour been vain,
Had not dexterous hand and outspeeding foot
Been steered by the ready brain.

The lusty men of the English line
Were they troubled about the past?
Did they waste a thought on our three times nine
Or easily yield the last?
No! Goals were registered, lines were crossed,
But still as their race doth use,
They played like men who had never lost
And never would stoop to lose.

So from two ends of an Empire met
Stocks of the self-same brand.
All Blacks, All Whites, they were twain, but yet
Sons of one brave old land.
She'll laugh—'Good Lads!' when, as seasons turn,
Our sons to their sons relate
How the jersey black and the famous Fern
Won through unto Twenty-Eight.

Weave them a crown, for they gained it there,
Winning achievement's aim.
Twine them a wreath of the fern they wear,
Famed, since they gave it fame.
For the forest-leaves that our champions earn
Tell best of the glory great
Of the conquering sons of the Silver Fern,
And the Last of the Twenty-Eight.

WILLIAM PEMBER REEVES

W. P. Reeves.

A New Zealander of many talented parts, William Pember Reeves was at the test dinner at the Café Royal in London after the All Blacks beat England on 3 January 1925 to end the British and Irish section of the tour. Reeves wrote this poem celebrating the Invincibles' feat and timed it 10 p.m. the night of the dinner. The All Blacks won two matches in France and two in Canada after this.

Punch cartoonist Bernard Partridge (who was knighted a year later) saw the humour in a comparison between the black jerseys of the footballers then conquering all in Britain and Ireland, and the black shirts of Benito Mussolini's followers. *PUNCH*, 26 NOVEMBER 1924

to take advantage of opponents' mistakes rather than any superior individual or collective skill. Others would differ; New Zealanders obviously but so too people in Britain who, as in 1905, saw New Zealand play a game at a level beyond what they were used to seeing. This would have been one of the reasons why *The Times* published its own lift-out guide to the way the All Blacks played.[52] Unlike in 1905, England in 1924 were at a rugby peak and earlier that year had won the grand slam – beating each of the other countries in the Five Nations competition – for the second year in a row. Corbett's view notwithstanding, New Zealand also had individuals who were dominant in their positions for much of the 1920s and whose names have not been forgotten – players such as Maurice Brownlie, Bert Cooke, Mark Nicholls and, beyond all others, George Nepia. It was an English novelist and sports writer, Denzil Batchelor, who wrote a quarter of a century after the tour:

> If Mark Nicholls failed, there were others to improvise fresh attacks – if Nepia failed, the castle was taken, the side was beaten. . . . It is not with me a question of whether Nepia was the best fullback in history. It is a question as to which of the others is fit to loose the laces of his Cotton Oxford boots.[53]

The tour by the All Blacks in 1924 and that by the league team in 1926 were a study in contrast and did much to determine the standing of both sports. The rugby team was triumphant; it went one better than its 1905 predecessors and acquired the nickname of the Invincibles, while the league team was on a tour that, according to league journalist and historian John Coffey, 'died of shame'.[54] New Zealand rugby in the 1920s stopped trying to follow league innovations or worry about what

The All Blacks in both 1905 and 1924 visited Watcombe pottery in Devon and were given personalised samples of Torquay ware, the distinctive style of domestic pottery made in the area for about a hundred years. This waisted mug was given to forward Ron Stewart.

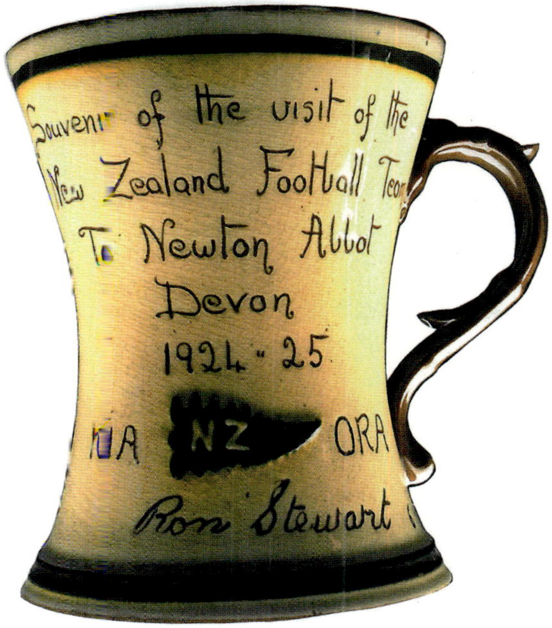

The Invincibles pose at Colombes Stadium in Paris before their match against a French Selection. The grim looks on the faces of the players confirm it is a pre-match photo. The photographing of teams immediately before a match was common in Britain and Europe, but seldom happened in New Zealand.

Among the spectators when the Invincibles played in Paris was Winston Churchill, who applauds while his companion, lawyer and politician Vincent Moro-Giafferi, is more demonstrative. But Churchill showed an interest in rugby because three years later he painted his impression of a lineout when New South Wales played in Toulouse in 1927. The painting now hangs at Chartwell in Kent, Churchill's home that is preserved by the National Trust. FRÉDÉRIC HUMBERT COLLECTION

the other sport did. It just got on and did what it did. Part of the reason for this confidence was the public acclamation for the successful tour, partly because rugby felt threatened by league mainly only in Auckland, and to some extent because the All Blacks had to forget about 'the Auckland game' law variations and play according to the laws as laid down in London.

During the 1924 tour, neither the International Rugby Board nor the English union was impressed by arguments by the team's manager, Stan Dean, and a Christchurch referee, Len Simpson – who was one of the touch judges in the England test – for changing laws to make the game more attractive. Neither did the London bodies want an advisory board that would have been a platform for the non-British unions to express their views. A conference convened by the RFU was, as noted earlier, practically a waste of time. The NZRFU's

Jack Gilmour, signing himself as 'Jno Gee', had much fun with a reported casual remark by a French cabinet minister after watching the All Blacks play a French Selection in Paris in 1925. The senator for the Gironde whose portfolio included the Ministry of Fine Arts, Guillaume Chastenet, talked to a vice-president of the French Rugby Federation after the match at the Colombes Stadium. Rugby, he considered, was an admirable vision of art. 'What a fine picture of agile and graceful athletic gestures the New Zealanders made,' Chastenet was quoted as saying. 'In my report on fine arts I shall advocate a closer union between art and sport.' This was reported with evident glee in New Zealand and was seized upon by Gilmour of the *Free Lance*. This sketch was the result and it carried the caption: 'M. France with enthusiasm: "Behold the grace, the exquisite beauty of this glorious New Zealander! An Englishman called him an Angel. By gar, he is more; he is an Artist! He is a new Hercules, a grand Apollo! And has he not drawn together again the loving bonds of the Entente Cordiale?"'

representative in England, Cecil Wray, wrote to Stan Dean a month after the team's arrival home and brought him up to date with how rugby officialdom had moved since:

> The amendments to the rules have been pretty well strangulated; the kick into touch rule has been knocked out; the Advisory Board idea has been tomahawked and 1926 tour to New Zealand is kamate. The amendments are in such a muddle that it is no use dealing with them . . . [Adrian] Stoop attacked the RFU representatives on the International Board very bitterly for the way they had handled the rules; and really gave them a pretty bad roasting and they made a very feeble show in reply.[55]

No one, it seemed, entertained great hopes of getting a British team to New Zealand in 1926, which would have been the first since 1908. There were many factors against such a plan, some of which Wray spelt out: 'I never thought they would get a Touring Team to New Zealand in 1926. For one thing they are afraid of getting a deuce of a beating; for another thing, times are very bad and men cannot get away; and then it comes too soon after the South African Tour.' (A combined British team, retrospectively the British and Irish Lions, toured South Africa in 1924.)

The British tour eventually came about in 1930 and with it more accusations against New Zealand's way of doing things. New Zealand also reciprocated the 1921 South African tour and this brought its own recurring issue – race.

The power of the shield

Some time in May 1902, the Governor, Lord Ranfurly, fired off a telegram to the New Zealand Rugby Football Union that said, in effect: 'Instead of a cup for rugby competition, I think a shield would be better.' The union had already been talking about what form the competition for the Ranfurly Cup would take; now it planned for the Ranfurly Shield. The gesture by the governor, the first gift of a trophy to the national union, changed the game forever.

Ranfurly, an Anglo-Irish aristocrat who had been governor since 1897, had first raised the idea of a rugby trophy the year before when he told the NZRFU secretary, Alf De Costa, that he would donate a cup for an annual match between the champion team of the North Island and the 'cracks' of the South.[1] It was the thought that counted, but rugby people could see the drawbacks of such an arrangement. How it should be played for was discussed at the union's annual meeting in April 1902 and the first plan, put forward by a Wellington delegate, George Goldie, was that the Ranfurly Cup should be contested annually between New Zealand, New South Wales and Queensland.[2] This too had obvious drawbacks and the ultimately successful plan was raised first by the union chairman, George Dixon, and treasurer, Neil Galbraith. In the way that rugby officialdom sometimes operates, the pair had likely discussed this before the meeting and agreed on a way forward. The annual meeting decided that the cup be presented at the end of the year to the union with the best record and that thereafter, the holder could be challenged by any other union.

While Ranfurly reconsidered his offer and came up with a shield instead of a cup, an NZRFU subcommittee worked on rules. Initially, it wanted just one challenge a year but decided such a limiting rule would shut out smaller provincial unions from getting a look-in.[3] Another controversial provision was that challenges could be made only by representative teams of unions affiliated to the NZRFU. This may be a self-evident truth, but it was not so clear then. Thames, for example, was a strong rugby area, but because it was a sub-union of Auckland, it could not challenge for the cup in its own right. Similarly, Rotorua at the time was also part of the Auckland union and it could not challenge until the Bay of Plenty union was formed eight years later. The rule ensured the growth and consolidation of provincial union boundaries for more than a century. The acceptance of the shield also provided an interprovincial competitive edge that was to serve New Zealand rugby well for at least a century; England, as an example, did not have structured competitions until the early 1980s.

Ranfurly's shield arrived in Wellington in June and through the back-slapping and self-congratulation dawned the horror that a representation of a game engraved on it was of a soccer match. A writer for the *Evening Post* rather unkindly remarked: 'It may be assumed that either His Excellency was under the impression that the game was the same as that which has such a great hold on the Old Country, or that the engraving artist perpetrated the "bull".'[4] Ranfurly was both an Eton and a Harrow man with an inherited title, but he was no monocled toff.[5] He had worked and lived in Victoria for some years and had been in New Zealand long enough to know the difference between versions of football and he was in fact a

IN TIME OF PERIL.

First Auckland Rugby Union Official: We ought to get it photographed, Mac. We might never see it again.

Second A.R.U.O.: Bah! Vic, let us nail it to the wall and make them come and take it.

Cartoonist William Blomfield ('Blo') illustrates the increasing value of rugby's greatest provincial prize, the Ranfurly Shield. *OBSERVER*, 7 SEPTEMBER 1907

regular at rugby matches. Ranfurly was also on close terms with a Wellington journalist, Malcolm Ross, who had played rugby for Otago and been the Otago union's secretary for a time. It seems likely that the artist's briefing included just the word 'football' and therein lay the confusion. Anyway, it was changed quickly enough for it to go on show in a shop window in Lambton Quay.

Auckland were unbeaten in 1902 and at halftime in the interisland match in Wellington in September, Ranfurly presented his shield to George Dixon, representing Auckland. Ironically, the North Island, including eight Aucklanders and wearing the blue and white hooped jerseys of Auckland, was beaten 20–14 by the South. The winners included nine players from Canterbury and wore Canterbury jerseys. As the *Evening Post* rugby writer remarked: 'In the popular mind, the contest resolved itself largely into a Canterbury-Auckland fight and Southerners were delighted at securing a set-off to the Ranfurly Challenge Shield on the day of its presentation.'[6]

The Ranfurly Shield became 'the rugby goldmine' as administrator and coach Norman McKenzie called it, but it was even more than that.[7] It provided a focus for provincial rugby and helped consolidate rugby's unofficial status as the national game. The All Blacks provided the external polish to the game, the shield the internal. It was only with the advent of the multi-tiered national provincial championship in 1976 that provinces were given another focus beyond 'friendly' matches. There were occasional whinges that the shield was more trouble than it was worth and one Auckland president, Albert Devore, once famously remarked that it would be a good thing if someone took the shield from them and lost it on the way to Wellington.[8] The gist of his complaint was that the shield's presence had a detrimental effect on club rugby (through players having to put their province ahead of club). Auckland, who had lost the shield to Wellington in the first challenge in 1904 but regained it the following year, were in the midst of their first great shield era. As reluctant as they may have been at times, they had what every other province wanted.

McKenzie rubbished the idea that the shield took a while to catch on. 'That is scarcely correct,' he wrote, 'because immediately Wellington began its defence of the shield the pounds, shillings and pence began to roll in in considerably increased numbers.' Crowd figures before all-seating matches were notoriously unreliable (and can still be when every seat can be accounted for), but for the interisland match in 1902 – the game at which the shield was handed over – reporters estimated a crowd of between 5000 and 6000.[9] In 1904, when Auckland lost the shield to Wellington, a crowd of 9000 was given and a record gate of £505

Hawke's Bay dominated all in 1926 as Alan Peterson's cartoon so graphically shows.

announced, and in Wellington a year later when Auckland took it back again, 6000 were said to be at Athletic Park. These were more than respectable crowd figures for the time.[10]

The shield also produced a variant of the chicken and egg argument. Did provinces have successful shield eras because they had great players or did the fact of having the shield produce the great players? There could be arguments both ways. When Auckland's first hold on the shield was prised off by Wellington, the Auckland team included eight who had played for New Zealand and Wellington had four. And when Auckland regained the shield in 1905, they did so while seven Aucklanders, including captain David Gallaher, were away with the 1905 All Blacks. Whatever the inherent or inculcated quality of the players, it was generally acknowledged that the added tension and competitiveness of shield rugby hardened players for the still sterner requirements of the international game. Players of course welcomed the shield: far better to play a game with a purpose than one just for the fun; and far better to win. A Hawke's Bay player, Albert Downing, moved to Auckland in time to play shield rugby before it was lost to Taranaki. He was so enamoured of the chance he got he had an image of the shield tattooed on his left forearm.[11]

While the early years of the shield largely justified the fears of those who worried that it would be the sole property of the bigger unions, Taranaki provided one exception before the First World War and Southland provided another immediately after when Wellington took the shield on tour. But the Taranaki and Southland reigns were relatively brief, just enough to give a taste of the

The power of the Ranfurly Shield. Hawke's Bay took the shield to Christchurch in 1926 and nearly regretted giving such a formidable opponent as Canterbury a home challenge. The Bay retained the shield, but only by two points, saved by a missed kick in the last minutes. They lost it in the first challenge of the following year. Lancaster Park was packed for the shield match, just the second to be played in the city. The first was in 1919 when Wellington won an away challenge. CCL-IMPHFr-2015-001, CHRISTCHURCH CITY LIBRARIES

fizz that the shield could bring. The main 'small union' beneficiary of the shield before the Second World War was Hawke's Bay. From August 1922 until September 1926, the Bay roared. The era began when Hawke's Bay were given little chance in a challenge against Wellington, even though the Wellingtonians were weakened by having four players away with the All Blacks. But coach Norman McKenzie could call on four who had just returned from a Māori tour of Australia, Wattie Barclay, Jack Blake, Jack McGregor and Sam Gemmell, and he also had six who would become All Blacks. The 19–9 result was seen as an upset at the time, but in retrospect it was seen as just the first success in one of the shield's most scintillating eras. For the next four years, Hawke's Bay could be brilliant (as in successive wins of 58–8 against Wellington and 41–11 against Auckland) or lucky (6–0 against Wairarapa and 9–8 against Canterbury).

In both of the 'lucky' matches, McKenzie could see in action the once-in-a-lifetime player he had picked from school: George Nepia. McKenzie first saw Nepia in 1922 when he was seventeen and put him on a wing in an early-season game. McKenzie thought: 'Well, that is quite sufficient for you this year. I'll put you aside and perhaps next year you'll be more experienced.'[12] Nepia kicked a penalty into the teeth of a wind from the touchline to help with the win against Wairarapa the next year and alongside him was his great mate, also from the Māori Agricultural College in Hastings, Lui Paewai. Another Māori McKenzie found and nurtured was the halfback, Jimmy Mill, and all three were on the Invincibles' tour of 1924–25. Also on that tour were the stoic Brownlie brothers, crucial to the success of both the All Blacks and Hawke's Bay. Maurice Brownlie, one of the most withdrawn of men, would have been embarrassed by the clamour he sometimes unwittingly caused, such as a time in a Southland challenge when he tangled with a future Southland All Black, Bill Hazlett. The referee, Bill Meredith, who apparently was a bit of a chatterbox in games and liked to be on good terms with the players, walked up to Hazlett and told him: 'Now then Hazlett, you leave Mr Brownlie alone.' This prompted a rhymester on the weekly newspaper, *NZ Truth*, into action:

The southerners all stood a-trembling with fear
As the referee strode up the ground.
In Richardson's eye stood a glittering tear:
His emotion, though deep and profound
Could find no expression in gesture or word –
Could his team such an error atone?
And this was the sentence the Southlanders heard:
'You leave Mister Brownlie alone.'

As Maurice came down at the head of a rush
Young Hazlett dived in at his knees.
His skipper reproved him, 'Young fellow, don't brush
'Into Maurice, I beg of you please.'
'You may tackle Falwaser, or Grenside, or Mill;
'But surely you ought to have known
'You may jump on Bill Irvine, or Nepia Kill;
'But – you leave Mister Brownlie alone.'

The crowd on the bank were quite merry and gay;
And they cheered themselves hoarse with delight,
As they gladly predicted a win for the Bay
And a filling of tankards at night.
But look! He is down! Who has rashly presumed!
From the 'fans' comes a sorrowful moan,
When up swaggered Bill, and then angrily fumed,
'You leave Mr Brownlie alone!'

But Maurice just grins and caresses his shins
Then jumps for the ball on the line.
Down the field like a flash in a rattling good dash
With his team mates all backing up fine.
But he suddenly gasps, as he lands on his head,
And says in a comical tone,
'Now didn't you hear what the referee said?
'Just buzz off, and leave me alone.'

So all other forwards take warning from me:
When you meet the Bay team at its best,
In the heat of the fray, should you mix it that day
Don't put your own prowess to test.
Be gentle; don't tackle your foeman too hard,
Lest the side line unto you be shown.
The goal-line your full-back can easily guard;
And you – leave Mister Brownlie alone.[13]

The Bay's era ended, and all eras must, when they were beaten 15–11 by Wairarapa on King's Birthday, 1927. Wairarapa were coached by Norman McKenzie's brother Ted, and he knew as well as his brother that the Hawke's Bay team was not what it had been. What was more, Wairarapa included two Invincibles, Bill Irvine and Bert Cooke, who had previously played for the Bay. Wairarapa beat Bush 53–3 in their first challenge and then prepared to meet Hawke's Bay in Masterton in what for years was the most talked about shield match played. It was dubbed 'the

Battle of Solway' because it was played at the Solway Showgrounds, but the name may owe more to cute phrasing than to being an accurate description of the tone of the match. Referee Bert McKenzie – brother of the two coaches – sent Maurice Brownlie and Quentin Donald off because he thought the competitiveness was getting out of hand, but no players afterwards thought the game could be described as dirty or vicious. It was just good, hard shield rugby and Hawke's Bay, by general consent, deserved their 21–10 win. Brownlie and Donald apparently saw out the game yarning to each other.

The battle began after the final whistle. It concerned Wattie Barclay who had played all his football in Hawke's Bay until early in 1927, when he went briefly to Auckland. He was back in Hawke's Bay in time to be chosen for the Masterton match, McKenzie believing he had fulfilled the fourteen days' residency rule. But there was a New Zealand union rule that required three weeks' residency. McKenzie did not know of it and neither, apparently, did anyone else because it was not mentioned before the game in which Barclay played. Hawke's Bay and Wairarapa officials agreed before the game that Barclay was eligible. But after the game, the chairman of the NZRFU, Stan Dean, who was in Masterton, pointed out the law had been infringed. McKenzie's view was that if Dean did not see fit to mention it beforehand, he should 'forever have held his tongue'. But Barclay was deemed ineligible and the Bay had to forfeit the shield.

While that was being ruled on in Wellington, Wairarapa were beaten by the short-lived combined union of Manawhenua (Manawatu and Horowhenua) and it took the shield. Needless to say Dean's standing in Hawke's Bay was not high; it was never explained why he said nothing until after the game. There was speculation that the autocratic Dean, chairman of the NZRFU from 1922 until 1948, was not fond of Norman McKenzie because he thought McKenzie had dangled financial inducements in front of players to get them to go to Hawke's Bay (Bert Cooke especially). But if that were true, Ted McKenzie should have been in Dean's bad books as well because Cooke was by then a Wairarapa player. There seems to have been backdoor payments and blind-eye administration throughout the amateur era, confined usually to players of outstanding merit.

In its negative, perverse way, the 'Battle of Solway' summed up the power of the Ranfurly Shield every bit as much as the great matches played in its name or the great crowds attracted by it. Lindsay Knight, a journalist reared on tales of the shield who was to become its leading expert and the only author of a narrative history of it, summed up its lure:

> For all the anomalies . . . for all the shabby deeds committed in its name by administrators, for all the blind parochialism it has stirred and for all the casual profiteers, the Ranfurly Shield has been one of New Zealand rugby's basic strengths. Outside the international arena, it has been the closest approach to a test. But above all else it has been a tangible means by which many a young New Zealander has come by his love of rugby . . .[14]

All Blacks strike ballet-like poses during a training session at the Sydney Cricket Ground before the first test of 1929.

8 Lessons on tour

New Zealand's best have donned their boots,
And pants and jerseys black;
We hope their belts are lined with scalps
When they come sailing back[1]

When the Wellington-based management committee of the New Zealand Rugby Football Union met for the first time in 1910, the business on the agenda seemed routine. Since it was still summer, there was no 'live' rugby to concern the administrators and business consisted of receiving and replying to correspondence. One letter was from Wiremu Teihoka Parata, a garage proprietor in Rotorua and a man who would have been known to the NZRFU chairman, George Dixon, and the other four members present.

Parata, originally from the Ngāi Tahu stronghold of east Otago and a cousin of the pioneering Māori footballers Tom Ellison and the Taiaroa brothers, Jack and Dick, wanted the union's approval to take a Māori team to Australia. The idea, he said in his letter, was not to make money but to 'play rugby and also for the educative purposes of the players'. He said he had chosen players with care and their conduct on and off field could be relied upon. Parata wanted the NZRFU to give its blessing and to ask the New South Wales union to organise fixtures.[2]

The management committee agreed to approach the union in Sydney and if it were happy, the tour could proceed. In the context of the times, it was a significant decision for two reasons: it was the first official involvement by the NZRFU in the organisation of Māori-only teams and it came just two years after a privately organised Māori visit to Australia had degenerated into farce, litigation and embarrassment. That tour was organised by an All Black of 1903, Albert Asher, who was probably better known by his nickname, 'Opae', sometimes spelt as 'Opai'. This was the name of a horse that won the Great Northern Hurdles in 1893 and Asher supposedly was able to hurdle opponents with equal ability.[3] Australian newspapers kept it simple and just called him 'the India Rubber Man'. Anyway, Asher took his hand-picked team to Australia to play league, but in the course of the tour fell out with the New South Wales Rugby League over money and refused to play. The *Observer* in Auckland said of Asher, who was a fireman when not trying to run a football tour: 'Opai was better off when he was cleaning boots at the Aurora Hotel or squirting water on behalf of the City Fire Brigade than he

Wiremu ('Ned') Parata, the instigator, underwriter and manager of Māori teams for more than twenty years.
MS-1262, W. T. PARATA ALBUM, HOCKEN COLLECTIONS

is at the present time when Australia is giving him the cold shoulder.'[4] The Māori ended their tour by playing a benefit match in Sydney to raise enough funds to get home.[5] The NZRFU would have been understandably wary of any new idea of a team to go to Australia.

Parata had no interest in league. Educated at Te Aute College, he had played rugby in his youth and had formed a team at Karitane on the east coast of Otago that played against other teams in the area. He also played club rugby in Dunedin and organised a combined Otago-Southland Māori team that played several times against the leading club in Dunedin at the time, Alhambra. The team included such notables as the All Black first five-eighth from Southland, Billy Stead, Peter Buck (later Sir Peter or Te Rangi Hīroa), and a later Methodist minister and singer, Hemi Papakura. Buck and Papakura were students and flatted together in Dunedin. Parata became seriously ill towards the end of the first decade of the twentieth century – tuberculosis was assumed to be the ailment – and he moved north to Rotorua and what he hoped was more propitious weather. He made the move in 1909 and the following year was elected president of the Rotorua Rugby Union, which was then a sub-union of Auckland. He started up his own business as a garage proprietor and car salesman, and it was income he generated from that which bankrolled Māori teams for nearly twenty years. The NZRFU approved the tour to Australia in 1910 and tours followed in 1913, 1922 and 1924. National Māori teams under Parata's control also made internal tours and played visiting teams such as the South Africans in 1921. Throughout this period, the responsibility for the Māori teams was entirely Parata's; the NZRFU role was only to approve his plans for each tour, to assist with liaison with other unions such as New South Wales, and to oversee his accounts to ensure they were in keeping with their own practice and did not include payments to players.

For the first tour in 1910, Parata prevailed upon two 1905 All Blacks, Stead and Bill Cunningham, who had last played for New Zealand in 1908, to come out of retirement. He chose a widely respected Māori player, Ariki ('Alex') Tākarangi, from Wanganui, as his captain. Born in 1876, Tākarangi first played for both Hawke's Bay and Manawatu in 1896, then for Wanganui in 1898,

Some of the Māori players relax on the P&O liner *Narkunda*, which took the team from Melbourne to Marseilles. Given the clothing the players wear, this may have been taken when the whole team assembled for a disembarkation photo at Marseilles. MS-1262, W. T. PARATA ALBUM, HOCKEN COLLECTIONS

missing only the 1902 season because he was in London on military duty at King Edward VII's coronation and the 1907 season because of a broken jaw. Age and experience saw him progress from fullback to the forwards. Other notables in the first team were George Sellars, who played for New Zealand in 1913 and who was killed in action in 1917, and Roger Dansey, who played for New Zealand Universities on their first tour of Australia in 1908. Dansey was a captain in the Māori Contingent in 1915 and was said to have led his troops in the 'Ka mate!' haka before the assault on Chunuk Bair. The first tour was a playing success, the Māori winning seven of eleven matches, but Parata came home with a financial loss reckoned at about £500. The following year, when he was in Gisborne organising an internal tour, the local paper said of him: 'Mr Parata is considered by all to be the best of sports and the champion of the Māori race in regard to football.' It added that he bore the cost and the losses.[6]

While Parata had said in his original letter to the NZRFU that his planned tour was for 'educative' purposes, there was also clearly an intention to give Māori opportunities in rugby so they would not be tempted, as were Asher's men, to league. Parata spelt this out once when he was in Palmerston North. He said most of the Māori players recruited by league were from the Bay of Plenty area and that it would be a perpetual recruiting ground were it not for rugby.[7] Parata also found time to form the Bay of Plenty

Rugby Union and his original intention had been to confine it to Māori players and clubs, again as a deterrent to league inroads. That became impractical, however, as the NZRFU could not approve of a new union based on racial grounds. Parata borrowed from his old province of Otago the colours for his new one, blue and gold.[8]

It was also in 1911 that Parata first raised the prospect of emulating the prolonged odyssey of the Natives in 1888–89. He did not entertain anything on such a grand scale, but did propose that a Māori team should be dispatched to Britain. The time was not right because of the difficulties within the British Isles about teams from pesky 'colonies' such as New Zealand and Australia that insisted on doing things their way. Then the First World War intervened. It was only in the first decade after the war that the idea came up again. This time, the New Zealand union was more disposed, especially after the much-publicised Māori 'prophet' of the 1920s, Tahupōtiki Rātana, argued that Māori were not fairly represented in New Zealand teams and his followers might take over the administration of Māori rugby. This prompted an editorial reaction from the *Auckland Star*: 'This suggestion looks rather like somebody butting in to take the credit and honours of the years of hard spade work put in by Mr E. Parata . . .'[9] The NZRFU had entertained hopes since 1920 of bringing a French team to New Zealand and it seemed in prospect towards the end of 1925 when the French federation secretary, Cyril Rutherford (a Scot), said the federation agreed in principle. But both New Zealand and Australia also wanted to go to France and something had to give: in the end, the French agreed to accept a Māori team in 1926 and a French visit to New Zealand would have to wait (it did – until 1961).

The Māori team of 1926–27 played 40 matches compared with the 119 of their 1888 predecessors, but in its way it was still a tour of staggering proportions, lasting from the end of July 1926 until the end of February 1927 and with games in New Zealand, Australia, Sri Lanka (or Ceylon as it was), France, Wales, England, France again, Wales again and Canada. Of the 40 matches, 30 were

This undated ticket was most likely issued for a reception hosted by the French Rugby Federation for the Māori team in Paris in 1926. MS-1262, W. T. PARATA ALBUM, HOCKEN COLLECTIONS

Members of the Māori team pose on one of the artillery pieces at the Honourable Artillery Company Ground in London. Visiting teams frequently trained at the 380-year-old ground, which is surrounded by City of London office buildings. It is also a first-class cricket venue.

The striking poster produced by French commercial artist Joe Bridge for the Māori match against France at Colombes Stadium in Paris on Boxing Day, 1926. Bridge, whose real name was John Steer, was from New York but spent most of his working life in Paris. NZ RUGBY MUSEUM

won, two were drawn and eight were lost. The most significant victory was 12–3 against France at the Colombes Stadium in Paris. Managed by Parata but with assistance from an NZRFU appointee, Harry Harris, the tour was a success on and off the field. The team gained friends in high places – the Prince of Wales (later King Edward VIII) arranged for each of the players to be given a specially struck medal and his brother, the Duke of York (King George VI) happened to be on the same train as the team going to Wales. As the captain, Wattie Barclay, later recalled:

> During the journey Ned Parata and I were invited to meet His Royal Highness. He asked us how we were enjoying our stay, smoked a cigarette with us, and was most friendly. The passage way outside the carriage was soon filled with Maori players all holding out notebooks for His Highness to sign. He very kindly signed every one I handed him with a very shaky 'Albert' – the train was travelling flat out and rolling quite a bit I remember.[10]

The royal brothers were also present at a reception in London to which Parata and Barclay were invited – complete with top hats, walking sticks and spats. Winston Churchill popped in as well. So too Bernard Freyberg, still a relatively junior officer. It was amid such a conducive environment that Parata seized the chance to suggest to the Prime Minister, Gordon Coates, that it would be a fine gesture for the government to repeat its offer to the 1905 All Blacks and send the team home via Canada. Coates, who was in Britain for an imperial conference, agreed.[11]

The names of some of the players on the tour are retained in memories. Barclay himself, one of the greatest players never to be an All Black; Sam Gemmell, who was compared favourably with

New Zealand Prime Minister Gordon Coates, a keen rugby man, pictured at the French Rugby Federation offices in Paris in 1926. He presented a shield, which had been carved by Māori, to the French Federation. BIBLIOTHÈQUE NATIONALE DE FRANCE

Maurice Brownlie and who had an astonishing record for Māori and Hawke's Bay through the 1920s; Wiremu ('Bill') Rika, who was described as a 'colossal chap'; Eruera Te Whiti o Rongomai, otherwise known as Tiwi Love, who became the first Māori commander of the 28th (Māori) Battalion in the Second World War and was killed in action in 1942; the extraordinarily versatile man of Marlborough, Jack Macdonald, who also played rugby for the South Island, rowed for New Zealand at Olympic and Empire Games, played a 'services international' for England during the war and had a career in league in England as well.

The players represented the flower of Māori rugby of the 1920s with one exception. George Nepia was not among them. For reasons which remain a mystery, Nepia was not in Wellington when the players embarked. Parata had asked Nepia to join the tour and he replied he would. The players assembled in Auckland for a first match and Nepia, who had recently been married, asked if he could miss that match but join the team in Wellington. He did not hear back and went to see his mother before heading for Wellington. But when the players were at a farewell in Wellington, NZRFU chairman Stan Dean read out a telegram which said Nepia was not able, after all, to join them. No explanation was given. Nepia said later he never sent a telegram. His version of events was:

> I called at my mother's place, near Napier, and there read in the paper that the team had sailed that day. You could have knocked me over with a straw at that moment. I could hardly believe what I read and, as you may well imagine, there was, to say the least of it, considerable surprise on the East Coast when I got back there a few days later. Everyone – including my wife – thought I was on the high seas, bound for the second tour of my rugby career.[12]

Within eighteen months at the most of the departure of the Māori team for Australia, Nepia had it confirmed for him that he would be missing another tour: the All Blacks' visit to South Africa in 1928. The NZRFU chairman, Stan Dean, mentioned at a union management committee meeting in May 1927, when discussing other details of the tour, that Māori would not be eligible. It was not headline news at the time and no one expressed any surprise. Indeed, the *Auckland Star* noted 'this decision was really made as far back as 1925 and has been more or less an open secret in Rugby Union circles'.[13] The paper backgrounded the decision by saying it was caused by the South Africans' attitudes to Māori in 1921 and the NZRFU executive 'realised that the viewpoints of South African residents from centres where the racial threat is a daily shadow must of necessity be considered'. And although the union made no formal decision at the time, and nothing appears in its minutes, there seemed to have been a tacit understanding that the Māori tour of France and Britain was organised, at least in part, as compensation. The *Star*'s point was a good one. There

Straw that had been on the ground to protect it from frost was piled over the touchline before the Māori 'test' against France in Paris in 1926. It was a warmer and more comfortable position for the players at halftime, who otherwise would have had to remain on the ground, according to the rules at the time. The Paris newspaper, *Match*, reported spectators stamped their feet at halftime to get warm. It was apparently one of the coldest winters in France and on the day of this match, a temperature of 16°C below was recorded east of Paris. *MATCH*

Caricatures of some of the Māori rugby players in the English weekly tabloid magazine, the *Bystander*. The page is signed 'Mac', which could indicate the artist was Helen McKie, who worked for the *Bystander* from 1914 until 1929. MS-1262, W. T. PARATA ALBUM, HOCKEN COLLECTIONS

has been much in rugby, as in other activities, that has been discussed and is generally known but without it being made public. These sorts of things are generally neither recorded nor reported, either at the time or later because of a lack of a source to acknowledge or an absence of evidence. Knowledge exists in an abyss of anonymity and because nothing has been written down, later recollections, if there are such things, are often imperfect.

The union, after meeting prominent Māori rugby people and Members of Parliament, set up a Māori Advisory Board in 1922. This was, in effect, a subcommittee of the union's management committee and its function was to make recommendations to the union about Māori rugby and to act as a conduit between the national union and iwi. Parata became first chairman of the board and, as such, became a member of the union's management committee. The union's position in 1927 vis-à-vis the South African tour was that it discussed the selection of Māori with the board and that it and the union were in agreement. If the South African Rugby Board requested the All Black team be all-white, no evidence of that remains, and there were no published suggestions at the time that was the case. The decision not to pick players such as Nepia and Jimmy

George Nepia, a mysterious absentee from one tour and not wanted for another because he was Māori. CROWN STUDIOS

Mill and perhaps other Māori appears to have been solely the New Zealand union's. Another probably excluded from consideration, although there is now no way of knowing, was the first Tongan-born All Black, Walter Batty. He played for New Zealand in 1928 against New South Wales. Dean and others on the union undoubtedly would have known that the South Africans asked for only white players in the 1919 army team.

It was only towards the end of the 1927 rugby season, when trials were held for the South African tour, that there was some reaction from the public. As New Zealanders were to find over the next 65 years, opinion was polarised and tolerance of an opposing view was scant. One reader who used the nom de plume 'Pakeha' wondered in the *Auckland Star* why 'Dutchmen' should dictate the composition of a New Zealand team: 'Here is Batty, undoubtedly one of the finest forwards playing the game . . . stopped from wearing an All Black jersey because he has black hair and dark skin.'[14] And the contrary view was aired:

> . . . enthusiasts should remember that it is not long since a Maori team was allowed to go abroad and play in England, France and Canada. The fortunate players who were given that trip owed it to the fact that they were Maoris and to nothing else. It ill becomes them now to protest that because they are Maoris they have been denied the opportunity of going to South Africa.[15]

A reporter for the *Star* went to George Graham, an Auckland accountant who was a leading Pākehā ethnologist in the first half of the twentieth century, for his view. New Zealand should have replied, he said, that a team containing only white people would not be a representative New Zealand team. 'A New Zealand team should contain our best players, and without the Maoris it cannot do that; therefore, it should not be called a New Zealand team if the Maoris are excluded.'[16] But another New Zealander, who was not identified but was said to have had experience in South Africa, thought New Zealanders could have no idea of how non-white people were regarded there. 'The Maori commands the respect of his pakeha footballer friend and it was to save him from the insult that the all-white All Black idea was adopted.'[17]

A Northumberland-born journalist for the *Cape Times*, Joe Sherwood, was quoted as saying he was not surprised Māori would not tour. He knew South African rugby people had a high opinion of Māori, he wrote, and the issue was how the non-white population in South Africa might react to a Māori presence. 'It is almost certain that the coloured population of Capetown would be affected – they would regard it as an occasion for rejoicing and trouble might follow.' That was also why South Africa had never played the West Indies at cricket, he said.[18]

Nepia, denied one trip for a reason that remains obscure and denied another because he was Māori, said nothing publicly at the time. In his newspaper column in *Truth* nine years later, he repeated the view of the union that 'it would not be desirable to have Maori players in the team . . .'. He commented: 'More unutterable nonsense was never advanced as a reason for anything than that stipulation about Maori. I need hardly say the whole of New Zealand was highly indignant, not only at my exclusion from the team but also at the slur on her Maori citizens.'[19]

One of the outstanding All Blacks of the 1920s, Mark Nicholls, did not mention absent friends in his book about the South African tour, but that did not mean the players were indifferent to the plight of the teammates they left behind.[20] A journalist, John Thomson, recounted how he became friendly with the 1928 captain, Maurice Brownlie, years later in Gisborne.[21] Thomson wrote that Brownlie in 1948 had been told by an NZRFU official in Wellington that he should make himself available to be the manager of the team going to South Africa in 1949. Brownlie was quoted as saying:

> Not for a sizeable fortune would I ever return to that country in an official rugby capacity. As captain in 1928 I had nothing but worry over the attitude of many South African officials in the game. They seemed to have an uncanny knack of putting it across us in various ways – to their own advantage, of course.

Two- or three-day journeys by train during tours of South Africa were common until the 1960s. Players could still smile during this stop for a photo opportunity on the 1928 tour ALISON WAGHORN COLLECTION

One leader meets another. The 1928 All Black captain, Maurice Brownlie, shakes hands with Jan Smuts, South African soldier and politician.

Thomson said Brownlie did not elaborate on the all-whiteness of the 1928 party but did say: 'It was ridiculous to think we were a truly representative side without George Nepia and Jimmy Mill. It was bad enough to be without Bert Cooke [who made himself unavailable for business reasons], but the absence of the two Maori stars who had served us so well on the 1924–25 tour . . . was an additional handicap.' This was loquacity for Brownlie, who was noted as being a man of very few words, and this was acknowledged by Thomson. 'He could seldom be induced to talk about rugby but one late afternoon in the sociable atmosphere of the nineteenth hole [at the Poverty Bay club] he became quite voluble.' Generally, even when among teammates and friends, he had little to say. At an Invincibles reunion in 1950, for example, he was called up to a microphone and asked by his old manager, Stan Dean, if he was well and if he was enjoying himself: 'Fine thanks. I'm very pleased to be among them again.' Dean: 'You were always a bit backward, you know. Are you looking forward to the next day or so?' 'Yes, indeed.' 'Thank you Morry.'[22]

Thomson recalled Mill as a spectator in Gisborne and wrote: 'His last appearance was touchingly sad . . . he was nearing the end of his life and was so weak that . . . Brownlie carried him up to a seat in the grandstand and supported him tenderly throughout the match.'[23] Mill died in 1950, aged 50.

If the tour of South Africa in 1928 was a Rubicon for New Zealand in terms of supinely acquiescing to the racist dictates of South Africa – however noble the motivation – it was no less significant in a playing sense. This was the tour during which New Zealand's forward methods, and specifically its scrum formation, confronted South Africa's developing formation, and the New Zealand method was found wanting. The tour was the beginning of the end for the two-three-two scrum and the wing forward; it was the beginning of the now-familiar three-four-one scrum, a concept so unremarkable in the twenty-first century that it is seldom referred to as three-four-one. But for many years after 1928, players who knew the old two-three-two system were in no doubt which was better. Even as relatively late as 1974, Cliff Porter, the captain of the All Blacks in Britain in 1924, was adamant in a radio interview that the old scrum formation was better for both players and spectators. 'Would you favour a return to two-three-two?' he was asked. 'Most certainly,' was the immediate reply.[24]

The All Blacks knew as early as the second match of the tour, a loss to combined Cape Town Clubs, that they would need to make a fundamental change. The Cape Town team won because its forwards gained almost a three to one advantage in scrum possession and because the team's first five-eighth, Bennie Osler, dictated the pattern of play, mostly through tactical kicking.

When a test was not a test

Australian rugby records show that by the end of 201[illegible], the Wallabies had played the All Blacks on 176 occasions. But the New Zealand record shows only 152 matches – a difference of 24. The discrepancy came about because the Australian Rugby Union in the 1980s took a benevolent retrospective look at games in the 1920s and belatedly called them test matches.

For much of the 1920s, rugby in Queensland barely existed and no national teams were fielded. Instead, New South Wales carried the rugby banner on its own, including most famously the Waratahs' tour of Britain and Ireland in 1927–28.

A Sydney sports historian and journalist, Jack Pollard, first proposed to the ARU in 1986 that the Waratahs' matches against the 'home countries' in 1927–28 should be deemed tests. Emboldened by the ARU's agreement, he then proposed that any New South Wales matches outside of Australia should be similarly upgraded. When they were, he then urged the ARU to go the whole hog and add New South Wales home matches, which it did, even deciding matches against New Zealand Māori were tests.[1]

The Australian hindsight view was that rugby in Victoria was hardly worth considering, and as there was hardly any or no rugby in Queensland, New South Wales represented Australia.

The national union, which didn't exist until 1949, eventually bowed to pressure and accorded all the New South Wales matches the full status of internationals. They seemed to ignore the argument that Victorian rugby did exist in the 1920s and was still a force in the 1930s, when the state beat New South Wales. Thirteen Victorians played for Australia before the Second World War, the most notable of them being Sir Ernest ('Weary') Dunlop, who played in the first Bledisloe Cup series in 1932. Another Melbourne club player in that series was Dave Cowper, who had made his debut against New Zealand in Auckland the year before.

A full-page colour plate from the *Boy's Own Annual* of 1921 that correctly shows the Australian cap in the light blue of New South Wales. Emerald green was adopted for the Australian jersey in 1929 and the gold jersey was first used in 1961. Green and gold were first used as the national Australian colours by cricketers in the nineteenth century and Olympic teams (including New Zealanders) followed suit in 1908. The Australian Government decreed by order-in-council in 1984 that green and gold are the national colours.

Tom Lawton moved from Queensland to New South Wales in the 1920s so he could continue to play rugby. He was also once a reserve for England and was one of the leading players in the revival of Australian rugby in 1929. This is Lawton kicking in the first test against New Zealand in Sydney.

The New Zealand union has never followed suit, although matches in the 1920s between the All Blacks and New South Wales were sometimes referred to in newspapers as 'tests' and players were given caps. But the most consistent thing about the games was their inconsistency. Sometimes New South Wales were up against the full New Zealand team, but on other occasions matches against the state were just fill-ins on the calendar; at the end of the Invincibles' tour in 1925, for example, each of the players was ruled out of an All Black tour of New South Wales. But later in the year, New Zealand played New South Wales in Auckland and the team was almost entirely Invincibles.

One of the most notable of the Australians in the non-test era was Tom Lawton, a five-eighth of exceptional talent who went under the occasional nickname of 'the Loping Ghost'. He was a Queenslander and played for the state in 1919 and 1920, but when the union closed up shop, he moved to university in Sydney and played for New South Wales. He was back in Queensland in 1921 and played league for the University club. He went to Oxford as a Rhodes Scholar and won a rugby blue but was temporarily suspended while

English authorities investigated his flirtation with league. Satisfied, the English union promptly made him a reserve for an England match against Ireland. Lawton returned to Australia and captained New South Wales in New Zealand in 1925, made the Waratahs' tour of 1927–28 and was captain when a full Australian team returned to the field in 1929. Two of his grandsons, Tom and Rob, played for Australia in the 1980s.

Even before the First World War, some matches against Australia were reduced in status by New Zealand, even though they were still regarded as tests. On the first occasion, in 1905, a test against Australia was played in Dunedin after the 1905–06 team had left for Britain; in 1913, the Australians played three tests against the All Blacks but the second and third of them were after the main New Zealand team had left for California.

The 24 matches that are seen as tests by Australia but not by New Zealand are shown in the following table.

Matches seen as tests by Australia (but not by New Zealand)

DATE	VENUE	NZ	NSW	COMMENTS ON NZ COMPOSITION
24.7.1920	Sydney	26	15	
31.7.1920	Sydney	14	6	
7.8.1920	Sydney	24	13	
3.9.1921	Christchurch	0	17	Between 2nd and 3rd tests against South Africa; included three test players
29.7.1922	Sydney	26	19	
5.8.1922	Sydney	8	14	
7.8.1922	Sydney	6	8	
25.8.1923	Dunedin	19	9	Nine new players in NZ team
1.9.1923	Christchurch	34	6	Six changes
15.9.1923	Wellington	38	11	14 new players in NZ team
5.7.1924	Sydney	16	20	
12.7.1924	Sydney	21	5	
16.7.1924	Sydney	38	8	
13.6.1925	Sydney	26	3	Invincibles not considered for selection
20.6.1925	Sydney	4	0	Invincibles not considered for selection
23.6.1925	Sydney	11	3	Invincibles not considered for selection
19.9.1925	Auckland	36	10	13 Invincibles, two others
10.7.1926	Sydney	20	26	
17.7.1926	Sydney	11	6	
20.7.1926	Sydney	14	0	
29.7.1926	Sydney	28	21	
5.9.1928	Wellington	15	12	Played while main players returning from South Africa
8.9.1928	Dunedin	16	14	Played while main players returning from South Africa
15.9.1928	Christchurch	8	11	Played while main players returning from South Africa

On the train the next day from Cape Town to Kimberley, the decision was made to play the South Africans at their own game; in other words, to abandon New Zealand's long-held way of doing things in the forwards. One of the newspaper correspondents with the team, Graham Beamish of the *Auckland Star*, saw the significance: 'This match [against Griqualand West] will be historic in the rugby history of New Zealand for the reason that it is the first time in the All Black era that a New Zealand team has abandoned its own style of play for that of its opponents.'[25] One of the All Blacks, Jim Burrows, was frank: 'To say there was alarm and despondency in our camp would be to put things mildly. The writing was now clearly on the wall because the trouble lay not so much in our lack of match practice as in our inability to get the ball from the scrums.'[26]

A coach at Stellenbosch, August Frederick Markötter, known as 'Mr Mark' or 'Oubaas', an Afrikaans word that means elder or doyen, was regarded as the brains of South African rugby in the first half of the twentieth century. He had devised the three-four-one scrum formation which the All Blacks saw first in Cape Town. It was clearly superior to their own two-three-two with a wing forward standing off. The South African scrum proved in the long run to be superior as well to the British three-two-three system and formed the basis of South African successes until the three-four-one became the rugby world's gold standard. Markötter's idea was simple. He moved the two outside players, the breakaways, from the back row of the three-two-three up a row so they pushed in on an angle on the front row men rather than on the locks. The effect was to create a tight wedge and with three in the front row it had a broader front than New Zealand's two-man front row. Under the New Zealand system, the front row men were both hookers and of the three in the second line, the middle one 'locked' the forwards in position, and hence the name. By moving up a row, Markötter's change also meant the outside men, now the modern flanker, were closer to the action when the opposition had the ball. Their ability to detach also meant they could protect their halfback, thus overcoming the need for a wing forward. (Curiously, loose forwards are sometimes still called 'back-row forwards' even though a scrum has not had a back row for many years.)

New Zealand adopted the Markötter scrum and beat Griqualand West 19–10 and Burrows became the first modern All Black hooker, that is, the middle man of the front row. But while there was success in Kimberley, the All Blacks still had a lot to learn as their next match, against Transvaal in Johannesburg, proved. They again used the three-four-one scrum but the five men who packed down behind the front row were all specialist side or back-row men rather than locks. Neither of the team's locks, Geoff Alley and Ian Harvey, played in the game. Burrows, at hooker again, recalled the scrums often collapsed into an untidy heap, tempers frayed and, worst of all, the New Zealanders could not win enough ball. The short tempers led to one of the All Blacks, 'Bunny' Finlayson, being held in a stranglehold and having his face deliberately squashed into the ground. When he rose, Finlayson punched the offender, but the referee saw only the punch and Finlayson was sent off. Burrows recalled he and his teammates were angry because Finlayson was not known as a dirty player and had been provoked beyond reason. It also meant that the All Blacks, already struggling in the forwards, were a man down. So the All Blacks, confused, annoyed, frustrated, were beaten again. What was worse, Burrows had ribs damaged so severely he had to be out of action for several weeks. The All Blacks also went back to their two-three-two scrum on the basis that occasional quickly heeled ball was better than more frequent slowly heeled ball.

The first test in Durban became a contest between the new world and the old world of scrum formations. The new was the victor. But it was not just the writhing, heaving mass of forwards.

Cartoonist Stuart Peterson links the two great kickers of the 1928 series in South Africa, Bennie Osler and Mark Nicholls. Peterson had Osler handing a boot to Nicholls while saying: 'Take it, Mark. It was your turn with the boot today.'

Bennie Osler punished the All Blacks from start to finish with the frequency and accuracy of his kicking. It was not pretty rugby, certainly not the attractive rugby New Zealand had been striving for, especially in Auckland, but it was winning rugby; it was ten-man rugby, meaning the ball seldom got beyond the first five-eighth. South Africa have relied on a string of outstanding kickers at No. 10, and Osler was among the best of them. Mark Nicholls, who watched the first test from the grandstand and who was no mean kicker himself, was refreshingly objective: 'Bennie Osler was the hero of the day, fourteen points coming from his wonderful boot. He rose nobly to the occasion, his kicking being magnificent and his tactics correct.'[27] The South Africans won 17–0, with a try to wing Jack Slater and Osler kicked two dropped goals (worth four points each then) and two penalty goals. It was New Zealand's heaviest defeat until 1999, when Australia won 28–7 in Sydney. Nicholls thought the South Africans would have scored even more but for the All Blacks' 'great defence'.

These were desperate times and New Zealand found a desperate measure for the second test in Johannesburg. The All Blacks devised a move that involved their wing forward, Ron Stewart, joining the front row on New Zealand's put-in almost at the last second, after it had packed down. This automatically gave New Zealand the loose head. It was a solution of sorts, as Burrows called it.[28] At other times, Stewart packed down on South African put-ins and robbed them of the loose head; on others, he stayed out of the scrum altogether. The scrum outcomes were vastly different. According to an expatriate South African journalist living in New Zealand, Graeme Barrow, the All Blacks had heeled sixteen times to the South Africans' 36 in the first test; in the second, the All Blacks still heeled sixteen times, but the South Africans were reduced to 29. It could have been even better for New Zealand had they not lost hooker Bill Hadley to injury and thus been reduced to fourteen men, at which point they reverted to two-three-two scrums. The South Africans were angry, bemused and beaten, although only by a point and all points were through kicks.[29]

New Zealand scored two tries in the third test in Port Elizabeth while South Africa scored three and Osler added a conversion for an 11–6 Springbok win. It was at least a better game for the spectator because there was more running with the ball and less control from what the French call 'the hinge', the halfback–first five-eighth combination. The South Africans were dominant in the forwards again and this prompted a writer in the *Cape Argus* to comment: 'With two tests lost and the narrowest of victories in one, their form makes it impossible to predict anything but a South African victory tomorrow.'[30] But the confidence, not entirely unjustified, of South Africans did not account for the belated inclusion in the New Zealand team of Mark Nicholls. He was every bit as talented and skilful as Osler and was one of the outstanding backs of the 1920s. He was vice-captain and a tour selector, but for some reason he could not get into the test team until the last match in Cape Town. There was a personality difference – and eventually bad blood – between the confident, extroverted Nicholls and the quiet, introverted Brownlie. Nicholls made no mention in his book about why he was not chosen for the first three tests or what he thought of Brownlie. The final test came to be called 'the umbrella test' because rain bucketed down to create similar conditions to those in the drawn 1921 test in Wellington. It could also be called Nicholls' test. 'We went on to the field with the knowledge that South Africa thought they could not lose,' Nicholls wrote.

> If we had failed, then New Zealand's great name in the rugby world would have been lowered to second place . . . this match will always live as an example of what determination and confidence can achieve with the biggest odds facing a team. Our forwards, who played as if inspired, won the match because they dominated play, called the tune while the Springboks danced to it.[31]

The walking wounded in Scuth Africa in 1928, Frank Kilby and Swin Hadley. ALISON WAGHORN COLLECTION

A hint of what was to come occurred on a training ground at Sea Point, a beachside suburb not far from the centre of Cape Town. The All Blacks did not train as a team for the fourth test, but individuals went out as they pleased. Among them were halfback Bill Dalley and Mark Nicholls, who had been chosen – belatedly – at second five-eighth. But at the training, Dalley practised firing out passes from the base of the scrum to Nicholls in the first rather than second-five position. 'I had visions of taking passes from Dalley and dropkicking goals and I wanted to get used to his passes which I had not taken on tour,' Nicholls wrote in an unpublished book.[32]

It became clear that Nicholls ran the game rather than Brownlie. When Brownlie as captain won the toss in the terrible conditions, he turned to Nicholls and sought his advice. Nicholls told him to take the wind and said that he might try to kick a goal while the ball was still dry. 'This was the first time that Morry had asked me my opinion on a decision he had to make . . . it was most satisfying to me when within a few minutes of the commencement of the game I kicked my first penalty goal . . .'[33]

Nicholls wrote that there was only one incident between him and Brownlie during the tour and that was in the final test when New Zealand

The lost art of rugby

Until sevens was included in the programme for the Olympic Games in Rio de Janeiro, rugby in New Zealand had had little to do with the Olympics. Rugby administrators served on the games association but taking part in a games was contemplated only rarely and when it was, firmly rejected. But a competitive entry did come close. There is a rare tale of a statue of an All Black being sculpted for the art competitions in the Olympics in Amsterdam in 1928, but it appears never to have been entered.

There were brief mentions in newspapers of the period that a Welsh artist, Vincent Evans, who was head of art at Wanganui Technical College, had created the statue as a tribute to the 1924 All Blacks and that the New Zealand Olympic Committee (or New Zealand Olympic Association as it was at the time) had agreed to enter it in the art section.[1] Arts competitions still form part of the Olympic programme, but without the emphasis and publicity they had in former years. The official report of the games in Amsterdam noted that the founding president of the International Olympic Committee, Pierre de Coubertin, 'wholeheartedly promoted and propagated the unity of sport and art with the greatest fervour'.[2] The sculpture category in Amsterdam comprised awards for statues and for reliefs and medallions. Evans's statue would have qualified for the competition in which the three medallists were Paul Landowski of France ('Boxeur'), Milo Martin of Switzerland ('Athlete au repos') and Renée Sintenis of Germany ('Footballeur'). There were 112 entries from eleven other countries, but none from Evans and none from New Zealand.

The sculpture 'All Black', by Vincent Evans, which was intended to be entered in the arts section of the Olympic Games in Amsterdam in 1928. DAI GEORGE

What happened to his entry – what happened to his statue – is not known. Intriguingly, a photo of Evans's statue exists.

An early history of the Olympic organisation in New Zealand noted: 'It was reported on 16 January 1928 that a request by a Mr Vincent Evans of Wanganui to have a statuette of an "All Black" entered in the art competition of the Amsterdam Olympiad had been agreed to.'[3]

Luxembourg artist Jean Jacobys' winning entry, 'Rugby', in the drawing section of the Olympic Games art competition in 1928. OFFICIAL REPORT, 1928 OLYMPIC GAMES

Rugby did feature in the arts competition: Jean Jacoby, a newspaper illustrator and stamp designer from Luxembourg, won the painting gold medal at the preceding Olympics in Paris with three sports studies that included one of rugby; in 1928, he defended his title with a drawing simply called 'Rugby'.[4]

Evans was no passing palette. Born in 1895 in the Welsh mining village of Ystalyfera, about 20 kilometres north of Swansea, he did what most other boys in the Welsh-speaking village had to do and went down into the mines. He had a talent for drawing and gained a scholarship to Swansea School of Art when aged 22. In 1920, he went on to the Royal College of Art and graduated from there in 1922. He was hired by the Wanganui Technical College and remained there until 1932, when he returned home. While in New Zealand, he painted a portrait of Mother Mary Aubert, the founder of the religious charity order, Daughters of Our Lady of Compassion. The portrait hangs in the Home of Compassion in Island Bay in Wellington. Back in Britain, he became noted for portraits of British prime ministers David Lloyd George and Harold Wilson, as well as paintings of mining and colliery scenes. He is sometimes known as 'the miner artist'. The Lloyd George painting was executed in 1936 and hardly seen until borrowed in 2008 by the George museum at Llanystumdwy, a coastal village in north-west Wales.

Evans died in 1976 and more than thirty years later a fellow Welshman, Dai George, began researching Evans's life and lost works and travelled to New Zealand on his quest. He thinks many of Evans's paintings and sculptures remain unknown. He was unable to establish the whereabouts of the All Black statue or who, if anyone, it was modelled on. George thought it may have been the captain of the Invincibles, Cliff Porter, but the likeness is more akin to Jock Richardson, who stood in for Porter on occasions.[5]

were given a penalty and Nicholls picked the ball up and was about to kick. Brownlie said to him, 'Who's captain of this team?' so Nicholls gave him the ball. Brownlie told Ron Stewart to take the kick. Later, there was another penalty in a similar spot and when Nicholls went to pick up the ball, Stewart told Brownlie to leave Nicholls alone.[34] That at least was the Nicholls version of events. Brownlie, as ever, said nothing. In the event, the All Black forwards did all that could be expected of them, Nicholls as planned moved into first five-eighth and kicked a dropped goal from a pass by Dalley. To top it all off, Jack Swain scored a try and New Zealand won the game 13–5 and squared the series. The South African captain, Phil Mostert, said if Nicholls had played in the other three tests, New Zealand would have won the series. It would have made a difference too if the best of the Invincibles centres, Bert Cooke, had been available, or if the NZRFU had allowed the selection of George Nepia and Jimmy Mill. But ifs are the hurdles of life.

If there was something of an air of contentment after the drawn series against South Africa – or perhaps just relief at squaring a series that could so easily have been lost – a shock awakening came the following year when Australia re-emerged as a united force in world rugby. During the wilderness years of the 1920s, New South Wales almost alone carried the rugby flag, though the game still had a small minority presence in Victoria. New Zealand had done much to keep the game going on the other side, agreeing to play New South Wales at least once a year and the All Blacks played in Melbourne on their way to South Africa in 1928. New South Wales sent a team to Britain in the northern winter of 1927–28 and its success quickened interest in the game in Sydney and helped bring about a revival in Queensland. Among its best players was the Rhodes Scholar, Tommy Lawton, a Queenslander who had moved south in search of rugby. Once the 'great public schools' decided in 1928 to revive rugby among themselves,

The All Blacks may have arrived in Australia in 1929 as the world's greatest footballers, as this advertisement asserts, but by the end of the tour the title may have been Australia's. The New Zealanders were beaten three–nil in the first test series played by an Australian team since 1914. *SMITH'S WEEKLY*, 6 JULY 1929

administrators saw the opening, reformed the Queensland union and attracted Lawton home to play, coach and foster interest in the game.[35] New South Wales sent a team to New Zealand in 1928, but it included only three of those who had toured Britain, halfback Syd Malcolm, centre Cyril Towers and lock Geoff Bland.

It seems scarcely credible that a team that one year played for the 'world's championship' of rugby (a title bestowed on the 1928 series by reporters) could the next year be beaten by a country fielding a full national team for the first time in fifteen years.[36] There was no denying the

Australia returned to test rugby in 1929 after an absence of fifteen years and surprised New Zealand with a three–nil test series win. In this photo from the first test in Sydney, All Black flanker Wattie Reside tackles Australian halfback Syd Malcolm. Ruben McWilliams is in the background.

talent and reunified zeal of the Australians, but the New Zealanders had an unlucky run with unavailabilities and injuries. The captain, Cliff Porter, was injured before the tour and did not play until the second test; halfback and vice-captain Bill Dalley hurt a shoulder in the second game and did not play again; George Nepia had a recurring back problem then spent time in hospital in Armidale with influenza. (George Slade, a Wellington printer and a former chairman of the national union, followed the tour and looked forward to seeing Queensland for the first time. But instead of continuing north, he stayed in Armidale to be with Nepia.)[37] One reporter called the tour 'a tour of misfortune' and said that 'there has been some sort of a hoodoo or Indian sign on it'.[38] The overnight train carrying the team to Brisbane being involved in an accident seemed, to the reporter anyway, ample proof. Three carriages overturned when the locomotive hauling them left the line at a way station called Black Mountain in the New England Range. No one was injured and some of the All Blacks were said to have continued sleeping while things went bump in the night. One of the players, Taranaki forward Alf Kivell, had been in an earlier railway accident just a few weeks before when travelling to join the team to Australia.

The All Blacks lost a three-test series for the first time and the general view seemed to be that the Australians deserved to win. 'Jerry' Portus, historian and educator, wrote in the *Sydney Mail*: 'We won the rubber . . . very largely because we held them in the van. Despite all that has been said about the scintillating play of the Waratah backs, it was on our forwards that we relied when the pinch came . . .'[39] If the writing had been on the wall in 1928 about the dwindling power of the New Zealand scrum, it was underlined in 1929.

Maurice Brownlie leads New Zealand on to the ground at Newlands in Cape Town
for the fourth test in 1928, the match the All Blacks had to win to draw the series. They did.

15

9 The shadow of the wing forward

I'm sure I fairly dealt with you,
With me then fairly deal;
I played the game, just do the same,
Don't raise a bally squeal[1]

In the early evening of Wednesday, 31 May 1930, a Cheshire insurance company manager, James Baxter, walked into a dinner at the Grand Hotel in Wanganui. He was manager of the British rugby team that had just begun its 21-match tour of New Zealand with a 19–3 win against the local side at Cook's Gardens. The words he spoke in his first formal speech in New Zealand echoed down the years and sometimes he has been blamed for the death of the wing forward, that distinctive if controversial position that was seen as central to the All Blacks' success in the first third of the twentieth century.

This was the first visit by a British team since 1908, and it is possible that it might have slipped some minds in the intervening years that rugby as it was played in New Zealand was not exactly as it was played in England. The wing forward was one of the main differences, but far from the only one. The position was adapted from what the Natives saw in northern England in 1888 and developed primarily by Tom Ellison. The wing forward was like a second halfback because, so the theory went, the ball went into and out of the New Zealand two-three-two scrum so quickly that two halfbacks were needed – one to put the ball in and the other to take it from the back of the scrum and give it to the backs. The second halfback, the wing forward, was also handily placed to prevent opponents from reaching the opposing halfback. Some exponents of the role, such as the 1905 pair of David Gallaher and George Gillett and the 1924 captain Cliff Porter, were expert at staying on the correct side of the fine line between being on or offside. Less polished or less scrupulous practitioners were not. New Zealand referees wanted rid of it. But as long as the unique New Zealand two-three-two scrum existed, so too did the wing forward. By the time of the 1930 tour, the New Zealand scrum's drawbacks had been exposed, especially in South Africa, and change was in the air. The British manager, Baxter, changed nothing, but he unwittingly

In isolated splendour, as such a great player often was, George Nepia kicks a restart when playing for New Zealand Māori against Great Britain in Wellington in 1930. The Māori, like the All Blacks, had to change to white jerseys to avoid a clash with Britain's dark blue. 1/2-023841-G, NEW ZEALAND RAILWAYS COLLECTION, ALEXANDER TURNBULL LIBRARY created a national mood that was a catalyst for change.

He watched his team beat Wanganui and was appalled by what he saw of the play of Wanganui's wing forward, Maurice Waldin. Baxter was not the type of manager who saw his job only as counting heads to ensure all his players were on the bus or picking up wet jerseys from a dressing-room floor before heading for the nearest bar. He was a man of experience and influence in rugby and the epitome of the middle-class self-made man.[2] He played three tests for England and 27 times for his county, Cheshire, and, unusually for a rugby player, had a yachting silver medal from the Olympic Games in 1908. He served throughout the First World War as a lieutenant-commander in the Royal Naval Volunteer Reserve and when rugby resumed he pursued refereeing and had control of six test matches. He became an England selector and president of the Rugby Football Union in the 1926–27 season. He was also manager of a British side that toured Argentina in 1927, a team that retrospectively has been rebranded as one in the series of 'British and Irish Lions' tours. Baxter would have seen the All Blacks in Britain in 1924–25 and may have had other gaps in his New Zealand knowledge filled during the Argentine tour by one of the halfbacks, Jules

British players, later to be known as Lions, assemble at Waterloo Station in London at the start of their 1930 tour of New Zealand.

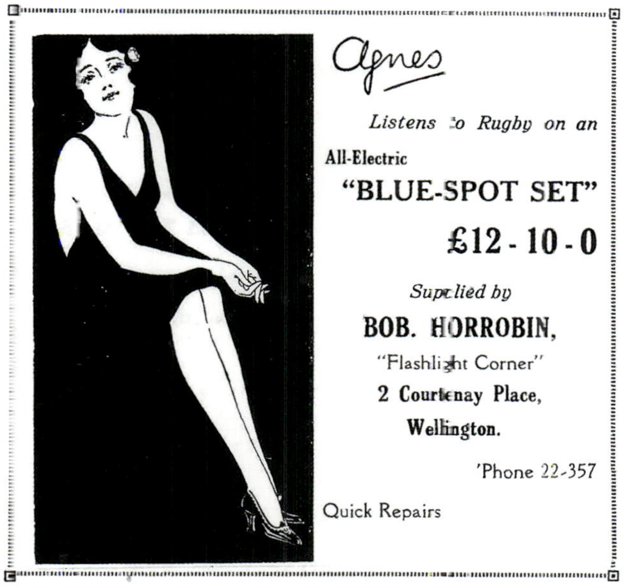

Rugby a man's game? Not for Agnes, who according to this 1930s advertisement likes to follow it on the radio.

Malfroy, a Hokitika-born lawyer who had played rugby for Wellington before gaining a scholarship to Cambridge.

Baxter was very well aware of New Zealand's continuing grievance that it had no say in the international running of the game or in the framing of its laws. Rugby had slowly changed and the RFU had ceded its self-appointed role as arbiter of the laws to the International Rugby Board. But none of the outriders, 'the colonies' as they were still sometimes known, was allowed to exercise any influence. Baxter had this in mind when he rose at the dinner to respond to a toast to his team:

> I watched this game today very carefully. I know that some gentlemen sitting at this table [he meant NZRFU officials] are hoping for certain events to come to a head and one of the best means of arriving at an understanding is to have one universal law and to play exactly the same game to the best of our ability. I am not going to criticise tonight but there is one thing I dislike and that is your wing forward play. I am sure that the gentleman who had the misfortune to play there, if he looked into his own heart, didn't like it either. I won't say he is on the borderline; he is over it, and must be discouraged. He causes irritation to both sets of forwards. I am not speaking about the man who played there today, but speaking of a man playing in that position. It is contrary to the spirit of rugby football.[3]

Baxter's comments created an immediate flurry of reactions, some supportive, some opposed, and they continued after the following game, against Taranaki, when he called the wing forward a cheat. There seemed more emotion than logic in Baxter's argument. It cannot be a position, *per se*,

This advertisement linking the 1905 captain, Dave Gallaher, with the promotion of Player's cigarettes appeared in several British newspapers in the 1930s. It is assumed the advertisers did not have the permission of either Gallaher's widow, Nellie, or the New Zealand union (and they probably were not aware of it). Gallaher and his vice-captain, Billy Stead, warned about the potential harmful effects of smoking cigarettes in their 1906 book on the tour, *The Complete Rugby Footballer*.

Geoff Alley, former All Black and future national librarian, wrote this book about the British team's tour in 1930.

that cheats but a player in that position at any particular time. A 1928 All Black, Geoff Alley, made this point in his book about the 1930 tour. Baxter's strictures, he wrote, could be reduced to a simple form such as:

> 'The wing forward today appeared to be offside and generally a nuisance.' Therefore all wing forwards have been, are and will be offside and general nuisances. 'This is a pig and it is brown – therefore all pigs are brown.' Of course one may convince oneself by this kind of reasoning but something a little less ambitious is generally looked for in analysing statements made in public by men other than politicians.[4]

The most biting response to Baxter came later in the tour, at the dinner after the third test in Auckland. The manager of the All Blacks, Ted McKenzie, who was both chairman of the national selectors and a member of the NZRFU management committee, was noted, as were his illustrious brothers, for not holding back on expressing an opinion. Speeches at test dinners and after-match functions were normally as bland as thanking captains and referees and, at after-matches, the ladies for bringing a plate. But not on this occasion. McKenzie was forthright and blunt. 'The wing forward has been described as the wolf of the game,' he said. 'We appreciate this criticism, coming as it does from a man so high in the rugby world in England.' But he had seen the majority of the British team's games and had some criticisms of his own:

> There have been points in the British play to which strong exception can be taken. I have noticed frequently cases of obstruction and what we in New Zealand know as shepherding. . . . I must say that some of the instances of obstruction appeared to have been deliberately studied. Shepherding a player with the ball so that he cannot be tackled has also been common. Frequently members of opposing teams have been held by their jerseys after they have got rid of the ball. . . . I will not pretend that our own players are perfect . . . I will say that the British team is a fine enough side to win matches without resorting to obstruction and similar tactics which may or may not be intentional.[5]

McKenzie's unexpected tirade was greeted, apparently, with astonishment, and at one point the captain of the British test team, Carl Aarvold, had a muttered conversation with a fellow lawyer, the president of the NZRFU, Jim Prendeville. They were, like McKenzie, at the top table. McKenzie looked along at them and said: 'I am speaking at present, Mr Aarvold, not you.' It's unlikely that Aarvold, who became a senior Old Bailey

Part of the crowd of about 40,000 at Eden Park in Auckland for the third test against Great Britain in 1930. The All Blacks' 15–10 win put them two–one up in the four-match series. They also went on to win the fourth test in Wellington. PH70/3.25, AUCKLAND WAR MEMORIAL MUSEUM

judge and was knighted, was spoken to in such a way very often. Stan Dean, the chairman of the NZRFU and chairman of the dinner, quickly restored proceedings to the more orthodox when he invited the New Zealand captain, Cliff Porter, to speak and he began in predictable fashion: 'It was a great pleasure to me to lead the New Zealand side against Britain.'

The McKenzie incident, as it became known, was relevant because in the opinion of journalist Gordon McLean (who was at the dinner and whose brother Hugh was a member of the New Zealand team), McKenzie would never have spoken as he did had Baxter held his tongue at the beginning of the tour. McLean said Baxter's comments on the wing forward were ill-timed, but to his credit, he realised he was on delicate ground and thereafter kept to non-controversial topics. The damage had already been done, however. Baxter seemed as upset by McKenzie's comments as the reverse and, according to McLean, vowed not to speak again and not allow the fourth test to proceed unless McKenzie apologised. 'Fortunately, he was mollified by the conciliatory attitude

Preparing 'the bible' in prison

The *Rugby Almanack* is to New Zealand rugby what *Wisden* is to world cricket. That is not overstating the value of either in recording the statistics of their sports. For a record of who did what and when in New Zealand rugby, the *Almanack* is as necessary to the game as a pair of goalposts and a ball.

Modern methods of data assembly and dissemination such as websites and blogs, even so-called official ones, do not remotely approach the breadth of material available in the *Almanack*. A list of first-class games in New Zealand on the web? Forget it. Obituaries of former players? Rarely. Even details available on the web of All Blacks are unreliable.

The *Rugby Almanack of New Zealand*, to give it its full title until 1995, first appeared in 1935, just a Johnny-come-lately when compared with the first edition of *Wisden Cricketer's Almanack* in 1864 (which changed the apostrophe to the collective after the 's' for the 1869 edition).

But the *Almanack* can boast something *Wisden* cannot: one edition was worked on while its editor was in jail.

A need to record the game's statistics has always been recognised. Sam Sleigh, who underwrote and managed the first New Zealand team in 1884, recorded the team's deeds in the *New Zealand Rugby Football Annual 1885*, which he published himself. The next attempt at a national annual came in 1920 when the treasurer of the New Zealand Rugby Football Union, Tom ('Ponty') Jones, embarked on the task. He produced seven until 1932 when he moved from Wellington to Auckland and became a columnist on the *Auckland Star* as 'Ponty'.

Arthur Herbert Carman, a young man who worked for the Government Audit Department (and whose boss was George Campbell, who turned down a chance to be an All Black), saw the value of Jones's *Annuals* and thought one day he would pick up the publishing torch.[1] In the meantime, he paid his own way as a journalist to follow the 1924–25 All Blacks in Britain, France and Canada. His younger brother, Walter, did the same with the Māori tour of France, Britain and Canada in 1926–27.

Carman knew he could not do it on his own and he turned first to a friend and a referee, Arthur Swan, who had a similar liking for keeping a record of the game. Carman and Swan, who moved from Gisborne to Wellington in 1935, hit it off so well that they ended up in a bookselling business together. (Swan became the only official historian the New Zealand Rugby Football Union appointed and on its behalf he produced several volumes of official records.) They were not business partners in the normal sense; Carman owned the shop and Swan spent his days there, selling newspapers, books and smokes while at the same time tending to rugby matters.

As the pair worked on the first *Almanack* over the 1934–35 summer, Carman thought the name of a well-known player might help the new publication's credibility (and sales). He wrote to the Canterbury lock, Read Masters, whom he knew from 1924 and whose diary of the Invincibles' tour had been published. 'I was wondering if you would care to have your name associated as an associate editor,' Carman wrote. 'We have most of the record stuff ready and as soon as proofs are out you could have them for comment . . . I want immediately to know your answer. You would have a share in profits, if any.'[2]

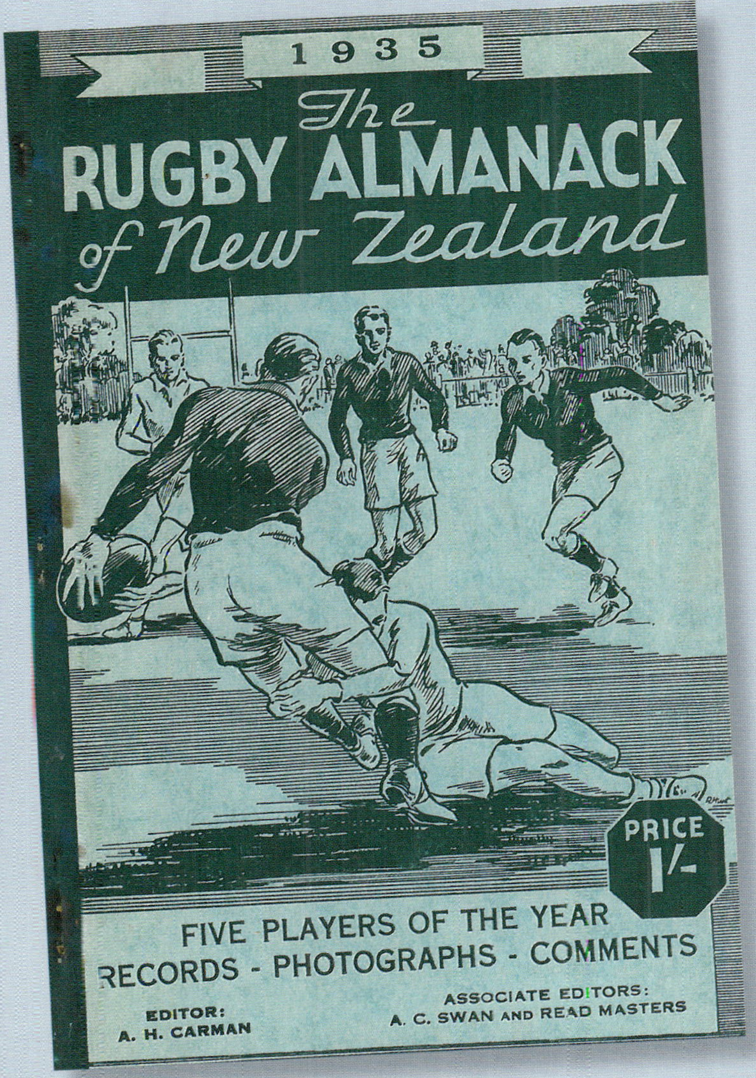

The first *Almanack*, edited by Arthur Carman with assistance from Arthur Swan and Read Masters.

Masters was keen and the trio produced the *Almanack* each year until Masters's death in 1967. Swan died in 1973 and Carman was left on his own until 1981, when he agreed to pass on the responsibility to Aucklanders Rod Chester and Neville McMillan, who by then had already published their magnum opus, *Men In Black*, and the first edition of the *Rugby Encyclopedia*. Publication moved from Carman's own Sporting Publications to Moa Publications, which later was absorbed by Hachette New Zealand. (The *Almanack* now has three editors again: Clive Akers, Geoff Miller and Adrian Hill, and is published with the support of the New Zealand union.)

It was never a profitable venture. 'We always sought to cover our costs, the costs of printing and travelling,' Carman once said in a radio interview. 'We've never made a profit and if there was any surplus it just went into the business.'[3]

He initially had no contact with the New Zealand union and never sought its approval. In later years, when Swan was the official historian, the union provided team sheets from first-class matches and unofficial assistance but not much else.

For a time in 1941, Carman must have wondered if the *Almanack* could be produced. Not for any rugby reasons, although the war had severely

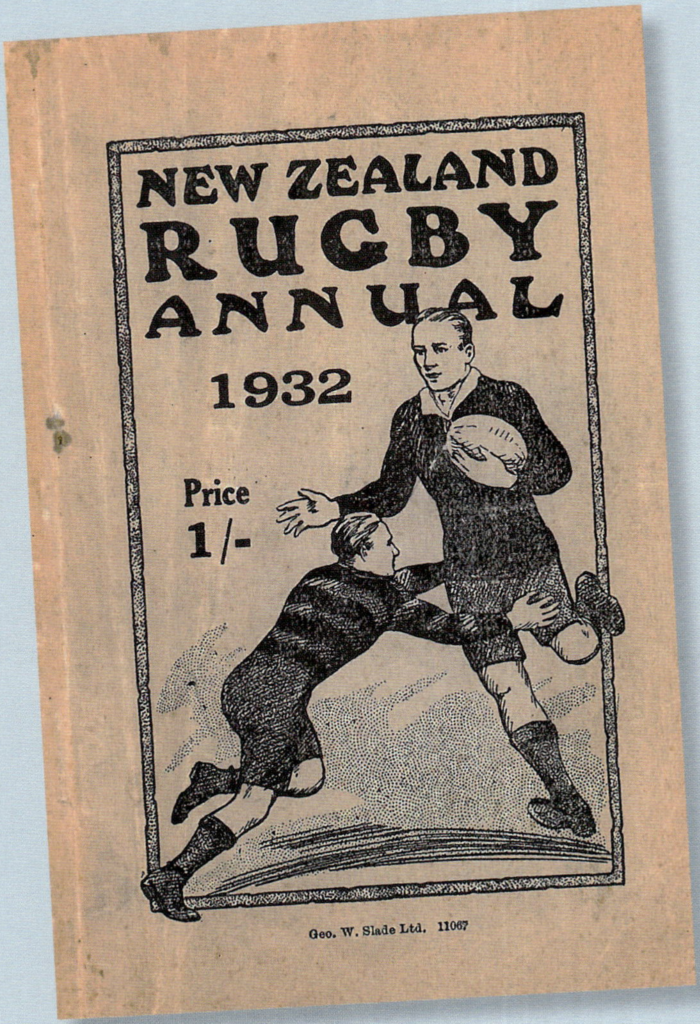

The last of the *Rugby Annuals* produced by the former treasurer of the New Zealand union, Tom ('Ponty') Jones.

restricted the game. What put it in doubt was Carman's attitude to the war.

Carman, 37 when the war began, was one of several members of the Christian Pacifist Society who faced subversion charges in early 1941. Another was Ormond Burton, who was a decorated veteran and author from the First World War but who had turned against war and co-founded the society. Carman was arrested and appeared in the Supreme Court in Wellington charged with publishing a subversive statement, attempting to publish it and taking part in a prohibited meeting, or attempting to. Carman defended himself and on the second day of the trial, the jury found him guilty after a 20-minute deliberation. All the charges were laid under a wartime measure, the Emergency Regulations Act 1939.

A day after being found guilty, Carman was sentenced to twelve months' imprisonment by the Chief Justice, Sir Michael Myers.[4] (Such was Carman's rugby knowledge he probably knew the man on the bench as Mickey Myers, keen rugby man and onetime member of the Wellington College First XV.)

Carman was taken to Mt Crawford prison overlooking Evans Bay in Wellington and remained there until he was freed on Christmas Eve, 1941. While in prison, he carried on his 'outside' life as best he could. He continued to be a candidate for the Wellington City Council after the city's solicitor said there was no reason his sentence should stop him.[5] (There was a precedent: a Wellington lawyer, George Barton, was elected to Parliament in 1878 while behind bars for contempt of court.) Carman, an independent candidate for the council, received 2239 votes – nowhere near enough.[6]

Swan ran the shop at 80 Lambton Quay for him while he was in prison. Both before and after 1941, the shop was a well-known place for catching up on rugby or political gossip. After Carman's sentence, Prime Minister Peter Fraser was said to have 'blasted' Labour MPs for calling in to it. (The shop was not far either from another well-established rugby gathering point, the Grand Hotel; the owner of the former would never be seen in the latter but many in the latter would seek out the former to settle rugby arguments.)

The two Arthurs and Masters in Christchurch continued to work on the *Almanack* through 1941 and, perhaps fortunately, the reduced rugby meant the 1942 and 1943 *Almanack*s were combined. Swan was calculated to have written 23 letters to Carman during the seven months he was in jail, although few survived. One that did read in part:

> I see, when you referred to Rugby you meant the Rep. Games. I took it you desired results of the Club contests. How will this work: I will send in the file and a duplicate cover, and you could make a copy for your own use and return the original for me to keep up to date? I cannot see any better method and will post in the necessary today. The file I will give to Mrs C [Arthur's wife Edith]. I am waiting reply for a North Otago and an Otago team to bring that game into line with the others. Yes, I caught up with the Almanack settings. That will always happen with last minute changes. You see, time only allows for the line or paragraph to be lifted. Any further alteration to the page would have to be charged for. Actually such changing about of matter means unlocking frames and re-making up . . .[7]

Carman was trapped by New Zealand's conscription in 1942, but he was eventually excused military service because of poor eyesight. By then, he was 40 years old and supported a wife and four children. He also stood as an independent in the safe Labour seat of Wellington North in 1943 and gained 298 votes. From the early 1930s until the late 1970s, Carman took an active interest in local government; he served on several authorities and wrote several local histories in addition to his rugby work. He sold his bookshop in 1959 and worked from his home in Linden where he produced both the *Rugby Almanack* and its cricket equivalent, which he had begun in 1948.[8] He was a familiar figure in Tawa, at NZRFU gatherings and in the press box at Athletic Park until his death in 1982.

The blue jersey of the British team in 1930 that forced the All Blacks to wear white for the first time.

of other of the New Zealand union's officials,' McLean wrote.[6]

Another disagreement in 1930 between New Zealand and Britain was also portentous in its way, although much more superficially. The British arrived with blue jerseys bearing three golden lions 'passant guardant' and to dismayed comments that they clashed with black, Baxter replied that blue was the British team's 'traditional colour'. The first two British teams to New Zealand, in 1888 and 1904, wore jerseys of red, white and blue hoops, and the third, in 1908, wore red and white hoops (the blue stayed at home with Scotland). The only British teams to wear dark blue were in South Africa in 1924 and the quasi-official team in Argentina. Both sides said the other would need to change, then both sides changed their minds and offered to change. The final word was by the NZRFU which, in the week of the match against Wanganui, told Baxter the All Blacks would wear white jerseys with a 'silver' fern on a black shield, black shorts and black socks with two white hoops.[7] In some reports, the All Blacks became the All Whites. The British adopted their now-familiar scarlet jerseys for their tour in 1950.

There were other minor, even comical, differences in the way New Zealanders and Brits read the laws. At halftime in Wanganui, the local players trooped off Cook's Gardens for a sit-down in the dressing room and a lemonade, a cup of tea and for those who did, a smoke. The British players, made to look larger than life by the knee-length size of their voluminous shorts, stayed on the field for what they called 'lemon time'. Baxter complained and New Zealand teams thereafter had to comply with the law and stay on the field. It was a common occurrence for curious spectators to wander on to the ground at halftime and have a close-up look at the players or listen to what was being said. No one seemed to be bothered.

The background to all of this was New Zealand's desire to get a say in framing the laws and England's desire that everyone do it their way. The previous November, the NZRFU secretary, Alf Neilson, sent a letter to all provincial unions asking for their views of an English resolution which said, in effect, 'the dominions' must play by England's laws if they want a future say in framing laws. The provincial unions delivered a collective view at their annual meeting in 1930: 'That in New Zealand all games in future be played under the rules of the international board if and when we are given satisfactory representation in the framing of such rules.'[8] The differences were as much a question of national attitude or characteristics as they were a rugby issue. Alley noticed this:

> The lack of desire to change anything in the game is a most galling thing to New Zealanders, who are freed from the bonds of tradition in a way that the English mind is not, and we should be false to the idea of progress if we abandoned our attitude. Growth is the only excuse for life, or at any rate one of the strongest of reasons for it, and we must be prepared to scrap anything that can be superseded by something better.[9]

Away from the longer-term issues of laws and who ran the game, the British team was enormously popular with the public. Record crowds watched it play and, off the field, the players' every move was followed with intense interest. The tour made a profit for the NZRFU of £22,000 (about $1.9 million today). 'Every home, every dance-hall and every picture show in the country was thrown open to them,' McLean wrote. 'They played on practically every golf course in New Zealand and never had to pay a penny in green fees.' Unlike their predecessors of 1904 and 1908, 'intemperance was not one of their faults', as McLean neatly put it. In Dunedin, two of the players received a letter in which two women detailed their charms and offered to meet them at any time at any place.[10] The public interest in the tour, more intense than it had been with the South Africans in 1921, set the pattern for major tours for the next sixty or so years, until professionalism reduced tours to a rump of a test or two. Everywhere the team was referred to as Great Britain or the British team, never the Lions although that nickname had been acquired six years previously in South Africa because of the lion lapel badge that was worn. Strangely, the 1950 team in New Zealand was seldom – if at all – referred to as the Lions either, and it was only in 1959 that the term came into general use in New Zealand.

A touring team was most likely to be popular if it did not beat the All Blacks and if it took its defeats with cheery demeanour (at least publicly). As became the norm with British teams on three-month tours in the twentieth century, many players were unavailable because of work, injury or simply because they did not want to be away from home for so long. For New Zealanders then and now, long trips and long tours were commonplace; for the British, they were a significant undertaking.

The 1930 British team manager, James Baxter, insisted that teams had to stay on the field at halftime, contrary to the New Zealand practice of returning to the dressing room. This is the British team at halftime in the fourth test in Wellington. At least two women have joined the players, one taking particular notice of a player on the ground; at least three policemen are there and a local St John man treats one of the players.

Among those who did not come to New Zealand in 1930, and it may have been a different tour if he had, was the England captain from 1924, Wavell Wakefield (later Lord Wakefield). He was named as captain when the touring squad was first made public, but later withdrew because of a chronic groin injury. For all Wakefield's influence on the game through the 1920s (and beyond), McLean thought he may have been more a hindrance than a help. (Wakefield had not played for England since 1927.) He wrote:

> From remarks made by several members of the team during the tour, it is doubtful if the loss of Wakefield was a serious one. Not only was he said to be past his best playing days, but also he was considered to be something of a martinet, and a man who would not have been conspicuously tactful in his dealings either with the team or with New Zealanders.

This was the man who, as England captain, showed not the slightest interest in preventing the sending off of Cyril Brownlie at Twickenham in 1925. There were others who could not tour, but one who did and played only in the first game may have been missed most of all. He was the England halfback, Wilf Sobey, who had formed a relationship with his first five-eighth, Roger Spong, not unlike that of Gareth Edwards and Barry John 41 years later. But Sobey twisted a knee in the opening game against Wanganui and never played again. He had set up two tries for the British when the injury happened but he stayed on, hobbling around. The British fullback, George Bonner, left the field to have a cut attended to which meant that poor Sobey had to soldier on. Had replacements been allowed, to which Baxter was strongly opposed, Sobey could have been treated and may have eventually played a full part in the tour. But he was thereafter a non-playing member.

Of the 21 matches played by the British, they lost six, including three of the four test matches. The test they won, the first by a British side in New Zealand, was the first in appalling conditions in Dunedin. The All Blacks selectors had hoped for wet weather and a muddy ground to slow the British backs and that was what they got: snow, sleet, rain. But the backs were not noticeably slowed and the British won 6–3, two tries to one. In better conditions for the remaining three tests, the New Zealanders were the better side. This series marked the end of some outstanding All Black careers, most notably a trio of Invincibles, George Nepia, Bert Cooke and Cliff Porter. The British also lost to Wellington, Canterbury and Auckland.

For all the financial health the game found itself in because of the British tour, plus the fact the series had been won, there was disquiet. Delegates to the 1931 annual meeting of the NZRFU talked again about the possibility of severing the relationship with Britain but, being coldly realistic, a majority realised it made more sense to comply with laws as laid down by the IRB and not as changed in Wellington. There has arisen a belief that this stricture included abandoning the wing forward, but it did not. All that the laws required at the time were that the ball when being put into a scrum had to pass three feet before it could be hooked; New Zealand's two-man front row could accommodate this. The offside law at the time said a player was offside if he, not being in the scrum, remained with either foot in front of the ball. New Zealand's configuration could accommodate this too. The laws as framed made no specific mention of a wing forward (or whatever name it sometimes went by, including 'halfback-forward').

The wing forward disappeared from the game because New Zealand wanted it to. This came about at the 1932 annual meeting, by which time several provinces had dispensed with the position anyway. Delegates to the 1932 annual meeting filed into the new premises of the Commercial Travellers' Club on Customhouse Quay in Wellington. These days, the building houses a café-bar called Pravda, which is the Russian word for truth. The truth of the matter at the building in 1932 was that the NZRFU's management committee wanted the wing forward abolished for the sake of uniformity in the rugby world. Provincial delegates voted in favour of the abolition by 50 votes to 21 and thus ended a distinctive period of New Zealand rugby's playing history. The vote indicated a sizeable minority for retention of the position. A feature of the annual meeting debate was that in addition to the dark-suited older delegates, there were also former players, some of them recent. Three of great standing, Billy Wallace, Cliff Porter and Mark Nicholls, took turns at a blackboard demonstrating with diagrams the pros and cons of the wing forward. Wallace and Nicholls were in favour of the abolition; Porter was opposed. The NZRFU chairman, Stan Dean, moved the successful motion: 'That with a view to securing uniformity, this conference approves of the management committee's recommendation that the three front-row scrum be adopted and the

The cup that cheers

The annual report of the New Zealand Rugby Football Union for 1931 appeared in the *New Zealand Rugby Annual* edited by a former treasurer of the union, Tom Jones. The report by chairman Stan Dean contained this passage:

> Bledisloe Cup
> Prior to the test match between New Zealand and Australia last year [1931], our Patron, His Excellency the Governor-General, Lord Bledisloe, donated a cup for competition between the two Rugby playing countries. The cup, which is not yet to hand, is of a very handsome design and will be a very valuable trophy. The thanks of the New Zealand union is due to His Excellency for his generous gift. New Zealand, by their win in the test match, is the first holder of the trophy.[1]

This sounds like Dean retrovision. There is indeed a small plaque on the cup showing it was won by New Zealand in 1931 and the hallmark on the plaque suggests it was made when the cup was. But Bledisloe's suggestion for a trans-Tasman rugby trophy was first made to the New Zealand Rugby Football Union eleven days *after* the 1931 test.

The 1931 test in Auckland was on 12 September. The union's management committee minutes for 23 September record:

> The chairman reported that His Excellency the Governor-General had expressed a wish to present a cup for competition between Australia and New Zealand and that after consultation with the New South Wales union, the offer was accepted . . . a letter be sent to the Governor-General thanking him for his generous donation and informing him that the trophy, which will be known as the Bledisloe Cup, will be played for in test matches between the two countries.

Nelson Isaac, the head of the art school of Wellington Technical College, designed the cup and it was made at Walker and Hall in London. It arrived in Auckland in 1932. As it happened, the All Blacks were in Australia at the time and their first test – which was won by the Wallabies – was on the Saturday after the cup's arrival in Auckland.

That test on 2 July 1932 at the Sydney Cricket Ground was the first for the Bledisloe Cup even though the cup was still in Auckland. The *Auckland Star* on 29 June, stating the cup was on show at the Milne & Choyce department store, also said: 'The first contest for the trophy, to be known as the Bledisloe Cup, takes place at Sydney on Saturday.'[2]

The cup was then parcelled up and sent, arriving in time to be exhibited in the window of the New Zealand Government office before being taken to the SCG for the third test. 'Attracting great attention, the cup is much admired,' a New Zealand journalist in Sydney reported.[3]

The cup was on a table at halfway during the third test, in which the New Zealanders ensured they would be the first holders, but it was not presented until the following Friday at a farewell function in the Hotel Wentworth. The players sailed for home the next day and arrived in Wellington to learn they had to go to Government House for lunch with Bledisloe and his wife and have the cup presented to them. On being told the cup had already been presented, Bledisloe said there was no point doing it twice but come to lunch anyway. And they did.[4]

The 1932 New Zealand team went to lunch at Government House in Wellington the day after arriving home from Australia in possession of the Bledisloe Cup for the first time. The donor of the cup, Lord Bledisloe, and his wife Alina pose with team manager Billy Wallace and the players.

Bledisloe knew his rugby. He came from the small village of Lydney in Gloucestershire not far from the Welsh border and he was elected president of the local rugby club in its first year in 1887, when he was just twenty. He remained president until he died in 1958, aged 90. Bledisloe, or Charlie Bathurst as he was, was educated at Sherborne School, one of England's noted rugby schools.

He gained a bachelor's degree at Oxford in 1890 and worked as a lawyer until he entered Parliament as a Conservative member in 1910 and remained there until 1928, by which time he was Baron Bledisloe of Lydney. He became Governor-General two years later.

He maintained his links with New Zealand and rugby at the end of his term, by which time he had been made Viscount Bledisloe. He went to several matches played by the 1935–36 All Blacks and six of the players stayed with him for a time at his model pig farm at Lydney Park. The *New Zealand Free Lance* noted in its coverage of the visit: 'The guests were thrilled with the deer in the park and with Lady Bledisloe's own pet one, which comes to her every morning to be fed. Lord Bledisloe took the boys shooting every day and they found him an excellent shot.'

At a farewell function for the team in London, Bledisloe presented each of the players with an inscribed silver ashtray.

His rugby cup ensured that Bledisloe outlived his nickname of 'Chattering Charlie', evidently gained because he was forever badgering newspaper editors about inaccuracies in coverage about him. Bledisloe left more than just a cup for rugby in New Zealand. He bought the Treaty House at Waitangi and gave it to the government and he and his wife Alina also donated trophies for golf, chess, photography, apple growing and dairy farming. Alina donated a cup to Ranger Guides and one for 'tribal efficiency in aspects of Maori culture'.

Feed them till they want no more

When the All Blacks led by Jack Manchester, a Canterbury stock and station agent, arrived in Wales in 1935, the score stood at one-all. Wales won the first match against New Zealand, in 1905, and the All Blacks won the second, in 1924. Now it was time for the decider. Welsh rugby was not at a peak then, but neither was New Zealand's game, yet each were regarded almost in the same breath as South Africa as the best rugby countries in the world.

The Welsh pack leader was Arthur Rees, a Cambridge student who later became chief constable of Staffordshire. He knew the reputation of Welsh rugby – the very fate of Wales – rested on the outcome of the match on 21 December 1935. 'I felt I had been born and bred for this very day,' he later recalled.

The Arms Park was packed like it had never been packed before. These were still the days when people poured down from the valleys and east from the iron and steel and tin industries; when double-decker buses belched their way round narrow roads and over hump-backed bridges, every available space taken by fervent followers who wanted to be fed until they could want no more; when trains strained with every huff and puff from Paddington, from Birmingham, from Swansea. This was the match when the English referee, Cyril Gadney, turned up at the main gate without a ticket and was refused entry. 'But I'm the referee!' he complained, to which the gatekeeper responded: 'We've had twelve of them already!'

The Welsh had generation-bridging players in the backs: Vivian Jenkins, who spent his last days reminiscing and watching occasional matches in Queenstown; Cliff Jones and Haydn Tanner, an inside back pairing that could be mentioned in the same sentence as Gareth Edwards and Barry John; there was Wilfred Wooller, who could seemingly play for Wales or England at any sport he chose.

Before the game, Rees reminded his forwards how good the backs were and it was the responsibility and duty of the forwards to see the ball was sent out to them. He also let on he knew well the reputation of the All Blacks, justified or not: 'No rough stuff unless they start it,' he told his players. 'I'll tell you "when" if they start it and then everybody in – and I mean everybody.'[1] As the game unfolded, Rees recalled, his forwards played as he wanted, but Manchester must have been concerned about his players because he was heard to shout: 'Come on New Zealand, get stuck into these Welsh bastards!'

Glyn Prosser, a flanker on the field, a blacksmith on working days and a Sunday School teacher on the seventh day, was aghast. He turned to his forward leader: '*Now*, Mr Rees?' Rees recalled that he fully understood the meaning behind Prosser's question:

> In a flash, eight New Zealanders were either rocking or down. I connected with a huge sheep farmer, [Athol] Mahoney, all 17 stone of him, a veritable giant. He recovered just in time to hear Cyril Gadney say to me: 'What on earth is going on here?' Rees pointed to Manchester: 'He called us Welsh bastards.' 'Ah,' said the learned referee, 'that's only a term of endearment in New Zealand.'

The game then settled down and Rees said it continued hard but fair, no fighting. All players knew what could happen: one in, all in. With ten minutes to go and New Zealand 12–10 up, Wales lost a player. Hooker Don Tarr lay motionless as play moved on. Gadney was quickly to him and advised others not to move him until he could be placed face down on a stretcher. (It was found later he had a broken vertebra; the spinal cord was not affected but Tarr never played again.) The All Blacks, two points and one man up, should have been able to hang on. But the Welsh attacked, Wooller kicked over the head of New Zealand fullback Mike Gilbert and the ball bounced into the dead ball area and into a pile of straw that had been put there the night before to ward off frost. Geoff Rees-Jones, who had already scored one try for Wales, raced over the line and onto the ball before it drifted dead. Wales won 13–12.

'We had won a splendid, rip-roaring sporting game, never to be forgotten,' Rees recalled. 'Wales erupted that night. Coal output leapt for months. The world was young again . . .'

It was the second and second-last Welsh victory over New Zealand.

wing forward position be abolished, and recommend acceptance to all affiliated unions.'[11]

The last match by a New Zealand team in which a wing forward was employed was the 1931 test against Australia in Auckland. The last wing forward was Frank Solomon, who had been born in American Samoa and was thus one of the first Pacific Islanders to play for the All Blacks. When next the All Blacks appeared, for the first Bledisloe Cup series in 1932, they packed down a three-four-one scrum for the first time (aside from the experiment in South Africa) and the first specialist hooker to play for New Zealand was, ironically, an Australian, Evan Jessep. Solomon had been converted to a loose forward. The two-three-two scrum was gone forever, although its passing was frequently mourned over the following years, especially when New Zealand demonstrated during the 1930s and late 1940s how difficult it was to adapt to the new formation. The new scrum wiped out the two-three-two and gradually supplanted the British three-two-three. Contemporaries blamed the losses that followed on New Zealand's adoption of the new scrum formation but, as always, there were other reasons. When the Australians beat New Zealand in 1934 to win the Bledisloe Cup for the first time they had talented players whose skill outweighed any forward disadvantage that may have been attributed to New Zealand.

On the long tour of Britain in 1935–36, when the players carried the burden of their predecessors and were expected to go through unbeaten, British rugby had improved. Even so, the forward formation was a factor. The veteran British journalist, Edward Sewell (always known as E. H. D. Sewell), was then 63 and had seen all the previous New Zealand matches in Britain, including the 1919 army team's. 'The present team is playing in the new formation of eight forwards and seven backs,' he wrote, 'to which we, and not they, are accustomed. Remember that fact well and never

London Transport produced posters in 1935 to encourage people to use its services to get to Twickenham. The poster for the Boxing Day match and the test was the work of artist Hyman Segal. It is not known who drew the earlier poster, promoting the first of the two matches the All Blacks played against London Counties.

forget it when you are comparing notes since to forget it is to be unfair to our visitors.'[12]

The All Blacks played 30 matches and lost just three – a first loss to a British club team when they lost to Swansea, plus test losses to Wales and England. But judged by the standards of the past, the tour was seen as failure. Even though the manager, celebrated lawyer Vin Meredith, thought the tour should be judged successful because winning should not be the sole objective, he still saw the scrum as the bogey. 'We packed three in the front row as the New Zealand union agreed to do and found that we had a deal to learn about this method of packing,' he wrote.[13] The theme that the old ways were the best ways was taken up by others, including two of the players. Dan McKenzie, a journalist and rugby follower of long standing in New Zealand, had this to say: 'It seems to me that the lesson to be learnt . . . is that New Zealand's old method of playing the game will have to be reverted to as far as the scrummage is concerned.'[14] Jack Griffiths, a member of the team who was an All Black captain and later a national administrator, wrote: 'I would like to see the old 2–3–2 scrum and a wing forward adopted

Barely a month into their tour, Jack Manchester's All Blacks of 1935–36 aroused the interest of a cartoonist for the weekly satirical magazine, *Punch*. PUNCH, 9 OCTOBER 1935

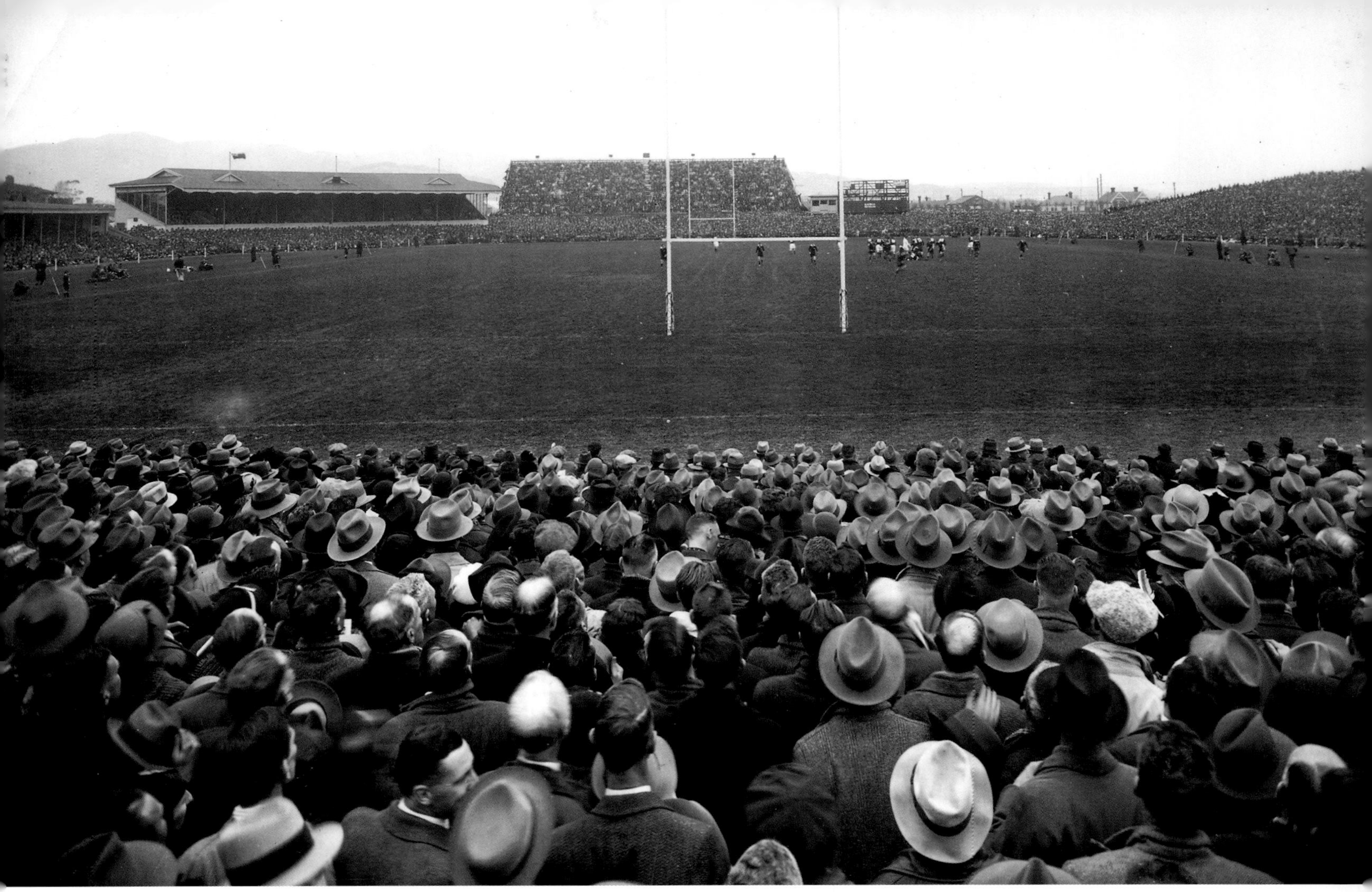

One of the Invincible All Blacks of 1924, Alan Robilliard, described this crowd for the second test against South Africa in 1937 as the biggest he had seen at Lancaster Park in Christchurch. The crowd was estimated at 45,000. This photograph was taken from the city, or Memorial Gates, end.

universally for the simple reason that it lends more for bright, open back play.'[15] And another player, Nelson ('Kelly') Ball, said: 'From a back's point of view, I feel that the abolition of the wing forward has not been in the interests of good back play . . . today we have several fast-breaking forwards continually harassing inside backs.'[16]

The nadir of the post-wing forward days, the 1930s, came when the South Africans toured in 1937. The All Blacks won the first test but were beaten in the second and third and, as the old joke goes, the Springboks were the best team to leave New Zealand. Some of the British sides in 1935–36 detected a weakness in the New Zealand scrum and took advantage of a law that allowed the side with the throw-in to a lineout to take a scrum instead. This was exploited even more by the South Africans. Paul Roos, the captain of the first South Africans to tour Britain in 1906–07, told the players before they left Durban: 'Let the spirit be the spirit of the Charge of the Light Brigade, "Theirs was not to reason why, theirs was but to do or die".' Roos had a more immediate (and practical) message after the Springboks lost the first test, largely because of the goal-kicking of the first five-eighth, Dave Trevathan. 'Scrum, scrum, scrum,' were the only words in a cable sent by Roos from Cape Town.[17] Another cable arrived for the captain, Philip Nel, from his home town of Greytown in rural Natal: 'Ji kumulayo!' This was, Nel explained to those who did

League to the financial rescue

When a London businessman and sports entrepreneur, Sydney Parkes, decided to make maximum use of the dog tracks he owned by making them rugby league venues as well, he needed to look beyond Britain for players.

It would not have taken much business or sporting acumen to look to New Zealand rugby players and especially George Nepia, one of the headline acts of the Invincibles of 1924–25.

Parkes gained approval from league authorities to start two clubs, Acton and Willesden north of the Thames, and Streatham and Mitcham to the south. He appointed an Auckland journalist, Eric Bennetts, as his agent.

Attempts had been made before to lure Nepia to league, but this time the time was ripe. The Depression still had New Zealand in its grip and Nepia's playing powers were on the wane; it was five years since he had played for New Zealand and a recall was unlikely.

Some Māori thought they were getting a raw deal from the NZRFU. Only one Māori, lock and/or flanker Tori Reid, had been chosen for the 1935–36 tour of the United Kingdom and Ireland. Some who had been obvious successes on a Māori tour of Australia, especially midfield back Charlie Smith and lock Jack Macdonald, were said to have been disappointed at being overlooked by the national selectors. Later in the decade, a Hawke's Bay Labour Member of Parliament, Edward Cullen, farewelled the league team going to England and noted there were six Māori in the team. 'There is no colour bar there,' he was quoted as saying. 'And if there was not so much colour bar in rugby we would have more Maoris wearing the silver fern than in the past.'[1]

Inevitably, there was a chorus of dissent from within rugby, including from the president of the Wanganui union, Ariki ('Alex') Tākarangi, who had played for a variety of teams, including the first national Māori team.[2]

By the end of October 1935, both Smith and Macdonald, along with another from the Māori team, George Harrison, had left for a new career in England.[3] Nepia had jokingly told his great friend Smith, 'When you get to Auckland and see that agent, you can tell him I'll play rugby league too.' Not long after, by Nepia's account, an offer arrived by telegram from Bennetts: 'I said to myself, I'll fix this bloke. My reply was, "Offer accepted £500 or nothing." I said to my wife Huinga, "I do not think we will hear another word." Two days later, Bennetts telegraphed that the price was accepted.'[4] Thus trapped, Nepia had no choice but to honour his word. But he was also a practical man. 'To us on that farm, £500 was like a million pounds. Immediate debts could be paid, some definite plans could be laid for the future, most of our anxieties about the welfare of the children would be dispelled . . .' (The Reserve Bank calculates £500 in 1935 as being the equivalent of about $[illegible]0,000 in 2013.)

League offered Nepia the one thing that rugby would not and could not: money. When he was in Gisborne en route to Auckland to join a ship to Britain, Nepia dispelled rumours that he was going to league because he was dissatisfied with rugby. 'I have not the slightest feelings of dissatisfaction with the Rugby Union people, and my non-selection had nothing to do with my decision. . . . one cannot live by football in later years and I have to think of my family.'[5]

George Nepia is a picture of elegance as he sips tea while waiting for questions from reporters on his arrival in England to play league.

It was the money rather than the game that attracted Nepia, just as it had his Invincibles teammate Bert Cooke, four years earlier. Almost despite himself, because he said he went unwillingly, he enjoyed it. He found it fast and exhilarating and the four fewer players on the field gave him more room that he relished. But Parkes's plans were not a success. Professionally promoted sports need people to pay to watch them and not enough went to watch the two London clubs. Parkes first began to sell off his Acton and Willesden players and Smith went to Halifax and another of the Māori players, Eddie Holder, a 1934 All Black, went to Wigan. Nepia during the first year became manager as well as captain of the side, but by the end of 1936, he too was on the market. Some of the New Zealanders in the club during 1936 had not been paid for a month.

Nepia followed Smith to Halifax and played three months there before returning home to his wife, family and farm. He continued to play league in New Zealand, for Manukau in 1937 and 1938, and in 1937 he played in a New Zealand win against Australia. He also played for Hornby in Christchurch and for Canterbury in 1937, as well as the national Māori team.

Another New Zealander to turn to English league in the 1930s was Rex King from Timaru, who played rugby for Canterbury and New Zealand Universities. He played league for Warrington and wrote home of his try-scoring exploits against Leeds, the champion team of the time:

> We had not beaten them for years and here they were again with more champions in their side than ever. From the kickoff we scrummed down on their line. The ball was put in and the next thing anyone knew (myself included) I, who should still have been in the second row,

was over the line with the ball . . . before the end, I scored another stupid try. Besides these two tries I did nothing to compare with the great football that was played by both sides.[6]

King captained the New Zealand league team on its tour of England in 1939 that was cut short after two games because of the outbreak of war. He returned home and enlisted, and in 1940 on the way to Britain with the 2nd New Zealand Expeditionary Force Second Echelon, he played for the army against Cape Town Universities at Newlands. He also played army rugby in Britain before going to Crete where he won a Military Cross for his role in the famed counter-attack at Galatas. He was taken prisoner and spent the rest of the war in Germany, then spent the rest of his life in England.

Nepia, like King and practically all other league players before the war, could return to rugby because the army made no distinction between the two sports and the rugby authorities after the war, as they had done after the First World War, allowed an amnesty. Macdonald, the versatile forward who went to league just before Nepia, later played a rugby test for England during the war (they were known as services internationals). Macdonald also toured France and Britain with the Māori team in 1926 and rowed for New Zealand at the first Empire Games in 1930 and at the Olympic Games in Los Angeles in 1932.

Nepia, at the age of 45 years and 158 days, played his last game of rugby in 1950 for the invitation Olympians club in Gisborne against Poverty Bay.

Everything else went into the background when the South Africans arrived in 1937, according to this welcoming full-page cartoon by William Blomfield. *OBSERVER*, 22 JULY 1937

not know, a Zulu battle-cry, a defiant challenge that meant, in effect, 'Let them all come!'

The South Africans made a bit of a blunder with their first test selection by putting their halfback, Danie Craven, at first-five; they were also without their goal-kicking fullback, Gerry Brand. For the second test, Craven was back where he should have been, Brand was back wearing the No. 1 jersey and the Springboks won 13–6. It was some consolation, but not much, to New Zealanders that the fast Taranaki centre, Jack Sullivan, scored two tries. It was no consolation at all when Sullivan was shunted out to the wing for the third test, and as with every wing since the game began, it was irrelevant how good or fast he was unless he had the ball. The All Blacks lost the third test 17–6 and while that may not sound much of a margin now, it was recognised as a humiliation at the time. Not only did the All Blacks lose the

They each played for their country, coached their country and chaired their national unions – Danie Craven and Jack Sullivan vie for the ball in the third test of the 1937 series in Auckland.

test, they also lost a series to South Africa for the first time. The intensity of competition between the two teams, and the depth of passion felt by supporters, were significant contributors to the determination to keep playing each other in later years when much of the rest of the world cried for them to stop. Two of the principal administrators of those controversial years, Craven and Sullivan, had begun their rivalry – and yes, friendship – as players. For the time though, it was just the pain of losing. A Wellington lawyer and man about town, John Carrad, expressed his anguish in verse:

> A bloody staunch pig islander
> Stood up against the bar;
> His ruddy eyes were sombre
> And his thoughts were soaring far
> Away from bloody Auckland,
> From that gory Eden Park,
> And he drank his beer in silence
> While his brow was grim and dark,
> And he thought of other, golden days,
> When All Blacks were the tops . . .

His verse drifted through the winning days but eventually moved back to the present:

> . . . he sighed a sad and dismal sigh,
> A tear dropped in his drink,
> And sadly out into the night,
> He made his footsteps slink.
> And no one said a bloody word,
> So deep was their despair;
> And ghosts of other, bloody days,
> Stalked out and left them there
> To their bloody, bloody thoughts,
> And a half-drunk glass of beer.[18]

Historian Greg Ryan had a pertinent point to make about the 1937 tour. He wrote that almost without exception accounts of the debate about playing rugby with South Africa take the 1958–60 period as a starting point.[19] He was right. He also made the point that even when there is a more educated longer-term view, the 1937 tour of New Zealand is almost always ignored. He was right there too. The South Africans did not play a Māori team in 1937 and it has been generally assumed that was because of what happened in 1921. In a loose sense, it was. But there was more to it than that and Ryan recounts how the Arawa confederation told the national union that Māori should not be involved in matches against the South Africans. A 'memorial' (petition) given to the union by Tai Mitchell on behalf of Te Arawa sought to 'protect the Maori race from any possible recurrence of the unpleasant incidents which occurred during the previous visit' and specifically asked that no Māori player be called upon to play against South Africa and that

One of the Māori who played for New Zealand against South Africa in 1937, Tori Reid, leads a breakout in the first test in Wellington. Players from left: rival captains Danie Craven and Ron King, Springbok halfback Pierre de Villiers, All Black prop Doug Dalton, Reid, No. 8 Allan Parkhill and wing Dai Williams, who scored South Africa's only try in the match. The photographer was Charles Percy Samuel Boyer of the *Evening Post*.
MNZ-2323-1/2-F, MAKING NEW ZEALAND CENTENNIAL COLLECTION, ALEXANDER TURNBULL LIBRARY

no Māori representative match be played. As Ryan correctly deduced, this took the debate to a whole new level, from one involving purely rugby to one having an impact on the whole of race relations.

Te Arawa did not, of course, speak for all Māori and the union knew that. As always, debates within the union's governing council were private and only the outcomes were made public. In the end, it was rationalised by the union that a Māori match was one of the casualties of a shorter itinerary. It was two matches fewer than it had been in 1921 and adding to the time constraints was the fact the South Africans were given a clear week before each of the tests. In 1921, they had a clear week before only the third test.[20] Māori (as well as the Solomon brothers from the South Pacific) played for various provincial teams against South Africa and three Māori, 'Tori' Reid, Bill Phillips and Everard Jackson, played in the tests.

The series loss in 1937 cast a long shadow. Deliberately or not, consciously or not, the overriding aim of New Zealand rugby, in the widest sense of the phrase, was to avenge that loss, to beat South Africa and re-establish the All Blacks as the best team in the world. That was how series between the two countries were viewed – as world championships. All other series, even the Lions, were a rung down on the ladder of rugby aspiration. It was this obsession in the mind of New Zealanders who loved their rugby, or even just those who somehow lived under its influence, that dominated for years to come. It was why the shadow extended as far as into the 1980s and plunged the country into some of its darkest days.

The All Blacks went to Australia in 1938 and completed the task set them without a blemish, but it was no more than an interim tour until the one that mattered came around again: a series against South Africa. There were players in the series against Australia who, wise heads argued, should have played against the Springboks the year before. One of them was the rangy wing, Tom Morrison, and another the small and fast halfback, Charlie Saxton. Each was a man of influence on the field and each extended that influence in the years beyond their playing days. The NZRFU wanted the All Blacks to go to Australia in 1939 because that would have been ideal preparation ahead

Kerwin Maegraith began his career as a sketch artist and caricaturist in Adelaide, where he was schooled on drawing Australian rules footballers. But he adapted to rugby players when he moved to Sydney as this collection of the 1938 All Blacks shows. The Wallabies, as Maegraith correctly depicts, wore gold jerseys with a broad green band, and black shorts.

of naming a team to go to South Africa in 1940; equally, it would have been good for the Wallabies because they were due to go to Britain on a long tour over the 1939–40 summer. But the Australian union did not want to change the agreed timetable so 1938 it was. It became a stepping-stone tour, between one South African series and the next.

The All Blacks were scheduled to arrive in Durban on 2 June 1940 and, as with the 1928 tour, the NZRFU decided it would select its team after trials the previous year. It seems more than a little bizarre, at least in hindsight, that the interisland match and trial matches in 1939 were played in September and October – after New Zealand had joined Britain and the rest of the Empire in war against Germany. The rationale was that rugby would go ahead as normal for as long as it could in the hope – a hope not confined to rugby – that the war would be over by Christmas. After the trials, chairman Stan Dean thanked the players for making themselves available 'in difficult times' and added that footballers knew where their duty lay 'and they would serve their country just as nobly as soldiers'.[21] Since the war was not over by Christmas, the NZRFU told the South Africans they would not be touring until peace returned. The sole selector of the team that never toured was Ted McKenzie and although it is not known if he ever chose a touring squad, there was ample speculation in following years about who was in it or who may have been in it. Charlie Saxton had been the All Black halfback in 1938, but in 1939 he played both halfback and first five-eighth. Ted McKenzie, like good selectors until the loquacious years of television, kept his thoughts to himself, but it was known he was concerned about a lack of quality at first five-eighth. McKenzie's brother Norman published his own team – he carefully avoided saying if he had spoken to his brother about it – and had Saxton at first five-eighth while he had Eric Tindill, whose only test had been at first-five, at halfback.[22] Saxton was often mentioned in later years as being the likely captain in South Africa in 1940, but hindsight could have been responsible for that because of his leadership of the 2nd New Zealand Expeditionary Force team after the war. Tindill was also a possibility as captain, as was a Wanganui centre, Dave Barton. The captain in Australia the year before, 'Brushy' Mitchell, was not available. Other men who would have an enduring influence on New Zealand rugby, men such as Jack Sullivan and Ernie Todd, joined Saxton and Morrison in Norman McKenzie's paper-only team.

Rugby and South Africa had to wait.

White Russian, red rose

Of all the tries scored against the All Blacks in tests, something approaching 600, it seems unlikely that any one of them could have had as much impact and enduring publicity as the two scored for England in 1936 by a Russian prince.

For a start, the two scored by Alexander Sergeevich Obolensky, the White Russian who embraced the red rose, enabled England to beat New Zealand for the first time – and the only time for another 37 years. A rugby history website says there were two reasons Obolensky's day of glory became so celebrated: one was that the tries were unorthodox and the other the simple fact that the match was filmed (and therefore the tries could be seen again and again).[1] The website quoted New Zealand rugby writer Terry McLean as saying 'Obolensky's try' was 'a stupendous exhibition of the hypotenuse in rugby'. McLean's brother Hugh, who played in the match, was less mathematically descriptive and merely mentioned that the second try, which came from a diagonal run across the field and against the grain of New Zealand's defence, 'might not come off again in a hundred years'. The first try, which was England's first score, was more orthodox with Obolensky in the backline as an extra man and he beat the New Zealand defence by sheer pace.

The *Morning Post* described Obolensky's try-scoring:

> Runners we have seen before but never such a runner with such an innate idea of where to go and how to get there. His double swerve to gain his first try was remarkable enough but the extraordinary turn-in and diagonal right to left run which won him his second and which drew forth that great Twickenham rarity, a double roar of applause, will never be forgotten by anybody who saw it.[2]

(A remarkably similar angled run gave David Campese a try against New Zealand in the World Cup semifinal in Dublin in 1991.)

It is tempting to dismiss glowing reports of Obolensky's tries as flights of historical fancy or of heart-warming nostalgia obscuring the reality. Fortunately, the game was filmed by cameraman Leslie Murray of British Movietone News using a six-inch lens from a vantage point of 10 metres above ground; both tries are preserved on YouTube.[3] Even allowing for the eccentricity of early cine film, Obolensky's speed is astonishing and his move that led to the second try a remarkable example of vision and pace. His tries live with the best of any era.

There were more reasons for Obolensky's fame to last. One was that he introduced a touch of the exotic to English rugby: not just a Russian émigré whose family fled the communists, but one of noble blood. The Prince of Wales, just sixteen days away from becoming King Edward VIII, was introduced to both teams before the match and the tale has grown up that when he shook the Russian hand, he asked Obolensky by what right he could play for England. Obolensky apparently answered immediately and haughtily: 'Your Highness, I am an Oxford man.' So he was. So too was another of the England team, Harold ('Tuppy') Owen-Smith, who was a South African, and the Oxford team was captained by a New Zealander, Malcolm ('Mac') Cooper, who played for Scotland.

But Obolensky was much more than just an Oxford man. His family background was rooted in

Alex Obolensky throws the ball into a lineout while playing for Middlesex, probably in 1938. He played for Rosslyn Park and Middlesex after leaving Oxford.

the Russian imperial court. His father was Prince Sergei Alexandrovich Obolensky, an aide-de-camp to the Moscow governor-general and a captain in the Tsar's Horse Guards. Prince Sergei was said to have been a confidant of the last tsar, Nicholas, but their nobility did not rest solely on royal patronage. The Obolenskys could trace their ancestry back to Saint Vladimir, the ruler who introduced Christianity to Russia in the tenth century, and before that to the ninth-century founder of Kiev, Rurik the Viking chief of the Russ tribe (who put the 'Russ' into Russia). The younger Obolensky was a child of the revolution, born in St Petersburg in 1916, but during the communist uprising the following year, the family fled to the Crimea and later were taken on a British warship to France. The move to England followed and young Alex went to Trent College in Nottingham, where he

Eric Tindill, the All Blacks' first five-eighth, grabbed the ball at the end of the England test in 1936. It became Tindill's ball, but it was forever Alex Obolensky's match. NZ SPORTS HALL OF FAME

gained a mention in national newspapers for his sprinting ability, and then on to Oxford, where he gained his rugby 'blue' in 1935.[4]

Obolensky played for England only three more times after the New Zealand match and never scored another try. But more than seventy years later, the two he did score were still written about as the best at Twickenham, as this paragraph from the *Guardian* demonstrates:

> Better than the merry dance England's Peter Jackson led Australia in 1958 or the dazzling Twickenham brace by two other Englishmen – both against Scotland: Richard Sharp's string of dummies in 1963 or Andy Hancock's marathon gallop two years on. Yep, better even than David Duckham's spring-heeled solo, a Barbarian sinking the Springboks in 1970; or [Philippe] Saint-André's sealing of France's epic against England 20 seasons later. Or Rory Underwood's polished gem against Scotland in 1993; Obo even bettered the day Jonah Lomu left white shirts floundering, flattened in his wake with his fearsome 50-yarder in 1999.[5]

The manner of his going also heightened the Obolensky story. When war began, he joined the Royal Air Force and in 1940 went on a training course on flying Hawker Hurricanes. Just before it, Obolensky was on leave in London and he ran into his fellow Oxford blue and rugby international, Vivian Jenkins. 'How's the training going?' Jenkins asked. 'It's going absolutely fine, great fun,' Jenkins reported the reply. But then Obolensky added: 'Except I still haven't got the hang of landing.' He was killed when his aircraft flipped and burned on landing at Martlesham in Suffolk on 29 March 1940. He became the first (of fourteen) England rugby internationals to die while on service in the Second World War. He was buried at nearby Ipswich cemetery, and among the wreaths at his funeral was one from the New Zealand Rugby Football Union and another from the All Blacks he had helped beat. Seventy years later, the local borough council decided a statue of the Russian who played and died for England was called for and it sought donations. The money was raised, helped along by another Russian émigré, billionaire Roman Abramovich, better known for his ownership of the Chelsea soccer club, and the statue in Cromwell Square in Ipswich was unveiled in 2009.

If Obolensky's two tries were against Wales, or Scotland or Ireland or Australia, would they have so long endured in the public memory, and especially England's? Perhaps not. As Will Carling remarked 57 years later after he had led England to victory over New Zealand at Twickenham: 'There is a special bond that comes with beating New Zealand . . .'[6]

10 Defeat at home and abroad

The rugby winger nowadays
Is showing signs in lots of ways
Of getting quite dejected –
He's woefully neglected[1]

Rugby continued as best it could during the years of the Second World War and the best was better than it had been during the First World War. In one year of the first, 1916, no representative rugby was played at all and in other years the game at first-class level was restricted to players under twenty years of age. The New Zealand union's policy for the second war was summed up by its chairman, Stan Dean, at the annual meeting in 1940: 'We should not play any matches which are going to be a discouragement to recruiting. We should carry on with our football as far as we can . . .'[2] Interisland and Ranfurly Shield matches were suspended for the duration of the war (the interisland game resumed in 1944) and the union decided to abandon tours, which would have become impossible anyway. Some provincial unions organised only club competitions at various stages during the war and did not field representative teams. The national union encouraged school rugby and gave a grant of £750 to assist schools with equipment and clothing.[3]

The years between 1940 and 1945 also saw the advent of services teams in club and interprovincial competitions. The union relaxed residential rules to allow servicemen to play without needing special permission in the areas in which they were stationed. A future All Black captain and coach, Fred Allen, who had already played for Canterbury, thus found himself playing for Marlborough; a staunch Aucklander, Eric Boggs, played for Wellington; a true-blue Otago man, Jim Kearney, had to don the red and black of Canterbury. The changed nature of rugby was evident with the opening match of the 1940 season in Auckland. The Māori Battalion, which had been in camp at Palmerston North, played a Combined Fifteen from the Ngaruawahia and Papakura camps. The latter included All Black Cyril Pepper, who was to die in Wellington in 1943 after being invalided home from North

New Zealand soldiers play in what appears to be an impromptu match in Egypt in 1941, given the lack of playing gear and unmarked field. Such games abounded wherever there were enough men, and sometimes not, and enough time. DA-00793-F, ALEXANDER TURNBULL LIBRARY

This is the way we kick the ball in New Zealand, a member of the Divisional Cavalry might be saying to some locals he ran into in Syria in 1942. DA-02505-F, ALEXANDER TURNBULL LIBRARY

Africa, and two members of the national league team whose tour of England had to be abandoned the year before, Jack Campbell and Ivor Stirling.[4] The inclusion of the latter two in a showcase rugby match demonstrated that, as in the first war, animosities between the two versions of rugby would be suspended during the greater animosity. This allowed players who had had league careers in England, including luminaries George Nepia, Rex King and Jack Macdonald, back into rugby. King, captain of the 1939 league team, played for a Second Echelon team in a hastily arranged match against a University of Cape Town team. The Second Echelon, which included the Māori Battalion, although none of its members seemed to have played in the game, was in Cape Town for three days on its way to Britain in 1940. The game, which was played at Newlands, attracted a crowd of 'some thousands' according to a report published in New Zealand. The New Zealanders were led by the 1935 All Black – and national cricketer – Eric Tindill and among them were several players with provincial experience. The side was, though, 'a far remove from what would have been but for the war'.[5]

In the Second World War, unlike the first, the air force and navy entered provincial competitions; the New Zealand Army played the Royal New Zealand Air Force for the first time in 1943 and in 1944 in Wellington, a New Zealand XV played Combined Services. The Wellington game, which had a sprinkling of All Blacks through both sides, attracted a crowd of about 18,000.[6]

An indication of the different shape first-class rugby took in the two world wars is amply shown by the following table.

Wartime matches comparison

	INTER-UNION	OTHERS	TOTAL
1915	13	2	15
1916	0	0	0
1917	8	6	14
1918	16	5	21
1940	54	18	72
1941	49	8	57
1942	21	35	56
1943	29	13	42
1944	39	9	48
1945	52	11	63

A. C. Swan, *History of New Zealand Rugby Football*, vol. 1 (Wellington: A. H. & A. W. Reed, 1948), p. 257.

Wherever New Zealand men found themselves overseas, most commonly in North Africa and Italy but also in Fiji and New Caledonia, they played rugby. Some of it was organised officially on a unit basis, culminating in the selection of 2nd New Zealand Expeditionary Force or divisional or combined services teams, and some of it organised haphazardly wherever there happened to be some flat ground, a ball and a lull in the fighting. And sometimes not even that. Royal Air Force aircraft once roamed the skies above a rugby ground to allow the game to proceed unhindered.

Jack Finlay leads the 2nd New Zealand Expeditionary Force team on to the field in Alexandria on Sunday, 1 February 1942 to play Rest of Egypt. The New Zealanders, who included pre-war All Blacks Tom Morrison, Artie Lambourn and Athol Mahoney, won 22–0. Finlay became vice-captain of the 2NZEF Kiwis in 1945, was an All Black in 1946 and later a national selector. DA-02380-F, ALEXANDER TURNBULL LIBRARY

Two significant teams were the Kiwis, the 2NZEF team captained by 1938 All Black Charlie Saxton, and the lesser known New Zealand Services team.[7] Both toured Britain, Ireland and France after the war while the Kiwis also played in New Zealand. Several New Zealanders played in what were known as 'services internationals' during the war; that is, matches involving England, Scotland, Ireland and Wales.

Among the myriad of matches in Britain while servicemen were waiting for ships home was one at Richmond between Pākehā and Māori, the latter captained by Jack Macdonald. There were oddities in the wartime rugby. One was at Bradford between a 'Rugby Football Union XV' and a 'Rugby League XV'. This was no scratch match thought up on the spur of a moment. Both teams were made up of the best available players, many of them internationals and, ironically, the rugby side included two future custodians of the amateur ethic, secretaries of the RFU, Robin Prescott and Bob Weighill.[8] The game was played according to rugby rules and the league team won. During the 1970s, when rugby was going through one of its periodic searches for players who had dabbled with money, Weighill was reminded of the match. Had he been caught going down in a scrum with a professional, he would have been instantly banned. A jovial former air commodore, Weighill laughed: 'Ah but that was wartime. You can get away with

Sport and war come together through the pen and ink of *Observer* artist Alex Garmonsway as he links rugby with the first confrontation of the Second World War between New Zealand and German troops, in Greece. *OBSERVER*, 16 APRIL 1941

anything when there's a war on.'[9] That was around the time that the England captain, Bill Beaumont, was banned for taking proceeds from a biography, a clear breach of amateur regulations.

Surely one of the oddest wartime rugby matches was in the Cassino area of Italy at a time of prolonged and difficult fighting. The New Zealand Division's chief engineer, Fred Hanson, told the story at a reunion of army rugby players in Wellington in 1961.[10] Hanson related how he went to see a company of his sappers working on a section of Allied ground held by the Free French. Among Hanson's listeners was a 1928 All Black and later brigade commander, Jim Burrows, and he related Hanson's tale:

> As he approached the area where his sappers were working he saw that under the shelter of some high ground a game of rugby was in progress. There were no rugby posts and the sidelines were made by the soldiers in the uniforms of France and New Zealand, all shouting and cheering their respective teams. The players themselves were also dressed in the uniforms of France and New Zealand but the game lost nothing because of this. Play swept up and down the field and the spectators had worked themselves up to a high pitch of excitement. As Fred drew near he began to wonder why, so far, no one had kicked the ball. . . . Suddenly he realised why. The football was a dead fowl.[11]

The French team was in Wellington for the second test against New Zealand at the time of the reunion and among the guests was the French manager, Marcel Laurent, and a few other members of the touring party as well as French journalists. Burrows recalled how one of the Frenchmen turned to him and said:

This book was produced by a Wellington rugby player and returned soldier, Paul Donoghue, for a 2nd New Zealand Expeditionary Force rugby reunion in 1961.

Members of the 22 Battalion team celebrate winning the Freyberg Cup at Forli in Italy in December 1944. The 22nd, captained by Wellington five-eighth Lin Thomas who is pictured in the centre holding the base of the cup, beat the Divisional Ammunition team in what turned out to be the last rugby tournament of the war for the New Zealanders. DA-07858, WAR HISTORY COLLECTION, ALEXANDER TURNBULL LIBRARY

> What is it about sport that it can bring people together in this way? Here at Cassino, under conditions that . . . could only be described as dangerous, two armies from foreign countries, neither speaking the other's language, suddenly decide to play a game of football. They have no jerseys or studded boots, no marked field and no football posts. They have no football. But does that bother them? Never. They take the field as if they were at Twickenham. Tell me, what is the appeal, what is the magic of this game called rugby, that under such conditions grown men will play it with a dead fowl?[12]

Another example of how seriously soldiers took their wartime rugby was the determination to broadcast a battalion's match that not all its members could get to. In Italy, the 22 Battalion team was scheduled to meet Divisional Signals in a semifinal of the divisional championship for the Freyberg Cup. The 22 Battalion team, which was coached by a 1936 All Black, Jock Wells, was withdrawn from the line ahead of the rest of the battalion. One of the battalion officers, Stuart McKenzie, a Palmerston North accountant in peacetime and a son of Norman McKenzie of rugby renown, borrowed a wireless-telegraphy truck from brigade headquarters and throughout the match progress scores were passed on by field telephone to the men in the line. As the battalion's history noted: 'At every telephone in the battalion (no matter how remote or exposed the position) a listener took down the latest score and relayed it to the expectant group around him.' Wells said: 'That was one broadcast which fooled the Hun intelligence.'[13]

Even before the war was over, rugby administrators again turned their minds to tinkering with the laws of the game. Germany was beaten but Japan resisted over the New Zealand winter months of 1945, and in Dunedin, the Otago union urged the national union to allow referees to put the ball into scrums.[14] They had been doing this, off and on, in various provinces for years, and Otago wanted it to be official. The reason was that referees, being objective and impartial by definition, would put the ball in fairly and the game would be rid of time-wasting resets and accusations of cheating. Some chance. The NZRFU

From war to sport

In January 1940, the Second World War had barely begun. An advance party of New Zealand troops had arrived in Egypt and their recently appointed general officer commanding ('GOC' as they knew him), Major-General Bernard Freyberg, had just arrived from London. Among the ten officers of the advance party was a captain, Allan Andrews, who had been a noted rugby player and who was just as well known for having turned down a chance in 1934 to be an All Black. Rather than go to Australia with the New Zealand team, he chose to stay in Christchurch for university exams. It was a decision he regretted for the rest of his life.

Freyberg knew Andrews, who was a professional soldier, either personally or by reputation. Either way, the general invited the captain to his Cairo flat for dinner. 'After dinner and over a brandy and cigars,' Andrews recalled, 'he first propounded his vision of a 2NZEF rugby team touring the UK after the war, as happened in 1919.'[1]

Bernard Freyberg, the general officer commanding the 2nd New Zealand Expeditionary Force, played senior club rugby in Wellington and Dunedin before the First World War as well as being a national champion swimmer. He encouraged rugby among troops during the Second World War and his orders led to the formation of the 2NZEF Kiwis team. Freyberg is pictured among spectators at a match in Egypt. DA-00956-F, ALEXANDER TURNBULL LIBRARY

In January 1940, there was still more than five years of war to come. In those five years, the New Zealand army men under Freyberg's command would fight in Greece, Crete, North Africa and Italy. Many would die, many would be taken prisoner. 'Right throughout the war the General, even in the black days when the Division was being mauled and hammered,' Andrews wrote, 'never lost sight of his great ambition to see his rugby team march through the British Isles after the war playing rugby of a quality that would be an inspiration to all rugby players who either played against the Kiwis or watched them play.' On 13 May 1943 near Enfidaville in north-eastern Tunisia, Freyberg waited to accept the surrender of the senior German and Italian commanders in North Africa. While waiting, Andrews recalled, the conversation went back to rugby. 'It became clear to me that a successful 2NZEF rugby team playing rugby of a high standard was almost as important to the General as winning the war.'[2]

A 2NZEF Kiwis jersey. The Kiwis were a team organised by the army and paid for by the government but, as a courtesy, asked the NZRFU if they could use the silver fern. The device was not registered then, but the union said yes anyway. 1997.222, STAN YOUNG COLLECTION, NATIONAL ARMY MUSEUM NZ

Two years later, when the New Zealand soldiers were having a break after helping rid Florence of Germans, Freyberg sat down at a table with some of his senior rugby men. There was Jim Burrows, a brigadier who had been an All Black in 1928; Andrews, who had risen to lieutenant-colonel; Captain Jack Griffiths, a 1930s All Black who had been aide to Freyberg for much of the war; Captain Charlie Saxton, a 1938 All Black who had got into all manner of scrapes as a member of the Long Range Desert Group; Captain Murray Sidey, who like Griffiths had been by Freyberg's side for much of the war; Lieutenant Mac Cooper, a lieutenant from Auckland who had played for Cambridge and Scotland; Lieutenant John Wade, who had played for Canterbury; and Gunner Ron Stewart, an Invincible from 1924 who also went to South Africa in 1928 and played his last test against the British team in 1930.[3]

Freyberg said he hoped they were not being over-optimistic in talking about a rugby tour when the war was far from over. But he said it was necessary to get to work and get the machinery set up. It was to be a 2nd New Zealand Expeditionary Force team and not just the division, which meant troops back in Cairo and scattered over various parts of North Africa and Italy would also be eligible. 'Every unit or detached unit must have a chance,' Freyberg told his men. The minutes of the meeting then recorded:

> GOC went on to say that we should produce as good a team as ever left New Zealand – team should have good combination after a long period of training. On the other hand the men were soldiers, not sports specialists, and would have to continue their duties as soldiers in the meantime . . . the question of including New Zealanders in England was considered but decided against as New Zealand personnel there were mainly air force and navy. As this was an army team professional and league players would be eligible.

It was fine to tell the troops; not so fine to tell the world. Bill Brodie, one of the 2NZEF war correspondents, fired off a story to London to be sent on to New Zealand. In the money-saving 'cablese' of the day, Brodie wrote: 'Initial steps have been taken proselection rugby team representing 2NZEF primarily adplay sixth south african armoured division but cumpossibility in mind of tour postwar stop.' And it did stop. Freyberg's personal assistant, John White, called a halt to the message: 'The GOC has considered this matter and feels that at the present moment it would be unwise to give the report publicity . . .' It would be

The Kiwis before their first 'test' against France in Paris, which they won 14–9. Charlie Saxton (front, third from left) and Fred Allen (second from left) may be sharing a joke about the ball on Saxton's left which bears the legend 'Allen'. Rugby balls made by the Allen company in France were common and had nothing to do with the Kiwis' first five-eighth (and later All Black and coach). NZ SPORTS HALL OF FAME

a few months before sport could come before war. Even in April 1945, when the war in Europe was all but over, the South Africans suggested a game against the New Zealand Division in Florence. Freyberg himself wrote by hand on the message form: 'Top secret. Cable to say we are not able to take any part in sport as we shall be operationally employed.'[4]

But all bad things, just like the good, must come to an end. By the time the Germans surrendered, Andrews had done his general's bidding and sought nominations from every 2NZEF unit, wherever it may have been. Three former All Blacks, Jack Hore, Ron Stewart and Vic Butler, were designated selectors: this was the army – they were not asked, they were not elected, they were told. It was a reflection of the New Zealand army that Hore was a warrant officer, Stewart a non-commissioned officer and Butler a major. Ranks never mattered. During the tour, fullback Bob Scott said that, within the team, there were no worries about rank. There were three majors, two captains, three lieutenants 'and the rest of us were also-rans, but it was not unusual to hear the famous word "dumb" accompanied by other words, pass among all without distinction of rank'.[5]

Despite Freyberg deciding league men could be chosen, two were not. Scott had played league before the war and his only rugby was with army teams; similarly with Johnny Simpson, the prop known as 'the iron man'. The word got about and a message came back down the chain of command: 'If they're good enough, include them.' Some players who were nominated had cruel luck. George Newland would have been a certainty for the team. In one of the last river crossings of the war, he drove

Jim Sherratt scored 23 tries for the Kiwis on their post-war matches in Europe and New Zealand. He was a particular favourite in France where his galloping style of running earned him the nickname 'le beau grand cheval' (the beautiful big horse). This caricature which he signed was drawn in Paris in 1946. NZ SPORTS HALL OF FAME

his truck loaded with assault boats into the River Po, intending to ford his way across. An American Thunderbolt fighter-bomber roared down and attacked the truck, which caught fire. Newland was dead before he could be dragged clear. Mick Kenny, a Wellington fullback also considered a certainty, was almost killed by a burst from a German machine-gun and took years to recover. Remarkably, he reappeared on the rugby field again for Wellington and New Zealand Māori.[6]

Gradually the team took shape. The army held trials at Klagenfurt in Austria, a half-day's ride in the back of a three-tonne truck from Trieste, and the New Zealanders played a couple of scratch matches against a British army combination and a French team, which comprised mainly members of the resistance. More trials were held at Margate at the eastern extremity of Kent that sticks out into the English Channel. Players stayed at the grand old Norfolk Hotel in Margate, which was convenient because it was one of several reception areas for repatriated New Zealand prisoners of war. Three of them, Pat Rhind, Jack McLean and Neil McPhail, who had all been captured on Crete in 1941, had been playing for the Wasps club in London and were included in the trials. From 396 nominations from army units in Italy and Cairo, the number was whittled down to 66 who assembled in Margate for a series of eight trial matches. Finally, in mid-October 1945, a squad of 29 was chosen: it included just four pre-war first-class players, the three former prisoners of war and the captain, Charlie Saxton. The majority of the players had been late reinforcements for the division in Italy because soldiers in the first and second echelons of 1940 or earlier replacement drafts, which included pre-war All Blacks and provincial players, had been killed, wounded, imprisoned or returned home after service of four and a half years.

One of the British reporters who watched the trials at Margate, Hylton Cleaver of the *Evening Standard*, was prescient: 'The New Zealanders are going to be a tonic to our rugby. There is no doubt about that. They do not pretend to reach the standard of peacetime All Blacks, but they will delight the crowds with their long accurate passing, speed of thought, strength of limb and good backing up.'[7]

The team's official title was 'the New Zealand Army Touring Team (Rugby)', but the players among themselves decided to reduce the military mouthful to 'the Kiwis', and the Kiwis they became. The tour was entirely an army venture and had nothing to do with the New Zealand Rugby Football Union, although its chairman, Stan Dean, agreed the silver fern could be used on jerseys (not that he could have prevented its use).[8] The New Zealand Government underwrote the cost of the tour (as it funded all other post-war sports tournaments) and also ensured the team would be well publicised. A war correspondent who had formerly been chief of staff of the *Free Lance*, Jim Gasson, was assigned to the tour and an extrovert warrant officer on the staff of the Army Education Welfare Service in Wellington, Winston McCarthy, was sent to provide broadcasts of matches.[9] The tour turned McCarthy, and the Kiwis, into household names.

From late October 1945, when the Kiwis made their debut against Swansea, until early August 1946, they played 38 matches in the British Isles and New Zealand and won 32 of them; they drew three and lost three. They scored nearly three times as many points as their opponents. But it was not a tour whose qualities could be illuminated by statistics. It was the manner of the Kiwis' play rather than their win–loss ratio that attracted attention wherever they went. As Andrews wrote: 'I venture to say that no All Black touring team before or since our tour has ever had such a percentage of its tries scored by its wing threequarters.'[10] When the tour was nearing its end in Britain, another war correspondent, Tom Mahony, wrote a special article for the *Auckland Star* and the *Sports Post* in Wellington: '. . . no better service could have been rendered to New Zealand football than by this team whose purpose was to play bright, open rugby and at the same time preserve the Dominion's proud reputation in this country as the world's most successful exponents of the game.'[11]

It was no coincidence that Saxton, the captain of the team, during the 1950s helped develop a 'code of conduct' for Otago rugby that was based on an open, exciting game and that he wrote

Jack Finlay, vice-captain of the 2NZEF Kiwis, heads home with the team's bag of 605 points (they conceded 185). This was drawn by an unidentified cartoonist in Paris at the time of the last match, against L'Ile de France, the administrative region that includes Paris. NZ SPORTS HALL OF FAME

The ABC of Rugby, the opening sentence of which reads: 'Rugby is an attacking game and players can make a success of the game only if they think about it or talk about it in terms of attack.'[12] Neither was it a coincidence that Saxton managed the 1967 All Blacks, who were coached by one of the leading players of the Kiwis and the first post-war All Black captain, Fred Allen. The 1967 team was one of the best New Zealand teams to tour the United Kingdom.

When the Kiwis were chosen, Saxton was the only All Black. Sixteen more went on to play for New Zealand, some of them such as Bob Scott among the best in their positions; Allen captained the All Blacks in the tests of the 1940s but gained a greater fame as a coach of Auckland during the Ranfurly Shield era of the 1960s and an unbeaten coach of the All Blacks.

knew it could not agree to any such thing unless it was agreed first in London, and that was not likely. New Zealand and New South Wales had proposed in 1920 for referees to put the ball in, but the idea got short shrift and the shrift had not got any longer in the intervening years.[15] The great player of the 1920s, Mark Nicholls, deemed it remarkable that some unions – he mentioned Otago, Auckland and Wairarapa – set such an example of law-breaking. 'The referee is not a player and has no right to participate in the game,' he wrote. 'It is beyond my understanding that the referees have accepted the responsibility of influencing the result of the game.'[16]

On the other side of the world, the rugby authorities emerged from their wartime hibernation – the services rugby matches were organised by the services – and the IRB confirmed a change that was proposed in 1939, but war prevented its confirmation. This was to abandon the provision for a side with the throw-in to a lineout being able to have a scrum instead. Since South Africa exploited that to the full in 1937 and pushed the All Blacks out of the series, the change was not a cause for dismay in New Zealand.

For all the deprivations of the war years – including the deaths of many first-class players – the game reflected both prosperity and popularity when it returned in full in 1946. King's Birthday Monday in early June was a popular day for traditional matches; that is, matches between near neighbours which were played home and away annually. In 1946, Auckland went to Hamilton for a 10–9 win against Waikato in front of a crowd of about 10,000; Manawatu beat Wellington 11–10 in Palmerston North with about 5000 watching; in Napier, where there was a competing Napier Park Racing Club winter meeting, a crowd of 6000 showed up at McLean Park to watch Hawke's Bay being beaten 13–8 by Wairarapa; Canterbury went over the Alps to Greymouth and were beaten 11–9, no doubt to the delight of a parochial crowd of 3000. The *Greymouth Evening Star* seemed to take great pride in reporting the home side had 'definite superiority' in the forwards.[17]

The Greymouth match was refereed by a Coaster, Arthur Fong, who three months later refereed the first test after the war, against Australia in Dunedin. As a player, Fong was a midfield back for the West Coast, played for the South Island in 1933 and had a New Zealand trial in 1934. He took up refereeing in the late 1930s. He became the first person, and one of the few, of Chinese parentage to play and referee rugby at first-class level. A member of 22 Battalion, he also refereed when he could while on active service in North Africa and Italy.

The New Zealand team that played Australia in the test resumption comprised fifteen debutants, the first time that had happened since New Zealand's first test match in 1903. Even the first test in 1921, the first after the First World War, had one player who had played before the war. Seven All Blacks died as a result of war service between 1939 and 1945 (compared with thirteen in the First World War) and upwards of 200 who had experience of first-class rugby for provinces also died.[18] Many more who might have featured in post-war rugby were wounded out of contention and others had their careers ended by the war. One of the latter was the try scorer against South Africa in 1937 and later selector and chairman of the NZRFU, Jack Sullivan. Shrapnel from a German shell in the Western Desert in June 1942 ended Sullivan's playing days.

The tests against Australia in 1946 and 1947 re-established rugby at an international level and prepared New Zealand for its tour of South Africa and Australia for the British Isles. The tests also saw the introduction of members of the Kiwis, the army team that toured Europe, including men who would have a profound influence on the game. One was the fullback, Bob Scott, who by his retirement in 1954 was regarded as an equal of George Nepia's, and the other was the post-war captain, Fred Allen, whose influence was much greater as

Bob Scott, one of the great All Black full-backs and a favourite of his day.

a coach than it was as a player. Allen's time as a coach would come; in the 1940s, the coach most talked about was Victor George Cavanagh, coach of the Otago team that dominated the Ranfurly Shield in the last years of the decade. He and his father, Vic senior as he was known, first coached Otago together in 1936 when they held off eight shield challenges. The father had coached the University club and the son Southern and it was the club final between their two sides in 1936 that was the subject of one of the most evocative pieces of literature about rugby, a short story called 'The Big Game' by A. P. Gaskell.[19] This was ostensibly a work of fiction, but Gaskell was the pen-name of Alexander (Alec) Gaskell Pickard, who played in the match, which was won by 'young' Vic's Southern.[20]

More than their familial rivalry, though, and more even than the Ranfurly Shield, the Cavanaghs – 'the twa Vics' as they were described at the time in Dunedin when Scottish accents were still common – were known for their creation and advocacy of rucking. This method of attacking forward play was devised by 'old' Vic as a means of getting the most effective use out of his lighter university forwards against heavier opponents. The procedure was succinctly described by Dunedin writer and historian George Griffiths:

> To counter the disadvantages of the lightweight student pack, he had devised by 1929 the loose scrum technique, in which the first forward to a breakdown in play stepped over the tackled player, supporting forwards binding on, to ruck 'ball and all' back and start the new attack, the process being repeated until gaps appeared in the opponents' defence.[21]

Occasional critics of rucking, usually British, took the view that it created a forward-dominated game or ten-man rugby, but the Cavanaghs' intention, and invariably the result, was quite the opposite. (Teams which had bigger forwards used their bulk to gain and retain possession, making a forward-dominated game more likely.) Having enveloped the opposition forwards and fractured the defensive lines of the opposition backs, the object was to get the ball quickly out to the wings,

'Old' Vic and 'young' Vic – the Cavanaghs father and son, who gave rugby the ruck. ALLIED PRESS

It's in The Book!

This could be one of those stories covered by the phrase 'You just had to be there'. Apparently, during the latter years of the Second World War in North Africa and Italy, a bond developed between New Zealanders and South Africans. It had its roots in rugby rivalry and an unshakeable belief by one or the other that their country was superior on the rugby field.

For a generation of New Zealand and South African men, 'The Book' meant just one thing. 'The Book,' according to radio broadcaster and writer Wallie Ingram, 'was one of the most famous things to come out of the war and represented a comradeship between South Africans and New Zealanders that will stand the test of time.'[1]

Towards the end of 1942 and into 1943, New Zealand and South African troops began to have more contact, and invariably conversations began and ended with rugby. As Ingram put it, they would talk over 'a glass of Pig's Ear or some Gyppo [Egyptian] concoction' and discuss the great matches that had been and the even greater ones to come. South Africans liked to remind New Zealanders of who won the last test between the two – the Springboks did and clinched the 1937 series – and New Zealand memories mysteriously stopped a little bit short of that. Talk would get around to the merits of the three-four-one scrum versus the two-three-two and, frequently, the talk needed to be backed up by action. They'd pack down wherever they happened to be and as Ingram remarked: 'Many an Egyptian bar-tender was sure that the South Africans and New Zealanders had been out in the midday sun too long and too often.'

One of the South African soldiers, Pat Swanepoel, wrote that such rugby talk was not confined to committed rugby men. It seemed to happen whenever the soldiers of the two nations ran into each other.[2] 'Somewhere between Cassino and the Alps out of all the chaff and ragging about rugby, there came into being an imaginary volume containing the rules and general hints of the game which each side began to recommend to the other for intensive study. This volume became known as The Book.' The first real book, more of a pamphlet, was printed in July 1945, after the war in Europe was over, when a South African artillery regiment played what was left of the Milan Amatori club, a rugby offshoot of the soccer club, Inter Milan. Most Italians knew little about rugby so the book was written to explain, in simple language, what the game was all about. A noted artist among the troops, Ginger Townley Johnson, added the illustrations. 'The Book' showed befuddled-looking New Zealanders being instructed by an Afrikaner-looking man with the South African 6th Division's crest on his breast. And it carried lines such as: 'And the Springbok did verily overpower and smite the Kiwi tribesmen, saying to them "Go ye to the men of Iti land and first practice the art of Rugby with them, learning from the great and wise script which is called De Book".'

The New Zealand troops responded in kind with the assistance of official war artist Peter McIntyre. They produced a similar-looking pamphlet, with the words: 'THIS is the book!' on the cover, and within was contained the response: 'Lo! The teams moved on the face of the field and there were Kiwis crying in the scrum, "Suffer, Little Springboks and come unto us and we shall teach you the Laws of the Book".'

'The Book' was the subject of much boasting and banter during the last couple of years of the war. On the left is a page from the South African version by Ginger Townley Johnson and a New Zealand page on the right by Peter McIntyre.

All the talk in the bars was put to the test on the rugby field. The New Zealanders and South Africans played first at Rapallo on the coast near Genoa and next at Florence. In the first, the teams were merely listed as Green and Gold, and Black. In the second, they were listed as South Africa and New Zealand. 'Boy' Louw, whom Danie Craven reckoned was the best forward to play for the Springboks, coached the South Africans. They won both of the matches, although for the first, the New Zealand team had to travel overnight in an old bus that kept breaking down and they did not get to Rapallo until a couple of hours before the start. In any case, the best of the New Zealand rugby players still on active service had gone to Britain for trials for the 2nd New Zealand Expeditionary Force team – the Kiwis – or the lesser known New Zealand Services team.

Ingram described 'The Book' (whichever version it was) as being 'one of the most treasured souvenirs of the Italian campaign and no lucky Springbok or Kiwi who managed to secure a copy will ever be persuaded to part with it'.

The rugby mania permeated other sports as well. A New Zealand soldier wrote in a letter home how he was at the Eighth Army tennis championships in Trieste. 'Every time you run into a South African,' he wrote, 'he has some caustic remark to make about football, such as lending us a book on how to play . . .' He related how he watched a New Zealand private beat a 'Tommy' officer in singles and a South African leaned over and said: 'Why the hell don't you blokes stick to tennis?'[3]

Charlie Saxton and Vic Cavanagh junior with Otago and New Zealand forward Peter Johnstone.

whose job was to score tries. It was an astoundingly simple tactic in what the Cavanaghs, and their disciples, always maintained was a simple game. This was the basis of the rugby played by the Kiwis under the tutelage of captain Charlie Saxton, who had played for Otago when both Cavanaghs were in coaching harness, and which formed the underlying precept of his book, *The ABC of Rugby*.[22] Fred Allen, a member of the Kiwis, became an Auckland convert to the Otago way. Saxton and 'young' Vic Cavanagh combined in the 1950s with the development of a 'code of conduct' that was designed to encourage faster, brighter fifteen-man rugby throughout the country.[23] Saxton was a delegate to the IRB annual meeting in 1963 and reported when he returned home that he had discussed the Otago code with some members who expressed an interest in adopting part of it. Ahead of its time, it recommended among other things that loose forwards stay attached to scrums until the ball was out and that scrums called as a result of lineouts be held 15 metres in from touch.[24]

Otago won nineteen matches under the younger Cavanagh, one of the most notable eras of shield dominance. But the shield could have been lost in the second defence, against Auckland in 1947. Shield historian Lindsay Knight rated that midweek match at Carisbrook before a crowd of about 26,000 as one of the most memorable, along with the 'Battle of Solway' in 1927 and the Canterbury–Auckland match in 1985. Otago trailed 12–3 at halftime, and what helped build one of the legends of the game was not so much what happened on the field but what Cavanagh said to his players in the dressing room at halftime. Various versions have been bandied about over the years, usually passed on in the knowing rugby way by people who 'have it on good authority' but really we can only guess. One version had it that Cavanagh just looked stonily at his players until time was up and then said: 'Out you go again, girls.' Another view was that he ranted and raved in the way coaches are imagined to act but seldom do. Cavanagh himself told Knight: 'The gist of what I had to say was that in the first half they produced a second class effort, that if

At last, a seat at the top table

In 1949, more than 50 years after the formation of the national union and 45 years after the All Blacks first played a test, New Zealanders were finally allowed to sit at the International Rugby Board's table.

Even then, it was not on equal terms. England, Scotland, Ireland and Wales still had two delegates each but the newcomers, New Zealand, Australia and South Africa, were allowed just one each. It was another decade before equality was achieved.[1]

The IRB was formed in 1886 to control matches between the four 'home' countries. At other times, each of the countries could play by any old rules they liked. The IRB's early days were noted for disputes as Scotland, Wales and Ireland refused to accept English dominance. In some years, England had no one to play. In the 1888–89 season, for example, England's only international fixture was against the New Zealand Natives because the others would not bow to England's wishes. Arbitrators were called in and they decided that the playing laws that would apply in international matches would be those framed by England and that the IRB would comprise twelve members, six of them from England and two each from the other three countries. When Scotland fell out with England about arrangements for the New Zealand and Australian tours of 1905 and 1908, it proposed that each of the four countries should have equal representation. Scotland never achieved what it wanted, but it did have some success because the board decided in 1909 that England's representation would be reduced to four.

New Zealand, New South Wales, Queensland and South Africa all went to the IRB at various times before the Second World War, sometimes with proposed law changes, but generally seeking some sort of say in the running of the international game. The Anzac unions in particular gained small concessions, such as dispensation to alter some laws for domestic matches, but gained little change at all on the broader aim of equal status of all national unions. During this period, the southern hemisphere unions were members of the English union, giving them the status effectively of an English county. A significant breakthrough came in 1930 when it was agreed that the IRB would be responsible for the laws for all matches, not just internationals, and that England could no longer have the final say. They decided to form a 'Rugby Football Commission' on which each of the 'home' countries would have two delegates and the 'overseas dominions' one each. The commission's discussions would be restricted to the laws of the game only. New Zealand's chairman, Stan Dean, said the aim was a seat on the IRB and nothing less would do and it wanted nothing to do with any commission. The idea lapsed.

Throughout this period, New Zealand had to conform with the British way of playing the game or face not having any international opponents. It was this need for conformity that led to the abolition of the wing forward. Some New Zealanders wanted to go their own way and 'cut the painter', as they expressed it, rather than bow to wishes from London.

One passionate friend at court for the southern hemisphere unions was an Australian doctor, Leonard ('Bruno') Brown, who was an ear, nose and throat specialist at the North Middlesex and Charing Cross hospitals after serving with the Royal Army Medical Corps in the First World War. He combined rugby playing and administration with his medical work and became a member of the Rugby Football Union, taking over as president in 1948. He represented New South Wales on the RFU. The IRB eventually agreed with Brown's advocacy and decided in Dublin on 27 February 1948 that Australia, South Africa and New Zealand could be members. This meant an Australian union had to be formed; previously, New South Wales and Queensland (and Victoria) were colonial unions that had not joined together when the country federated in 1901. A solicitor and businessman from Durham County, Eric Watts Moses, wrote a brief history of the IRB in which he said: 'The changed attitude of the Home Unions towards the Dominions arose in part from the closer ties forged under wartime conditions, but perhaps even more from the retirement of administrators who were strongly opposed to any widening of the Board's constitution. No individual strove more keenly on the Dominions' behalf than Dr L. G. Brown . . .'[2]

The expanded board held its first meeting in March 1949 when New Zealand's sole delegate was the national union president and All Black of the early 1930s, Don Max, a farmer from Nelson. Watts Moses went to Sydney to assist in the negotiations between the Australian states for the formation of a national union, which was agreed late in 1949, and the whole new board met for the first time in March 1950. England had given up another two of its seats, which meant it was then on a par with the other 'home' unions. New Zealand's delegates thereafter argued almost annually for all countries to be represented equally and that eventually came to pass in 1958. The crowning acknowledgement of New Zealand's persistence came in 1959, when the board met in Wairakei, its first meeting outside of the British Isles.

they continued with it they would certainly be beaten . . .'[25] Otago won 18–12.

It was matches like this that brought Cavanagh's name forward when discussion turned to who should coach the New Zealand team to South Africa. The tour was originally scheduled for 1940 but cancelled because of the war. It was then scheduled for 1948 but delayed a year because of a lack of shipping in the immediate post-war years. Even though there were series against Australia in 1946 and 1947, South Africa took precedence. As the NZRFU president, Harry Strang, who managed the All Blacks in Australia in 1947, said after a union meeting: 'Only one thing will stop us going to South Africa and that is lack of transport. South Africa is the first priority.'[26]

When the tour in 1949 was confirmed, the NZRFU decided to do what it did for the 1928 tour and choose its team late the year before, based obviously on the previous year's form. There was speculation that Vic Cavanagh junior, as the most successful coach in the country at the time, should go as assistant manager – the euphemism employed in the amateur era for the position of coach. It seems to have become an article of remembered faith that rugby politics in Wellington intervened and 65-year-old Alex McDonald, one of the 1905 All Blacks, was preferred ahead of Cavanagh, who was then 39, and that the Otago man forthwith decided he wanted nothing more to do with New Zealand rugby.

That was not how it happened. When Cavanagh died in 1980, Terry McLean wrote in the *New Zealand Herald* that McDonald had intended applying for the manager's job and that he wanted Cavanagh as his coach. But the 1924 All Black, Jim Parker, who was a member of the powerful NZRFU inner circle, decided he wanted to be manager and the chairman, Alan ('Slip') Belcher, compromised by making Parker the manager and McDonald the coach.[27] When McLean wrote this, no one was left to confirm or deny whether this was in fact what happened. Just

The three men who chose the New Zealand team that went to South Africa in 1949 – Alex McDonald, Harry Strang and Norman McKenzie.

to confuse the issue, it was reported in Dunedin in 1947, a year before the decisions were made, that 'old' Vic had just returned from the national bowls tournament and while 'up north' had been shoulder-tapped to manage the All Blacks, but had declined. ('Old Vic' had also been talked about as a possible coach of the 1940 team.)[28] In any case, did young Cavanagh really want the job of coach? His widow Bessie told the Southern club historian, Winston Cooper, that when her husband heard the announcement of the two administrative appointments, he said, 'Thank goodness.' She said he never liked being away from home and that he was at the time suffering from an ulcer.[29] What really soured Cavanagh against the NZRFU was not South Africa at all, but the failure of the union to reappoint him to its South Island selection panel in 1949. He was replaced by a coach from Buller, Vernon ('Bull') Goodall, who was on the panel for two years. The decision to appoint McDonald and Parker was made in November 1948, nearly a month after the touring squad was chosen by the three national selectors, McDonald, Norm McKenzie and Harold Strang. It included eleven of Cavanagh's Otago team and, while they were away, Cavanagh still coached their replacements to retain the shield.

The NZRFU, as it had twenty years earlier, decided that the team should not include Māori because of South Africa's attitude toward non-whites, an attitude that was at the time in the process of being hardened by Daniel Malan's Nationalist Party, which had been elected in June 1948. New Zealanders did protest but not in the concerted, organised manner that would be characteristic of later years. One of the first comments in fact came eight years before the tour. Charles Bennett, a son of the first Bishop of Aotearoa, went to war as a lieutenant with the Māori Battalion. It was a part of the Second Echelon that stopped at Cape Town on the way to England. In a letter home, Bennett wrote that racial discrimination was not as bad as 'New Zealand make it out to be'.[30] He continued:

> I can't help smiling when I think . . . of all the squabbles and controversies we used to have . . . over the question of whether we should send a Maori in an All Black team for South Africa or not. After my experience here I am of the firm opinion he would be as well received here as he would be in any other country. The whole thing is a bogey of our own creation.

Around the time the all-white All Black team was chosen in 1948, a much more senior soldier than Bennett let fly. Major-General Sir Howard Kippenberger was a much-respected brigade commander during the war and had occasional command of the New Zealand Division. He had one foot blown off by a mine at Cassino in 1944 and the other had to be amputated. Kippenberger returned to service in Britain to supervise the repatriation of New Zealand prisoners of war and, in peacetime, he became editor-in-chief of the Official War Histories. But it was with another hat on, that of president of the Returned Services'

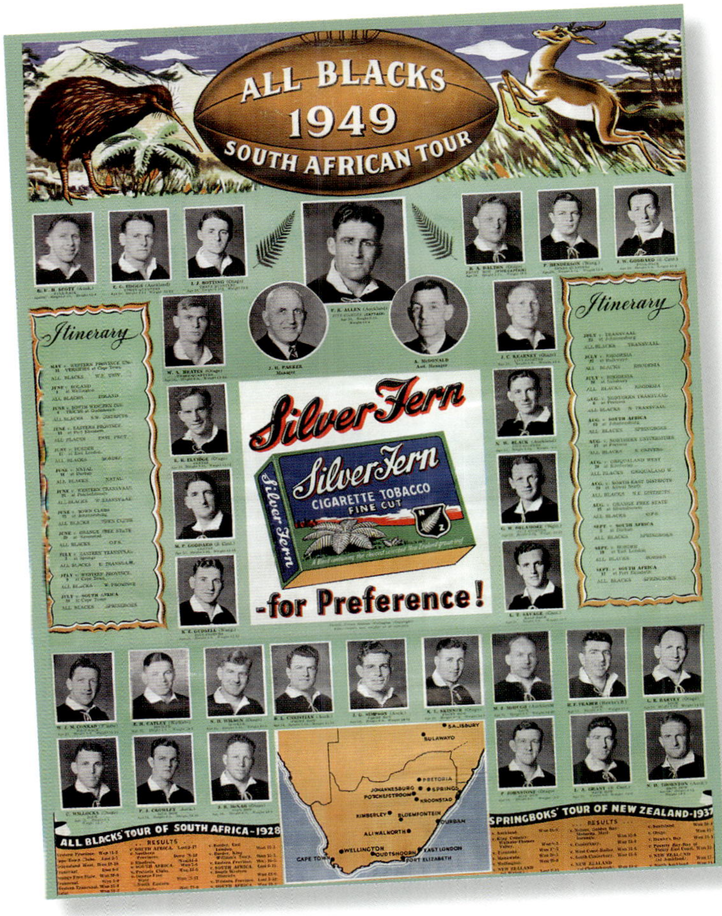

A poster and a tour fixtures card produced for the 1949 tour. Both were typical of their type and given away as promotional items. They did not have to be authorised by the New Zealand union.

Association, that he made his views known about the rugby tour. Speaking at a private function in Christchurch for ex-servicemen, he said the RSA seemed to be the only body standing for the rights of equality for Māori and he intended to make a personal protest to the NZRFU: 'I had Maoris under my command for two years and in that time they had 1500 casualties and I am not going to acquiesce in any damned Afrikanders saying they cannot go. To hell with them.'[31]

Kippenberger had to field a range of responses, some of them supportive, some not. He received a telegram from Opotiki saying: 'Maori RSA send congratulations and thanks for a useful stonk.' Author and former parliamentary librarian Guy Scholefield wrote: 'I feel very strongly that it is much more our duty to play the game with the Maoris than to pander to racial feeling in another Dominion. We have no right to send a team at all.' From the other extreme came a letter from an E. J. R. Roberts on Union Club of South Africa letterhead: 'In the name of all Afrikanders I say "to hell with you" and no damned Maoris will be allowed to enter this country.'[32] Kippenberger apologised a few days later because he said the reference to 'damned Afrikanders' was quite improper. 'I am very sorry indeed that I allowed myself to make these objectionable remarks,' he said.[33] The apology was published on the same day as reactions from two pro-Nationalist Afrikaans-language newspapers were reported. One, *Die Transvaler*, said the tour 'could no longer be considered as an attempt to strengthen friendly ties between the countries', while the other, *Die Burger*, hoped a man 'with the exceptional name of Kippenberger' was satisfied with the

All Blacks in head-on train crash

About 9 p.m. on Sunday, 31 July 1949, the night after the All Blacks had drawn 3–3 with Rhodesia in Salisbury, the train carrying the team on the 1000-kilometre trip to Pretoria rolled out of the station. Five hours later, in the rural Midlands area of Rhodesia, the steam locomotive slammed head on into a mail train heading in the opposite direction. Both drivers realised they were on a collision course and had been able to slow their trains, otherwise the result of the crash might have been much worse than it was.

One carriage was telescoped, another flung onto an embankment and the two locomotives were locked in a steely embrace; several people were injured and a coal trimmer on the train carrying the All Blacks was trapped amid steel and steam and died before he could be extracted.

Most of the passengers, including the All Blacks, were thrown from their beds or seats.

This was 1949: what the players knew as Rhodesia was in fact the crown colony of Southern Rhodesia that 30 years later became Zimbabwe, and Salisbury became Harare; in 1949 in a rugby sense, the country was regarded as a province of South Africa; eight players from there were chosen for South African teams.

When the trains hit, manager Jim Parker did what all good managers would have done and began counting heads, making sure his charges were all right. Some were shaken, but they were mostly fine. The worst of them was lock Charlie Willocks, who had a sore shoulder that cost him a place in the test team a fortnight later. Midfield back Ron Elvidge, in the last year of his medical studies, went to the front of the train to see if he could help.

The All Blacks were probably fortunate they were in three carriages at the rear of the train. Two of the South African journalists, C. J. Ferreira and John du Toit, were in a carriage in front of the team. Ferreira wrote he heard three piercing whistles from the locomotive before a terrific crash. He remembered saying to du Toit the locomotive must have hit an elephant. They put clothes on over their pyjamas and went out into the night. 'We could see the fiery glow of two engines with steam clouds rising heavenwards,' he wrote. 'The engines were intertwined and wrecked.'[1] They joined others at the point of impact trying to free the driver while rescuers, including Elvidge, did what they could for the driver's assistant. 'Ron really put up a magnificent show that night,' Ferreira wrote. 'He was helping all over the show and he tried his utmost to free

The morning after. The locomotives locked together as daylight shows how serious the 1949 crash was, and how lucky the All Blacks were. NZ SPORTS HALL OF FAME

the trapped native. They were going to amputate his leg when the necessary supplies arrived, but the native died just before that.'

Ferreira himself later collapsed and was treated by Elvidge, who diagnosed cracked ribs and delayed concussion. Ferreira stayed with the team, but other injured were taken to the nearby town of Que-Que (now Kwekwe, about 200 kilometres south-west of Harare).

A news agency report said the mail train heading towards Salisbury appeared to have overshot a siding where it was supposed to have waited while the trains crossed. The driver was apparently aware of that and applied his brakes when the engines were a few hundred yards apart. The driver of the All Blacks' train was assumed to have seen the light ahead of him and also applied his brakes. 'Fortunately the speed of both trains was thus considerably reduced,' the story said.[2]

Relief trains arrived at about six in the morning and the All Blacks were taken to Gwelo (now Gwero) about 60 kilometres away, where Parker could send a message to New Zealand saying what had happened and that no one was seriously hurt. The team finally arrived in Pretoria on the Wednesday morning, about eighty hours after leaving Salisbury. Since the players had also had a game in Bulawayo, where they were beaten by Rhodesia, they had been in trains eight nights out of eleven.

The crash came twenty years after the All Blacks in Australia in 1929 were also involved in a train crash.

publicity he had enjoyed.[34] It echoed the view of the NZRFU: 'The decision to invite only white All Blacks is . . . in the interests of the Maoris themselves . . .'

Die Transvaler had editorialised on the subject two years earlier when the tour was still scheduled for 1948 and there was a brief bout of speculation that Māori might be included. 'A team like that will not be accepted in South Africa and the New Zealand authorities should know it,' the editorial said. '. . . the Black team of New Zealand may safely stay at home. This island dominion must not think that South Africans . . . will sacrifice their principles just to be able to play a few matches.'[35] The editorial was circulated by the British Dominions Office to its diplomatic missions. The British high commissioner in Wellington, Sir Patrick Duff, wrote to the deputy under-secretary of the Dominions Office, Sir John Stephenson, and said there was a general view it was in the interests of Māori for them not to go. He then added:

> The controversy also tends to confirm New Zealanders in the complacency which they already feel at the allegedly perfect equality between Maori and pakeha. In fact of course the Maori is treated with tolerance (a more accurate description than equality) by the New Zealander because the latter is not afraid of him. He is at present no threat either in point of numbers, or by reason of his industry, education or intelligence, to the white man's supremacy.[36]

A hand-written comment on the letter, from an otherwise unidentified person with the initials 'CRP', added: 'It seems that the New Zealanders are likely to play for safety and not include any Maoris in their tour. They will probably be wise to follow this course in the interests of the Maoris themselves. There is a great deal of force in the last 2 or 3 sentences of Sir P. Duff's letter.' Duff, a former secretary to Winston Churchill, was sent to Wellington from Ottawa, where he had been deputy high commissioner. In recommending Duff to Churchill for the Wellington post, the head of the Dominions Office, Viscount Cranborne (the fifth Marquess of Salisbury), apparently said that 'one does not need a very big gun there'.[37]

The NZRFU was as silent about Kippenberger's comments and the reactions as it had been about its original decision. An *Evening Post* editorial made the point that the public still did not know how the invitation from South Africa was framed. But whatever the wording, 'New Zealand would be wise to send no team at all until a fully representative team can be received . . .'[38] A prominent Māori politician, Eruera Tirikatene, was later reported to have said the team should be known as a New Zealand European team rather than the All Blacks.[39] Perhaps he did, but when the team was farewelled from Wellington in April 1949 he was quoted as telling the players: 'You are representing New Zealand and that means you have the best wishes of my people. Perhaps on this trip of yours you will be able to convey to those you meet on the field of play our very best wishes and say "kia ora" from the Maori people.'[40] His boss, Prime Minister Peter Fraser, expressed regret 'that the exclusion of Maoris . . . had been necessary because of conditions over which New Zealand had no control'.[41]

As the tour progressed, it became even more evident – in a purely rugby sense – there were other conditions over which New Zealand had limited or no control. The tour was a disaster. Not only did the All Blacks lose each of the four tests, but a second national team picked from the stay-at-homes lost two tests to Australia. The year was the worst in terms of results for New Zealand rugby. On no other occasion has New Zealand lost six test matches in a row. The mere listing of the results in South Africa indicates that the All Blacks were not good enough; they were outplayed. That seems axiomatic when four tests have been played and four have been lost. But the mere results were too simplistic an indication of

The Rhodesia Herald

Established 1891
THE OLDEST ESTABLISHED NEWSPAPER IN RHODESIA

SALISBURY, THURSDAY, JULY 28, 1949

Price 3d.
REGISTERED AT THE GENERAL POST OFFICE AS A NEWSPAPER

RHODESIA BEAT ALL BLACKS

Two Tries Scored By Home Team

10-8 VICTORY AT BULAWAYO

From Our Correspondent
Bulawayo, Wednesday.

THE sporting prowess of Rhodesians reached its highest pinnacle in Bulawayo this afternoon, when at Hartsfield, the Rhodesian Rugby XV, playing with magnificent teamwork, convincingly defeated the All Blacks by ten points (two goals) to eight points (a goal and a try).

The highlight of their victory was the fact that although the New Zealanders had thrice previously been beaten in South Africa on their present tour, the Rhodesians are the only opponents who have so far crossed the All Blacks' line more than once.

J. Pretorius

10,000 PEOPLE SAW THE GAME

EXCELLENT CROWD CONTROL

From Our Own Correspondent
Bulawayo, Wednesday.

The orderly assembly and the dispersal of the biggest crowd Bulawayo has ever seen was a feature of a red letter day today when Rhodesia beat the All

Allen, their captain, broke through once but was checked before a dangerous move could develop by the hard tackling Rhodesian centres, Brune and van Schoor. Shortly afterwards they were awarded a penalty and Goddard just failed with his kick.

Goddard, with a good touch kick, put the New Zealanders on the attack but from a loose ruck which followed a line-out right on the home team's line, the Rhodesian forwards, with Morkel and du Rand in the van, shovelled them back. The half-time whistle went immediately afterwards.

Rhodesia 5 points, New Zealand 0.

At this stage Rhodesia had won nine scrums to the All Blacks' eight. The All Blacks had a slight advantage in the line-outs with 14 wins to Rhodesia's 12.

Tried A Drop

Rhodesia went into the attack again on the resumption and Karg tried a snap drop which went wide. Kearney finally cleared for New Zealand with a long raking touch but, nothing daunted, the home team moved on to the attack and pressed into the New Zealand half.

Here Morkel broke and bulldozed his way for some distance before flashing the ball out to Jones who was well up in support. Jones swerved past the shaken New Zealand defence to score under the posts. Karg converted amid terrific applause to give Rhodesia a clear ten points lead. (Rhodesia 10, New Zealand 0).

Kidd's Effort

when he passed, however, and Brink relieved the pressure for Rhodesia soon afterwards with a free kick.

New Zealand were again dangerous when Boggs was sent streaking towards the line from an orthodox movement. He was forced out just before the corner flag. They scored a few seconds later when Conrad broke around the scrum, but Goddard failed with the kick and Rhodesia were still ahead by two points. (Rhodesia 10, New Zealand 8).

Dalton Injured

With ten minutes to go and play moving backwards and forwards, Dalton, the All Blacks vice-captain, was injured and had to be carried off the field. He was back again soon. Rhodesia's first injury came a few minutes later when du Rand, who was playing an inspired game in the forwards, hurt his shoulder and left the field.

A penalty was awarded to New Zealand about 40 yards in front of the posts but Goddard was short with the kick.

In the last four minutes of play Rhodesia suddenly swung into the attack from a forward rush. Du Rand came back at this stage and joined in a hot attack on the New Zealand line.

Fighting Hard

The All Blacks now, instead of being able to level matters, were fighting hard to prevent Rhodesia scoring again. The home team forwards were playing with terrier-like ferocity and the final whistle went with them right on the New Zealand line. (Rhodesia 10, All Blacks 8).

The final tally of set scrums was: All Blacks 17, Rhodesia 17; Line-outs: All Blacks 29, Rhodesia 21.

The All Blacks lost all four tests to South Africa in 1949 and went down to lowly Rhodesia as well. The country (now Zimbabwe) in a rugby sense was effectively a province of South Africa and matches against it were never considered test matches.

Today the 1949 All Blacks will arrive in Wellington after their tour of South Africa. They will be given an official State "welcome home" this afternoon and, later, after a cocktail reception they will start making their way home. Auckland farewelled them on the tour; Wellington welcomes them home. Mack and Iti give these souvenir sketches to mark the return of a team that deserved greater success, but one that earned the respect of the opposition. From left (and then clockwise): F. R. Allen, J. C. Kearney, R. R. Elvidge, L. T. Savage, G. W. Delamore, P. Henderson, K. E. Gudsell, E. H. Catley, R. W. H. Scott, D. L. Christian, R. A. Dalton, H. F. Frazer. "[illegible]" is N. L. Wilson.

The All Blacks of 1949 receive a sympathetic welcome home from the Wellington morning newspaper, the *Southern Cross*. The souvenir sketches, it said, 'mark the return of a team that deserved greater success'. *SOUTHERN CROSS*, 14 OCTOBER 1949

what happened. For a start, the All Blacks were not, as the bare results indicate, outplayed. None of the test match deficits were embarrassing – four points in the first, six in the second and third and three in the fourth. Overall, New Zealand scored more tries than South Africa. The New Zealand players returned home feeling they had been let down by the NZRFU, they had had the wrong team management foisted on them and had been out-thought off the field – rather than outplayed on it – by the South Africans.

It was an unhappy bunch of All Blacks on the ship home, but they agreed to captain Fred Allen's plea to present a united front and not complain publicly. What happened on tour stayed on tour. Allen himself broke his silence only in the last year of his life. He told a tale, familiar to later teams, of lavish hospitality by the South Africans and of itineraries that had them travelling up and down the vast country by train; of referees chosen with South African interests in mind, not impartiality or neutrality. Allen listed all sorts of factors, but perhaps the most telling was that they had the wrong coach. 'The man the All Blacks desperately needed,' he was quoted as saying, 'was . . . Vic Cavanagh. We'd have certainly drawn the series and maybe won it if we'd had him with us.'[42] Another aspect of the tour that saddened Allen and the other players came to be typical of series between the two countries, especially the series in 1956 in New Zealand and 1960, 1970 and 1976 in South Africa. Allen said that the South African captain, Felix du Plessis, told his players just before the start of the first test: 'Today South Africa plays New Zealand so consider your country at war.'[43] (Du Plessis's son Morné was captain in the 1976 series.)

This was not just a melancholic look back by an All Black captain in the late evening of his years. The *Natal Mercury* said in an editorial after the third test in Durban it was an event best forgotten: 'It was not sport. It was a facet of nationalism.'[44] The leader writer presumably meant national

Evening Post cartoonist Neville Colvin seems to illustrate what most New Zealanders thought in 1949 – that the All Blacks were penalised out of the series. *EVENING POST*, 10 SEPTEMBER 1949

reputation took precedence over the good of the game; in other words, win at all costs. The same charge was levelled against the All Blacks by 'Boy' Louw, who had played against the All Blacks in 1928 and 1937. 'They have cramped their true style of game by making it subservient to victory.'[45] This was the series in which the goal-kicking of the South African prop, 'Okey' Geffin, and the marauding play of their No. 8, Hennie Muller, were most dominant. Claude King, the sports editor of the *Dominion* in Wellington, covered the tour for the New Zealand Press Association. He felt the South Africans were negative in their play and played not to lose rather than to win and that the New Zealanders were too orthodox. This was an implied criticism of McDonald's coaching. 'There was little entertainment value in the matches. The dour, grim, puritanical spirit of one side was matched by orthodoxy. The glorious spirit of adventure that makes Rugby one of the greatest of ball sports was lacking.'[46]

The South Africans forsook their usual reliance on eight heavy men in the pack and rested their strategy instead on five, employing three loose forwards to scavenge among the backs. This had the immediate effect of stifling the All Blacks' back play while gainful employment of the South African backs was not a priority. Sid Nicholls, older brother of Mark, the great All Black of the 1920s, had been in South Africa and argued that the Springbok flankers and No. 8 were nothing but the old wing forward 'rearing his ugly head again and killing the game'.[47] The South Africans had won, but Nicholls thought he knew at what cost:

> I say clearly that if such methods were adopted in New Zealand and Australia the game would die a natural death in a season because nobody would go to watch play so low in spectator value, while they could go across the road and see a match played under the league code in which emphasis is placed on the more attractive features of the game.

That was the type of argument that enveloped rugby before and after the First World War and would again in the second half of the twentieth century. Rugby authorities in different eras strived to make their game more attractive for spectators.

Broadcaster Winston McCarthy's book about the 1949 tour. The jacket was designed by James Berry, whose greater fame was as an artist and designer of postage stamps.

The All Blacks' fullback, Bob Scott, was not as sure as a goal-kicker as he usually was. There were many reasons for the All Blacks' losses, but Scott felt keenly his lack of success with kicks at goal. At one point, he recalled, he sat down in the dressing room, said, 'I'm sorry, fellows' and had 'the biggest howl of my life since childhood'.[48] The All Blacks were also handicapped by poor form or indecision or both in the inside backs. The selectors' first-choice halfback was said to have been the Aucklander, Percy Tetzlaff. But he had decided his trip to Australia in 1947 was enough of the touring life for him and he declared himself unavailable.[49] Larry Savage was halfback in three of the four tests and the captain, Fred Allen, was dropped for the last two tests after playing at second five-eighth in the first two to accommodate Jim Kearney at first-five. More than just his own play, Scott also worried about the state of the New Zealand game. He had seen the best of exciting rugby with the Kiwis in 1945–46, now he saw the worst of it with the safety-first but win-at-all-costs attitude of 1949. He could have been talking about a great span of years when he wrote: 'So decisive has been the hold of "safe" [conservative] rugby in New Zealand in the decade since the war that the great lesson of the Kiwi tour, that attack is the first virtue of rugby, has not yet wholly regained its old status in the New Zealand game.'[50]

As a broadcaster, Winston McCarthy was known for his spontaneous judgements and a seeming ability to talk long and often. But he proved he could also think about the game and, significantly, the good of the game. Like Nicholls, Scott and many others, he saw bad times ahead for rugby. 'Make no mistake about it, defensive football will come and when it does let us hope the Cavanaghs, the Saxtons, the [Merv] Corners and the other "thinkers" of rugby will plan to defeat the defeatists of open play.'[51]

Cavanagh and Saxton later developed what they called a code of conduct, but which could have been more descriptively termed 'method of play', to counter these defeatists. The aim, which they inculcated in club and provincial teams in the south, was for forwards to win the ball and for backs to have the space and time in which to run and pass. Fred Allen also adopted this method for his Auckland and New Zealand teams. But balanced against the need for enjoyment for players and entertainment for spectators was what many saw as the greater desire to win.

The British Isles visited in 1950 and New Zealand's test losses in succession nearly became seven when the first Lions test ended 9–9. The Lions – although the name was not then

Welsh and British sprinter Ken Jones fends off Ron Jarden in the British team's match against Wellington in 1950.

He would also show it again in Cardiff three years later when he scored the try that led to New Zealand's defeat against Wales. The British team in 1950 also had a first five-eighth – or out-half as the position was known in Ireland – from Belfast called Jackie Kyle whom many good judges who saw him play swore was among the best in his position to play in New Zealand, better even than the 1971 'king', Barry John.[52] The British had talented backs and were willing to use them, providing they could get the ball to them.

So too did New Zealand in 1950 and some of the rugby was spectacular. But there was one yardstick for South Africa and another for the rest of the rugby world. This point was picked up by the British team manager, 'Ginger' Osborne, in his non-rugby life a dental surgeon-captain in the Royal Navy. He said New Zealand might be in the doldrums so far as its rivalry with South Africa was concerned, but the strength of the game

First five-eighth in New Zealand, out-half in Ireland, stand-off elsewhere; whatever his position was called, Jackie Kyle was regarded as one of the greatest. WORLD SPORTS

in common use – were a team of all the talents, especially in the backs, and they showed how entertaining rugby could be, but New Zealanders wanted it to be winning rugby as well.

The All Blacks managed to win the series, which had its spectacular moments: one was when the injured New Zealand captain, Ron Elvidge, returned to the field in the third test in Wellington and scored the try that made the difference and ensured the series could not be lost. The other was a try by the Welsh wing, Ken Jones, in the fourth test in Auckland. Jones was a semifinalist in the 100 metres at the Olympic Games in London in 1948 and a silver medallist in the sprint relay: he showed his speed over 50 yards at Eden Park.

Man of war now in peace. Governor-General Sir Bernard Freyberg shakes hands with one of his Kiwis players, Johnny Simpson, before the first test in 1950. Captain Ron Elvidge is behind Freyberg making the introductions and waiting his turn is Lester Harvey.

astonished his team.[53] He was not talking about the All Blacks, but about New Zealand footballers generally:

> When they come on the field they show a sustained and intense concentration. This is most marked when they are in an attacking position. We had this impression confirmed in match after match. . . . We will always recall the complete disregard for self with which a New Zealand forward charges for the line – almost as if there were no one to stand in his path.

The British team was enormously popular on and off the field and gave the game a lift when it needed it. People wanted to see them play: in Whangarei, which then had a population of 10,000, newspapers reported 12,000 crowded into Rugby Park to see the match against North Auckland. Osborne said he was introduced to a schoolboy who had ridden 36 miles on a bike to see the team play.[54] Praise for the British team and its manner of play came also from knowing and sometimes cynical judges such as the veteran Paddy Sheehan in Auckland: 'The memory of their games remains a delicious joy. A hundred stodgy teams have come and gone since and been forgotten.'[55] Praise too from opponents: 'The highest compliment I could pay the tour of New Zealand by the British Isles team of 1950 would be to say that it was the Kiwi tour in reverse.'[56] When the New Zealand team arrived in London at the start of the 1953–54 tour, both manager Arthur Marslin and captain Bob Stuart remarked that if their tour could be regarded as half as successful and half as enjoyable as the British tour of New Zealand in 1950, they would be very satisfied.

Many of the players of 1950 and 1953 had been through the war; some had served together and some of the New Zealanders had served with British forces (Bob Stuart was in the Royal Navy, for example). Men of one country had gone to the assistance of the other. Some of the British had

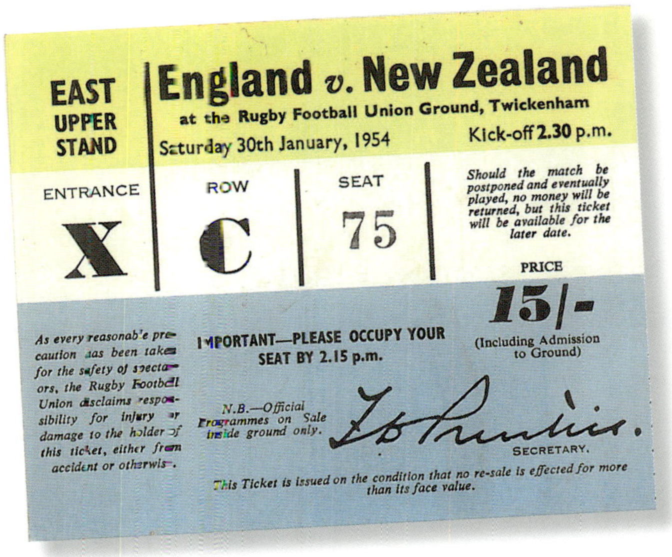

A ticket for the test at Twickenham in 1954. Note that the secretary's signature is F. D. Prentice, who was the captain of the 1930 British team in New Zealand.

been sustained by food parcels from New Zealand; New Zealand as the farm for Britain was the unquestioned pillar of the national economy; a New Zealander in a British expedition had just reached the top of the world's highest mountain. The men of rugby fraternised and were friends and remained friends for the rest of their lives. It was why a crowd of 40,000 at Athletic Park in Wellington could stand, hold hands and sing 'Auld Lang Syne' and 'Now is the Hour' as the British players stood around out on the ground, as if reluctant for their tour to end. It was why a crowd of 56,000 at the Arms Park in Cardiff could do likewise after the All Blacks had played the British Barbarians for the first time as a curtain call to their tour; why the players from both sides stood in a huge circle, holding hands (Welshman Clem Thomas with the ball stuffed up his jersey); why after the singing the crowd chanted 'We want Scott! We want Scott!' A Welsh crowd wanting a New Zealander. And as J. B. G. Thomas, who could be a helpful colleague and an acerbic critic, wrote: 'Onto the field of play went the crowd and up onto their shoulders went Scott and his captain, Bob Stuart.'[57]

Bob Scott shows off his barefooted kicking prowess in Eastbourne in 1953.

All Black wing Morrie Dixon kicks for touch against the Barbarians in Cardiff in 1954, forcing Barbarians wing Gareth Griffiths to turn back.

This was the tour on which a journalist was sceptical of reports of Bob Scott being able to kick goals barefooted so he challenged him to do so in front of a photographer. 'What will you give me?' asked Scott. 'Three attempts for a bob [a shilling]?' 'Certainly,' said the reporter. The first attempt from halfway was short; Scott moved a little to the right for the next kick, but still on halfway. As soon

Lock Nelson Dalzell, a lone ranger against England in 1954. Dalzell was rugby's equivalent of aristocracy – he was father-in-law of one All Black, Graeme Higginson, brother-in-law of another, Alan Elsom, and grandfather of three more, the Whitelock brothers Sam, Luke and George.

as he'd kicked the ball, he said: 'That's it. That's it.' And it was. The journalist offered Scott half a crown. 'No, no,' he said. 'Professionalism!'[58]

By the demanding standards of New Zealand rugby, standards which require all matches be won, the tour of 1953–54 was a failure: four matches were lost, two in Wales and two in France, and two were drawn. That was out of 36 matches over five months. By the end, the concern of the 'assistant manager' (coach), Arthur Marslin, and the manager, Norm Millard, was not so much the results but how they were achieved. Too many of the sides they played, they thought, adopted spoiling tactics, which was a common enough strategy when playing touring sides. Plenty of New Zealand provincial teams did it over the years too. It was all designed to stop the other team from scoring. Larry Montague, sports editor of the *Manchester Guardian* and therefore more conscious of 'the other game' than London-based writers, wrote that the only way rugby could resist the challenge of league would be by pursuing open attack.[59] That was precisely the argument of Scott, Saxton, Allen and others reared on the qualities of the Kiwis. But even more than that, the overriding ambition of New Zealand rugby was to win and never was this more evident, more compelling, than in 1956.

Above: Richard ('Tiny') White reaches high in a lineout in the crucial third test in Christchurch in 1956. The man of the test, Kevin Skinner, is No. 13. The masses of spectators at the tests were replicated in the provincial games, such as Wellington (below) where wing Tom Katene tackles South African wing Tom van Vollenhoven.

11 Springboks, race and a new era

On the Tour, on the Tour, on the Tour,
You can play if you're racially pure.
All Whites together, we're Birds of that Feather,
That's how we got picked for the Tour.[1]

That indefatigable campaigner against racism wherever he found it, Trevor Richards, once remarked that even the Communist Party was in favour of the tour by South Africa in 1956.[2] Richards gave no source for this belief, but there is no reason to doubt him. The only surprise would be that the party even had a view in 1956 about whether the Springboks should or should not tour. Arguing against going to South Africa without Māori was one thing; having the South Africans in New Zealand was quite another. If there were voices raised in protest about the 1956 tour, they were but whispers compared with the thunder of a perceived national need to welcome and beat the Springboks. Thousands of people – 'ordinary' New Zealanders – lined streets, gathered outside hotels or rugby grounds and waited at railway stations to see and hear the South Africans; crowds were frequently described as being the biggest since the first visit by the Queen and Prince Philip three summers before.

It could not have been so, but everyone seemed to have a passionate interest in the tour; every small boy, and some not so small, seemed to know the name of every South African player (and one small boy, Warwick Roger, recalled the tour years later with great fondness).[3] Everyone who had eyes to read and ears to hear seemed to have an opinion about who should be in the local team to confront the Springboks and, most important of all, who should be in the New Zealand team. At stake was provincial pride and national honour. From the first week in June until the first week in September, New Zealand was engrossed in the outcome of a series of rugby matches. By the standards of earlier years, and by those of years yet to come, the rugby was often stodgy and pallid; the ball seemed forever

A familiar sight to railway porters and passengers during the heyday of rail travel.

Crowds said to be surpassed only for the Queen's visit two years before lined New Plymouth streets for a procession of floats on the morning of Taranaki's match against South Africa. More than 50 floats, including one from neighbouring Waikato, were involved. The players watched it all from their hotel balcony (top left).

to be within the forwards and the outside backs were nothing more than necessary appendages. But not knowing the outcome provided the excitement and tension rather than the quality of play.

From the first match, against Waikato in Hamilton, to the last, the fourth test in Auckland, people slept outside grounds to buy tickets. When the gates opened, usually between ten and eleven o'clock in the morning, they raced in to get a 'possie', the closer to halfway the better. They had with them their own refreshments – sandwiches wrapped in brown paper and tied with string; sometimes in tin lunch boxes, often accompanied by Thermoses of tea. Some more experienced in the ways of the world laced the tea with spirits, some brought in crates of beer and, when the beer was finished, the crates could be mounted for an elevated view and for the men, the bottles could be used to avoid a struggle through the crowds to the toilets. Small boys and girls, their lapels draped with black and white ribbons sometimes topped by a rosette of the same colours or sometimes with a small metal badge bearing a photo of the team, made their way through the forests of legs collecting the empties.

After the games, people might hang around for a glimpse of the players in the late afternoon sun, then they'd head home and there wait until it was time to go to the corner shop to buy a copy of the 'sports special' – the late Saturday edition of the afternoon paper that would have all the stories and photos about the big game in the afternoon. It was the *8 O'Clock* in Auckland, the *Sports Post* in

Wellington, the *Star-Sun Sports* in Christchurch, the *Star Sports* in Dunedin, others in other towns and cities. If the game was in a distant town, people would gather round radios and listen to the commentary on the YA network. If it was a New Zealand game, or the Universities or the Māori team, the commentator would be Winston McCarthy and his familiar voice – 'List-en . . . wait for it . . . it's a goal!!!!' Otherwise the commentator would be a local, getting broadcast around the country for perhaps the first time.

Grounds then, and for a good many years after, did not provide only allocated seating. The more people could be crammed into a ground, the happier the administrators were. But the urge to watch the South Africans, or to watch them get beaten, led to passages in newspapers like this, which could have been from 1981:

> People were crushed and trampled in wild scenes of near-panic at the gates of Lancaster Park early this afternoon. All available police reinforcements were rushed to the park when hundreds of people tried to storm the turnstiles in the face of a nearly equal number who were struggling to leave the jam-packed ground. People dropped like flies in the struggling crowd, said police officers.[4]

People wanted to get out because it was too dangerous to stay in; people wanted in because it was unbearable to be out. Police said some were taken to hospital and that 'dozens' fainted. They estimated the crowd at 51,000; the public address announcer said 53,000; the controllers of the ground, the Victory Park Board, went for a much more conservative 45,000. There are two remarkable aspects to the story. This was not the

Standing room only at Rugby Park in New Plymouth in 1956 when the South Africans came to play.

The crowd spills on to the ground after the epic third test against South Africa at Lancaster Park in Christchurch.

test match, but the game against Canterbury. And the three separate stories about the crowding and the fainting and the panic were on the back page of the Saturday evening sports paper, not the front page. That was reserved for the game. Always the game.

Journalist Terry McLean, who covered Springbok tests that year for the first time, later wrote it was the year that New Zealanders 'went to bed praying that their men would beat those bastards of Boers, one match after another. In terms of nationalist fervour mounting to hatred, it was the worst tour rugby has ever known.'[5]

For all the burning desire to beat the South Africans, New Zealanders felt the need to maintain the polite courtesy of a host, to welcome the visitors as friends. The programme for the third test in Christchurch, the match that effectively decided the series and represented the apex of New Zealand emotion, carried a bold heading: 'Our friends – the Springbok players'. This courtesy and an official aversion to any incidents similar to the 1921 Māori game were apparently the motivation behind an entreaty to the Māori team to 'take it easy'. The South Africans had been beaten in their previous two matches, in the

'TP' always at the front of a ruck of writers

Hundreds, perhaps thousands of people, mostly men but more than a few women, have made it their business over nearly 150 years to write about rugby in New Zealand. Some have been cynical professionals, some enthusiastic amateurs; some have been uncompromising critics, some mere acolytes; some have been knowledgeable, others less so. They wrote for newspapers, magazines, books and sometimes just for their own enjoyment. Some who wrote have shelves of books as their legacy, while others have just a fading clipping or a blog that few may or may not read. Then there were all those living in other countries who found the need, and sometimes the urge, to write about rugby in New Zealand. They were fewer in number, but there were still the good, the bad and the indifferent; the informed, the misinformed and the ill-informed.

Terry McLean pictured in the 1980s. NORMAN SMITH

It would be impractical to attempt to canvass the rugby writers from such a long period. But there is one name that any serious history of New Zealand rugby cannot ignore: Terence Power McLean, 'TP', 'Terry', 'Teepers' as he was sometimes irreverently called, or Sir Terry as he was known in his final years. McLean wrote about rugby for the best part of half a century and, for about thirty of those years, he was the best-known rugby writer in New Zealand. In that part of the country that called the *New Zealand Herald* its morning newspaper, McLean's name was practically synonymous with rugby. Wherever the game was played by New Zealanders, he was there; whatever the issue, whether team selection or the tackle ball law, McLean had an opinion on it. To the rest of the country, at least from 1954, he was the cove – a McLean word – who wrote books about rugby tours. If it was the All Blacks in Britain or South Africa, or the Lions and others in New Zealand, the tour did not seem complete until McLean's book was published, the last word on a tour.

McLean's first taste of the rugby reporting life came in 1930 when he was just seventeen and he assisted older brother Gordon, who covered the Great Britain team tour for the British news agency, Reuter. The McLean name in rugby was already well established through another brother, Hugh, who was an All Black between 1930 and 1936. Terry had the singular experience at his first test, at Eden Park on 26 July 1930, of watching brother Hugh score two tries in New Zealand's 15–10 win. When McLean left school and entered

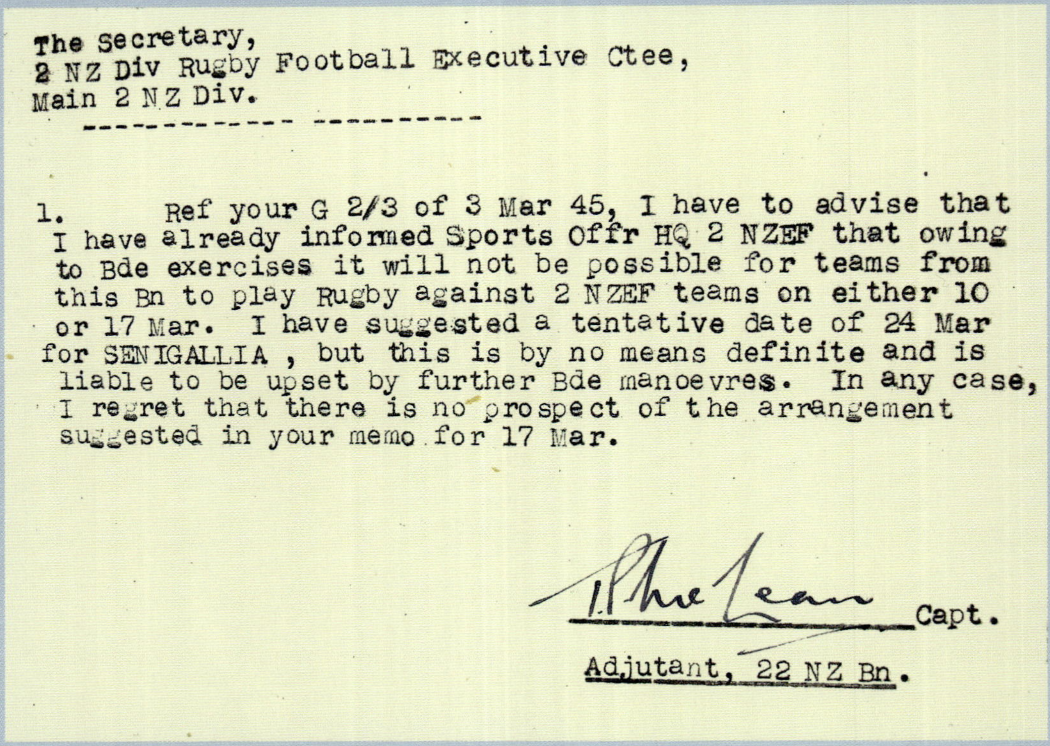

The Secretary,
2 NZ Div Rugby Football Executive Ctee,
Main 2 NZ Div.

1. Ref your G 2/3 of 3 Mar 45, I have to advise that I have already informed Sports Offr HQ 2 NZEF that owing to Bde exercises it will not be possible for teams from this Bn to play Rugby against 2 NZEF teams on either 10 or 17 Mar. I have suggested a tentative date of 24 Mar for SENIGALLIA , but this is by no means definite and is liable to be upset by further Bde manoevres. In any case, I regret that there is no prospect of the arrangement suggested in your memo for 17 Mar.

T. P. McLean Capt.

Adjutant, 22 NZ Bn.

The adjutant of 22 Battalion of the 2nd New Zealand Expeditionary Force, Captain Terry McLean, tells the division's sports office that the war must come before rugby. 2ND NEW ZEALAND EXPEDITIONARY FORCE RUGBY (DA 21.1/9/G2/3/1, PARTS 1 AND 2), ARCHIVES NEW ZEALAND

daily journalism, he turned to the bright but brief *Sun* in Auckland where brother Gordon was a leader writer. The *Sun* set after just three years and one of its luminaries, Robin Hyde, noted the young McLean in passing, saying he went on to the Hastings *Tribune* 'and had a hectic time in the quake four months later'.[1] The 'hectic time' included McLean losing his job and, for the rest of the 1930s, he led a peripatetic life, popping up at newspapers here and there; he was grinding out all manner of sports stories by the end of the decade for the Wellington Saturday-night paper, the *Sports Post*. It and its equivalents around the country were eagerly awaited in the early Saturday evenings because they contained the first news of all the day's sport (and racing) and generally had magazine-style sections as well.[2]

Army service during the Second World War helped shape the rest of McLean's life. In its most literal sense, the war led to Ron Horton (later chairman and managing director of the *Herald*-owning family firm, Wilson and Horton) being impressed by McLean's writing for services papers and offering him a job. McLean signed on with the *Herald* and stayed with it the rest of his working life. He also wrote for innumerable other publications under various pseudonyms, perhaps the most transparent being Phil Allan in the weekly *Rugby News*. McLean also used the name 'Harold Power' at times but chose not to in Britain in 1978 when a New Zealand reporter with the real name of Terry Power (nicknamed 'TP2') also covered the tour – and on one occasion Terry Power scooped the former Harold Power. McLean seemed never to go to any lengths to conceal his style along with his identity – when a report about accusations of thuggery against the All Blacks ended with the line, 'Over to you, Eliza Doolittle', other rugby journalists had no doubts about who was the author.[3]

As with thousands of others, the war left its mark on McLean: for the rest of his life, he talked, walked and acted like a returned serviceman, a type recognisable then but not so much now.

He – and they – carried on their lives with a sense of duty, a view of nationhood and a code of behaviour that may seem quaint by modern standards. There was also an invisible but unshakeable bond between men of the same calibre. McLean during his later journalism career had an enormous advantage over other rugby writers not necessarily because of his prodigious talent and output (although that was enough in itself) but also because he was a contemporary of men who were running rugby: he served with the likes of Jack Sullivan, Tom Morrison and Charlie Saxton, and he had the same military training as Ces Blazey. They may have played together in army teams, drank together in Italian bars, fought together from river to river in the northern advance in Italy. He and they came from an era in which one dressed for dinner and one wore a tie more often than not.

McLean did not always benefit from such contacts – there were frequently disagreements between them – but they gave him an understanding and knowledge that was beyond younger and less experienced reporters. McLean's relationship with Sullivan when the latter was the NZRFU chairman was more frosty than friendly, but there was a mutual respect. It may have been significant that McLean had been an officer, Sullivan not; equally it may have been that Sullivan knew well that McLean was a selector of army teams during the war and, by being a journalist later, had somehow crossed a line.

McLean's first overseas venture with a New Zealand team was the 1953–54 tour of the United Kingdom and other places. He was seconded to the Press Association for the tour and he and radio commentator Winston McCarthy were the only New Zealand 'pressmen' throughout the long tour. It led to McLean's first tour book and the beginning of a pattern that lasted until 1978 and his retirement from daily journalism, although he continued writing books until 1991. (McLean's long association with McCarthy also led to his being interviewed at length by lawyers when McCarthy sued a South African journalist, Fred Labuschagne, for defamation. The case was settled out of court and McCarthy benefited financially.)[4] His last tour was to Japan in 1987 when he was 74 and, while still active, he was beginning to show the wear and tear of the touring life. Much against his will, his colleagues helped him with his luggage. One of the All Blacks at one point asked one of the younger journalists: 'Who's that old bloke with you guys?' By then, he'd seen more rugby than that player was ever likely to see, certainly more All Black games than anyone, written more books about rugby than anyone, and knew more about the game. By then, he was well known among the press at least as 'the doyen'. He modestly complained about such a title, but secretly he was chuffed. Likewise, he was outwardly modest and inwardly delighted with his knighthood, though he would have preferred to have been a knight of one of the ancient British orders rather than the new-fangled New Zealand one.

McLean wrote eighteen tour books, a genre that is now practically extinct, three books with players or coaches (George Nepia, Fred Allen, Bob Scott), one tour book with a British broadcaster, Ian Robertson, two general rugby books (*Great Days in New Zealand Rugby* and *Rugby Legends*), an eclectic collection of newspaper stories published as *The Best of McLean* and his final book, a history of the All Blacks published in England that was designed to cash in on the second World Cup. Among other writing there was a general history of New Zealand sport, *Silver Fern*.

Spectators at Eden Park fill in the time on Māori rugby's big day in 1956. It turned out to be a match to forget; the South Africans won 37–0. EP/1956/1793-F, EVENING POST COLLECTION, ALEXANDER TURNBULL LIBRARY

third test in Christchurch and by New Zealand Universities in Wellington, when they went to Eden Park to play a Māori team for the first time since 1921. The Māori included two who had played in the third test, captain Bill Gray and lock Stan Hill, plus another two who were in the test reserves, Pat Walsh and Keith Davis. Great things were expected of the Māori and thousands made the trip to Eden Park, there to be marshalled into designated iwi seats by Rangi Royal, a Maori Battalion hero from the Second World War, and twenty-year-old Howard Morrison, a promising entertainer and son of Temuera, who played for New Zealand Māori.[6] But the Māori threat proved to be empty. The South Africans recorded their biggest win of the tour, 37–0.

Fifty-four years later, in 2010 when the centenary of formal Māori rugby was marked, the 1956 fullback, Muru Walters, told a radio host, Willie Jackson (himself a descendant of an All Black), that the players had been told they must not win 'for the future of rugby'. The bearer of the message, according to Walters, was the Māori Affairs Minister, Ernest Corbett. But Stan Hill did not have the same recollection as Walters. He said he knew Ernie Corbett personally and never saw him before the match, either at Titirangi where the Māori players gathered or at Eden Park. Corbett's intervention, if it occurred, seems likely to have been a ham-fisted effort to avoid any type of incident à la 1921, when reports of and comments after the Springboks–Māori game inflamed the race relations issue.

The public face of friendship between the visitors and visited was not always all it seemed. Ces Blazey, then a rugby administrator on the rise, was chairman of the Universities Rugby Council, whose team beat the South Africans. He arranged at the after-match function that the two teams would get together later that night. The Springboks were at the Hotel St George and the students at the Midland, a now-demolished hotel just an easy stroll

The two men who led the South Africans, manager Danie Craven and captain Basie Viviers.

Bench seats from cars pressed into service for the first South African test in Dunedin.

away down Willis Street and along Lambton Quay. But the students waited in vain. Blazey eventually went to the St George and found that the South African manager, Danie Craven, was furious at his players for losing and had confined them to barracks. Rather than let them socialise with the students, he gave them a blackboard lecture of where they went wrong. For all the public portrayal of the Springboks being affable chaps mixing in with New Zealanders – a poi dance here, a hongi there; a vintage car parade here, a sing-song there – newspapers also reported that they were clannish and standoffish, speaking Afrikaans in front of their New Zealand hosts. But most New Zealanders did not come into contact with them; they merely observed or listened from afar. For the people of Waikato and Canterbury (where the Springboks lost) or Taranaki (where they drew), the days of 1956 were memorable days. But the most talked-about match was the third test because it was the one upon which the series outcome depended.

The All Blacks had won the first test in Dunedin, a dull affair brightened only by an intercept try by the New Zealand wing, Ron Jarden – and the South Africans won the second in Wellington. On the Thursday after the second test, the ruling council of the New Zealand union had a special meeting with the selectors present. Newspaper reporters suspected the rugby politicians wanted a say in the selection but Cuth Hogg, the chairman, said the selectors had already decided on their third test team before they went to the meeting. 'No attempt was made to discuss the team or the merits of individual players,' he said. '. . . there was no suggestion that there should be any influence on the selectors . . .'[7] So why the meeting seemed a reasonable question.

Among the changes was the introduction of the big-kicking Waikato fullback, Don Clarke.

N. Z. Rugby Football Union
TEMPORARY SEATING TICKET
(UNRESERVED)
ON THE WESTERN SIDE ON GROUND
ATHLETIC PARK
SOUTH AFRICA v. NEW ZEALAND
SATURDAY, 4th AUG., 1956
15/-
Secretary: N.Z.R.F.U.
Holder of Ticket to be admitted at North or South end, Rintoul Street entrance.
This portion to be retained by holder and shown on demand.

A 1956 second test ticket to a reserved part of the western bank at Athletic Park. The ticket valued at 15 shillings is equivalent to about $70 today.

The tale of the tape

When the New Zealand team to play South Africa in the first test in 1956 was announced, the forward pack was described as the most powerful yet selected. The *Dominion*'s sports editor, Claude King, who made the observation, reckoned the selectors' intention was to 'pound the opposition in the forwards'.[1] King said the forwards averaged 15 stone 3 pounds (96.6 kilograms) and seven of the eight forwards were more than six feet (1.82 metres). The biggest of the forwards was the Lyttelton accountant, Bob Duff, at 104.8 kilograms and 1.9 metres. The only forward who did not make it to six feet was Morrinsville farmer Ian Clarke, a prop. Huge in its time, no doubt, but not so big when compared with the team chosen to play the first test against South Africa in 2013. Comparisons of height and weight can be seen in the table opposite.

All Blacks 1956 and 2013

POSITION	PLAYER	HEIGHT	WEIGHT
Fullback	Pat Walsh	1.75	78.5
	Israel Dagg	1.86	86
Left wing	Ron Jarden	1.72	83.9
	Julian Savea	1.93	105
Centre	Ross Brown	1.75	73.5
	Conrad Smith	1.86	94
Right wing	Maurie Dixon	1.72	73.5
	Ben Smith	1.86	90
2nd 5/8	Bill Gray	1.8	74.4
	Ma'a Nonu	1.82	105
1st 5/8	Robin Archer	1.75	73.5
	Dan Carter	1.78	96
Halfback	Pat Vincent	1.75	78.5
	Aaron Smith	1.71	81
No. 8	Stan Hill	1.87	99.8
	Kieran Read	1.93	109
Flanker	John Buxton	1.85	90.7
	Sam Cane	1.89	103
Lock	Ray White	1.89	101.2
	Sam Whitelock	2.02	115
Lock	Bob Duff	1.9	104.8
	Brodie Retallick	2.04	119
Flanker	Don McIntosh	1.87	94.3
	Liam Messam	1.9	105
Prop	Ian Clarke	1.77	92.1
	Owen Franks	1.85	119
Hooker	Ron Hemi	1.82	90.7
	Dane Coles	1.84	108
Prop	Mark Irwin	1.83	97.1
	Tony Woodcock	1.84	119

The All Blacks line up for a team shot before the second test in 1956 against South Africa. Back row: Don McIntosh, Nev MacEwan, Morrie Dixon, Ron Jarden, Ross Brown, Bill Clark, Bob Duff, Pat Vincent. In front: Ian Clarke, Richard White, 'Mick' Bremner, Pat Walsh, Dennis Young, Bill Gray, Frank McAtamney.

A monthly magazine of the time reflects the standing of Ron Jarden, New Zealand and Wellington wing.

Previously, the All Blacks had relied on a part-time goal-kicker, Jarden. Now they decided a specialist was needed. But another change also had a much talked about significance: the return of the prop, Kevin Skinner, who had come out of retirement a few months before. Two of the selectors, Tom Morrison and Jack Sullivan, separately travelled to watch him play and satisfy themselves of his readiness. The folklore has grown up since that New Zealand won the third test because Skinner (a boxer who won the national heavyweight championship in 1947) 'sorted out' the South African front row. These were the days when it was freely understood that players administered justice if referees did not. The Springbok forwards in the first two tests had been allowed to get away with intimidation; in the third, Skinner drew the line. When a South African prop, Chris Koch, tried to interfere in the New Zealand lineout, Skinner hit him. When the other prop, Jaap Bekker, tried to illegally disrupt Skinner in a scrum, he hit him too. 'It led to a scuffle which was soon sorted out and

One of the significant test debutants in the series against South Africa was Don Clarke. This photo of him preparing to kick was later in his career, on tour in 1963. At right, Clarke and the South African captain, Basie Viviers, swap jerseys after the fourth test. In the background, forwards coach Bob Stuart chats to Peter Jones and obscured in the background at left is the New Zealand union chairman, Tom Morrison.

that was that,' Skinner said.[8] New Zealand won the fight and the test.

The All Blacks could not lose the series after Christchurch; with victory in Auckland, they could win it. New Zealand's only try in the winning scoreline of 11–5 was scored by Peter Jones, a Northland fisherman who burst from a lineout with the ball and ran . . . and ran. It was about 35 metres, but it is the way of such things that they can be often exaggerated. In some retellings, Jones ran 50 metres. The try contributing to South Africa's first series loss in 60 years was memorable enough. But Jones's after-match comment on staid state radio made it unforgettable. The crowd chanted for Don Clarke and Jones to go to the microphone after the game. Clarke got there first: 'Thanks everybody,' was his complete 'speech'. Then it was Jones: 'I hope I never play in as tough a game again. I'm absolutely buggered.' The crowd roared with laughter and the announcer, after a bit of a titter, said: 'Well, we'll ignore that.'[9] But of course it could not be ignored and Jones had found his place in rugby legend.

What the series win in 1956 meant to New Zealand. Cartoonist Tom Mayne in the Christchurch Saturday-night paper, the *Star-Sun Sports*, explains.

Eden Park at the end of the fourth test against South Africa. E. A. WHITE COLLECTION

So too did the All Blacks of 1956 because they beat the Springboks; it was New Zealand's first series win against South Africa. There remained just one task left: to beat the South Africans there. The losses of 1949 ran deep and New Zealand rugby people, of the 1956 generation and later, would not rest easy until that task was completed. New Zealand rugby would not be seen as the best in the world – by New Zealanders themselves – until victory was achieved under the hot sun and on the hard grounds of South Africa. There were other opponents, of course, Australia most frequently and the Lions every so often; even the individual European countries began touring, but South Africa always waited in the rugby shadows.

Even at the time of the next big tour, the 1959 British team that was known, finally and universally as the Lions, South Africa still lurked. A fortnight before the Lions' first game, the NZRFU council decided against including Māori in its team for the tour of South Africa the following year. As for the 1928 and 1949 tours, the union argued it was in the best interests of Māori players. By this time, unlike the earlier occasions, a growing number of people disagreed and said so. Opposition to sport with South Africa gained organisation, most notably with the formation of the Citizens' All Black Tour Association, led by a Wellington surgeon, Rolland O'Regan (father of the later Ngāi Tahu leader, Sir Tipene O'Regan). Opposition too came from the New Zealand Council of Churches, whose secretary was a Presbyterian minister, Alan Brash (father of the later National Party leader and Reserve Bank governor, Don Brash). 'It is an almost unbelievable

Bard of the Happy Isles

Tom Pearce was a prop and a trucker who had a reputation for speaking in a manner that left no doubts about his meaning. He played 40 games for Auckland, three national trials, played for the North Island twice and was a reserve for the All Blacks in 1937. After his playing days, he took his prop's pragmatism to administration and served both the Auckland and New Zealand unions for many years. He was also chairman of the Auckland Regional Authority for a time.

He had the nuggety build and cauliflower ears of a prop, but beneath the barrel chest beat the heart of a poet. This became most evident when he was manager of the team going to South Africa in 1960 and, amid the politicians and diplomats of a typical Wellington farewell to a rugby team, he rose to speak.

Pearce, who was then 47, stunned and impressed his audience when he talked of the task confronting the team in South Africa, and then launched into the last third of the stirring monologue, 'Ulysses', written by Alfred, Lord Tennyson:

> Come, my friends,
> 'Tis not too late to seek a newer world.
> Push off, and sitting well in order smite
> The sounding furrows; for my purpose holds
> To sail beyond the sunset, and the baths
> Of all the western stars, until I die.
> It may be that the gulfs will wash us down:
> It may be that we shall touch the Happy Isles,
> And see the great Achilles, whom we knew.
> Tho' much is taken, much abides; and tho'
> We are not now that strength which in old days
> Moved heaven and earth; that which we are, we are;

The 'bard of the happy isles', Tom Pearce, with the ruler of South African rugby, Danie Craven, in 1960.

> One equal temper of heroic hearts,
> Made weak by time and fate, but strong in will
> To strive, to seek, to find, and not to yield.

The crescendo Pearce reached on the last line almost brought the house down, in the words of a reporter present.[1] The captain, Wilson Whineray, and the coach, Jack Sullivan, both expressed their appreciation of Pearce's oratory and their gratitude that he would bear the speaking load in South Africa, and not them.

When the team arrived in Sydney a few days later, the players were all but ignored but the manager was not. Pearce was described as 'Wild Tom Pearce' and the reporter went on to relate how he used Tennyson's words to describe the challenge of their tour. 'Don't make me out to be an arty type,' Pearce was quoted as saying.[2]

His eloquence took on a different tack later in the tour in Potchefstroom in the Afrikaner heartland about 100 kilometres south of Johannesburg. The local mayor spoke to the players at a reception in Afrikaans and then repeated himself (it was assumed) in English. Pearce thought he could do the same and the *Weekly News* reported:

> With imposing gestures and impressive mien, he reeled off a string of Maori placenames. At each pause, he would remark, 'Which means, Mr Mayor . . .' Waipapakauri . . . Hikurangi . . . Whakatane . . . Aotearoa . . . kia ora katoa . . . they all came out. It was, in fact, a remarkable feat on Mr Pearce's part to remember so many names on the spur of the moment.[3]

Pearce was cornered by a Durban journalist and, unusually for a manager of the All Blacks, the talk was not about rugby. Pearce spoke of his love of the sea, his exploits in the surf for which he was known in New Zealand, and how he used to go out and catch 200 or 300 snapper in an hour. And of course the talk turned to poetry. His favourite, he thought, might be Tennyson or Shakespeare and the best Australian was Banjo Paterson. 'But don't go calling me what the boys do – the Travelling Bard.'[4]

Pearce had decided views on how rugby should be played. The key, of course for a prop, was the forwards, always the forwards. One of his daughters, Sandra Coney, once quoted him as writing, 'What is this bright open rugby (but) the froth on the beer, the icing on the cake?' Without surging forwards, Auckland rugby 'will have all the glitter and glamour of a modern jerry built house on a rotten foundation'.[5]

A 1959 poster advertising a meeting of the Citizens' All Black Tour Association which sought merit selection of the New Zealand team to go to South Africa the following year. Chairman Rolland O'Regan, the father of future Māori leader Sir Tipene O'Regan, advertised the presence of former All Blacks George Nepia, Lui Paewai and Vince Bevan and Manahi 'Doc' Paewai, a halfback who played for several provinces and New Zealand Māori. The protest meeting was on the Wednesday night before the first British Isles test in Wellington. EPH-D-RACIAL-1959-01, ALEXANDER TURNBULL LIBRARY

example of blindness to all human values,' Alan Brash said when he learnt of the NZRFU decision.[10] But a Māori member of the council, Ralph Love, supported the decision. The fact he was a noted Labour Party supporter and worker (he was secretary to the member for Southern Māori and cabinet minister Eruera Tirikatene at the time) demonstrated how the vexed issue of South Africa did not follow predictable party lines.

At least with the Lions the rugby could be appreciated for its own sake without accompanying controversy, aside from an odd murmur about Irish dislike at being lumped under the name British. It helped too that New Zealanders believed, grounded in the tours of 1930 and 1950, that while the Lions represented the best of British (and Irish) they were not quite the playing threat the Springboks were. The Lions off the field were also like 'us', even given their regional or Home Counties accents. The team of 1959, captained by an Irishman, Ronnie Dawson, proved to be more formidable than was expected. In fact, were it

The Lions' nemesis in Dunedin, Don Clarke, scores his try in the second test at Athletic Park in Wellington. Lions defenders are Dickie Jeeps (left), Malcolm Price and John Young (right). Referee Cecil Gillies is obscured by Young.

not for the big-kicking fullback from Waikato, Don Clarke, the Lions might have won the series.

The Lions, who had been beaten only by Otago in the first weeks, should have won the first test. They scored four tries – in 1959, four tries was a lot. The All Blacks had had four tries scored against them in a test only three times previously (twice by Australia and once by South Africa). But the 17 points gained from the four tries, a conversion and a penalty goal were not enough to beat New Zealand, for whom Clarke kicked six penalty goals. A final score of 18–17 was seen as a gross injustice. The capacity crowd at Carisbrook made known its feelings. For a time, the crowd chanted 'Red! Red! Red!' as it collectively realised the injustice of a team scoring four tries to none being on the losing end. Ironically, Clarke put the All Blacks in a winning position in the second test as well, but this time with a diving try. Only in the third test in Christchurch, which was won 22–8, could New Zealand be said to be dominant. They lost the fourth test by the Lions scoring three tries (nine points) to two penalty goals from Clarke.

New Zealand was still twenty years away from agreeing to 'neutral' referees – by definition, referees should be neutral so the term should be 'third-country referees' – and inevitably, there was criticism. Bryn Thomas, the much-travelled sports editor of the *Western Mail* in Cardiff, said he would not call New Zealand referees biased, but he

The call of the wild

Wherever and whenever the All Blacks have played, they have been accused of cheating. Sometimes the accusations have been justified, sometimes not. Take the match against Combined Western Province Universities in Cape Town on the tour in 1960, for example. The referee, a W. J. Beckman, came from the South-West Districts, in the Western Cape. The principal town in the area is Oudtshoorn, best known for its ostrich population. This is the bird that lies flat and hides its face in the child-like belief it makes itself invisible.

The All Blacks did not play all that authoritatively for their 14–3 win, but it was decisive enough and no one queried which side was the better. But Beckman had no doubt which side's players were the most prolific infringers. He gave 18 penalties against New Zealand and just two against the local side. Even that on its own was not all that significant. The All Blacks had encountered home-town refereeing many times before.

But Beckman came up with a novel explanation for the constant cheating (as he saw it). He told an Afrikaans-language newspaper, *Vaderland*, that the All Blacks deliberately broke the laws when they, ostrich-like, thought he could not see them.[1] When a scrum went down early in the match, he said he heard the cry, 'Socks! Socks!' come from the depths of the black pack.

'They were warning each other that they could see my yellow socks and would be wise not to attempt anything illegal,' he told the paper. Beckman gave the paper a list of infringements for which he had awarded penalties and most of them were for offences in or around scrums or rucks.

A tour card for 1960 produced by a Wellington company, Hope Bros.

Tom Pearce, the All Blacks' manager, later castigated Beckman for speaking publicly. Referees are supposed to suffer in silence. But the players just laughed. 'Socks' was one of those words that players dream up as a call to others, mostly in lineouts but frequently in other play as well. The call 'socks', rather than drawing attention to the referee's attire, was a signal for a move by the halfback and first five-eighth.

Usually, such calls stay within a team and are rarely published. But on this occasion, one of the reporters, Fred Boshier of the *Evening Post*, knew all about it because he typed out all the calls for the players. Even when he knew the joke was on him, Beckman still described the match as the toughest of his career.[2]

Spectators queue for tickets to the new temporary stand on the western bank at Athletic Park for Wellington's match against the British Isles in 1959. The 'tubular steel stand', as it was described, was replaced by the towering Millard Stand two years later. EP/1959/2661-F, EVENING POST COLLECTION, ALEXANDER TURNBULL LIBRARY

did say they were either incompetent or the Rugby Referees Association, which controlled them, misinterpreted the laws of the game.[11]

The issue of refereeing was a constant of rugby, continuing even after New Zealand reluctantly agreed to the third-country principle in 1979. Referees in different countries interpreted laws in different ways or had different refereeing styles. Third-country referees may have been the ideal, but in practical terms it was another example of British administration of the game according to conditions applying in Britain but not elsewhere. In the amateur days, when referees like players had day jobs, it was easy for an English referee to take a train from Paddington to referee a game in Cardiff between, say, Wales and Scotland, and be back home the night of the game. The nearest third-country referees to New Zealand were in Australia and getting across the Tasman would have involved at least a couple of days, probably more. And would third-country referees have stopped criticisms and arguments? Time and experience have shown they have not.

There were also differences in the fundamental approach to the game. The difference centred on a British reluctance to accept the principle of the ruck. In New Zealand and to a lesser extent in Australia and South Africa, players of whatever level understood that when a tackled player hit the ground, his role was to place his body between the opposing forwards and his own oncoming teammates. His job was to retain the ball and his teammates would then ruck it back. As soon as the ruck began, the tackled player and the tacklers rolled clear or got up and out of the way or joined the forming ruck. As Bob Stuart, captain of the 1953–54 All Blacks and a coach of understated merit, once wrote: 'If they had any sense, they certainly did not try to hold the ball or adopt any body position to impede arriving forwards obtaining quickly rucked ball for their backs to exploit a possibly disorganised backline.'[12] If they did, the consequences were inevitable. Players would be rucked out of the way 'with minimum mercy and maximum vigour'. Generally speaking, southern hemisphere players and referees accepted this as an integral part of the game; not so in Britain where rucking, the raking back of the feet, was often seen as kicking or as 'stomping' or 'stamping' by British reporters anxious for their stories to be newsworthy enough to drive soccer off the back pages. British players, whether at home or on tour in New Zealand, were frequently characterised as being habitual offenders for lying on the ball or lying on the wrong side of a ruck. To New Zealanders, there was only one way to stop that.

In purely domestic terms, rugby seemed in as fine a fettle as it had ever been. Rugby aspiration had a triangular shape, with clubs and schools at the base, provinces and teams such as national Māori or Universities or age grade national teams halfway up and, at the apex, the All Blacks. It was

Captains Wilson Whineray and Ronnie Dawson lead their sides out on to Athletic Park in Wellington for the second test of the 1959 British Isles series. The crowd at the park that day was estimated at a record 53,000. EP/1959/2878-F, EVENING POST COLLECTION, ALEXANDER TURNBULL LIBRARY

simple and uncluttered. Players aspired to rise from one level to another, but even if they did not, they were happy enough where they were and this was also the era when players returned from the apex to play again at the lower levels. It seemed not to matter that while club competitions – for 'the shield' or 'the flag' or 'the pennant' – were popular with the public and keenly contested, provincial matches were just for the pride and glory. The only exceptions were regional contests for the Seddon Shield (northern South Island and West Coast) or the Coronation Shield (the northern third of the North Island) and similar regional trophies. Then there was the Ranfurly Shield, providing a pinnacle all of its own. Even though many provinces had never won it, and it stayed in some areas long enough for the years to become known as 'shield eras', it was still seen as the ultimate trophy in New Zealand rugby. Its status, shared equally by players and spectators and loved by administrators

The match was just an end-of-season frolic in 1957 between Wellington's second team, the Bs, and the invitation club, the Centurions, but a crowd of 9000 showed up at Athletic Park to pay tribute to one man, Wellington and All Black wing Ron Jarden. Just 27, he decided to retire from the game because he wanted to do other things in life. The Wellington union chairman, Norm Millard, probably spoke for most people when he said: 'I think it is ridiculous that a boy of his age should be retiring.' But Jarden was adamant and it was his final first-class match. Wellington B won the match but that seemed irrelevant – Jarden scored nineteen points for the Centurions. The photo shows two spectators carrying Jarden in his last exit from a rugby field. EP/1957/3711-F, EVENING POST COLLECTION, ALEXANDER TURNBULL LIBRARY

with an eye on balance sheets, brought out the best of rugby. An ordinary provincial match might be ambling along to a finish, one side knowing it had enough points and the other accepting it would have to wait another day for victory. But a shield match was different. Players lengthened their stride, jumped so much higher, tackled so much harder, pushed more vigorously, rucked more intently. If the game was getting near the end and the scores were close, tension was high – for spectators and for players.

Such a game occurred on 28 September 1960, the last rugby weekend of the year. Auckland had taken the shield from Southland in the last game of the previous year, had lost it to North Auckland in its third defence, then regained it eleven days later. Since then, it had defended it against Manawatu, Bay of Plenty (just), Wellington and Taranaki. The final challenge of the year came from Canterbury, a team as steeped in shield history and lore as Auckland itself. Thirty thousand people were at Eden Park.

With thirteen minutes to go, Auckland led 11–9. Kel Tremain had scored a try for Auckland and the fullback, Mike Cormack, had kicked the conversion and two penalty goals. Canterbury's nine points came from three penalty goals kicked by their centre, Stuart ('Buddy') Henderson. With twelve minutes to go, Henderson scored a try in the corner for Canterbury to lead 12–11. With nine minutes to go, Cormack kicked another penalty goal and Auckland led 14–12. With five minutes to go, Henderson kicked another penalty goal: Canterbury 15, Auckland 14. With two minutes to go, Henderson again: Canterbury led by four points. Down in front of the main stand, someone in an Auckland blazer went out to the touchline and took the shield from the table where it had sat during the game. He anticipated a handover up in the members' area. But the Auckland players would not have noticed. Their intentions were different. They thrust forward from the kick-off and referee Pat Murphy ordered a scrum, red ball. Somehow, the Auckland hooker, Colin Currie, struck first and gained that most precious of prizes, a tighthead. Des Connor, the Australian halfback for Auckland, grasped at the unexpected riches and gave the ball to his first-five, Mac Herewini. The Auckland left wing, Warren Moran, seemed unmarked and Herewini toed the ball across in his direction. Moran and Canterbury defenders raced for it but a rugby ball's bounce is one of its infuriating charms. It bounced into the in-goal area and Waka Nathan, the Auckland flanker, pounced, just ahead of the Canterbury No. 8, Hugh Burry. 'I didn't take much notice,' Nathan recalled. 'I just had to get there. I could hear Wilson Whineray behind me. He was shouting, 'Under the posts, Waka! Under the posts!' Nathan obliged and threw himself on the ground, just behind the right upright. Whineray threw his

Waka Nathan scores and Wilson Whineray celebrates. The Ranfurly Shield stayed in Auckland.

Rugby through the lens

Modern followers of rugby know what players of earlier generations looked like mainly through the actions of a man with one leg who was born in Yorkshire. He was Frank Thompson, whose skill as a photographer lives on in images that bear the credit of Crown Studios in Wellington.

Thompson was born on a farm in the dairying country of Wensleydale on the slopes of the Pennines in North Yorkshire in 1895. His mother moved to Burnley in Lancashire, and young Francis, known as Frank, had a hankering to start a new life in New Zealand. In 1914, he bought a £10 passage on a ship and after arriving in Wellington with five shillings in his pocket, he found a job as a labourer on a farm near Palmerston North.

Frank Thompson of Crown Studios organises the 1970 All Blacks into a team shot.

When he first tried to enlist for service in the First World War in 1915, he was turned down because he had 'hammer toes', which had been amputated six years previously. 'The country doctor did the operation on the kitchen table,' Thompson recalled.[1] The examining army doctor noted the amputation of the deformed toes but said Thompson should still be fit for duty.[2] The army did not want him immediately though because, as Thompson thought, he was not much good at marching. But a year later, when the need for manpower was greater, Thompson was drafted into the Medical Corps as a stretcher bearer and left Wellington in July 1916. After training, he was an orderly for a time at the Walton on Thames hospital, one of several in southern England that were for New Zealand patients, but by mid-1917 he was in the thick of action in the Third Battle of Ypres. He was caught by machine-gun fire that ripped through both legs and one arm. His left leg was amputated at a field ambulance and he underwent a series of operations in England to save the other. Thompson knew he could not go back to labouring so was sent to a prominent London photography firm, Speight Ltd, in New Bond Street, where he learnt the basics of photography and the specialised art of retouching. After being fitted with an artificial leg, Thompson returned to New Zealand in 1920 and gained a job with the photography firm of S. P. Andrew. A few months later, Andrew took over Crown Studios in Cuba Street and installed Thompson as manager. The rest became rugby history.

Thompson recalled that the first All Black team he photographed was the team that drew the third test against South Africa in 1921. Three years later, he was asked to take a studio photo of the 1924 team about to leave for Britain and that was the start of his life's work. Very few All Blacks, either individually or in a team, between then and 1970 would not have gazed into Thompson's lens. As well as All Blacks, he took photos of interisland match teams and head and shoulders shots of All Black trialists. He was also for a time the official photographer for Olympic and Commonwealth Games teams.

Sport was just one side of his business. Groups and studio shots were his speciality and he said the record number of people in a group shot in his Cuba Street studio was 150. During the Second World War, he also operated a studio at Trentham and was kept busy with shots of New Zealand soldiers as well as American marines. 'I had ten to fifteen assistants in those days,' he recalled.

Thompson announced his retirement in 1969, although it is thought that he was persuaded to carry on another year and took a group shot of the 1970 All Blacks who went to South Africa. His son Francis, also known as Frank, took over the care, cataloguing and preservation of his father's work and, when he died, the photo library went to the Alexander Turnbull Library.

arms in the air. The noise was incredible and didn't abate as Cormack lined up the conversion which would decide whether the shield stayed or went. It stayed.[13]

Auckland resisted a record 25 challenges during their shield tenure from 1960 to 1963, a record that was matched by Canterbury between 1982 and 1985, and one more match than the previous record set by Hawke's Bay in the 1920s. The 1960s may have been the peak of the amateur era or the last of the summer wine. Not only was the shield the prize all wanted, another opportunity arose for provincial teams with the much-delayed decision by the individual northern hemisphere countries to tour. The attitude of the British had always been that they could not afford time away from their jobs for tours so far away (let New Zealanders do it) and, in any case, they offered the Lions to the rugby world. France had been on New Zealand's shopping list ever since the army matches in 1917–19: a tour was proposed in the early 1920s and then another in the early 1950s, but always something seemed to get in the way. At last, in 1961, it happened.

The first French tour was important because it took New Zealand rugby followers beyond the old Empire for the first time and showed a different way of playing and touring. It showed another side of New Zealand journalists too, given the phrases and exclamations in French they contrived to get into their copy and headlines. Right from the start, the French were the 'menace formidable'.[14] The monthly magazine, *Sports Digest*, helpfully ran a dual-language glossary: readers could learn what the French called a halfback (*le demi de melee*) and what the French were said to be especially good at, *la passé croisee* (the scissor pass).[15] A vice-president of the French Rugby Federation, Jean Delbert, was quoted as telling the players on the eve of their departure for Auckland: 'You are . . . ambassadors of French muscle.'[16] Champagne (the word) and rugby were regularly juxtaposed as the French made their first journey through New Zealand.

Provincial teams saw wins against touring

The cover of the monthly *Sports Digest* that reviewed the French tour of 1961. The All Black pictured is halfback Des Connor. Behind him are French forward Michel Crauste and referee Alan Farquhar.

teams as something to fondly remember over the years, and the touring teams sometimes brought out the unexpected from spectators. In one of the great upsets, South Canterbury beat the first French team. It was a bad-tempered game – 'dirty' was a word frequently used – and the manager, Marcel Laurent, tried to laugh it off later when he said a local brass band's rendition of 'La Marseillaise' before the game was too stirring and his players got all worked up.

It was not just the French who got worked up as the match wound down with South Canterbury in front. As the big hand of the old clock at Fraser Park neared fulltime, South Canterbury second five-eighth Eddy Smith ran down the grandstand touch and seemed headed for a clinching try. But he was taken down, some say illegally, by a French forward. Flanker Michel Crauste, with a visage that required only a beret and a protruding Gauloise for French perfection, happened along and picked Smith up, then dropped him. This was altogether too much for a 51-year-old grandmother in the crowd, Hilda Madsen. She'd made the trip across the Waitaki River from Oamaru with her husband, two sons and a nephew to see the game

Taranaki's Ferdinand is introduced to French rugby, according to cartoonist Douglas Nankivell.
TARANAKI HERALD, 11 JULY 1961

Eager Wellington kids press against a Wellington airport window to get a view of the first French players to visit New Zealand. The objects of their attention are Guy Boniface, Claude Vidal and Michel Celaya.

and was not going to tolerate any Frenchman taking liberties. Wearing a fur coat and with a walking stick in one hand, she marched on to the ground and, to the delight of the crowd and the astonishment of players and officials, she punched Crauste on his back. 'I was so mad I didn't know what I was doing,' she said later. 'I hit him hard but I don't think it hurt. I think he got a bit of a shock, though.' A St John man who was tending Smith pushed Madsen off and two policemen went on to the ground and took her away. They decided against charging her with anything on the grounds it would have seemed ridiculous. They left her in the care of husband Rex and sons Joe and Pye and nephew Stu Birtles. 'I suppose I would do the same thing again, I don't know,' she said. Madsen told Graeme Jenkins, the New Zealand Press Association man on the tour, 'That sort of play spoilt rugby. It was not good for young boys to see that sort of example.'[17]

England toured New Zealand for the first time on its own but only for five matches, two of which were tests. The rushed, crowded itinerary indicated that the English union had reluctantly acceded to New Zealand requests for a tour after years of All Blacks taking a third of the year off work to go there. The English won only their first match, against Wellington, but went tantalisingly close to upsetting the All Blacks in the second test in Christchurch. The scores were tied at 6–6 with only about five minutes to go when the New Zealand fullback, Don Clarke, claimed a fair catch (a 'mark') on halfway near the left touchline. He decided to kick for goal, which was allowed under the laws then. Clarke took the ball back to firmer ground and whistled up brother Ian, the All Blacks' prop, to hold it for him. As Clarke prepared to kick, the English players charged and referee Pat Murphy reckoned they charged too soon so Clarke was allowed a fresh start. The kick of about 65 metres went over and New Zealand won 9–6. It was the last goal from a mark for New Zealand in a test match. (The practice was

Charlie Saxton's ABC

The captain of the army Kiwis and a later coach and administrator, Charlie Saxton, worried so much about the state of New Zealand rugby in the 1940s and 1950s he did something about it. With the co-operation of the New Zealand union, he wrote a mini-classic among rugby books, *The ABC of Rugby*, in which he restated fundamentals and principles that he thought had been lost along the way.

Saxton's argument was straightforward: rugby is a simple game. His arguments were in an era when rugby was an amateur game and when marketing was confined to newspaper and magazine advertisements. Yet they are as valid now in an intensely marketed professional era as they ever were.

Saxton saw the game's fundamentals as:

1. Ability to take and give a pass correctly.
2. Dribbling.
3. Ability to take the ball in the air and from the ground.
4. Ability to kick with either foot.
5. Tackling.
6. Rush-stopping.

Charlie Saxton pictured during the prime of his administrative career. F-206283-1/2 CROWN STUDIOS COLLECTION, ALEXANDER TURNBULL LIBRARY

Saxton wrote: 'It is not too much to ask of a player that he master these few individual fundamentals.' He then listed the team's fundamentals: (1) Backing up, (2) Teamwork.

The fundamentals were linked to Saxton's three Ps of rugby: position, possession and pace.

Position: 'Every forward and every back must know his positional play. He must know what should be his correct position to suit every given moment of play. He must say to himself: "I must keep my position. I must keep my position".'

Possession: 'It is necessary to have the ball to score tries. Get it from rucks, scrums, lineouts, the opposition's bad kicks and bad play. When possession has been gained, keep it.'

Pace: 'Rugby is a game which should be played at speed all the time. The speed at which it moves depends on the individual player and it is in his hands to dictate the tempo at which it will move.'

Aside from the disused art of dribbling, no modern coach could quibble with any of Saxton's points.

Wilson Whineray's All Blacks of 1963–64 out for a run in one of London's royal parks, Green Park, across Constitution Hill from Buckingham Palace.

abolished in 1977. The last goal from a mark in a first-class match anywhere was by Kit Fawcett for Waikato against Wairarapa-Bush on 10 September 1977.)

Tours of Britain by New Zealand were then still ten years apart and Wilson Whineray led his side to the 'home countries' and France over the 1963–64 summer with prop Ian Clarke the only survivor of the previous tour. Half a century later, rugby players crossed the globe as frequently as they crossed Cook Strait. Whineray's team played 36 matches and won 34 of them, a loss to Newport and a surprising scoreless draw with Scotland detracting from a perfect score. Before the last of their British Isles tests, against Scotland, manager Frank Kilby was even quoted as saying 'the boys' were 'quietly determined and have high hopes of

It is not just modern All Blacks who become celebrities and feature in women's magazines. The captain in 30 tests, Wilson Whineray, with his wife Beth and children James and Kristen pictured at their home in Henderson in 1964.

completing the grand slam'.[18] It was a surprising comment from such an experienced former player and national administrator as Kilby. Much better to act first and talk second. The aspirations to be the first New Zealand team to achieve a grand slam in Britain – victory against each of the 'home' countries – came unstuck on the thawing warmth of the surface at Murrayfield, with its newly installed 'electric blanket' (underground heating). New Zealand would have to wait another fourteen years for a grand slam (on the same ground, as it happened). The All Blacks had been in such imperious form, including an emphatic win against Wales, that Scotland seemed to be regarded as barely a hurdle. But there's a proverb south of Hadrian's Wall that says there's many a slip twixt cup and lip and so it proved. The Glasgow *Evening Times* summed up the match neatly: 'Great Scots! All Blanks!'[19] The All Blacks have not been held scoreless in a test since. The paper's reporter remarked: 'It was a really grand game, full of thrills and excitement.'

The final match in Britain, against the invitation Barbarians club in Cardiff, provided the climax. It was won 36–3 by the All Blacks, but the manner of the winning deserved to be remembered. Even the cynics rose to the All Blacks and especially to their captain, Wilson Whineray. Perhaps the president of the Barbarians, Brigadier Glyn Hughes, spoke for all when he said to Whineray at the dinner after the match: 'As a leader you have achieved even more than as a player and

Wilson Whineray heads for his farewell try against the Barbarians in Cardiff in 1964.

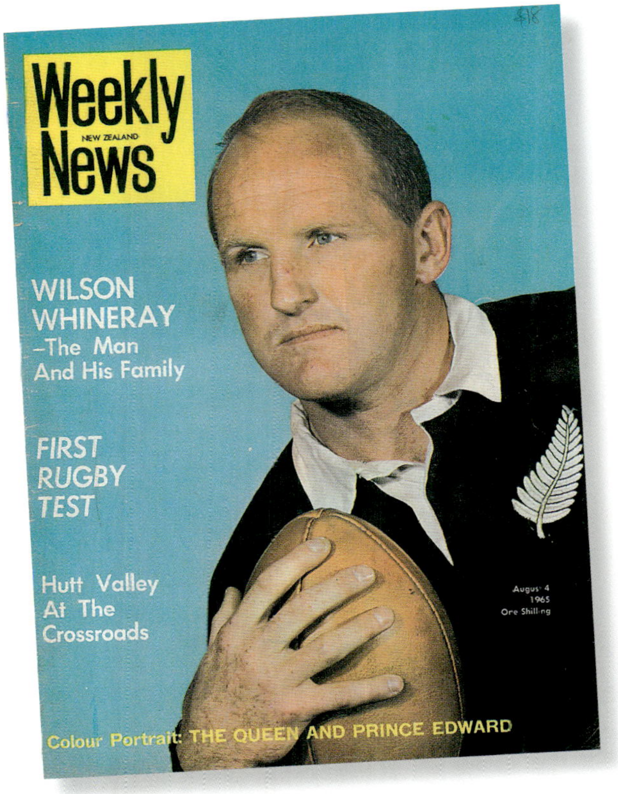

The face of a leader: Wilson Whineray pictured in his last year as New Zealand captain.

I am sure that many victories on this tour have been attributable to your controlled discipline and mastery of tactics.'[20] It helped the Whineray image, and the warm end-of-tour glow, that the captain himself scored a runaway try (a rare enough event for props). He took the ball from the New Zealand centre, Paul Little, and charged for the line. He had only the Barbarians fullback, Stewart Wilson, to beat and he had an unmarked Colin Meads outside him. Wellington journalist Alex Veysey described what happened next: 'Ten yards from the line Whineray sold Wilson a dummy of such outrageous cheek that even Meads studied him with some concern. The crowd rose as one as Whineray sprinted around behind the posts to secure his first try of the tour.' When the game was over and the players ambled around as if reluctant to leave the arena, the crowd of 60,000 still stood and sang 'For He's a Jolly Good Fellow', 'We'll Keep a Welcome in the Hillside' and, to round off the tour, 'Now is the Hour'.[21] It was a remarkable demonstration that the All Blacks are not always painted black in Britain.

Even in such sunlit times for rugby, however, South Africa lurked in the dark. Since the Sharpeville massacre in March 1960, when police killed 69 people for demonstrating against an element of the apartheid laws, eyes were opening around the world to what was happening in South Africa. A month before that, the British prime minister, Harold Macmillan, had made his 'wind of change' speech to parliamentarians in Cape Town: 'The wind of change is blowing through this continent and whether we like it or not, the growth of national consciousness is a political fact . . .'[22] Macmillan was predicting an end to white minority rule throughout Africa, but the white South African government headed by the Dutch-born and Rhodesia-raised prime minister, Hendrik Verwoerd, saw things differently. New Zealand rugby officials went with the wind of change, despite the blind ignorance and occasional arrogance often attributed to them. Two members of the NZRFU council, the retiring chairman, Cuth Hogg, and his successor, Tom Morrison, went to an International Rugby Board meeting in Edinburgh in March 1962 and there gained agreement that New Zealand teams should be fully representative or they would not tour (the IRB controlled the international tour schedule). Two years later, Morrison and another council member, Ces Blazey, went to London for an IRB meeting on the laws of the game. While there, they told the two South African delegates, Danie Craven and G. J. Potgeiter, that Māori should be included in the New Zealand team scheduled to tour in 1967. The two South Africans agreed.

Later that year, the South African Rugby Board marked its seventy-fifth anniversary and two Māori, administrator Ralph Love and recently retired player Pat Walsh, went as guests of the board. This was regarded as a breakthrough at the time, but it

Four of the men influential in the decision to abandon a scheduled New Zealand tour of South Africa in 1967: New Zealand union chairman Tom Morrison; Māori Advisory Board chairman Ralph Love; the union president in 1965, Tom Pearce (who was also manager of the team in South Africa in 1960); and a delegate to the International Rugby Board (and future chairman), Ces Blazey.

was hardly that. They went as feted guests, not as 'ordinary' non-whites. Morrison and Tom Pearce went to an IRB meeting in Cape Town at the same time and the Māori message was reinforced. None of these behind-the-scenes moves by New Zealand rugby people was made public at the time, or even later. A report on the 1964 talks stated (with underlining in the original): 'This report must be kept strictly confidential to Council Members as any publicity at this stage could jeopardise the South African Rugby Board's proposal.'[23] The result of this series of meetings was that the New Zealanders thought they had agreement from their South African counterparts that the invitation to tour in 1967 would not be qualified.

In the meantime, another all-white South African team toured New Zealand and while there were some protests, they were restrained and had no effect on the progress of the tour, which was largely reported as all previous incoming tours had been: the emphasis was on how formidable South African rugby players can be and how New Zealanders, whether playing for province or country, needed to be at their best to win. The Springboks lost the first two tests and they had also lost to Wellington and to Auckland. They came good in the third test and won 19–16, lock Jacobus ('Tiny') Naude kicking a penalty goal in the last minutes. The unrestrained joy for the South Africans was leavened somewhat by a speech the same day in eastern Transvaal (now Mpumalanga) by Verwoerd that killed off any chance of progress. Known as the Loskop Dam speech, Verwoerd reiterated the apartheid policy of his Nationalist Party. He specifically mentioned rugby and said that while South Africans are in another country, they must honour the laws, customs and traditions of that country. And equally so in reverse. His government's position was unambiguous, he said. That effectively was the end of the planned New Zealand tour of South Africa in 1967. Six months after Verwoerd's final word, the IRB again met in Edinburgh and Craven, whose turn it was to chair the meeting, reported the 1967 tour could not happen under the conditions agreed in 1962. The minutes of the meeting record:

Dr Craven explained that unfortunately the intention stated in Minute 10 of Board Meeting of 16th March 1962 that Maoris could be included in future New Zealand teams visiting South Africa could not be fulfilled at this time, notwithstanding the unanimous wish of the South African Rugby Board. The Board agreed that in the circumstances the New Zealand decision to cancel the tour should be approved.[24]

The All Blacks went to Britain instead. B. J. Vorster, who replaced Verwoerd as prime minister, said in April 1967 that South Africa, at least as far as cricket and rugby were concerned, would no longer tell countries who they could select for visits there.[25] That opened the way for the inclusion of Māori (and a Samoan New Zealander) for the first time when the All Blacks went to South Africa in 1970. The South African cricket team, as isolated from international competition as the rugby players came to be, did not play any non-white team until apartheid was abolished even though the West Indies, Pakistan, India and Sri Lanka were all members of the International Cricket Council to which South Africa also belonged. Conveniently for South African rugby, all of the member countries of the IRB were old-empire white (old-empire until France was added in 1978).

There have been reports over the years that the New Zealand prime minister, Keith Holyoake, had a hand in the cancellation of the 1967 tour. It is entirely likely that he and rugby officials discussed it at some stage, but to suggest the NZRFU somehow bowed to Holyoake's wishes would be going to an extreme for which there is no evidence. The contrary evidence is that the rugby people themselves initiated the small dent in apartheid (because of the protests preceding the 1928, 1949 and 1960 tours), something for which they have never been given credit. Holyoake and rugby people in Wellington were frequent conversationalists, partly because he was a sociable person but also because he played rugby himself at first-class level as a hooker.[26]

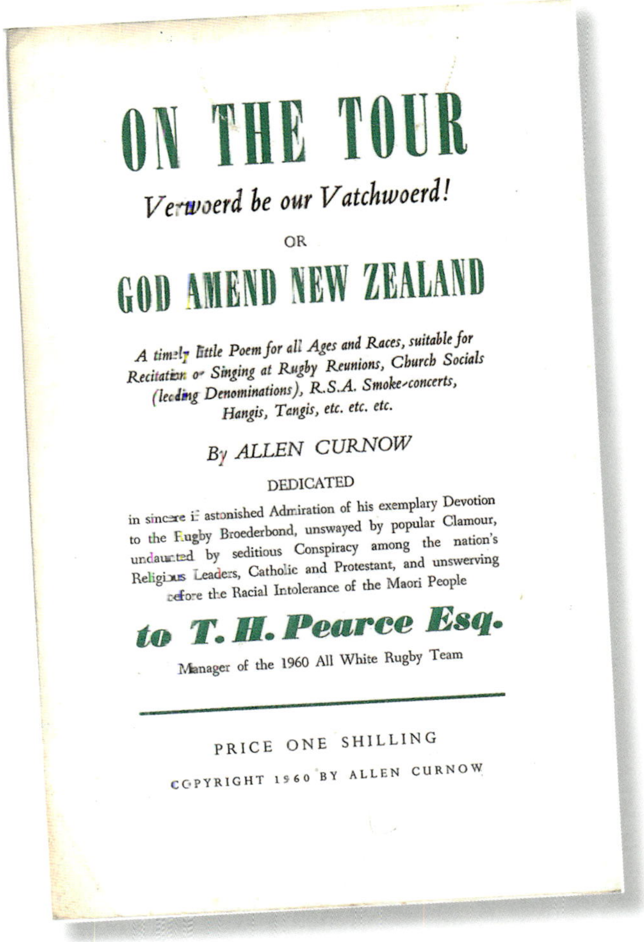

Poet Allen Curnow's pointed parody of a rugby standard, 'On the Ball'.

The cradle of rugby

School rugby has an equivalent of the Ranfurly Shield, but it has had such a chequered history that school days may have come and gone for some boys without their knowing of its existence. The Moascar Cup came, as its name implies, from the fag end days of the First World War. Troops were left in Egypt until the early months of 1919, partly to keep an eye on restless Egyptians and partly because there were not enough ships available to get thousands of men home to North America and the South Pacific from Europe and the Middle East. Interested British, New Zealand and Australian soldiers camped at Moascar in Ismaila, at the northern end of the Suez Canal, east of Cairo, formed the Ismaila Rugby Union and organised a competition. Five Australian, four British and two New Zealand teams played, but the full records of the matches were lost on a returning transport.

The New Zealand Mounted Rifles Unit and Depot had entered two teams but, according to one report, any men who had been wounded or who had had malaria could not play, so the two teams combined. This was seen by some New Zealanders as a British ploy to weaken them. With soldierly skulduggery, some of the men ordered out simply re-entered with different names. The Moascar union organised a cup – described as 'a handsome Irish cup' (actually, a loving cup – a two-handled cup traditionally used at weddings and banquets) – and had it mounted on a piece of a wooden propeller from a German aircraft shot down in Palestine. Thus, the Moascar Cup came into being, and it was won by the New Zealand team, which won nine of its ten matches. The rugby was not just an idle kick-around in the sand. 'When the competition first started,' an *NZ Truth* reporter (who seems to have been a returned man) wrote, 'the teams were regarded as slightly superior club teams might have been regarded in New Zealand . . . but rapidly the contest assumed an international aspect both because of the personnel of the teams and the high standard of play attained.'[1]

Eventually, the cup was carried home in triumph and the captain, Herb Quarterman from Wanganui, and the senior officer on the troopship home, Edward Hulbert, presented it to the New Zealand Rugby Football Union. Their condition was that it be a challenge trophy for secondary schools. The union liked the idea and promised to donate a shield upon which would be engraved the names of the winning schools. The two schools to contest the cup for the first time, Christchurch Boys' High School and Palmerston North Boys' High School, were determined by their record in recent years. They met to contest for the cup at Athletic Park in Wellington in 1920 in appalling conditions. 'Driving rain across a ground that was a shallow lake made team play almost impossible,' one of the Christchurch players, Jim Burrows, later wrote.[2] Prime Minister William Massey and several cabinet ministers, having adjourned Parliament for the afternoon, 'sat miserably' in the main grandstand. The game ended with no score so extra time was played and the referee ruled that if there was no score, 'force-downs' (that is, a touch-down in goal) would count. A Palmerston North player kicked the ball dead and that was deemed, much to the dismay of the Palmerston North players and supporters, a force-down. Christchurch Boys' thus became the first holders.

The Christchurch Boys' High School team that won the first Moascar Cup match.

The cup aroused enormous interest among secondary schools in the early 1920s, but the competition seemed to become a victim of its own success. It was such a prize that schools used up money and boys' holidays in pursuit of it, and there were concerns that the cup was becoming a trophy for which only the rich could compete.

Journalist Gordon McLean, in recalling the glory days of the cup, once wrote: 'The interest that was aroused may be gauged from the fact that the Christchurch Boys' High School first XV travelled to Auckland to play Grammar . . .'[3] A school trip from one island to the other may sound nothing by twenty-first-century standards, but it was an undertaking of some magnitude in the 1920s. Some schools came to believe that too much emphasis was placed on the winning rather than on the playing and that the pursuit of the cup had got a bit out of hand. Several of the leading rugby schools, Christ's in Christchurch, Nelson College, Wellington College and Wanganui Collegiate, all decided to give Moascar matches a miss.

There was also talk of Te Aute College, the Māori college in Hawke's Bay, being too strong for most schools because Māori boys matured earlier than Pākehā boys and were bigger and stronger – a forerunner of a similar argument applying to boys of Pacific Island heritage more than half a century later. A North Auckland delegate to the annual meeting of the New Zealand union in 1928, Alex Charters (who was also principal of Whangarei High School), said his and other schools had pulled out of cup competition because 'they could not meet a side such as Te Aute and give away a great deal of weight'.[4] This led to an accusation by an East Coast delegate, Bob Macfarlane, that 'the colour line was being drawn' because the cup was held by a Māori school. Charters responded by saying his school's first XV included three Māori.

Another school trophy, the Vancouver Cup, which was given to the All Blacks of 1925 when they were in Canada, was played for on a similar basis by primary schools. Like the Moascar Cup, its worth was questioned on the basis that playing sport for trophies should not be encouraged among school pupils.[5]

The place of rugby in schools was also questioned in the 1920s. The soccer authorities, the New Zealand Football Association, introduced a trophy named for its president, Charles Skerrett, who was Chief Justice, and decided it, like the Moascar Cup, would be a challenge trophy for school teams. But not many of the leading schools allowed winter sports teams other than rugby. The principal of Wellington College, Thomas Cresswell, said rugby was the only recognised winter sport for boys at his school because of insufficient playing grounds and because of 'difficulties in organisation'.[6] In other schools, smaller rolls meant they could not entertain more than one winter sport. Cresswell, himself educated at another noted rugby school, Christchurch Boys' High School, continued:

St Bede's boys in rugby action in 1934. PB1706 5, V. C. BROWNE AND SON

Mt Albert Grammar School won the Moascar Cup in 1991. Pictured with it are future All Black Andrew Blowers, coach Bevan Whiting and Teri'i Rahui. Rahui played sevens for the Cook Islands at the 1998 Commonwealth Games in Kuala Lumpur.
ARTHUR REEVE COLLECTION

> Most of our masters have never played anything but Rugby themselves and consequently they feel that that is the game which they are most competent to teach the boys. . . . I am not prepared to say which is the better game for boys; no doubt Soccer is a very fine game, but that is the position at the Wellington College.[7]

It was the position too at Southland BHS, Christchurch BHS and Auckland Grammar, and perhaps others. Boys at those schools did play soccer, but for local clubs rather than for their schools. Auckland YMCA soccer club, for example, was seen as the de facto Auckland Grammar team.

By the 1930s, it seemed the Moascar Cup was all but forgotten and the *Truth* writer thought its decline in popularity may have been a factor in a general deterioration of play at schools and in senior club grades. This was also at a time when New Zealand rugby generally took time to adapt to the changed scrum formation (the present three-four-one from the old two-three-two) and the effect this had on back play.

These changes themselves coincided with the Great Depression when, for most of the 1930s, spending hard-to-come-by money on travel for sports teams would not have been a priority. The *Truth* writer said if schools could not afford to challenge for the cup, or did not want to, it should be returned to Herb Quarterman in Wanganui or be given to a museum.

The cup seemed to be the permanent property of Te Aute because of a lack of interest from other schools until 1951 when Northland College challenged and won 11–9. For the next twenty or so years, the cup was played for only in the north of the North Island and the rest of New Zealand seemed to neither know nor care about it. But one man did. Arthur Reeve was a Wellington man interested in many sports but especially schools rugby and he wrote about it diligently and frequently, for any newspaper that could be bothered to take his copy.

A coloured plate from the *Boy's Own Annual* in 1926 showing British, mainly English, school colours and caps.

Mostly, the *Dominion*, the *Sunday Times* and the *Sports Post* published his reports. Around the fiftieth anniversary of the first Moascar Cup game, Reeve wrote about how sad it was such a prized trophy no longer seemed of much interest. Someone in Napier read it and Napier Boys' High School challenged and went north and took the cup from Pukekohe High School.

'During my years of reporting on college rugby, I made it my business to revive and promote Moascar Cup games,' Reeve later wrote.[8] Reeve died in 2002, aged 89, knowing that the Moascar Cup had been restored if not to its former glory, at least to a status in schools rugby as a prize worth having.

Given the significant role of schools in New Zealand rugby, it was out of kilter that New Zealand was the last of the established rugby countries to field a national schools team. That did not happen until 1978, by which time New Zealand rugby administrators looked enviously at Australia's schoolboy record and decided they too

Typical of the 'rugger' stories for boys, usually based on English public schools where there was equal measure of pluck, chums and bounders, was this by Walter C. Rhoades.

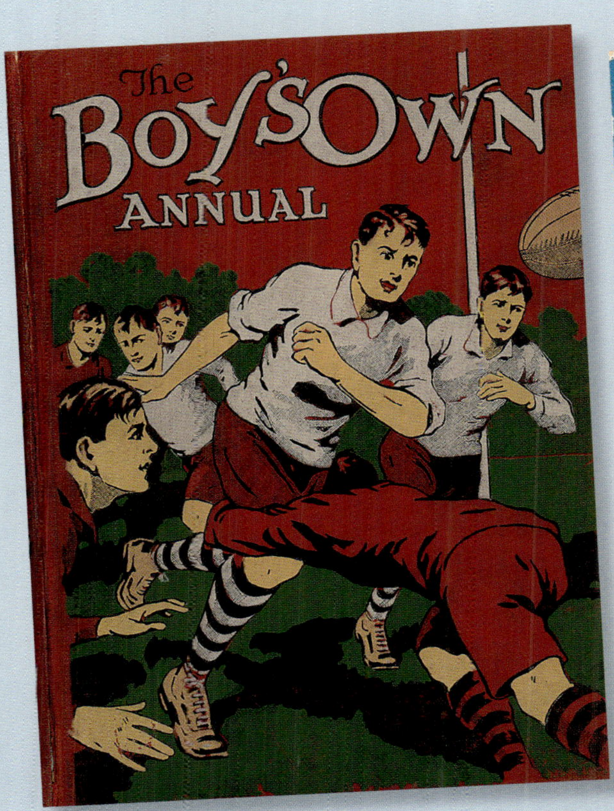

Typical examples of rugby books for boys. The *Boy's Own Annual* from 1926; and one of the few of the genre written by a New Zealander, but set at mythical Ruckington School in England.

needed to act. The first New Zealand team won 7–6 against an Australian side that was largely the hugely popular team that had toured Britain and Ireland earlier the same year. It included such players as the Ella brothers, Michael O'Connor and a man destined to be a synonym for excellence in league, Wally Lewis.

It seemed strange too that New Zealand did not have the same tradition of rugby stories for boys that prevailed in Britain, especially in publications such as *Boy's Own*. The *Boy's Own* paper and its *Annuals* were distributed in New Zealand and so generations of boys (and perhaps girls) were reared on English tales of pluck and luck at rugger rather than New Zealand stories.

One of the few came late in the piece and, ironically, featured a New Zealand boy at an English school named, appropriately, Ruckington, rather than be set in New Zealand. *The Boy from New Zealand* was written by a Wellington man, Mervyn Elias, who soon after its publication in 1940 became an official photographer with the 2nd New Zealand Expeditionary Force.[9] One of New Zealand's most celebrated children's authors, Margaret Mahy, once wrote she read it with interest though with restricted enthusiasm.[10] Elias's hero, Bradshaw, is amazed when he learns that sport is not compulsory at the school: '"Do you mean to say," he blurted out, "that most of the chaps here are loafers? They don't play rugger or cricket? Don't go in for any kind of sports?"' No wonder, Mahy noted, his school chum Grenville reddened at the shattering summation. As Mahy wrote: 'The prospect of the hero's final victory is implicit in the beginning and sustains us through the days when, due to the machinations of some bounder, the hero's honour is impugned.'[11]

Ken Gray secures the ball in an attacking lineout against Wales. Kel Tremain and Sam Strahan (centre) look as if they are about to start a drive from the lineout and halfback Chris Laidlaw (No. 9) waits. Other All Blacks are Graham Williams, Brian Lochore, Brian Muller, Colin Meads and Bruce McLeod.

12 End of an era approaches

But we always turn back to rugby,
When our worst is never too bad,
And the argument goes on unceasingly,
As to the best side we ever had.[1]

When Russ Thomas was a highly regarded manager of the national team, it was his habit in speeches to talk about the inherent qualities of rugby, as if it were a higher calling than sport. Travelling journalists who knew Thomas well, and liked him for his honesty and genuineness, had heard the speeches often and gleefully muttered the phrases among each other a few seconds before they came from Thomas. It behoves us all, he used to say, to preserve those qualities 'for the sake of our children and our children's children'. One of those qualities was amateurism, which his and earlier generations saw as a defining characteristic of rugby. It was amateurism that created a point of difference between rugby and other sports, the argument used to go. That was not quite so. What Thomas and others meant was that amateurism was the point of difference between rugby and other versions of football, especially league, a game so disliked they frequently dared not speak its name.

By the late 1960s and early 1970s, the days of amateurism were coming to an end. Cricket had led the way when in 1962 the Marylebone Cricket Club (MCC), which then ruled the game, abolished the distinction between amateurs and professionals on the grounds that it was increasingly difficult to tell the difference. The gentlemen amateurs were a breed of the past and amateurs who were not gentlemen made more money from the game than did the professionals. Jim Laker, the professional England spin bowler, worked out that if he toured as an amateur, the collection of various allowances would give him a better income than he could get as a professional. He applied to the MCC to be an amateur for a tour, but his novel, honest approach was turned down. The annual Gents versus Players game was abolished, and all cricketers could take to the field through the same gate. What applied to cricket applied eventually to all other sports, including rugby.

A politician, writer and cricketer of some note, Lord Williams of Elvel (just plain Charles Williams on his book jackets), thought that the changes in sport reflected changes in British society and that the debacle of the Suez crisis in 1956 was when general public opinion finally

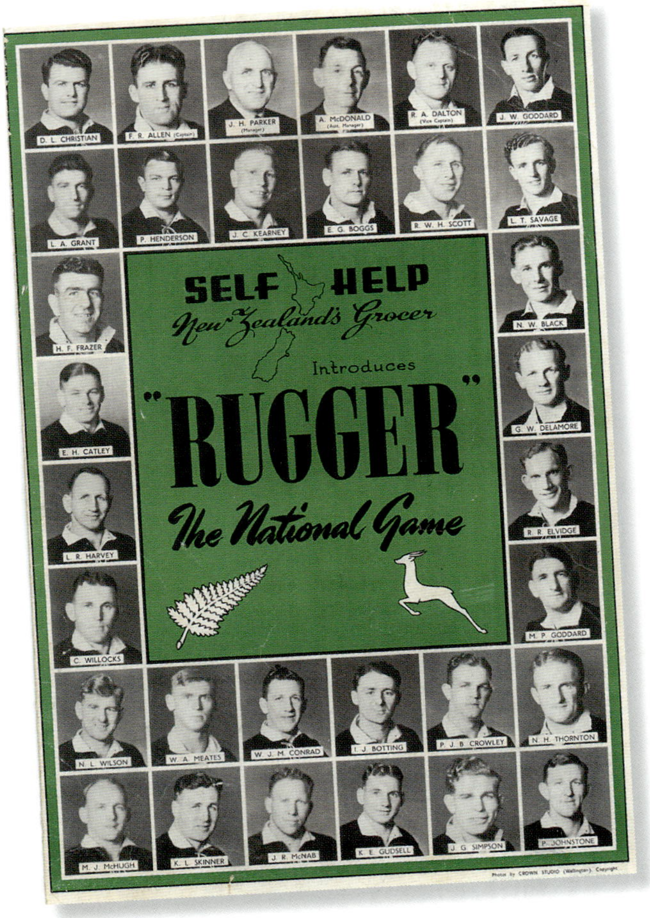

Many companies associated themselves with the All Blacks or just with the game itself, especially when they were free to do so. The grocery chain Self Help produced this board game.

abandoned its respect for 'gentlemen':[2] 'Those of us who were alive at the time . . . recall vividly the humiliation that the "gentlemen" had brought on Britain.' If that were so, it took a little more time in New Zealand for the amateur ramparts to be breached, even allowing for the absence of a class born to rule. But the war generation brought with it a societal change just as irreparable. By the late 1960s and into the 1970s, there were those who fought in the war, or at least lived through it, and those who did not. The new generation, labelled flippantly as 'baby boomers' by Americans, had a different set of values, a different attitude to life and living. Thomas was the last chairman of the New Zealand union to have served in the Second World War; Fred Allen was the last coach of the All Blacks to have donned a uniform in wartime. Others prominent in rugby for a generation such as Cuth Hogg, Tom Morrison, Charlie Saxton, Jack Sullivan and Ces Blazey were either gone or going. Rugby, as always, was a cross-section of society. The last prime minister to have served in the war was Robert Muldoon who, like Allen, was in Italy in the last days. There seemed a distinctive line drawn between men of war and men of peace. Trevor Richards, no admirer of any of the men mentioned, thought the paroxysm of protests from the 1970s to the mid-1980s stemmed in some part from the clash between the traditional values of what he called old New Zealand and those of the generation of the 1960s.[3] The clashes about playing against racist South Africa were the lightning rod, he thought.

A casualty of the collision between generations was amateurism; it was a long and drawn-out battle with many skirmishes along the way, but there could only ever be one winner: a Corinthian spirit, a Victorian era ideal, as difficult to grasp as moonbeams, was at odds with the practical need to earn money. It was no different from the argument in England in 1895 when rugby was split, or even in 1906–07 when some players in New Zealand began league, but now the numbers had changed. When cricket declared all players to be merely cricketers, the editor of the *Wisden Almanack*, Norman Preston, recorded the facts with a sorrowful tone: 'We live in a changing world. Conditions are vastly different from the days of our grandparents; but is it wise to throw everything overboard?'[4]

Such weighty issues as the moral force of the game, even its future, were not likely to have been on the minds of players as they went about their winter business in the late 1960s. Some All Blacks would have, as some always had, worried about where the next pound (or dollar, after New Zealand changed to decimal currency in 1967) was coming from; some would have had to take yet more leave from work so they could play rugby

Cartoonist Paul Clarkson drew this when he was a seventeen-year-old pupil at Christchurch Boys' High School. He features in bold two of the school's masters who were All Blacks, Pat Vincent and John Graham. Both, incidentally, also captained the All Blacks. PAUL CLARKSON

and a few would have had to pay someone to do their job while they were away. Others would have said simply they could not afford to play for their country. These were the practical considerations of the theoretical rules enforced from London. The vast majority of rugby players would have just played and trained as they always did: club training Tuesday and Thursday nights, games on Saturdays and if they were lucky and good enough, 'rep' (representative) training and even 'rep' games later in the season. And after that, there was always the chance of a few social or festival matches, matches in which the results mattered to no one – except of course the players.

Rugby was never just 80 minutes of endeavour, though. It was a shared lifestyle, even if lives were led in different ways. Students and labourers, lawyers and truck drivers, doctors and shop workers, all were the same in the freemasonry of rugby. There was generally an after-match function at which sandwiches or saveloys were eaten and beers were drunk, after which there might be a bit more drinking and a dance in the clubrooms. It was a man's world into which women were not just admitted, but welcomed. Mothers, sisters, wives, girlfriends, all were as part of the club as a father, a son, a brother and his mates. Mothers whose childhood weekends had been spent in rugby clubrooms now took their daughters along. In some areas, especially in the country, the rugby club served also as community hall. It was not because rugby tried to lord it over other sports, but because rugby was the main sport, a focal point for a community and provided a tribal camaraderie. Some clubs diversified into other sports to boost membership numbers and spread the financial load, but also to provide a service. Squash clubs were frequently an adjunct to rugby clubs, but so were a range of other sports. When women's rugby began to develop fully in the 1990s, the women's teams became an important feature of club activity.

Most clubs or teams had their tours: perhaps an early-season away trip at Easter, maybe a quick couple of days away at Queen's Birthday weekend, most likely something in early October to mark the end of the season. Rep teams, the name by which provincial teams were universally known, had a routine to their seasons even before the national provincial championship began in 1976. Over the years, home and away fixtures gradually became accepted parts of the calendar and they were played always strictly in turn. Auckland, for example, would make a southern tour every second year and play provinces with which it had a traditional arrangement – at least Wellington, Canterbury and Otago; sometimes more. That was a tradition dating back to the first provincial tour in 1875. Until the 1970s, travel on such tours was by train and interisland ferry (which meant usually the overnight voyage between Lyttelton and Wellington). Fixture lists for the year were thrashed out in hurried and sometimes acrimonious discussions between provincial delegates, usually on the night before the New Zealand union's annual meeting in Wellington. This became known as 'the wool sale' because so many voices were going at once: 'I've got Saturday the third free in the South – any takers? Tuesday or a Wednesday on the fourth, anyone?' Many years later, there was a move in the 'modern' New Zealand union to revert to the old ways of choosing members of the governing body; that is, nominations and votes at the annual meeting. One delegate argued against such a practice, saying he did not want to see a return to the old wool sale, clearly not knowing what the old wool sale was. It was a sad commentary on the modern game not to know what had preceded it.

Like amateurism, the South African issue never went away; it was just in remission from time to time. Ironically it was that issue that gave New Zealand rugby one of its best teams and tours – the All Blacks' tour of Britain in 1967. The union mounted the tour when it decided it could no longer go to South Africa without Māori. For years afterwards, the 1967 All Blacks were looked upon fondly as a tour worth remembering. Even the prickly *Daily Telegraph* rugby writer, John Reason, gave the team a glowing reference:

One of the biggest men in the New Zealand team, Brian Lochore, looks set to confront the smallest man in the French team, Jean Gachassin, during their 1967 test in Paris. Gachassin went by the nickname of 'Peter Pan', apparently because of his size (his height was about 1.55 metres). *MIROIR SPRINT*, 20 NOVEMBER 1967

> The All Black team was so powerful in certain specific areas that it was exactly the technical stimulus the players of the four home countries needed. In addition, the All Blacks played a type of Rugby [many newspapers still capitalised the name of the game] which was far more expansive than anything New Zealand had attempted for forty years . . .[5]

This team could have become the first to achieve a grand slam in the British Isles, the defeat of each of the 'home' countries on one tour, but could not because of an outbreak of foot-and-mouth disease in England. This meant restrictions on travelling to Ireland and agriculturally sensitive New Zealanders readily understood. The players under Brian Lochore, who had taken over the leadership the year before for a four–nil dispatching of an under-strength Lions team, were a modern version of the army Kiwis of just over twenty years before. Their manager was the Kiwis' captain, Charlie Saxton, and their coach was Fred Allen, one of the Kiwis and a willing convert to the Saxton and Vic Cavanagh principle of fifteen-man rugby based on forwards winning the ball and backs scoring with it. The All Black forwards may not have had the majesty of the year before or of two years before when they beat the Springboks, but they were still strong enough against the individual British sides. They did not have backs of a lifetime such as the Invincibles had more than forty years before, but they had men of merit and spirit. At one extreme they had at the base of the scrum a halfback, Chris Laidlaw, with one of the finest passes seen in the game and a brain that was as quick, and at the other the most resolute and fearless of fullbacks, Fergie McCormick. This was the first year of test rugby for Gareth Edwards, the best halfback to wear the scarlet of Wales, who would later write:

Fred Allen during a training session with the All Blacks in 1967.

> There is something about the blackness of an All Black jersey which sends a shudder through your heart. Fifteen of them look dark and sinful; eight snorting bulls and seven black panthers. It takes a success or two of your own before you know they are saying the same about you. I simply stood and stared in the autumn of 1967.[6]

So did a lot of people stand and stare. The All Blacks of 1967 were at their most imperious, beginning with a match against Australia in Wellington to mark the seventy-fifth anniversary of the New Zealand union and ending with an unbeaten tour in Britain and France.

The only thing that took the gloss from the tour was the sending off of Colin Meads in the match against Scotland. It was just the second dismissal in a test between established rugby countries after Cyril Brownlie in 1925. It was no coincidence that both players were competitive forwards whose hard and uncompromising approach to the game was not always as well understood elsewhere as it was at home. Meads and other All Blacks have always been adamant that Meads kicked out at the ball as it headed for the arms of the Scottish first five-eighth, David Chisholm. The Irish referee, Kevin Kelleher, had earlier warned against indiscriminate rucking and he stopped play and told Meads to go. Saxton, the epitome of integrity, watched replays of a film of the incident in a BBC outside broadcast van in the Murrayfield carpark and he was convinced there was nothing in it. Kelleher reacted because the crowd bayed for Meads, Saxton thought. He had to go to a hearing at the team's next stop, in Cardiff, where Kelleher gave evidence, but there was no provision for

With the Band of the Grenadier Guards as silent witnesses behind them, the All Blacks reach the climax of their haka before the test against England at Twickenham in 1967. The Queen and Prince Philip stand on the edge of the ground (lower left).

Meads to do so. Saxton was on a panel sitting in judgement: with him were Cyril Gadney, a former referee, and the president of the Welsh union, Glyn Morgan. They decided that Meads would be suspended for two matches.

'This was particularly hard for me,' Saxton wrote in a report to the New Zealand union, 'as I said I would accept the referee's statement along with the others. I had to anyway, but I fought hard for no further penalty or suspension. Unfortunately, I was on my own and eventually had to compromise for a penalty of a suspension for the next two games.'[7] At an IRB meeting in Edinburgh a few months later, a report from the disciplinary hearing said Saxton turned down a chance for Meads to appear. This led to what politicians would call a frank exchange of views with the New Zealand delegate, Ces Blazey, saying Saxton did no such thing. Blazey ensured the addition of a rule to the IRB's disciplinary procedures which said that 'the player ordered off shall have the right to be heard if he so desires'.[8]

The 1967 halfback, Chris Laidlaw, had this to say when Saxton died in 2001: 'The 1967 All Blacks were given an impossible itinerary and survived it largely on the strength of the pride and determination to win with style that Saxton and Fred Allen instilled. They were a perfect combination, these two. Saxton, the organised, disciplined, principled leader, and Allen the emotional, volatile and intensely creative coach.'[9] A future prime minister, Geoffrey Palmer, was doing postdoctoral research at Cambridge at the time of the tour and he was so incensed by the Meads incident that he wrote a letter to the editor of *The Times*. 'There are a number of things about New Zealand rugby that followers of the game in the British Isles do not understand,' Palmer wrote.[10] 'Rugby is one of the central ingredients of New Zealand culture. The physical contact element has always been important in New Zealand rugby. There has been a tendency over here to regard this type of play as ungentlemanly and rough. New Zealanders for their part regard the style of rugby here as soft and effete.'

One of the little-known ironies was that the chairman of the New Zealand union, Tom Morrison, had not wanted Meads on the tour anyway. He had told Allen that Meads, prop Ken Gray and hooker Bruce McLeod should be left out to avoid any risk of offending the British with rough play. Allen rightly told Morrison to stick to his knitting. Allen's unbeaten run as coach of the All Blacks continued until the end of 1968, along the way gaining series victories against Australia and France. But Allen, as he revealed late in his life, was aware of a Wellington clique who thought him too big for his coach's boots, even though he had not lost a game.[11] Such petty campaigns did, and probably still do, happen. Despite the burning desire to go to South Africa and make up for the losses there as captain in 1949, Allen quit. It was a shock to the rugby community, but those close to him knew it was coming. Allen was no man's puppet.

The Welsh toured New Zealand for the first time in 1969 and while there were stars of the future in the side, players such as Edwards, Barry John and J. P. R. Williams, the New Zealanders were as unstoppable as they had been in Britain. This led again to South Africa and the tour there in 1970. This time, three Māori and a Samoan New Zealander were included so the 'no Māoris no tour' protests were stilled, but the argument had moved on to one against playing South Africa as long as its teams were racially selected. This was the message of a few thousand protesters who were at Wellington Airport to 'farewell' the team.

How the *Weekly News* portrayed the selection of the first non-white All Blacks to tour South Africa in 1970. The players are Blair Furlong, Sid Going, 'Buff' Milner (top) and Bryan Williams. *WEEKLY NEWS*, 8 JUNE 1970

For the first time, some players took the side of the protesters – mentally if not physically. Ken Gray, a Wellington prop who had been an All Black since 1963, said at the end of 1969 that he was retiring. It was later learnt that he retired because he did not want to go to South Africa to play racially selected teams. Another of similar mind was not an All Black, but would be the following year. Bob Burgess was teaching in Southland and showed sufficient promise as a rugby player to be nominated for the All Black trials. (In those days, provinces nominated as many players as they wished and the selectors would then choose their trial teams, and consequently their national teams, from nominated players.) When someone from the

Colin Meads against Western Province in 1970, his second game back after breaking his left arm. Note the strapping on his wrist which held in place a specially fitted arm guard.

Southland union told Burgess he was to be nominated, rather than be met with the unalloyed joy that would normally accompany such a statement, Burgess said he did not want to be nominated, thanks all the same.

Allen was replaced as coach in 1969 by a 1955 All Black prop, Ivan Vodanovich, who was in partnership in a menswear shop in Wellington with Allen's arch-foe, Morrison. Vodanovich, for all his personal charm and humour and his work for rugby until his death in 1995, was not a success as a coach. The All Blacks lost the series three to one and, as always, it was the test results that mattered most. But the fact the series was lost obscured the quality of the team – all the provincial matches were won and some players, especially Bryan Williams, Brian Lochore, Grahame Thorne and Colin Meads, were regarded as outstanding. Meads of course was in the news more than most. On this tour it was because he played a test match with a broken arm – another building block in the storied legend of Meads.

Perhaps partly because of the departure of Allen but also because of the unrelenting process of age, the All Blacks entered a new era in the 1970s. Most of the players who had been part of the Allen unbeaten run in the 1960s had retired. Some were still there, especially Meads as captain in 1971, and Ian Kirkpatrick and Sid Going, but largely it was a new generation of players who carried the New Zealand flag. The decade did not begin auspiciously. After losing three tests to South Africa in 1970, the All Blacks then lost two and drew one in 1971 to lose a series to the British Isles for the first time. The tour remains in memories not so much because of the All Blacks – and they were not outclassed – but because of the Lions, who at last and for the only time in

New Zealand realised the potential that lies in the combination of four rugby-playing countries (even if rugby is the main sport in only one of them, Wales). It was the Welsh who provided the playing brilliance with men in their prime such as Barry John and Gareth Edwards, a man gifted in captaincy, John Dawes, and most of all the best coach the Lions have had, Carwyn James. But it was not just a Welsh expedition. The shrewd manager was a Scottish doctor, Doug Smith. Managers were far more publicly influential people on tours then than they are now and Smith was canny enough to bind the four nations into one at the same time as confusing New Zealanders when he said such things as the Lions had worked out who the All Blacks' weak link was. The Lions also had forwards, Willie John McBride, Gordon Brown, Ian McLauchlan, John Pullin, among others, who could fulfil the prime task of delivering the ball to their clever backs.

Vodanovich made the point afterwards that of course the Lions were good but the All Blacks scored more tries than them. That was true; they did. But the Lions won the series and that, for New Zealanders, was really all that mattered. The tour also had a sour note injected by foul play, especially in the Canterbury match. The men regarded as the Lions' two best props at the time, Ray McLoughlin of Ireland and Sandy Carmichael of Scotland, could play no more after Canterbury. Carmichael had two black eyes and it was plain he had been deliberately set upon, but

Ian Kirkpatrick leads the All Blacks towards the field at Ravenhill in Belfast for the 1972 match against Ulster. Police and soldiers patrolled inside and outside the ground because of the sectarian 'troubles' that beset Northern Ireland, but there were no incidents. Earlier in the year, Wales and Scotland had refused to play in Dublin for fear of violence. Players immediately behind Kirkpatrick are Joe Karam and Sid Going (obscured), Ron Urlich, Jeff Matheson, Keith Murdoch and Ken Stewart. PETER BUSH

Llanelli artist Ron Jacobs painted this representation of players leaving the field after Llanelli's 9–3 win against the All Blacks in 1972. He shows a triumphant captain, Delme Thomas, being carried off just behind dejected New Zealanders. The painting was featured seventeen years later on the front of the match programme when Llanelli again met the All Blacks, but this time New Zealand won 11–0.

Carmichael remained loyal to the front rowers' code and would not say who his attacker was (even though most people close to rugby, including reporters, knew the culprit's name).

Aside from a three-test thumping of an Australian team in 1972 – an Australian team that was also beaten by West Coast-Buller – the All Blacks' stocks did not rise. They had a long tour of the British Isles and France over the summer of 1972–73, and while they went close to being the first All Black team to achieve the grand slam, they have been consigned to the failure file in rugby history. That is a harsh judgement because opinions of them seemed to have been formed more on the basis of off-field imagery and rumour than on-field performance. Such a judgement is also a sad way to remember one of the finest of players, and gentlemen, of rugby, Ian Kirkpatrick. This was the tour from which prop Keith Murdoch was banished through his own behaviour (assaulting a hotel security guard) coupled with poor management. Other instances of poor supervision of the players included allowing some to buy hats and be photographed as pretend gangsters, which negatively affected the team's image. The peak of the tour was not one of the tests but the match against the Barbarians. It is still referred to as one of the greatest matches of all time and the try scored by Edwards as one of the finest. That was a cracker of a try, but it should not be overlooked that the All Blacks contributed as much to that game as did the Barbarians (who were more or less the Lions of the year before).

For the next few years, the All Blacks lurched from one controversy to the next and, for a time, the standing of New Zealand rugby had never been lower. The two issues of the twentieth century, South Africa and amateurism, drove rugby down. The downward trajectory accelerated sharply in 1973 when Prime Minister Norman Kirk told the New Zealand union to withdraw its invitation for a South African team to tour. The union did as he asked. Kirk had said the year before that a Labour Government would not stop the proposed tour, but he changed his mind because of a lack of progress towards merit selection in South Africa and because of police concerns about protests in New Zealand.[12] It was not widely reported that Kirk in fact warned that if the tour went ahead the government might need to declare a state of emergency to allow soldiers to act as police: 'I cannot see that any government can contemplate the probability of having to invoke a state of emergency with such sweeping authority in order to discharge an invitation in respect of sport.'[13]

Another factor in the cancellation was that Christchurch at the time was organising the Commonwealth Games for 1974 and games organisers and politicians were concerned that if the rugby tour went ahead African countries would not attend the games. This was probably a justifiable concern, and the contrasting views of South Africa on one hand and the rest of Africa on the other became a constant factor as long as apartheid remained.

It became a strange rugby year in 1973. England cancelled a planned tour of Argentina because of concerns about the country's political stability and the safety of their players. This was at the end of a period of military rule and the return from eighteen years' exile in Spain of the former president, Juan Peron. England toured

Brian ('Stack') Stevens scores England's second try in the 1973 test in Auckland. Bryan Williams, Ian Hurst and Sid Going were too late. It was just the second win by England over the All Blacks.

Wrong place, wrong time, wrong decision

Ernie Todd, the manager of the New Zealand team in Europe in 1972–73, died about eighteen months after the tour, in 1974. The chairman of the New Zealand union at the time of the tour, Jack Sullivan, died in 1990. John Tallent, Sullivan's equivalent in Britain, died in 2004. Stanley Couchman, the English union's liaison man on the tour, died in 1992. With them all died a little piece of one of the most publicised yet most mysterious stories about rugby: the sending home from the tour of the All Black prop, Keith Murdoch.

Others too have died, especially one of Murdoch's closest teammates, Lin Colling, and the journalist who was there in Cardiff in 1972 and who confronted Murdoch in Western Australia in 1974, Terry McLean.

All had pieces of the jigsaw that contributed to the Murdoch tale. It is a story that now cannot be fully told, even in the improbable event of Murdoch himself breaking the habit of a lifetime and talking willingly and openly about himself. Therein lies the continuing fascination with the

Keith Murdoch prominent in his last rugby match: the test against Wales in 1972. PETER BUSH

Murdoch story: the attraction and lure of the unknown and unknowable.

The bare essentials are known: Murdoch went to the kitchen of the Angel Hotel in Cardiff at some late stage during the night after New Zealand had beaten Wales 19–16 at the Arms Park (and Murdoch himself had scored the All Blacks' only try). Some sort of argument with security guards ensued and Todd was summoned from a function room of the hotel by Colling: 'You gotta come down below, Keith's in trouble.'[1] He was indeed. He and the security guards were separated, but somehow Murdoch punched one of them, Peter Grant, whose resulting black eye became a badge of outrage and a target for photographers. Murdoch was reprimanded by Todd the next morning. Although he'd been chosen by the coach, Bob Duff, in the team to play in Birmingham two days later, Todd changed his mind and told Murdoch, by then in Birmingham, to go. Murdoch poked his head in the door of the team bus and told his teammates, 'Hooray boys, I'm off.'

Couchman, the liaison man, accompanied Murdoch by train from Birmingham to Euston Station in London, and then to Heathrow, where Murdoch was put on board a Qantas flight for Sydney, via Singapore. (One of the pettier sidelights to the whole affair was that the British Airports Authority complained Murdoch was given a VIP departure without its authority.)[2] Photos show Murdoch in his All Black blazer without the silver fern pocket badge. Some reports said he was 'stripped' of the badge, but players said later he picked it off himself. The badge had been stitched on, rather than embroidered.

He was booked to fly on from Sydney to Wellington. But he left the flight in Singapore, pleading fatigue to airline staff. 'Passenger requests press not advised,' the Qantas cable from Singapore to Wellington said. 'Please treat as confidential.'[3] He spent the night in the Mandarin Hotel in Singapore as 'Mr Oliver' and was sitting at the airport the next day when he was found by David Barber, the New Zealand Press Association's correspondent in Singapore. Barber, his wife Frances (who was also a journalist), Alan Graham, an NZPA London correspondent returning home who was staying with Barber, and a *Daily Mail* reporter had gone to Changi Airport in search of Murdoch. 'I couldn't believe it when we immediately found the man sitting alone in the terminal building, instantly recognisable even though he had shaved off his Viva Zapata moustache,' Barber recalled.

'Murdoch denied his identity when we approached him,' he said, 'but I saw he was wearing a big wristwatch with the words, "New Zealand Rugby 1972" on the face. He said he didn't want to talk and when I said, "Well, let's go and have a drink," he said something like, "No, that's how this all started."'[4] The *Mail* reporter told Murdoch that Todd had said the British press had conducted a deliberate campaign against him. 'Well, you said it,' Murdoch replied. When told it was Todd who said it, Murdoch smiled and shrugged.

Murdoch boarded the flight (to Sydney via Darwin) and was not heard of again until the president of the Western Australian Rugby Union, Joe Lord, told New Zealand journalists in Adelaide in 1974 that Murdoch was working 'in the bush in the west'. Lord gave more or less precise details of the location.[5] Murdoch had meanwhile cabled his mother Ellen in Dunedin on 11 February 1973, two months after he left Britain: 'Staying here. Will write later. Keith.'[6]

Murdoch has stayed there, although he has made several return visits to New Zealand, on one occasion saving a friend's child from drowning in a residential pool in Timaru.[7] He has also made a few cameo appearances in front of journalists, but said nothing of note or substance. He was required to appear at a coronial hearing in the Northern Territory in 2001 into the death of an Aboriginal man and was as non-committal outside the court as always. He apparently tore up a $50,000 offer from a rugby magazine.[8]

Daily Mail, Tuesday, December 5, 1972 PAGE 15

Exit the wild man, leaving one all-black eye behind

BY MERVYN THOMAS AND AUBREY CHALMERS

TOUGH security guard Peter Grant rubbed his blackened left eye yesterday and told of the night he found himself on the wrong end of a punch from 18-stone Keith Murdoch, 'Wild Man' of the All Blacks Rugby team.

What happened that night—it was described by bearded Mr Grant as like a brawl in a Western saloon — led to Murdoch being sent back to New Zealand in disgrace by his tour manager, Mr Ernie Todd.

Murdoch was on his way by air last night while 29-year-old Mr Grant was giving his account of a celebration party held at the Angel Hotel in Cardiff after the All-Blacks 19—16 victory over Wales.

He said: 'I was called to the kitchen because Murdoch was terrorising waitresses and other members of the staff. He was standing against the oven, trying to get food or drink and behaving like a wild animal.

'Another security officer was with me, and we asked Murdoch to leave without using any force whatsoever. I did not think he was drunk, but we could see he was not going to leave peacefully, so we sent for Mr Todd.

'These blokes are supposed to respect their manager, but when Mr Todd arrived and put a hand on Murdoch's shoulder the player drew his fist back with the intention of hitting him.

'We restrained Murdoch, but some of his friends came along and said they could handle him. We withdrew, but as they came out of the kitchen Murdoch said to me: "You IRA bastard." I'm not even an Irishman. I come from Nuneaton.'

Then came the punch. Said Mr Grant: 'I was talking to one of the other players. I thought Murdoch had gone, but suddenly—clock! He struck me from behind a pillar with a right-hander that gave me a left-eye shiner.

'I was dazed but ready to have a go at him. Fortunately other security men held me back. They probably thought all hell would break out if they let me go.

'I'm a reasonably big man'—he's 6ft. 3in. and weighs 17st. — 'but this bloke Murdoch has hands like shovels and his arms and wrists make mine look matchsticks. You can see where the violence comes from into this game if this is what one player can do.'

Shocked

Mr Grant went on: 'Murdoch had been causing trouble before, tipping beer over waiters in the bar as well as the kitchen. One waiter was carrying a large tray of glasses. Murdoch knocked them over.

'Murdoch said the British Lions left a pile of glasses 3ft. deep before leaving New Zealand at the end of their tour. I [illegible] had the same idea.'

Tour manager Todd, who investigated the hotel incident, announced the decision to send home Murdoch to a shocked All Blacks team, who were in Birmingham for tomorrow's game against Midland Counties. Murdoch left immediately for Heathrow Airport in London.

Mr Todd said later: 'He is going home because we feel it would be in the best interests of the team and for Keith himself. I intend to apologise to the security guard, although Murdoch has not asked me to do so.

'Murdoch has accepted the decision to send him home like the wonderful man he is. He accepted the situation, probably to a better degree than most other men would have done. I will miss him from the team. My word I will.'

Hazard

Murdoch, who plays prop forward, said on the way to the airport: 'It was the management's decision to send me home. It had nothing to do with me. This will not affect the tour. The team will still win without me.'

Last night another row broke when Murdoch was smuggled aboard a Qantas Jumbo jet from a side door at Heathrow. The British Airports Authority protested in a statement that the move was made without their knowledge or authority. They said they were taking the matter up with the police, immigration authorities and Qantas airline at 'the earliest possible moment.'

Last word from bruised security guard Grant: 'The whole thing has cast a smear on players representing their countries abroad—and it has certainly finished my wife and I with New Zealand lamb chops!'

Security man Grant, with his black eye

Murdoch in London yesterday

Picture by RONALD FORTUNE

Terry O'Connor writes . . .

Bad boy Murdoch should never have been selected

KEITH MURDOCH should never have been included in the All Blacks team. His dismissal from the party leaves a smear on Rugby and will overshadow the New Zealand party until the end of the tour.

Bad man Murdoch arrived with a reputation which made it certain he would turn any row into a brawl. What happened at Cardiff was always likely.

Ernie Todd, the manager, had no choice but to send him home. Todd should never have been put in the position by the selectors.

During the 1970 All Black tour of South Africa, Murdoch hit the little Springbok fly-half Piet Visagie in a bar because he didn't like something which was said. Following this Murdoch was attacked by Visagie's friends and injured to such an extent he did not play for a month.

Last year when the British Lions were in New Zealand, Murdoch became a mystery man. Three times he was selected to play against the Lions but never turned out, claiming he was unfit.

These snubs still did not deter the New Zealand selectors from including him in the prestige tour of the British Isles.

They were prepared to overlook the many unsavoury fights he had been involved in. Yet they must have realised his ungentlemanly manner would place him in a number of difficult situations.

This was typified when he ended up swearing at Sir William Ramsay during what should have been a normal Rugby conversation.

'Come and have Christmas dinner with me and we will see who can swear the most,' said Sir William, who was knighted for his work for Rugby.

It is impossible to converse with Murdoch. I have tried but he refuses, or is unable, to contribute.

In Dunedin, where Murdoch lives, he pulls pints and acts as a bouncer in a tough dock-side pub. This is just one of the many unskilled jobs he has tried.

As a player, Murdoch is exceptionally strong and fast for a prop but his ability as a scrummager has been frequently exposed by British teams.

Excuse

What talents he may have are countered by his uncontrolled use of fists and feet. The Welsh captain, Delme Thomas, now has a black eye because Murdoch took a poke at him during the international last Saturday for no reason at all.

This should now be the end of Murdoch's unsavoury Rugby career. He can never be selected for New Zealand again and surely his own team, Otago, cannot again use the excuse that they need a tough man to protect their own players.

The 'wild one' is coming . . .

What O'Connor said in the Mail on September 25.

The *Daily Mail*'s farewell treatment of Keith Murdoch. *DAILY MAIL*, 5 DECEMBER 1972

While no one knows the whole truth about what happened and what Murdoch's version of events may be, he probably does not know the whole story either. It seems unlikely that Todd told him why he had changed his mind about not sending him home. The reason was pressure from the Four Home Unions Committee (an umbrella group for the British countries and Ireland). It transpired later that Todd on the Sunday, the morning after, told the chairman of the committee, Tallent, that Murdoch was being sent home. Tallent was satisfied. But the team then went to Birmingham and Todd told Tallent that Murdoch was not going home after all. With Tallent at the time, according to Tallent, were the secretary of the Four Home Unions, Albert Agar, and the veteran treasurer and former president of the Welsh Rugby Union, Ken Harris. Tallent phoned Jack Sullivan in Wellington on the Monday (Sunday for Tallent) and although there is no written record of what was said, Sullivan two days later recalled that Tallent had promised him a full report by cable 'of the Murdoch incident and the views of Mr Tallent and his Committee in relation thereto'.

Tallent, an England centre in the 1930s, a stockbroker and an army colonel, among other achievements, did not send the promised cable and Sullivan booked a call to him on the afternoon of Wednesday, 6 December. Sullivan had with him his deputy chairman, Ces Blazey, and the union secretary, Ray Morgan. He had Morgan record a transcript of the conversation, made possible by Sullivan repeating Tallent's words for Morgan's

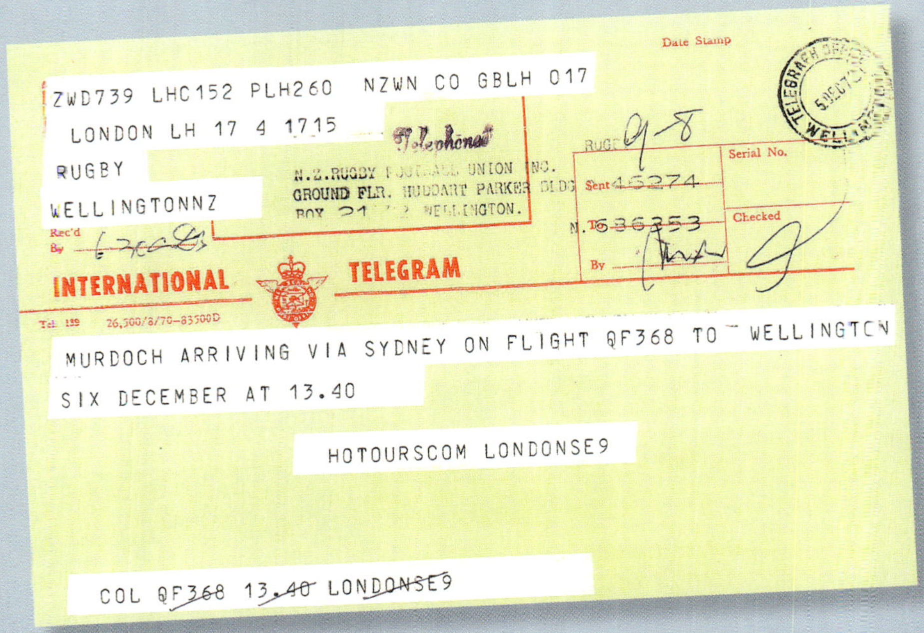
ZWD739 LHC152 PLH260 NZWN CO GBLH 017
LONDON LH 17 4 1715
RUGBY
WELLINGTONNZ
INTERNATIONAL TELEGRAM
MURDOCH ARRIVING VIA SYDNEY ON FLIGHT QF368 TO WELLINGTON
SIX DECEMBER AT 13.40
HOTOURSCOM LONDONSE9
COL QF368 13.40 LONDONSE9

The telegram giving details of Keith Murdoch's arrival. It arrived; he did not.

benefit. It was this conversation that starkly set out why Todd changed his mind.[9] Morgan's transcript reveals towards the end of the conversation:

> Mr Sullivan said 'to recap the whole position once more and to confirm the telephone conversation of two days ago, was this the position? A. Unless Murdoch went home, the tour was in jeopardy? Answer – yes. B. If Murdoch did not go home the manager was in jeopardy? Answer – yes. They would ask for a replacement of the manager.'

Fleet Street, meanwhile, could not get enough of the story. Murdoch was dubbed 'the wild man' and the *Daily Mail* cartoonist, Jon, pictured Murdoch in a cage being shipped back to New Zealand.[10] This raised the ire of an English woman living in Wellington, Joan Kaye, who wrote to the paper in defence of the All Blacks in general and of Murdoch in particular: 'Keith Murdoch's punishment is in itself enough, without the added insults of your cartoon . . . excerpts from articles in British papers . . . indicate that the British Press has contributed more to the increase of tension than anything.'[11] Practically all stories carried emotive descriptions such as '18-stone prop', 'burly bar bouncer', and 'disgraced giant'.

There was a suggestion that Murdoch may have been sent home to forestall police action against him, but the police themselves denied that. A Cardiff police spokesman confirmed that police went to the hotel and spoke to Todd before the team left for Birmingham. But no other police action was taken. 'It was one of numerous incidents we get on international rugby nights,' a spokesman was quoted as saying.[12] Anyone who has been in the Angel Hotel the night of a Cardiff test knows the place is shoulder to shoulder with rugby people.

Five years after Todd died of cancer, his widow Pat made public a tape recording Todd made in Birmingham, which revealed that there was more than just the Angel Hotel incident behind the dispatch of Murdoch. Todd talked to his wife on the tape:

> It was sad seeing the boys say goodbye to him. I know they think I'm a prize ratbag but darling, I had to do it – I really did. He'd been in quite a bit of trouble . . . not quite a bit of trouble, but on

> three or four occasions he's been in trouble and . . . John Tallent . . . virtually demanded that I send him home. We tried to get out of it but the more I thought about it the more I thought, 'Well, there's no guarantee that he wouldn't do the same thing again if he had the same amount of drink' and Keith admitted this. So he had to go home . . .[13]

This did not tally with a comment made by Todd at the annual meeting of the New Zealand RFU in Wellington in April 1973: 'I took the decision personally,' he told delegates, 'and I take all responsibility. The decision was mine alone, there was no direction to me from any source.'[14] At least three people in the room, Sullivan, Blazey and Morgan, knew this comment to be wrong, but nothing was said publicly. There had been speculation before the meeting that members of the ruling council might be discarded because of dissatisfaction with the national union on a number of fronts, including its handling of Murdoch. But only two lost their seats – Jack Griffiths, a former All Black captain, and Morrie Ingpen.

Typically, there was much anecdotal talk among journalists about what Murdoch had done on this or other tours; some of the stories found their way into print, some have not; some of the stories may have been true, some not. Terry McLean recounted a few of them in 1990 at the time of the screening of a TVNZ documentary which purported to tell the 'true' story about the sending home of Murdoch, but of course did no such thing.[15] Many of the stories about Murdoch related to journalists, which should be no surprise given that it was journalists who kept the stories in circulation. The *Auckland Star* journalist on the 1972–73 tour, Roy Williams, was said to have been upended out of his bed in Belfast by Murdoch; a former *New Zealand Herald* writer and colleague of McLean's, Norman Harris, was apparently thrown to the floor by Murdoch in Peebles; there was another story about one of the NZPA men in London, Mike Robson, being confronted in some way by Murdoch in Cardiff. There was an older story about a *Truth* reporter, Chris Gaskell, being held fully clothed under a shower in Dunedin. Such incidents occur on tours but whenever they involved Murdoch they seemed to cross the line, either at the time or in the retelling, from horseplay to assault, from high jinks to low acts. McLean believed that the assault on Harris, reported anonymously in the *Sunday Times* the morning after the Welsh match, was instrumental in the sending home. 'I waited in the hotel foyer for Todd to return from mass. Was there any truth in the story, I asked, that he intended to send Murdoch home? "Too bloody right there is," said Todd. And that, despite the recommendation of the tour committee . . . was about that.'[16]

McLean seemed to have got himself ahead of evidence and events.[17] Another journalist who was there at the time was the sports editor of the *Western Mail* in Cardiff, J. B. G. (Bryn) Thomas. He had a close relationship with Welsh union officials and was in no doubt why Murdoch was banished: 'If the real truth of the Murdoch case was to be published, as I have received it from official sources, it would shock the whole New Zealand nation. It was never a question of the Manager sending him home voluntarily. He was given orders to send him. This I know to be true.'[18] (Thomas could not have known, but the recording of the conversation between Tallent and Sullivan confirmed his view.)

Once the news of what happened in Cardiff was published, many other incidents related to Murdoch, or thought to, were regurgitated. Among them was a comic tale of Murdoch hitting the South African first five-eighth, Piet Visagie, by mistake in 1970. Peter Devlin, sports editor of the *Auckland Star*, had been in South Africa and related how a persistent local annoyed the All Blacks at Upington after the match against North-West Cape.[19] The All Blacks were on their bus and about to leave the after-match function when someone thumped on the bus door.

Two men central to the Keith Murdoch saga: manager Ernie Todd at left and the NZRFU chairman, Jack Sullivan.

Murdoch, Devlin reported two years later, thought the thumper must have been the annoying man from the function. 'Murdoch opened the door and threw a punch only to find that . . . the man on the receiving end was . . . Visagie.' He was trying to say goodbye to the All Blacks. It was something Murdoch did two years later – forever.

Murdoch was let down by the New Zealand Rugby Football Union, which cravenly bowed to the wishes of the British tours committee. That committee's chairman, John Tallent, was perfectly entitled to complain to Todd or Sullivan about the behaviour of one or more of the players. But to then demand the expulsion of Murdoch or the expulsion of Todd or the abandonment of the tour went too far. Sullivan should never have agreed. But Sullivan, like Tallent, was reared and educated in a different way to those who sit in later judgement. Questioning the hegemony of Britain came from a later generation, not from Sullivan's. Wellington journalist Alex Veysey, who was not on the tour, alluded to this in a piece he wrote for the *Sunday Times* in London:

> It is not stretching the longbow to align the tenderness of New Zealanders over the British immigration legislation to a further deterioration in their mental relationship to what they once called the mother country because of press bombast on rugby matters. It seems to them that while it is a highly desirable thing in British eyes for colonials to follow the gentle courtesies of ambassadorship while in Britain the reverse compliment need not apply.[20]

Veysey also mentioned numerous well-publicised 'wrecking' (and worse) incidents by various Lions teams in New Zealand and South Africa over the years that had not resulted in any disciplinary action; in fact some 'antics' gained tacit approval from the team management. The action by some New Zealand newspapers, notably the low-market *Sunday News* and *Truth*, against the Lions in 1977 (the 'lousy lovers' tour), was in part a reaction to the excesses of the British press on the Murdoch affair.

There may have been earlier, but there were certainly later, off-field incidents of the same order as Murdoch's. At least three All Blacks spent time in police custody for forms of assault but were able to rejoin their teams and continue their tours, virtually unpunished other than the stain of a brief flurry of publicity. In all the time Murdoch has had for contemplation in the vastness of the Australian outback, he would justifiably have felt hard done by.

England captain John Pullin speaks to the crowd after the upset win at Eden Park in 1973. The loss is reflected in the faces of the All Black captain, Ian Kirkpatrick, and selector Ivan Vodanovich (seated in the centre).

New Zealand instead and provided great joy for the provinces they played because England lost to each, but then great sorrow for the country because the All Blacks were badly beaten in the single test. The NZRFU also organised an internal tour to try to make up for the loss of the Springboks and this included two matches, one in Wellington and the other in Auckland, as de facto farewell matches for Meads. A President's XV captained by Meads in fact beat the All Blacks in Wellington, and just to emphasise the low state of the national team, they were also beaten in Dunedin by the national under 23 team, the Junior All Blacks.

Rugby in this period of trial gained support from an unexpected, even unlikely, quarter, the editorial in the weekly *Listener*, the broadcasting programme magazine that was transformed into a thinking listener's journal. Its editor at the time, novelist and broadcaster Ian Cross, argued that rugby was central to New Zealand:

> Rugby is also being exposed to doubt these days because it is alone in carrying the full weight of a change in our policy of international relationships. This is quite a burden for it. The time has come to pay some compensatory recognition to a game that has given us a unifying pride and more regard for ourselves in relation to other nations.[14]

Cross's words were written in 1973. The burden became infinitely heavier in the following years and in the polarising climate of contact with South Africa, 'compensatory recognition' for the good rugby has done was almost totally absent. Rugby could hardly complain because it brought most of what it suffered through the 1970s and 1980s upon itself. Whether at the administrative, playing or just the support level, rugby found itself being pulled by competing forces – one way to keep playing against South Africans and finally win a series there; the other way to march in step with most of the rest of the western world and shun the South Africans until white rule was exposed as the untenable expedient that it was.

If there were a Richter-type scale to measure the magnitude of shock and revulsion to accompany each rugby tour during this period, 1981 would be of the greatest order and 1976 would be second. In 1976, the All Blacks were

A cartoonist in the weekly *Rugby News* comments on Prime Minister Norman Kirk's instruction to the New Zealand union to call off the South African tour in 1973. *RUGBY NEWS*, 28 MARCH 1973

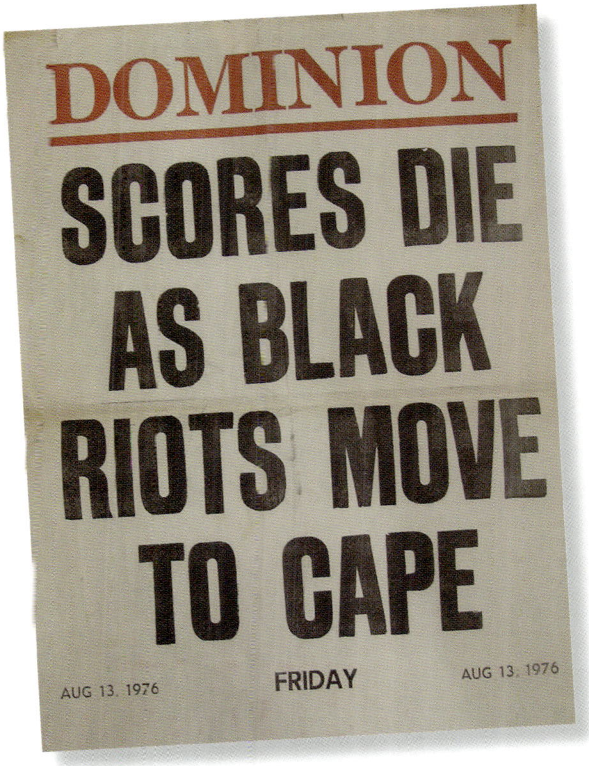

A *Dominion* billboard tells potential readers of the South African riots spreading from Soweto in Johannesburg to Cape Town.

dispatched to South Africa and travelled by a ludicrously circuitous route to avoid possible trade union action in Australia (and how ironic that would have been, given the ambivalence if not reluctance of unions in New Zealand to support their ideological cousins in the Labour Party). The tour in a rugby sense ended much the same way as the others had – easy wins against provinces, complaints about itineraries, travelling and referees, and a loss in the test series.

The consequences of this tour reached around the world for the first time, however, thanks in the main to Abraham Ordia, a Nigerian who was president of an umbrella political organisation, the Supreme Council for Sport in Africa. Whatever its other aims, Ordia ensured the council focused on ridding South Africa of apartheid, and one way he saw to do that was to deny the Afrikaners their cherished confrontations with New Zealand rugby. Early in the year, Ordia said if the All Blacks went to South Africa, he would ensure a boycott of the Olympic Games in Montreal later in

All Blacks Ian Kirkpatrick and Bryan Williams were caught in the crossfire when police responded to rioters in Cape Town in 1976 with teargas. Police rescued the two players, plus journalist Bob Howitt and photographer Ross Wiggins, and put them in the safety of one of their vans. Wiggins took this photo of Kirkpatrick in the van. *NZ HERALD*

The two Robertsons, Bruce for New Zealand and Ian for South Africa (he was actually a Zimbabwean), pictured in the fourth test in South Africa in 1976. They were the two central figures in the match's most controversial incident. Bruce Robertson kicked ahead into the South African in-goal area and, while following up, was obstructed by Ian Robertson. The All Blacks were given a penalty, which Bryan Williams turned into three points, but New Zealanders argued it should have been a penalty try. South Africa won the match 15–14. *DB RUGBY ANNUAL*, 1976 (MOA PUBLICATIONS)

the year. This was rugby, a minor sport in most countries, being kicked up into the big league by its association with South Africa. Ordia began the era of Olympic boycotts by seeking New Zealand's suspension from the Olympics because of the All Blacks' tour. In a rash of meetings in the Queen Elizabeth Hotel in Montreal the International Olympic Committee member in New Zealand, Lance Cross, successfully persuaded the IOC that rugby had nothing to do with the Olympics and the New Zealand team in Montreal was blameless. The IOC agreed so the boycott began. First it was just African countries, then a few Asians and then some Caribbean. Some of the 'boycotting' countries had reasons of their own for not being in Montreal, and it was easy to be cynical about the undemocratic nature of most of them. Ordia had been bold enough to go to New Zealand to preach his concerns, and underlying his Montreal anger was an antipathy between him and the New Zealand Prime Minister, Robert Muldoon. It had not helped the All Blacks that shortly before their tour began, school children in Soweto, the rambling non-white outer southern suburb of Johannesburg, began rioting. Nearly 200 were believed to have been killed in the government crackdown and rioting continued spasmodically throughout the tour.

A few players vowed never to go to South Africa again, but it was hard to determine whether that was because of apartheid or because a referee, Gert Bezuidenhout, had not awarded the

Cartoonist Eric Heath drew this caricature of Prime Minister Robert Muldoon (later Sir Robert) during the South African controversy. *SPORTS DIGEST*, AUGUST 1977

All Blacks a penalty try in the fourth test when he ought to have. The whole tour certainly soured the New Zealand coach, J. J. Stewart, who had taken over the job in 1974. He became an unrelenting critic of South Africa, its politics and its rugby. He disliked the way the South Africans played the game – 'it's a kicking game, let's all go and surf' – and during the tour he made no attempt to hide his contempt for the country's political system. But he still had the grace to enter the referees' room after the last test and present Bezuidenhout with an All Black blazer. Bezuidenhout, so it was reported, burst into tears.[15] New Zealanders cried for a different reason.

The 1970s in rugby were not all unrelieved gloom, however. One of the arguments against the anti-apartheid protesters was their inconsistency and their lack of opposition to countries such as Romania which, under the communist rule of Nicolae Ceausescu, was as oppressive as any. Such arguments missed the point. The Romanians toured New Zealand for the first time in 1975 and some of their players were astonished when, at their first port of call, the NZRFU's liaison man with them, Ivan Vodanovich, grabbed a bunch of forwards in the hotel corridor and showed them how to pack and go down in scrums. The Romanians who avoided the impromptu practice looked on with eyes wide in wonder. The Romanian team had with them 33-year-old Valeriu Irimescu, who had played the last of his 32 tests four years before. His role on the tour was vague and he seemed to do an awful lot of wandering around with hands behind his back and with an enigmatic smile on his face. He professed not to speak English, but he knew very well that the English speakers had dubbed him 'the KGB man' or the commissar. Despite his known playing background, he rarely trained with the team and took the field just once, as a replacement in the last minutes in Blenheim against Marlborough. His one contribution was to calmly kick a conversion from wide out. His enigmatic smile got wider.

All Black teammates, provincial rivals. Graham Mourie (right) and Kevin Eveleigh lead out their Taranaki and Manawatu teams for a National Provincial Championship match in 1977. Behind Eveleigh is another All Black teammate, Doug Rollerson.

The NZRFU introduced structure and a national element to provincial rugby with the start in 1976 of the national championship. Previously, provinces organised their own matches with nothing more at stake than a provincial pride and the trophies that were available in regional contests such as the Coronation Shield (Auckland, Bay of Plenty, Counties, King Country, Northland, Thames Valley and Waikato). An Auckland administrator, Barry Smith, is most often regarded as the man who led the campaign for a national championship, but there were others in other areas.[16] The national union, innately conservative, took some persuading to adopt the scheme partly because it knew the international board and the British unions were opposed to what they called

The poster produced for the first tour of Argentina by a national New Zealand team in 1976. The illustration also served as the cover for match programmes.

'leagues'. But by the mid-1970s it was an idea whose time had come, and the first winners of the first division were Bay of Plenty; it was no coincidence that four of their players were in a second New Zealand team later in 1976 that toured Argentina for the first time. The championship thus proved in its first year that it provided an automatic stepping stone for players from provincial to national level. The original eleven first-division unions were chosen based on performances in the previous five years. The first competition in 1976 comprised the first division plus a second division based on each of the North and South Islands. That format continued until 1984 and the championship has undergone various changes since, including the introduction of semifinals and finals in 1992. One of the ironies of the first year was that it was sponsored by Radio New Zealand, a medium which the NZRFU had long regarded with suspicion. Ever since the first broadcast of a rugby match in 1926, administrators had worried about radio exploiting the game and having the potential to keep spectators away. These concerns were transferred to television for a later generation of administrators. The first test was telecast only in 1972.[17]

The national game seemed to have returned to a semblance of its old self in 1977 when the Lions toured and the All Blacks won the series. But it was a Lions team captained by the gifted Welshman, Phil Bennett, who had not wanted to be captain and did not like being away from home. It was coached by another Welshman, John Dawes, who found coaching in New Zealand quite different to captaining as he had in 1971, and managed by a Scot, George Burrell, popular when he managed Scotland on their first tour in 1975 but less so with the Lions. Some sections of the New Zealand press were especially virulent and harmed the general standing of both the newspaper industry and of the Lions. This was the tour that included one newspaper headline: 'Lions lousy lovers'. The *Sunday News* quoted a woman as saying she had had sex with four of the Lions and found them boring and self-centred and anything but exciting. *Sunday News* and its weekly partner in grime *Truth* maintained an anti-Lions outrage for much of the tour, which did little for

The climax to the Lions series in 1977. Lawrie Knight scores the try that gave New Zealand the test and the series. The Lions captain, Phil Bennett, is on his knees after a vain attempt to stop Knight. The other Lions are Scots Doug Morgan (left) and Ian McGreechan (13). PETER BUSH

the equanimity of Burrell or Dawes, or the players. But they were still nearly good enough to beat the All Blacks and could have squared the series with a win in the fourth test at Eden Park. The Lions were in front 9–6 as the end approached but their hooker, Peter Wheeler, lost control of the ball in a tackle by Graham Mourie. The ball bobbed up into the arms of No. 8 Lawrie Knight and he trotted over the line unthreatened for the winning try. This was also the test in which the All Blacks were embarrassed by being outplayed in the forwards and at one point put down a three-man scrum. Strong men in the stands put their heads in their hands, John Reason wrote.[18] It was not quite as bad as it was painted. Prop John McEldowney left the field injured and play continued while his injury was assessed and before replacement Bill Bush could take the field. When a scrum was ordered and only one prop available, captain Tane Norton made Knight a makeshift prop and withdrew the other forwards.

South Africa's pariah status led to the decade highlight for New Zealand rugby, just as it had created the opportunity for the 1967 team. In late 1977, while the All Blacks squared a series in France, the British and Irish unions (which

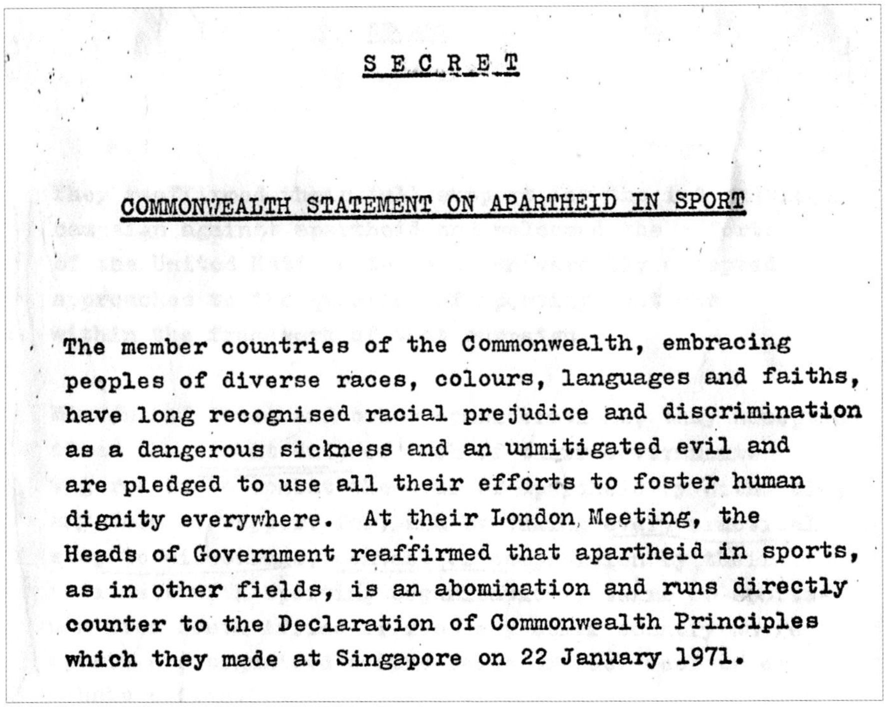

SECRET

COMMONWEALTH STATEMENT ON APARTHEID IN SPORT

The member countries of the Commonwealth, embracing peoples of diverse races, colours, languages and faiths, have long recognised racial prejudice and discrimination as a dangerous sickness and an unmitigated evil and are pledged to use all their efforts to foster human dignity everywhere. At their London Meeting, the Heads of Government reaffirmed that apartheid in sports, as in other fields, is an abomination and runs directly counter to the Declaration of Commonwealth Principles which they made at Singapore on 22 January 1971.

A copy of a draft of the 1977 Gleneagles Agreement, before it was approved by a full session of the Commonwealth heads of government meeting in London.

collectively met as the Four Home Unions) decided they could not agree to the scheduled tour of the British Isles by South Africa in 1978–79. A Labour government was in power in Britain and Commonwealth heads of government (including Britain's James Callaghan) had reached what was known as the Gleneagles Agreement under which they would in their own ways discourage sports contact with South Africa. Britain also had the recent memory of disruption of the 1969–70 South African tour. The British and Irish turned to New Zealand for their replacement tour. This became known as the grand slam tour, the first by an All Black team to beat each of the British Isles countries on the one tour. Russ Thomas, a grocery chain manager in Christchurch, managed the team and its playing side was led by coach Jack Gleeson and captain Graham Mourie, the pair who had been together in Argentina in 1976 and France in November 1977. It was a modern version of the Kiwis and of the 1967 team – characterised by a desire to play attractive, disciplined rugby and to enhance, or rebuild, New Zealand's rugby reputation on and off the field. Gleeson's coaching mantra was 'play the game at pace and be a thinker'. This was largely what the All Blacks did in their opening matches until they ran into a brick wall in Limerick. For the only time, a New Zealand rugby team was beaten in Ireland. The Munster team was too committed, too strong, too desperate for an All Black team that wondered what had hit it. Gleeson the morning after the game talked about Munster's 'kamikaze tacklers' but they were not that, because they got up and tackled again. And again. It was one of those matches that become rugby folklore. The match programme was reprinted after the game – and sold out. Bumper stickers in Limerick read: 'Munster 12 New Zealand 0'. They too sold out.

Before Munster, the fifth match of the tour, there had been some sotto voce talk of an unbeaten tour. The match following Munster was the first test, against Ireland, and after that had been won in the last minute, there were whispered comments within the New Zealand party about a grand slam. Players themselves dared not entertain such

Munster wing Jimmy Bowen on the attack that led to Christy Cantillon's try against the All Blacks in Limerick in 1978. Munster won 12–0, New Zealand's only loss to an Irish team. 'Once they got ahead,' captain Graham Mourie said later, 'they became fanatical.' *LIMERICK LEADER*

distant goals, at least not publicly, but it was in the backs of minds. It came closer after the win against Wales, the match that was won by replacement Brian McKechnie's penalty goal (which was not awarded for Andy Haden's theatrical dive from the lineout, as often presumed), and closer still after a surprisingly comfortable win against England. It came finally in the gloaming at Murrayfield and people in the stand could barely see Bruce Robertson as he ghosted through the dusk to score the winning try. Haden's attempt to gain a penalty aside, such a celebratory tour was marred only by the Bridgend game when J. P. R. Williams, second only to Gareth Edwards in Welsh affections at the time, had a cheek gashed open by one of New Zealand prop John Ashworth's boots.

When the Welsh union marked its centenary two years later, in 1980, the All Blacks were there as playing guests. That tour too had its controversy. All Black lock Graeme Higginson was ordered off in the match against Llanelli by Scottish referee Allan Hosie, but entreaties by the New Zealand captain, Graham Mourie, and Welshmen Ray Gravell and Phil Bennett, forced a judicious change of mind. The way the All Blacks played and the results they achieved had them high in public esteem. But soon they were at the other end of the scale.

It's not just a game for men

A hundred years after the first public proposal in New Zealand that women could and should play rugby, the first official World Cup for women was played in Wales in 1991. The centenary was entirely coincidental. For most of those hundred years, the idea that women might play a man's game was often derided as preposterous, ridiculous and dangerous. It was only in the last twenty or so years of the twentieth century that the women's game showed any formal organisation and only in the last decade that it gained official approval.

Football for females made a fleeting appearance in the press as early as 1888 when it was suggested that Wellington schoolgirls might play a modified form of rugby. Nothing seems to have come of it.[1] A more definable beginning came in 1891 when Nita Webbe proposed the formation of two teams with a view to playing exhibition matches around New Zealand and Australia. Little is known about Webbe, who lived at the time in Ponsonby, but her cameo role in the genesis of women's rugby has been mentioned, if briefly, in most histories. A noted chronicler of women's history, Sandra Coney, herself reared in a rugby household, noted that Webbe formed a team that she planned to tour. 'This was vigorously condemned as unwomanly and it is not clear if the tour ever went ahead,' Coney wrote.[2] The tour did not go ahead, but even more remarkable than Webbe's idea that women could play the game was the fact she proposed a travelling troupe of paid players, something not proposed for men until the half-hearted attempts to promote professional rugby in the 1970s and 1980s. She planned to pay her players 10 shillings a week (about $85 today). Webbe's idea, however bold and pioneering it was, got no further than the similar plans put forward by 1970s men such as David Lord in Sydney and Lew Pryme in Auckland. (It is possible that Nita Webbe was Oamaru-born Mary Anita White, who married Frederick Cleaver Webbe in Wellington in 1887. He died in Sydney in 1918 and she also in Sydney in 1930. Her death notice said she was also known as Netty.)

According to the *Auckland Star*, Webbe had 30 women in training and they 'have already obtained a fair degree of proficiency in manipulating the leather'.[3] But the newspaper's editorial writer or perhaps his boss, the civic-minded editor Thomson Leys, did not like the idea and though he professed that 'every sphere in which women are fitted to take their part should be as freely open to them as men', women were 'constitutionally unfitted' for rugby and such games would be 'essentially unwomanly'.[4] He wondered whether men and women would encourage sisters to enter the life of an itinerant footballer and also raised doubts about the financial security of the promoters. Webbe wrote in reply with several examples of women entering spheres previously deemed unfit for them – law, medicine and sports such as cricket and swimming – and said the women's game could be better than the men's: 'Strict observance to the rules will be enforced and when they play in public I am confident that the verdict will be not only that there has not been the slightest breach of propriety, but that a cleverer game has seldom been seen here.'[5]

But they never played in public. About a month later, newspapers reported the scheme had been abandoned and the weekly *Observer* recorded, without further explanation, 'a certain action for damages having broken down, the projected team

The first match played by the 'British ladies football team', as depicted in the *Graphic* by artist Henry Paget. *GRAPHIC*, 30 MARCH 1895

of female footballers has come to nought'.[6] The uncompleted action may have been related to the *Star*'s questioning of the Webbes' finances, but that can be only speculation. Some later reports recorded the tour was abandoned because of public outrage – Coney's 'vigorously condemned'; the *Star* leader writer would be flattered if he could know he spoke so loudly for the public. In fact, reports of Webbe's plans and the scrapping of them did not dominate newspapers. If there was public outrage, it was not expressed in newspapers.

Webbe's plans, although they did not come to fruition, preceded similar moves in Britain that have attracted more scholarly attention than Webbe has. The advent of the British Ladies Football Club in 1895 was, according to author James F. Lee, 'a cultural expression of change . . . another example of growing opportunities for women in sport in the 1890s'. The game the women played was soccer, but the same concerns were raised whenever women played, or wanted to play, a game that was deemed by men to be unsuitable for them. The advent of women's football in England and Scotland was reported in New Zealand newspapers.[7]

It is impossible to know when women first played rugby, and probably irrelevant when they did so. Of all the football matches of indeterminate types played before rugby was organised, it is reasonable to assume that some females took part, whether in picnic or fete matches or in something a little more organised. Not all women of course were in favour of the game. Annabella McLean wrote to her older brother, the Lands Minister, Sir Donald McLean, in an undated letter (but in the early 1870s): 'Football has commenced. I wish it would pour of rain every Saturday for it is a rough game.'[8] (As was common at the time, the type of football was not given.)

In the selective, retrospective expertise that rugby marketing has developed, a ten-year-old Ulster girl, Emily Valentine, was promoted at the women's World Cup in 2010 as 'the first lady of rugby'. She was evidently watching a school match at Portora Royal School in Enniskillen in 1887 when she persuaded the boys to allow her to take part. In later life, as Emily Galwey, she remembered: 'I got the ball – I can still feel the damp leather and the smell of it . . . I grasped it and ran dodging, darting . . .'[9] This female version of William Webb Ellis at least had the benefit of recorded evidence, but there is no reason to suppose she was the first or only girl to join in a game somewhere at some time.

The issue is not when females first played, but when the women's game was organised. The slow emergence of women's rugby needs to be seen in a contemporary context and not through a prism of political correctness. The sports for women that developed first and most rapidly were those which

A stereotypical view of women's rugby in its early years, although this sketch by French illustrator Fabien Fabiano from *Fantasio* magazine in 1924 could have been about *barette*, supposedly a non-contact rugby-like sport played by French women. The captain commands her players to press on with the melee while she touches up her make-up. FRÉDÉRIC HUMBERT COLLECTION

were not dominated by men or seen as men-only sports. Of team sports, basketball (netball from 1970) and hockey were two; other sports such as athletics, swimming, cricket, golf and bowls took longer to acquire organisation and standing. Athletics in New Zealand had no championship races for women until 1926 and then only a couple until 1939; swimming had only one national title event for women from 1912 until 1921 when extras were added intermittently over following years. Internationally, women were so frustrated by the lack of events allowed them by men that a French professional interpreter, Alice Milliat, organised world women's games until the International Olympic Committee reluctantly caught up.[10] The IOC's president, Henri de Baillet-Latour, visited Wellington after the Olympic Games in Los Angeles in 1932 and ventured the opinion that women should still have their own games rather than be admitted to the quadrennial event he controlled. His predecessor and founder of the IOC, Pierre de Coubertin, was also against women competing at the Olympics.[11] Milliat also had a role in the women's sports club, known as Fémina-Sport, which had been formed (by a man) in 1911 and arranged a variety of sports for women. Included among them was *barette*, which had some characteristics of rugby and some of touch football, and was said to be a southern offshoot of the earlier game based in Normandy and Picardy, *la soule*. French rugby historian Philip Dine called *barette* a genteel alternative to the full-contact game.[12] It seems to have faded out in the 1930s.

In New Zealand, women's exhibition rugby matches or early attempts at an organised club competition owed little if anything to the men's established clubs, but there was still a rugby-playing male influence. For example, at a fundraising sports day in Wellington in 1915, two women's teams played an exhibition of 'rugby as it should be played' at halftime of a men's match. Despite the limited duration, each team scored a try.[13] A hint at the male influence came from the referee, who was named only as Mrs du Chateau. But people in the know would have been aware she was May, the daughter of the 1884 All Black, Harry Roberts, and sister of Teddy Roberts, who was the New Zealand halfback both before and after the First World War.[14] The match was played to raise money for war-related purposes and those involved, as well as spectators, probably saw nothing beyond the novelty of women playing rugby for a good cause. But a similar occurrence in Western Australia, where women first played Australian football to raise money, has been elevated by scholarly re-evaluation. A Melbourne historian and authority on Australian sport, Rob Hess, said the women's innovative venture 'is an important element in overall understandings of how both masculine and feminine ideals were being challenged and redefined by sporting practices, especially those associated with football codes played by women, in a time of tremendous social flux'.[15]

Scholarly analysis has also zeroed in on attempts to establish women's football teams in New Zealand in the 1920s (especially 1921). One theory was that women would have figured they had to do men's jobs in wartime so why not play men's games in peacetime? But that seems to have been more applicable to industrial Britain than New Zealand. An Auckland scholar, Barbara Cox, herself an international soccer player, suggested that as the beginning of the 1920s was a significant time of social change, including 'new forms of dance, movies, less desire for early marriage and more freedom for women', the women who wanted to play various versions of football were no different to any other women of their time.[16] Cox muses about various reasons why the 'girl footballers' made their entrances in 1921 and made their exits after just a few months. One possible reason she does not mention is that the 'girls' could have been inspired or influenced by the South African rugby players in New Zealand at the same time, filling reels of newsprint, but her focus was on league and soccer as well as rugby. Cox suggests netball emerged as the 'appropriate' game for women as a counterpoint to the football experiments. It is true the first national netball tournament was played only in 1926 (to coincide with an international exhibition in Dunedin), but the game had been played increasingly since the early 1900s.

A young Wellington woman, Phyllis Dawson, was at the heart of the move for women's rugby.[17] It was reported she was born in England, which was true enough, but she was born of New Zealand parents and her mother's brother was the man known as the father of New Zealand cricket, Daniel Reese, and another brother, Tom, wrote two volumes recording the early years of cricket in New Zealand. The Reese family was well known in a variety of sports in Canterbury and Daniel had also played rugby for the province. The announcement of Dawson's plans used language that was usually employed when the words 'women' and 'rugby' were juxtaposed:

> Miss P. Dawson of Wellington is now going to prove that girls can play Rugby. Not silly Rugby, you know, with a lot of hysterical maidens tripping over their skirts and pulling each other's hair, but the real thing, with the fair Rugbeians tricked out in jerseys, shorts, caps to cover their hair and all other furnishings necessary to the fit and proper exposition of New Zealand's national game before the critical eye of a referee.[18]

Wednesday, July 13, 1921. *New Zealand Free Lance* 15

OUR PICTURE GALLERY.

A WELLINGTON LADY RUGBY CAPTAIN.

MISS P. DAWSON.

Captain of the new Ladies Rugby Football Club that was formed in Wellington last week, who says she doesn't see why girls should not be able to enjoy Rugby as well as the boys. (See letterpress.) —Sarony, photo.

Instigator and intended captain of a women's team in Wellington, Phyllis Dawson, pictured in the *Free Lance*.
ALEXANDER TURNBULL LIBRARY/*FREE LANCE*, 13 JULY 1921

This photo labelled 'the New Zealand Women's Rugby Team' was believed to have been taken in 1926 and it was sold at auction in Auckland in 2011. It is something of a mystery. There was no national women's team until more than 60 years later and the auctioneers, Art + Object, could offer no information other than that the photographer was H. K. Fox of Gloucester, wherein may lie a clue. According to British rugby historian John Griffiths, Fox was well known in Gloucester as a photographer between the wars and his name was often associated with events at the Gloucester club's Kingsholm ground. Although the women's jerseys look authentic for the period, the material seems almost satin, too light to stand up to the rigours of a rugby match, and the women, as far as it is possible to deduce such things, look more English than they do New Zealander. It is possible they were dressed for some theatrical performance. The photo appears to have been taken in a garage – vehicles can be seen in the background and the corrugated iron wall behind the women bears a barely legible legend, 'Smoking strictly prohibited'. PACOLL-9944, ALEXANDER TURNBULL LIBRARY

A woman identified only as 'L. M.' wrote in *NZ Truth* that women should value their 'true womanhood' ahead of their quest for something exciting, to which Dawson replied: 'I will ask her which is better for a brand of young girls: to be out in the open air, playing games, or sitting in a stuffy drawing room with no other aim in view but to look genteel?'[19]

The women did not play in 1921 because of a lack of suitable grounds and made another attempt in 1922, with fifteen women attending a pre-season meeting at the end of March. Again, there was a tinge of the demeaning to the reporting: 'The girls would play in proper boots – no high heels. A girl: "Will we be allowed to powder and paint?"' Dawson said 37 women had signed up in 1921 and she expected as many again, but there was a need for financial backing and for guaranteed use of grounds.[20] Neither could have been forthcoming because Dawson's plans faded from the public prints. Women around the same time began playing soccer in Wellington and league in Auckland but, again, without conspicuous success or longevity.[21]

Attempts to establish women's rugby, as with some other sports, were accompanied by warnings of dire consequences from medical men. A Christchurch doctor, William Simpson, was among the most outspoken: 'Football for girls,' he intoned, 'would prove deleterious from both the physical and temperamental standpoint . . . they are not built for it . . . the scrum work and the tackling alone are too dangerous for women.'[22] Another, Albert Orchard, was quoted as saying that, anatomically, females would be taking a risk 'and would be liable to feel the bad effects in later years'.

The Second World War, as with the First, brought women's teams out on to the field to raise funds for welfare and patriotic purposes. In one game at Carisbrook in Dunedin, teams recruited from swimming, basketball (netball) and hockey played in a game that apparently raised thousands of pounds.[23] One of the teams was captained by Islay Purdie, who was a national champion swimmer and who had just missed qualifying for the 1938 Empire Games. Her team was coached by an Otago (men's) forward, Mervyn Phelan (who was killed on air operations in Britain two years later). Rugby was back at Carisbrook after the war, but with a difference: rather than just a single game, a knockout competition was played in 1946 and while the women took it seriously, the compiler of the match programme could not resist the usual language: 'The girls have been instructed that hair-pulling, gouging and scratching are strictly illegal and the official referees have been asked to nip unmaidenly conduct in the bud by giving the first offenders their marching orders.'[24] The writer did concede, though, that some women had more than a passing knowledge – one, Maude Jolly, was a daughter of the Otago RFU chairman David, and later married Willis Perriam, a midfield back for Otago and services teams.

In what seems to have been the first competitive tournament to be played by women in New Zealand (all previous outings having been single matches) four teams were involved in a knockout tournament that was won by a team named, but not necessarily representative of, St Kilda. It and Dunedin North were tied on points at the end of the game and St Kilda were awarded the game, according to a report in the *Otago Daily Times*, 'on the touch down system'.[25] (This presumably meant the team that had to force the ball least in its own in-goal.) 'Some of the players gave the appearance of knowing the general idea of playing Rugby football, but the majority were more willing than scientific and the referees could do little about it,' the paper noted. One of the referees in the tournament was Iain Gallaway, lawyer and sports broadcaster who was a qualified rugby referee and, as such, lent the tournament added credibility. Among the players was eighteen-year-old Mayzod Reid, who became a three-time national springboard diving champion and competed at the Empire Games in Auckland in 1950.

For all that, progress thereafter was so slow as to be almost moribund. Women played occasional 'fun' matches and as long as they were not part of rugby officialdom, that was all they could be. Until they could be part of the male rugby administrative infrastructure, fledgling women's teams would struggle for numbers, money and grounds. This they continued to do until the mid-1980s. There was more positive action elsewhere. A women's competition was developed in the Netherlands, and in June 1982 the first women's international was played when France beat the Netherlands 4–0 in Utrecht. France seemed to be the leader as one of the Dutch players, Wim Peperkamp, remembered. 'I can't recall who actually set up the match but I remember that the French were better organised than us with their own federation and championship.'[26]

For all the enthusiasm of women in New Zealand for the game – for the women's game, that is – and for all the serious intent of its players, it was a man who made the difference and established women's rugby within the male infrastructure. Laurie O'Reilly, yet another significant Timaru contribution to the New Zealand sporting landscape, was a lawyer in Christchurch and coached the Canterbury University men's team. A Canterbury women's team was chosen

Not much was recorded about this scene – not the year, not the venue, not the names, not the occasion, but it is clearly women enjoying playing rugby.

in 1984 and the players complained about the level of coaching they could get. O'Reilly, as a coach accredited by both the Canterbury and New Zealand unions, became involved and by the end of the season was, in his words, 'impressed but not convinced'. The following year, his daughter Lauren told him she wanted to hook for the university women's team. 'No daughter of mine will play in the front row without proper coaching,' O'Reilly exclaimed, and that committed him. He became the Canterbury coach in 1985 and the first New Zealand coach in 1989.[27] O'Reilly wrote that he had a clear understanding with all teams with which he was involved: 'You are rugby players who happen to be women – not women who happen to be rugby players.'

The game flourished with the enthusiasm of women in Canterbury, Auckland and Taranaki and the expertise of O'Reilly. The breakthrough was noted in Canada, where women became keen converts:

> He [O'Reilly] believed that women are physically and psychologically suited to rugby and that they find a spirit and freedom in rugby that is absent in other sports. It is O'Reilly's opinion that the game is safe for women and that when good coaching is available, it is relatively injury free. He emphatically stated that the coaching style and process should be the same for men and women.[28]

O'Reilly's position and influence forced the New Zealand union to take notice, and senior administrators such as Russ Thomas, the union's chairman and (significantly in the context) a Canterbury man, and a former All Black coach, J. J. Stewart, became passionate advocates. The Canterbury University team, named the Crusadettes, toured Europe in 1988. (New Zealand rugby had the Crusadettes ten years before it had the male Crusaders.) A first New Zealand team was chosen in 1989 and made its debut at Lancaster Park in Christchurch against an

The first official game played by a New Zealand women's team, one that was under the control of the national union, was against an American Pacific Coast team that was known, like the male version, as the Grizzlies. The game was played in Christchurch in 1989 as a curtain-raiser to an Argentina match against Canterbury. Not then the Black Ferns, the New Zealanders won 13–7. In this photo, New Zealand flanker Nina Sio breaks from a scrum and the grasp of Californian halfback Deb Dennis.

American Pacific Coast team. The game, won 13–7 by the New Zealanders, was a curtain-raiser to the Canterbury men playing Argentina.

Women's rugby made even greater strides the following year when 'RugbyFest 1990' was organised in Christchurch with New Zealand playing teams from the United States, the Netherlands and the Soviet Union. The tournament had no official standing, although the Americans apparently regard the games played by their team as official tests. A first World Cup for women was played in Wales the following year, 1991, and a New Zealand team organised and coached by O'Reilly was eliminated in a semifinal by the United States, who beat England in the final. Despite the support of men such as O'Reilly, Thomas and Stewart, among others, that first cup did not have the blessing of the NZRFU because it had not been approved by the International Rugby Board. New Zealand was not represented at the next cup, in Scotland in 1994, but returned as an official entry in 1998 for the first of four successive wins. (The soccer women's World Cup also began in 1991 and the World Cup for women's league was first played in 2000.)

The sexist and demeaning language that used to always be associated with women's rugby has largely gone, although a serious, supportive article in 1992 written by a woman perhaps had a male subeditor because it was headed 'Boobs'n'all'.[29] Women gained proper status within the rugby hierarchy even to the extent of gaining an officially registered and protected nickname, the Black Ferns. Originally, the team was known as 'the Gal Blacks' because the name 'Black Ferns' (the logical and the union's preferred choice) had been registered by a Dunedin businessman, Pat McCarrigan. But the NZRFU negotiated and the logical name won out over the crass.

One of the most celebrated women players, Anna Richards, about to pass during the national championship final in Auckland in 2007 in which Auckland beat Otago 32–27. Richards played for New Zealand at four World Cups and played 37 tests between 1990 and 2010. About to confront her is another Black Fern, Otago centre Claire Richardson, and on the right is yet another, Huriana Manuel, who was part of the 2010 team that won the World Cup. Huriana Manuel's mother Liza Mihinui also played for New Zealand, making them the first mother and daughter Black Ferns. CHRIS SKELTON/PHOTOSPORT

An example of sexist trivia in a Sunday newspaper was a suggestion the team be named the 'She Bs' and other historians pointed out that the name of every player in the Black Ferns was identified through her association with males.[30]

Acceptance did not mean the women's game was at the same level as the men's, however. A women's national provincial championship was begun in 1999 – dominated by Auckland ever since – but was not played in 2010 because the NZRU was cutting costs. The annual players' awards, handed out at a year-end dinner, usually in Auckland, have not historically been kind to women. In 2006, when the women won the World Cup for the third time, the team of the year award instead went to the All Blacks, who won twelve of thirteen tests. The Tom French Cup, awarded annually to the outstanding Māori player of the year, in fact goes to the outstanding male Māori player.[31] One historian worried that the national union did nothing to get the 1998 World Cup final live on television (that was beyond its power), and while women were playing sport in ever-increasing numbers, 'lack of media coverage and financial support obscures this trend'.[32] An objective response is that news media coverage of women's rugby in New Zealand, without going into a media studies method of measurement and timing, is better than anywhere else. Any reader will have a lengthy search in newspapers in Australia or Britain or the United States for a mention of women's rugby.

While much new information has been revealed here, especially about the efforts of Webbe and Dawson, one looking for profit, the other for pleasure, there is undoubtedly a need for a comprehensive history of women's sport in New Zealand, not just rugby. Two histories of soccer in New Zealand, for example, do not have women playing the game until the 1970s. Too often the history of women in sport comes across as being merely anti-rugby or anti-male.

Official rugby catches up with the game for women. *IRB WORLD OF RUGBY*, 2002

Most writing on women's rugby has been about the playing of the game, and when there has been criticism of the game (especially by women) it has usually been because of its male dominance. This criticism had several feeders during the 1980s when rugby's clinging to apartheid South Africa gave its critics even more ammunition. There was even a Women Against Rugby organisation which, according to one historian, 'allegedly represented a significant campaign against male domination'.[33] But women have always been involved with rugby as long as the game has been played. Players had mothers and sisters who may, or may not, have encouraged their men to play; when male players married, or were responsible for children, there may have been female influence on whether they could continue to play. There is no evidence to support or rebut this view; but every male who has had anything to do with the game knows what the women closest to him thought of it. Rugby has never been played and followed in a male-only vacuum. This is not just the view of someone who has been around rugby and its players for most of his life. It is also the view of a female historian. Jennifer Curtin, speaking at the winter lecture series at Auckland University in 2011, noted that women had been encouraged to watch early football matches and their presence was usually noted in newspaper reports.[34] (General crowd photos from rugby matches in any era show women spectators). Curtin suggested there were three reasons why women embraced rugby from the earliest times and 'assisted in its ascendancy and ultimate claiming of the title of New Zealand's national game'. One was the place rugby came to hold in the social life of many towns and communities; another was what she called 'eager watching' or 'male gazing'; and the third was that it was likely many women had an independent interest in or passion for the game.

Auckland theologian George Armstrong speaks to police as they approach protesters on the field at Rugby Park in Hamilton in 1981. The scheduled match between South Africa and Waikato was eventually abandoned. EP/1981/2598/28A-F, DOMINION POST COLLECTION, ALEXANDER TURNBULL LIBRARY

13 Conflict and money

The new All Black winger
Who made the new model –
A muscular athletic runner
Who could rarely be stopped by one tackle[1]

Rugby and South Africa in the apartheid years were an uncomfortable coupling, like the quarrelsome husband and wife who could not live together but who could not live apart. Most international sports bodies had shunned South Africa, but the International Rugby Football Board had not. Such was the power and attraction of South African rugby: the rest of the world, and especially New Zealand, wanted it when it knew it should not. Some in New Zealand just wanted the Springboks anyway, come what may, arguing the old impossible line about sport and politics being separate or believing that New Zealand was being picked on by those who wanted equality and justice for the majority of the population in South Africa.

South Africa's rugby power was evident at the beginning of the 1980s and again just over a decade later, when between them the repentant last white president, F. W. de Klerk, and the newly freed and first black president, Nelson Mandela, ushered in the new 'Rainbow Nation'. New Zealand rugby for different reasons embraced the South Africans at either end of the political roller-coaster. In the middle, the NZRFU chairman, Ces Blazey, and the white rugby chief, Danie Craven, had a falling out and for a time the New Zealand union and the forces against South African contact unexpectedly and bizarrely found themselves on the same side.

New Zealand rugby has had to deal with several status-threatening crises through its organised life: the rise of league before the First World War; the dislocation of the rebel tour of South Africa in 1986; the attempted expansion of league and the subsequent threat of an anti-establishment rugby 'circus' in 1995; the World Cup sub-hosting shambles of 2001–02; but none more serious or as widely spread as the tour by the South Africans in 1981. The potential effect of other crises was mainly on rugby itself, whether it could continue as the dominant game or whether it would be split asunder. The tour in 1981 affected the whole country.

In 1973, Prime Minister Norman Kirk told the national union to 'postpone' a tour by South Africa partly because he thought that if it proceeded, his government might have to declare a state of emergency and invoke sweeping powers that no democratic government should want. That included the possibility of soldiers being drafted in as extra police. The New Zealand union reluctantly obeyed. No similar instruction was forthcoming in 1981 from Robert Muldoon, who had been elected in 1975 on the promise, among other things, of no political interference in the affairs of sports bodies. The juxtaposition of words such as 'promise' and 'politicians' can be an oxymoron. In 1980, Muldoon and his government tried to prevent New Zealanders from competing at the Olympic Games in Moscow, but he knew he could not legally stop them.[2] Muldoon saw the rugby tour as one that the union was entitled to mount without government interference. In 1981, he could legally prevent South Africans entering New Zealand, but he chose not to do so. One of the reasons was that he knew a vast number of New Zealanders agreed with him. While the protests that accompanied the tour indicated how strongly a great many New Zealanders did not want it, the crowds inside the grounds indicated quite the opposite, as the following table shows.[3]

A poster for a 1981 anti-tour rally in Christchurch three weeks before the tour began. CCL-EPHEMERA-SPRINGBOK-1981-07-03-EPH06-02, CHRISTCHURCH CITY LIBRARIES, COURTESY OF MARY BAKER

Estimated crowd figures, 1981

MATCH	VENUE	CROWD
Poverty Bay	Gisborne	15,000
Waikato	Hamilton	28,000
Taranaki	New Plymouth	28,000
Manawatu	Palmerston North	20,000
Wanganui	Wanganui	12,000
Southland	Invercargill	15,000
Otago	Dunedin	15,000
NZ (1)	Christchurch	41,000
Nelson-Bays	Nelson	7500
NZ Māori	Napier	22,000
NZ (2)	Wellington	32,000
Bay of Plenty	Rotorua	30,000
Auckland	Auckland	26,000
Northland	Whangarei	20,000
NZ (3)	Auckland	49,000

Those figures give a total of 360,500, which represented about 11 per cent of New Zealand's population of about 3.2 million in 1981. It is reasonable to assume that the majority of the crowds in each case were drawn from the areas in which the games were played. Only the test matches were likely to have attracted people from throughout New Zealand.

Figures for protesters were more difficult to pin down than those for matches because they were not in any controlled space such as a rugby ground and did not have to pay. Protesters in each case were also probably drawn from local areas, but a difference from the rugby numbers was that on the days of matches, there were frequently

Percy Bush had a bob each way when the Māori played South Africa in 1981. He told protesters he was with them, then produced a match ticket so he could watch nephew Bill play.
EP/1981/2914/2A-F, DOMINION POST COLLECTION, ALEXANDER TURNBULL LIBRARY

protests throughout the country, just as there had been before the tour. The vast majority of New Zealanders may well have had a view on the tour but neither attended games nor actively protested. Some people had a bob each way and both protested and watched games, though the figure is not likely to have been high. One who put himself in that category was a 63-year-old Hawke's Bay man, Percy Bush. He joined in the protests in the streets of Napier before the South Africans' match against New Zealand Māori. At one point, he grabbed a megaphone, identified himself and said he was of one mind with the protesters. He then carried on to the ground, produced a match ticket to get past police and security, and went in to McLean Park to watch the Māori, who were captained by nephew Bill.[4] 'Billy' Bush had also been an All Black in the 1970s.

There was no way of accurately and objectively working out which side was in the majority. The *New Zealand Herald*, the morning paper in Auckland, tried with a poll conducted in the first fortnight of the tour. Pollsters asked the question: 'Should a Springbok rugby team have come to New Zealand?' Overall, the poll showed 42 per cent in favour and 49 per cent opposed, with the majority of opposition in metropolitan areas and most support in the country.[5] It was sufficient to know that there was more opposition to a rugby tour than before and that it had long since ceased to be a rugby issue. There were suggestions that some of the protesters were motivated for other reasons and that some saw the tour as an opportunity to have a go at the police in a quasi-legitimate way. That was undoubtedly true of some, but not of the majority. It was the worst, most widespread disorder New Zealand had seen, worse than the 1932 Depression riots, worse than the riotous labour dispute in Waihi in 1912, worse than anything 'Massey's Cossacks' tried to quell in Wellington in 1913.

Before, during and after the tour, the attitude of the New Zealand Rugby Football Union was that its role was to promote the game and that it saw a series against South Africa as doing just that and other considerations were not theirs to worry about. Its chairman, Ces Blazey, made a lengthy statement at the time of the union's annual meeting in Wellington in April, three months before the tour: 'It is necessary to remind ourselves of our function and our responsibilities. They are to administer an amateur sport; not to seek to change the political system in any country.'[6] The union's annual report stuck to the same theme in this passage (probably written by Blazey): 'The sole objective was to play games of Rugby against traditional opponents. The tour had nothing to do with support for the political situation in South Africa, any more than our contacts with some other countries indicates support for systems in those countries.'[7]

There was no public dissension from any of the 26 provincial unions, although there were individual rugby people, in an official capacity or otherwise, who opposed the tour. The most prominent of them was the successful captain of the All Blacks for the previous four years, Graham Mourie. He decided over the 1980–81 summer he would not make himself available to play against South Africa on moral grounds. One of his team-mates, Bruce Robertson, who had toured there in 1976, decided the same and a former All Black, Merv Jaffray, who coached Nelson at the time, said he would take no part when the South Africans were in the city. Someone with a sense of humour, or irony, or something, must have designed the front of the union's annual report for 1981. Rather than depict anything from the most controversial tour rugby had seen, the cover had a Peter Bush action photo of Mourie from the preceding tour, by Scotland.

The South African tour was organised along the same lines as all recent tours in the amateur era: the hosts bore all the costs, including the overseas travel of teams, and took all the profits. When the All Blacks went to South Africa, therefore, the NZRFU did not gain a bean. When the South Africans toured in 1981, total expenditure by the NZRFU was $687,420 (about $2.4 million today according to the Reserve Bank inflation calculator) and it gained a net income of $132,185 (about $463,000).[8] But the tour for rugby was never about making money.

There was much talk in the lead-up to the tour about the Gleneagles Agreement, which Commonwealth heads of government reached in 1977. It required all Commonwealth countries to discourage sports contact with South Africa, and Muldoon had been one of the small group at the Scottish golfing resort of Gleneagles who had drafted it. But the rugby argument was that the union was not itself a signatory to the agreement, which was not part of New Zealand law. The Gleneagles Agreement had been reaffirmed at the following Commonwealth heads of government meeting, in Lusaka in Zambia, in 1979. Muldoon was there too. In June, a month before the tour, the House of Representatives passed a resolution which urged 'the New Zealand Rugby Football Union to observe the terms of the Gleneagles agreement and to reconsider its invitation to the Springbok rugby team . . .'.[9] On almost the eve of the tour, Muldoon made his last pre-tour comment. He did so on television 'because I want all the people of New Zealand to know exactly what I have said'.[10] He reiterated that the Gleneagles Agreement gave sports bodies the right to make their own decisions but with that right came responsibility. He continued:

NEW ZEALAND RUGBY FOOTBALL UNION INC.

SOUTH AFRICA v. WAIKATO

Saturday, 25th July, 1981

Frankton or Whitiora GATE ENTRANCE

$4.00

Admit Bearer

This portion to be surrendered to the Gatekeeper at Entrance to Rugby Park.

B. R. USMAR, Secretary, N.Z.R.F.U.

NEW ZEALAND RUGBY FOOTBALL UNION INC.

South Africa v. Waikato

Sat. 25th July 1980 — Rugby Park, Hamilton

Ground Admission

Standing Room Only

This ticket is purchased subject to the conditions printed on the back hereof.

This portion to be produced to usher and RETAINED by the Ticketholder, but on its own DOES NOT ADMIT to ground. This portion to be produced on demand.

B. R. USMAR, Secretary, N.Z.R.F.U.

The programme for the match that never happened, Waikato against South Africa in Hamilton, and a ground ticket for the same game. Note the incorrect year on the main portion of the ticket. TICKET: GEOFF MILLER

> The Government will not order the Rugby Union to abandon the tour any more than we ordered sports bodies to refrain from participating at Moscow last year. To do so would be to take away the fundamental freedom that I successfully argued for at Gleneagles. To do this in face of pressure and threats from other countries would be cowardice. . . . the issue now rests with the New Zealand Rugby Union and I say to them: think well before you make your decision.[11]

The union did not change its view and the South Africans arrived about a fortnight later, beginning their tumultuous tour in Gisborne. The police warnings beforehand of what might happen were amply justified. Protesters stormed their way on to one ground, Rugby Park in Hamilton, and forced the cancellation of that game. The face of the ugly New Zealander was seen on both sides – in the shouted abuse by protesters at police and tour supporters; and by the rugby followers at protesters and, bizarrely, by throwing beer cans at reporters in the rickety old press box. The message was clear, the messenger was shot. One of the news media recipients of a beer missile was a 34-year-old South African, Trevor Quirk, who covered the tour as a broadcaster. A wicketkeeper for Northern Transvaal in more than forty matches, he neatly caught a can aimed at him and shouted to the thrower: 'Hey, I'm a South African!' Back came the rejoinder: 'Enjoy the beer then.'[12] Few other beers would have been enjoyed that night.

The NZRFU cancelled another match, against South Canterbury in Timaru, for 'security reasons', the union said. But a union council member, Russ Thomas, later told the South Canterbury union it was to give police some respite from the constant drain of confrontations.[13] The Counties union was initially assigned a match, but rather than play it at vulnerable Pukekohe, the NZRFU thought Eden Park in the neighbouring Auckland union would be a safer bet. Auckland protested about hosting a game for someone else so the Auckland team played the game instead. The NZRFU had to pay compensation to Counties.

Police tried to fortify grounds by surrounding them with jumbo bins and trucks and stringing barbed wire around the perimeter of the playing surface. The most concentrated demonstrations, when police lines were most sorely pressed, were in Wellington and Auckland. The phrase 'pitched battle' was frequently used in newspapers. In Auckland, a protester dressed as a referee managed to get on to the field before the Auckland match and kicked the ball away; a light aircraft droned over Eden Park for most of the third test, its occupants occasionally dropping bags of flour. One of the few funny incidents of the tour followed. One of the so-called 'bombs' hit the All Black prop, Gary Knight, and a St John man raced on to treat him. Knight was covered in flour and the referee, Clive Norling of Wales, quickly told the first aider not to use water 'or he'll become paste'. The All Blacks won the three-test series

A familiar scene from the 1981 tour by South Africa: police and barbed wire. This was at Athletic Park in Wellington during the second test. PETER BUSH

An Anglican priest, Geoff Walpole, dressed in white shorts and a Suva referee's jersey, got past police and rugby officials to grab the match ball and kick it in the general direction of the main stand before Auckland's match against South Africa.

thanks to a last-minute penalty goal in Auckland by fullback Allan Hewson; the Springboks otherwise had a successful tour, winning each of their provincial matches and having a draw against the Māori side. But the playing results to all but the most committed rugby supporters were incidental.

The man ultimately responsible for the policing of the tour was the Police Minister, Ben Couch. Thirty-two years before, he had been an All Black, playing against Australia at home. Were he not Māori, he would have been considered for selection in the New Zealand team that went to South Africa that year. He was asked his thoughts after the 1981 tour and he declined. But persistence brought its own reward and eventually he issued a written statement in which he largely repeated the government line and included these comments:

> The Springbok tour showed us some ugly facets of our own nature. We discovered we are not a passionless people; not as tolerant or law-abiding as we had thought. We learnt, also, that there are those among us who are prepared to break the law to get their own way, with no thought for others; and there are also those of us who will use any pretext to encourage violence safely, in an

Wing Stu Wilson scores New Zealand's first try in the deciding third test against South Africa in 1981. He wrong-footed Ray Mordt (right) and was too quick for Naas Botha. PETER BUSH

anonymous group. These are things we needed to know, although the learning was an ugly shock. We should have learnt, also, that if democracy has rights, it has corresponding responsibilities; and one of these is that no one is above the law. Whether or not the Rugby Union was wise in inviting a South African rugby team to come to New Zealand is a matter of opinion. What is certain is that the union acted legally and that the police had a duty to uphold that legal right.[14]

Other tours came and went, other rugby carried on, but always in the background was the threat of more South African disruption. The IRB schedule had included since 1970 a tour by New Zealand to South Africa in 1985 and the union showed every sign of wanting to go ahead, despite 1981. Others were not so sure, however. A Labour government had been elected in 1984 and Prime Minister David Lange was vehemently opposed to the tour but reluctantly had to admit he could no more stop it

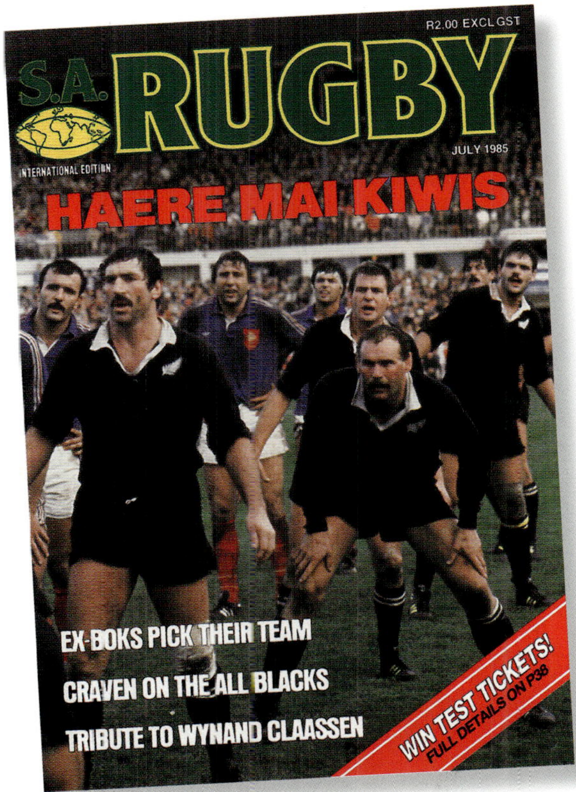

A South African rugby magazine welcomes the All Blacks in 1985. But they did not arrive. *SA RUGBY*, JULY 1985

than Muldoon could have stopped athletes from going to Moscow (or South Africa in 1976). Chris Laidlaw, an outstanding halfback of the 1960s who was a key member of the All Blacks in South Africa in 1970, was on Lange's staff at the time. He drafted a letter for Lange saying that in the country's wider interests, the tour must not proceed.[15] Lange, with Laidlaw in tow, backed that up with a visit to the NZRFU headquarters where Blazey asked him if the government was instructing the union not to send the team. Lange could not go that far. Laidlaw dressed up his account somewhat by referring to the councillors as 'beefy' – which men such as Ron Don and Peter Wild and even Blazey himself were emphatically not – but conceded he had never seen Lange give a more appalling performance.[16] Some of the councillors were well known to Laidlaw, including Ivan Vodanovich, who had chosen and coached him in 1970.

The opposition within rugby had grown in the few years since 1981 and the Auckland union argued against the tour on the basis that it would do more harm than good to the game.[17] The previous chairman of the Auckland union, Ron Don, was a staunch and public advocate of playing against South Africa. His successor, Malcolm Dick, who had toured there as a player in 1970, was not. It was coincidental to the union's stand that two members of Auckland rugby clubs affiliated to the Auckland union brought the legal action that eventually killed off the tour. Patrick Finnigan and Philip Recordon offered themselves as plaintiffs in an action against the union that challenged the tour decision on the grounds that the tour would infringe rule 2a of the union: 'The objects of the Union shall be: (a) to control, promote, foster and develop the game of amateur Rugby Union Football throughout New Zealand.'[18]

Most reports since have talked of the tour being stopped by legal action, which is true as far as it goes. But no court found the tour itself wrong or that the NZRFU in making its tour decision

Ron Don, the most outspoken advocate among rugby administrators of continued contact with apartheid South Africa. PETER BUSH

was legally wrong. When Finnigan and Recordon brought their case, the NZRFU's lawyers applied for it to be struck out on the grounds that the two plaintiffs lacked 'standing'; that is, that they had no legal authoritative position in rugby to challenge the union. The Chief Justice, Sir Ronald Davison, agreed. The plaintiffs appealed and the Appeal Court held that the plaintiffs did indeed have standing as club members and allowed the appeal. The case went back to the High Court and it soon became evident it could not be completed by the scheduled departure date of the team. Accordingly, the plaintiffs applied for an interlocutory injunction, a device that would have the effect of delaying the tour until the case could be heard. The High Court judge, Maurice (later Sir Maurice) Casey, allowed the injunction but said the union could still make arrangements for a tour after the substantive action was completed. In the event, the union said it had run out of time and abandoned the tour. The NZRFU mounted a legal footnote later in the year when it applied for leave to test the Appeal Court's decision on standing with the judicial committee of the Privy Council. It was refused.[19]

One of the dominant administrators in the second half of the twentieth century, Ces Blazey, stands in front of his Wellington home. NZ SPORTS HALL OF FAME

Blazey was not a trained lawyer – he was the national manager of AMP Insurance – but personally briefed the NZRFU's lawyers and was present throughout the hearings. He later commented privately, without a trace of bitterness or irony (given the occupations of the plaintiffs), that the only winners in the whole affair were lawyers. He had a point. Legal fees paid by the union in the calendar year 1984 amounted to $6,150. In 1985, they were $160,552.[20] But Blazey acknowledged that lawyers for 'the other side' had largely acted for no fee.

That effectively was the end of official New Zealand rugby's love affair with South Africa until the end of apartheid. Most of the All Blacks who were packed and ready to go to South Africa went instead on a replacement tour to Argentina, and those close to rugby knew there was a seething resentment among the players about how their big trip had been stopped. There was talk of them going independently anyway, but lawyers warned of the legal consequences for people such as Andy Dalton, who was the captain, and any others who could be deemed to be 'servants' of the union (to whom the injunction applied). Plans were made over the summer for a tour in 1986 without the knowledge or approval of the union, and in dribs and drabs after the first matches in a new pre-season competition involving Canterbury, Auckland, Wellington, New South Wales, Queensland and Fiji, selected players crept away. It helped the clandestine nature of the organisation of the tour that seven of the rebels had been dispatched on official business to Britain, where they played in special matches to mark the centenary of the International Rugby

BERRYMANS TOTAL OFFICE SUPPORT
Free Offstreet Parking
77 Ferry Road

THE PRESS

Nihil utile quod non honestum

LAMBSWOOL SEAT COVERS
FOR MOST CARS
BOWMANS MOTOR SUPPLIES

CHRISTCHURCH, NEW ZEALAND. MONDAY, APRIL 14, 1986. Price 35c

All Blacks sidestep off to South Africa

By JOHN BROOKS

Eluding demonstrators and television cameras at Christchurch Airport last evening proved far easier for five Canterbury All Blacks than breaching the Auckland rugby cover defence at Lancaster Park an hour or two earlier.

Quitting the country, New Zealand style, proved to be no more than a leisurely stroll along a near-deserted footpath for the footballing quintet.

Only a few yards away, banner-carrying demonstrators and news media representatives were milling round with Sydney-bound passengers, their friends and relatives, airline officials and policemen in a jam-packed departure vestibule.

Ironically, the demonstrators opposing the visit by the New Zealand rugby players to South Africa were in the ideal position to harass the Canterbury players until five minutes before the footballers arrived, showered and deodorised, from Lancaster Park.

But the wind was chilly, the police had formed a ...

... into the airport compound in two private cars, there was no-one to greet them but a traffic enforcement officer.

Obviously not in on the cloak-and-dagger arrangements, the officer, who was busy writing out tickets for expensive cars, told Hobbs he could not park in that area. Hobbs said he had news for him.

Anderson and Simpson tried a side door to the overseas arrival building, but it was locked. Far from the maddening crowd, they sauntered along the footpath until directed into a side entrance of the departure lounge by a policeman.

Hobbs, who captained New Zealand on the Argentinian rugby tour last year, said he and his colleagues would be part of a squad from which an international team would ...

Deans said he and the other players were looking forward to the tour, and would be back in Christchurch to beef up the Canterbury team's effort in late May or early June.

Two other Canterbury players, Wayne Smith and Warwick Taylor, flew to Brisbane last week to participate in the International Rugby Board centennial games. Their involvement in the South African project has not been confirmed.

The players were ensconced in the departure lounge before the demonstrators and the news media folk came hot-footing out the main entrance. The demonstrators were too late to make their protest.

Earlier, the Aucklanders, Alan and Gary ...

... unmarked van or bus, and anxious eyes turned skywards when a helicopter hovered into view at 5 p.m.

After all that, the Qantas flight left for Sydney on time at 5.45 p.m.

Five Canterbury All Blacks at Christchurch Airport last evening after successfully eluding demonstrators and television cameras. From left, they are Craig Green, Victor Simpson, Albert Anderson, Jock Hobbs, and, in the foreground, Robbie Deans.

Wyllie: I can't blame them

The Canterbury rugby coach, Mr Alex Wyllie, is disappointed that seven of his players have left for ...

Just before the Canterbury players left the team's dressing-room at Lancaster Park yesterday, ...

How the morning newspaper in Christchurch reported some of its favourite players slipping away to play in South Africa. Craig Green, Victor Simpson, Albert Anderson, Jock Hobbs and Robbie Deans are pictured at Christchurch Airport. *PRESS*, 14 APRIL 1986

Board. It was a simple matter for them to leave from Heathrow for Johannesburg. Those leaving from New Zealand had to evade protesters and disapproving rugby people who had got a whiff of the departure plans. Only two members of the All Black team chosen the year before did not go to South Africa as rebels or, as they called themselves, Cavaliers: John Kirwan and David Kirk. (It was not recorded if the instigators had a sense of irony, naming their team after a group loyal to the establishment during the seventeenth-century English civil war.)

A part of the IRB centenary celebrations was a congress attended by delegates from 54 countries in which rugby was played (although only eight of them were full members of the IRB). As they gathered at an eighteenth-century stately home, Heythrop Park, in Oxfordshire for talks and pats on the back, the significance of the rebels' action (and the insignificance of the IRB) became clear as *The Times* rugby writer, David Hands, noted:

> The New Zealand authorities know they have to take punitive action (and will not need other delegates at Heythrop to tell them so) otherwise we will be approaching a state of anarchy. How sad it is that an occasion which should be a cause for celebration will now be completely overshadowed; how necessary the whole affair suggests a world authority for the game is required.[21]

As the intentions of the players became clear, and when it was known that a national selector, Colin Meads, had gone as coach, Blazey's anger mounted. As he later recalled, he searched out Craven and told him that the 'unauthorised tour', as Blazey always called it, was simply unacceptable. Blazey recounted that Craven affected a puzzled expression on his face and, in his best Afrikaans-accented English, said: 'What does unacceptable mean?'[22] Craven had four doctoral degrees and was almost as fluent in English as Blazey was. He knew very well that the Transvaal union, which had organised the rebel tour with help from the players in New Zealand, had crossed the Rubicon. So too had the players the instant they took the field for their first game. Most of the members of the ruling NZRFU council were at the congress, but Blazey waited until he was home before mounting a response. All he could do from Oxfordshire was to fire off a telegram to Meads telling him that seven players had been given approval to play in a celebration match in Johannesburg and only they could play; 'the other New Zealand players should not be allowed to play in the matches in South Africa'.[23]

Craven did his chameleon-like best to disassociate himself from the tour, letting the Transvaal union and its strong-willed president, Louis Luyt, take the blame. But Blazey always believed Craven knew what was going on and so did Blazey's successor as chairman, Russ Thomas. (It was entirely coincidental that Blazey had carried out his previously announced intention to step down in 1986.) Thomas towards the end of the year wrote to Craven summarising various conversations he and Blazey had had with him and it was clear Craven was no innocent party. At one point Thomas wrote: 'I covered with you the point that although you disassociated yourself with the tour, you did welcome the team to South Africa and in fact, somebody must have organised the four tests.'[24]

For all the anger and dismay expressed by men such as Blazey and Thomas, there was little they could do simply because the union did not have rules to cover such an eventuality. It was an indication to men of integrity (however wrong-headed they may have seemed at times to others) that an amateur game could no longer be run on trust, handshakes and the words of people; contracts, rules and lawyers were needed. In the event, the union charged each of the players with two counts of misconduct: one that they left to play in South Africa without first gaining a clearance; the other that they did not comply with a request from the NZRFU to complete an application for clearance. The rebels' captain, Andy Dalton, and one of the players who was also a lawyer, Jock Hobbs (both captains of the All Blacks as well), appeared on behalf of all the players. The union's council found the players guilty of the first charge but not of the second.

Most reports of this sorry episode in New Zealand rugby show the players were banned for 'only' two games. It is necessary to understand that the union's constitution and disciplinary procedures in 1986 were not geared for such activities. Lawyers for the most part were people with law degrees who played the game, not acted for or against it. The players were not 'banned' at all for two games. They had been declared ineligible for a test against France – the 'Baby Blacks' test of 1986 in Christchurch – because they had not fulfilled well-understood residential requirements; they were not back in New Zealand in time to be considered. On the charge on which they were found guilty, they were 'declared ineligible for the NZRFU National Representative Team to play the First Test against the Australian RFU team in the year 1986'.[25] The distinction between being ineligible on grounds of residence and being ineligible as a penalty is important because it demonstrated how porous and ill-equipped the union's regulations were. The union also mounted a separate and tortuous investigation into whether the players had been paid in South Africa. Predictably, the union had to concede it had no evidence of payments. Few people seemed concerned enough to prolong the probe. (A 'World XV' played in South Africa in 1989 and a Welsh union inquiry found that the ten Welsh players involved were paid £30,000 each.)[26]

Andy Haden, an All Black for an astounding 117 matches, deserves to be remembered for

Shield of desire

So many Aucklanders wanted to be in Christchurch on Saturday, 14 September 1985, that Air New Zealand put on a special flight and used a Boeing 747 for it. It was a Jumbo aircraft for a jumbo occasion. Auckland were challenging Canterbury for the Ranfurly Shield. They were the two best teams in the country. Canterbury had had the shield for 25 successful defences, exactly matching the record held by Auckland in the 1960s.

Two years before, Auckland went to Christchurch confident of a win but were thrashed 31–9. The next year, when the two met in a national championship match at Eden Park, the result was reversed – Auckland won 32–3. The two provinces had by and large the best players in the country and, at least in the view of their parochial supporters (which combined made up a majority of rugby supporters in New Zealand), they had the two best coaches: John Hart for Auckland and Alex Wyllie for Canterbury. Hart was the corporate world personnel manager coupled with the characteristic talkativeness of a first-class halfback; Wyllie was the former All Black loose forward hard man who revelled in the nickname of 'Grizz'.

There was even more to this match for the ages. It was what rugby needed after months, years, of self-harm and squabbling about South Africa, about accusations and finger-pointing. The rebel Cavaliers were still several months away in a vague future. Rugby needed a rugby occasion to lift the national spirit, to help restore its bruised standing.

But there was more. In the week preceding the match, the New Zealand Rugby Football Union showed impeccably poor timing by announcing that, henceforth, the Ranfurly Shield would bear the name of a Japanese electronics company.

Boys admire the Ranfurly Shield on the touchline at Carisbrook in 1948. ALLIED PRESS

The deal had been brokered by none other than the Auckland captain, Andy Haden, who had been hired by the union – which two years before had carpeted him for supposed breaches of the amateur regulations – to improve its marketing. There were weasel words around the deal – it was the shield series being sponsored, not the shield itself – but the rugby public saw the devil not the detail. Barry Clarke, an enterprising Christchurch reporter, phoned the latest Lord Ranfurly to ask what he thought. He was not happy.[1]

There was yet more. State television (there was no other at the time) was desperate to provide live coverage of the match, but the NZRFU said no, the effect on the gates of other provincial matches being played at the same time would be disastrous. Lights at rugby grounds were still a decade away, but such clashes could be avoided by imaginative

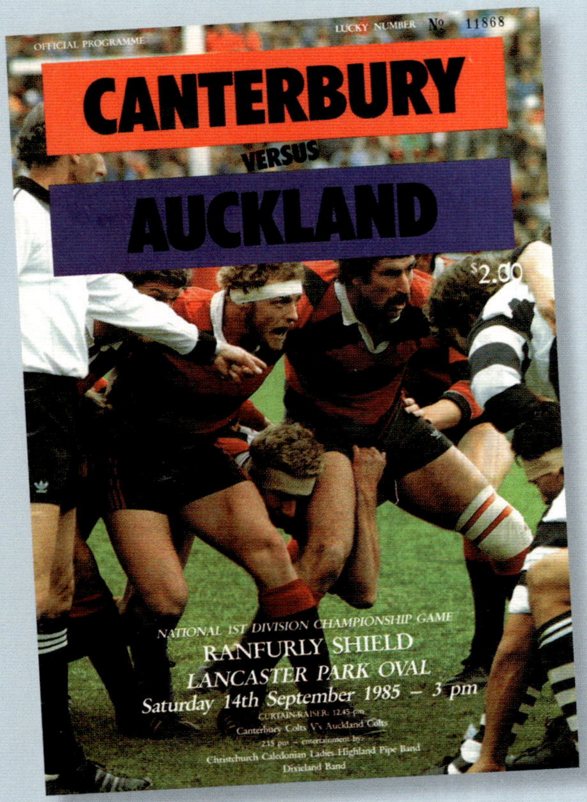

A contender for match of the century: Canterbury's Ranfurly Shield defence against Auckland in 1985.

scheduling of games, such as late morning starts. This had happened at other times, but not on this occasion. Hence the Jumbo and capacity demand for scheduled flights, hence crowded roads, all leading to rugby's Rome. The attendance was estimated at 52,000, but that was a guess as good as any other. It was probably more; certainly not less. The crowd spilled out of the stands and off the bank and lined the touchline; police and security guards, such as there were, made no attempt to keep the crowd back. They wanted to see the game too.

Before the big game at 3 p.m., the crowd could watch Auckland and Canterbury Colts and perhaps speculate on the futures of some of the players – the brothers Stephen and Graeme Bachop in red and black and the brothers Robin and 'Zin' Brooke in blue and white (Stephen Bachop was halfback, brother Graeme at first five-eighth in a role reversal of their later All Black time); Auckland also had a flanker called 'Mike' Jones, who came to be better known as Michael. Spectators could also flick through the programme that carried no mention of a shield sponsor; in fact, the only mention of the sponsoring company's name came in a full-page advertisement in which the virtues of an NEC Advanced Personal Computer were extolled by Andy Haden under the heading: 'So, what does a professional writer like me know about personal computers?' His job description was the artifice that allowed him to laugh at the amateur regulations.

It was Haden's real job as a rugby player, though, that took him and thousands of others to Lancaster Park for what was billed as 'the match of the century' as had been so many others, before and since. But, for once, it was not misplaced hope. The match, the occasion itself, was one of those rugby days which remain in the memory for all who saw and experienced it. For some reason, the Canterbury captain, Don Hayes, gave Auckland the benefit of a stiffish breeze when he won the toss. That was all Auckland needed. Try, try and try again in the first half as the Auckland score mounted. When players and spectators took a breath after 40 minutes that seemed like five, Auckland led 24–0. Teams stayed on the field during the break then and coach Wyllie moved among his players. He had a ball in his hands. 'This,' he said, 'is what it's all about. Get it and use it. If they can score 24 points in the first half, so can you in the second.'[2] He and his assistant, Doug Bruce, then walked off.

Spectators in the main stand squinted into the lowering sun, programmes held up to eyes, as Canterbury set about their retaliation. It began with the halfback, Bruce Deans, when he scored after charging down an attempted clearing kick by Grant Fox. Craig Green ran onto a pushed-through kick from the other Deans, Robbie, and scored. A penalty was added. Prop Steve McDowell rather smudged the fairy-tale page when he scored for Auckland, but Canterbury were not done. With five minutes to

Bruce Deans scores and gives hope to spectators close to the touchline as he begins the Canterbury comeback in the second half of the epic Ranfurly Shield match at Lancaster Park in 1985. Auckland halfback David Kirk is the tackler. PETER BUSH

go, Wayne Smith lobbed a kick to a corner, and somehow it was retrieved by Jock Hobbs who gave it back to Smith for a try. The unlikely began to look possible. With the score at 28–17 and the big hand on the clock at the south-eastern end of the ground almost at its final resting place, Robbie Deans kicked high from a penalty – his brother gained possession and Albert Anderson scored. Robbie Deans converted. Auckland 28, Canterbury 23. The crowd was in a frenzy and when referee Bob Francis from Masterton called it off just a minute or so later, everyone knew they had seen something special.

Alex Veysey tapped away in the press box in the No. 3 stand and wrote: 'Too often rugby occasions which have had the element of potential greatness have in the event wallowed into anonymity. This was a magnificent exception.'[3] Lindsay Knight, who five years before had written a book about the history of the shield, wrote in the *8 O'Clock*, the *Auckland Star*'s sports paper: 'It was a game that throbbed with drama from the first thunderclap roar of the massive . . . crowd to Canterbury's rousing and glorious fight to the death.'[4]

The after-match function was supposed to be an invitation-only affair, but it was so crowded the

The Southland Times
Home of the Ranfurly Shield
Friday, October 23, 2009
$1.10
YES!

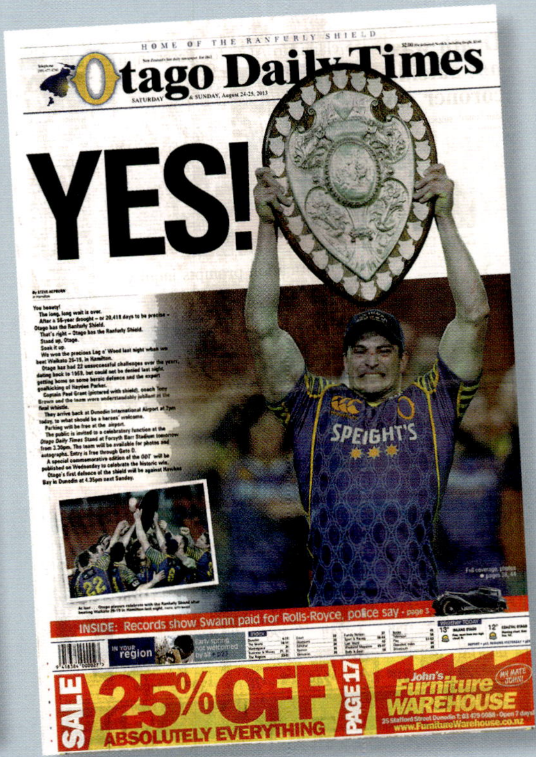
HOME OF THE RANFURLY SHIELD
Otago Daily Times
SATURDAY & SUNDAY, August 24-25, 2013
YES!
INSIDE: Records show Swann paid for Rolls-Royce, police say - page 3
SALE 25% OFF ABSOLUTELY EVERYTHING
PAGE 17
John's Furniture WAREHOUSE

Similar front pages greet the end of long Ranfurly Shield droughts in the south.

players could hardly squeeze their way in. The talk was about what a great occasion it was, how it was just what rugby needed and how the NZRFU had got it wrong. In his speech, the Canterbury union president, Merv Barnett, said he hoped Canterbury would go north to challenge for the Ranfurly Shield and not for one with a sponsor's name. Wyllie lamented that the NZRFU had wasted a great chance to promote the game by not having the match on television. 'We would have agreed to play on Sunday to avoid disruption to those other matches,' he said.

Such was the magic and attraction of the shield, a trophy without peer in world rugby.

The public had been enchanted and enraptured with the shield twelve years before on the same ground, when little Marlborough challenged mighty Canterbury and went back to Blenheim with the prize. Marlborough as a union had been in existence since 1888, but in the 71 years of the shield, it had challenged only three times previously: beaten 32–0 by Auckland in 1908, 26–8 by Wairarapa in 1928 and 30–3 by Hawke's Bay in 1968. The 1973 challenge was thus the first in the South Island and as many as 3000 people from Marlborough, including the Blenheim Municipal Band, made the trip south. All would have hopes, but most would have understood the reality. By late afternoon on Saturday, 28 July 1973, the reality was that Marlborough had won in one of the great sporting upsets. This was a Canterbury side with as much All Black pedigree as the one in 1985 that lost the shield to Auckland. The 1985 coach, Alex Wyllie, was the 1973 captain; there were players of renown such as Hamish Macdonald and Doug Bruce, Fergie McCormick and Duncan Hales, Lin Davis and Billy Bush, Tane Norton and Kerry Tanner. Marlborough could boast just one All Black, Alan Sutherland, but they had some tough and tenacious players

Before 2004, Bay of Plenty had played eighteen Ranfurly Shield matches and won none. Then it all changed. The Bay won rugby's greatest prize for the first time when it was taken from Auckland.

(such as Alan's brother Ray and Jim Joseph), a clever and crafty first five-eighth, Tony Goddard, and speedsters like Brian Ford (later an All Black). John Brooks in the *Press* thought Canterbury lacked a vital spark, but Marlborough lacked nothing.[5] They scrapped and they fought and when Goddard dropkicked a goal from 30 metres with nine minutes to go, his side gained a 9–6 advantage. Four minutes from time, Ford received the ball around his own 10-metre mark and slipped past his marker, Junior All Black (and later senior All Black) Terry Mitchell. Ford, a summer sprinter, was too quick for the cover defence and he raced around McCormick for the shield-winning try.

Wyllie's farm bordered the main road in North Canterbury and when rugby people drove past the signpost that says Omihi, they gave it a glance, acknowledging a man who has achieved most things in rugby and been unaffected by them all. On the night of the shield loss in 1973, Wyllie arrived home to find that Marlborough people, not for the first time that day, had got there first: his letterbox was wrapped in ribbons of Marlborough's red.

As it had done in other cities and towns since before the First World War, the shield lifted spirits, buoyed optimism and filled the union's bank accounts. Its presence was a boost to provincial pride; it brought a gleam to the eye and a lift to the step.

Even in the professional era, the shield lost none of its attraction, none of its lure, none of its effect on a community. Just when people may have been tiring of it being held too long by the rich provinces such as Auckland, Canterbury or Waikato, just as people were beginning to say the shield had lost its meaning, that there was no place for it in the modern game, along would come a challenger to rekindle the fever. It went to Taranaki and people gaped and marvelled, and the shield spent a night in a cowshed. It went to Bay of Plenty and became immersed in an eligibility row that was a reminder of 'the Battle of Solway' of so many years before. The Bay won the shield for the first time when they beat Auckland 33–28 in 2004, but questions were raised almost as soon as the players had left the field about the eligibility of one of the Bay players, Colin Bourke, who had played in Hawke's Bay earlier in the year. The NZRFU mounted an inquiry and it found that Bourke indeed was ineligible and the Bay union was fined $3,000. It could have lost the shield and the national championship points it gained from the match. Auckland asked only to ensure the rules were adhered to and said for it to retain the shield in such circumstances would be inappropriate.[6] Such decency and common sense had not always prevailed when the shield was involved.

The power of the shield again began to be questioned as the professional game took hold and

Patricia Rose, fifteen, of Blenheim, leaves no doubt about her allegiance and interest.

as the best players were increasingly not allowed to play for their provinces. The 'Super' series of rugby provided another level in the apex of aspiration and provincial rugby was shunted down a peg; provinces were increasingly places from which players came but seldom went back to. But those who were left savoured the shield just as much as if they had all the stars in the galaxy. Evidence of this has been provided in recent years with the shield going to North Harbour (formed in 1985) for the first time and places such as Southland after a gap of 50 years, to Otago after 56 years, to Hawke's Bay after 44 years and to Counties-Manukau for the first time.

A Counties supporter longed so much for the shield that he took it while it was on display in a Wellington bar in 2009. He videoed himself with it in his flat before the police arrived to retrieve it. He avoided conviction with a donation to charity and a letter of apology.[7] Had he waited four years, he could have avoided the publicity as well and just revelled in it being in Pukekohe for the first time.

When the shield was on one of its long spells in Hamilton, the Waikato union dropped it off at Bonham's, antique dealers, for a valuation. As a result, a precise description of the shield was produced for probably the first time:

> The Ranfurly Shield – a pressed copper backing overlaid with silver electroplating in an Art Nouveau style. Inscribed on the top of Shield 'Ranfurly Challenge Shield 1902' and beneath on a panel supported by two Art Nouveau styled maidens, 'Presented to the New Zealand Rugby Football Union by the Earl of Ranfurly.' Having a raised cartouche edged in a shell and star border of a rugby match. The shield is decorated in the Art Nouveau style with heart shaped pattern to lower part as well as foliant decoration. Mounted on an oak backing with a hinged stand. Surrounding the shield are twenty-two shield shaped sterling silver medallions all but three engraved. Width 51 cms. Length 71 cms.[8]

The company calculated the replacement value at $11,000 and noted drily, 'No allowance has been made for historic value.'

Any New Zealand rugby follower could add: 'Irreplaceable and priceless.'

Even the pie bags in Taranaki reflected Ranfurly Shield pride.

more than just his tilting at windmills for most of his career. There was a notable occasion in London in 1978 when Haden meandered into the opulent Park Lane Hotel in Piccadilly and Micky Steele-Bodger, a veterinarian who had held just about every position in rugby it was possible to hold, spied him. Haden pretended to hide behind a pillar and Steele-Bodger, the most charming of men, wagged a finger and intoned: 'One day I'm going to get you Haden, one day.' He never did, despite Haden's hobby of overtly brushing aside rugby's off-field laws and conventions whenever he could. He was even hauled before an NZRFU judicial hearing in 1984 and charged with, among other things, advocating professionalism. Haden could see the new era of rugby and his inquisitors and critics either could not or could and did not like what they saw. He was not alone, although his name invariably popped up whenever there was talk of professional teams, usually promoted by people with big ideas but little money.

Haden's last hurrah as a player was the rebel tour and by then, the IRB had reluctantly agreed to a joint proposal from New Zealand and Australia to launch a World Cup. Ireland and Scotland opposed a cup, but the vote got through with the support of South Africa, even though it was clear that its playing days were over until apartheid ended. The IRB used to meet at the East India Club in St James's Square in London, a place reeking of English tradition and history. The IRB was suitably clubby for its first hundred years and was forced to change only because a modern sporting world ruled by money and television demanded it. It and the dominant British and Irish components had several times rejected the prospect of any form of international tournament such as a world cup. It also strongly opposed any involvement with the Olympic Games. The advent of the cup in New Zealand and Australia changed not just rugby but the IRB itself.

While the British may not have understood this, New Zealanders did. It was articulated best by John ('J. J.') Stewart, the academic in gumboots who had coached the All Blacks in South Africa in 1976 and then moved into administration. Stewart was not the type who sat and said little at meetings; at annual meetings which were public, he was frequently the star of the show, saying things that others dared only think. At one stage after the rebels' tour, Ron Don at a meeting mounted his usual advocacy of South Africa and Stewart interrupted: 'The final whistle's been blown . . . can't you hear it, Ron?'[27] To other councillors such as Peter Wild, who had argued in vain against the 1985 plans, it was like the tolling of joyous bells. It was Stewart who wrote for an NZRFU subcommittee a paper proposing a form of trust funds for senior players, similar to what had applied for some years in athletics. In the paper, Stewart criticised the IRB for tenaciously clinging to its principles of amateurism and referring to them as the cornerstone of the game. In the next sentence, he tartly pointed out that when the IRB was established, it was there just to rule on disputes about the playing laws between the British countries. No principles of amateurism were proposed, accepted, implied or even discussed.[28]

By the time of the first World Cup in 1987, change was inescapable. South Africa was not invited because of its unwanted status both in New Zealand and elsewhere; the Lange government would not have allowed the South Africans in, the Hawke government in Australia would probably have done the same, and other countries may not have wanted to play against the South Africans anyway. But the rest of the small rugby world came to play, united in a tournament for the first time. Besides the other IRB countries, also taking part were Japan, Tonga, Zimbabwe, the United States, Fiji, Argentina, Italy, Canada and Romania. The IRB's reluctant hands were forced by matches in the cup being full internationals – how could they be otherwise? If the All Blacks playing Australia was a test match, so would have to be

A flag carried by touch judges during the first World Cup in 1987 reflecting the symbols of the two host countries.

the All Blacks playing Fiji, or Italy or Argentina. The rugby world expanded rapidly because of the cup. For the first time, administrators had to organise a tournament rather than just a tour; the old way of meeting all the costs and taking all the profits could not work any more. New systems had to be worked out, new financial backers had to be found and, inevitably, the IRB needed a slice of the tournament it did not really want.

The first tournament was a resounding success given the short time in which New Zealand and Australia had to organise it and given the novelty of the whole thing. It was a success too for rugby because it helped restore the game's standing in the eyes of the public after the odorous years. Parochially, it helped of course that New Zealand won; not just won, but dominated. Perhaps the majesty of an end-to-end try in the opening game against Italy by John Kirwan showed the rest of the world that the All Blacks were the pre-eminent team. The cup opened more eyes than just those of administrators. Some All Blacks, notably Dalton, appeared in television commercials as they were entitled to do according to the New Zealand rules, even if not associating Dalton with the All Blacks was a bit disingenuous. There was a difference,

Wayne Shelford leads the haka before a World Cup match in 1987. The haka before 1987 was not always performed and, when it was, players sometimes looked self-conscious. Shelford told his teammates in 1987 that if it was to be done, it had to be done properly. NORMAN SMITH

Michael Jones makes his debut in the first match of the 1987 World Cup against Italy. He was the first player to score in both this cup and in the next in England in 1991. NORMAN SMITH

however, between the New Zealand and IRB rules and even with the World Cup participation agreement, the defining 'bible' for the teams. When Russ Thomas, as chairman of the NZRFU and a director of the new company Rugby World Cup, had a press conference in his Christchurch office, it became a slanging match between 'them' and 'us' about the legality of the commercials; 'us' were the enlightened ones from New Zealand and Australia and 'them' were those from the northern hemisphere.

These two different views of a changing world became evident two years later when the All Blacks were in Britain and it was learnt that captain Wayne Shelford had been hired to open a supermarket or two during the tour. This outraged the British press and the Four Home Unions, the domestic offshoot of the IRB, had to make soothing noises. But while the All Blacks were in Britain, a Scottish newspaper carried a report that some members of the Scottish union, that most conservative of bodies, had come around to the view that players should be allowed to make money from their status as international players and even be compensated for lost wages.[29] This view was echoed publicly by the Welsh captain, Robert Jones.

By the next cup in 1991, when the English were the hosts, the unions previously opposed to

David Kirk signals triumph for New Zealand in the first World Cup in 1987. NORMAN SMITH

a cup had bowed to the inevitable (and had also seen a cash cow). In 1987, the gross income for the cup was £3.3 million, according to the IRB's own figures; four years later it was seven times that at £23.6 million. The potential television audience (the magnet for potential sponsors) for 1991 was estimated at 1.75 billion. There is nothing like large dollops of money coming in to overcome long-held principles. The IRB moved from a one-man band at the East India Club to new offices in Bristol and then subsequently, for tax reasons, to Dublin, capital city of the country that voted against the cup in the first place. It set up a subsidiary company to run the cup and found tax havens to maximise the profits.

Rugby could not remain an amateur game at the same time as so much of it changed. The rugby change was not in isolation. Other sports changed too as the reality of satellite transmission of television led to sport – a relatively cheap form of programme – becoming a global commercial commodity. The Olympic Games, as much an amateur bastion as rugby, allowed professionals after the games in Seoul in 1988; sports such as athletics, riddled with 'shamateurism', dropped all the pretence.

The end for rugby was inevitable and, true to form and precedent, change was forced upon it rather than initiated from within. The catalyst was Rupert Murdoch, the news media overlord who had branched from newspapers into broadcasting, among other things, and he (or his minions) wanted better and sole ownership of programmes for his television channels. He began a new rugby league competition that his News Corporation called Super League; it was in opposition to the established Australian Rugby League, for which Murdoch's rival Kerry Packer had rights. More players were needed to accommodate two competitions, if both survived, and rugby was the obvious source. By this time South Africa was back in the rugby fold – with the advent of majority rule and the abolition of apartheid, tours had resumed in 1992 and with almost indecent haste, the IRB meeting in Wellington voted South Africa as the next World Cup host. (An indication of how players valued tests between New Zealand and South Africa came after the first resumption test in Johannesburg in 1992. Springbok hooker Uli Schmidt told the after-match function at Ellis Park that there were two types of Springboks: 'Those who play the All Blacks and those who don't. Thank you for making us real Springboks.')

As the 1995 World Cup approached, worried rugby administrators from New Zealand, Australia

25

TENNIS
27
Exhausted Sampras crowned king at Queen's

CRICKET
30
Stewart to call the opening shots at Lord's

CYCLING
33
Master to turn wheel of fortune for Boardman

BOXING
35
Bowe's attack proves his best defence

TIMES SPORT

MONDAY JUNE 19 1995

All Blacks sweep into World Cup final with dismissive display

Lomu runs England ragged

THE TRY THAT BROKE ENGLISH HEARTS

Put all your debts in one basket

Jonah Lomu had as big an impact in Britain as he did in New Zealand. This is how it began. *THE TIMES*, 19 JUNE 1995

and South Africa went as supplicants to Murdoch, the man who began the crisis. In a remarkably short time – a little over a month – they put together an arrangement under which Murdoch's company would pay the three unions $US555 million over ten years in return for the television rights to all test matches between the three, a new provincial-level competition involving all three, and the domestic competitions of each. In offices and apartments in Johannesburg and London during this frenetic period, professional rugby took shape. It was not called that then, but that was what it was. The three national unions unveiled the deal on the eve of the World Cup final, won by South Africa in extra time against New Zealand. This was the time of the Rainbow Nation, of Mandela attending the final and donning a Springbok No. 6 jersey, symbolically bringing black and white together. It seemed South Africa's destiny to win. The Springboks triumphed and so too did rugby because it had been saved from Murdoch's league predators.

Even then, some of the players and others involved knew there was another threat, not yet public. This came from another Australian, Ross Turnbull, a former Wallaby prop (in his playing days he was known as 'Mad Dog') and national administrator who had plans of his own for professional rugby. He was backed, so it was said, by Murdoch's rival in the media and sports business, Packer.[30] Murdoch's deal with the three unions was conditional that their best players be involved, and from a New Zealand perspective, especially the sensation of the time, Jonah Lomu, the blockbusting wing who had been practically unstoppable in the cup matches. But Turnbull was confident his own scheme could give the players more money than could the establishment and he began extracting promises from leading players.

Little of what unfolded in the following weeks became public, but those close to rugby knew that Turnbull had some players as allies and agents and that others in the game were ready to go with

A cartoonist in *The Times* gives an English view of the World Cup in 1995. *THE TIMES*, 20 JUNE 1995

How *Dominion* readers learnt how serious was the intention of some players to turn their back on New Zealand rugby in 1995.

whichever side won. Brian Lochore, who had been the campaign manager for the All Blacks at the cup, and Jock Hobbs, by then a lawyer and member of the New Zealand council, had the task of ensuring the leading players remained loyal to the union.[31] It became evident the top 150 or so players could be lost to New Zealand. New Zealand rugby would have been decapitated if Turnbull's plans had worked or, so it was later learnt, if the majority of players got their way. More than a hundred years of tradition and development, more than a hundred years of establishing New Zealand rugby as among the best in the world, would have been jeopardised.

The World Cup-winning former captain, David Kirk, linked the money-chasers with the rebels of nine years before, the team he had refused to join on its illicit visit to South Africa.[32] He argued that rugby would survive: 'After all, we have done it all before. If you doubt this, ask the Cavaliers who went to South Africa in 1985 [actually, 1986], believing New Zealanders supported them and would stand by them. None of them enjoyed finding out they were wrong.' Kirk then delivered a very clear message: 'To the older players and some coaches and administrators who are leading the charge to the WRC [World Rugby Corporation], I say go. Get out, leave, remove the stain, the blot you are on the spirit of rugby. Take whatever money you can get, from whoever you can get it, but leave before you do any more damage.'

All Blacks asked Lochore and Hobbs for breathing space so they could properly prepare for tests in Auckland and Sydney; at the same time the players continued negotiating with Turnbull. The tests over, the All Blacks, Lochore and Hobbs returned to New Zealand and an extraordinary round of meetings began, the two men going separately from provincial union to provincial union, putting their case, which was essentially backing loyalty with money. Some players listened in silence; some were truculent. At one point, the All Blacks gave a statement to a Sunday paper – no individual names were attached – which said, among other things: '. . . we want to assure them [the rugby public] that at all times the traditions, the culture and the future viability of the game are paramount in our thinking'.[33] No one was fooled. Kirk summed it up: 'The selfishness of a few will not dim the light of those who are prepared to give to the spirit of rugby rather than [take] from the trough of financial gain.'[34]

The breakthrough came in August when the first two All Blacks, Jeff Wilson and Josh Kronfeld, signed with Hobbs and the New Zealand union. Several provincial players followed on the same day. The Turnbull dam had been breached and, eventually, twenty of the World Cup All Blacks signed. Others went to Japan or to league. This had been a greater crisis for the game than the 1907 arrival of league in New Zealand; greater

Loyal to New Zealand rugby. Jeff Wilson and Josh Kronfeld in a promotional photo for the World Cup in 1999. HODDER MOA BECKETT

than any purely rugby issue. Hobbs has often been described as the man who saved rugby; that might have been going a bit far but he might have saved the All Blacks in the short term. There was no question that he was the main person in keeping the top level of players within New Zealand. He had gone, as he himself once remarked with a rueful smile, from rebel to rebel-catcher; poacher to gamekeeper. Hobbs agreed part of his motivation in his work for rugby in 1995 was to make up for his role with the rebels of a decade earlier.[35]

Seventeen days after Wilson and Kronfeld began the move back, the International Rugby Board caught up and after three days of negotiations in Paris, it declared the game 'open'. Its president, Frenchman Bernard Lapasset, said: 'We have adopted principles which will effectively make the game open and ensure its development around the world. It's a revolution.'[36] It was no such thing. It was evolution, an evolving outcome that had been apparent for years; the IRB was among the last to acknowledge it. It was fitting that the meeting was in France, a country that had seldom held the same lofty view of amateurism as the British unions had.

The Times, frequently over a hundred years the mouthpiece for the rugby establishment, was frank. It said in an editorial: 'A veil of dishonesty has now been lifted: rugby union players may now be paid the salaries they deserve, without subterfuge, rancour or any decline in standards. There is an ethos, after all, for every age.'[37]

Rugby entered the modern era. It did so without Hobbs. The annual meeting in 1996 introduced a new 'corporate-style' board for the national union – its corporate world architects not knowing or forgetting that most senior rugby administrators for a hundred years had been successful businessmen, some of them running large companies. Most of the country saw Hobbs as a saviour; the delegates to the meeting did not see him as saviour enough to give him a seat on the new board.

A rugby phenomenon. Jonah Lomu, almost unstoppable when at his best, played 73 matches for New Zealand between 1994 and 2002 – then had a kidney transplant. PETER BUSH

14 The more things change . . .

McCaw lifts the Webb Ellis Cup,
Tired joy is on their faces:
It's a hard road to win the cup.[1]

In the dying days of amateurism and the wondering early days of pay for play, there was some speculation that New Zealand would suffer. The argument, one that some national administrators had used in favour of staying amateur, went along the lines that in rugby as in war, god would be on the side of the big battalions. New Zealand, then with a population approaching four million and geographically remote, could not hope to compete for players and money against countries such as England and France with their greater playing numbers and commercial pull. Even Australia, despite rugby on the other side of the Tasman still being seen as an elitist game, would gain from money in the game while New Zealand would be the loser.

How could a couple of island dots – or 'poxy little island' as Wales's Australian assistant coach, Scott Johnson, in 2004 described New Zealand – continue to be successful in rugby when success was determined not by the ability to take time off work to play, but by money and market?[2] They were valid concerns that proved to be without foundation. As the money years unwound, New Zealand showed it could adapt and dominate the game in the professional era as much as it did when the game was amateur.

In international rugby, the All Blacks have a greater success rate as professionals than they did as amateurs. The figures are illuminating. By the end of 1993, six years after the first World Cup and when the end of amateurism was nigh, the All Blacks had played 277 test matches and won 199 of them with 64 losses and 14 draws. That gave them, from their first test in 1903 until their last in 1993, a winning percentage of 71.8. From their first test of 1994, a loss against France, until the end of 2014, they had played 229 matches for a winning percentage of 81.92. No other national team is close. The All Blacks' success rate in the professional era of 82.83 per cent is about 20 percentage points better than the next best, South Africa. It could be – and probably will be – argued that in the professional era New Zealand have played many of the game's lesser lights such as Portugal, Fiji, Samoa and Romania, and that is true. But so have all the other countries. In the same period the leading countries, and especially New Zealand, Australia and South Africa, have also played each other much more frequently than they ever did.

England, for all their playing resources and money, have made little impact on New Zealand under professionalism. The two countries have met on 40 occasions and England have won only seven of them – and only three of those wins (2002, 2003 and 2012) have been in the professional era. Wales have not beaten New Zealand since 1953 and Scotland and Ireland have never done so (though both have gone close). The Lions, that marketing dream of the British and Irish countries combined, have toured New Zealand just once as professionals, in 2005, and were a failure. The following table demonstrates New Zealand's continued dominance.

Leading countries in the professional era (from 1 November 1995 until 31 December 2014)

COUNTRY	TESTS	WON	LOST	DRAWN	% WINS
New Zealand	233	193	36	4	82.83
South Africa	238	152	82	4	63.86
Australia	244	150	87	6	61.47
England	216	131	81	4	60.64
France	224	133	87	4	59.37
Ireland	203	112	87	4	55.17
Wales	228	111	113	4	48.68
Scotland	195	76	116	3	39.74

Source: ESPN Scrum

theguardian Saturday 16.11.13

The secrets of Spain's success Page 2 »

sport

Barney Ronay Retire to your shed and savour the joys of cricket through the small hours Page 14 »

The Ashes In search of the real David Warner Page 10 »

Are the All Blacks unstoppable?

Steve Hansen's New Zealand are two games away from a perfect season. Andy Bull, page 8 »

Fraser-Pryce threatens strike action over a lack of support

Taylor faces fine after mocking black team-mates on Twitter

This was how the *Guardian* newspaper in England saw the All Blacks in 2013, when they became the only team in the professional era to win every test in a calendar year. *GUARDIAN*, 16 NOVEMBER 2013

The All Blacks went through the 2013 calendar year unbeaten, the only country in the professional era to do such a thing. While they were in London for the second-last match of the year, a *Daily Telegraph* reporter was invited into their hotel team room and someone overlooked the potential embarrassment of motivation slogans plastered around the walls reaching the public's eyes and ears. The All Black of the past was generally humble and modest, hanging his head as he trotted back after scoring a try. But the high-fives and emotive jubilation of the modern era have been matched by words off the field. 'We are the most dominant team in the history of the world,' one of the slogans read.[3] Such things, if they must exist, are best left unseen. Most players would cringe at such a trite comment and just let their record speak for itself. And it does.

Much changed in rugby after the momentous decisions of 1995, but there was much that stayed the same. The game was still played by fifteen people on either side with an odd-shaped ball that added chance to enthusiasm and skill. People still talked about the game, people still watched it and it remained by far the most dominant sport in the country. The effects of the game going professional were not fully apparent for several years; it was as if rugby could continue more or less as before, with the only difference being that players could be paid.

The most obvious public change was the introduction of the Super 12, the tripartite (Australia, New Zealand and South Africa) competition that was part of the deal reached with News Corporation. It was an expanded version of early-season competitions that had been played since 1986 with benefits for the provincial unions involved but of minimal interest to those which were not. The first of them, involving Auckland, Wellington and Canterbury of New Zealand unions, was grandly named the South Pacific Championship, but with changes and additions it became the Super Six and finally the Super 10. It required not a hint of original thought for the new Murdoch-funded competition to become the Super 12. The plan was idealistically sound but flawed in a practical sense. To overcome the parochial disinterest that characterised the earlier competition, the new one introduced new teams with new names and called them 'franchises', owned by the national union with administration delegated to specially created boards.

They were, and remain, based in Auckland, Hamilton, Wellington, Christchurch and Dunedin, but their 'franchise' extended to other provincial unions, from which they could – in theory – draw their players. In addition the union introduced a draft system. The idea was that the best players in the country would play in the competition and return to their home provinces at the end of it. In the initial years, there were even 'commissioners' to ensure this happened. But they soon became superfluous when it became apparent that the unions in which the 'Super' teams were based held most of the strings, including those attached to the purse.

During the settling-down period, the teams were known by their provincial names as well as their contrived ones: the Wellington Hurricanes, the Waikato Chiefs and so on. This did not sit well with other unions – for example, Taranaki people found it hard to get enthusiastic about a team called Wellington (Taranaki later became part of the Chiefs). Gradually, the provincial names were dropped and they became just the Highlanders, the Chiefs etc. This has always confused rugby journalists and commentators in other countries, especially Australia where there was more of a nickname tradition. After nearly twenty years of the competition, references are still made to 'the Otago Highlanders' or 'the Wellington Hurricanes' or whatever.

The original intentions were good – it was thought that at the end of the Super 12, the top 25 or so players would go on to the international games, including the new Tri Nations series with Australia and South Africa, but that the rest would go back to club rugby. This would have meant a lift to the game at all levels, but it did not work out that way. The gradual expansion of both the 'Super' series (first 12, then 14, now 15, soon 17) and the Tri Nations into the Rugby Championship had quite the opposite effect. The best players do not play club rugby, many probably do not belong to clubs; most of them do not even play provincial rugby.

The top rugby officials would admit there were faults as they adapted to the new world, but New Zealand seemed to take the more sensible and manageable course by contracting players centrally; that is, the best players owed their pay packets and their contractual allegiance to the New Zealand union first. In some other countries, most notably England, rugby followed the soccer model and players were contracted to clubs, which meant they had the final say on when players could be freed for internationals (or not). It took years of negotiations, arguments and the intervention eventually of a reorganised International Rugby Board to bring some order. Friction between unions and clubs in Europe simmers away still. It seems to have become a characteristic of rugby that precedents in other sports are followed rather than rugby itself initiating something. Sirens indicating half and fulltime were confined to Australia until professionalism saw them added elsewhere;

Farmers and footballers

New Zealand's rugby players at whatever level they play come from all sections of society and, in the amateur days, top level players were from a wide range of occupations. Farmers or workers in the broader agricultural industry have always had a considerable presence. At least twenty All Black captains have been farmers or in farm-related work, and included among them are some of the most illustrious rugby names: Wilson Whineray, Colin Meads, Brian Lochore, Sid Going, Alex Wyllie, Dave Loveridge, Graham Mourie . . . if rural workers such as stock and station agents are added, the list goes on. Joe Warbrick, who played in the first New Zealand team and organised and led the Natives tour in 1888, was a farmer. As Terry McLean once wrote: 'Down through the years, the boys from the waybacks have contributed an enormous amount of players, a tremendous amount of enthusiasm and a goodly quantity of outstanding talent to the cause of rugby in this country.'[1]

A sheep under each arm, Colin Meads at work. Meads and his brother Stan came to be the epitome of the hard farmer All Blacks, trained to perfection on rough farmland rather than in a gymnasium. *SPORTS DIGEST*, JULY 1968

Colin Meads, whose farming brother Stan was also an All Black, reckoned the rural life gave him basic rugby training that no sedentary occupation in the city could ever provide. He did not always wander round his King Country farm with a sheep under each arm, as he was once pictured doing, but in the days before quad bikes, he frequently ran rather than used tractors or horses on his property.[2] Brian O'Brien, editor of the monthly *Sports Digest*, once recalled a Christmas visit to Meads's farm: 'I could see with half an eye that even then, four months before the rugby season, he was fine and lean. He was working his guts out.'[3]

Another All Black farmer, Ken Gray, told O'Brien: 'I find the farm environment is a tremendous help. Carting fence posts on your shoulders up steep hills can't, in my opinion, be excelled for your legs.' Gray said that during the South African tour of New Zealand in 1965, he took a Springbok centre, Francois Roux, a farmer from Griqualand, to his farm in the hills north of Porirua. Gray said:

> Roux gave me his opinion that New Zealand is the last country on earth, in a rugby-playing sense, where men who play the game also sweat and work hard. He said to me: 'All the old brand of Boer farmer is gone now. Kaffirs do all the hard work.

In New Zealand, the farmers still do it themselves and these are the men who wear All Black jerseys.'

(Gray retired at the end of 1969 because he was opposed to the 1970 tour of South Africa.)

Terry McLean went through a list of notable farmer-footballers and reckoned among the strongest was a Canterbury lock of the 1950s, Nelson Dalzell:

> They used to swear that he could pick up 44-gallon drums (loaded) and sling them on to the back of a truck. . . . I always used to doubt its practicality – after all, that would have made 'Dad' the strongest cove in the world – but the last man I would ever have expressed the doubt to would have been Nelson himself.[4]

Since professionalism, all players have listed their occupations as 'rugby player'. Only Andy Haden, another brought up on a farm, did that in the old days. But the farming background and genes are still there. Richie McCaw was brought up on a farm and enrolled at Lincoln College on a rugby scholarship, intending to do an agricultural science degree until rugby took over. Three of his teammates, the Whitelock brothers Sam, George and Luke, are all prime farming stock: they are grandsons of 'Dad' Dalzell.

McLean wrote his piece on footballer-farmers in 1964 just after Brian Lochore's first season as an All Black. Professionalism then was in an unimaginable future. McLean worried about a farmer-less time: 'When the day comes when New Zealand rugby can no longer rely on its farmer boys, New Zealand rugby will really be in the cart.'[5] Not quite yet. All Black hooker Andrew Hore played his last game for his country during the unbeaten year of 2013 and when it was all over, he went back to the family farm in the Maniototo.

For all the rural influence, rugby's playing population has reflected the overall population; that is, cities and towns provide more players than do country areas, although there are doubtless many examples of areas that once were rural and are now urban, Manurewa or Papakura for example. Of the 495 players to play for New Zealand before 1950, 182 were born in Auckland, Wellington, Christchurch, Dunedin or Invercargill, about 37 per cent. But such statistics are indicative rather than conclusive.

Not all forwards were farmers and not all farmers were forwards. One of the best of fullbacks, George Nepia, heads off for a day's work on his Rangitukia farm, accompanied by his son George. Young George was accidentally killed while serving with the Fiji Battalion in Malaya in 1954.

Just how rural New Zealand rugby was, especially in its first fifty or so years, has been a matter of interest to those few professional historians who have ever bothered about the game. One of them, Jock Phillips, saw the origins

A long-established farmers' magazine, *Straight Furrow*, featured one of the farmer-All Blacks, recently retired captain Graham Mourie, on its front page in 1982.

of a New Zealand 'type' in a frontier rural setting and the poor chaps who lived in towns had to compensate. 'Men who pursued sedentary urban occupations therefore felt a special urgency to prove their virility on their Saturday afternoons off.'[6] That theory belongs almost in the same category as the Phillips belief that 'the scrimmage was rather like an organised hug' or that in a society that was short of women, men found solace in a scrum.[7] Greg Ryan delivered the urban riposte to Phillips and backed his comments up with a range of tables which included players' occupations, the provincial origins of All Blacks, the main centre dominance of national touring teams and compared occupations of All Blacks of one era with another.[8] The cumulative effect was that New Zealand rugby has always been weighted towards the towns and Ryan's work provided the actuality to override the myth. This is not to detract from the quality and contribution of some of those players from country areas.

Super rugby teams get competition points even during their bye week, a practice introduced by league in Sydney; most of the myriad of rules surrounding the World Cup have been used by soccer.

The strength of New Zealand rugby had always been the organisational pyramid, with the clubs at the base, then provincial rugby, island and national rugby such as trials and Māori, then the national team at the apex. Professionalism introduced the new level of the 'Super' competition, which pushed provincial down a level, but societal and demographic changes had their effect too. The interisland game, for so long a season staple and seen at times as just below test level, lost its allure before the advent of professionalism because of the perceived strength of the North and because players increasingly saw it as a waste of time (and could not be compelled to play in it). A contrived effort to have an interisland game in 2012 based on franchises as a financial boost for Otago rugby was marked by public disinterest. Trials during the professional era have become occasional matches to suit the desires of national coaches, while national Māori matches, despite the marketing elevation to being 'Māori All Blacks', are usually the next-best Māori after the All Blacks have been excluded. Various other national teams have come and gone – 'Emerging Players' in the dying years of amateurism when many of the players chosen had emerged long since, and in the professional era, New Zealand A (which meant 'B') and New Zealand Juniors or 'Junior All Blacks' (another marketing contrivance that had nothing to do with age or with the earlier team of the same name but prouder provenance).

Provincial unions took time to find their place in the new order. For a time, the unions that were used as a base for the Super teams were seen as the rich getting richer while the others were poor and getting poorer. It was never that simple. Provinces had to pay players and, in the case of All Blacks, the Super provinces had to pay them to keep them, even though they seldom if ever played for their provinces. Their retention was necessary for their Super eligibility. Several provinces, notably Otago, Southland, Counties-Manukau and Bay of Plenty, went to the brink of dissolution. A salary cap was introduced to provincial rugby to prevent financial excesses and in the case of Super rugby, each of the teams became centrally funded to make its own purchases of players rather than rely on provinces. Private investment in the franchise teams was also sought to spread the load and risk.

The Super 12/14/15 and whatever it ends up did not replace provincial rugby, the level of the game that remains largely based on settlement patterns and political decisions from the nineteenth century. It provided a new level, a series of games that its promoters hoped would appeal beyond the traditional rugby supporter, and with that hope came all the show business and marketing paraphernalia such as night games, pop music, pre-match 'entertainment' and giant TV screens. Beneath the frippery there was serious business and no coach or player could ever have taken Super rugby less than seriously. The dynasty of success achieved in Christchurch by the Crusaders has been one of New Zealand sport's remarkable success stories; the success of New Zealand rugby has in large measure been founded on that. Auckland used to be seen as the real strength of New Zealand rugby, but that mantle was taken over by Christchurch, and while Auckland's population and ethnic mix grew, its relative rugby success went in the reverse direction to such an extent that the New Zealand union singled it out for remedial treatment.

Auckland is at the heart of another of rugby's distinctive features over the past thirty or so years – the so-called 'browning' of the game. Māori representation in the All Blacks historically has usually been around the same proportion as Māori of the population as a whole. But the vast increase in players of Pacific Island origin or ancestry altered the face of New Zealand rugby. Players of

Robin Brooke charges off for one of his two tries for the Auckland Blues against the Otago Highlanders in Dunedin in 1997. The Blues won 45–28. That's Brooke's New Zealand teammate, Josh Kronfeld, on the ground. Teams later dropped their provincial prefixes.

Samoan or Tongan or Fijian (and Tahitian and Niuean) background could be counted almost on one hand until the 1980s. Frequently, white players are now in the minority, and there are occasional stories that mothers won't allow their sons to play rugby because of the greater size and strength of early-maturing players of South Pacific ethnicity (as there were too in the 1920s when Māori had a dominant period). All this led to frequent moans

Samoan-born Eroni Clarke of the Auckland Blues with support from Carlos Spencer during the 1997 Super 12 final against the ACT Brumbies at Eden Park. The Blues won 23–7, giving them the first two Super 12 titles after they beat Natal in the first final the year before. Clarke was one of the players in the 1990s associated with the so-called 'browning' of rugby.

from the northern hemisphere that New Zealand and, to a lesser extent, Australia had plundered the island countries for their rugby talent. An aspect that concerns those with the interests of the game at heart (rather than merely money) is that the increased number of Polynesian players is not matched by a proportionate increase in coaches or administrators. Neither has rugby made any serious effort to benefit from the increasing Asian population of New Zealand.

Sevens rugby used to be a pre-season or post-season frolic when not enough players could be found for the full game (and that was why it began in the Scottish Borders in the nineteenth century). The IRB and various national unions gave short shrift to sevens (New Zealand wanted nothing to do with the Hong Kong sevens when it first began) until they realised that it could make money for them and it was their ticket to the marketing nirvana that is the Olympic Games. Of course, sevens is more about public spectacle than rugby and for spectators, it's more a fancy dress party.

With the expansion of both Super rugby and the increased number of international matches, the new-style provincial competition was a level

The committed and the curious. Spectators ring the main ground at Peter Johnstone Park in Mosgiel when Brad Thorn, multi-tasking rugby and league international, turned out for the local club, Taieri. *OTAGO DAILY TIMES*

down from where it had been. All Blacks played in it only for convenience or when needing games as part of rehabilitation from injury.

Club rugby could never regain the popularity it had in the 1950s. A whole range of factors – weekend shopping, less drinking and even less drink-driving, increased leisure alternatives – combined to limit any growth in club rugby. Some diehard clubs, anecdotal evidence says, continued to pay players money or in kind, but even that seemed to be on the wane by the early years of the twenty-first century. Rugby clubs had long since ceased to be the community focal points they once had been, but many remained powerful magnets for community allegiance and feeling. It is unlikely that another A. P. Gaskell could happen along to play in and write about 'The Big Game', but there are areas in New Zealand, mostly outside big population areas, where a club game is still a matter of interest to people beyond the players, their families and other club members. If an All Black, for whatever reason, plays for a club the crowd swells enormously. When Richie McCaw or Dan Carter played for their Christchurch clubs as a first step back on the road to the top, the games became national television events. When Brad Thorn played for Taieri, it was almost the biggest thing to happen in Mosgiel since the Queen went walkabout. In the amateur days, the appearance of the mighty among the masses was commonplace; it was not unusual for a player to play a test on a Saturday and turn out for his club on the Sunday. Players frequently played for both club and province in the one week. This interchange of levels is now rare. After domestic tests, the national union announces which players

Hardly any spectators, lousy day, muddy ground, but still all in an afternoon's fun for All Black halfback Dave Loveridge, here playing for his Inglewood club.

from the All Black squad have been 'released' to be available for provinces.

The riches the sport now brings are not necessarily at odds with a love for the game. When the Highlanders had a weekend off in 2013, two of their All Blacks, Andrew Hore and Tony Woodcock, turned out for Hore's home team, Maniototo, charmingly nicknamed the Maggots. The game was an important one in the club's calendar against Wakatipu in Queenstown. The home team's coach was Justin Marshall, the 81-test halfback for New Zealand who agreed to play 'the odd game'. Marshall recalled his first pass as being a bit wobbly, which brought a comment from Hore: 'Nothing's changed, eh Marshy?' Of course, when a lineout throw from Hore went awry, Marshall responded in kind. But the final word was with Marshall's ten-year-old son, Lachlan, who was a ball boy. Marshall was stepped by a Maniototo attacker and was on the ground by the touchline when the try was awarded. Lachlan looked down at his father and said: 'You should have made that tackle, Dad.'[4]

The nature of international rugby changed once players were paid, as it had to. International rugby was founded on the concept of the tour, dating from 1888 when the Natives went to Britain and an English team toured New Zealand and Australia. Later tours were not as arduous as those two, but they nevertheless followed the general pattern with two matches a week for up

All Blacks Tony Woodcock (centre) and Andrew Hore (left) enjoy a return to the grass roots with Hore's club, Maniototo, for a match in Queenstown against Wakatipu, coached by former All Black Justin Marshall. TEAUKURA MOETAUA/MEDIA SPORT

to three months and with three or four tests along the way. This was distinctively rugby; only cricket among other sports could match it.

Colin Meads played 133 times for New Zealand, but 'only' 55 of those matches were tests. At the other extreme in the professional era, Tony Woodcock and Dan Carter each topped a century of matches for New Zealand and every one of them was a test match. Occasional efforts were made to restore some aspect of the old tours to the professional era, but they were more lip service than serious intent. The New Zealand union tried to make a genuine attempt at reintroducing the tour concept with the Lions in 2005 and seven matches were played against provincial sides, plus New Zealand Māori and the three tests. But the Lions coach, Clive Woodward, rather undercut the plan by bringing 48 players on tour plus 30 assorted coaches, officials and various off-field workers, including a chef and British Prime Minister Tony Blair's spin doctor. The Lions were a national joke rather than, as in the past, a team to admire. The tour did have the advantage, however, of showing the IRB that New Zealand could still stage big rugby events, especially in terms of hotel and flight requirements. Without the Lions tour as evidence, New Zealand may not have won the right to host the World Cup in 2011.

The All Blacks overseas have occasionally tried to fit in midweek matches as in days past, but they have been rare. The most common non-test opponent has been the Barbarians, that invitational remnant of when England ruled the rugby world, and the most spectacular opponent was Munster in 2008, a game arranged as a thirtieth anniversary celebration of the province's dramatic win against the All Blacks in 1978. That game remains the only New Zealand loss in Ireland, but the 2008 version nearly joined it, the All Blacks winning by just 18–16. It was sandwiched between tests against Ireland and Wales and consequently the two teams were not the best the country and province could field.

Dan Carter, one of the outstanding players of the early twenty-first century and by far the All Blacks' highest points scorer. He is pictured here kicking his one conversion in the 21–11 win against Ireland in wet and windy conditions in Wellington in 2008. PETER BUSH

The inevitable with tours happened when France in 2013 played the Blues midweek rather than Auckland or some other provincial team, and the following year, England played the Crusaders. Since both were midweek matches during the 'international window' when Super rugby was not played, top players were rested. Professionalism had reduced a rugby institution, the tour match, to something approaching a marketing exercise. While players play those games for their own personal reasons, usually with the intention of being chosen for the next level up, the element of team or provincial pride and satisfaction is

Job done. Zinzan Brooke, Justin Marshall and captain Sean Fitzpatrick leave the field after New Zealand won a series in South Africa for the first time. DAVID ROGERS/GETTY IMAGES

either missing or not as important as it used to be. Rugby loses part of its soul when it is reduced to a box-ticking exercise.

One of the most celebrated events in New Zealand rugby came in the second year of professionalism, when the All Blacks won a series in South Africa for the first time. It was an odd visit, combining as it did elements of the old-style tour and of the new Tri Nations competition. The first match could have come from the itinerary of any of the tours of the amateur era. It was played at Worcester in the Western Cape, about an hour and a quarter up the motorway from Cape Town, a town known more as the boyhood home of Nobel Prize winner J. M. Coetzee than as a rugby centre. The All Blacks beat a Boland Invitation XV there on the Tuesday then beat the Springboks in Cape Town on the following Saturday in the last of the Tri Nations matches. That business attended to, the team then had three more provincial matches and a three-test series. Coach John Hart had had the wisdom, and the New Zealand union had the sense to agree, to seek an enlarged touring party on the basis that one team could play the tests and the other the rest of the games. There were some murmurings about why they couldn't do it the old way, with players doubling up from Saturday to Tuesday or Wednesday. The reason was that tests in 1996, and frequently ever since, were just a week apart. Winning the series in South Africa was a momentous achievement. This was against a South Africa that had won the World Cup the year before and was high on confidence both through its playing achievements and by being embraced as a focal point of Nelson Mandela's new Rainbow Nation.

The New Zealanders had their own high emotion; there was no professionalised cynicism for them. Much was made of how the teams of 1928, 1949, 1960, 1970 and 1976 had strived and struggled in South Africa, only to be denied their prize by a variety of means and for a variety of reasons. The 1992 All Blacks went to Johannesburg and won their one test, but it was not a series and, in any case, the Springboks then were still emerging from their apartheid chrysalis. This was different and the All Blacks were told how they were playing a hardened, successful South African team for themselves, yes, but also for all those who had gone before. When the win came by 33 points to 22, the reactions showed what it meant to the players. The captain, Sean Fitzpatrick, was down on his knees when the French referee, Didier Mene, blew his last. He pounded the turf in relief and ecstasy. Halfback Justin Marshall jumped around like a demented chimpanzee, Zinzan Brooke adopted the more traditional victory posture of arms aloft; that devotee of American basketball, Jeff Wilson, high-fived whoever was near. Older men remembered when they were younger. Don Clarke was there in 1960 when the All Blacks were beaten, and now here he was again, 63 years old, and he wiped away a tear as the players stepped lightly back into the dressing room. There were men back in New Zealand, in the half-light of dawn, doing the same thing.

All Blacks are expected to win; it's part of their implicit charter with the people of New Zealand. No other national sports team has ever carried that burden. For some others, it's a pleasant surprise when they win; more common for them to lose. But not the All Blacks. To show how special this win in South Africa was, the team was given an American-style triumphal parade on Queen Street in Auckland when they got back. Only the 1905 All Blacks when they arrived back in Auckland or the 1924 team when they got back to Wellington had had similar receptions.

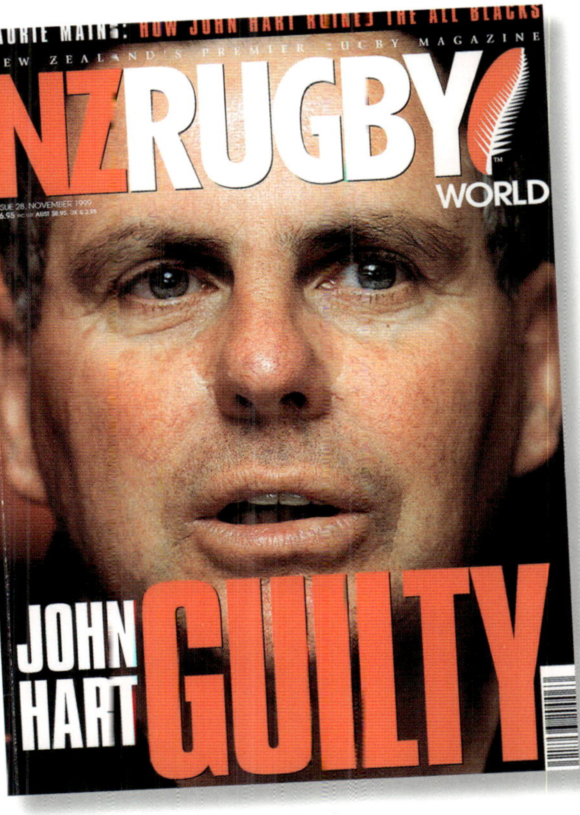

It was only a game. Coach John Hart is harshly treated for New Zealand's World Cup semifinal loss to France in 1999. *NZ RUGBY WORLD*, NOVEMBER 1999

The professional era was also the age of the cult of the coach. If a team won, it was because of the players; if a team lost, it was the coach's fault. As the game became increasingly complex as the twentieth century became the twenty-first, its observers still drew simplistic conclusions. The World Cup has defined eras. John Hart had been co-coach in 1991 with Alex Wyllie; from 1992 to 1995 it was Laurie Mains, and from 1996 Hart was back, this time on his own. When his All Blacks were beaten by France in a cup semifinal in 1999, Hart was vilified. It was unjust. It was the players who lost a game in which they had control; with about half an hour of the game to play, New Zealand led by fourteen points. It was not Hart who let that lead fritter away; it was not Hart who missed tackles. But he got the blame. A national rugby magazine carried an appalling front cover, calling Hart 'guilty' and giving him more public condemnation than many criminals receive. When Hart went to a harness race meeting in Christchurch not long after the cup, he was spat at. The whole reaction to the All Blacks' loss seemed to say more about an immaturity or inherent nastiness of New Zealanders than it did about the abilities of the players or their coach.

Hart was replaced by one of his assistants, Wayne Smith, who himself was assisted by the successful Highlanders coach, Tony Gilbert. But Smith towards the end of his second year said he did not think he was right for the job and his employer should look for someone else. That led to the appointment of John Mitchell, and he fared hardly any better in public than Hart, though the fact he was not as articulate made life more difficult for him than it should have been. Just to show that the World Cup had become the new measuring rod for international rugby, the New Zealand union chairman, Jock Hobbs, said publicly before the cup was even over that Mitchell's job would be advertised. Hobbs himself was in the chairman's job because the national union had got itself into a pickle coping with the modern commercial demands of rugby and had botched the chance of hosting some of the 2003 cup matches.

Australia decided in 1997 it wanted to run the cup in 2003 and it suggested to New Zealand that it be a sub-host and have one pool of matches, two quarterfinals, a semifinal and the game no one wants, the play-off for third. The NZRFU agreed and things seemed to be progressing until two years before the cup when New Zealand reacted against demands for unscheduled payments and against change in cup regulations. IRB chairman Vernon Pugh ran the organisation because it had not had a chief executive for more than a year and governance and management merged into confused unison. The three major issues for New Zealand were that it not make a loss on the tournament, that the national provincial competition still proceed even though it overlapped, and what the precise definition of 'clean' (absence of advertising) was in relation to rugby grounds. A private note from within NZRFU headquarters read in part: 'Our beef is not with the ARU (even though they are leaking information and clearly enjoy the predicament we're in) but with the IRB. We believe there has been a lack of leadership from the IRB on this issue.'[5]

Primary school players had their own World Cup in 2011, with chosen schools playing in the names of competing cup countries. It was one of the ways the organisers chose to fulfil their marketing slogan, 'a stadium of four million'. In this photo of a Rippa World Cup game at Albany, eleven-year-old Julian Hikiwai-McIntyre, playing for 'Japan' (Parkvale Primary in Hastings), attacks against 'Tonga' (Fairfield Primary, Hamilton). *NZ HERALD*

New Zealand administrators were frequently exasperated. At one stage, when they were discussing whether the NPC could still be played at the time of the cup, the NZRFU told the IRB that the last scheduled game of the NPC was the day of the cup opening game in Sydney and therefore there would be no clash. The IRB thought this was deliberately misleading, not understanding that the time difference between Sydney and Wellington would have allowed it to happen. It was a modern version of the age-old issue of Anglocentric administration with little understanding of what happened beyond Land's End. This ignorance endures; provinces in New Zealand are frequently referred to as 'clubs' by the people on the other side of the world; jerseys are shirts and grounds are pitches. Even soccer's 'captain's armband' has found its way into New Zealand rugby reports.

In the event, Pugh got his way, New Zealand was dropped as a sub-host and the NZRFU had a humiliating cleanout at the elective top and lost its chief executive, David Rutherford. This led to the return of Hobbs, who had been dumped when the old council was replaced by the new board in 1996. He became chairman towards the end of 2002 and remained in the position until he knew his failing health would not allow him

World Cup 2003 timeline: the slips twixt cup and lip

1998

FEBRUARY: The International Rugby Board accepted a proposal that Australia host the 2003 World Cup with New Zealand as a sub-host; applications were also received from France and Italy. It was agreed 23 matches, comprising two pools, two quarterfinals, a semifinal and the play-off for third, be played in New Zealand.[1]

2001

FEBRUARY: The IRB said the hosts would have to pay travel and accommodation costs for teams and VIPs, including every national union president and members of the International Olympic Committee (rugby was not then part of the Olympics). The increase was estimated at $A20 million.

MARCH: The NZRFU received a copy of the host agreement, including the demand for 'clean' stadiums and advertising-free zones around stadiums. The NZRFU said the definition of 'clean' was constantly changing.

MAY: In light of changed circumstances and revised forecasting, the NZRFU estimated a loss of about $A12 million.

AUGUST: The NZRFU board decided to continue as sub-host providing there was no financial loss; and that it adopt an 'all or nothing' approach, including non-participation.

SEPTEMBER: The NZRFU accepted a draft draw and designated Albany, Auckland, Christchurch, Dunedin, Hamilton, Invercargill, Napier, Palmerston North, Rotorua and Wellington as venues. New Zealand rejected an Australian proposal that it stage both semifinals and the play-off.

OCTOBER: The New Zealand and Australian unions and Rugby World Cup officials met in Singapore to discuss concerns over money and scheduling. They failed to reach agreement. The demand for 'clean' stadiums was raised to 100 per cent. For the 1999 cup, stadiums had to provide only half of their corporate boxes for RWC use, according to the NZRFU.

Agreement was reached between New Zealand and Australia over match splits – New Zealand was left with two pools, two quarterfinals and a semifinal.

NOVEMBER: The NZRFU was told by the IRB chairman, Welsh lawyer Vernon Pugh, that a compromise could be reached and that a pragmatic approach would be adopted. This 'gentleman's agreement' was not confirmed in writing.

DECEMBER: The ARU, at Rugby World Cup insistence, agreed to pay $12 million to the NZRFU for the play-off match and to limit any New Zealand financial loss.

2002

FEBRUARY: The NZRFU disagreed with the expansion of the Super 12 competition, apparently much to the disgust of Australia, which said New Zealand's cup role could be affected.

A team of 'inspectors' from the IRB toured New Zealand grounds, voiced concerns about the lack of corporate boxes and said, privately at least, the 'gentlemen's agreement' between Pugh and NZRFU chairman Murray McCaw was unreliable.

By the IRB's 8 March deadline for the sub-host agreement to be signed, the NZRFU offered an alternative agreement, expressing concerns about cup demands for 'clean' stadiums and the requirement that the NPC not overlap with the cup.

The IRB asked the Australian union for a proposal to stage the cup on its own, saying it had 'reluctantly been forced into this action by the NZRFU's failure to conform to or to accept its obligations'.

Sponsors Coca-Cola and Heineken both wrote to the cup's commercial arm expressing concern about the disagreements and about the prospect of games not being played in New Zealand.

8 MARCH: The NZRFU signed the sub-host agreement with three changes, including no guarantee of 'clean' grounds. The ARU and the RWC company said that meant New Zealand could not be involved. NZRFU chairman Murray McCaw said Pugh was acting outside of his mandate.

10 MARCH: The *Sunday Times* in London said the game's greatest tournament had made a sacrifice on its commercial altar of its finest nation.

11 MARCH: The government supported the NZRFU stance on stadiums and said the union could not legally sign a contract containing conditions it knew it could not meet.

McCaw said the IRB's power was consolidated in one person, Pugh. 'He has too much power,' he said.

17 MARCH: McCaw met Pugh in Beijing and recorded it was 'a strange meeting in many ways', saying Pugh had very little to say.

24 MARCH: The NZRFU apologised in writing for comments made about Pugh.

APRIL: The NZRFU discussed for the first time, but did not say so publicly, the possibility of withdrawing its team from the cup. (The IRB said New Zealand had first raised the possibility of the All Blacks not playing before the Singapore meeting the previous year.)

3 APRIL: Rugby World Cup Ltd (RWC), the cup subsidiary of the IRB, accepted Australia's sole bid.

Pugh said in a lengthy summation of the position as he saw it that 'the credibility of the IRB, RWC and rugby as a sport in the international commercial sports market is probably at its lowest ever'.

18 APRIL: The IRB accepted the RWC recommendation that Australia be the sole host. It said: 'Generous accommodations made by RWCL to meet the needs and problems of the NZRU were repaid with consistent failures and wholly inappropriate behaviour.'

19 APRIL: Sports Minister Trevor Mallard said he would like to perform a sensitive operation on Pugh and on Australian Rugby Union chief executive John O'Neill using 'Heinekens in particularly uncomfortable places'. He later said he regretted the comment.

25 APRIL: The NZRFU said it had asked retired

Michael James Bowie Hobbs, otherwise known simply as 'Jock', first became a national figure in 1983 when he was selected for New Zealand as a flanker against the Lions. He played in each of the four tests and was made captain the following year in Fiji, an early indication of how his leadership qualities were regarded. He played in 21 tests, four of them as captain (two against Argentina and two against France). Hobbs went on the rebel tour of South Africa in 1986 and retired the following year. It was as an administrator that he left his most enduring legacy: in 1995 he was mainly responsible for contracting players on behalf of the New Zealand Rugby Football Union and thus warding off a proposed Sydney-led professional troupe. He took over as chairman of the national union in the wake of the fiasco about the sub-hosting rights for the 2003 World Cup and restored New Zealand's international standing by leading the successful bid to stage the 2011 cup. He died of leukaemia just under five months after the cup final, won by the All Blacks. Hobbs is pictured in the third test against the Lions in 1983 at Carisbrook in Dunedin, sizing up a tackle on the Lions' first five-eighth, Ollie Campbell. PETER BUSH AND NZ SPORTS HALL OF FAME

Chief Justice Sir Thomas Eichelbaum for an independent review of the circumstances in which the sub-host rights were lost.

12 JULY: The NZRFU received reports from a public relations firm and a law firm about possible consequences of the cup fiasco.

23 JULY: McCaw and Rutherford resigned their positions when Eichelbaum's report was published. Eichelbaum found that the NZRFU adopted a cautious approach to sub-hosting the cup; it created the impression that it did not properly value the cup and there was a breakdown in relations between the principal parties. 'Administrative deficiencies' in the cup company also contributed.

Rob Fisher, a previous chairman and one of the two New Zealand members of the IRB, took over from McCaw as chairman of the NZRFU.

30 JULY: Several provincial unions said the whole NZRFU board should have resigned. Canterbury union chairman Mike Eagle said the whole board had to be accountable. (Eagle became chairman of the NZRU board a decade later.)

6 AUGUST: Provincial unions forced a special general meeting of the NZRFU and, as a result, Fisher recommended that all board members resign.

18 SEPTEMBER: A special general meeting of the NZRFU elected five new members on to its governing board. One of them, Jock Hobbs, had previously been on the forerunner council, and was elected chairman.

16 DECEMBER: A recent deputy chief executive of Fonterra, Chris Moller, was appointed NZRFU chief executive. Fonterra's founding chief executive, Craig Norgate, had been a member of the previous NZRFU board.

The road to 2011

When rugby officials set off around the world in 2005 in search of support for their bid to stage the 2011 World Cup in New Zealand, one of the cards they played was that of influence. They did their homework thoroughly and took with them personal knowledge of how New Zealand or New Zealanders had benefited rugby in the countries they visited.

The national union chairman, Jock Hobbs, and chief executive, Chris Moller, criss-crossed the globe with reminders of New Zealand's standing in the rugby world. Their argument was never about how good the national team had been or might be; it was always about the often unsung roles played by New Zealanders in all sorts of rugby corners. The message was that rugby was in the blood of New Zealanders and the only other nationality that could be similarly described would be the Welsh.

Hobbs and Moller had assistance from people at home and away during their lobbying tour.

They had prepared arguments on the pressing issues, such as commercial arrangements, ticketing and stadium capacities, and in this they had the lessons from the flawed sub-host campaign of four years earlier. There was some humble pie to be chewed as they went because mistakes of the past were acknowledged, apologies delivered.

Often, though, they let history do their talking. For example, New Zealand rugby has often been accused of doing little or nothing for the South Pacific region from which it benefits in terms of players and general support. Any number of island tours could be mentioned in rebuttal, including by the All Blacks. The Fijian union was begun by a New Zealander with a little help from his friends, some of them also expatriates. Paddy Sheehan was a Dunedin plumber who had been in the forwards for Otago when he was hired in 1913 to do some work on the Grand Pacific Hotel being built in Suva. He set about establishing a rugby club, the Pacific, and then he and a friend, Otto Strachey from Christchurch, formed the union with Sheehan its founding chairman. He also organised a match in Suva between Fiji and the All Blacks who were on the way home from their tour of California (Sheehan played for Fiji and scored the side's only points, a penalty goal). Sheehan also persuaded the island group governor, Ernest Bickham Sweet-Escott, to provide a trophy for interclub competition. The centenary of the Escott Shield was marked in 2013. Fijian rugby, which also benefited from island chiefs being educated in New Zealand, never looked back.[1]

The New Zealand Rugby Union sent this cartoon drawn by Tom Scott to people who had helped with the country's successful bid to stage the 2011 World Cup. It depicts three of the principals involved in the final presentation to the International Rugby Board in Dublin: Prime Minister Helen Clark being chaired by All Blacks Colin Meads and Tana Umaga.

The All Blacks have several times played in Fiji, sometimes with unexpected outcomes. This match against Nadroga in 1980 was called off two minutes early when spectators liked a scrap so much between Graeme Higginson (No. 5) and local players that they joined in. Gary Knight on the far left seems to have also attracted attention. A policeman and a touch judge whisked the referee, Rod Jepsen, off the ground, and the players more or less called the game off themselves.

Another close neighbour, Australia, was also gently reminded of New Zealand's enduring influence. Not that it did much good, because the Australians supported Japan's bid. Nevertheless, the Australians were reminded how several times their rugby had been dug out of financial holes by the New Zealand union.

And so it went on, this odyssey of influence as country after country was gently reminded of what New Zealand and New Zealanders had done for them. How influential it all was when the International Rugby Board council members cast their votes cannot be known. Bolstering the bid for the showdown in Dublin were Prime Minister Helen Clark, All Black captain Tana Umaga and Colin Meads. Meads took the chance to have a beer with an old opponent and mate, Syd Millar, the onetime Irish prop who had become IRB chairman. Millar himself did not have a vote, but Ireland's two could have been critical.

Voting figures were not made public and all that was known was that New Zealand won narrowly, Japan were second and South Africa were eliminated after the first round of voting. The decision delighted New Zealanders, of course, but not everyone else.

Stephen Jones, the veteran rugby writer for the British *Sunday Times* who has a track record of baiting New Zealand, remarked that the decision 'may well have set the world game back by decades'.[2]

There were published accusations of countries being offered tests against the All Blacks in exchange for votes, of delegates not following their mandates and of the voting somehow being rigged. A tentative bid to force a revote two months later was made by a London law firm, but that failed when it became known that the law firm's instructions came from someone with no standing.[3]

A colleague of Jones's, Mark Souster, wrote that New Zealand's bid appeared to lose steam because of concerns about stadium size and 'infrastructure' (which seemed to be a euphemism for hotel beds and flights), but 'they played heavily on the emotion and tradition of New Zealand rugby. It worked.'[4] But Jones had a different view: 'The idea of New Zealanders as god's travelling global gift to rugby is too sick-making for words.'

Hobbs, Moller and the others in Dublin were delighted with the win, understandably, but annoyed that they did not have Australia's support. Publicly, Hobbs was diplomatic and talked only about it being 'concerning'; privately, he was furious. Less than a month after the vote, the Australian union chairman, Dilip Kumar, resigned.[5]

How the voting for 2011 may have gone

		1ST BALLOT			2ND BALLOT	
	VOTES	NZ	JAPAN	SA	NZ	JAPAN
Africa	1			1	1	
Argentina	1			1	1	
Asia	1		1			1
Australia	2		2			2
Canada	1		1			1
England	2		2			2
Europe	1			1		1
France	2			2		2
Ireland	2	2			2	
Italy	1	1				1
Japan	1					
NZ	2					
Oceania	1	1			1	
Scotland	2	2			2	
SA	2				2	
Wales	2	2			2	
		8	6	5	11	10

The bidding countries could not vote in the first round; only South Africa, because it was eliminated, could vote in the second.

Impromptu signs of support for the All Blacks popped up all over the country during the World Cup in 2011. The decorated hedge at top was in inland Canterbury and that proclaiming Richie McCaw's birthplace was on State Highway 1 just south of Oamaru.

to continue. But he lived long enough to inject new energy and purpose into both the NZRFU – which dropped the 'F' along the way – and the IRB. He and another former All Black captain, Graham Mourie, did much to transform the IRB from an ineffective old boys' club into a more truly representative international governing body.

The 2003 World Cup fiasco also introduced Chris Moller as the new chief executive. He had been deputy chief executive at the Fonterra dairy group and was said to have the skills and business acumen required by the modern game. It was thanks to him and Hobbs, along with staff work, that New Zealand won the right to hold the 2011 World Cup, despite opposition from Australia and a growing international feeling that the cup should go to Asia for the first time. (It will do that in 2019.) This new duo at the top had the sense to go to the government for both practical and financial assistance and so the pursuit of the cup, and its eventual staging, became a project for New Zealand as a whole rather than just rugby. When the cup bid was won, the government's involvement and that of the tourism industry ensured local authorities, especially in areas where games were played, were enthusiastic promoters. Rugby was not just rugby any more.

The cup had become a national obsession. Brian Lochore, the coach of the All Blacks who won the first cup in 1987, warned before the semifinal in Brisbane that year against Wales that he was worried about rugby following the Olympics and soccer and others in adopting a four-year cycle. It would mean, he thought, that rugby in the future would be organised and judged in four-year increments and that what happened outside the cup might be seen as less important. His comments were eight years before the end of amateurism and not even he, sage rugby man that he is, could have predicted the 1995 upheavals and the resulting new competitions.

Throughout rugby's history, what happens at the apex of the game percolates through the lower levels: if the national team is successful, so too is the rest of New Zealand rugby. When the All Blacks are not winning as regularly as their record and reputation demands, the game as a whole suffers. It is not entirely frivolous to ask which had a greater impact on New Zealand over the period 2007–08, the global financial crisis or the All Blacks being eliminated from the World Cup in 2007 for the first time at the quarterfinal stage and then in 2008 losing two test matches, to be followed by four more in 2009? This was also the period when rugby's finances were sorely tested by the world economy

Captain Richie McCaw and first five-eighth Aaron Cruden after New Zealand beat Argentina in a quarterfinal of the World Cup at Eden Park in Auckland in 2011. Cruden had gone on during the match as a replacement for Colin Slade. *NZ HERALD*

allied with the need to commit millions to the 2011 cup. Something had to give and other national teams suffered such as the women, Māori and the inappropriately named 'Juniors'.

The success of the cup in 2011, both the staging of it and the winning of it, restored rugby's faith in itself and reasserted its place in New Zealand life. It was more than a rugby event over a few weeks of 2011. It involved people who otherwise would not care who won or lost, although as New Zealanders, part of their identity was because of rugby. The challenge for rugby is to ensure that continues.

Rich in tradition and steeped in lore . . . Colin Meads charges during the first test against the Lions in Dunedin in 1971. With their captain are Sid Going, Ian Kirkpatrick, Brian Muller, Tane Norton and Richie Guy. PETER BUSH

Epilogue

So over, all over: the whistle peals 'Time!'
The field lies bare to the last of the light.
Too late to tell what you might have done;
The goal is kicked, and a stronger has won.
To you is only the glow of the fight;
To you is only the soreness and grime.

What matter, so long as you played the game?
What matter, provided you filled your place,
And took the fall, the kick, the blow,
And tackled the foeman clean and low –
Blind sun in your eyes, wet wind in your face –
What matter, so met ye the luck as it came?[1]

It was a fairly astute national administrator who once said that rugby had become too important a business to be regarded as mere sport, but too important a sport to be regarded as mere business. By the first decade of the twenty-first century, the New Zealand union had an annual turnover of something more than $100 million and its wages bill for players was somewhere around $30 million. Rugby in New Zealand as a whole industry, the national and all the provincial unions plus those Super teams that now attract private-sector investment, is a significant business. No sport in New Zealand is bigger.

On a world scale in financial terms, New Zealand rugby is not big at all. Big in reputation and standing certainly, but not when it comes to dollars. Some clubs in Europe spend more money a year on players than the NZRU does. Rugby has come a long way since Saturday afternoon games on open grounds when players brought their own jerseys, if they had any, made up the rules as they went along, and when they took time off work to play (and sometimes took more time off work to recover from playing).

The game that is seen now is the latest view of a game that goes back centuries, some of it recognisable, some not. It is a game that is rich in tradition and steeped in lore; it remains a game whose core elements set it apart from other games. At its heart is that it is a contest for possession – it has always been both as simple and as complicated as that. Neither team by right is given the ball;

each team by tradition and practice has to compete for it. Logic says the team that has the possession the longest should be the winner, though that is not necessarily so. That is because another essential element of the game is once possession is obtained, the team with the ball has to work out how to keep it and score. It has always been thus.

A wise New Zealand coach once wrote that rugby was different in two significant aspects from other sports: that rugby skills could be acquired by anyone, they were not the preserve of naturally gifted athletes; and that people of all physical sizes could play the game.[2] He foresaw that in a modern era of professional rugby that is centred as much on the gymnasium as it is on the rugby ground those unique elements would one day be lost. At the highest level, aside from the odd exception, that day has come.

But rugby is not just about the highest level, although it sometimes seems so. When rugby is judged, when it is analysed, whether it is in newspapers or on television or radio or on what is loosely known as social media, invariably the subject is the high end. When people say rugby is not the same now as it was, when it's said to be more like league, when it's said to be boring, when referees are said to have too much of a role, invariably the game being talked about is the international game or the level immediately below. Perhaps too often the eyes and minds are on the summit rather than on the base camp, and maybe too often the real heart of rugby is forgotten.

Some of those things may be true and if they are true in the twenty-first century, they were equally true in the twentieth century. Take any medium, take any era, there were critics of the game; rugby always was better in the old days, no matter whose old days were meant. Here is a former player of high standing in a letter to the editor: 'With the close of the rugby season, may

A wet afternoon, a muddy ground, a trudge back to the dressing room where there may, or may not, be hot water for a shower. Life at the heart, or the base camp, of rugby. PETER BUSH

Carisbrook in Dunedin during the first test after the Second World War, against Australia. The All Blacks won 31–8.

I have space to point out a very growing menace to the hold rugby has in New Zealand. It must be very apparent how easy it is for a referee to make or mar a game, as he has supreme and final control.'[3] This was Billy Stead, superlative first five-eighth at the beginning of the twentieth century, writing in 1947. His main concern was that scrums went ahead only if the referee was happy. (This was just after several unions had been told off by the national union for allowing referees to put the ball into scrums.) Here is another, even older, example. It comes from 1899 and the writer was predicting the end of the wing forward (which happened 30 years later): '. . . anything more barbarous than to see two pair of men engaged in a purely personal rough and tumble encounter in a game supposed to be one of skill and dexterity, it is difficult to imagine'.[4] He was writing about wing forwards, but he could have been writing about today's 'guard dogs', those vigilantes who stand-to on the edges of breakdown. There was this comment from a respected sports editor of *NZ Truth*, Morrie Mackenzie, in 1958: 'Out of the plethora of changes that have been made in the rules in recent years, how many have actually resulted in a more enjoyable and attractive game? The answer is: very few.'[5]

Rugby has always been a changing game, right from the start when men who had recently been schoolboys got together in 1863 and decided their rules were better than those of the other boys-to-men who formed the Football Association. Not many sports are played now as they were a hundred or more years ago. Rugby certainly is not. As the game took hold and evolved, players' techniques and skills developed, and as those changes

A remnant of rugby history. A brick building dating from 1926 that used to house turnstiles is all that remains of the former test venue of Carisbrook in Dunedin.

took place, rules changed too. Other changes were made to make the game popular with the public. Still more changes were made to keep the game popular with television executives who made money decisions. And as people such as J. J. Stewart have pointed out, as the game evolved so the laws had to change to keep pace. 'The game will continue to change as a consequence of law change (and referee interpretation), and the thinking of those at the current work face – the players and coaches,' Stewart wrote. 'The two – law changes and game patterns – are forever following each other.'[6]

Part of the criticism of rugby now is not about rugby at all, but about the way in which it is presented, as if it were some sort of rock concert or beer festival.

But that is just one level of rugby. It may be the rugby that everyone can see, but it is not necessarily the rugby for which people feel. There is occasional talk that the New Zealand union concerns itself too much with the All Blacks and money-making, to the detriment of the game as a whole. Obviously the union needs to pursue income, and it would probably say it has the balance right. As a university master's thesis commented, 'To support growth in the national game, the NZRFU must retain the interest in rugby across all parts of society.'[7] There are people who love their rugby, who never miss a club match, who seldom miss a 'rep' match, who go to Super matches if they can and if the weather is right, but who feel sad and even guilty that they wonder if they can afford to go to test rugby. There is a level of understanding and support for rugby that escapes the notice of the public opinion pollsters, of the marketing experts, of the ratings game players, even sometimes of those who are responsible for content of newspapers. These unsung and unacknowledged people are those who reminisce and remember; not because they think the game is not the same, but because they used to gain a great deal of enjoyment and satisfaction from the game at an earlier time, either as player or spectator. These are people who enjoy yarning about the game, reading about it, perhaps watching old footage and marvelling at the space there used to be on a rugby field (not that the players then thought so), or admiring again the skills of yesterday's players. Today's players are fitter, faster, stronger, bigger and the game is harder and faster, but it's all relative. Today's champions might have been champions yesterday, just as yesterday's might have been today's. There is no way of knowing. But the ordinary rugby people, keen followers, average players, they have just kept going through the generations.

One of New Zealand rugby's challenges is to keep earning enough money so it can keep its players and keep its high standing in the world game. The other, contrasting but not necessarily contradictory challenge, is to keep the game within reach of the people in a nation that has embraced it more than any other.

A football timeline

Pre-1800	Various games, some named as football, played in China, Greece, the Roman Empire and eventually western Europe.
1815	Sir Walter Scott wrote of 'a great foot-ball match' in the Scottish Borders. It was a handling game.
1827	Thomas Arnold began as headmaster at Rugby School, beginning the movement to 'muscular Christianity' and greater discipline in schools and more attention to games.
From 1840	Periodic reports of football matches in New Zealand, but no descriptions were published.
1854	Dublin University Football Club, a rugby club, was founded.
1857	*Tom Brown's Schooldays* by Thomas Hughes was first published. It contains a description of football at Rugby School.
	Academical Football Club (rugby) founded in Edinburgh.
	Sheffield FC (soccer) founded.
1858	Blackheath FC founded as the first rugby club in England.
1863	The (English) Football Association was formed by clubs which agreed on no-hacking (kicking an opponent on the shins) rules (handling was initially allowed).
	Christchurch Football Club formed.
1866	Guy's Hospital FC founded in London. (The club itself says it was formed in 1843 but concedes evidence in support of that is only circumstantial.)
1869	Newspapers reported football matches according to rugby rules in Wanganui.
1870	Clubs which remained outside the FA met in a London restaurant and formed the Rugby Football Union, based on a game using the rules laid down at Rugby School in the 1840s.
	First games played in Nelson (14 May) and in Wellington (12 September).
1875	First interprovincial match (Auckland Clubs v Dunedin Clubs).
1876	First interschool match (Nelson College v Wellington College).
1879	Canterbury and Wellington became the first provincial unions.
1882	The first overseas team, New South Wales, toured New Zealand.
1884	The first New Zealand team was chosen; it played in New South Wales.
1886	The International Rugby Football Board was formed (its initial purpose was to rule on disagreements between the British countries and Ireland).
1888	The first visit to New Zealand by a British team.
	The Natives became the first overseas rugby team to tour the British Isles.
1892	The New Zealand Rugby Football Union (NZRFU) was formed.
	The founding member unions were Auckland, Hawke's Bay, Manawatu,

Marlborough, Nelson, South Canterbury, Taranaki, Wairarapa, Wanganui and Wellington.

1893 The NZRFU at its first annual meeting decided the national team's playing uniform would include a black jersey with a silver fern motif.

The national team was referred to as the All Blacks for the first time.

1895 Rugby clubs in Yorkshire and Lancashire left the (English) Rugby Football Union because of disagreements about payment and formed the Northern Union (later the Rugby Football League).

1897 The first interisland game was played.

A subcommittee of the Old Rugbeian Society in England concluded, contrary to evidence it received, that the game of rugby football had begun in 1823 when William Webb Ellis supposedly handled the ball.

1902 The Ranfurly Shield was inaugurated.

1903 New Zealand's national team played a test for the first time (v Australia).

1904 The first test was played in New Zealand (v Great Britain).

1905 An official New Zealand team went to the British Isles for the first time.

1907 A New Zealand rugby league team was formed and played in Australia and Britain; the first game in New Zealand was in Wellington the following year.

1910 The first official national Māori team was chosen.

1915 The first known game by women in New Zealand was played in Wellington.

1919 A New Zealand army team, comprising players who had completed service in the First World War, became the first New Zealand team to tour South Africa.

1921 New Zealand played South Africa for the first time.

1931 The NZRFU accepted the offer of a cup from the Governor-General, Lord Bledisloe, for matches against Australia.

1948 New Zealand gained a single seat on the International Rugby Board (IRB).

1958 New Zealand and all other member countries of the International Rugby Board were each given two seats on the board, achieving equality for the first time.

1959 The International Rugby Board met in New Zealand for the first time.

1982 The first women's test was played (The Netherlands at home v France).

1987 New Zealand and Australia staged the first World Cup; won by New Zealand.

1989 The first New Zealand women's team played.

1991 The first women's World Cup was staged in Wales (New Zealand did not take part).

1995 The IRB abandoned its amateurism regulations.

1998 New Zealand played in the women's World Cup for the first time – and won.

2002 The NZRFU lost sub-hosting rights to World Cup.

2011 New Zealand hosted World Cup for the second time and the All Blacks won it for the second time.

The challenging power of the haka. New Zealand flanker Mike Brewer in the climax to the haka against Ireland in Dublin in 1989. The Irish team advanced to within touching distance of the All Blacks and prop Nick Popplewell on the end of the line did his best to look unmoved. It was after this that match officials decided a space needed to be kept between the teams.

Notes

Introduction

1 Seaforth MacKenzie, quoted by 'Cyrano' (Alan Mulgan) in the *Auckland Star*, 5 May 1923, p. 17.
2 The statue was erected outside the State Services Commission building in Molesworth Street; the NZRU moved in there in 2013.
3 Wild's speech, and introductory remarks by the NZRFU chairman, Tom Morrison, were recorded for the NZRFU by His Master's Voice (NZ) Ltd (LO 35885 PR539).
4 Yale commencement address 11 June 1962, from Arthur M. Schlesinger Jr., *A Thousand Days: John F. Kennedy in the White House* (London: Andre Deutsch, 1965), p. 560.
5 *Auckland Star*, 5 May 1923, p. 17.
6 John Mulgan, *Report on Experience* (Oxford: Oxford University Press, 1947), p. 7.
7 Ibid., p. 8.

Chapter 1: A fork in the football road

1 Thomas Hughes, *Tom Brown's Schooldays* (London: Thames Publishing, Regent Classics, 1950), p. 88.
2 For biographical details of Giles, see *The Times*, 14 and 16 February 1935, p. 17; and Janette Ryan, 'Giles, Herbert Allen', *Oxford Dictionary of National Biography*, Oxford University Press, Online Edition (http://www.oxforddnb.com), <accessed 14 September 2011>. The pinyin system, devised in the second half of the twentieth century, replaced the Wade-Giles system for romanising Chinese.
3 Herbert A. Giles, 'Football and Polo in China', *The Nineteenth Century and After*, vol. 59 (January 1906), p. 508.
4 W. J. Stead, *Billy's Trip Home: The Remarkable Diary of an All Black on Tour* (Dunedin: New Zealand Sports Hall of Fame, 2005), pp. 39–40.
5 *Age*, 17 February 2012, p. 1.
6 *Press*, 24 March 2012, p. 1.
7 *The Times*, 12 November 1880, p. 4.
8 Giles, pp. 510–11.
9 It is mistakenly written in some sources as 'cu ju', which appears to be an attempt at an English phonetic pronunciation independent of the authorised version.
10 Giles, *The Civilization of China* (London: Williams and Norgate, 1911), Nalanda Digital Library (http://www.nalanda.nitc.ac.in) <accessed 24 October 2011>.
11 David F. Elmer, 'Epikoinos: the Ball Game Episkuros and *Iliad* 12.421–23', *Classical Philology*, vol. 103, no. 4 (October 2008), p. 414.
12 H. A. Harris, *Sport in Greece and Rome* (London: Thames and Hudson, 1972), p. 87.
13 G. E. Marindin, 'The Game of Harpastum or Pheninda', *The Classical Review*, vol. 4, no. 4 (April 1890), p. 145.
14 Ibid., p. 146n.
15 D. H. Craven, 'The Evolution of Major Games', doctoral thesis, University of Stellenbosch, 1978.
16 Sir Charles Tennyson, 'They Taught the World to Play', *Victorian Studies*, vol. 2, no. 3 (March 1959).
17 Eric Dunning and Kenneth Sheard, *Barbarians, Gentlemen and Players: A Sociological Study of the Development of Rugby Football* (Oxford: Martin Robertson, 1979), p. 21.
18 Ibid., p. 26.
19 Joseph Strutt, *The Sports and Pastimes of the People of England*, New edition enlarged and corrected by J. Charles Cox (London: Methuen and Co., 1903), p. 97.
20 William fitz Stephen, *Fitz-Stephen's Description of the City of London, newly translated from the Latin original; with a necessary commentary. A dissertation on the author. Ascertaining the exact year of the production is prefixed; and to the whole is subjoined a correct edition of the original, with the various readings, and some useful annotations.* By an antiquary (London: 1872). Eighteenth Century Collections Online <accessed 10 October 2011>.
21 Montague Shearman, *Athletics and Football* (London: Longmans, Green, 1887); *The Badminton Library of Sports and Pastimes*, edited by His Grace the Duke of Beaufort, assisted by Alfred E. T. Watson.
22 Shearman, p. 251.
23 Dunning and Sheard, p. 23.
24 *Spectator*, 10 June 2000, p. 24.
25 Shearman, p. 262.
26 Strutt, pp. 93–4.
27 This was from Scott's 'Song, on the Lifting the Banner of the House of Buccleuch at a great Foot-ball match, on Carterhaugh', in Scott, *The Poetical Works of Sir Walter Scott, with Memoir of the Author* (Boston: Little, Brown and Co., 1857), p. 266.
28 C. L. R. James, *Beyond A Boundary* (London: Serpent's Tail, 1994).
29 A. J. H. Reeve, 'Arnold, Thomas (1795–1842), headmaster and historian', in *Oxford Dictionary of National Biography* online edition (http://www.oxforddnb.com) <accessed 23 September 2011> (hereafter *ODNB*).
30 James, pp. 161–2.
31 *Sunday Times*, 22 May 1960, p. 32.
32 Sheard, 'Ellis, William Webb (1806–1872), Church of England clergyman and supposed originator of rugby', *ODNB*.
33 *Illustrated London News*, 29 April 1854, p. 400; see John Ward, 'Beard, Richard (1801–1885), photographic entrepreneur', *ODNB*.
34 The Rev. F. Marshall, *Football: The Rugby Union Game* (London: Cassell, 1892).
35 *Meteor*, 22 December 1880, pp. 155–6.
36 For the definitive account of the split, see Tony Collins, *Rugby's Great Split: Class, Culture and the Origins of Rugby League Football* (London: Frank Cass, 1998).
37 Hughes letter of 14 March 1895 to Old Rugbeian Society (ORS), in *The Origin of Rugby Football (1897), Report (with appendices) of the Sub-Committee of the Old Rugbeian Society appointed in July 1895* (Rugby: ORS, 1897), pp. 12–13.
38 Lincoln Allison and Rusty Maclean, 'There's a Deathless Myth on the Close Tonight: Reassessing Rugby's Place in the History of Sport', *International Journal of the History of Sport*, vol. 29, no. 13 (September 2012), p. 1869. See also Jennifer Macrory, *Running with the Ball: The Birth of Rugby Football* (London: CollinsWillow, 1991).
39 H. J. Stevenson, letter to the editor, *Scotsman*, 26 November 1937, p. 13. See also John McI. Davidson, *Rugby Union: The Game Comes to Scotland* (Edinburgh, Scottish Rugby Union, 2000), pp. 2–3.
40 David Barnes, *The Accies: The Cradle of Scottish Rugby* (Edinburgh, Birlinn, 2008). The Scottish Rugby Union was the Scottish Football Union until 1924.
41 Trevor West, *The Bold Collegians: The Development of Sport in Trinity College Dublin* (Dublin: Lilliput Press, 1991).
42 Andrew Carpenter, *Verse in English from Eighteenth-Century Ireland* (Cork: Cork University Press, 1998), pp. 90–8.

43 Dunning and Sheard, pp. 100–101.
44 See Tony Mason, 'The makers of association football', in *ODNB*.
45 *Spectator*, 6 February 1953, p. 14.

Chapter 2: Rugby comes to New Zealand

1 Ernest Leonard Eyre, 'Rugby', *Colonist*, 16 April 1920.
2 *New Zealand Spectator and Cook's Strait Guardian*, 12 November 1847, p. 3.
3 *New Zealand Colonist and Port Nicholson Advertiser*, 24 March 1843, p. 4.
4 Geoffrey Blainey, *A Game Of Our Own: The Origins of Australian Football* (Melbourne: Information Australia, 1990), p. 81.
5 T. W. Reese, *New Zealand Cricket 1841–1914* (Christchurch: Author, 1927), pp. 150–3. The Australian game was certainly played for much of the nineteenth century and a New Zealand team even entered the first interstate carnival – in 1908, but by then it comprised mainly Australian expatriates.
6 A. C. Swan, *History of New Zealand Rugby Football, Volume 1, 1870–1945* (Wellington: A. H. & A. W. Reed, 1948), p. 1.
7 Ibid., p. xi. A fact little known about Swan, and probably not published before, was that his surname technically and legally was not Swan. When he enlisted in 1917, he told the army his father was Richard Bluett and that he was Arthur Cameron Bluett. But Richard died in 1902 and Arthur's mother, Alice, remarried in 1904, this time to Hector Percy Swan. Arthur Swan, 19 when he enlisted in 1917, told the army man that using the Swan surname was his choice and he wished to continue doing so.
8 *Wanganui Herald*, 2 June 1869, p. 1.
9 Ibid., 21 June 1869, p. 2.
10 *Wanganui Chronicle*, 22 June 1869, p. 2.
11 *Wanganui Herald*, 13 July 1869, p. 2.
12 T. Eyton, *Rugby Football Past and Present: The Tour of the Native Team* (Wellington: Author, 1896), p. 5.
13 Ernest D. Hoben, 'The National Game of Maoriland', *Review of Reviews*, 20 July 1895, pp. 37–46.
14 D. McKenzie, *The History of Rugby Football in Wellington and Wairarapa* (Wellington: NZ Times, 1911), p. 3.
15 William McKenzie letter to Sydney Hoben, 10 February 1918.
16 *Wellington Independent*, 29 September 1868, p. 9.
17 Jack Pollard, *Australian Rugby Union: The Game and the Players* (Sydney: Angus & Robertson in association with the Australian Broadcasting Corporation, 1984), pp. 912–13.
18 R. T. Brittenden, *'Give 'em the axe': The First Hundred Years of the Christchurch Football Club* (Christchurch: Christchurch FC, 1963), p. 4.
19 Harper's father was the first Anglican Bishop of Christchurch; a son, Eric, was a member of the 1905–06 New Zealand team. For a recounting of the early days of football in Christchurch, see Geoffrey T. Vincent, '"To Uphold the Honour of the Province": Football in Canterbury c1854–c1890', in Greg Ryan (ed.), *Tackling Rugby Myths: Rugby and New Zealand Society 1854–2004* (Dunedin: University of Otago Press, 2005), pp. 13–30.
20 *The School List of Christ's College from 1850 to 1965* (Christchurch: Christ's College Old Boys' Association, 1966), p. 511.
21 *Press*, 1 April 1905, p. 11.
22 Swan, pp. 38–40.
23 *Press*, 17 April 1905, p. 8.
24 Tony Murdoch, *The Old Club: The History of the Christchurch Football Club 1863–2013* (Christchurch: Christchurch FC, 2013), p. 18.
25 *Hutt News*, 6 September 1928, p. 7.
26 *Dominion*, 27 June 1928, p. 14.
27 Ibid., 5 July 1928, p. 15.
28 Some of the Tennent family history is in Reed, *100 Years of Rugby* (pp. 25–7), but see also James Bertram (ed.), *The Letters of Thomas Arnold the Younger (1850–1900)* (Auckland: Auckland University Press/Oxford University Press, 1980).
29 A. P. Stanley, *The Life and Correspondence of Thomas Arnold, DD, Late Head-Master of Rugby School and Regius Professor of Modern History in the University of Oxford, vol. II* (London: B. Fellowes, 1845), p. 194.
30 *Evening Post*, 18 August 1904, p. 6.
31 Ibid., 11 August 1930, p. 4.
32 Ibid., 1 May 1875, p. 2; 3 May 1875, p. 2.
33 Swan, p. 47.
34 The most complete, if sometimes contradictory, story of rugby's earliest days in Auckland was written by one of the participants, William Wills Robinson, for *Pall Mall Gazette* in 1905. His articles were turned into a small book which was republished with additions in 2012. See *W. W. Robinson's Rugby Football in New Zealand: Its Development from Small Beginnings with an Introduction by Rowan Gibbs and Notes on Robinson's Life and his Sporting Career* (Wellington: Smith's Bookshop, 2012).
35 Swan, p. 38.
36 Pilling's death was widely covered by Auckland newspapers, especially the *Auckland Star* of 11 and 12 June 1875 and the *NZ Herald* of 12 and 13 June.
37 *Lancet*, as reprinted in *Evening Post*, 9 June 1875, p. 2.
38 *Sporting Review*, 10 September 1891, p. [illegible].
39 *Auckland Star*, 27 July 1889.
40 Samuel Sleigh, *Northern Tour of the Dunedin Football Club* (Dunedin: R. T. Wheeler, 1877), p. 27.
41 The official version of events surrounding the first Scotland–England match was detailed in a booklet compiled and published by the Scottish Rugby Union, *Scotland v England 1871*. Hamersley played four times against Scotland – in each year 1871–74, the last as captain.

The opening blast

1 A. C. Swan, *History of New Zealand Rugby Football, Volume 1, 1870–1945* (Wellington: A. H. & A. W. Reed, 1948), p. 94.
2 http://www.nzedge.com
3 Atack letter to Massey, 3 February 1916, Archives New Zealand (AD1 51/217).
4 *Dominion*, 17 September 1945, p. 8; *Evening Post*, 17 September 1945, p. 6.
5 *Brisbane Courier*, 15 August 1883, pp. 4–[illegible]. This was also noted by Sydney rugby historian Sean Fagan – 'Whistling Rugby's Tune', jottingsonrugby.wordpress.com (12 June 2013).
6 *Otago Daily Times*, 11 June 1884, p. 4.
7 Admiral Sir Percy Royds, *The History of the Laws of Rugby Football* (London: International Rugby Football Board, 1949), p. 34.
8 *Referee* (Sydney), 28 June 1899, p. 8.

Chapter 3: Thinking nationally – sometimes

1 Augustus William Hurry, 'Football', *Auckland Star*, 27 July 1889.
2 *Star*, 9 August 1877, p. 2.
3 *Timaru Herald*, 28 July 1879, p. 2.
4 Lewin obituary, *Press*, 11 May 1931, p. 1[illegible].
5 Larry Saunders, *The Canterbury Rugby History 1879–1979* (Christchurch: CRFU, 1979), pp. 10–1[illegible].
6 James Bertram (ed.), *New Zealand Letters of Thomas Arnold the Younger (1850–1900)* (Auckland: Auckland University Press/Oxford University Press, 1980), p. 41.
7 *Sydney Morning Herald*, 18 February 1884, p. 8.
8 *Otago Daily Times*, 20 December 1883, p. [illegible].

9 *Southland Times*, 17 May 1884, p. 3; *Otago Daily Times*, 17 May 1884, p. 2.
10 *Referee* (Sydney), 3 July 1901, p. 8; *Sydney Morning Herald*, 2 May 1942, p. 18.
11 *Otago Daily Times*, 16 May 1884, p. 2.
12 See for example Greg Ryan, 'Rural Myth and Urban Actuality: The Anatomy of All Black and New Zealand Rugby 1884–1938', in Ryan (ed.), *Tackling Rugby Myths: Rugby and New Zealand Society 1854–2004* (Dunedin: Otago University Press, 2005).
13 Full details of the tour are in S. E. Sleigh, *The New Zealand Rugby Football Annual for 1885* (Dunedin: Otago Daily Times, 1885).
14 For this and other details on Stoddart, see David Frith, *'My Dear Victorious Stod': A Biography of A. E. Stoddart* (Guildford: Lutterworth Press, 1977).
15 *Illustrated London News*, undated clipping, 1888.
16 *Sunday Times*, 20 May 1888, p. 3.
17 Tony Collins, *A Social History of English Rugby Union* (London: Routledge, 2009), p. 31.
18 Letter reproduced in the *Maitland Mercury and Hunter River General Advertiser*, 8 November 1888, p. 3.
19 That and other letters were reproduced in the *Otago Daily Times*, 21 November 1888, p. 4.
20 *Sunday Times*, 19 August 1888, p. 3.
21 Irwin Hunter, *New Zealand Rugby Football: Some Hints and Criticisms* (Dunedin: Whitcombe & Tombs, 1929), p. 6.
22 *Evening Post*, 10 May 1888, p. 2.
23 *NZ Referee*, 18 May 1888, p. 307.
24 Ibid., 18 January 1889, p. 104.

When mind and muscle met

1 *NZ Herald*, 11 September 1882, p. 5.
2 *Otago Daily Times*, 30 April 1888, p. 2.
3 *Otago Guardian*, 23 September 1875, p. 2.
4 *Evening Star*, 22 September 1875, p. 2.
5 *Otago Daily Times*, 30 April 1888, p. 2.
6 T. R. Ellison, *The Art of Rugby Football* (Wellington: Geddis and Blomfield, 1902), p. 64.
7 *Evening Star*, 30 April 1888, p. 2.
8 Irwin Hunter, *New Zealand Rugby Football: Some Hints and Criticisms* (Dunedin: Whitcombe & Tombs, 1929), p. 5.
9 R. A. Barr, *British Rugby Team in Maoriland: True Story of the Tour* (Dunedin: Otago Daily Times and Witness, 1908), frontispiece.

Sale of the nineteenth century

1 *Otago Daily Times*, 23 September 1875, p. 3.
2 Biographical details about Sale can be found in the *Dictionary of New Zealand Biography* online (http://www.teara.govt.nz/en/biographies). Sale's was written by John Barsby of the Department of Classics, Otago University, who also gave a talk to the Classical Association of Otago on 13 June 2002. The text is available on the university website (http://www.otago.ac.nz/classics/scholia11(2002).pdf).
3 For more on academic influence on early rugby, see Rex W. Thomson, 'Provincial Rugby in New Zealand: Otago's Academic Pioneers', *Journal of Sport History*, vol. 23, no. 3 (Fall 1996), pp. 211–27.
4 Jed Smith, Introduction, *The Original Rules of Rugby* (Oxford: Bodleian Library, 2007), pp. 21–2. (Smith was at the time of publication curator of the Rugby Football Museum at Twickenham.)

Chapter 4: The first and the greatest

1 T. Eyton, *Rugby Football Past and Present: The Tour of the Native Team* (Wellington: Author, 1896), p. 6.
2 *The Times*, 26 May 1868, p. 5.
3 John Mulvaney and Rex Harcourt, *Cricket Walkabout: The Australian Aborigines in England* (Melbourne: Macmillan, 1988).
4 Leslie Frewin (ed.), *The Poetry of Cricket* (London: Macdonald and Co., 1964), p. 113.
5 Most amply covered by Chris Bolsmann of Aston University in Birmingham in a presentation to a North American Society for Sports History conference in 2009.
6 Rev. Frank Marshall, *Football: The Rugby Union Game* (London: Cassell, 1892), pp. 504–506.
7 *Scotsman*, 29 August 1888, p. 7. The Taiaroa at the time who was a lawyer was Jack, who played for the first New Zealand team in 1884. His brother Dick, who was in the Natives team, was a surveyor and farmer.
8 'To the Maori Football Team', *Punch, or the London Charivari*, 20 October 1888, p. 185.
9 Macaulay, Lord, *Edinburgh Review*, October 1840.
10 Greg Ryan, *Forerunners of the All Blacks: The 1888–89 New Zealand Native Football Team in Britain, Australia and New Zealand* (Christchurch: Canterbury University Press, 1993).
11 *Daily Telegraph* (Napier), 16 January 1888, p. 3.
12 *New Zealand Referee*, 4 May 1888, p. 285.
13 *Evening Post*, 15 June 1925, p. 3.
14 Eyton service record, AD32, box 49, 2758, Archives New Zealand.
15 Eyton, p. 5.
16 Ibid., p. 78.
17 T. R. Ellison, 'The Prospects of a New Zealand Rugby Team Visiting England', *Wellington Rugby Annual 1898* (Wellington: Wellington RFU, 1898), pp. 53–7.
18 Eyton, p. 112.
19 *Manchester Weekly Times*, 9 February 1888, p. 6.
20 *Bulletin*, 24 July 1897.
21 *Liverpool Mercury*, 22 October 1888.
22 Eyton, p. 72.
23 *Courier*, 22 July 1889, p. 6.
24 *Otago Daily Times*, 6 August 1889, p. 3.
25 Ibid., 10 August 1889, p. 3.
26 Otago Rugby Football Union (ORFU) minutes, 30 May 1891 (Hocken Collections).
27 ORFU match programme, 4 May 1940, p. 3.
28 *Rau Tau: One Hundred years of Māori Rugby* (Wellington: NZRU, 2010), p. 4.
29 Ellison, *The Art of Rugby Football* (Wellington: Geddis and Blomfield, 1902), p. 66.
30 E. B. Osborn, 'New Zealand Football', *The Nineteenth Century and After*, January 1906, p. 108.
31 Ellison, *Art*, p. 53.
32 E. D. Hoben, 'Ake, Ake, Kia Kaha', *Countess of Liverpool's Gift Book* (Wellington: Whitcombe and Tombs, 1915), p. 132.
33 Ryan, 'Athletic Warriors or a Social Elite: the Formative Years of Maori Rugby 1870–1914', paper presented to Australian Society for Sports History conference, Australian Catholic University, Sydney, July 2003. See also Ryan, 'The Paradox of Maori Rugby 1870–1914', in Ryan (ed.), *Tackling Rugby Myths: Rugby and New Zealand Society 1854–2004* (Dunedin: Otago University Press, 2005); the latter seems to have been based on the former.
34 Harry Dansey, 'Tradition Moulds Character of Maori Rugby', *Rugby Weekly*, 28 August 1965, p. 7. Dansey was a writer and cartoonist and race relations conciliator.
35 *Silver Fern*, 1 July 1965, p. 13.

Some Natives did not live long to tell their tales

1 Alfred Warbrick, *Adventures in Geyserland* (Dunedin: A. H. & A. W. Reed, 1934), pp. 122–3.

2 *Leader Supplement*, 5 October 1895, p. 18.
3 *Otago Daily Times*, 4 November 1889, p. 1; *Auckland Star*, 12 November 1889, p. 8.
4 Ibid., 4 January 1890, p. 6.
5 *Evening Post*, 16 September 1922, p. 14.
6 *Poverty Bay Herald*, 25 August 1893, p. 2.
7 *Auckland Star*, 12 August 1899, pp. 7 and 8 (Madigan); *Observer*, 9 November 1901, p. 4 (W. Warbrick); *Sydney Morning Herald*, 14 January 1904, p. 6 (F. Warbrick).
8 T. Eyton, *Rugby Football Past and Present: The Tour of the Native Team* (Wellington: Author, 1896), p. 13.
9 *Thames Star*, 15 January 1892, p. 2.
10 *Poverty Bay Herald*, 25 January 1897, p. 2.
11 *Manawatu Standard*, 30 October 1900, p. 3.
12 *Auckland Star*, 22 September 1902, p. 5.
13 *Evening Post*, 12 July 1904, p. 1 (Lee); *Thames Star*, 3 December 1909, p. 2 (Stewart); Ron Palenski, *The All Blackography* (Auckland: Hodder Moa, 2007), p. 144 (Ellison).
14 *NZ Herald*, 17 April 1958, pp. 1, 14.

The Natives and Jack the Ripper

1 http://www.met.police.uk
2 Amid the infinite variety of books about the murders, try Patricia Cornwell, *Portrait of a Killer: Jack the Ripper – Case Closed* (London: Little, Brown, 2002).

Rugby and music often in tune

1 Allan Thomas, 'On the Ball: New Zealand's Rugby Song', in Brad Patterson (ed.), *Sport, Society and Culture in New Zealand* (Wellington: Stout Research Centre, Victoria University of Wellington, 1999), p. 119.
2 Nepia on radio station 1ZB, 13 September 1974, Sound Archives/Ngā Taonga Kōrero.
3 Michael Brown, 'And Everybody Sang: Community Singing in Wellington', paper presented at 'New Horizons: New Zealand Folklore Symposium', 1 December 2007, Victoria University.
4 M. F. Nicholls, *With the All Blacks in Springbokland* (Wellington: L. T. Watkins, 1928), p. 17.
5 'Hiraeth' has no direct translation into English but gives a general sense of loneliness, longing and love.
6 Gordon Spittle, *Counting the Beat: A History of New Zealand Song* (Wellington: GP Publications, 1997), p. 3.
7 *Evening Post*, 18 July 1907, p. 7.
8 Letter to author, 4 December 1987.
9 *Evening Post*, 7 September 1956.
10 The author is indebted to Max Cryer for his assistance on this subject. See Max Cryer, 'Sing a Song of Rugby', *New Zealand Listener*, 10 September 2011.

Chapter 5: The grand tour

1 Alfred Benjamin Cooper, 'The New Zealanders: A Fragment of a Tennysonian Epic', *Boy's Own Annual*, 1906.
2 *Observer*, 23 February 1918, p. 4.
3 For the most thorough account of Hoben's Hawke's Bay days, there's nothing better than Frank Long's *Magpie Magic*, vol. 1 (Napier: Author, 2007).
4 *Otago Witness*, 26 November 1891, p. 30.
5 For correspondence between Otago, Hoben and the RFU, see *Otago Daily Times*, 5 May 1893, p. 4.
6 The full story of the *Wakatipu* contretemps is in Ron Palenski, *All Blacks: Myths and Legends* (Auckland: Hodder Moa, 2008), pp. 150–4.
7 *Otago Witness*, [illegible] August 1893, p. 32.
8 The best works on English rugby's self-flagellation are both by Tony Collins – *Rugby's Great Split: Class, Culture and the Origins of Rugby League Football* (London: Frank Cass, 1998) and *A Social History of English Rugby Union* (London: Routledge, 2009).
9 See for example *Otago Witness*, 7 September 1899, p. 42; *Referee* (Sydney), 13 September 1899, p. 5.
10 *Referee* (Sydney), 27 September 1899, p. 8.
11 *Evening Post*, 7 May 1904, p. 5.
12 Ibid., 2 October 1903, p. 2.
13 *Strand Magazine*, vol. XXV, no. 146 (February 1903), pp. 176–7.
14 Gallaher, 'Secret of Our Success', in J. A. Buttery (ed.), *Why the All Blacks Triumphed!* (London: Associated Newspapers, 1905), p. 7.
15 *Arrow*, 19 October 1917, p. 2; *Referee* (Sydney), 24 October 1917, p. 12. The same story appeared in both papers.
16 *Evening Star* (Dunedin), 12 May 1930, p. 6.
17 Rudyard Kipling, 'The Islanders', *The Complete Verse* (London: Kyle Cathie, 2006), pp. 240–2.
18 *The Times*, 10 October 1905, p. 15. Vaile wrote a similar letter to the *Daily Mail* – *Daily Mail*, 10 October 1905, p. 6.
19 P. A. Vaile, *Modern Lawn Tennis* (London: William Heinemann, 1904), p. viii. Vaile also wrote books on golf and later practised as a lawyer in Chicago, where he died in 19[illegible]. See *Golfdom*, August 1940, p. 22.
20 Jock Phillips, *A Man's Country? The Image of the Pakeha Male – A History* (Auckland: Penguin, 1987), p. 1[illegible]8.
21 *Evening Post*, 8 February 1910, p. 11.
22 Caroline Daley, 'The Invention of 1905', in Greg Ryan, *Tackling Rugby Myths: Rugby and New Zealand Society 1854–2004* (Dunedin: Otago University Press, 2005). She was referring to Phillips, *A Man's Country?* and Sinclair, *A Destiny Apart: New Zealand's Search for National Identity* (Wellington: Unwin Paperbacks in association with the Port Nicholson Press, 1986).
23 Daley, p. 69.
24 Ryan, *The Contest for Rugby Supremacy: Accounting for the 1905 All Blacks* (Christchurch: Canterbury University Press, 2005), p. 78.

The art of the footballer

1 S. E. Sleigh (ed.), *The New Zealand Rugby Football Annual for 1885* (Dunedin: Otago Daily Times, 1885), p. [illegible].
2 *Observer*, 19 December 1891, p. 9.
3 *Sporting Review*, 17 March 1892, p. 5.
4 Pierre Lafond and Jean-Pierre Bodis, *Encyclopédie Du Rugby Français* (Paris: Dehedin Editions; online www.lnr.fr).
5 *NZ Herald*, 20 May 1893, p. 1.
6 For a summary of Ryan's artistic career, see Iain Sharp, *Real Gold: Treasures of Auckland City Libraries* (Auckland: Auckland University Press for Auckland City Libraries Tāmaki Pātaka Kōrero and the Auckland Library Heritage Trust, 2007), p. 66.
7 For the full story of this extraordinary visit, see Brian Mackrell, *Hariru Wikitoria! An Illustrated History of the Maori Tour of England, 1863* (Auckland: Oxford University Press, 1985).
8 Obituary, *Auckland Star*, 24 February 1[illegible], p. 3.

All Blacks adopted by twins

1 Lappe Laubscher and Gideon Nieman, *The Carolin Papers: A Diary of the 1906–07 Springbok Tour* (Pretoria: Rugbyana Publishers, 1990), p. 220.
2 Music Australia (http://www.musicaustralia.org).
3 Christopher Martin-Jenkins, *World Cricketers: A Biographical Dictionary* (Oxford: Oxford University Press, 1996), p. 146.
4 *Evening Post*, 10 March 1911, p. 9.
5 *New York Clipper*, 3 September 1919, p. 4.

6 Details of the twins in Hong Kong come from Gwulo: Old Hong Kong (http://gwulo.com).
7 *China Mail*, 29 September 1960.

The try that never was

1 David Smith and Gareth Williams, *Fields of Praise: The Official History of the Welsh Rugby Union* (Cardiff: University of Wales Press, 1980), p. 163.
2 Wallace's memoirs were published over several weeks in the *New Zealand Sportsman* newspaper in 1932 and the parts relating to Wales were republished by the New Zealand Sports Hall of Fame in 2011.
3 A drag was a step up in comfort from a coach.
4 Smith and Williams, p. 157.
5 *South Wales Argus*, 16 December 1905.
6 Billy Stead, *Billy's Trip Home: The Remarkable Diary of an All Black on Tour* (Dunedin: NZ Sports Hall of Fame, 2005), p. 52.
7 *Daily Mail*, 18 December 1905, p. 8.
8 *New Zealand Graphic*, 17 March 1906, p. 23.
9 *Dominion*, 5 August 1922, p. 18.
10 E. H. D. Sewell, *Rugby Football Up to Date* (London: Hodder & Stoughton, 1921), p. 87.
11 *Evening Post*, 26 July 1958, p. 16.
12 *Weekly News*, 23 July 1948, p. 40.
13 *Magnet*, no. 53, 13 February 1909.

The Minister for Football

1 *NZ Herald*, 19 October 1905, p. 5.
2 Ibid., 20 October 1905, p. 4.
3 *Auckland Star*, 18 October 1905, p. 5.
4 *Southland Times*, 19 February 1906; Stead's newspaper columns were republished as *Billy's Trip Home, The Remarkable Diary of an All Black on Tour* (Dunedin: NZ Sports Hall of Fame, 2005).
5 Dixon letter to Wylie, 11 January 1906.
6 *Evening Post*, 7 March 1906, p. 6.
7 Seddon's involvement in 1905 is fully covered in Greg Ryan, *The Contest for Rugby Supremacy: Accounting for the 1905 All Blacks* (Christchurch: Canterbury University Press, 2005) and Ron Palenski, *All Blacks: Myths and Legends* (Auckland: Hodder Moa, 2008).

They gained a following; they already had the name

1 *Daily Mail*, 28 August 1906, p. 6.
2 John A. Buttery, *Why Kruger Made War – or Behind the Boer Scenes* (London: William Heinemann, 1900).
3 *Daily Mail*, 18 September 1905, p. 8.
4 Ibid., 22 September 1905, p. 6.
5 *Star* (Christchurch), 29 June 1906, p. 1. The author is grateful to John Griffiths in Britain for tracking Buttery's movements through the UK Census.
6 J. A. Buttery (ed.), *Why the All Blacks Triumphed! 'Daily Mail' Story of the Tour* (London: Associated Newspapers, 1905).
7 *Express and Echo*, 16 September 1905.
8 *Referee* (Sydney), 26 June 1889, p. 6. The author thanks Sean Fagan in Sydney for the reference.
9 *Evening Post*, 31 August 1889, p. 3.
10 *New Zealand Observer and Free Lance*, 29 July 1893, p. 5.
11 W. J. Wallace, *Reminiscences of a Famous NZ International: W.J. ('Carbine') Wallace Writes Rugby History* (Dunedin: New Zealand Sports Hall of Fame, 2005), p. 19.
12 Recording of speeches at the reunion from Sound Archives/Ngā Taonga Kōrero (ID35461).
13 *Northern Daily Mail*, 11 October 1905.
14 *Daily Mail*, 12 October 1905, p. 7.
15 *Evening Star Sports Special*, 10 September 1927, p. 3.

A Stuart restoration

1 Reprinted in *Otago Witness*, 28 February 1906, p. 60.
2 Gareth Williams, 'The 1905 All Blacks Tour of Britain', Rugby Football Union (England) (http://www.rfu.com).
3 Billy Wallace, 1955 reunion, Midland Hotel, Wellington, Sound Archives/Ngā Taonga Kōrero (ID35461).
4 W. W. Robinson, *Rugby Football in New Zealand: Its Development From Small Beginnings* (London: The Pall Mall Press, 1905); the text was first published in the *Pall Mall Gazette* in October and November 1905. The book was republished in New Zealand in 2012 with the addition of *With An Introduction by Rowan Gibbs and Notes on Robinson's Life and His Sporting Career* (Wellington: Smith's Bookshop, 2012).
5 For biographical details of Hoatson, see the *Press*, 18 November 1891, p. 6; 13 May 1910, p. 7.
6 Reprinted in *Auckland Star*, 24 February 1906, p. 14.
7 *Free Lance*, 11 July 1914, p. 24.

Rugby at the Olympics

1 The most complete statistical record of rugby at the Olympics is Pierre Vitalien, *Le Rugby Aux Jeux Olympiques* (Paris: Author, 2004). See also Bill Mallon and Anthony Bijkerk, *The 1920 Olympic Games: Results for All Competitors in All Events, With Commentary* (Jefferson, North Carolina: McFarland, 2003).
2 Pierre de Coubertin, 'Notes about Foot-ball', originally written in 1897 and republished in *Total Rugby: The Bulletin of the International Rugby Board*, issue 9, 2005.
3 Mark Ryan, *For the Glory: Two Olympics, Two Wars, Two Heroes* (London: JR Books, 2009), p. 160.
4 This was reported in an undated American account, 'No Quarter Asked, No Quarter Given – the US and the 1924 Olympic Games', by Ivan Calhoun in the American *Rugby* magazine. A slightly different version appears in Ryan, p. 198.
5 Ibid., p. 200.
6 George Orwell, *Orwell: The Collected Essays, Journalism and Letters of George Orwell, Volume 4, In Front of Your Nose 1945–1950* (London: Penguin Books, 1970), pp. 62–3.

Chapter 6: The game splinters

1 *Observer*, 17 August 1907, p. 5.
2 For the most complete account of what came to be known in rugby as 'the great schism', see Tony Collins, *Rugby's Great Split: Class, Culture and the Origins of Rugby League Football* (London: Frank Cass, 1998).
3 *Daily Mail*, 14 December 1905, p. 8.
4 F. W. Cooper, 'Northern Union Comparisons', in J. A. Buttery (ed.), *Why the All Blacks Triumphed! 'Daily Mail' Story of the Tour* (London: Associated Newspapers, 1905), p. 83.
5 He was registered at birth as Albert Henry Baskiville, but he used the Anglicised spelling of the French surname.
6 *Dominion*, 9 October 1907, p. 6.
7 For a first-person account of the inconsistencies in cricket's 'them and us', see Charles Williams, *Gentlemen & Players: The Death of Amateurism in Cricket* (London: Weidenfeld & Nicolson, 2012).
8 A. H. Baskerville, *Modern Rugby Football: New Zealand Methods* (London: Gordon & Gotch, 1907).
9 Ian Heads and David Middleton, *A Centenary of Rugby League 1908–2008: The Definitive Story of the Game in Australia* (Sydney: Pan Macmillan, 2008), p. 9.
10 *Evening Post*, 6 May 1907, p. 7.
11 See John Haynes, *From All Blacks to All Golds, Rugby League's Pioneers* (Christchurch: Ryan and Haynes, 1996).

12 *Truth*, 4 May 1907, p. 3.
13 Ibid., 25 May 1907, p. 3.
14 *NZ Free Lance*, 1 June 1907, p. 6.
15 *Observer*, 10 August 1907, p. 2.
16 *Otago Witness*, 5 June 1907, p. 40. The first reference to 'All Golds' seems to have been in the *Sydney Morning Herald* on 7 August 1907, p. 9.
17 Letter from Kathleen Holmes to Bruce Montgomerie, 3 August 1964, NZ Sports Hall of Fame.
18 For details of the beginnings of league in Sydney, see Sean Fagan, *The Rugby Rebellion: The Divide of League and Union* (Sydney: RL1908, 2005). Fagan also delivered the annual Tom Brock lecture at the NSW Leagues Club on 27 September 2007 with the topic: '"Nothing But a Nine-Day Wonder" – the founding of rugby league – Australia's first professional code'.
19 *Spectator*, 18 September 2010.
20 *Dominion*, 17 October 1907, p. 5.
21 William Greenwood, 'Class, Conflict and the Clash of Codes: The Introduction of Rugby League to New Zealand 1908–1920', doctoral thesis, Massey University, 2008.
22 *Spectator*, 6 February 1953, p. 14.
23 *Dominion*, 28 October 1907, p. 9.
24 RFU committee minutes 23 October 1906, 15 March 1907, 21 December 1907.
25 Comments by Harnett, Galbraith and others associated with the tour are in R. A. Barr, *With the British Rugby Team in Maoriland: True Story of the Tour* (Dunedin: Otago Daily Times and Witness, 1908). See also G. T. Vincent, 'Practical Imperialism: The Anglo-Welsh Rugby Tour of New Zealand, 1908', *International Journal of the History of Sport*, vol. 15, no. 1 (April 1998).
26 *Evening Post*, 19 May 1908, p. 3.
27 Letter to Neil Galbraith from Sydney, 12 September 1908, author's collection.
28 *West Coast Times*, 11 June 1909, p. 3.
29 *Otago Witness*, 23 September 1908, p. 61.
30 For the league and dismissal from the tour aspects, see Barr, p. 82; Ron Palenski, *All Blacks v Lions* (Auckland: Hodder Moa, 2005), p. 36; Tom Mather, *Rugby's Greatest Mystery: Who Really Was F S Jackson?* (London: London League Publications, 2012). For family background and the Jackson family, see 'Rugby in the Blood', *Sports Digest*, January 1976, p. 35; *Gisborne Herald*, 16 October 2012, p. 25 and 23 October 2012, p. 28.
31 *Auckland Star*, 28 July 1908, p. 4; *NZ Herald*, 28 July 1908, p. 5.
32 *Truth*, 1 August 1908, p. 5.
33 *NZ Herald*, 18 July 1908, p. 6.
34 *Otago Witness*, 11 November 1908, p. 62.
35 Galbraith's financial accounting is in Barr, pp. 154–5.
36 *Dominion*, 25 April 1908, p. 9.
37 *Observer*, 1 August 1908, p. 3.
38 *Evening Post*, 9 October 1908, p. 2.
39 *Report of Imperial Rugby Conference held at the Great Northern Hotel, King's Cross, London, on the 12th Day of December 1924* (Dublin: published by the secretary, 1925). See also Bob Luxford, 'Report of Imperial Rugby Conference', *Points Unlimited*, vol. 14, no. 1 (March 2007), pp. 12–14.
40 Eric Watts Moses, *A History of the Proceedings of the International Rugby Football Board, 1886–1960* (London: IRFB, 1961), pp. 12–13.

Amateurs cash in

1 *NZ Herald*, 18 July 1908, p. 8.
2 *Wanganui Chronicle*, 17 December 1908, p. 5.
3 *NZ Herald*, 11 October 1905, p. 7.
4 *Otago Witness*, 31 July 1907, p. 60.
5 *Auckland Star* 5 November 1918, p. 6.
6 RFU Committee minutes, 18 August [illegible]3.
7 *Truth*, [illegible]3 February 1909, p. 3.
8 *Sydney Morning Herald*, 10 February 1909, p. 9.
9 *Observer* (UK), 17 January 1909, p. 7.
10 *Scotsman*, 13 January 1909, p. 11; 14 January 1909, p. 4.
11 *Evening Post*, 21 January 1909, p. 7.
12 Palliser letter to J. D. Avery, 5 February 1909.
13 Ibid., 12 February 1909.

California, here we come

1 *San Francisco Call*, [illegible]4 August 1910.
2 Jack Pollard, *Australian Rugby Union: The Game and the Players* (Sydney: Angus & Robertson/ABC, 1984), pp. 4–5.
3 *San Francisco Chronicle*, 2 October 1913
4 Unidentifiable, undated newspaper clipping.
5 *Los Angeles Times*, 6 November 1913.
6 Greg Ryan, 'Brawn Against Brains: Australia, New Zealand and the American "Football Crisis", 1906–13', *Sporting Traditions*, vol. 20, no. 2 (May 2004) p. 33.
7 *Auckland Star*, 19 December 1913, p. 8.
8 Rupert Brooke, 'From A New Boy', in Peter Miller (ed.), *The Irregular Verses of Rupert Brooke* (Lechlade, Gloucestershire: Green Branch Press, 1997), p. 13.

From trenches to touchlines

1 The best documented report of such actions was by Captain Wilfred Nevill of the East Surrey Regiment, who was said to have kicked a ball marked 'East Surreys v Bavarians' towards the German lines before beginning an attack on the Somme in 1916; he was shot dead soon after. A drawing of the feat by noted war artist Richard Caton Woodville appeared in the *Illustrated London News* on 27 July 1916. The ball, one of two bought by Nevill, was a soccer ball. When Nevill's letters were deposited in the Imperial War Museum in London, the *Daily Telegraph* on 11 January 1979 reported the inscription on the ball read 'East Surreys v Barbarians', which may have given rise to a belated belief it was a rugby ball. There was also a published reference to Australians dribbling a rugby ball and the Germans mistaking it for a new type of grenade. See *Windsor Magazine*, vol. 47, 1918, p. 69.
2 *Northern Advocate*, 28 July 1921, p. 3.
3 *Chronicles of the NZEF*, 16 May 1917, p. [illegible]9.
4 *Poverty Bay Herald*, 13 December 1915, [illegible].
5 *Evening Post* 4 June 1917, p. 2.
6 *L'Image*, April 1917, from collection of Frédéric Humbert.
7 Details of Boyau and all rugby internationals killed in the war are in Ron Palenski, *Last Post: Rugby's Wartime Roll Call* (Dunedin: NZ Sports Hall of Fame, 2011).
8 *NZ Herald*, 30 June 1919, p. 4.
9 *Dominion*, 4 November 1919, p. 5.
10 J. A. Mangan, 'Tragic Symbiosis: Distinctive Anglo-Saxon Visions and Voices', *International Journal of the History of Sport*, vol. 28, nos. 3–4 (2011); Mangan's seminal work as it is often described, was *Athleticism in the Victorian and Edwardian Public School: The Emergence of an Educational Ideology* (Cambridge: Cambridge University Press, 1981). Another significant work was Mangan's *The Games Ethic and Imperialism: Aspects of The Diffusion of an Ideal* (London: Viking, 1985).
11 Scott A. G. M. Crawford (ed.), *'Serious Sport': J. A. Mangan's Contribution to the History of Sport* (London: Frank Cass, 2004).
12 Wray Vamplew, 'Exploding the Myths of Sport and the Great War: A First Salvo', *International Journal of the History of Sport*, 2014, available online at http://www.tandfonline.com/loi/fhsp20.

Chapter 7: From war to the Invincibles

1 Robert J. Pope, 'The All Blacks', *Free Lance*, 11 March 1925. The author is grateful to poet and anthologist Mark Pirie for bringing this to his attention.
2 *Rugby in Auckland 1883–1967: Official History of the Auckland Rugby Football Union* (Auckland: Auckland Rugby Football Union, 1967), p. 53. Laurie Knight was an All Black in 1925; a younger brother, Arthur ('Bubs') played fourteen matches for New Zealand between 1926 and 1934; Laurie's son Lawrence Gibb Knight (Lawrie), played 35 matches between 1974 and 1977.
3 D. Gallaher and W. J. Stead, *The Complete Rugby Footballer on the New Zealand System* (London: Methuen & Co., 1906), p. 233.
4 *Evening Star*, 13 April 1928, p. 5.
5 *NZ Herald*, 6 August 1902, p. 6. J. T. Ferreira, J. P. Blignaut, P. K. Landman, and J. F. du Toit, *Transvaal Rugby Football Union: 100 Years* (Johannesburg: Transvaal RFU, 1989), p. 255.
6 Auckland Museum Cenotaph Database (muse.aucklandmuseum.com/databases/Cenotaph/33946.detail), *New Zealand Herald*, 13 August 1901, p. 5. The cup carries an inscription, 'Zeeurst. Rugby League Cup', and this has led to a belief it was a rugby league match, but the sport was not known as rugby league until many years later and the reference is more likely to league in a competition sense.
7 The board's decision was recounted by Gideon Nieman and Lappe Laubscher, 'W P Schreiner and his role in the 1919 New Zealand Services tour of South Africa', *Points Unlimited*, vol. 7, no. 2 (September 2000), pp. 24–7; F. J. G. Van Der Merwe, 'Race and South African rugby: A Review of the 1919 "All Black" Tour', African Journals Online (http://www.ajol.info); Ron Palenski, *All Black Myths and Legends* (Auckland: Hodder Moa, 2008), pp. 204–14.
8 *The Times*, 30 June 1919, p. 16.
9 Ibid., 2 July 15.
10 *Poverty Bay Herald*, 5 November 1919, p. 2.
11 Tureia was later an interpreter for the Native Department; he enlisted again in 1939, was commissioned and killed in action at El Alamein. Service record, New Zealand Defence Force Archives.
12 See for example Douglas Booth, *The Race Game: Sport and Politics in South Africa* (London: Frank Cass, 1998), p. 23. Booth gave as his source Finlay Macdonald, *The Game of Our Lives* (Auckland: Viking/Allen Lane, 1996).
13 *Natal Witness*, 26 August 1919, p. 5.
14 Ibid., 27 August 1919, p. 5.
15 Fred Boshier, *All Blacks in South Africa* (Wellington: Blundell Bros, 1960), p. 111.
16 Bob Luxford, *Alex the Bruce* (Palmerston North: Rugby Museum Society, 1994), pp. 17–18.
17 Greg Ryan, 'Anthropological Football: Maori and the 1937 Springbok Tour of New Zealand', in Ryan (ed.), *Tackling Rugby Myths: Rugby and New Zealand Society 1854–2004* (Dunedin: Otago University Press, 2005), p. 106.
18 Van Der Merwe.
19 *Evening Star Sports Special*, 18 August 1932, p. 3. Brown did in fact play for New Zealand Māori in 1913, but he was categorised as a guest player in a benefit match in Auckland aimed at raising money for a player, Sammy Piki. He was in hospital in Sydney after suffering a broken leg in the first match of the Māori Australian tour that year.
20 *The Klink*, troopship magazine produced on the *Turakina*, July 1917, p. 34.
21 Cavanagh's views of the evolution of rugby were published in a series of articles in the *Evening Star Star Sports* in 1950. His 'bounce out' comments were published on 6 May 1950, p. 3.
22 *The Times*, 23 October 1926, p. 7; 13 November 1926, p. 5.
23 *Evening Star*, 10 September 1926, p. 11.
24 *Evening Post*, 28 April 1922, p. 11.
25 Ibid., 22 April 1922, p. 12.
26 *Observer*, 29 July 1937, p. 9.
27 Mark Nicholls, unpublished manuscript.
28 Theodore Wright Leslie was invariably known as Dorrie; he first helped train a rugby team when he was with the All Blacks before their first test at home, in 1904. He was also the first New Zealander to officiate at an Olympic Games. See *NZ Sportsman*, July 1949, pp. 51–3.
29 *Evening Post*, 13 September 1921, p. 7.
30 Ibid., 11 June 1921, p. 9.
31 Norman McKenzie, *On With the Game: The Rugby Reminiscences of Norman McKenzie* (Wellington: A. H. & A. W. Reed, 1961), p. 91.
32 *Auckland Star*, 24 May 1924, p. 7.
33 *Evening Post*, 29 March 1923, p. 6.
34 Ibid., 3 April 1923, p. 8.
35 Carroll was reinstated to rugby in 1967, although he had coached teams while still banned. Two sons, Joe and Jim, played for Manawatu; Jim was a test match reserve and in the NZ Under 23 team that beat the All Blacks in Dunedin in 1973. See Bob Luxford entry on Carroll in the *Dictionary of New Zealand Biography* (http://www.teara.govt.nz/en/biographies). Luxford was curator of the New Zealand Rugby Museum in Palmerston North.
36 Historian Greg Ryan wrote about the connection between military defaulters and sport and covered the RSA's requests to sports bodies in 'Men Who Defaulted in the Greatest Game of All: Sport, Conscientious Objectors and Military Defaulters in New Zealand 1916–1923', *International Journal of the History of Sport*, published online (http://www.tandfonline.com/loi/fhsp20).
37 McKenzie, p. 22.
38 J. M. Mackenzie, *All Blacks in Chains* (Wellington: Truth (NZ) Ltd, 1960), pp. 48–9. For Mussen's obituary, see *Southland Times*, 26 February 1943, p. 4. For more on Booth's role in Southland, see Lynn McConnell, *Something to Crow About: The Centennial History of the Southland Rugby Football Union* (Invercargill: Craig Printing, 1986).
39 George Nepia, *Rugby Every Time: George Nepia's Own Story* (Dunedin: NZ Sports Hall of Fame, 2009), p. 21. Nepia's comments were originally published in a series of columns in *NZ Truth* over eight weeks in 1936.
40 McKenzie, p. 78.
41 Read Masters, *With the All Blacks in Great Britain, France, Canada and Australia 1924–5* (Christchurch: Christchurch Press, 1928), p. 89.
42 *Evening Post*, 7 March 1925, p. 6.
43 A. H. Carman, *Diary of the Experiences of A. H. Carman during his travels through Australia, South Africa, Great Britain, Belgium, France and Italy from June 27th 1924 to March 24th 1925* (Wellington: Carman family, 2010).
44 W. C. Dalley, unpublished diary, collection of Alison Waghorn.
45 Ron Palenski, *Century In Black: 100 Years of All Black Test Rugby* (Auckland: Hodder Moa, 2003), p. 35; Douglas Myers email to author.
46 *Daily Mail*, 6 February 1998, p. 71. This was also recorded in Dalley's diary.
47 William Pember Reeves, 'The Last of the Twenty-Eight, 3rd January 1925 10pm'.
48 *Evening Post*, 16 February 1925, p. 7.
49 Ibid., 2 April 1925, p. 6.
50 Len Corbett, 'England Rally Too Late', in Wilfred Wooller and David Owen, compilers, *Fifty Years of the All Blacks: A Complete History of New Zealand Rugby Touring Teams in the British Isles 1905–54* (London: Phoenix House, 1954), pp. 36–7; Wooller played for Wales against the 1935 New Zealand team and Owen was a pseudonym for J. B. G. (Bryn) Thomas, the sports editor and rugby writer for the Cardiff *Western Mail*.

51 Terry McLean, *Great Days in New Zealand Rugby* (Wellington: A. H. & A. W. Reed, 1959), pp. 46–7.
52 'Rugby Football. The All-Blacks' Game – Methods and Men', *The Times*, 31 January 1925.
53 Denzil Batchelor, *Days Without Sunset* (London: Eyre & Spottiswoode, 1949), pp. 214–15.
54 John Coffey, *Strike! The Tour That Died of Shame* (Leeds: Scratching Shed Publications, 2012).
55 Cecil Wray letter to Stan Dean, 7 April 1925, author's collection.

Death of a captain

1 *Press*, 11 December 1917, p. 8. (The dispatch from London was dated 16 October.)
2 Gallaher service record, Archives New Zealand (AABK 18805 W5515 0001971). See also Matt Elliott, *Dave Gallaher: The Original All Black captain* (Auckland: HarperCollins, 2012).
3 War diary, No. 3 Australian Casualty Clearing Station, October 1917, Australian War Memorial (AWM4, 26/64/13).
4 Launceston *Examiner*, 2 June 1942, p. 4. Muschamp's service record, Australian Archives.
5 A. D. Carbery, *The New Zealand Medical Service in the Great War 1914–1918* (Auckland: Whitcombe & Tombs, 1924), pp. 333–40.
6 Guyton service record, New Zealand Defence Force, Trentham.
7 *Referee* (Sydney), 9 January 1918, p. 12.

The infamous 1921 cable

1 *Daily Telegraph* (Napier), 9 September 1921, p. 5.
2 Ibid., 10 September 1921, p. 5.
3 *NZ Herald*, 13 September 1921, p. 6.
4 Ibid., 14 September 1921, p. 8.
5 *Auckland Star*, 15 September 1921, p. 8.
6 Ibid., 16 September 1921, p. 7.
7 *NZ Truth*, 17 September 1921, p. 6.
8 A. C. Wilson, *Wire & Wireless: A History of Telecommunications in New Zealand 1890–1987* (Palmerston North: Dunmore Press, 1994), pp. 210–11.
9 Blackett's 'career' details are listed on http://www.espn.cricinfo.com.
10 Blackett service record at Australian Archives, http://recordsearch.naa.gov.au. Other Blackett biographical information was supplied by a descendant, Yvonne Airey, to whom the author is grateful.
11 *Evening Post*, 6 September 1938, p. 4.
12 Ivor D. Difford, *The History of South African Rugby Football (1875–1932)* (Wynberg, South Africa: The Specialty Press of SA, 1933), p. 709.

When the All Blacks became Invincibles

1 Stanley Cohen, *Dodgers! The First 100 years* (New York: Birch Lane Press, 1990), p. 8.
2 *New Zealand Free Lance*, 7 January 1925.
3 *Evening Post*, 2 December 1933, p. 19.
4 *Press*, 6 February 1951, p. 1.
5 *Auckland Star*, 12 October 1927, p. 14.
6 *Evening Post*, 7 March 1928, p. 10.

The power of the shield

1 *Evening Post*, 12 September 1901, p. 5.
2 Ibid., 26 April 1902, p. 6. One of the obvious drawbacks was that in the second year of Australian federation, some people in New Zealand still saw themselves as being the constitutional equivalent of the former colonies rather than of the new Commonwealth.
3 Ibid., 3 May 1902, p. 5.
4 *Evening Post*, 28 June 1902, p. 6.
5 Gavin McLean, *The Governors: New Zealand's Governors and Governors-General* (Dunedin: Otago University Press, 2006), p. 144.
6 *Evening Post*, 15 September 1902, p. 2.
7 Norman McKenzie, *On With the Game: The Rugby Reminiscences of Norman McKenzie* (Wellington: A. H. & A. W. Reed, 1961), p. 94.
8 *NZ Herald*, 2[illegible] April 1910, p. 8.
9 Ibid., 15 September 1902, p. 7.
10 Ibid., 8 August 1904, p. 3; 28 August 190[illegible], p. 7.
11 Albert Joseph Downing army service record, Archives New Zealand (http://www.archives.govt.nz); Downing was killed on 8 August 1915 on Gallipoli and thus became the first All Black to be killed in action in the First World War.
12 McKenzie, p. 100.
13 *NZ Truth*, 29 August 1925.
14 Lindsay Knight, *The Shield: A Century of the Ranfurly Shield* (Auckland: Celebrity Books, 2002), p. [illegible]

Chapter 8: Lessons on tour

1 Unattributed, 'The Opun Road', Otago University Capping Carnival Programme, 1928.
2 *Dominion*, 25 February 1910, p. 6.
3 His full name was Albert Arapeta Asher; the nickname was sometimes rendered as 'Opai' but the horse's name was Opae.
4 *Observer*, 5 September 1908, p. 6.
5 The team's woes were summed up in *Sydney Morning Herald*, 3 August 1908, p. 7; 4 August 1908, p. 7; 13 August 1908, p. 10.
6 *Poverty Bay Herald*, 17 June 1911, p. 4.
7 *Manawatu Times*, 3 June 1911, p. 5.
8 For background on Māori rugby and Parata, see *Rau Tau: 100 Years of Māori Rugby* (Wellington: NZRU, 2010); and Arthur H. Carman, *Maori Rugby 1884–1979* (Wellington: Sporting Publications, 1980).
9 *Auckland Star*, 18 April 1925, p. 15.
10 D. J. C. Pringle, *The New Zealand Maori Rugby Tour 1926–27* (Akaroa: Akaroa Mail, 1971), pp. 70–1.
11 Ibid.
12 Nepia column, *NZ Truth*, 18 November 1936. Nepia's series of columns were reproduced as *Rugby Every Time: George Nepia's Own Story* (Dunedin: NZ Sports Hall of Fame, 20[illegible]).
13 *Auckland Star*, 31 May 1927, p. 10.
14 Ibid., 21 September 1927, p. 14.
15 Ibid., 21 October 1927, p. 6.
16 Ibid., 11 October 1927, p. 9.
17 Ibid., 19 October 1927, p. 14.
18 *Evening Star Sports Special*, 18 June 1927, p. [illegible].
19 Nepia column, 18 November 1936.
20 M. F. Nicholls, *With the All Blacks in Springbokland* (Wellington: L. T. Watkins, 192[illegible]).
21 John Bell Thomson, Words of Passage – a journalist looks back, Hocken Collections (Misc-MS-1059), p. 91.
22 Invincibles reunion 4 July 1950, Sound Archives/Ngā Taonga Kōrero (ID25473). Mark Nicholls spelt the diminutive of Brownlie's given name as 'Morry' rather than the more usual 'Maurie'.
23 Thomson, p. 92. Thomson's manuscript, unpublished in print, has been published as an e-book: J. B. Thomson, *Words of Passage: The Original*, Xlibris Corporation, 2012 e-book (http://www.xlibris.co.nz).
24 Talkback with George Nepia on radio station 1ZB, 13 September 1974, Sound Archives/Ngā Taonga Kōrero (ID[illegible]4595).
25 *Auckland Star*, 7 June 1928, p. 7.
26 J. T. Burrows, *Pathway Among Men* (Christchurch: Whitcombe & Tombs, 1974) p. 4[illegible]
27 Nicholls, p. 108.
28 Burrows, p. 45.

29 Graeme Barrow, *All Blacks versus Springboks* (Auckland: Heinemann, 1981), p. 34.
30 Quoted in Ron Palenski, *Century in Black* (Auckland: Hodder Moa Beckett, 2003), p. 200.
31 Nicholls, pp. 166–7.
32 Nicholls unpublished autobiography, p. 14.
33 Ibid., p. 20.
34 Ibid., p. 22.
35 John G. Mulford, *Guardians of the Game: The History of the New South Wales Rugby Union 1874–2004* (Sydney: ABC Books, 2005), pp. 85–7.
36 The previous time a full Australian side took the field was on 15 August 1914, when it lost 22–7 to New Zealand.
37 Match programme, NZ v Australia, 27 July 1929, p. 8.
38 *Auckland Star*, 30 July 1929, p. 10.
39 Quoted in Spiro Zavos, *The Gold and the Black: The Rugby Battles for the Bledisloe Cup* (Sydney: Allen & Unwin, 1995), p. 43. Garnet Vere (Jerry) Portus played three times for England while he was a Rhodes Scholar before the First World War.

When a test was not a test

1 Letter from Australian Rugby Football Union executive director Bob Fordham to Jack Pollard, 21 September 1988; letter from Pollard to Rod Chester, 27 December 1988.

The lost art of rugby

1 *Evening Post*, 17 January 1928, p. 14; *Auckland Star*, 2 June 1928, p. 15.
2 *Official Report, Games of the Ninth Olympiad* (Amsterdam: Netherlands Olympic Committee, 1929), p. 877. Available online at http://library.la84.org/6oic/OfficialReports/1928/1928p1.pdf.
3 *The Olympic and British Empire Games* (Wellington: New Zealand Olympic and British Empire Games Association, 1954), p. 68; no author was named, but the book was written by the association's secretary, George Craig.
4 Results details from a research website, http://www.olympedia.org, operated by the International Society of Olympic Historians (http://www.isoh.org). See also Bernhard Kramer, 'In Search of the Lost Champions of the Olympic Art Contests', *Journal of Olympic History*, vol. 12 (May 2004).
5 Conversations and email correspondence with author.

Chapter 9: The shadow of the wing forward

1 Blair Swannell, 'Swannell's Reply', *Observer*, 24 August 1907. Swannell was a British player who also played for Australia; he was killed at Gallipoli.
2 For the most complete details of Baxter's career, see Philip J. Beacall, *Birkenhead Park: The First Hundred Years* (Birkenhead: published by the club, 1971).
3 *Evening Post*, 22 May 1930, p. 11.
4 G. T. Alley, *With the British Rugby Team in New Zealand 1930* (Christchurch: Simpson and Williams, 1930), p. 46.
5 *Auckland Star*, 28 July 1930, p. 9.
6 McLean's comments were in a wide-ranging review of the tour published in the Auckland *Sun*, 13 September 1930.
7 *Evening Post*, 23 May 1930, p. 6.
8 Ron Palenski, *All Blacks v Lions* (Auckland: Hodder Moa Beckett, 2005), p. 42.
9 Alley, p. 28. Alley was an educator and librarian and became New Zealand's first national librarian in 1964.
10 *Sun*, 13 September 1930.
11 *Dominion*, 15 April 1932, p. 17.
12 Ron Palenski, *Our National Game* (Auckland: Moa Beckett, 1992), p. 59.
13 *Weekly News*, 19 February 1936, p. 64.
14 *The All Blacks of Jubilee Year* (Wellington: L. T. Watkins, 1936), p. 13.
15 Ibid., p. 14.
16 Ibid., p. 16.
17 Reg Sweet, *Springbok and Silverfern: The Great Tests Since 1921* (Wellington: A. H. & A. W. Reed, 1960), p. 94.
18 John Carrad, 'September the 25th One Nine Three Seven', reprinted in Ron Palenski (ed.), *Touchlines: An Anthology of Rugby Poetry* (Dunedin: NZ Sports Hall of Fame, 2013), p. 102.
19 Greg Ryan, 'Anthropological Football: Maori and the 1937 Springbok Tour of New Zealand', in Ryan (ed.), *Tackling Rugby Myths: Rugby and New Zealand Society 1854–2004* (Dunedin: Otago University Press, 2005), p. 105.
20 *Evening Post*, 6 November 1936, p. 10.
21 *Dominion*, 2 October 1939.
22 *Free Lance*, 4 October 1939.

Preparing 'the bible' in prison

1 *Sports Digest*, January 1977, p. 31.
2 Quoted in *R. H. Chester & N. A. C. McMillan, 1984 DB Draught Rugby Almanack of New Zealand* (Auckland: Moa Publications, 1984).
3 Arthur Carman interviewed by Peter Sellers, 1970, Sound Archives/Ngā Taonga Kōrero (T745).
4 *Evening Post*, 10 May 1941, p. 7.
5 Ibid., 14 May 1941, p. 11.
6 Ibid., 19 May 1941, p. 9.
7 M. G. Carman, R. M. Carman, and E. E. Jones, *The Prison Letters: Letters Written to Arthur H. Carman while he was imprisoned for subversion in Mt Crawford Prison Wellington 1941* (Wellington: privately published, 2008), p. 59.
8 See David Grant's entry on Carman in the *Dictionary of New Zealand Biography* (www.teara.govt.nz/en/biographies).

The cup that cheers

1 *NZ Rugby Annual 1932* (Wellington: Geo. W. Slade Ltd, 1932), p. v.
2 *Auckland Star*, 29 June 1932, p. 3.
3 Ibid., 22 July 1932, p. 7.
4 *Evening Post*, 2 August 1932, p. 9.

Feed them till they want no more

1 *Rugby World*, December 1974, pp. 8–10.

League to the financial rescue

1 *Evening Post*, 31 July 1939, p. 7.
2 Ibid., 5 August 1939, p. 23.
3 *Auckland Star*, 28 October 1935, p. 13.
4 George Nepia and Terry McLean, *I, George Nepia: The Autobiography of a Rugby Legend* (London: London League Publications, 2002), p. 125.
5 *Auckland Star*, 7 November 1935, p. 22.
6 *Timaruvian* (Timaru Boys' HS old boys' magazine), April 1940, p. 59.

White Russian, red rose

1 http://www.rugbyfootballhistory.com; the tries can be seen at http://www.youtube.com/watch?v=2XhAS_Bieo0.
2 Quoted in the *Daily Telegraph*, 2 November 2006.
3 Leslie Murray, 'Reel Rugby,' in H. B. T. Wakelam (ed.), *The Game Goes On* (London: Sportsman's Book Club, 1954), pp. 133–6.
4 Obolensky family background supplied to the author by a nephew, Nick Obolensky, in a series of emails in 2002.

5 http://www.guardian.co.uk, sport blog, 24 March 2010.
6 Ron Palenski, *Century in Black* (Auckland: Hodder Moa Beckett, 2002), p. 42.

Chapter 10: Defeat at home and abroad

1 Nicholas Aufrere Fenwick, 'The Starving Winger', *Rhyme or Reason* (Alexandra: Central Otago News, 1949).
2 *Evening Post,* 2 May 1940, p. 17.
3 Ibid., 3 May 1940, p. 12.
4 *Auckland Star*, 26 April 1940, p. 11.
5 *Evening Post Sports Post*, 13 July 1940, p. 6.
6 *Evening Post*, 2 October 1944, p. 3.
7 For match details of the Services team, see Arthur C. Swan and Arthur H. Carman, *Five Seasons of Services Rugby: The History of the New Zealand Services Team in Great Britain, Ireland and France, 1941–46* (Wellington: Sporting Publications, 1948).
8 *The Times*, 18 April 1944, p. 2.
9 Conversation with author.
10 This was the reunion for which Paul Donoghue's book, *Rugby Versus Rommel*, was published: Paul Donoghue, *Rugby Versus Rommel* (Wellington: Author, 1961).
11 J. T. Burrows, *Pathway among Men* (Christchurch: Whitcombe & Tombs, 1974), pp. 196–7.
12 Ibid.
13 Jim Henderson, *22 Battalion: Official History of New Zealand in the Second World War* (Wellington: War History Branch, Department of Internal Affairs, 1958), pp. 393–5.
14 *Evening Post*, 1 June 1940, p. 19.
15 Percy Royds, *The History of the Laws of Rugby Football* (London: International Rugby Football Board, 1949), p. 75.
16 *Weekly News*, n.d.
17 *Greymouth Evening Star*, 4 June 1946; crowd figures from *Free Lance*, 12 June 1946.
18 Calculations by Clive Akers, co-editor of the *Rugby Almanack*, show 183 provincial players were killed. Email correspondence with author.
19 A. P. Gaskell, *The Big Game and Other Stories* (Christchurch: The Caxton Press, 1947).
20 Pickard obituary, *Waikato Times*, 9 December 2006, p. 13.
21 G. J. Griffiths, Business, research and personal papers, Hocken Collections (ARC-0320).
22 C. K. Saxton, *The ABC of Rugby* (Wellington: NZRFU, 1959).
23 Griffiths papers.
24 *Otago Daily Times*, 25 March 1963, p. 5.
25 Lindsay Knight, *The Shield: A Century of the Ranfurly Shield* (Auckland: Celebrity Books, 2002), pp. 58–9. From the author's own experience, Cavanagh was a man of strong views which he was not afraid to express.
26 *Dominion*, 1 March 1947, p. 8.
27 Terry McLean, *The Best of McLean* (Auckland: Hodder & Stoughton, 1984), p. 180.
28 ORFU weekly programme, 17 May 1947, p. 11.
29 Griffiths papers. See also Winston Cooper, *Once A Southern Man: The History of the Southern Rugby Football Club 1884–1984* (Dunedin: Southern RFC, 1984), pp. 143–4.
30 *Observer*, 11 June 1941, p. 19.
31 *Evening Post*, 2 September 1948. Kippenberger's comments were reported in the *Press* in Christchurch the morning after he made them, but with the direct quotes omitted.
32 Maoris excluded from South African rugby tour – September–October 1948, Archives New Zealand (IA77 3).
33 *Evening Post*, 7 September 1948, p. 8.
34 Ibid.
35 *Die Transvaler*, 27 August 1946.
36 Sir Patrick Duff letter to Sir John Stephenson, 13 September 1946, 'New Zealand Maoris – Visit to South Africa of All Black Football Team', the National Archives (UK) (DO 35/122).
37 Joe Garner, *The Commonwealth Office 1925–68* (London: Heinemann, 1978), p. 182.
38 *Evening Post* 3 September 1948, p. 6.
39 Richard Thompson, *Retreat from Apartheid: New Zealand's Sporting Contacts with South Africa* (Wellington: Oxford University Press, 1975), p. 16.
40 *Evening Post* 12 April 1949.
41 *NZ Herald*, 12 April 1949.
42 Alan Sayers and Les Watkins, *Fred the Needle: The Untold Story of Sir Fred Allen – The Authorised Biography* (Auckland: Hodder Moa, 2011), p. 51.
43 Ibid., p. 52.
44 *Natal Mercury*, 5 September 1949.
45 *Cape Times*, 10 September 1949.
46 Winston McCarthy, *The All Blacks on Trek Again* (Wellington: Sporting Publications, 1950), p. 211.
47 Ibid., p. 209.
48 R. W. H. Scott and T. P. McLean, *The Bob Scott Story* (Wellington: A. H. & A. W. Reed, 1956), p. 91.
49 *Baa Baa News*, Barbarians club newsletter, October 2009, p. 4.
50 Ibid., p. 47.
51 McCarthy, p. 222.
52 This was the view of statisticians Rod Chester and Neville McMillan. See *Men In Black* (Auckland: Moa Publications, 1978), p. 158.
53 *Evening Post*, 3 August 1950.
54 Ibid.
55 Quoted in D. J. Williams, *1950: The Year of the Lions* (Hamilton: Author, 1988), p. 10.
56 Scott, p. 95.
57 *Western Mail and South Wales News*, 22 February 1954.
58 *Evening Post*, 2 November 1953. A bob was slang for a shilling, worth 12 pence; half a crown was two shillings and sixpence, i.e. 30 pence.
59 *NZ Sportsman*, April 1954, p. 42. The *Guardian* dropped Manchester from its title in 1959 and moved to London in 1964.

From war to sport

1 Andrews' unpublished notes on tour, NZ Sports Hall of Fame.
2 Ibid., p. 2.
3 2NZEF – Headquarters 2 NZ Division – Sporting Activities – Rugby, 1944 (DA 21.1/9/G2/3/1, part 1), Archives New Zealand.
4 Ibid., part 2.
5 R. W. H. Scott and T. P. McLean, *The Bob Scott Story* (Wellington: A. H. & A. W. Reed, 1956), p. 29.
6 The most comprehensive story of the Kiwis is Mike Whatman, *Khaki All Blacks: A Tribute to the Kiwis – the 2nd NZEF Army Rugby Team* (Auckland: Hodder Moa Beckett, 2005).
7 *Evening Post*, 20 October 1945, p. 7.
8 Ibid., 10 October 1945, p. 8.
9 *Press*, 24 October 1945, p. 10.
10 Andrews, p. 8.
11 2NZEF Rugby, part 2.
12 C. K. Saxton, *The ABC of Rugby* (Wellington: NZRFU, 1959), p. 5.

It's in The Book:

1 *Southern Cross*, 15 July 1949.
2 *Outspan*, 6 May 1949, p. 37.
3 *Auckland Star* 7 September 1945, p. 4.

At last, a seat at the top table

1 Eric Watts Moses, *A History of the Proceedings of the International Rugby Board, 1886–1960* (London: IRFB, 1961).
2 Ibid., p. 15.

All Blacks in head-on train crash

1 *Evening Post*, 31 August 1949.
2 *Dominion*, 3 August 1949.

Chapter 11: Springboks, race and a new era

1 A stanza from the poem by Allen Curnow, 'On the Tour – Verwoerd be our Vatchwoerd! Or God Amend New Zealand' (Auckland: The Pilgrim Press, 1960). Permission to reproduce from the copyright owner, Tim Curnow, Sydney.
2 Trevor Richards, 'Thou Shalt Play! What 60 Years of Controversy over New Zealand's Sporting Contacts with South Africa Tells us about Ourselves', *New Zealand Studies*, July 1996.
3 Warwick Roger, *Old Heroes: The 1956 Springbok Tour and the Lives Beyond* (Auckland: Hodder & Stoughton), 1991.
4 *Star-Sun Sports*, 21 July 1956, p. 32.
5 Terry McLean, *Goodbye to Glory: The 1976 All Black Tour of South Africa* (Wellington: A. H. & A. W. Reed, 1976), p. 20.
6 Match programme, NZ Māori v South Africa, Auckland, 25 August 1956, p. 7.
7 *Evening Post*, 11 August 1956, p. 1.
8 Bob Howitt, *New Zealand Rugby Greats*, vol. 1 (Auckland: Moa Publications, 1975), pp. 257–8.
9 *8 O'Clock*, 1 September 1956.
10 *The Times*, 13 June 1959, p. 7.
11 *Evening Star*, 20 July 1959.
12 *Oval World*, December 1998, pp. 14–15.
13 Various match reports from *8 O'Clock, Auckland Star, NZ Herald, Dominion*, 28–30 September 1960.
14 *Evening Post*, 4 July 1961.
15 *Sports Digest*, July 1961, pp. 13–14.
16 *Dominion*, 29 June, 1961.
17 *Evening Post*, 16 August 1961.
18 Ibid., 18 January 1964, p. 21.
19 *Evening Times*, 18 January 1964.
20 *Evening Post*, 17 February 1964.
21 *Dominion*, 17 February 1964.
22 Saul Dubow, 'Macmillan, Verwoerd and the 1960 "wind of change" speech', *The Historical Journal*, vol. 54, no. 4 (December 2011).
23 Undated NZRFU report headed 'Report on discussions in London – January 1964'. Author's collection. For details of NZ representation at IRB meetings, see NZRFU annual reports 1962 and 1964.
24 Minutes of IRFB annual meeting, Edinburgh, 18 March 1966. Author's collection.
25 Juan Klee, 'Multinational sport participation replaces apartheid sport in South Africa – 1967–1978: the role of BJ Vorster and PGJ Koornhof', Department of Historical Studies, University of Johannesburg (http://dspace.nwu.ac.za); for an overview of the sport and racism issue, see Douglas Booth, *The Race Game: Sport and Politics in South Africa* (London: Frank Cass, 1998).

'TP' always at the front of a ruck of writers

1 Robin Hyde, *Journalese* (Auckland: National Printing Co., 1934), p. 198.
2 McLean's career was detailed in Paul Lewis with Jock McLean, *TP: The Life and Times of Sir Terry McLean* (Auckland: HarperCollins, 2010).
3 *The Times*, 10 November 1972, p. 14.
4 Papers relating to Winston McCarthy libel case, Alexander Turnbull Library (MS-Papers-8944-018).

The tale of the tape

1 *Dominion*, 9 July 1956, p. 10.

Bard of the Happy Isles

1 *8 O'Clock*, 18 June 1960.
2 *Evening Post*, 20 June 1960.

The call of the wild

1 *Evening Post*, 9 May 1960.
2 Ibid., 12 May 1960.
3 *Weekly News*, 15 June 1960.
4 *Sunday Times* (Johannesburg), 29 May 1960.
5 *Dominion Sunday Times*, 30 August 1987.

Rugby through the lens

1 *Evening Post*, 21 March 1969, p. 14.
2 Thompson service record, Archives New Zealand.

The cradle of rugby

1 *NZ Truth*, 24 November 1937.
2 J. T. Burrows, *Pathway Among Men* (Christchurch: Whitcombe & Tombs, 1974), p. 16.
3 *Observer*, 7 July 1943, p. 27.
4 *Auckland Star*, 4 May 1928, p. 5.
5 Ibid., 19 April 1928, p. 10.
6 *Evening Post*, 29 June 1921, p. 9.
7 Ibid.
8 Arthur W. V. Reeve and Lynn McConnell, *Cradle of Rugby: The History of New Zealand College Rugby* (Wellington: Inprint, 1992), p. 52.
9 Mervyn D. Elias, *The Boy from New Zealand: The Story of a New Zealand Boy at an English Public School* (Wellington: Whitcombe & Tombs, 1940).
10 Margaret Mahy, *A Dissolving Ghost: Essays and More* (Wellington: Victoria University Press, 2000), p. 70.
11 Ibid.

Chapter 12: End of an era approaches

1 Sir Richard Wild, in an address to the New Zealand Rugby Football Union's seventy-fifth anniversary dinner, Wellington, 19 August 1967; reproduced in Ron Palenski (ed.), *Touchlines: An Anthology of Rugby Poetry* (Dunedin: New Zealand Sports Hall of Fame, 2013), pp. 115–17.
2 Charles Williams, *Gentlemen & Players: The Death of Amateurism in Cricket* (London: Weidenfeld & Nicolson, 2012), p. 31.
3 Trevor Richards, 'Thou Shalt Play! What 60 Years of Controversy over New Zealand's Sporting Contacts with South Africa tell us about Ourselves', *New Zealand Studies*, July 1996.
4 *Wisden Almanack*, 1963 (London: Sporting Handbooks, 1963), online edition: http://www.espncricinfo.com/wisdenalmanack.
5 John Reason and Carwyn James, *The World of Rugby: A History of Rugby Union Football* (London: British Broadcasting Corporation, 1979), p. 159.
6 Gareth Edwards, *Gareth* (London: Stanley Paul, 1978), p. 59.
7 C. K. Saxton report to the NZRFU, Report No. 4, 7 December 1967.
8 Minutes IRB meeting, Edinburgh, 14–15 March 1968.
9 *Otago Daily Times*, 9 July 2001, p. 19.
10 *The Times*, 9 December 1967, p. 7. Sir Geoffrey Palmer succeeded David Lange as leader of the Labour Party and prime minister in 1989 and was himself replaced by Mike Moore in August 1990. Palmer

acknowledged to the author that he was indeed the writer of the letter to the editor.

11 Alan Sayers and Les Watkins, *Fred the Needle: The Untold Story of Sir Fred Allen – The Authorised Biography* (Auckland: Hodder Moa, 2011), pp. 121–8.
12 *Otago Daily Times*, 10 May 1972, p. 1. *New Zealand Foreign Affairs Review*, April 1973, pp. 22–8.
13 *Review*, p. 26.
14 *Listener*, 27 August 1973.
15 T. P. McLean, *The All Blacks* (London: Sidgwick & Jackson, 1991), p. 111.
16 Lindsay Knight, *NPC: The Heart of Rugby* (Auckland: Penguin Books, 2001).
17 Background on radio and rugby, see *NZ Sportsman*, August 1951, p. 8.
18 Ron Palenski, *All Blacks v Lions* (Auckland: Hodder Moa Beckett, 2005), pp. 135–6.

Wrong place, wrong time, wrong decision

1 *Sunday Times*, 25 November 1979, p. 2.
2 *The Times*, 5 December 1972, p. 1.
3 Cable received by Qantas Wellington from Qantas airport traffic staff in Singapore. Author's copy.
4 David Barber emails to author, 29 June 2003, 22 February 2013.
5 Personal knowledge.
6 *Otago Daily Times*, 11 February 1973.
7 Ron Palenski, *New Zealand Rugby: Stories of Heroism and Valour* (Auckland: Cumulus, 2002), p. 49.
8 *NZ Herald*, 28 July 2001.
9 Transcript of conversation between J. L. Sullivan and John Tallent, 6 December 1972. Author's copy.
10 *Daily Mail*, 5 December 1972, pp. 14–15.
11 Ibid., 21 December 1972, p. 23.
12 *The Times*, 4 December 1972, p. 1.
13 *Sunday Times*, 25 November 1979, pp. 1–2.
14 NZPA report published in various newspapers, 19 April 1973.
15 *NZ Herald*, 25 June 1990.
16 Ibid.
17 McLean, after talking to *Sunday Times* columnist Dudley Doust, reported the Harris incident in the Sunday *Herald*, 3 December 1972.
18 Thomas letter to Warwick Larkins, 11 May 1973. Author's copy.
19 *Auckland Star*, 6 December 1972, p. 52.
20 *Sunday Times*, 10 December 1972, p. 28.

It's not just a game for men

1 *Evening Post*, 13 February 1888, p. 2; 20 February 1888, p. 4.
2 Sandra Coney, *Standing in the Sunshine: A History of New Zealand Women Since They Won the Vote* (Auckland: Penguin, 1993), p. 247. Coney's father was Tom Pearce, Auckland rugby player and administrator and manager of the national team in 1960.
3 *Auckland Star*, 2 June 1891, p. 8.
4 Ibid., 5 June 1891, p. 2.
5 Ibid., 8 June 1891, p. 4.
6 *Observer*, 1 August 1891, p. 4.
7 See James F. Lee, *The Lady Footballers: Struggling to Play in Victorian Britain* (Oxford: Routledge, 2008).
8 McLean Papers, object 1026027, MS-Group-1551, Alexander Turnbull Library.
9 RFU poster, World Cup 2010.
10 Ghislaine Quintillan, 'Alice Milliat and the Women's Games', *Olympic Review*, vol. 26, no. 31 (Feb–March 2000); Mary H. Leigh and Thérèse M. Bonin, 'The Pioneering Role of Madame Alice Milliat and the Fédération Sportive Féminine Internationale in Establishing International Track and Field Competition for Women', *Journal of Sport History*, vol. 4, no. 1 (1977).
11 *Evening Post*, 20 September 1932, p. 4.
12 Philip Dine, *French Rugby Football: A Cultural History* (Oxford: Berg, 2001), p. 32.
13 *Dominion*, 14 June 1915, p. 3.
14 The author gratefully acknowledges the help of Peter du Chateau of Rotorua.
15 Rob Hess, 'Playing With "Patriotic Fire": Women and Football in the Antipodes during the Great War', *International Journal of the History of Sport*, vol. 28, no. 10 (July 2011).
16 Barbara Cox, 'The Rise and Fall of "the Girl Footballer" in New Zealand during 1921', *International Journal of the History of Sport*, vol. 29, no. 3 (March 2012).
17 *Free Lance*, 13 July 1921, p. 15.
18 Ibid., p. 31.
19 *NZ Truth*, 23 July 1921, p. 9; 13 August 1921, p. 6.
20 *Evening Post*, 30 March 1922, p. 4.
21 See Cox.
22 *Evening Post*, 11 July 1921, p. 8.
23 *Weekly News*, 11 April 1941, p. 35.
24 Otago Rugby Football Union programme, Ladies Competition, 28 September 1946, p. 2.
25 *Otago Daily Times*, 30 September 1946, p. 3.
26 *IRB World of Rugby*, issue 2, 2002, p. 18.
27 Laurie O'Reilly, 'Women's Rugby: A Coach's View', *Journal of Physical Education New Zealand*, vol. 26, no. 3 (1993), p. 11.
28 John Arthur O'Hanley, 'Women in Non-Traditional Sport: The Rise and Popularity of Women's Rugby in Canada', master's thesis, Queen's University, Ontario, 1998.
29 *Sports Alive*, spring 1992, p. 34.
30 Angela Burroughs and John Nauright, 'Women's sports and embodiment in Australia and New Zealand', *International Journal of the History of Sport*, vol. 17, nos 2–3 (2000).
31 Award winners are listed annually in the *New Zealand Rugby Almanack*.
32 Ann Cleary, 'Rugby Women', *Annals of Leisure Research*, vol. 3, no. 1 (2000).
33 Charlotte Hughes, 'Moira's Lament? Feminist Advocacy and the 1981 Springbok Tour of New Zealand', in Greg Ryan (ed.), *Tackling Rugby Myths: Rugby and New Zealand Society 1854–2004* (Dunedin: Otago University Press, 2005), p. 140.
34 Jennifer Curtin, 'More than a Man's Game – Women and Rugby Union in New Zealand', Winter Lecture Series, University of Auckland, Maidment Theatre, 2 August 2011.

Chapter 13: Conflict and money

1 'John Kirwan', by Bill Sutton, published in Ron Palenski (ed.), *Touchlines: An Anthology of Rugby Poetry* (Dunedin: New Zealand Sports Hall of Fame, 2013), p. 123.
2 Most Olympic sports either caved in to the government's pressure or its administrators were enthusiastic supporters of the government. The crucial point is, though, that the New Zealand Olympic and Commonwealth Games Association (as it then was) voted in favour of competing. Only two sports, canoeing and modern pentathlon, stayed in and went to Moscow.
3 Crowd figures were merely estimates, often just by journalists. The figures have been taken from various sources and, in each case, the lowest number is listed. Neither the provincial unions nor the national union gave definitive crowd figures, as some do now, mainly because grounds were not all seating. Analysis of the figures should also take into account the difference between Saturday and midweek games. In some cases, notably the second test in Wellington, the crowd was said to be several thousand fewer than the number of tickets sold.

In the case of the Waikato game, which was not played, the figure given was of the crowd estimated to be in Rugby Park when the game was cancelled.

4 *Auckland Star*, *Daily Telegraph*, *NZ Herald*, 26 August 1981.
5 http://www.nzhistory.net.nz/media/photo/opinion-on-the-springbok-tour-around-new-zealand.
6 Blazey statement, 'Tour: South Africa to NZ 1981', 9 April 1981.
7 NZRFU Annual Report 1981, p. 11.
8 Ibid., p. 52.
9 NZPA report, 19 June 1981.
10 Prime Minister's statement, 6 July 1981, p. 1.
11 Ibid., p. 3.
12 Bob Howitt (ed.), *DB Rugby Annual* (Auckland: Moa Publications, 1981), p. 20.
13 *NZ Herald*, 18 November 1981.
14 'Visit of South African Rugby Team, 1981', Office of the Minister of Police, undated.
15 Chris Laidlaw, *Rights of Passage: Beyond the New Zealand Identity Crisis* (Auckland: Hodder Moa Beckett, 1999), p. 116.
16 Ibid.
17 Auckland Rugby Football Union letter to NZRFU and provincial unions, 21 December 1984.
18 As quoted in David Baragwanath, 'The Tour', *New Zealand Law Journal*, Oct. 1985, p. 222.
19 Vol. 2 *New Zealand Law Reports* 1985, High Court, Finnigan v NZRFU, pp. 159–75; Appeal Court, Finnigan v NZRFU, pp. 175–80; High Court, Finnigan v NZRFU (2), pp. 181–9; Appeal Court, Finnigan v NZRFU (3), pp. 190–208.
20 NZRFU Annual Report, 1985, p. 74.
21 *The Times*, 15 April 1986, p. 40.
22 Conversation with author.
23 *The Times*, 19 April 1986, p. 40.
24 R. W. Thomas letter to D. H. Craven, 14 November 1986.
25 NZRFU statement, 18 July 1986.
26 Tony Collins, '"The First Principle of Our Game": The Rise and Fall of Amateurism: 1886–1995', in Greg Ryan (ed.), *The Changing Face of Rugby: The Union Game and Professionalism Since 1995* (Newcastle: Cambridge Scholars Publishing, 2008), p. 14.
27 *Dominion*, 13 August 1989, p. 43.
28 Ibid.
29 *Herald Scotland*, 7 November 1989.
30 For a full if Australian-slanted account of the events of 1995, see Peter FitzSimons, *The Rugby War* (Sydney: HarperSports, 1996).
31 For Lochore's account of the negotiations, see Alex Veysey, Gary Caffell, and Ron Palenski, *Lochore: An Authorised Biography* (Auckland: Hodder Moa Beckett, 1996).
32 *Sunday Star-Times*, 6 August 1995, p. B3.
33 Ibid.
34 Ibid.
35 Conversation with author.
36 *The Times*, 28 August 1995, p. 1.
37 Ibid., p. 15.

Shield of desire

1 *Weekend Star*, 14 September 1985, p. 1.
2 *New Zealand Rugby News*, 18 September 1985, p. 2.
3 *New Zealand Times*, 15 September 1985, p. 23.
4 *8 O'Clock Shield Special*, 15 September 1985, p. 4.
5 *Press*, 30 July 1973.
6 NZRFU inquiry decision, 19 August 2004.
7 *Dominion-Post*, 20 June 2009, p. 1.
8 Bonham's letter to Waikato RU, 19 March 1994.

Chapter 14: The more things change . . .

1 Mark Pirie, 'The Cup', reproduced in Ron Palenski (ed.), *Touchlines: An Anthology of Rugby Poetry* (Dunedin: New Zealand Sports Hall of Fame, 2013), p. 130; stanza reproduced with permission.
2 Context is needed for Johnson's comment. He said first that New Zealand was 'a poxy island in the Pacific' and after humourless outrage by New Zealanders, he apologised and said he got it wrong: he really should have said two islands. When Johnson delivered his 'apology', under his red Welsh tracksuit top he wore a black T-shirt with words on the back: 'I love Kiwis – when they are in New Zealand'. His initial comments and the reactions were widely reported.
3 *Daily Telegraph* online, 11 November 2013 (http://www.telegraph.co.uk).
4 *Mountain Scene*, 2 May 2013.
5 Note to author.

Farmers and footballers

1 *Sports Digest*, July 1964, p. 13.
2 Ibid., July 1968.
3 Ibid., August 1969, p. 29.
4 Ibid., July 1964, p. 14.
5 Ibid., p. 16.
6 Jock Phillips, *A Man's Country? The Image of the Pakeha Male – A History* (Auckland: Penguin, 1987), p. 92.
7 Ibid., p. 93. Phillips used the word 'scrimmage' rather than scrummage or scrum.
8 Greg Ryan, 'Rural Myth and Urban Actuality: The Anatomy of All Black and New Zealand Rugby 1884–1938', *New Zealand Journal of History*, vol. 35, no. 1 (2001); an essay based on that and with the same title appeared in Ryan (ed.), *Tackling Rugby Myths: Rugby and New Zealand Society 1854–2004* (Dunedin: Otago University Press, 2004).

World Cup 2003 timeline: the slips twixt cup and lip

1 Chronology compiled from newspaper accounts and from IRB, ARU and NZRFU statements, all in author's collection.

The road to 2011

1 Derek Robinson (ed.), Rakavi *60: 60 Years of History of the Fiji Rugby Union* (Suva: Fiji Rugby Union, 1973).
2 Times Online, 20 November 2005.
3 IRB media statement, 8 January 2006.
4 Times Online, 18 November 2005.
5 NZRU statement, 9 December 2005.

Epilogue

1 Seaforth MacKenzie, 'L'Envoi'. This rounded off W. F. Alexander and A. E. Currie, *New Zealand Verse* (London: Walter Scott Publishing, 1906), p. 253.
2 J. J. Stewart, *Rugby: The Game – Understanding Developments in the Field of Play* (Palmerston North: Department of Management Systems, Massey University, 1995), p. 80.
3 *Star Sports*, 20 September 1947, p. 4.
4 *New Zealand Illustrated Magazine*, 1 October 1899, p. 75.
5 *NZ Sportsman*, March 1958, p. 9.
6 Stewart, p. 76.
7 Gerard John Martin, 'The Game is not the Same: A History of Professional Rugby in New Zealand', master's thesis, Auckland University of Technology, 2005.

Bibliography

Primary sources

Archival

1st New Zealand Expeditionary Force service records, various, Archives New Zealand.

2nd New Zealand Expeditionary Force rugby (DA 21.1/9/G2/3/1, parts 1 and 2), Archives New Zealand.

2nd New Zealand Expeditionary Force service records, New Zealand Defence Force, Trentham.

Andrews, Brigadier Allan. Notes on 2NZEF rugby, New Zealand Sports Hall of Fame.

Australian service records, Australian Archives.

Baskerville archive, New Zealand Sports Hall of Fame, Dunedin.

Griffiths, G. J., Business, research and personal papers, Hocken Collections (ARC-0320).

McLean Papers, MS-Group-1551, Alexander Turnbull Library.

Match programmes, miscellaneous correspondence. Author's collection.

'New Zealand Maoris: Visit to South Africa of All Black Football Team', the National Archives (UK) (DO 35/1122).

Otago Rugby Football Union minutes, Hocken Collections.

Parata, W. T., Album of Māori Rugby Football Team Tour Overseas 1926–27, Hocken Collections (MS-1262).

Rugby Football Union (England), committee minutes, various, Twickenham.

Sound Archives/Ngā Taonga Kōrero, various items as cited in endnotes.

Stead, J. W., papers, Hocken Collections (MS-1205).

Thomson, John Bell, Words of Passage – a journalist looks back, Hocken Collections (Misc-MS-1059).

Published

All Blacks of Jubilee Year, The, 1935: an interesting account of all matches played in the United Kingdom, with comments and criticism of the play and players, photographs of teams, records of players, matches, etc., L. T. Watkins, Wellington, 1936.

Alley, G. T., *With the British Rugby Team in New Zealand 1930*, Simpson and Williams, Christchurch, 1930.

Barr, R. A., *With the British Rugby Team in Maoriland: True Story of the Tour*, Otago Daily Times and Witness, Dunedin, 1908.

Baskerville, A. H., *Modern Rugby Football: New Zealand Methods – Points for the Beginner, the Players, the Spectator*, Gordon & Gotch, Wellington, 1907.

Bennett, Phil, and Williams, Martyn, *Everywhere for Wales*, Stanley Paul, London, 1981.

Boshier, F. W., *All Blacks in South Africa*, Blundell Bros, Wellington, 1960.

Burrows, J. T., *Pathway Among Men: An Autobiography*, Whitcombe & Tombs, Christchurch, 1974.

Buttery, J. A., *Why Kruger Made War – or Behind the Boer Scenes*, William Heinemann, London, 1900.

Buttery, J. A. (ed.), *Why the All Blacks Triumphed! 'Daily Mail' Story of the Tour*, Associated Newspapers, London, 1905.

Carbery, A. D., *The New Zealand Medical Service in the Great War 1914–1918*, Whitcombe & Tombs, Auckland, 1924.

Carman, A. H., *Diary of the Experiences of A. H. Carman during his Travels through Australia, South Africa, Great Britain, Belgium, France and Italy from June 27th 1924 to March 24th 1925*, published by the family, Wellington, 2010.

Carman, M. G., Carman, R. M., and Jones, E. E., *The Prison Letters: Letters Written to Arthur H. Carman while he was Imprisoned for Subversion in Mt Crawford Prison Wellington 1941*, privately published, Wellington, 2008.

Cooper, Alfred Benjamin, 'The New Zealanders: A Fragment of a Tennysonian Epic', published in *Boy's Own Annual*, 1906.

Coubertin, Pierre de, 'Notes about Foot-ball', originally written in 1897, republished in *Total Rugby: the Bulletin of the International Rugby Board*, issue 9, 2005.

Elias, Mervyn D., *The Boy from New Zealand: The Story of a New Zealand Boy at an English Public School*, Whitcombe & Tombs, Wellington, 1940.

Ellison, T. R., *The Art of Rugby Football*, Geddis and Blomfield, Wellington, 1902.

—— 'The Prospects of a New Zealand Rugby Team Visiting England', *Wellington Rugby Annual 1898*, Wellington RFU, Wellington, 1898.

Eyton, T., *Rugby Football Past and Present: The Tour of the Native Team*, Author, Wellington, 1896.

Fenwick, N. A., *Rhyme or Reason*, Central Otago News, Alexandra, 1949.

Gallaher, D., and Stead, W. J., *The Complete Rugby Footballer on the New Zealand System*, Methuen & Co., London, 1906.

Gaskell, A. P., *The Big Game and Other Stories*, The Caxton Press, Christchurch, 1947.

Hoben, E. D., 'Ake, Ake, Kia Kaha', *Countess of Liverpool's Gift Book*, Whitcombe & Tombs, Wellington, 1915.

—— 'The National Game of Maoriland', *Review of Reviews*, 20 July 1895.

Hughes, Thomas, *Tom Brown's Schooldays*, Regent Classics, Thames Publishing, London, 1950.

Hunter, Irwin, *New Zealand Rugby Football: Some Hints and Criticisms*, Whitcombe & Tombs, Dunedin, 1929.

Hyde, Robin, *Journalese*, National Printing Company, Auckland, 1934.

Jones, Tom (ed.), *NZ Rugby Annual 1932*, Geo. W. Slade Ltd, Wellington, 1932.

Kipling, Rudyard, *The Complete Verse*, Kyle Cathie, London, 2006.

Laidlaw, Chris, *Rights of Passage: Beyond the New Zealand Identity Crisis*, Hodder Moa Beckett, Auckland, 1999.

Laubscher, Lappe, and Nieman, Gideon, *The Carolin Papers: A Diary of the 1906–07 Springbok Tour*, Rugbyana Publishers, Pretoria, 1990.

McCarthy, Winston, *The All Blacks on Trek Again*, Sporting Publications, Wellington, 1950.

McLean, Terry, *Goodbye to Glory: The 1976 All Black Tour of South Africa*, A. H. & A. W. Reed, Wellington, 1976.

Marshall, the Rev. Frank, *Football: The Rugby Union Game*, Cassell, London, 1892.

Masters, Read, *With the All Blacks in Great Britain, France, Canada and Australia 1924–5*, Christchurch Press, Christchurch, 1928.

Miller, Peter (ed.), *The Irregular Verses of Rupert Brooke*, Green Branch Press, Lechlade, Gloucestershire, 1997.

Mulgan, John, *Report on Experience*, Oxford University Press, Oxford, 1947.

Nepia, George, *Rugby Every Time. George Nepia's Own Story*, New Zealand Sports Hall of Fame, Dunedin, 2009.

Nicholls, M. F., *With the All Blacks in Springbokland*, L. T. Watkins, Wellington, 1928.

Origin of Rugby Football, the (1897). Report (with appendices) of the Sub-Committee of the Old Rugbeian Society Appointed in July 1895, ORS, Rugby, 1897.

Orwell, George, *Orwell: The Collected Essays, Journalism and Letters of George Orwell, Volume 4: In Front of Your Nose 1945–1950*, Penguin Books, London, 1970.

Osborn, E. B., 'New Zealand Football', published in *The Nineteenth Century and After*, January 1906, p. 108.
Report of Imperial Rugby Conference held at the Great Northern Hotel, King's Cross, London, on the 12th Day of December 1924, published by the secretary, Dublin, 1925.
Robinson, W. W., *W. W. Robinson's Rugby Football in New Zealand: Its Development from Small Beginnings, with an Introduction by Rowan Gibbs and Notes on Robinson's Life and his Sporting Career*, Smith's Bookshop, Wellington, 2012.
Rugby Almanack of New Zealand, various issues, edited by Carman, A. H., Swan, A. C., and Masters, R. R., from 1935 until 1967; by Carman and Swan until 1973; by Carman until 1982; by Chester, R. H., and McMillan, N. E. C., from 1983 until 1994; by McMillan and Akers, from 1995 until 1998; by Akers and Geoff Miller from 1999. Published by Sporting Publications, Wellington, 1935–82; Moa Publications, Auckland, 1983–92; Moa Beckett, Auckland, 1993–95; Hodder Moa Beckett, Auckland, 1996–2005; Hodder Moa, Auckland, 2006–13.
Saxton, C. K., *The ABC of Rugby*, NZRFU, Wellington, 1959.
Schlesinger Jr., Arthur M., *A Thousand Days: John F. Kennedy in the White House*, Andre Deutsch, London, 1965.
School List of Christ's College from 1850 to 1965, The, Christ's College Old Boys' Association, Christchurch, 1966.
Scott, R. W. H., and McLean, T. P., *The Bob Scott Story*, A. H. & A. W. Reed, Wellington, 1956.
Scott, Sir Walter, *The Poetical Works of Sir Walter Scott, with Memoir of the Author*, Little, Brown and Co., Boston, 1857.
Sewell, E. H. D., *Rugby Football Up to Date*, Hodder & Stoughton, London, 1921.
Sleigh, S. E., *Northern Tour of the Dunedin Football Club*, R. T. Wheeler, Dunedin, 1877.
Sleigh, S. E. (ed.), *The New Zealand Rugby Football Annual for 1885*, Otago Daily Times, Dunedin, 1885.
Stanley, A. P., *The Life and Correspondence of Thomas Arnold, DD, Late Head-Master of Rugby School, and Regius Professor of Modern History in the University of Oxford*, vol. II, B. Fellowes, London, 1845.
Stead, W. J., *Billy's Trip Home: The Remarkable Diary of an All Black on Tour*, New Zealand Sports Hall of Fame, Dunedin, 2005.
Vaile, P. A., *Modern Lawn Tennis*, William Heinemann, London, 1904.
Warbrick, Alfred, *Adventures in Geyserland*, A. H. & A. W. Reed, Dunedin, 1934.
Watts Moses, Eric, *History of the International Rugby Football Board 1886–1960*, IRFB, London, 1961.

Newspapers, magazines etc.

(Country or city of origin is given if not obvious)
Advertiser (Adelaide)
Age (Melbourne)
Auckland Star (also known for a time as *Evening Star*)
Baa Baa News (Auckland)
Cape Times (Cape Town)
Chronicles of the NZEF (London)
Courier (Brisbane)
Daily Mail (UK)
Daily Telegraph (Napier)
Daily Telegraph (UK)
Die Transvaler (Johannesburg)
Dominion (Wellington)
Edinburgh Review
Evening Dispatch (Edinburgh)
Evening Post (Wellington)
Evening Star (Dunedin)
Evening Star Star Sports (Dunedin)
Examiner (Launceston)
Foreign Affairs Review (New Zealand)
Guardian (also *Manchester Guardian*)
Gisborne Herald
Golfdom (US)
Graphic (UK)
Guardian (UK)
Hutt News
Illustrated London News
IRB World of Rugby (Dublin)
Listener (NZ)
Liverpool Mercury
Los Angeles Times
Maitland Mercury and Hunter River General Advertiser
Manawatu Times (Palmerston North)
Natal Mercury (Durban)
New York Clipper
New Zealand Graphic (Auckland)
New Zealand Spectator and Cook's Strait Guardian (Wellington)
NZ Sportsman (Wellington)
NZ Truth
Nineteenth Century and After (UK)
Observer (UK)
Otago Daily Times (Dunedin)
Outspan (Johannesburg)
Pall Mall Gazette (UK)
Points Unlimited (Auckland)
Poverty Bay Herald (Gisborne)
Press (Christchurch)
Punch (UK)
Referee (Christchurch)
Referee (Sydney)
Review of Reviews (Australian edition)
San Francisco Call
San Francisco Chronicle
Scotsman (Edinburgh)
Silver Fern (Wellington)
Southern Cross (Wellington)
Southland Times (Invercargill)
Spectator (Australian edition)
Spectator (UK)
Sporting Review (Auckland)
Sports Alive (Auckland)
Sports Digest (Wellington)
Star (Christchurch)
Strand Magazine (UK)
Sun (Auckland)
Sunday News
Sunday Star-Times
Sunday Times (UK)
Sydney Morning Herald
The Times (UK)
Timaru Herald
Wanganui Chronicle
Wanganui Herald
Weekly News (Auckland)
Weekly Times (Manchester)
Wellington Independent
West Coast Times (Hokitika)
Western Mail (also *Western Mail and South Wales News*) (Cardiff)
Windsor Magazine (UK)

Secondary sources

Akers, Clive, *The Life and Times of the Man Who Gave New Zealand Rugby*, Author, Palmerston North, 2008.

Alexander, W. F., and Currie, A. E., *New Zealand Verse*, Walter Scott Publishing, London, 1906.

Barnes, David, *The Accies: The Cradle of Scottish Rugby*, Birlinn, Edinburgh, 2008.

Barrow, Graeme, *All Blacks versus Springboks*, Heinemann, Auckland, 1981.

Batchelor, Denzil, *Days Without Sunset*, Eyre & Spottiswoode, London, 1949.

Beacall, Philip J., *Birkenhead Park: The First Hundred Years*, published by the club, Birkenhead, 1971.

Bertram, James (ed.), *The Letters of Thomas Arnold the Younger (1850–1900)*, Auckland University Press/Oxford University Press, Auckland, 1980.

Blainey, Geoffrey, *A Game of our Own: The Origins of Australian Football*, Information Australia, Melbourne, 1990.

Booth, Douglas, *The Race Game: Sport and Politics in South Africa*, Frank Cass, London, 1998.

Brittenden, R. T., *'Give 'em the axe': The First Hundred Years of the Christchurch Football Club*, Christchurch Football Club, Christchurch, 1963.

Carman, Arthur H., *Maori Rugby 1884–1979*, Sporting Publications, Wellington, 1980.

Carpenter, Andrew, *Verse in English from Eighteenth-Century Ireland*, Cork University Press, Cork, 1998.

Chester, Rod, and McMillan, Neville, *Men In Black*, Moa Publications, Auckland, 1978.

Coffey, John, *Strike! The Tour That Died of Shame*, Scratching Shed Publications, Leeds, 2012.

Cohen, Stanley, *Dodgers! The First 100 years*, Birch Lane Press, New York, 1990.

Collins, Tony, *A Social History of English Rugby Union*, Routledge, London, 2009.

—— *Rugby's Great Split: Class, Culture and the Origins of Rugby League Football*, Frank Cass, London, 1998.

Coney, Sandra, *Standing in the Sunshine: A History of New Zealand Women Since They Won the Vote*, Penguin, Auckland, 1993.

Cooper, Winston, *Once a Southern Man: The History of the Southern Rugby Football Club 1884–1984*, Southern RFC, Dunedin, 1984.

Cornwell, Patricia, *Portrait of a Killer: Jack the Ripper – Case Closed*, Little, Brown, London, 2002.

Crawford, Scott A. G. M. (ed.), *'Serious Sport': J. A. Mangan's Contribution to the History of Sport*, Frank Cass, London, 2004.

Davidson, John McI., *Rugby Union: The Game Comes to Scotland*, Scottish Rugby Union, Edinburgh, 2000.

Difford, Ivor D., *The History of South African Rugby Football (1875–1932)*, The Specialty Press of SA, Wynberg, South Africa, 1933.

Dine, Philip, *French Rugby Football: A Cultural History*, Berg, Oxford, 2001.

Donoghue, Paul, *Rugby Versus Rommel*, Author, Wellington, 1961.

Dunning, Eric, and Sheard, Kenneth, *Barbarians, Gentlemen and Players: A Sociological Study of the Development of Rugby Football*, Martin Robertson, Oxford, 1979.

Edwards, Gareth, *Gareth*, Stanley Paul, London, 1978.

Elliott, Matt, *Dave Gallaher: The Original All Black Captain*, HarperCollins, Auckland, 2012.

Fagan, Sean, *The First Lions of Rugby: The First British Lions and their Dramatic 1888 Tour of Australia and New Zealand*, Slattery Media Group, Melbourne, 2013.

—— *The Rugby Rebellion: The Divide of League and Union*, RL1908, Sydney, 2005.

Ferreira, J. T., Elignaut, J. P., Landman, P. J., and du Toit, J. F., *Transvaal Rugby Football Union: 100 Years*, Transvaal RFU, Johannesburg, 1989.

FitzSimons, Peter, *The Rugby War*, HarperSports, Sydney, 1996.

Frewin, Leslie (ed.), *The Poetry of Cricket*, Macdonald and Co., London, 1964.

Frith, David, *'My Dear Victorious Stod': A Biography of A. E. Stoddart*, Lutterworth Press, Guildford, 1977.

Garner, Joe, *The Commonwealth Office 1925–68*, Heinemann, London, 1978.

Giles, H. A., *The Civilization of China*, Williams and Norgate, London, 1911.

Griffiths, George, *W. G. Rees and His Cricketing Cousins*, Author, Dunedin, 1971.

Harris, H. A., *Sport in Greece and Rome*, Thames and Hudson, London, 1972.

Haynes, John, *From All Blacks to All Golds: Rugby League's Pioneers*, Ryan and Haynes, Christchurch, 1996.

Heads, Ian, and Middleton, David, *A Centenary of Rugby League 1908–2008: The Definitive Story of the Game in Australia*, Pan Macmillan, Sydney, 2008.

Henderson, Jim, *22 Battalion: Official History of New Zealand in the Second World War*, War History Branch, Department of Internal Affairs, Wellington, 1958.

Howitt, Bob, *New Zealand Rugby Greats*, vol. 1, Moa Publications, Auckland, 1975

James, C. L. R., *Beyond A Boundary*, Serpents Tail, London, 1994.

Knight, Lindsay, *NPC: The Heart of Rugby*, Penguin Books, Auckland, 2001.

—— *Playground to the World Cup*, Author, Auckland, 2011.

—— *The Shield: A Century of the Ranfurly Shield*, Celebrity Books, Auckland, 2002.

Lee, James F., *The Lady Footballers: Struggling to Play in Victorian Britain*, Routledge, Oxford, 2008.

Lewis, Paul, with McLean, Jock, *TP: The Life and Times of Sir Terry McLean*, HarperCollins, Auckland, 2010

Long, Frank, *Magpie Magic*, vol. 1., Author, Napier, 2007.

Luxford, Bob, *Alex the Bruce*, Rugby Museum Society, Palmerston North, 1994.

—— 'Report of Imperial Rugby Conference', *Points Unlimited*, vol. 14, no. 1, March 2007, pp. 12–14.

McConnell, Lynn, *Something to Crow About: The Centennial History of the Southland Rugby Football Union*, Craig Printing, Invercargill, 1986.

Macdonald, Finlay, *The Game of Our Lives*, Viking/Allen Lane, Auckland, 1996.

Mackenzie, J. M., *All Blacks in Chains*, Truth (NZ) Ltd, Wellington, 1960.

McKenzie, Dan, *The History of Rugby Football in Wellington and Wairarapa*, NZ Times, Wellington, 1911.

McKenzie, Norman, *On With the Game: The Rugby Reminiscences of Norman McKenzie*, A. H. & A. W. Reed, Wellington, 1961.

McLean, Gavin, *The Governors: New Zealand's Governors and Governors-General*, Otago University Press, Dunedin, 2006.

McLean, Terry, *Great Days in New Zealand Rugby*, A. H. & A. W. Reed, Wellington, 1959.

—— *The All Blacks*, Sidgwick & Jackson, London, 1991.

—— *The Best of McLean*, Hodder & Stoughton, Auckland, 1984.

Mackrell, Brian, *Hariru Wikitoria! An Illustrated History of the Maori Tour of England, 1863*, Oxford University Press, Auckland, 1985.

Macrory, Jennifer, *Running With the Ball: The Birth of Rugby Football*, CollinsWillow, London, 1991.

Mahy, Margaret, *A Dissolving Ghost: Essays and More*, Victoria University Press, Wellington, 2000.

Mallon, Bill, and Bijkerk, Anthony, *The 1920 Olympic Games: Results for All Competitors in All Events, with Commentary*, McFarland, Jefferson, North Carolina, 2003.

Mangan, J. A., *The Games Ethic and Imperialism: Aspects of The Diffusion of an Ideal*, Viking, London, 1985.

Markovits, Andrei, and Hellerman, Steven, *Offside: Soccer and American Exceptionalism*, Princeton University Press, Princeton, 2001.

Martin-Jenkins, Christopher, *World Cricketers: A Biographical Dictionary*, Oxford University Press, Oxford, 1996.
Mather, Tom, *Rugby's Greatest Mystery: Who Really Was F S Jackson?* League Publications, London, 2012.
Mulford, John G., *Guardians of the Game: The History of the New South Wales Rugby Union 1874–2004*, ABC Books, Sydney, 2005.
Mulvaney, John, and Harcourt, Rex, *Cricket Walkabout: The Australian Aborigines in England*, Macmillan, Melbourne, 1988.
Murdoch, Tony, *The Old Club: The History of the Christchurch Football Club 1863–2013*, Christchurch FC, Christchurch, 2013.
Nepia, George, and McLean, Terry, *I, George Nepia: The Autobiography of a Rugby Legend*, London League Publications, London, 2002.
NZ Rugby Annual 1932, Geo. W. Slade Ltd, Wellington, 1932.
Olympic and British Empire Games, The, New Zealand Olympic and British Empire Games Association, Wellington, 1954.
Palenski, Ron, *All Blacks v Lions*, Hodder Moa Beckett, Auckland, 2005.
—— *All Blacks: Myths and Legends*, Hodder Moa, Auckland, 2008.
—— *Century in Black: 100 Years of All Black Test Rugby*, Hodder Moa Beckett, Auckland, 2003.
—— *Last Post: Rugby's Wartime Roll Call*, NZ Sports Hall of Fame, Dunedin, 2011.
—— *New Zealand Rugby: Stories of Heroism and Valour*, Cumulus, Auckland, 2002.
—— *Our National Game: A Celebration of 100 years of NZ Rugby*, Moa Beckett, Auckland, 1992.
—— *The All Blackography*, Hodder Moa, Auckland, 2007.
—— *The Making of New Zealanders*, Auckland University Press, Auckland, 2012.
Palenski, Ron (ed.), *Touchlines: An Anthology of Rugby Poetry*, New Zealand Sports Hall of Fame, Dunedin, 2013.
Penn, Roger G. K., *Three Feathers and a Silver Fern: An Off-Field History of Wales and the All Blacks*, Gomer Press, Llandysul, Wales, 2013.
Phillips, Jock, *A Man's Country? The Image of the Pakeha Male – A History*, Penguin, Auckland, 1987.
Pollard, Jack, *Australian Rugby Union: The Game and the Players*, Angus & Robertson in association with the Australian Broadcasting Corporaton, Sydney, 1984.
Pringle, D. J. C., *The New Zealand Maori Rugby Tour 1926–27*, Akaroa Mail, Akaroa, 1971.
Rau Tau: One Hundred Years of Māori Rugby, NZRU, Wellington, 2010.
Reason, John, and James, Carwyn, *The World of Rugby: A History of Rugby Union Football*, British Broadcasting Corporation, London, 1979.
Reed, W. A., *100 Years of Rugby: Story of Nelson Rugby Football Club 1870–1969*, published by the club, Nelson, 1970.
Reese, T. W., *New Zealand Cricket 1841–1914*, Author, Christchurch, 1927.
Reeve, Arthur W. V., and McConnell, Lynn, *Cradle of Rugby: The History of New Zealand College Rugby*, Inprint, Wellington, 1992.
Robinson, Derek (ed.), *Rakavi 60: 60 Years of History of the Fiji Rugby Union*, Fiji Rugby Union, Suva, 1973.
Roger, Warwick, *Old Heroes: The 1956 Springbok Tour and the Lives Beyond*, Hodder & Stoughton, Auckland, 1991.
Royds, Sir Percy, *The History of the Laws of Rugby Football*, International Rugby Football Board, London, 1949.
Rugby in Auckland 1883–1967: Official History of the Auckland Rugby Football Union, Auckland Rugby Football Union, Auckland, 1967.
Ryan, Greg, *The Contest for Rugby Supremacy: Accounting for the 1905 All Blacks*, Canterbury University Press, Christchurch, 2005.
—— *Forerunners of the All Blacks: The 1888–89 New Zealand Native Football Team in Britain, Australia and New Zealand*, Canterbury University Press, Christchurch, 1993.
Ryan, Greg (ed.), *Tackling Rugby Myths: Rugby and New Zealand Society 1854–2004*, Otago University Press, Dunedin, 2005.
Ryan, Mark, *For the Glory: Two Olympics, Two Wars, Two Heroes*, JR Books, London, 2009.
Saunders, Larry, *The Canterbury Rugby History 1879–1979*, CRFU, Christchurch, 1979.
Sayers, Alan, and Watkins, Les, *Fred the Needle: The Untold Story of Sir Fred Allen – The Authorised Biography*, Hodder Moa, Auckland, 2011.
Sharp, Iain, *Real Gold: Treasures of Auckland City Libraries*, Auckland University Press for Auckland City Libraries Tāmaki Pātaka Kōrero and the Auckland Library Heritage Trust, Auckland, 2007.
Shearman, Montague, *Athletics and Football*, Longmans, Green, London, 1887; *The Badminton Library of Sports and Pastimes*, edited by His Grace the Duke of Beaufort, assisted by Alfred E. T. Watson.
Sinclair, Keith, *A Destiny Apart: New Zealand's Search for National Identity*, Unwin Paperbacks in Association with Port Nicholson Press, Wellington, 1986.
Smith, David, and Williams, Gareth, *Fields of Praise: The Official History of the Welsh Rugby Union*, University of Wales Press, Cardiff, 1980.
Smith, Godfrey (ed.), *Take the Ball and Run: A Rugby Anthology*, Pavilion Books, London, 1991.
Smith, Jed, Introduction, *The Original Rules of Rugby*, Bodleian Library, Oxford, 2007.
Spittle, Gordon, *Counting the Beat: A History of New Zealand Song*, GP Publications, Wellington, 1997.
Stewart, J. J., *Rugby: The Game – Understanding Developments in the Field of Play*, Department of Management Systems, Massey University, Palmerston North, 1995.
Strutt, Joseph, *The Sports and Pastimes of the People of England*, New edition enlarged and corrected by J. Charles Cox, Methuen and Co., London, 1903.
Swan, A. C., *The History of New Zealand Rugby Football*, 2 vols, A. H. & A. W. Reed, Wellington, 1948 and 1957.
Swan, A. C., and Carman, A. H., *Five Seasons of Services Rugby: The History of the New Zealand Services Team in Great Britain, Ireland and France, 1941–46*, Sporting Publications, Wellington, 1948.
Sweet, Reg, *Springbok and Silverfern: The Great Tests Since 1921*, A. H. & A. W. Reed, Wellington, 1960.
Thompson, Richard, *Retreat From Apartheid: New Zealand's Sporting Contacts with South Africa*, Oxford University Press, Wellington, 1975.
Thomson, J. B., *Words of Passage: The Original*, Xlibris Corporation, 2012, e-book.
Vitalien, Pierre, *Le Rugby aux Jeux Olympiques*, Author, Paris, 2004.
Veysey, Alex, Caffell, Gary, and Palenski, Ron, *Lochore: The Authorised Biography*, Hodder Moa Beckett, Auckland, 1996.
Wakelam, H. B. T. (ed.), *The Game Goes On*, Sportsman's Book Club, London, 1954.
Wallace, W. J., *Reminiscences of a Famous NZ International: W.J. ('Carbine') Wallace Writes Rugby History*, New Zealand Sports Hall of Fame, Dunedin, 2005.
West, Trevor, *The Bold Collegians: The Development of Sport in Trinity College Dublin*, Lilliput Press, Dublin, 1991.
Whatman, Mike, *Khaki All Blacks: A Tribute to the Kiwis – the 2nd NZEF Army Rugby Team*, Hodder Moa Beckett, Auckland, 2005.
Williams, Charles, *Gentlemen & Players: The Death of Amateurism in Cricket*, Weidenfeld & Nicolson, London, 2012.
Williams, D. J., *1950: The Year of the Lions*, Author, Hamilton, 1988.
Wilson, A. C., *Wire & Wireless: A History of Telecommunications in New Zealand 1890–1987*, Dunmore Press, Palmerston North, 1994.
Wooller, Wilfred, and Owen, David, compilers, *Fifty Years of the All Blacks: A Complete History of New Zealand Rugby Touring Teams in the British Isles 1905–1954*, Phoenix House, London, 1954.
Zavos, Spiro, *The Gold and the Black: The Rugby Battles for the Bledisloe Cup*, Allen & Unwin, Sydney, 1995.

Theses, academic articles

Allison, Lincoln, and Maclean, Rusty, 'There's a Deathless Myth on the Close Tonight: Reassessing Rugby's Place in the History of Sport', *International Journal of the History of Sport*, vol. 29, no. 13, September 2012, pp. 1866–84.

Burroughs, Angela, and Nauright, John, 'Women's sports and embodiment in Australia and New Zealand', *International Journal of the History of Sport*, vol. 17, nos. 2–3, 2000, pp. 188–205.

Cleary, Ann, 'Rugby Women', *Annals of Leisure Research*, vol. 3, no. 1, 2000, pp. 21–32.

Collins, Tony, '"The First Principle of Our Game", The Rise and Fall of Amateurism: 1886–1995', in Greg Ryan (ed.), *The Changing Face of Rugby: The Union Game and Professionalism since 1995*, Cambridge Scholars Publishing, Newcastle, 2008, pp. 1–19.

Cox, Barbara, 'The Rise and Fall of "the Girl Footballer" in New Zealand during 1921', *International Journal of the History of Sport*, vol. 29, no. 3, March 2012, pp. 444–71.

Craven, D. H., 'The Evolution of Major Games', doctoral thesis, University of Stellenbosch, 1978.

Dubow, Saul, 'Macmillan, Verwoerd and the 1960 "Wind of Change" Speech', *The Historical Journal*, vol. 54, no. 4, December 2011, pp. 1087–1114.

Elmer, David F., 'Epikoinos: The Ball Game Episkuros and *Iliad* 12.421–23', *Classical Philology*, vol. 103, no. 4, October 2008, pp. 414–23.

Giles, Herbert A., 'Football and Polo in China', *The Nineteenth Century and After*, vol. 59, January 1906, p. 508.

Greenwood, William, 'Class, Conflict and the Clash of Codes: The Introduction of Rugby League to New Zealand 1908–1920', doctoral thesis, Massey University, 2008.

Hess, Rob, 'Playing With "Patriotic Fire": Women and Football in the Antipodes during the Great War', *International Journal of the History of Sport*, vol. 28, no. 10, June 2011, pp. 1388–1408.

Kramer, Bernhard, 'In Search of the Lost Champions of the Olympic Art Contests', *Journal of Olympic History*, vol. 12, May 2004, pp. 29–34.

Leigh, Mary H., and Bonin, Thérèse M., 'The Pioneering Role of Madame Alice Milliat and the Fédération Sportive Féminine Internationale in Establishing International Track and Field Competition for Women', *Journal of Sport History*, vol. 4, no. 1, 1977, pp. 72–83.

Mangan, J. A., 'Tragic Symbiosis: Distinctive Anglo-Saxon Visions and Voices', *International Journal of the History of Sport*, vol. 28, nos. 3–4, 2011, pp. 435–57.

Marindin, G. E., 'The Game of Harpastum or Pheninda', *The Classical Review*, vol. 4, no. 4, April 1890, p. 145.

Martin, Gerard John, 'The Game is not the Same: A History of Professional Rugby in New Zealand', master's thesis, Auckland University of Technology, 2005.

Nieman, Gideon, and Laubscher, Lappe, 'W P Schreiner and His Role in the 1919 New Zealand Services Tour of South Africa', *Points Unlimited*, vol. 7, no. 2, September 2000, pp. 24–7.

O'Hanley, John Arthur, 'Women in Non-traditional Sport: The Rise and Popularity of Women's Rugby in Canada', master's thesis, Queen's University, Ontario, 1998.

O'Reilly, Laurie, 'Women's Rugby: A Coach's View', *Journal of Physical Education New Zealand*, vol. 26, no. 3, 1993, pp. 11–13.

Quintillan, Ghislaine, 'Alice Milliat and the Women's Games', *Olympic Review*, vol. 26, no. 31, February–March 2000, pp. 27–8.

Richards, Trevor, 'Thou Shalt Play! What 60 Years of Controversy over New Zealand's Sporting Contacts with South Africa Tell Us About Ourselves', *New Zealand Studies*, July 1996, pp. 26–32.

Richardson, Len, 'The Invention of a National Game: the Struggle for Control', *History Now*, vol. 1, no. 1, June 1995, p. 5.

Ryan, Greg, 'A Tale of Two Dinners: New Zealand Rugby and the Embrace of Empire 1919–32', *International Journal of the History of Sport*, vol. 28, no. 10, 2011, pp. 1409–25.

—— 'Athletic Warriors or a Social Elite: the Formative Years of Maori Rugby 1870–1914', Paper presented to Australian Society for Sports History conference, Australian Catholic University, Sydney, July 2003.

—— 'Brawn Against Brains: Australia, New Zealand and the American "Football Crisis", 1906–13', *Sporting Traditions*, vol. 20, no. 2, May 2004, pp. 19–37.

——'Men Who Defaulted in the Greatest Game of All: Sport, Conscientious Objectors and Military Defaulters in New Zealand 1916–1923', *International Journal of the History of Sport*, published online, http://www.tandfonline.com/loi/fhsp20

—— 'Rural Myth and Urban Actuality: The Anatomy of All Black and New Zealand Rugby 1884–1938', *New Zealand Journal of History*, vol. 35, no. 1, 2001, pp. 45–69.

Thomas, Allan, 'On the Ball: New Zealand's Rugby Song', in Brad Patterson (ed.), *Sport, Society and Culture in New Zealand*, Stout Research Centre, Victoria University of Wellington, Wellington, 1999.

Tennyson, Sir Charles, 'They Taught the World to Play', *Victorian Studies*, vol. 2, no. 3, March 1959, pp. 211–22.

Thomson, Rex W., 'Provincial Rugby in New Zealand: Otago's Academic Pioneers', *Journal of Sport History*, vol. 23, no. 3, Fall 1996, pp. 211–27.

Van Der Merwe, F. J. G., 'Race and South African Rugby: A Review of the 1919 "All Black" tour', African Journals Online, http://www.ajol.info

Vincent, G. T., 'Practical Imperialism: the Anglo-Welsh Tour of New Zealand, 1908', *International Journal of the History of Sport*, vol. 15, no. 1, April 1998, pp. 123–40.

—— '"To Uphold the Honour of the Province": Football in Canterbury c1854–c1890', in Greg Ryan (ed.), *Tackling Rugby Myths: Rugby and New Zealand Society 1854–2004*, University of Otago Press, Dunedin, 2005.

Walter, Brett, 'Effects of the All Blacks Test Results on the New Zealand Stock Market', master's thesis, University of Otago, 2000.

Ward, Tony, 'The Start of Australian Rules: Creation of a Dominant Sport', *Sporting Traditions*, vol. 31, no. 1, May 2014, pp. 17–34.

Online sources

Department of Internal Affairs, Births, Deaths and Marriages Online (https://bdmhistoricalrecords.dia.govt.nz)

Dictionary of New Zealand Biography (https://www.teara.govt.nz/en/biographies)

Encyclopédie du rugby français (http://www.[illegible].fr).

fitz Stephen, William. *Fitz-Stephen's Description of the City of London, newly translated from the Latin original; with a necessary commentary. A dissertation on the author. Ascertaining the exact year of the production is prefixed; and to the whole is subjoined a correct edition of the original, with the various readings, and some useful annotations.* By an antiquary (London: 1772). Eighteenth Century Collections Online (http://www.gale.cengage.co.uk)

Gwulo: Old Hong Kong (http://gwulo.com)

Metropolitan Police, London (http://www.met.police.uk)

Music Australia (http://www.musicaustralia.org)

Oxford Dictionary of National Biography (http://www.oxforddnb.com)

Papers Past (http://www.paperspast.natlib.govt.nz)

Rugby Football Union (England) (http://www.rfu.co.uk)

Rugby history (www.rugbyfootballhistory.com)

Trove – Australian newspapers online (http://www.trove.nla.gov.au)

Wisden Almanack 1963 (London: Sporting Handbooks, 1963), online edition (http://www.espncricinfo.com/wisdenalmanack)

Index

Page numbers in **bold** refer to illustrations.

First published 2015

Auckland University Press
University of Auckland
Private Bag 92019
Auckland 1142
New Zealand
www.press.auckland.ac.nz

ISBN 978 1 86940 836 7

Publication is kindly assisted by

A catalogue record for this book is available from the National Library of New Zealand

Front cover: Wraith-like, New Zealand halfback Sid Going drifts through the fog that enveloped Cardiff Arms Park for the match against East Glamorgan at the end of December in 1972. So thick was the fog that spectators, and sometimes even players, had to ask each other what had happened. The All Blacks won 20–9. PETER BUSH

Back cover: An estimated 45,000 spectators crowded into Lancaster Park in Christchurch for the second test of the South African series in 1937.

Cover design: Scott Crickett

Printed in China by 1010 Printing International Ltd